California Civil Procedure
BEFORE TRIAL

Procedure BEFORE TRIAL Califo
E TRIAL California Civil Proce
Civil Procedure BEFORE TRIAL
BEFORE TRIAL California Civil
ornia Civil Procedure BEFOR
edure BEFORE TRIAL California
California Civil Procedure
Procedure BEFORE TRIAL Calif
E TRIAL California Civil Proce
a Civil Procedure BEFORE TRIAL
e BEFORE TRIAL California Civil
fornia Civil Procedure BEFOR
edure BEFORE TRIAL California
L California Civil Procedure
l Procedure BEFORE TRIAL Calif
RE TRIAL California Civil Proc
a Civil Procedure BEFORE TRIA
e BEFORE TRIAL California Civil
lifornia Civil Procedure BEFOF

California Civil Procedure

BEFORE TRIAL
Volume 2

Edited by CEB attorneys:

CAROL S. BROSNAHAN, Supervising Editor
PAUL PEYRAT
JON A. RANTZMAN
ISADORE ROSENBLATT

CALIFORNIA CONTINUING EDUCATION OF THE BAR

Berkeley, California

Library of Congress Catalog Card No. 76-145875

© 1978 by The Regents of the University of California
Printed in the United States of America

 CALIFORNIA

CONTINUING EDUCATION OF THE BAR

By agreement between the board of Governors of The State Bar of California and the Regents of the University of California, Continuing Education of the Bar offers an educational program for the benefit of practicing lawyers. The program is administered by a Governing Committee through University of California Extension in cooperation with local bar associations and the Joint Advisory Committee made up of the State Bar Committee of the Continuing Education of the Bar and the Deans of accredited law schools.

Practice books are published as part of the educational program. Authors are given full opportunity to express their individual legal interpretations and opinions, and these obviously are not intended to reflect any position of The State Bar of California or of University Extension. Chapters written by employees of state or federal agencies are not to be considered statements of governmental policies.

California Continuing Education of the Bar publications and oral programs are designed to provide current and accurate information about the subject matter covered, to help attorneys maintain their professional competence. Publications are distributed and oral programs presented with the understanding that CEB does not render legal, accounting, or other professional service. Attorneys using CEB publications or orally conveyed information in dealing with a specific client's or their own legal matters should also research original sources of authority.

CALIFORNIA CONTINUING

Governing Committee
Chris R. Conway, of the Long Beach Bar, Chairperson
Jacques M. Adler, of the San Francisco Bar
Joanne M. Garvey, of the San Francisco Bar
Professor Edward C. Halbach, Jr., University of California
School of Law (Berkeley)
Professor Melville B. Nimmer, University of California
School of Law (Los Angeles)
Warren E. Schoonover, Director of Administrative Services—
Division of Agricultural Sciences, University of California
Keith Sexton, Dean, University Extension Programs,
University of California
William A. Carroll, Director, Continuing Education of the Bar
Joseph G. Hurley, North Hollywood, Liaison Governor
David J. Levy, Concord, Liaison Governor

State Bar Committee
Geraldine S. Hemmerling, Los Angeles, Chairperson
John B. Hook, San Francisco, Vice Chairperson
Justice Bernard S. Jefferson, Los Angeles, Advisor
David J. Levy, Concord, Liaison Governor
Theodore P. Shield, Los Angeles, Liaison Governor
Edwin J. Wilson, Long Beach, Liaison Governor
William J. Adams, Merced
D. Keith Bilter, San Francisco
Stuart D. Buchalter, Los Angeles
Robert R. Burge, Santa Ana
Jeffrey J. Carter, Berkeley
Gary E. Christopherson, Stockton
Patricia A. Cowett, San Diego
John S. Gilmore, Sacramento
Bruce L. Gitelson, Beverly Hills
Max Gutierrez, Jr., San Francisco
Hugh J. Haferkamp, Santa Barbara
Anne O. Kandel, Los Angeles
Albert M. Leddy, Bakersfield
William H. Levit, Jr., Los Angeles

EDUCATION OF THE BAR

Robert Y. Libott, Los Angeles
Ann G. Miller, San Francisco
James R. Moore, Santa Ana
M. Lea Cheryl Rhodes, San Diego
Walter J. Schmidt, Modesto
Herbert E. Schwartz, Century City
Stephen G. Valensi, Los Angeles
Mark Watterson, Toluca Lake
Edwin J. Wilson, Jr., Berkeley

Law School Deans
Dean George J. Alexander, University of Santa Clara
Dean Marvin J. Anderson, Hastings College of the Law
Dean Maxwell S. Boas, Western State University
Dean C. Boyack, Acting Dean, Southwestern University
Dean Robert K. Castetter, California Western University
Dean Eadie Deutsch, University of San Fernando
Dean Ernest C. Friesen, Whittier College School of Law
Dean Sanford H. Kadish, University of California (Berkeley)
Dean Pierre R. Loiseaux, University of California (Davis)
Dean John E. Loomis, San Joaquin College of Law
Dean Frederick J. Lower, Jr., Loyola University
Dean Paul L. McKaskle, University of San Francisco
Dean Judith G. McKelvey, Golden Gate University
Dean Charles J. Meyers, Stanford University
Dean Dorothy W. Nelson, University of Southern California Law Center
Dean Fred J. Olson, Ventura College of Law
Dean Mark Owens, Jr., San Francisco Law School
Dean Ronald F. Phillips, Pepperdine University
Dean Perry Polski, University of West Los Angeles
Dean C. Tom Reese, La Verne College School of Law
Dean Gordon D. Schaber, McGeorge School of Law,
University of the Pacific
Dean Carl R. Sederholm, Northrop Institute of Technology
School of Law
Dean Wiliam D. Warren, University of California (Los Angeles)
Dean Donald T. Weckstein, University of San Diego

Preface

This book completes the two-volume set that replaces CALIFORNIA CIVIL PROCEDURE BEFORE TRIAL (Cal CEB 1957). The books are intended to be practical and transactional guides to procedures, not exhaustive collections of citations. Frequent references are made to other treatises, particularly Witkin's CALIFORNIA PROCEDURE (2d ed), in which additional discussions and citations can be found.

Some parts of the new set are based on the 1957 book, but in addition to a discussion of current statutes, cases, and practice, a number of topics not covered in the old book are treated in both volumes. For example, this volume includes chapters on procedures either radically changed from the law in 1957 (*e.g.*, summary judgment) or newly enacted (*e.g.*, coordination of civil action).

The names of California practitioners who wrote for this volume are shown in the table of contents and on the first page of their chapters. A footnote at the beginning of each chapter identifies the CEB staff attorney who edited the manuscript. Supervisory editorial work on much of this volume was done by Carol S. Brosnahan.

All manuscript was reviewed by practicing lawyers, judges, and other consultants throughout the state. CEB extends special thanks to these consultants who are listed on the acknowledgment pages that follow.

Tribute should again be paid to J. N. De Meo of the Santa Rosa bar, who, as a contributor to the 1957 book and pioneer in the elimination of archaic language from forms, became a guiding spirit in the development of the CEB practice book, CEB style and CALIFORNIA CIVIL PROCEDURE BEFORE TRIAL in particular.

Production editing was handled by Rachel Ellis and Shirley Stark, assisted by Pamela Carter Sedransk. Ted Francis prepared the index.

William A. Carroll
Director

Acknowledgments

The following judges, attorneys, and others served as consultants on this book by reviewing and commenting on one or more chapter manuscripts. Their valuable suggestions have made the book more accurate, more practical, and more reflective of practice in the state. To each of them, our special thanks.

    Honorable Hollis G. Best, Fresno
    John H. Brinsley, Los Angeles
    Honorable Warren Deering, Los Angeles
    Honorable Leonard Dieden, Oakland
    J. N. De Meo, Santa Rosa
    Honorable Charles E. Goff, San Francisco
    Honorable August J. Goebel, Los Angeles
    Richard Field, Los Angeles
    W. Stuart Home, Fresno
    John B. Hook, San Francisco
    Catherine I. Hotchkiss, Los Angeles
    Patrick M. Kelly, Los Angeles
    Stephen J. Kennedy, Oakland
    Jay S. Linderman, San Francisco
    Mark W. Lomax, Los Angeles
    Honorable Eugene F. Lynch, San Francisco
    Thomas J. McDermott, Jr., Los Angeles
    Honorable Jay Pfotenhauer, San Francisco
    Daniel I. Reith, Monterey
    Charlene May Saunders, Los Angeles
    Bernard P. Simons, Los Angeles
    Gerald W. Stutsman, Fresno
    Robert H. Thau, Beverly Hills

ACKNOWLEDGMENTS

Honorable David A. Thomas, Los Angeles
Edwin J. Wilson, Jr., Berkeley
Charles S. Vogel, Los Angeles

Special research assistance was provided by:

José Aguilar
Joel Bludman
Terry Allen Bremner
Lorin Brennan
Robert Brockman
Thomas P. Corr
Leslie Corston
Brian Cragg
James Michael Curl
Paul M. Curry
Chris Dickson
Martin J. Elmer
Michael Fenger
Roy Geiger
Jeffrey Jaech
Nora Kronenthal
Elizabeth Read
Thomas Singman
Richard J. Taggi
Kathryn Tchopik
Kathy G. Teller
Mary I. Samuels

Contents

Part I. Motions, Orders and Special Actions

23. Motions and Orders 3
    SHELLEY M. MERCER, PETER I. OSTROFF, ARTHUR L. SHERWOOD

24. Declaratory Relief 61
    RICHARD M. MOSK

Part II. Bringing Case to Trial; Determining Scope of Action

25. Intervention 111
    MICHAEL HOLTZMAN

26. Setting Case for Trial 143
    RICHARD P. BYRNE

27. Consolidation and Severance 209
    RICHARD P. BYRNE

28. Coordination 225
    WILLIAM H. LEVIT, ALEXANDER B. YAKUTIS

Part III. Termination Without Trial

29. Summary Judgment 259
    ROBERT FAINER, JAN T. CHILTON

30. Default 323
    SANDOR T. BOXER

31. Dismissal 383
    PETER ABRAHAMS

32. Submitted Case 451
    JOHN E. HOFFMAN

33. Settlement 457
    KENNETH J. ARAN, MARIO CLINCO

34. Consent Judgment 485
    JOHN E. HOFFMAN

CONTENTS

Table of Statutes and Rules 499
Table of Cases 517
Table of References 553
Index 555

PART I
MOTIONS, ORDERS, AND SPECIAL ACTIONS

SHELLEY M. MERCER
PETER I. OSTROFF
ARTHUR L. SHERWOOD

Chapter 23
Motions and Orders

I. PRELIMINARY CONSIDERATIONS
A. Terminology; Scope of Chapter §23.1
B. Applicable Law; Local Practices §23.2
C. Applicant's Party Status §23.3
D. Place of Application §23.4
E. Notice: Need; Choice of Procedure
   1. Ex Parte Application §23.5
   2. Notice of Hearing; Waiver of Notice §23.6
F. Tactical and Economic Considerations §23.7

II. NOTICE OF MOTION PROCEDURE
A. Nature; Procedural Checklist §23.8
B. When To Serve and File
   1. Restrictions §23.9
   2. Service by Mail §23.10
   3. Tactical Timing; Laches §23.11
   4. Shortening Notice Time
      a. Reasons; Procedure §23.12
      b. Form: Application for Order and Order Shortening Time §23.13
   5. Extending Time
      a. Procedures §23.14
      b. Form: Stipulation Extending Time To Serve Notice of Motion (or Setting New Hearing Date) §23.15
      c. Form: Application for Order and Order Extending Time (or Setting New Hearing Date) §23.16
C. Motion Papers §23.17
   1. Form: Notice of Motion §23.18
      a. Caption; Introduction §23.19

SHELLEY M. MERCER, A.B., 1967, University of California (Riverside); J.D., 1970, University of Chicago. Ms. Mercer practices in Los Angeles with the firm of Nilsson, Robbins, Bissell, Dalgarn & Berliner.

PETER I. OSTROFF, A.B., 1964, Washington University, St. Louis, Mo.; J.D., 1967, University of Chicago. Mr. Ostroff is a member of the Los Angeles firm of Nossaman, Waters, Scott, Krueger & Riordan.

ARTHUR L. SHERWOOD, B.A., 1964, University of California (Berkeley); M.S., 1965, University of Chicago; J.D., 1968, Harvard Law School. Mr. Sherwood practices in Los Angeles with the firm of Gibson, Dunn & Crutcher.

CEB attorney-editor was PAUL PEYRAT.

MOTIONS AND ORDERS 4

        b. Time of Hearing §23.20
        c. Place of Hearing §23.21
        d. Nature of Order Sought §23.22
        e. Grounds §23.23
        f. Supporting Papers; Evidence §23.24
        g. Date; Signature §23.25
    2. Memorandum of Points and Authorities
        a. Requirement; Purpose §23.26
        b. General Format §23.27
        c. Caption §23.28
        d. Introduction §23.29
        e. Table of Contents; Index §23.30
        f. Headings §23.31
        g. Points; Arguments §23.32
        h. Authorities; Citations §23.33
        i. Conclusion §23.34
        j. Subscription §23.35
    3. Declarations and Affidavits
        a. Nature; Purpose §23.36
        b. General Format
            (1) Form: Declaration in Support of Motion §23.37
            (2) Form: Affidavit in Support of Motion §23.38
        c. Caption; Introduction §23.39
        d. Identity and Competence of Declarant §23.40
        e. Matter Stated; Admissibility §23.41
        f. Subscription
            (1) Declaration §23.42
            (2) Affidavit §23.43
    4. Other Documents and Exhibits §23.44
    5. Request That Court Take Judicial Notice; Form §23.45
    6. Proposed Order §23.46
    7. Proof of Service §23.47
D. Opposition Procedures §23.48
    1. Memorandum of Points and Authorities in Opposition to Motion §23.49
    2. Declarations in Opposition to Motion §23.50
    3. Collateral Response §23.51
    4. Time To File and Serve §23.52
E. Tentative Rulings §23.53
F. Reply and Supplementary Papers §23.54
G. The Hearing
    1. Attendance §23.55
    2. Argument §23.56
    3. Presenting Evidence §23.57
H. Rulings and Orders §23.58
    1. Form: Notice of Ruling §23.59
    2. Form: Order §23.60
I. Procedures After Motion Granted
    1. By Moving Party §23.61
    2. By Opposing Party §23.62
J. Procedures After Motion Denied §23.63

III. EX PARTE PROCEDURE
  A. Nature; When To Use §23.64
  B. Notice of Application; Procedural Guide §23.65
  C. Form: Ex Parte Application for Order and Order §23.66
IV. ORDER TO SHOW CAUSE PROCEDURE
  A. Nature; When To Use §23.67
  B. Notice of Application; Procedural Guide §23.68
  C. Form: Application for Order and Order To Show Cause §23.69

I. PRELIMINARY CONSIDERATIONS

§23.1 A. Terminology; Scope of Chapter

A motion is an application for an order; an order is a direction of a court or judge, made or entered in writing and not included in a judgment. CCP §1003. "Making a motion" is the process of applying for an order, commonly by filing a notice of motion, application, declaration for an order, or other paper. See CCP §1005.5 (a motion is deemed to have been made on the due service and filing of a notice of motion); *Weldon v Rogers* (1907) 151 C 432, 435, 90 P 1062 ("motion" and "application" are interchangeable). In a narrow sense, motion refers to an oral application to a judge for an order. See *Colthurst v Harris* (1929) 97 CA 430, 432, 275 P 868. Motions are made in pending cases, and usually relate to a question collateral to the main object of the action. *People v Sparks* (1952) 112 CA2d 120, 121, 246 P2d 64.

Statutes, court rules, and custom have created a variety of different orders that can be sought by parties to a lawsuit. The statute or rule that provides for an order may also prescribe or suggest the procedure to be used in applying for it. Failure to conform to statutory or court rule requirements for a particular motion is a ground for its denial. *People v Albin* (1952) 111 CA2d 800, 806, 245 P2d 660, 664.

This chapter discusses procedures, papers, and principles common to motions and orders generally. Other chapters of CALIFORNIA CIVIL PROCEDURE BEFORE TRIAL, volumes 1 and 2, discuss particular motions, applications, and orders appropriate to the subject matter of those chapters. Motion practice in appellate and federal courts is not covered in this chapter. See generally CALIFORNIA CIVIL APPELLATE PRACTICE chap 12 (Cal CEB

1966); Lavine & Horning, MANUAL OF FEDERAL PRACTICE chap 4 (1967).

§23.2   B. Applicable Law; Local Practices

Motion procedures are governed principally by statutes, the California Rules of Court, and local court rules, policies, and custom. Decisional law is more likely to relate to the merits of granting or denying a particular motion than to the procedures for making and opposing motions.

Code of Civil Procedure §§1003–1020 apply to motions, orders, and notices generally. An attorney preparing a motion must also check the code section that authorizes the particular order for additional or different procedural and substantive requirements.

California Rules of Court 203 (superior courts) and 503 (municipal and justice courts) are general rules for notices of motion; rules 235 and 523 concern orders extending time. Applications for orders in family law matters are covered in rule 1225. Other court rules deal with applications for particular orders. Section 15 of Division 1 of the Appendix of the California Rules of Court Appendix (Recommended Standards of Judicial Administration) applies to ex parte applications and orders. See §23.65. The California Rules of Court have the force of law unless contrary to express statutory provisions. *Cantillon v Superior Court* (1957) 150 CA2d 184, 187, 309 P2d 890, 892.

The courts in many counties and judicial districts have adopted local rules that relate to local motion practice. In addition to rules, some courts have adopted policy or procedure manuals that contain provisions relating to motions and orders in particular kinds of proceedings. Local policies and rules that represent requirements rather than mere guidelines, and that are fairly capable of being known by attorneys and parties, have the legal effect of procedural statutes unless they are contrary to higher law. *Wisniewski v Clary* (1975) 46 CA3d 499, 504, 120 CR 176, 180. County law libraries maintain collections of local rules from their own and other counties, and selected court rules are published by both the *Los Angeles Daily Journal* and the *Los Angeles Metropolitan News*. Superior courts in the Third Appellate District have adopted a set of rules applicable to all superior courts in that district as have superior courts in the Fifth Appellate District. Finding local municipal and justice court rules may require a call to the particular court or a law library in that district.

§23.3 C. Applicant's Party Status

Most orders must be applied for by or on behalf of a person who is a party in a pending action. See *Difani v Riverside County Oil Co.* (1927) 201 C 210, 214, 256 P 210, 212; *Beshara v Goldberg* (1963) 221 CA2d 392, 395, 34 CR 501. See generally 4 Witkin, CALIFORNIA PROCEDURE, Proceedings Without Trial §1(d) (2d ed 1971). However, nonparties can make certain motions. See, *e.g.*, *Ascherman v Superior Court* (1967) 254 CA2d 506, 513, 62 CR 547, 551 (deposition witness). For discussion of other applications made by nonparties, see, *e.g.*, 1 CALIFORNIA CIVIL PROCEDURE BEFORE TRIAL §2.81 (motion to quash service of process), chap 5 (petition for appointment of guardian ad litem), chap 6 (petition to sue in forma pauperis) (Cal CEB 1977), and in this volume, chap 25 (complaint in intervention). See also CALIFORNIA CIVIL DISCOVERY PRACTICE §2.28 (Cal CEB 1975) (motion to quash subpena duces tecum).

§23.4 D. Place of Application

Motions must be made in the court in which the action is pending. CCP §1004. But see CCP §2034(a) (motion to compel answers from nonparty deponent to be made in county where deposition is to be taken). Some applications may be heard and disposed of at chambers (CCP §166), while others should be scheduled for hearing in open court (see §23.6).

Applications for orders that request a hearing (*e.g.*, notices of motion) are normally filed with the clerk of the court in which the action is pending. In some counties and districts, local rules may require that all subsequent papers be filed with the clerk for the department of the court in which the motion is set for hearing.

E. Notice: Need; Choice of Procedure

§23.5 1. Ex Parte Application

An attorney who seeks a particular court order must first decide whether to apply for it by an ex parte or a notice procedure. An ex parte application does not set the motion for a hearing, although the moving party may be required to notify adverse parties that the application will be made, giving them a chance to state objections before the judge signs the order. See §23.65. The key difference between ex parte motions and noticed motions is not whether or when notice of the application is given, but whether a formal hearing must be scheduled before the order issues.

An ex parte application for an order (see §§23.64–23.66) is normally easier and quicker than a noticed hearing procedure (see §§23.64–23.66) and can be used when the order sought is one that affects only the moving party; adverse parties would have no legal basis or reason to object to its issuance (see §23.64). An ex parte procedure is also appropriate if the purpose of the order would be frustrated if notice of the application were given, as with certain restraining orders.

Ex parte applications are not permitted, *i.e.*, a hearing must be scheduled if the order sought would affect a substantial right of the adverse party. See §23.6. Rather than researching whether an ex parte procedure is appropriate for a particular motion, an attorney may: (a) ask a judge or court clerk whether orders of the kind sought are customarily granted in that court; or (b) skip the ex parte application and have the matter noticed for hearing. It is also possible to follow the ex parte procedure, and if that fails, serve and file a noticed motion.

§23.6 2. Notice of Hearing; Waiver of Notice

A notice procedure entails service and filing of a court paper that sets a date for a judge to hear argument for and against issuance of an order. The statute that provides for a particular order may specify whether notice must be given. Absent a statutory specification, the attorney may follow the general rule that no order that would affect the rights of an adverse party in the litigation should be granted unless that party has been given written notice and an opportunity to be heard. See *McDonald v Severy* (1936) 6 C2d 629, 59 P2d 98; *Caledonian Ins. Co. v Superior Court* (1956) 140 CA2d 458, 295 P2d 49. See generally 4 Witkin, CALIFORNIA PROCEDURE, Proceedings Without Trial §6 (2d ed 1971).

The procedure most commonly used in civil actions to notice a hearing is by noticed motion. See §§23.8–23.63. Also available is the order to show cause procedure that is used in domestic relations cases, requests for preliminary injunctive relief (see 1 CALIFORNIA CIVIL PROCEDURE BEFORE TRIAL §§15.36–15.41 (Cal CEB 1977)), and other situations (see, *e.g.*, 1 CIV PROC BEFORE TRIAL §§18.34, 18.35). See §§23.67–23.69.

Failure to give proper notice or any notice does not necessarily vitiate the proceeding or order. If the adverse party or his attorney actually appears at the hearing, he is considered to have waived notice unless he clearly states that he appears solely to object for lack of adequate notice. *Lacey v Bertone* (1949) 33 C2d 649, 651, 203 P2d 755, 757; *Tate v Superior Court* (1975) 45 CA3d 925, 930, 119 CR 835, 838. See generally 4 Witkin, CALIFORNIA PROCEDURE, Proc Without Trial §7.

§23.7   F. Tactical and Economic Considerations

Motions are tactical tools, and the decision to use them is made in the context of a party's overall litigation plan. For example, in response to a complaint, defendant might consider whether it is tactically better to demur for absence of jurisdiction, move to stay or to dismiss on grounds of inconvenient forum, move to transfer to another court, institute discovery preliminary to a motion for summary judgment, use other procedures, or not to make an immediate motion but answer and leave the case in the place and status set by plaintiff.

Making a motion entails time and effort for the moving party and sometimes alerts an adversary to defects in the case when there is still time to correct them. A kind of cost-benefit analysis underlies a decision to apply for an order. Will the predicted benefit of obtaining the order, discounted by the possibility that it will be denied and effect of educating the adversary, outweigh the expense of pursuing the procedure? What are the comparative cost-to-benefit ratios of alternative procedures? Often, the best alternative to an immediate motion is a discussion with opposing counsel to see whether there can be an agreement that achieves counsel's objective without need to resort to a court proceeding.

II. NOTICE OF MOTION PROCEDURE

§23.8   A. Nature; Procedural Checklist

The noticed motion procedure most often used to apply for an order (other than at trial) is initiated by serving and filing a notice of motion (a paper specifying a time and place for the motion to be heard) together with supporting papers. The motion is deemed to have been made and to be pending before the court, on all the grounds stated on due service and filing of the notice of motion. CCP §1005.5. In some circumstances, custom or statute may dictate that the order to show cause procedure be used (see §§23.67–23.69), but the effect of these two procedures is the same.

The following checklists show steps taken in a typical noticed motion proceeding:

By attorney for moving party:

(1) Consult statute or rule that authorizes motion for information on:

    (a) procedure required or permitted;

    (b) time limits for service or filing;

    (c) evidentiary showing required.

(2) Compute first and last day for service or filing (see §23.9). If period has passed, check statute or rule for late filing procedures;

(3) Check with court clerk for availability of hearing dates, and for any local rules or customs relating to the particular motion.

(4) Prepare moving papers (as required):

    (a) notice of motion (see §23.18);

    (b) memorandum of points and authorities (see §23.27);

    (c) declarations (if facts not already in the record are a basis for the motion; see §23.37);

    (d) exhibits (*i.e.*, documents or papers not yet on file in the action that bear on the motion; see §23.44);

    (e) requests that the court take judicial notice (see §23.45);

    (f) proposed order (see §23.46);

    (g) application for order extending or shortening time (see §§23.13, 23.16);

    (h) proof of service (see 1 CALIFORNIA CIVIL PROCEDURE BEFORE TRIAL §8.69 (Cal CEB 1977)).

(5) Serve and file moving papers (see §§23.9–23.11).

(6) Review opposition papers and serve and file supplementary papers, if needed (see §23.54).

(7) Check with court for tentative ruling if one has been made (see §23.53).

(8) Prepare for and attend hearing, and present argument (and evidence, if permitted) in favor of motion (see §§23.55–23.57).

(9) If a favorable ruling is obtained, prepare notice of ruling (see §23.59) or form of order (see §23.60) unless judge signs previously submitted proposed order, or will prepare the order.

(10) Present order to judge for signature (see §§23.58, 23.60).

(11) Serve and file notice of ruling or signed order (unless done by the court or otherwise unnecessary).

By attorney for party opposing motion

(1) Consult statute or rule that authorizes motion for information on:

(a) whether moving party has complied with procedural and time requirements;

(b) whether notice of motion and supporting papers meet form and content requirements;

(c) evidentiary or other bases for opposing the motion.

(2) Prepare opposition papers (as required):

(a) memorandum of points and authorities (see §23.49);

(b) declaration(s) (see §23.50);

(c) exhibit(s) which may be attached to the memorandum or declarations;

(d) proposed alternative order (see §23.60);

(e) stipulation or application for order setting new hearing date, if desired (see §§23.15–23.16).

(3) Serve and file opposition papers (see §23.52).

(4) Check with court for tentative ruling if one has been made (see §23.53).

(5) Prepare for and attend hearing, and present argument (and evidence, if permitted) against the motion or in support of a different or modified order (see §§23.55–23.57).

(6) If court issues an order denying the motion or favoring the responding party:

(a) prepare a notice of ruling (see §23.59) or form of order (see §23.60);

(b) present order to judge for signature (see §§23.58, 23.60);

(c) serve and file notice of ruling or signed order (unless done by the court or otherwise unnecessary).

As an alternative to opposing a motion on its merits, counsel may wish to use some form of collateral response, such as moving to quash service of notice or making a special appearance solely to challenge the adequacy of notice. See §23.62.

B. When To Serve and File

§23.9   1. Restrictions

Several restrictions affect an attorney's choice of date to serve and to file motion papers. The statute or rule that provides for a particular order may set a time period after an event within which a notice of motion must be served, filed, or both. If the notice of motion is served or filed later than the specified number of days from the event, the court can deny the motion as untimely, or ignore the application. An appellate court can overturn an order granted after such a time period has passed. An example of this time requirement is the notice of motion to strike, which must be served and filed by a defendant within 30 days after he has been served with the summons and complaint (see 1 CALIFORNIA CIVIL PROCEDURE BEFORE TRIAL §10.4 (Cal CEB 1977)).

Some motions are denied if the notice of motion is served too soon after an event. For example, a notice of motion for summary judgment under CCP §437c can be made no sooner than 60 days after the adverse party's appearance in the action (see §29.12), and a motion to dismiss under CCP §583(a), can be made no earlier than two years after the complaint was filed (see §31.35).

Counsel must also decide how long before the hearing on a motion the notice of motion must be served and filed. The general rule is that written notice of a hearing must be given (*i.e.*, served) at least ten days before the time appointed for the hearing, unless a judge has prescribed a shorter time. CCP §1005; but see §23.10 on service of notice by mail. Local court rules may also require that motion papers be filed a certain number of days before the hearing. See, *e.g.*, LA & SF LAW & MOTION POLICY MANUALS §16 (nine days). Local court rules may also specify a maximum time between date of service and date of hearing. See, *e.g.*, LA & SF LAW & MOTION POLICY MANUALS §16 (45 days).

The time within which to serve or file a notice of motion is computed by excluding the first day of the specified period and including the last day unless it is a holiday. CCP §12. If the last day is a Saturday, Sunday, or designated holiday, the notice may be served or filed before the close of the next business day. See CCP §§10, 12a–12b; Govt C §§6700, 6701.

§23.10 2. Service by Mail

Service of a notice of motion by mail is complete when the notice, in a properly sealed, stamped, addressed envelope is deposited in a mail box or other post office facility. CCP §1013(a). There is a question whether a notice served by mail must be mailed more than ten days before the date for hearing.

Code of Civil Procedure §1013(a) provides that if the adverse party must do an act or exercise a right within a given number of days after a notice or other paper is served by mail, the time within which the right may be exercised or act performed is extended, after deposit of the paper in the mail, by (a) five days if the place of address is within California, (b) ten days if outside California but within the United States, and (c) 20 days if outside the United States. Some lawyers thus conclude that if mailing is the method of service chosen the notice of motion must be deposited in the mail 15, 20, or 30 days before the date set for the hearing. See *Mather v Mather* (1943) 22 C2d 713, 719, 140 P2d 808, 811 (notice of motion for entry of judgment insufficient when date of hearing only ten days after date of mailing); *California Accounts, Inc. v Superior Court* (1975) 50 CA3d 483, 123 CR 304; *Shell Oil Co. v Superior Court* (1975) 50 CA3d 489, 123 CR 307 (extensions required for certain discovery procedures).

However, other lawyers conclude that a notice of motion deposited in the mail ten days before the date of hearing is valid They argue that the right to be present at the hearing on a motion is not "a right [that] may be exercised, or an act . . . to be done" as those terms are used in CCP §1013(a). See *Brown v Rouse* (1897) 115 C 619, 621, 47 P 601, 602 (extension not needed on notice of justification of sureties); *Welden v Davis Auto Exch.* (1957) 153 CA2d 515, 521, 315 P2d 33, 37 (notice of motion to dismiss cross-complaint for want of prosecution did not require extension of hearing date). See also *Cooper v Board of Medical Examiners* (1975) 49 CA3d 931, 942 n11, 123 CR 563, 570 n11. See generally Dobyns, *CCP §1013: The Pony Express Cenotaph* 3 Orange BJ 19, 21 (1976).

As long as this question remains unresolved, the safe course is either to deposit a notice of motion in the mail at least 15, 20, or 30 days before the hearing date, or to serve the notice by delivering it personally or to the office of adverse counsel and unrepresented parties. See 1 California Civil Procedure Before Trial §§8.61–8.63, 8.66 (Cal CEB 1977).

§23.11   3. Tactical Timing; Laches

When statutes and rules permit a motion to be made immediately or later during the lawsuit, tactical considerations may suggest a propitious time. In some cases, an early application saves the moving party effort and expense by, *e.g.*, gaining his dismissal from the lawsuit, transferring the action to a more convenient forum, narrowing issues that must be proved or met, or limiting discovery. In other cases, it is better to delay filing a motion until, *e.g.*, after investigation and discovery, or after an adversary is committed to a position.

Some motions can be postponed until it is too late for the adverse party to correct a defect in his case that the motion exposes. However, delay involves risk. Adverse counsel may oppose the motion on grounds of laches (see *Benjamin v Dalmo Mfg. Co.* (1948) 31 C2d 523, 531, 190 P2d 593, 598; *Leonis v Leffingwell* (1899) 126 C 369, 372, 58 P 940; *Corcoran v Los Angeles* (1957) 153 CA2d 852, 856, 315 P2d 439, 441), or the judge who rules on the motion may be unsympathetic to a delay intended to gain an advantage or create an inequity.

4. Shortening Notice Time

§23.12   a. Reasons; Procedure

To obtain a hearing date that is sooner than the ten days from date of service of notice of motion specified by CCP §1005, an attorney may apply for an order shortening time. Shortened notice time is appropriate if the order sought would otherwise be ineffective because of changing circumstances.

The application for an order shortening time may be typed at the end of the notice of motion, or on a separate sheet attached to and served with the moving papers. An order form is typed below the application. See form in §23.13. In some situations, a judge may sign an order shortening time on oral request without a written application.

The application is usually made, and the order granted, ex parte, by presenting the motion papers and application to a judge of the court in which the motion is to be made and immediately obtaining signature of the order shortening time. See §23.65 on the need to inform judge that other parties have been notified of the application, even if only by telephone. Normally, time will not be shortened to less than 48 hours, but some facts could justify a shorter time.

Although applications to shorten time are usually made by moving parties, the form in §23.13 can be adapted for use by a responding party that desires an earlier hearing date than that specified in the moving party's notice of motion.

§23.13   b. Form: Application for Order and Order Shortening Time

Copies: Original (presented to judge for signature and filed with proof of service); copies for service (one for each attorney of record and unrepresented party); office copies.

[Caption. See §§23.18–23.19]

No. _____

APPLICATION FOR ORDER AND ORDER SHORTENING TIME

____[Name]____ **declares:**

1. I am an attorney for ____[plaintiff / defendant]____ **in this action.**

2. It is necessary that the hearing on the ____[above / attached]____ **noticed motion for** ____[nature of motion]____ **take place, and the order issue,** ____[on _____, 19____ / no later than two days after service of the notice of motion]____ **for the following reasons:** _____.

3. I have notified ____[name]____, **attorney for** ____[name]____, **of this application for an order shortening time by** ____[describe method]____.

I declare under penalty of perjury that the foregoing is true and correct and that this declaration was executed on _____, 19____, **at** _____, **California.**

_____
[Signature of attorney]

[Typed name]
Attorney for ____[name]____

ORDER

Good cause appearing,

IT IS ORDERED that the motion of ____[plaintiff / defendant]____ ____[name]____ **for** ____[nature of order sought]____ **may be heard**

[When fixed date]

on _____, 19____, **provided that this order and the** ____[above / attached]____ **notice of motion and supporting papers are personally served on the attorney of record for each party, and each unrepresented party, in this action** ____[this day / on or before _____, 19____].

[When fixed notice]

_____ **days after service on the attorney of record for each party in the action of this order and the** ____[above / attached]____ **notice of motion and supporting papers.**

Dated: _____

_____
Judge

Comment: The notice of motion to which the application and order are attached should have "ORDER SHORTENING TIME" added to its caption.

5. Extending Time

§23.14   a. Procedures

An attorney who has reason to serve or file a notice of motion on a date that is after the last date prescribed by statute or rule (see §§23.9–23.10) may ask adverse counsel for a stipulation extending time to serve and file (see §23.15), or apply to the court for an extension of time (see §23.16). Code of Civil Procedure §1054 gives judges general authority to extend dates and requires them to honor stipulations extending time. See CCP §1054.1 on extensions of time for legislators. Any time set by the California Rules of Court may be extended by the court. Cal Rules of Ct 249(b), 534(b). See generally, 4 Witkin, CALIFORNIA PROCEDURE, Proceedings Without Trial §§2–4 (2d ed 1971). However, there is a question whether a court can grant an application to extend time to serve or file a notice of motion when that application is made after the prescribed time has expired.

California Rules of Court 235 and 523 require the application for an order extending time to be presented for determination to the judge before whom the action, motion, or other proceeding is pending, or, if that judge is absent or not able to hear it, to another judge of the same court. The application must disclose the nature of the case and any other extension previously granted by stipulation or court order. After the order has been signed, it must be filed immediately and copies served within 24 hours unless the judge has fixed a different time. Cal Rules of Ct 235, 523.

A party responding to a motion may wish to have the hearing set at a later date than the date specified in a notice of motion, *e.g.*, to allow more time to prepare responsive declarations and points and authorities, or to avoid a schedule conflict for the attorney who is to argue the responding party's position. The forms in §§23.15–23.16 may be used by a responding party as well as by a moving party.

§23.15   b. Form: Stipulation Extending Time To Serve Notice of Motion (or Setting New Hearing Date)

Copies: Original to file; one copy for each attorney or unrepresented party; office copies.

MOTIONS AND ORDERS §23.16

[Caption. See §§23.18– 23.19]

No. _____

STIPULATION____[EXTENDING TIME TO SERVE NOTICE OF MOTION / SETTING NEW HEARING DATE]____

The parties hereby stipulate and agree that

[When extending time]

____[name of party]____ **shall have until** ____[date]____ **to serve and file a notice of motion for** ____[nature of motion]____.

[When resetting time of hearing]

the hearing on the motion of ____[name of party]____ **for** ____[nature of motion]____ **previously set to be heard on** ____[old date]____ **shall instead be heard on** ____[new date]____ **at** ____[time]____ **in** ____[e.g., Department No.   ]____ **of this Court at** ____[address]____.

Dated: _____

[Signature of each attorney]

[Typed name]
Attorney for ____[name]____

Comment: Attorneys or parties who agree to reset a hearing date should inform the court clerk or judge immediately. The attorney who seeks the change should confirm that the clerk has recalendared the hearing and send a letter of confirmation to other counsel with a copy to the court. If the stipulation is not filed, local rule or custom may require a brief written notice to be filed. Such a notice, dated and signed, might read:

By agreement of the attorney for each party in this action, the date set for hearing on the motion of ____[name of party]____ **for** _____ **is changed from** ____[date]____ **to** ____[date]____.

§23.16   c. Form: Application for Order and Order Extending Time (or Setting New Hearing Date)

Copies: Original (to be presented to judge for signature and filed with proof of service); copies for service (one for each attorney of record and unrepresented party); office copies.

[Caption. See §§23.18– 23.19]

No. _____

APPLICATION FOR ORDER AND ORDER ____[EXTENDING TIME TO SERVE NOTICE OF MOTION / SETTING NEW HEARING DATE]____

§23.16 MOTIONS AND ORDERS

____[Name]____ declares:

1. I am an attorney for ____[plaintiff / defendant]____ ____[name]____ in this action.

2. This is an action for ____[nature of the case]____

[When extending time]

3. ____[Specify statute or rule]____ would normally require a notice of motion for ____[nature of motion]____ to be served before ____[date]____ in this action.

4. ____[Name of applicant]____ needs an extension of time until ____[date]____ to serve such a notice of motion for the following reasons: _____

[When resetting hearing date]

3. ____[Name of party who filed the notice of motion]____ has served on the undersigned a notice of motion for _____, that sets a hearing date of _____, 19____.

4. ____[Name of applicant]____ requests that the date of that hearing be changed to _____, 19____, for the following reasons: ____[State]____.

[Continue]

5. I have notified ____[name(s) of attorney(s) for other parties]____ that this application would be made by ____[describe method]____ and ____[he / she / they]____ ____[agreed / refused to agree]____ to setting the hearing on this new date.

[Add when appropriate]

6. The following extensions have previously been granted: (a) by stipulation of counsel, ____ days; (b) by the Court, ____ days.

[Continue]

I declare under penalty of perjury that the foregoing is true and correct and this declaration was executed on _____, 19____, at _____, California.

[Signature of attorney]

[Typed name]
Attorney for ____[name]____

ORDER

Good cause appearing,
IT IS ORDERED THAT

[When extending time]

____[name of moving party]____ have until _____, 19____, to serve and file a notice of motion for ____[nature of motion]____,

[When resetting hearing]

the hearing on ____[name of moving party]____'s motion for ____[nature of *motion*]____ **is changed from** ____[*old date*]____ **to** ____[*new date*]____ **at** ____[*time*]____ **in** ____[*e.g., Department No.* _____]____ **of this Court at** ____[*address*]____.

[*Continue*]

This order shall be served on all parties within _____ **days.**

Dated: _____   _____

                                                           Judge

Comment: If the applying party's attorney is unable to determine whether adverse counsel agree to the proposed extension or change, a statement of the reasons for this may be set out in paragraph (5) of this form.

A judge may decline to grant an ex parte application unless the applicant shows, as in paragraph (5), that notice was given to adverse counsel that the ex parte application would be made, or the reasons why such notice was not given. See discussion of Cal Rules of Ct Appendix, Div 1, §15 in §23.65.

§23.17 c. Motion Papers

A noticed motion proceeding is initiated by serving and filing a notice of motion (see §23.18) and supporting papers. Most notices of motion are accompanied by a memorandum of points and authorities (see §23.26) and one or more declarations or affidavits (see §23.36). The notice, memorandum, and declarations, are usually typed as separate papers, each with its own caption, but they are served and filed together with the notice on top, its caption specifying the other papers that are attached. When separate papers are bound together a tab at the bottom of the first sheet of each paper can be an aid to readers.

A copy of any paper on which the motion is based that has not already been served on the party to be notified must be served with the notice of motion. CCP §1010. Other papers can be attached as exhibits (see §23.44) to a memorandum of points and authorities or declaration.

§23.18 1. Form: Notice of Motion

Copies: Original (filed with court clerk with proof of service); copies for service (one for each attorney of record and unrepresented party); office copies.

§23.18   MOTIONS AND ORDERS

____[Name of attorney]____
____[Address]____
____[Telephone number]____
Attorney for ____[plaintiff / defendant]____ ____[name]____

[Title of Court]

[Title of case]

No. _____
NOTICE OF MOTION FOR
_____;
POINTS AND AUTHORITIES;
DECLARATION[S]; ____[SPECIFY OTHER ATTACHED PAPERS, E.G., ORDER SHORTENING TIME]____

[When required by local rule]
Hearing: ____[date and time]____
Department: _____
Estimated length: _____

To each party and attorney of record:
   PLEASE TAKE NOTICE that on ____[date set for hearing]____ at ____[hour when calendar is called]____ in ____[number or designation of Department or Courtroom]____ at ____[address]____, **California,** ____[plaintiff / defendant]____ ____[name]____ **will move the Court for** ____[description of the order sought]____.
   This motion is made ____[under code section(s) or rules that authorize the order sought]____ **on grounds that** ____[state]____.
   This motion is based on all pleadings, papers, and records filed in this action and on the attached memorandum of points and authorities ____[and declarations of ____[names of declarants]____]____ ____[and on such evidence as may be presented at the hearing]____.
Dated: _____

[Signature of attorney]

[Typed name]
Attorney for ____[name]____

Comment: The essential parts of a notice of motion are discussed in §§23.19–23.25. A notice of motion must conform to the general form and format requirements that apply to all court papers. Cal Rules of Ct 201, 501. These requirements are discussed and alternative forms are shown in 1 CALIFORNIA CIVIL PROCEDURE BEFORE TRIAL chap 22 (Cal CEB 1977). An illustrative typed notice of motion is shown in §22.22.
   Notices of motion must usually be supported by a memorandum of points and authorities, which is attached to the notice.

See §§23.23–23.35. In addition, one or more declarations are often attached to the notice. See §§23.36–23.43.

§23.19   a. Caption; Introduction

California Rules of Court 201 and 501 require the caption of a notice of motion to include the name, address, and telephone number of the moving party's attorney (see 1 CALIFORNIA CIVIL PROCEDURE BEFORE TRIAL §§22.12–22.14 (Cal CEB 1977)), the title of the court, the title and number of the case, and the nature of the paper. The title of the court includes the name of the court and county, and, if the notice is filed in a municipal or justice court, the name of the judicial district. See 1 CIV PROC BEFORE TRIAL §§22.16. Because a notice of motion is rarely the first paper filed in an action, the title of the case (names of the parties) may be in abbreviated form (see 1 CIV PROC BEFORE TRIAL §22.17), and the number already assigned to the case is typed on the form (see 1 CIV PROC BEFORE TRIAL §22.18). A defect in the title of the action does not render the paper invalid or ineffectual if it intelligibly refers to the action. CCP §1046.

The statement of the nature of the paper should embody a brief description of the nature of the order sought, *e.g.*, notice of motion for dismissal (CCP §581a), notice of motion for summary judgment. When other papers, *e.g.*, a memorandum of points and authorities or declarations, are attached to the notice of motion, these papers should be named in the caption of the notice, which will be the top sheet.

Some local rules require that the date and place of hearing be set forth below the caption of a notice of motion. See, *e.g.*, LA Super Ct R 28, §7; LA & SF LAW & MOTION MANUALS §2. While date and place of hearing are clearly required on supporting and opposition papers (see §§23.28, 23.39), it seems unnecessary on a notice of motion because the first page of the notice shows date, time, department, and address.

Other local rules require that the captions of motion papers state the length of time estimated for the hearing. See RIVERSIDE LAW & MOTION MEM §§2, 8 (March 7, 1977), which also requires that a special setting be arranged with the court in advance if the hearing is expected to take more than 30 minutes.

Attorneys customarily place below the caption of a notice of motion a line such as "To each party and attorney of record:" or

"To ____[names of parties]____." However, the line is not essential; an attached proof of service form (see §23.47) shows to whom notice is given.

§23.20   b. Time of Hearing

A notice of motion must state "when" the motion will be made (CCP §1010), and it is customary to specify the date set for hearing the motion and the hour when the hearing calendar for that day will be called. Failure to specify a date and time renders the notice ineffective. *Bohn v Bohn* (1913) 164 C 532, 536, 129 P 981, 983. See 4 Witkin, CALIFORNIA PROCEDURE, Proceedings Without Trial §9 (2d ed 1971).

When drafting a notice of motion, an attorney can determine the hearing date to use by (1) deciding when service will be effected (*i.e.*, the date of delivery or mailing to adverse counsel); (2) computing the minimum notice time required (unless an order shortening time is contemplated) and any maximum time; (3) and, if necessary, telephoning the court clerk or law and motion calendar clerk to learn the first available convenient calendar date within the period. See §§23.9–23.11 on computing notice time, and §§23.12, 23.14 on shortening and extending time.

§23.21   c. Place of Hearing

A notice of motion should specify the place where the motion will be heard. "Place" includes the address of the building in which the law and motion calendar is heard, and a designation of the department or courtroom.

§23.22   d. Nature of Order Sought

The notice of motion usually states the nature of the motion being made in terms of a description of the order sought. It is not necessary that the notice of motion spell out in detail all the terms of the order. For example, the notice might say, "a motion under Code of Civil Procedure section 437c for summary adjudication of issues" leaving it to the memorandum of points and authorities (see §§23.26–23.35), or proposed form of order attached to the moving papers (see §23.46) to state details. See *Cox v Tyrone Power Enterprises* (1942) 49 CA2d 383, 389, 121 P2d 829, 833 (order can be no more inclusive than motion requesting it).

§23.23 e. Grounds

A notice of motion must state the grounds on which the motion will be made. CCP §1010. The statement should define the issues for the adverse party and the court. *Hernandez v National Dairy Prods.* (1945) 126 CA2d 490, 493, 272 P2d 799. It is good practice to specify the code section or rule that provides for the order sought, but the notice of motion usually states grounds in a general or summary manner; the memorandum of points and authorities carries the argument and discusses relevant statutes and cases.

A total failure to state grounds for the motion may lead a trial judge to deny the motion, or an appellate court to vacate an order issued on a granted motion. See *Traders Credit Corp. v Superior Court* (1931) 111 CA 663, 665, 296 P 99 (dismissal vacated). Some courts have granted motions, or upheld orders, even though no grounds were stated in the notice of motion, if the grounds clearly appeared from papers filed with the notice. See 4 Witkin, CALIFORNIA PROCEDURE, Proceedings Without Trial §§10–11 (2d ed 1971).

Courts have also differed on whether grounds not stated in the notice of motion will be considered in support of the motion. Compare *Taliaferro v Riddle* (1959) 167 CA2d 567, 570, 334 P2d 950 (reversal of order not supported by either ground specified in notice); *Hernandez v National Dairy Prods., supra* (if new matter could be argued at hearing, purpose of notice of motion would be only to advise time and place) and *Westphal v Westphal* (1943) 61 CA2d 544, 550, 143 P2d 405, 408 (judgment of dismissal reversed) with *Tarman v Sherwin* (1961) 189 CA2d 49, 51, 10 CR 787 (affidavits, points and authorities, and other documents in court file, when referred to in the notice, can be considered in amplification of grounds). See also *Josephson v Superior Court* (1963) 219 CA2d 354, 362, 33 CR 196, 202 (statements in attached affidavits disregarded when consideration would have converted a special into a general appearance).

§23.24 f. Supporting Papers; Evidence

A notice of motion must "state" the papers, if any, on which it is to be based. CCP §1010. It is customary to state that the motion will be based on "all pleadings, papers, and records filed in the action." This may persuade the judge at the hearing to consider a document in the case file, the significance of which was not recognized when the motion papers were filed. However, if the attorney knows that part of a pleading, deposition, or other paper supports the motion, or provides basis for argument, it is a good practice to quote that part in an attached memorandum of points and authorities or declaration, or to attach a copy to the moving papers as an exhibit.

It is routine to refer to the "attached memorandum of points and authorities," because such a memorandum is usually required. See §23.26. Similarly, the evidence on which a motion is based is usually presented to the judge in the form of affidavits or declarations under penalty of perjury (see §23.26) and the notice of motion refers to each such document. For example: "the attached affidavit of Walter Johnson," or "the attached declarations of Walter Johnson, Charles Able, and George Smith."

Some attorneys routinely conclude the listing of papers on which a motion is based with a clause such as "and such oral and documentary evidence as may be presented at the hearing on this motion," may aid a later argument that testimony or a new exhibit should be admitted. However, many judges resist taking new evidence at the hearing and the clause is not a substitute for a presentation of facts and reasons to persuade the judge to accept the new evidence. See §23.57 on the judge's discretion to accept or reject testimony and new exhibits at the hearing. If a need to present evidence at the hearing arises, it is usually more effective to make a separate request for leave to present the evidence supported by a declaration of facts and reasons. If the need is known at the time the notice of motion is filed, the nature of the evidence should be specified in the notice and the reasons for its introduction stated in the attached declarations and memorandum. The notice should also state how much hearing time presentation of the evidence will require.

If the notice of motion mentions a paper that has not yet been served on adverse parties, a copy of that paper must be served and filed with the notice. CCP §1010; see §23.44.

§23.25   g. Date; Signature

The date that a notice of motion was served is normally shown on an attached proof of service form. See §23.47. Thus, although customary, it is not necessary to type a date on the notice. If the notice is served by mail, and is not accompanied by an affidavit or certificate of mailing, the date and place of mailing must be typed or written on the notice of motion itself. CCP §1013(b).

A notice of motion should be signed by the party's attorney of record, not the party. See *Jansson v National Steamship Co.* (1917) 34 CA 483, 486, 168 P 151; 1 CALIFORNIA CIVIL PROCEDURE BEFORE TRIAL §§1.40–1.41 (Cal CEB 1977) (attorney's right to control procedural matters). A subscription by the attorney's associate or office is normally sufficient. See *Caldwell v Geldreich* (1955) 137 CA2d 78, 82, 289 P2d 832 (vacationing attorney's name signed by associate). See also *Buell v Buell* (1891) 92 C 393, 396, 28 P 443 (newly employed attorney signed notice of motion to recall execution). However, no general statute or rule requires that notices of motion be signed, and the absence of a signature is ordinarily an irregularity that would not vitiate the notice. See 1 CIV PROC BEFORE TRIAL §7.33 (signature on complaint). See generally 4 Witkin, CALIFORNIA PROCEDURE, Proceedings Without Trial §8 (2d ed 1971).

2. Memorandum of Points and Authorities

§23.26   a. Requirement; Purpose

California Rules of Court 203(a) and 503(a) require a party filing a notice of motion to serve and file it with a memorandum of points and authorities to be relied on. The absence of a memorandum may be construed by the court as an admission that the motion is not meritorious and is cause for denial of the motion. Rules 203(a), 503(a). A court has discretion to hear and rule on a motion even though no memorandum is filed (*Kostal v Pullen* (1950) 36 C2d 528, 225 P2d 217; *Taliaferro v Coakley* (1960) 186 CA2d 258, 262, 9 CR 529), but a busy law and motion judge may find it easier to deny an unsupported motion.

A memorandum of points and authorities is not filed, however, merely because court rules require it. The party who makes a motion must convince the judge who hears it that the law supports issuance of the order sought. Persuasion should start with the memorandum even though the attorney will have a chance to present argument and cite authorities at the hearing on the motion (see §23.56). Some courts issue a tentative ruling based on the motion and response papers alone (see §23.53), and in other courts the judge will come to the hearing with a ruling already in mind.

§23.27 b. General Format

Local court rules may state, *e.g.*, that a mere list of code sections or case citations is insufficient and not in compliance with the rule requiring motions to be accompanied by a memorandum of points and authorities. See SF Super Ct R §6.2. Beyond this, no statute or rule prescribes a format for the body of a memorandum. An attorney drafting points and authorities must choose a format adapted to the nature and length of the argument to be presented.

If the right to the order sought clearly appears from a statute, it is usually sufficient to cite the statute, quoting relevant portions and adding a brief statement of its applicability to facts of the case. This brief memorandum can be typed under the heading "Points and Authorities" following the signature on a notice of motion, thus combining the notice and memorandum in a single paper. See *Kostal v Pullen* (1950) 36 C2d 528, 225 P2d 217 (citation of code sections in notice of motion sufficient compliance with rule requiring memorandum of points and authorities).

If more than one or two points and authorities are cited, it is better to draft the memorandum as a separate paper. Many attorneys use an outline format. See, *e.g.*, the illustrative memorandum in 1 CALIFORNIA CIVIL PROCEDURE BEFORE TRIAL §22.23 (Cal CEB 1977). Others prepare memoranda in the form of a written narrative with authorities cited in the argument, or use the format of an appellate brief.

§23.28 c. Caption

When a memorandum of points and authorities is typed at the end of a notice of motion, as part of that paper, it need be given no caption other than the heading "POINTS AND AUTHORITIES." When the memorandum is longer than one page, however, it is a good practice to prepare it as a separate paper with its own caption. This caption includes name, address, and telephone number of attorney, name of court, abbreviated title of case, case number, and nature of the paper. For example:

[*Name, etc., of attorney*]
Attorney for _____

[*Title of Court*]

[Title of Case]	No. _____ **POINTS AND AUTHORITIES** **SUPPORTING MOTION OF** ____[NAME]____ **FOR** _____ **Hearing:** ____[date and time]____ **Department:** _____

For a full discussion of caption requirements and alternatives, see 1 CALIFORNIA CIVIL PROCEDURE BEFORE TRIAL §§22.12–22.18 (Cal CEB 1977).

The local rules of many courts require that the date and time of hearing and the department number of the place of hearing be stated on the first page of all papers filed in connection with any noticed hearing. See, *e.g.*, LA Super Ct R §7, 28; LA & SF LAW & MOTION POLICY MANUALS §2. Although some local rules seem also to require that all motion papers show the length of time estimated for hearing (see §23.19), showing estimated time on the notice of motion should be sufficient unless the memorandum is filed later and gives a different estimate.

Even if not required by local rules, it is a good practice to indicate the date and place of hearing on the memorandum. Should it become separated from the notice of motion, it can then be more easily routed to the judge.

§23.29   d. Introduction

The body of a memorandum of points and authorities is often introduced by a statement such as "____[*Name of moving party*]____ submits this memorandum of points and authorities in support of his motion for an order ____[*nature of order sought*] ____." This introductory line serves no purpose unless it is used to describe more completely the nature of order or relief sought than was done in the caption.

A more useful introductory section or paragraph aids the judge by briefly identifying the parties, stating the present procedural status of the lawsuit, summarizing relevant pleadings, and otherwise placing the motion in context and showing the moving party's need for the order sought. Such an introductory section must be accurate and concise (normally no more than two pages), but can describe the litigation in a light favorable to the moving party.

§23.30 e. Table of Contents; Index

The reader of a lengthy or complex memorandum is aided by a concise table or index that shows topical headings or subjects discussed. The table should help the reader to locate separate discussions of different legal questions or issues, and may even provide a brief summary of the argument from point to point.

§23.31 f. Headings

It is helpful to subdivide the argument within a memorandum of points and authorities into separate sections and subsections and to give each section an appropriate heading. Headings should be as brief as possible, while characterizing the point being made in the section. They may be worded to forward the argument but should not be so lengthy as to be arguments themselves. For example, a general heading such as "The Law of Implied Indemnity," might be more effectively stated as "Cross-Complainant's Active Fault Precludes Implied Indemnity Recovery."

§23.32 g. Points; Arguments

The "points" in a memorandum of points and authorities are usually direct statements of points of law, or of the effect of legal rules on the facts of the case. The successive statements of points, each supported by one or more citations to a statute, case, or other authority (see §23.33), constitute the written argument being presented.

Points are sometimes presented in a textual format: sentences, followed by citations, organized in paragraphs. An outline format may also be used, with the argument being carried forward by a series of headings, statements of points, and paragraphs that quote from the authority cited, expand on the point, or note its particular applicability to the case at hand. For an example of points and authorities set out in one form of outline format, see 1 CALIFORNIA CIVIL PROCEDURE BEFORE TRIAL §22.23 (Cal CEB 1977).

Quotations should be as brief as possible without losing the point or becoming misleading. The memorandum should be persuasive and complete in itself; the judge cannot be expected to read texts or documents other than the moving papers.

§23.33 h. Authorities; Citations

Each point, or statement of a legal rule in a memorandum should be supported by citation to a statute, court rule, reported decision, textbook, law review article, or other authority. Generally, it is more effective to cite one statute or case, and point out its specific applicability, than to support a point with "string" citations.

A California Supreme Court opinion carries more weight than a Court of Appeal opinion unless the latter is more on point or more recent. Normally, one Supreme Court citation and the latest court of appeal case, provide all the support needed for a point unless the attorney needs to show how a rule has been applied in a variety of factual settings.

Local court rule or policy may set standards for the manner in which authorities are to be cited. LA & SF LAW & MOTION POLICY MANUALS §4, for example, states guidelines that could be used in any county:

A. *Citations.* Citation of California cases must be by reference to the Official Reports and West's California Reporter, and should indicate the volume number, the first page of the case, and the specific page or pages on which the pertinent matters appear in the Official Reports, and the year of such decision.

B. *Statutes.* Citation of California legislation should include the title of the code, the code section, and the effective date of enactment and/or last amendment.

C. *Reports of other jurisdictions.* If counsel offers case authority in support of his position other than California authority, it is better practice to attach a copy of any case upon which counsel primarily relies to the moving papers.

D. *Organization.* It is better practice to set forth a brief summary or quotation of the relevant substance of the cited authority and to point out in what way it bears on the matter before the court.

Copying of headnotes is bad practice. Each case cited for other than preliminary or elementary matters should be discussed in terms of its relationship to the case at bar.

Some local court rules suggest that citations to statutes, cases, and other authorities should be underlined. Otherwise, the use of capital letters and underlining is a matter of personal preference.

For a guide to citation style, see CALIFORNIA STYLE MANUAL (2d revised ed (1977) by Robert E. Formichi), available from the

Department of General Services, Publications Section, P.O. Box 1051, North Highlands, CA 95660.

§23.34   i. Conclusion

A concluding section that summarizes major points and stating the nature of the order sought will help the reader of the memorandum to arrive at the desired conclusion. This section should be a short aid to persuasion, not a verbatim repetition of points that only burdens the judge with additional reading.

§23.35   j. Subscription

There is no requirement that a memorandum of points and authorities be dated or signed. Most attorneys do so, however, perhaps to indicate that they take responsibility for the accuracy of its contents at least through the date indicated. A common subscription is:

Dated: _____   **Respectfully submitted,**
                                                [*Signature*]

                                                [*Typed name*]
                               Attorney for ____[*name*]____

3. Declarations and Affidavits

§23.36   a. Nature; Purpose

Declarations and affidavits are written statements used to present facts to the judge who must rule on a motion. Declarations are made and signed under penalty of perjury (CCP §2015.5; see §23.42), and affidavits are made under oath and attested to, ordinarily by a notary public (CCP §2003; see §23.43). ("Declaration" is used generally in this book to cover both a declaration under penalty of perjury and an affidavit.) These written statements are used in motion proceedings as a substitute for sworn oral testimony. See Evid C §§135, 225 (a declarant is a person who makes an oral or written verbal expression).

Motions are usually made and determined on declarations alone. See *Beckett v Kaynar Mfg. Co.* (1958) 49 C2d 695, 698 n3, 321 P2d 749, 751 n3. Declarations are used both to fill factual gaps in the record and as a means for stating facts in a direct and logical order, sparing the judge the need to ferret them out of the case record. Some motions are granted although not supported by a declaration. See *e.g., Black Bros. Co. v Superior Court* (1968) 265 CA2d 501, 507, 71 CR 344, 348.

Other sources of evidence and facts in a motion proceeding include allegations in verified pleadings, deposition transcripts, answers to interrogatories, admissions in pleadings or to requests for admissions, documents and exhibits filed with the motion papers or already on file in the action, and facts judicially noticed. See generally §§29.44–29.66 (evidence on summary judgment motions).

In California, the declaration form, which need not be notarized, is more widely used than the affidavit form. A declaration, in the form prescribed by CCP §2015.5, is as valid and effective in support of a motion as an affidavit, if the declaration is executed in California or another state that permits declarations under penalty of perjury. CCP §2015.5. If the statement is executed outside California, the affidavit form may be necessary. Even if the other state permits declarations under penalty of perjury, an affidavit may be more convenient because an out-of-state declaration must usually have attached to it a copy of the state law that authorizes declarations, to assure that the California judge will accept it.

Whichever form is used, it is important to conform strictly to content and execution requirements (see §§23.41–23.43). A judge may disregard a statement that is improperly phrased or executed. See *Palm Springs Alpine Estates, Inc. v Superior Court* (1967) 255 CA2d 883, 888, 63 CR 618, 621.

b. General Format

§23.37   (1) Form: Declaration in Support of Motion

Copies: Original (filed with court clerk); copies for service (one for each attorney of record and unrepresented party); office copies.

[Caption. See §§23.18–23.19]

No. _____

DECLARATION OF ____[NAME]____
IN SUPPORT OF MOTION

Hearing: ____[date and time]____
Department: _____

____[Name]____ **declares:**

1. **I am** ____[identity of declarant; see §23.40]____.

§23.38   MOTIONS AND ORDERS   32

2. ____[Continue with statements of fact in successively numbered paragraphs; see §23.41]____.

[If executed outside California]

____[8]____. ____[Citation to statute]____ **of the State of** _____, ____[a copy of which is attached]____ **permits declarations under penalty of perjury executed as below to be used as affidavits.**

[Continue]

I declare under penalty of perjury that the foregoing is true and correct and that this declaration was executed at ____[name of city or county and state]____ **on** ____[date]____.

_____
[Signature of declarant]

[Typed name]

Comment: A declaration should conform to the form and format requirements applicable to all court papers. See generally 1 CALIFORNIA CIVIL PROCEDURE BEFORE TRIAL chap 22 (Cal CEB 1977); for sample typed declaration, see 1 CIV PROC BEFORE TRIAL §22.24; see §§23.39–23.42 on form and content of declarations in support of motions.

§23.38   (2) Form: Affidavit in Support of Motion

Copies: Original (filed with court clerk); copies for service (one for each attorney of record and unrepresented party); office copies.

[Caption. See §§23.18–23.19]

No. _____
AFFIDAVIT OF ____[NAME]____
IN SUPPORT OF MOTION____

Hearing: ____[date and time]____
Department: _____

State of _____, **County of** _____
____[Name of affiant]____, **being sworn, says:**
  1. **I am** ____[identity of affiant; see §23.40]____.
  2. ____[Continue with statements of fact in successively numbered paragraphs; see §23.41]____.

_____
[Signature of affiant]

[Typed name]

Subscribed and sworn to before me on ____[date]____ **at** ____[state and county]____

[Signature of notary or officer]
───────────────────────────────
[Typed name]
----[Title, e.g., Notary Public]----
[Notary's or officer's Seal]

Comment: An affidavit should conform to the form and format requirements applicable to all court papers. See generally 1 CALIFORNIA CIVIL PROCEDURE BEFORE TRIAL chap 22 (Cal CEB 1977). See §§23.39–23.41, 23.43 on form and contents of affidavits in support of motions.

§23.39 c. Caption; Introduction

A declaration or affidavit is usually drafted as a separate paper and most attorneys use the caption prescribed for court papers by Cal Rules of Ct 201, 501, even though it is attached to a notice of motion. See generally, 1 CALIFORNIA CIVIL PROCEDURE BEFORE TRIAL §§22.12–22.18 (Cal CEB 1977). Because the declaration is filed after other papers in the case, the name of the first party on each side is sufficient. CCP §422.40. See 1 CIV PROC BEFORE TRIAL §22.17. A defect in the title of the action does not render the paper invalid or ineffectual if it intelligibly refers to the action. CCP §1046.

The local rules of many courts require that the date and time of hearing and the number or designation of the department to which it is assigned be stated on the first page of all papers filed in connection with any noticed hearing. See, *e.g.*, LA Super Ct Rule 28, §7; LA & SF LAW & MOTION POLICY MANUALS §2. Although some local rules seem also to require that all motion papers show the length of time estimated for hearing (see §23.19), showing estimated time on the notice of motion should be sufficient unless the declaration is filed later and gives a different estimate. Even if not required by local rule, it is a good practice to indicate the date and place of hearing on a declaration.

In an affidavit, it is customary to follow the caption with a line stating the "venue," the state and county (or other subdivision) where the affidavit was executed and notarized. Failure of the affidavit to show where the oath or affirmation of the affiant was administered does not by itself invalidate the affidavit. See *County Bank v Jack* (1906) 148 C 437, 440, 83 P 705 (venue line omitted). The venue line or lines may, with equal effect, be

§23.40   MOTIONS AND ORDERS

placed at the beginning of the jurat or notary's certification (see §23.43).

The body of a declaration is introduced with a line such as "John Jones declares:" or "I, Mary Smith, declare under penalty of perjury that:". Affidavits usually begin "John Jones, being sworn, says:" or "I, Mary Smith, being duly sworn, state as follows:".

§23.40   d. Identity and Competence of Declarant

The first paragraph of the body of a declaration or affidavit usually identifies the declarant by stating his or her title or relationship to the lawsuit. For example:

1. **I am the plaintiff in this action.**
1. **I am an attorney of record for the defendant Walter Johnson.**
1. **I am, and have been since July 4, 1976, the Vice-President in charge of marketing for the defendant, Widget Corporation.**

Generally, any person who would be competent to testify as a witness about a matter is competent to make a declaration or an affidavit. See *McLellan v McLellan* (1972) 23 CA3d 343, 359, 100 CR 258, 268. Evidence Code §700 provides that all persons are qualified to be witnesses unless disqualified by statute. See Evid C §701 (disqualification for inability to express oneself, or to understand the duty to tell the truth).

Competence to make a declaration usually refers to the requirement that statements about a matter are ordinarily inadmissible unless the witness has personal knowledge of the matter. Evid C §702; see generally §23.41 on admissibility of matter stated. Thus, one or more paragraphs of a declaration are often used to show that the declarant directly observed or had personal knowledge of the facts stated.

Some local court rules relating to summary judgment motions appear to require a declarant to state, *e.g.*,

2. **I have firsthand personal knowledge of all facts stated in this declaration, and if called as a witness I could and would testify competently to them under oath.**

See LA & SF LAW & MOTION POLICY MANUALS §72. Such a statement is a conclusion that may be held insufficient by a judge who feels that personal knowledge must be shown by factual statements. See *Fisher v Cheeseman* (1968) 260 CA2d 503, 506,

67 CR 258 ("That which is required is not a sworn statement that the affiant would so testify but a showing that he can competently do so.") LA & SF LAW & MOTION POLICY MANUALS §72 also state that declarations should "State facts which the declarant relies upon as establishing his personal knowledge of the substantive facts asserted. Whether or not the conclusory clause is used, facts showing personal knowledge should be stated in the declaration. For example:

> 3. I was at the corner of Fourth and Main Streets on April 1, 1977 and saw _____.
>
> 3. On May 1, 1977, I received a letter signed by John Smith that stated in part: _____.
>
> 3. I am the custodian of records for Mercy Hospital.

§23.41   e. Matter Stated; Admissibility

The body of a declaration or affidavit is a series of statements, usually set out in separately numbered paragraphs. The judge hearing the motion may decline to consider statements in a declaration on the same grounds that a trial judge would sustain an objection to proferred testimony. See *McLellan v McLellan* (1972) 23 CA3d 343, 359, 100 CR 258, 268; *Mayo v Beber* (1960) 177 CA2d 544, 551, 2 CR 405, 409. Admissible statements are evidence, but the judge is not bound to accept them as true except in some summary judgment situations. *Ware v Stafford* (1962) 206 CA2d 232, 238, 24 CR 153, 157 (affidavit is not proof until accepted as such by the court). Filing a declaration in support of a motion is normally the equivalent of offering it in evidence; it need not be offered formally in evidence at the hearing. See *Waller v Waller* (1970) 3 CA3d 456, 465, 83 CR 533, 538.

Declarations should state evidentiary facts rather than ultimate facts or legal conclusions. *Ware v Stafford* (1962) 206 CA2d 232, 237, 24 CR 153, 157. The facts should be set forth positively; a declaration that states only the conclusions or opinions of the declarant is insufficient. See *Tri-State Mfg. Co. v Superior Court* (1964) 224 CA2d 442, 445, 36 CR 750. One test for whether a statement in a declaration should be considered is whether a perjury prosecution could be based on the statement if it were false. See *Mack v Superior Court* (1968) 259 CA2d 7, 10, 66 CR 280.

Opinions stated in a declaration are sometimes considered when the declaration shows (1) the opinion is rationally based on the declarant's perception and is helpful to a clear understanding of his testimony (Evid C §800), or (2) the declarant is qualified to testify as an expert on the subject (Evid C §801). See Zack, *The 1973 Summary Judgment Act—New Teeth for an Old Tiger* 48 CAL SBJ 654, 657 (1973).

A declarant, like a witness (see Evid C §702), should normally state only facts personally known to him. The statute authorizing the order sought may also specify that matter in declarations must be based on personal knowledge. See, *e.g.*, CCP §437c (declarations on motion for summary judgment). Thus, a statement made "on information and belief" may be disregarded (*Franklin v Nat C. Goldstone Agency* (1949) 33 C2d 628, 631, 204 P2d 37, 39; *Judd v Superior Court* (1976) 60 CA3d 38, 43, 131 CR 246, 248) unless the fact stated is one that by its nature could not be known directly and positively (*e.g.*, another's intent). See *Brown v Happy Valley Fruit Growers, Inc.* (1929) 206 C 515, 520, 274 P 977, 979; *Fielder v Superior Court* (1963) 213 CA2d 60, 28 CR 597. Statements made in declarations and affidavits are presumed to be made on personal knowledge unless stated to be made on information and belief. *Weathers v Kaiser Foundation Hosps.* (1971) 5 C3d 98, 106, 95 CR 516, 521.

Hearsay statements may also be disregarded unless admissible under an exception to the hearsay rule. *Pacific Air Lines, Inc. v Superior Court* (1965) 231 CA2d 591, 42 CR 70. See also *Weathers v Kaiser Foundation Hosps.* (1971) 5 C3d 98, 105, 95 CR 516, 520 (although declarant's statement might have been based on hearsay, it might also have been based on observation, and could thus be considered under the presumption that it was made on personal knowledge).

An attorney drafting a declaration should consider not only the admissibility and persuasiveness of what is said, but also that the declaration may be used to cross-examine the declarant at a later deposition or at trial. Further, while the declaration must state enough factual matter to be persuasive in support of the motion, it should not be so detailed as to be tedious or unreadable. Litigation tactics may also dictate not volunteering some of the facts known to the declarant.

f. Subscription

§23.42 (1) Declaration

A declaration under penalty of perjury must be signed by the declarant and certified or declared to be true "under penalty of perjury." CCP §2015.5. The code section says that the certification or declaration may be in substantially the following form:

I certify (or declare) under penalty of perjury that the foregoing is true and correct.

This statement is normally placed at the end of the declaration. See *People v Pierce* (1967) 66 C2d 53, 59, 56 CR 817, 821 (end is preferred, not required, place). A statement declared to be made "under penalty of perjury" is acceptable even though the statutory words "true and correct" have been omitted. See *Pacific Air Lines, Inc. v Superior Court* (1965) 231 CA2d 587, 42 CR 68.

Either "certify" or "declare" can be used, but not both. Most lawyers use "declare" in all cases unless a particular statute calls for a certification or the paper is called a certificate. Other lawyers use "certify" when the declaration is signed by an attorney or court official.

The date and place of execution must be stated. CCP §2015.5; *People v United Bonding Ins. Co.* (1969) 272 CA2d 441, 443, 77 CR 310. Although an undated declaration may be disregarded, courts will not reject a declaration in which date and place of execution are somehow shown.

§23.43 (2) Affidavit

It is customary for the affiant to sign an affidavit, but an affidavit with a proper jurat is sufficient without the affiant's signature unless a particular statute or rule requires a signed affidavit. *Petaluma v White* (1907) 152 C 190, 195, 92 P 177; *Dodge v Free* (1973) 32 CA3d 436, 443, 108 CR 311, 316.

The jurat of an affidavit is a certificate stating when, where, and before whom the affidavit was sworn (or affirmed as permitted by CCP §2097). See form in §23.38. A statement without a jurat is not sufficient to serve as an affidavit. *People v United Bonding Ins. Co.* (1969) 272 CA2d 441, 443, 77 CR 310. The jurat may take different forms in other states or if made by an officer other than a notary public. Code of Civil Procedure §§2012–2015 specify the persons and officers in California ("any officer authorized to administer oaths") and elsewhere that may certify affidavits.

A notary's seal stamped near his or her signature should indicate the county in which the notary's bond is filed and the date on which the notary's commission expires. See Govt C §8207.

However, an otherwise sufficient affidavit is valid without the seal. See *Reclamation Dist. v Snowball* (1911) 160 C 695, 697, 118 P 514.

§23.44   4. Other Documents and Exhibits

Pleadings and papers on file in the action are before the judge and may be referred to in the memorandum of points and authorities and declarations. However, if the attorney wants the allegations of a pleading to be accepted as evidence in support of the motion, the pleading must have been verified and the allegations must be in the form of evidentiary facts rather than ultimate facts or conclusions. See *Continental Baking Co. v Katz* (1968) 68 C2d 512, 532, 67 CR 761, 773. Even though the clerk's file of the case will be given to the judge hearing the motion, a copy of the pertinent allegations or papers can be attached to the motion papers to save the judge the need to search the file.

Contracts, letters, business records, and other documents can be used to support a motion. The attorney should either (a) obtain agreement of adverse counsel that the document (or a copy) may be used; (b) include in supporting declarations authenticating statements that permit the document's admission in evidence over authentication (Evid C §1400), best evidence (Evid C §1500), and hearsay (Evid C §1200) objections. See *Dugar v Happy Tiger Records, Inc.* (1974) 41 CA3d 811, 815, 116 CR 412, 414. The declaration that authenticates a document may also incorporate it by reference. For example:

On April 12, 1977 I entered into a written agreement with Walter Johnson. A true and complete ____*[e.g., photocopy]*____ **of that agreement, marked Exhibit A, is attached to this declaration and is incorporated by this reference.**

If the document is in the control of the moving party, his attorney should attach copies to the motion papers and bring the original to the hearing to defeat any best evidence objection that might then be made. If the document is in the hands of an adverse party, a notice or subpena directing its production at the hearing can be served with the motion papers. CCP §1987(b)-(c); see §29.59. A copy, or other secondary evidence, may then be used if the original is not produced. Evid C §1503(a). A subpena duces tecum may be used to obtain production of originals controlled by nonparties (see CALIFORNIA CIVIL DISCOVERY PRAC-

TICE §10.6 (Cal CEB 1975)); copies may be used if the originals are not produced (Evid C §1502).

If a document is offered to prove the truth of matters stated in it, the document is hearsay evidence (see Evid C §1200) and the declaration that accompanies it should contain statements that establish its admissibility under one of the exceptions to the hearsay rule (see Evid C §§1220–1341). A document offered only to show its existence and terms is not subject to a hearsay objection. See generally Jefferson, CALIFORNIA EVIDENCE BENCHBOOK §§1.1–1.7 (1972).

§23.45 5. Request That Court Take Judicial Notice; Form

A moving party may ask that judicial notice be taken of facts that support a motion. See *Parker v Twentieth Century-Fox Film Corp.* (1970) 3 C3d 176, 181, 89 CR 737, 740 (motion for summary judgment). The court must take judicial notice of the matters specified in Evid C §451, but it is good practice in any case to give the notice of request that Evid C §453 states is a condition of requiring the court to judicially notice matters specified in Evid C §452. Local court rules may also prescribe procedures for obtaining copies of records to be judicially noticed. See *e.g.*, LA & SF LAW & MOTION POLICY MANUALS §§41–43. On judicial notice generally, see CALIFORNIA PERSONAL INJURY PROOF chap 20 (Cal CEB 1970); Jefferson, CALIFORNIA EVIDENCE BENCHBOOK §§47.1–47.6 (CCJ-CEB 1972); Witkin, CALIFORNIA EVIDENCE §§150–191 (2d ed 1966).

The request may be made by inserting a paragraph in the notice of motion or the memorandum of points and authorities. For an example, see 1 CALIFORNIA CIVIL PROCEDURE BEFORE TRIAL §9.13 (Cal CEB 1977). It is often more convenient to attach to the motion papers an additional paper called a Request for Judicial Notice.

[Caption. See §§23.18–23.19]

No. _____

REQUEST FOR JUDICIAL NOTICE

Hearing: ____[date]____
Department: _____

____[Name of moving party]____, **in support of his motion for** ____[nature of motion]____, **asks this Court to take judicial notice of the following:**

1. Under California Evidence Code section ____[451 / 452]____, ____[specify, in separately numbered paragraphs, each fact or document to be noticed and reasons why the court must or may take judicial notice of the item]____.

Dated: _____

[Signature of attorney]

[Typed name]
Attorney for ____[name]____

Comment: Caption requirements are discussed, with forms, in 1 CIV PROC BEFORE TRIAL §§22.12–22.19.

§23.46   6. Proposed Order

Attorneys often attach the form of a proposed order to the moving papers. This can aid the judge by showing exactly what the court is being asked to order and by requiring only a signature, not drafting time. The judge can also sign the order with confidence that adversaries served with the order form in advance had the chance to argue against even its harshest terms.

For discussion and a form, see §§23.58, 23.60.

§23.47   7. Proof of Service

The last paper in the group of papers served and filed to initiate a noticed motion proceeding is normally a proof of service form. On service and filing of the papers, see §§23.9–23.16. Motion papers are often served by mail (see §23.10) and a proof of service by mail form can be completed before the papers are mailed and filed. A conformed copy of the proof of service form is attached to each set of copies of the motion papers served. For a discussion of methods of service, and a form of proof of service by mail, see 1 CALIFORNIA CIVIL PROCEDURE BEFORE TRIAL §§8.59–8.69 (Cal CEB 1977).

§23.48   D. Opposition Procedures

A party on whom a notice of motion is served can either (1) do nothing, thus acquiescing in the issuance of the order sought; (2) contact opposing counsel to see whether a modified order, different procedure, or voluntary act would satisfy the moving party; (3) file and serve papers in opposition to the motion (see §§23.48–23.50) and attend the hearing to argue against issuance of the order, or for a modified order, (see §§23.55–23.57); or (4) use some form of collateral response (see §23.51).

There is no specific requirement that papers opposing a motion be filed or that the opposing party attend the hearing. The judge may deny the motion if the moving papers are deficient or an insufficient showing has been made. However, absent opposition papers, the judge will be inclined to make a tentative ruling (see §23.54) on the basis of the moving party's papers. Such a ruling is often difficult to change by argument or papers presented at the hearing. Some judges consider the failure to file opposition papers or to attend the hearing as a waiver of objection to issuance of the order sought.

§23.49   1. Memorandum of Points and Authorities in Opposition to Motion

The general principles for preparing a memorandum of points and authorities discussed in §§23.26–23.35 apply to preparation of memoranda in opposition to motions. The memorandum is captioned as are other court papers (see §§23.18–23.19) and the nature of the paper may be stated as, for example:

> No. _____
>
> **MEMORANDUM OF POINTS AND AUTHORITIES IN OPPOSITION TO** ____[NAME OF MOVING PARTY] ____'S **MOTION FOR** _____
> **Hearing:** ____[date and time]____
> **Department:** _____
> **Estimated length:** _____

The caption of an opposition memorandum should show the date and time at which the hearing is scheduled and the department where it is to be heard. Some local court rules require this information. See, e.g., LA Super Ct Rule §7, 28; LA & SF LAW & MOTION POLICY MANUALS §2. If there are multiple parties in the case, the caption must specifically identify the moving party and the nature of his motion. Cal Rules of Ct 201(c)(6), 501(c)(6). See §23.19 on local rules that require a statement of the estimated length of the hearing.

The organization of the body of the memorandum should be patterned to some extent as a rejoinder to the moving party's memorandum. If the moving party did not summarize the case for the hearing judge (see §23.29), the opposing party can aid the judge by doing so. Inaccuracies in the moving party's statement of issues or facts can be corrected. A table of contents or index can be as helpful in a lengthy opposing memorandum as in the memorandum of the moving party. See §23.30.

The opposition memorandum should be organized so that the judge can easily compare the points made in the moving party's memorandum with authorities and discussion that refute those points. Thus, the suggestions for paragraphing and headings in a moving party's memorandum (see §23.31) may be modified in an opposing memorandum to highlight the parallel sections of each. The attorney drafting an opposition memorandum can decide whether to follow the order of argument used by the moving party, or to lead with the opponent's best points or with points not discussed by the moving party. See §§23.32–23.35 for discussion of the manner of stating points and arguments, citing authorities, conclusions, and subscriptions.

An opposition memorandum can also state objections to all or part of the moving party's declarations or affidavits. Generally, the same objections that can be made to testimony and exhibits at a trial can be directed to declarations. See §23.41; CALIFORNIA TRIAL OBJECTIONS (Cal CEB 1967).

§23.50   2. Declarations in Opposition to Motion

Declarations and affidavits filed and served in opposition to a motion contain statements of the facts that are the basis for denial or modification of the order sought by the moving party, and may contain denials of facts stated in the moving party's affidavits. Motions may be opposed without filing a declaration. *Los Angeles v Superior Court* (1969) 271 CA2d 292, 295, 76 CR 256, 258. These denials are not the formal denials used in pleadings, but should be coupled with the declarant's positive statement of what is true. The declaration in opposition may also contain statements that call the judge's attention to conflicts between moving and opposing declarations and state facts showing why the latter should be believed and the former considered unpersuasive or not pertinent.

The general principles for preparing a declaration or affidavit discussed in §§23.36–23.43 apply to preparing declarations in opposition to a motion. The declaration is captioned as are other court papers (see §§23.18–23.19) and the nature of the paper stated as, *e.g.*:

DECLARATION OF
____[NAME OF DECLARANT]____
IN OPPOSITION TO
____[NAME OF MOVING PARTY]____'s
MOTION FOR _____

Hearing: ____[date and time]____
Department: _____

The caption of an opposition declaration should show the date and time at which the hearing is scheduled and the department where it is to be heard. Some local court rules require this information See *e.g.*, LA Super Ct R §7, 28; LA & SF Law & Motion Policy Manuals §2. See §23.52 on when opposition papers should be filed.

§23.51   3. Collateral Response

In addition to a direct response to the motion, an opponent may have available one or more forms of collateral attack. For example, the party may make a special appearance, filing papers and attending the hearing, not to argue the merits of the motion, but solely to contend that insufficient notice was given or that the court has no jurisdiction of the party. See, *e.g.*, *Bohn v Bohn* (1913) 164 C 532, 538, 129 P 981, 984; *Tate v Superior Court* (1975) 45 CA3d 925, 929, 119 CR 835, 837. See generally 1 Witkin, California Procedure, Jurisdiction §124 (2d ed 1970) and 4 Witkin, California Procedure, Proceedings Without Trial §7 (2d ed 1971).

§23.52   4. Time To File and Serve

Local court rules may require that memoranda of points and authorities and declarations in opposition to a motion be served and filed a specified number of days or hours before the hearing date. See, *e.g.*, LA & SF Law & Motion Policy Manuals §16B (filed at least two court days preceding the scheduled hearing). Even if no local rule controls, it is good practice to serve and file opposition papers several days before the hearing date so that they can be considered by the law and motion judge, or research assistant, at the same time as the moving party's papers.

If papers are not served at least 72 hours before the time of the hearing, service should be by personal delivery. See LA & SF LAW & MOTION POLICY MANUALS §16D. The judge can then be assured that by the time of hearing each side has had a chance to consider points made and evidence offered by the other side.

Counsel who wish to file or serve a paper at or soon before a hearing should be prepared to show reasons for delay, or the judge may decline to consider the papers. At the hearing, the judge may call for additional memoranda, declarations, or other papers, and set the terms for their filing and service.

§23.53   E. Tentative Rulings

Several courts have a policy of issuing tentative or proposed rulings on motions. These rulings show the judge's intended disposition of the motion based on conclusions drawn from the memoranda of points and authorities, declarations, and other papers filed by the parties. See, *e.g.*, LA & SF LAW & MOTION POLICY MANUALS §14. These tentative rulings are available to counsel on the day of the hearing or, in some courts, on the previous day.

The purpose of tentative rulings is to encourage counsel to waive argument at the hearing, or to focus argument on matters actually in dispute.

An attorney in whose favor a tentative ruling has been made may attend the hearing to argue for a further or different order, or to be sure that adverse counsel do not persuade the judge to reverse or change the tentative ruling. The attorney for a moving party favored by a tentative ruling who prefers not to attend the hearing, must notify the clerk of the appropriate department (*e.g.*, law and motion) that he is willing to submit the matter on the tentative ruling. Otherwise, despite the tentative ruling, the motion may be denied at the hearing if only the opposing party attends, or put off calendar if neither party attends or has notified the clerk.

An attorney who is not satisfied with a tentative ruling should attend the hearing to argue for a change or modification, and may offer to present additional points and authorities, declarations, or evidence. Even an attorney who acquiesces in an unfavorable ruling may wish to attend the hearing to be sure that the other party will not attend the hearing to ask for a different or further order.

§23.54   F. Reply and Supplementary Papers

A moving party's attorney who has been served with papers in opposition to the motion should consider whether there are arguments or facts in those papers that could be challenged or refuted, and whether to file reply papers or to rejoin orally at the hearing. When opposition papers have been filed shortly before the hearing (see §23.52), there is little time to file reply papers before the judge or a court research assistant begins to examine the motion and opposition papers. Further, some judges do not want to have to consider additional papers and may prefer counsel to present new points orally at the hearing along with an offer to supply additional written points and authorities and declarations. If reply papers are prepared, counsel should serve them on the attorneys for adverse parties as soon as possible and extra copies should be brought to the hearing in case last-minute service is not effected.

Either a moving or adverse party's attorney may consider whether additional papers should be filed to supplement the original moving or opposition papers. Another party in the action may even wish to file memoranda or declarations in support of a motion.

G. The Hearing

§23.55   1. Attendance

No statute or rule requires the attorney for the moving party, or for an adverse party, to attend the hearing on a motion. See *Ensher, Alexander & Barsoom, Inc. v Ensher* (1964) 225 CA2d 318, 325, 37 CR 327, 331. The motion is deemed to have been made when the notice of motion was served and filed (CCP §1005.5), and Cal Rules of Ct 202(c) and 502(c), relating to failure to attend the hearing on a demurrer, appear not to apply to motions. See generally, 4 Witkin, CALIFORNIA PROCEDURE, Proceedings Without Trial §22 (2d ed 1971). The parties themselves are not normally required to be present at motion hearings, and their presence may be a distraction.

An attorney who does not wish to attend a hearing should contact adverse counsel to see whether all will agree to submission of the motion on the papers filed. The attorney should also notify the clerk that the motion is submitted for decision without attendance of counsel. This permits the court to move more quickly through the calendar, and will assure that the judge will not put the matter off-calendar or interpret nonattendance as lack of interest in a ruling.

There are, however, several positive reasons for attorneys to attend a hearing. For example, adverse counsel may attend and present new arguments, authorities, or evidence that could be refuted. The judge may ask for clarification of some point raised in the motion or opposition papers. If the attorneys could not informally solve the dispute about which the motion was made, and it was worth counsel's time and effort to prepare motion or opposition papers, it should also be worth the time to attend the hearing.

A court's law and motion calendar for a given day normally lists several cases that will be called in the listed order beginning at a specified hour, and the attorneys on the first case should be ready to present argument at that time. Attorneys on subsequent cases should also be present and ready because early cases may be taken off the calendar or submitted without argument. Attorneys whose cases are low on the list can consult the court clerk to determine the time at which the case is likely to be called.

§23.56   2. Argument

The hearing gives counsel a personal chance to persuade the judge to decide the motion in the client's favor. It also permits counsel to see how the judge and adverse counsel perceive particular aspects of the case, and to clear up confusion and misconception. The argument should be planned, not merely a rehash of points made in the filed memorandum and declarations. Oral argument at a hearing is a privilege, not a right, and the court has discretion to limit argument or deny it. See *Gillette v Gillette* (1960) 180 CA2d 777, 781, 4 CR 700, 703.

If possible, the attorney who prepared the motion or opposition papers should attend the hearing and should be familiar with the facts of the case and all papers in the file. The judge may ask counsel such procedural questions as:

(1) Who are the parties and their attorneys?

(2) Have all parties been served?

(3) Is there an at-issue memorandum or certificate of readiness on file? Has there been, or been set, a trial setting, settlement, or pretrial conference? Is the case set for trial?

(4) Does the order sought affect the procedural status?

(5) Have all local rules applicable to the motion been complied with?

(6) Have all proofs of service and declarations or affidavits been properly executed?

(7) Has discovery been completed or is case within 30-days of trial?

(8) Is there any reason (*e.g.*, other motions, trial setting or settlement conference) why the file or any part of it may be unavailable to the court?

In preparing for oral argument at the hearing, the attorney should also consider such questions as:

(1) Were any arguments in favor (or against) the motion omitted from the memoranda?

(2) Is new evidence available or needed?

(3) What points in counsel's own memorandum or documents need to be highlighted?

(4) What points in the opponent's documents are easily or surely refutable?

(5) What reasons, if any, might give the judge difficulty in reaching a favorable conclusion?

(6) Are there points of compromise that might be suggested if the judge seems to be leaning the other way?

At the hearing, an attorney can begin the argument by stating points that support his position, but should be flexible, prepared to answer questions when they are asked, and ready to shift to issues that the judge wants discussed. Mention of a statute or case should include the page where the judge can find the citation in the motion or opposition papers, and it can be helpful to tab portions of declarations or documents to which reference may be necessary.

Ordinarily, no transcript will be made of oral argument on a motion unless one of the attorneys arranges before the hearing for a court reporter to be present.

§23.57 3. Presenting Evidence

Some courts have a policy against receiving evidence that is not in documentary form. Judges rarely welcome testimony at the hearing or exhibits that could have been, but were not, served and filed with the motion papers. A judge has the power to determine a motion on declarations alone and has discretion to refuse to hear oral testimony at the hearing on a motion. See

Beckett v Kaynar Mfg. Co. (1958) 49 C2d 695, 698 n3, 321 P2d 749, 751 n3; *Crocker Citizens Bank v Knapp* (1967) 251 CA2d 875, 880, 60 CR 66, 70; *Haldane v Haldane* (1962) 210 CA2d 587, 593, 26 CR 670, 673. On the other hand, the judge has discretion to receive testimony and exhibits at the hearing. See *Continental Baking Co. v Katz* (1968) 68 C2d 512, 524 n7, 67 CR 761, 769 n7; *Reifler v Superior Court* (1974) 39 CA3d 479, 485, 114 CR 356, 359. See generally, 4 Witkin, CALIFORNIA PROCEDURE, Proceedings Without Trial §25 (2d ed 1971).

If a party requests permission to put on testimony at the hearing, or to introduce an exhibit not previously mentioned, the judge must exercise the discretion to receive or to exclude; the judge cannot exclude solely because there is a local policy to consider declarations only. *Reifler v Superior Court, supra.* The judge should base the decision on the circumstances of, and reasons for, the particular request.

A party who wants a judge to consider oral testimony, or a new exhibit, or to permit cross-examination of a declarant or other person, should make that request as soon as possible so that calendar time can be scheduled. The reasons for the request should be stated, because the judge must be convinced to exercise the discretion to permit more than legal argument at the hearing. See §23.24.

§23.58   H. Rulings and Orders

An order is a "direction of a court or judge, made or entered in writing, and not included in a judgment." CCP §1003. (A judgment is a final determination of the rights of the parties in an action or proceeding; CCP §577.) Findings of fact need not be made in connection with the granting or denial of a pretrial motion (*Beckett v Kaynar Mfg. Co.* (1958) 49 C2d 695, 699, 321 P2d 749, 751) unless the order is the basis of a final judgment or a contempt judgment. See generally 4 Witkin, CALIFORNIA PROCEDURE, Trial §306 (2d ed 1971). However, some recitation of facts may be put in an order if it is necessary to provide guidelines to the persons who must obey it.

A judge ruling on a noticed motion may: make a tentative ruling (see §23.53) which, unless modified at the hearing, becomes the order; render an oral ruling at the hearing which the clerk will enter as a minute order; or take the motion under submission at the hearing and later issue a written order, or ask one of the attorneys to prepare an order to be signed. See §§23.64–23.66 on ex parte orders. An oral ruling becomes effective when the clerk enters it in the minutes (*Adam v Los Angeles Transit Lines* (1957) 154 CA2d 535, 540, 317 P2d 642, 646), and a written order, after it has been signed, becomes effective when it is filed (*Maxwell v Perkins* (1953) 116 CA2d 752, 756, 255 P2d 10, 13). See *Hollister Convalescent Hosp., Inc. v Rico* (1975) 15 C3d 660, 664, 125 CR 757, 760. See generally, 4 Witkin, PROCEDURE, Proc Without Trial §26.

Time within which to do an act after an order takes effect normally begins to run against a party when he is served with a notice of the ruling (see form in §23.59) or a conformed copy of the order (see form in §23.60). If the ruling is made orally at the hearing, in the presence of all counsel, and entered by the clerk in the minutes, counsel may be asked to waive notice. If counsel agree, no written notice of the order need be given. If any party is not present at the hearing, the attorney for a prevailing party can notify him by serving a notice of the oral ruling.

If the ruling on a motion is complicated, an attorney may be asked to prepare a written order for the judge's signature and for filing. Conformed copies (see §23.61) of the order can then be served on all parties.

If the judge takes the motion under submission and later rules on it, the court clerk must send notice of the ruling to the parties. Cal Rules of Ct 204, 504. However, notification by the clerk does not constitute service of notice, and the prevailing party usually prepares and serves on the parties an order form signed by the judge (see §23.60), or a notice of ruling (see §23.59). Cal Rules of Ct 204, 504. A notice of ruling is not itself an order, but only notification that a minute order has been entered.

§23.59   1. Form: Notice of Ruling

Copies: Original (for filing with court clerk with proof of service); copies for service (one for each attorney of record and unrepresented party); office copies.

[Caption. See §§23.18–23.19]

No. _____

NOTICE OF RULING ON MOTION

To each party and attorney of record:
   PLEASE TAKE NOTICE that the motion of ____[name]____ for ____[describe order sought]____ **came on regularly for hearing on** _____, 19____, **in this**

§23.60   MOTIONS AND ORDERS

court. Appearing as attorneys were _____. On ____[that date / _____,
19____]____, **Judge** ____[name]____, **of this Court,**

[When motion granted]

ordered that: ____[State terms of order]____

[Or]

made orders as set forth in a Minute Order dated _____, 19____, **a copy of which is attached to this notice.**

[When motion denied]

denied that motion.

[Continue]

This ____[order / order denying the motion]____ **was entered in the minutes of the court on** _____, 19____.
Dated: _____

Judge

Comment: Serving notice of an oral ruling may be necessary to begin the running of the time period prescribed by statute or rule for an adverse party to do an act. See generally §23.58. A proof of service form attached to and served with the notice should name each party of person served.

In multiple party cases, the notice must name the moving party and the party against whom relief was requested and specify the motion ruled on. Cal Rules of Ct 204, 504.

§23.60   2. Form: Order

Copies: Original (presented to judge for signature, then filed with proof of service); conformed copies for service (one for each attorney of record and unrepresented party); office copies.

[Caption. See §§23.18 – 23.19]   **No.** _____

ORDER ____[Nature of order]____

The motion of ____[plaintiff / defendant]____ ____[name]____ **for** ____[nature of order sought]____ **was regularly heard on** _____, 19____. **Appearing as attorneys were** ____[names of attorneys]____ **for** ____[name of party]____, **and** _____ **for** _____. **Parties appearing in person were** ____[names]____ **and** _____.

[When motion granted]

Satisfactory proof having been made and good cause appearing:

IT IS ORDERED that:
  1. ____[*Set out each term of the order in a numbered paragraph*]____.

[*If motion denied*]

THE MOTION IS DENIED.
IT IS ORDERED that:
  1. ____[*Set out any additional terms in numbered paragraphs*]____.
Dated: _____

_____
Judge

Comment: An attorney may prepare in advance a form of the order sought and attach it to the moving (or opposition) papers that are served and filed. See §23.46. Alternatively, the attorney may bring a form of the order to the hearing and present it for signature if the judge rules in the party's favor, or prepare the form after the judge has ruled on the motion or indicated what the ruling will be. The date and signature line in the original typed order, and sometimes also date and number spaces in the body of the order, are left blank for the judge to fill in. See, *e.g.*, sample form in 1 CALIFORNIA CIVIL PROCEDURE BEFORE TRIAL §22.25 (Cal CEB 1977). After the judge has signed the order, it is normally returned to counsel for the prevailing party to serve and file. See §23.61.

In some counties, the judge or clerk prepares the original order and mails copies to the parties.

The judge may request that an order prepared by counsel be approved as to form by adverse counsel before it is presented to the judge for signature. This may be done by asking adverse counsel to sign and date a line at the end of the order. *E.g.*:

Approved as to form
_____ _____, 19____
John Dough
Attorney for Defendant Johnson

An order is valid even though it does not contain recitals of when and how the motion came on for hearing, who appeared, and that proof was made and good cause appeared. However, it is customary to include these recitals, and at a later proceeding they will be regarded as true unless contradicted by other parts of the record. See, *E. M. Derby & Co. v Jackman* (1891) 89 C 1, 26 P 610; *Doran v Burke* (1953) 118 CA2d 806, 258 P2d 1078. The recitals also add clarity when several motions have been made in an action or there are multiple parties.

I. Procedures After Motion Granted

§23.61   1. By Moving Party

If the judge makes an oral ruling granting the motion at the hearing, counsel for the moving party may ask all attorneys or parties present to waive notice of the ruling. If any party does not agree, or if an attorney or unrepresented party is not present, the moving party's attorney can prepare a notice of ruling (see §23.59), serve copies, and file it with proof of service. It is important to serve a notice of an oral ruling on adverse parties who must perform some act within a specified time period. See §23.58.

The trial judge granting a motion may fill in and sign a written order form prepared by the moving party's attorney in advance (see §23.60), or may ask the attorney to prepare a written order form embodying specified terms. After a written order has been signed, the attorney should prepare conformed copies for service. These may be photocopies of the filled-in and signed original order, or copies of the original made before it was signed that have been conformed by writing or typing in the dates and numbers that the judge put in the original, and by writing or typing the judge's name on the signature line after the symbol "s/." E.g.:

s/ **Richard S. Row**
_____
Judge

Sometimes the court clerk will conform copies by rubber stamping the judge's name on the signature line. The conformed copies are then served on each other party, and a proof of service form is filed along with the original signed order if the latter was not previously filed.

§23.62   2. By Opposing Party

After a motion has been granted, an adverse party may pursue several possible courses of action. For example: (a) A statute may specify a means of review of a particular order (e.g., CCP §400 authorizing writ of mandate to review order granting or denying change of venue); (b) CCP §§904.1–904.2 provide for appeal from certain orders; (c) CCP §473 provides for relief from an order on the ground that it was taken against the party through his mistake, inadvertence, surprise, or excusable neglect. See

Los Angeles v Gleneagle Dev. Co. (1976) 62 CA3d 543, 553, 133 CR 212, 217 (mistake: failure properly to oppose motion). Further, the nature of the order, or the circumstances of its issuance (*e.g.*, a deficiency in the notice of the motion), may suggest other forms of attack on the order. See §23.51. The adverse party can even risk declining to obey the order, stating objections to it or the way in which it was obtained when enforcement of the order is sought.

Until an order given orally is entered in the minutes of the court, or a written order is signed and filed, the judge has authority to change his mind and to reverse or modify a ruling granting a motion. See *Adam v Los Angeles Transit Lines* (1957) 154 CA2d 535, 541, 317 P2d 642, 646; *Miller v Stein* (1956) 145 CA2d 381, 385, 302 P2d 403, 405. After the order has been entered or filed, however, there is no general statutory basis for a motion to reconsider or to vacate the order unless the reconsideration is sought under CCP §473, or some other specific statute. *Dunas v Superior Court* (1970) 9 CA3d 236, 239, 87 CR 719. See also *Farrar v McCormick* (1972) 25 CA3d 701, 705, 102 CR 190, 193 (*e.g.*, declarations supporting motion to vacate did not show mistake). See, however, 1 CALIFORNIA CIVIL PROCEDURE BEFORE TRIAL §§9.36, 9.40, 9.43 (Cal CEB 1977) (motions to reconsider after demurrer has been overruled or sustained).

§23.63   J. Procedures After Motion Denied

A party whose application for an order has been denied (or granted only in part, conditionally, or on terms) may make another application for the order originally sought, if new facts are shown. CCP §1008. See generally, 4 Witkin, CALIFORNIA PROCEDURE Proceedings Without Trial §§27–28 (2d ed 1971). The moving party must attach to the new application a declaration stating (1) what previous application was made, (2) when and to what judge, (3) what decision or order was made on that application, and (4) what new facts justify issuance of the order sought (even if the new facts are themselves shown in other documents).

The judge may (a) reject a second or subsequent application that does not comply with these requirements; (b) noncompliance may be punished as a contempt; and (c) an order issued on a noncomplying application may be revoked or set aside on ex parte motion or vacated by the judge who issued it or by another judge of the same court. CCP §1008. The penalties provided by CCP §1008 for failure to comply with its terms are not mandatory. *Moore v Moore* (1955) 133 CA2d 56, 60, 283 P2d 338, 342. However, the trial court has inherent power to impose sanctions on a moving party who makes a frivolous motion to reconsider. *Santandrea v Siltec Corp.* (1976) 56 CA3d 525, 529, 128 CR 629, 631.

A judge presented with a subsequent motion based on substantially the same grounds and seeking substantially the same relief as a denied motion may (i) deny it summarily without further reconsideration (*San Francisco v Muller* (1960) 177 CA2d 600, 603, 2 CR 383, 386), (ii) consider it and deny it (*Josephson v Superior Court* (1963) 219 CA2d 354, 358, 33 CR 196, 199); or (iii) reconsider the matter and reverse the prior decision (*Hover v MacKenzie* (1954) 122 CA2d 852, 857, 266 P2d 60). The court may not ignore the subsequent motion. *Muller v Tanner* (1969) 2 CA3d 445, 460, 82 CR 738, 784.

When a motion has been denied, the attorney for a party who opposed the motion may prepare a form of order denying motion (see §23.60) or notice of ruling (see §23.59) to inform other parties of the denial. This also assures commencement of any time period that begins to run against the moving party on denial of the motion.

III. EX PARTE PROCEDURE

§23.64   A. Nature; When To Use

An ex parte application (or application for an ex parte order) is a procedure for obtaining an order directly from a judge without scheduling or holding a formal hearing on the application. Motions may be made and granted ex parte when the order issued would affect only the moving party or at least would not affect a substantial right of any adverse party. See §23.5. Some attorneys and judges believe that an order may be issued ex parte unless a statute or rule specifically requires a noticed motion and hearing. Other judges believe that orders should be granted ex parte only when it is clear that requiring notice or a hearing would be impractical, or detrimental to the moving party's rights or to the purpose of the order. See generally, 4 Witkin, CALIFORNIA PROCEDURE Proceedings Without Trial §§6, 29 (2d ed 1971). Judges are generally reluctant to issue an order ex parte except on matters traditionally dealt with in that way, and local court rules may discourage the use of ex parte applications. See, *e.g.*, LA SUPER CT EX PARTE MAN §420.

§23.65 B. Notice of Application; Procedural Guide

The basic procedure for obtaining an order ex parte is to (1) prepare a written application with the proposed order appended; (2) present these papers to a judge and request that he or she sign the order; (3) serve conformed copies of the papers on other parties and file the original with a proof of service form. In addition, Cal Rules of Ct Appendix, Div 1, §15 (Recommended Standards of Judicial Administration) states:

Ex parte applications for orders should ordinarily not be granted unless:

(1) The applicant shows, to the satisfaction of the court, that reasonable formal or informal notice was given in sufficient time to permit the adverse party to make known to the court any opposition to the application, or the applicant made a reasonable good faith effort to notify the adverse party and further efforts to give notice would probably be futile or unduly burdensome; or

(2) It clearly appears from specific facts set forth in an affidavit, declaration or verified pleading that giving notice to the adverse party would be likely to result in a frustration of the proposed order or that the applicant would suffer immediate and irreparable injury before the adverse party could be heard in opposition; or

(3) It clearly appears from specific facts set forth in an affidavit, declaration, or verified pleading that no significant direct burden or inconvenience to the adverse party would be likely to result.

This standard of judicial administration recognizes that there are situations in which advance notice of the application need not be given to adverse parties. However, unless one of these exceptions applies, or the matter is so routine that other parties could have no objection to the order, and it is of a kind commonly granted ex parte, the following procedure should be followed:

(1) Prepare moving papers (see §23.66) including:

    (a) written application for the order, which may be in declaration form;

    (b) the proposed order, which should be appended or attached to the application;

    (c) memorandum of points and authorities if needed, usually brief and appended to the application;

(d) any other declaration or documents in support of the motion that are deemed necessary; and

(e) a proof of service form.

(2) Serve copies of the moving papers by delivery or mail on other attorneys of record and unrepresented parties, or, if service cannot be made or would not give time to oppose the motion, notify them by telephone when and where the ex parte application will be made;

(3) Present the papers to a judge and request that he sign the order (ordinarily, the attached proof of service form should show a sufficient lapse of time from the time other parties had notice that the judge is in compliance with the Cal Rules of Ct Appendix, Div 1, §15);

(4) Prepare conformed copies of application and signed order;

(5) Serve the copies on the other parties and file the signed original.

§23.66 C. Form: Ex Parte Application for Order and Order

Copies: Original (presented to judge to sign order, then filed with proof of service); copies for service (see comment, below); office copies.

[Caption. See §§23.18–23.19]

No. _____

EX PARTE APPLICATION FOR ORDER AND ORDER ____[NATURE OF ORDER SOUGHT]____

____[Name of attorney]____ **declares:**

1. **I am an attorney for** ____[plaintiff / defendant]____ ____[name]____.

2. ____[Continue in numbered paragraphs with statements of facts and reasons supporting issuance of the order, and issuance ex parte rather than on noticed motion]____.

[When notice of application has been given, see §23.65]

I have notified ____[name]____, **attorney for** ____[name]____, **and** _____, **attorney for** ____[name]____, **by** ____[describe method]____ **that this application would be made on** ____[date]____.

I declare under penalty of perjury that the foregoing is true and correct and that this declaration was executed on _____, 19____ **at** _____, California.

[Signature of attorney]

[Typed name]

Attorney for ____[name]____

[*Points and authorities, when brief, e.g., a citation to a code section or case, may be stated here*]

[*Continue*]

ORDER

Good cause appearing,
    IT IS ORDERED that ____[*terms of order*]____.
Dated: _____

_____
Judge

Comment: The caption of the application must conform to the requirements of Cal Rules of Ct 201, 501. See generally, 1 CALIFORNIA CIVIL PROCEDURE BEFORE TRIAL §§22.12–22.19 (Cal CEB 1977).

The application is in declaration form so that the attorney for the moving party can state facts that support issuance of the order. The declaration can also state reasons why the order should be issued and the facts and reasons that support issuance of the order ex parte, rather than after a hearing. Other declarations can be attached if there are facts that must be stated by other persons. See §§23.36–23.43.

Ex parte applications are often sufficiently routine that there need not be an extensive memorandum of points and authorities. A code section may be mentioned in the title of the paper (*e.g.*, APPLICATION UNDER CCP §1005 FOR ORDER SHORTENING TIME), or statutes or cases may be cited below the declarant's signature. If more is needed, a separate memorandum should be attached. See §§23.26–23.35.

If copies of the application are to be served on other parties before the application is presented for signature (see §23.65), counsel may wish to prepare an additional set of copies that can be conformed (see Comment to form in §23.60) and served after the judge has signed the order. Or, the attorney may make and serve photocopies of the signed order.

IV. ORDER TO SHOW CAUSE PROCEDURE

§23.67   A. Nature; When To Use

The order to show cause procedure is an alternative to proceeding by noticed motion. Basically, the moving party makes an ex parte application for an order that requires another party to

§23.68   MOTIONS AND ORDERS   58

attend a hearing and show cause why a specified order should not issue. Service of the order to show cause on the other party acts as the service of a notice of motion on him. The judge may order that the show cause hearing take place sooner than the ten days' wait normally required for a notice of motion (CCP §1005), thus eliminating the need for a separate application for an order shortening time.

Applying for an order to show cause is the customary method of obtaining an order in cases involving, *e.g.*, requests for a preliminary injunction (see CALIFORNIA CIVIL PROCEDURE BEFORE TRIAL §§15.36, 15.41 (Cal CEB 1977)), family law disputes (see Cal Rules of Ct 1225, 1226), contempt proceedings, provisional remedies, and extraordinary writs. See generally, 4 Witkin, CALIFORNIA PROCEDURE Proceedings Without Trial §§30–31 (2d ed 1971). The procedure may be used in other types of cases, the order to show cause being treated as if it were a notice of motion accompanied by a citation to a party to appear at a stated place and time. See *Green v Gordon* (1952) 39 C2d 230, 232, 246 P2d 38; *Difani v Riverside County Oil Co.* (1927) 201 C 210, 213, 256 P 210.

§23.68   B. Notice of Application; Procedural Guide

An order to show cause is obtained on ex parte application. However, it is rarely necessary to give advance notice of the application to adverse parties as is recommended for other ex parte applications by Cal Rules of Ct Appendix, Div I, §15. See §23.65. The order to show cause gives notice of a hearing, and the procedure is often used in cases in which it would be futile to try to give notice, a quick hearing is necessary, or giving notice would frustrate the purpose of the relief sought.

An attorney instituting an order to show cause procedure should normally:

(1) Prepare an application for order and order to show cause (see §23.69) attaching to the application and order additional declarations and points and authorities as needed, and a form of the order to be sought at the show cause hearing;

(2) Present the moving papers to a judge and request signature of the order to show cause;

(3) Serve conformed copies of the order to show cause and other papers on adverse parties and file the originals with a form of proof of service;

(4) Attend the show cause hearing to argue for issuance of the proposed order;

(5) If the proposed order is issued, serve and file copies as in a notice of motion proceeding (see §23.61).

The order to show cause, when signed by the judge, should be personally served on the adverse party if the order is to serve as a citation or summons that gives jurisdiction over that party, or as a basis for holding the party in contempt. The order may be served on the party's attorney, however, if the party has appeared in the action and the order serves merely as a form of notice of motion. *In re Morelli* (1970) 11 CA3d 819, 838, 91 CR 72, 84.

§23.69   C. Form: Application for Order and Order To Show Cause

Copies: Original (presented to judge to sign, then filed with proof of service); copies for service (see §23.68); office copies.

[Caption. See §§23.18–23.19]

No. ----------

APPLICATION FOR ORDER AND ORDER TO SHOW CAUSE

----[Name of attorney]---- **declares:**

1. I am an attorney for ----[plaintiff / defendant]--------[name]---- **in this action.**

2. ----[Continue in separate paragraphs with statements of facts and reasons supporting the need for the relief or order sought, the need to have an early hearing if that has been requested, and the need to proceed by order to show cause rather than by noticed motion]----.

I declare under penalty of perjury that the foregoing is true and correct and that this declaration was executed on ----------, 19---- at ----------, California.

[Signature of attorney]

[Typed name]
Attorney for ----[name]----

[Points and authorities, when brief, may be stated here]

[Continue]

ORDER

To: ----[Name of each party to whom order is directed]----:
Good cause appearing,
YOU ARE ORDERED to appear in Department No. ---------- **of this Court, located at** ----[room no. and address]---- **on** ----[date]---- **at** ----[time]----

to give any legal reason why the ____[following / attached]____ **order requested by** ____[name of moving party]____ **should not be made by this Court.**

[When form of the order sought is not attached,
it may be described here. E.g.]

If ____[moving party]____'**s motion is granted, you will be ordered to** ____[nature of order]____.

[When moving party also requests
other forms of interim relief]

IT IS FURTHER ORDERED that ____[nature of additional orders]____.
Dated: _____

Judge

Comment: The caption of the application must conform to the requirements of Cal Rules of Ct 201, 501. See generally, 1 CALIFORNIA CIVIL PROCEDURE BEFORE TRIAL §§22.12–22.19 (Cal CEB 1977). The application is in declaration form so that the attorney for the moving party can state facts that support issuance of the order.

Although this form gives general guidelines for drafting an application for an order to show cause, application in particular kinds of proceedings may differ. See, *e.g.*, 1 CIV PROC BEFORE TRIAL §§15.35–15.36 (Cal CEB 1977) (injunctions), 18.34 (receivers). See also Cal Rules of Ct 1285.10–1285.40, 1285.60 (family law).

RICHARD M. MOSK

Chapter 24
Declaratory Relief

I. INTRODUCTION
　A. Historical Background　§24.1
　B. Nature of Action　§24.2
　C. Statutory Authority　§24.3
　D. Purposes and Uses
　　1. General Purposes; Advantages　§24.4
　　2. Typical Uses
　　　a. Oral or Written Contracts　§24.5
　　　b. Other Instruments　§24.6
　　　c. Other Uses Under CCP §1060 and Govt C §11440　§24.7
II. DETERMINING AVAILABILITY OF DECLARATORY RELIEF
　A. Who May Obtain Relief　§24.8
　B. Requirement of Existence of Actual Controversy
　　1. Definition　§24.9
　　　a. Examples of Actual Controversy　§24.10
　　　b. Examples of No Actual Controversy　§24.11
　C. Effect of Availability of Other Remedies on Availability of Declaratory Relief.
　　1. Remedies Cumulative　§24.12
　　2. Availability of Other Forums or Procedures May Preclude Relief　§24.13
　D. Effect of Accrued Cause of Action on Availability of Declaratory Relief　§24.14
　E. Effect of Declaration That Party Has No Rights on Availability of Other Relief　§24.15
III. GROUNDS FOR DENIAL
　A. Lack of Jurisdiction　§24.16
　B. Lack of Actual Controversy　§24.17
　C. Lack of Standing　§24.18
　D. Judicial Discretion to Deny Relief
　　1. When Not Necessary or Proper　§24.19
　　2. When Complaint Does Not State a Cause of Action　§24.20

RICHARD M. MOSK, A.B., 1960, Stanford University; J.D., 1963, Harvard Law School. Mr. Mosk is a member of the firm of Mitchell, Silberberg & Knupp of Los Angeles.

CEB attorney-editor was ISADORE ROSENBLATT.

  E. Failure To Exhaust Administrative Remedies **§24.21**
  F. Underlying Claim Barred By Statutes of Limitation or Laches **§24.22**
  G. Mandatory Use of Other Forums or Procedures; Matters Within Exclusive Province of Another Government Branch or Agency May Preclude Relief **§24.23**
  H. Generally Not Available With Respect to Criminal Statutes; Exception **§24.24**
  I. No Declaration Regarding Future Conduct Sought **§24.25**
  J. Other Grounds for Denial **§24.26**
IV. PROCEDURE
  A. Commencing the Action
    1. Court in Which Action May be Brought
      a. Jurisdiction **§24.27**
      b. Venue **§24.28**
    2. Necessary, Indispensable, and Proper Parties; Governmental Entities **§24.29**
    3. Drafting the Complaint
      a. Requisite Contents **§24.30**
      b. Joinder of Causes of Action **§24.31**
    4. Form: Complaint for Declaratory Relief on Contract **§24.32**
    5. Form: Complaint for Declaratory Relief on Statute or Ordinance **§24.33**
  B. Responsive and Other Pleadings
    1. Methods of Responding
      a. Answer **§24.34**
      b. Cross-Complaint **§24.35**
      c. Demurrers **§24.36**
      d. Motion for Judgment on the Pleadings or Summary Judgment **§24.37**
      e. Form of Demurrer and Pretrial Motions **§24.38**
  C. Trial Aspects
    1. Precedence on Calendar **§24.39**
    2. Right to Jury Trial **§24.40**
    3. Burden of Proof **§24.41**
    4. Trial Court's Duty to Render Full and Complete Declaration **§24.42**
  D. Judgment
    1. Content and Effect **§24.43**
    2. Form: Judgment for Declaratory Relief **§24.44**
V. APPELLATE REVIEW **§24.45**

I. INTRODUCTION

§24.1 A. Historical Background

Under common law, declaratory judgment as a form of judicial relief generally was unavailable to a party involved in a controversy before his rights had actually been violated. The absence of such a remedy "was a defect of the judicial procedure which developed under the common law that the doors of the courts were invitingly opened to a plaintiff whose legal rights had already been violated, . . ." *Tolle v Struve* (1932) 124 CA 263, 271, 12 P2d 61, 64.

Despite the need for a procedure permitting a judicial determination of the rights and duties of parties actually engaged in a controversy before the invasion of a party's rights, until 1919 such procedures were available in this country only rarely, and then were often incomplete. See *King v Hall* (1855) 5 C 82; Harrison, *The Declaratory Judgment in California*, 8 CALIF L REV 133 (1920). In 1919, after Michigan passed the first broad declaratory relief statute (Michigan Public Acts 1919, No. 150, p 278), other state legislatures enacted such legislation. In 1921, California enacted declaratory relief legislation "based in part upon English practice and recent legislation in other states." Harrison, *California Legislation of 1921 Providing for Declaratory Relief*, 9 CALIF L REV 359 (1921).

In 1922, the Conference of Commissioners on Uniform State Laws approved the Uniform Declaratory Judgments Act (9A Uniform Laws), which has since been adopted in a majority of states. Almost all states now have statutes authorizing declaratory judgments. See AM JUR2d Desk Book, Doc. 129. Declaratory judgments have been available in federal courts since 1934. 28 USC §§2201–2202. See also Fed R Civ P 57. The validity of California declaratory judgment legislation has been upheld. *Blakeslee v Wilson* (1923) 190 C 479, 213 P 495. See generally, Note, *Developments in the Law, Declaratory Judgments—1941–1949*, 62 HARV L REV 787, 790 (1949); Borchard, DECLARATORY JUDGMENTS 150–203 (2d ed 1941).

§24.2   B. Nature of Action

The declaratory relief action in California is a statutory civil action generally brought to determine and establish rights before any actual invasion of those rights has occurred. See, however, §24.14 for discussion of declaratory relief after there has been an actual invasion of a party's rights.

At times courts have labeled declaratory relief actions equitable in nature requiring application of equitable principles. *Westerholm v Twentieth Century Ins. Co.* (1976) 58 CA3d 628, 632 n1, 130 CR 164, 166, n1; *Merigan v Bauer* (1962) 206 CA2d 616,

23 CR 872; see *Los Angeles v Glendale* (1943) 23 C2d 68, 142 P2d 289; *Adams v Cook* (1940) 15 C2d 352, 101 P2d 484; 3 Witkin, CALIFORNIA PROCEDURE, Pleading §705 (2d ed 1971). Yet, in other cases courts have suggested that declaratory relief is not strictly legal or equitable, but is sui generis. *Moss v Moss* (1942) 20 C2d 640, 128 P2d 526; see *Dills v Delira Corp.* (1956) 145 CA2d 124, 302 P2d 397. Because in a declaratory relief action a party is entitled to a jury trial of those issues that normally would be triable to a jury (*State Farm Mut. Auto. Ins. Co. v Superior Court* (1956) 47 C2d 428, 304 P2d 13; see §24.40), there has not been much controversy over whether the action is legal or equitable.

In all declaratory relief actions, however, courts exercise the same wide latitude in the formulation of judgments that is exercised in equitable actions (*Los Angeles v Glendale, supra; Westerhold v 20th Century Ins. Co., supra; Adams v Cook, supra; Munson v Linnick* (1967) 255 CA2d 589, 595, 63 CR 340, 343), and consider and apply equitable principles and doctrines (*Moss v Moss, supra; Merigan v Bauer, supra; Hollenbeck Lodge v Wilshire Blvd. Temple* (1959) 175 CA2d 469, 346 P2d 422; *Beeler v Plastic Stamping, Inc.* (1956) 144 CA2d 306, 300 P2d 852).

On the other hand the declaratory relief action is not subject to requirements of equity actions such as irreparable injury or inadequacy of a legal remedy, even though equitable defenses such as in pari delicto, unclean hands, or laches, may induce a court to exercise its discretion not to issue a declaration (see §24.19). See *Moss v Moss, supra.*

§24.3 C. Statutory Authority

The general statutory authority for declaratory judgments is contained in CCP §§1060–1062. See §24.39 for discussion of CCP §1062a.

The primary authority is found in CCP §1060, which states:

Any person interested under a deed, will or other written instrument, or under a contract, or who desires a declaration of his rights or duties with respect to another, or in respect to, in, over or upon property, or with respect to the location of the natural channel of a watercourse, may, in cases of actual controversy relating to the legal rights and duties of the respective parties, bring an original action in the superior court or file a cross-complaint in a pending action in the superior, municipal or justice court for a declaration of his rights and duties in the premises, including a determination of any question of construction or validity arising under such instrument or contract. He may ask for a declaration of rights or duties, either alone or with other relief; and the court may make a binding declaration of such rights or duties, whether or not further relief is or could be claimed at the time. The declaration may be either affirmative or negative in form and effect, and such declaration shall have the force of a final judgment. Such declaration may be had before there has been any breach of the obligation in respect to which said declaration is sought.

A number of other statutes provide for what amounts to declaratory relief in special instances. The following are some of those statutes:

CC §§7006, 7015   To determine the existence or nonexistence of parent-child relation.

CC §1203   To prove an instrument.

CC §4212   To test validity of a marriage.

CCP §386   To permit party against whom conflicting claims are made to compel the complainants to interplead and litigate their claims to determine which claim is correct.

CCP §§738–751.1   To determine conflicting claims to real and personal property (quiet title actions).

CCP §801.1   To determine adverse interests in real property titles affected by public improvement assessments.

CCP §§803–811   Quo warranto actions.

CCP §860   To determine validity of any matter of an in rem nature that is authorized to be determined under the procedure. See, e.g., Wat C §30066, providing for an action to determine the validity of certain assessments, warrants, contracts obligations, or evidence of indebtedness which may be brought under CCP §860.

CCP §1060.5   To determine residence for state personal income tax purposes.

CCP §1240.690   To obtain declaratory relief against state highway use.

CCP §1240.700   To obtain declaratory relief against road, street, and highway use.

Corp C §709   To determine the validity of the election or appointment of directors.

Corp C §1904   To determine matters concerning the winding up of the affairs of a corporation.

Ed C §§21180–21203   To determine any questions of law and fact affecting various aspects of grants founding educational institutions, the validity and legal effect of gifts or grants to such institutions, title to real and personal properties conveyed, and grants or surrenders of rights and duties of founders and others.

Elec C §407   To determine right of person to be registered to vote.

Elec C §§20000–20533   To settle contested elections.

Govt C §11440   To obtain declaration as to the validity of administrative regulations.

Govt C §71043   To determine whether population of judicial district is above or below 40,000 persons.

Health & S C §1055   To establish the fact of, and the time and place of a birth, death or marriage.

Prob C §588   To obtain instructions and directions by executor or administrator.

Prob C §§1080–1082   To determine heirship.

Prob C §1170   To establish fact of death when title to or interest in real or personal property is affected.

Prob C §1516   Proceeding by guardian to obtain instructions and directions.

Pub Res C §21167   To review or set aside acts or decisions of public agencies with respect to environmental impact reports.

Pub Res C §25454   To determine violations of Petroleum Resources Management chapter of the California Energy Conservation and Development Act.

Pub Res C §30803   To determine violations of the California Coastal Conservation Act.

Str & H C §741.8   Administrative proceedings with respect to rights in beds of mapped highway do not preclude an action for declaratory relief.

Str & H C §5265   To determine validity of contracts and proceedings relating to certain public works.

Wat C §7005   To determine rights in common conduit, well, and pumping plant.

Wat C §56090   To determine right of board to issue certain bonds.

Wat C Appendix §8–42.1   Action by bondholder to determine whether alteration of tax basis has impaired district's obligation under bond contract.

In addition, traditional actions can be used in certain circumstances to obtain what amounts to a declaration. See, *e.g.*, *Golden Gate Bridge Dist. v Felt* (1931) 214 C 308, 5 P2d 585 ("friendly suit" against administrative official to establish the validity of a bond issue); *Los Angeles v Dannenbrink* (1965) 234 CA2d 642, 645, 44 CR 624, 626 (mandamus proceeding to test city department's power to issue revenue bonds under amendment to the city's charter approved by city's voters.

D. Purposes and Uses
§24.4 1. General Purposes; Advantages

The purposes for which declaratory relief may be sought before actual injury are for the purposes of settling genuine disputes and determining the parties' rights and obligations in order to forestall infliction of harm and subsequent necessity for compensatory measures. The court pointed out in *Travers v Louden* (1967) 254 CA2d 926, 931, 62 CR 654, 658:

There is unanimity of authority to the effect that the declaratory procedure operated prospectively, and not merely for the redress of past wrongs. It serves to set controversies at rest before they lead to repudiation of obligations, invasion of rights or commission of wrongs; in short, the remedy is to be used in the interests of preventive justice, to declare rights rather than execute them.

See also *Rubin v Toberman* (1964) 226 CA2d 319, 38 CR 32; *Rimington v General Acc. Group of Ins. Cos.* (1962) 205 CA2d 394, 23 CR 40; Borchard, DECLARATORY JUDGMENTS 25 (2d ed 1941).

Although the form of declaratory relief varies with the nature of the particular enabling statute, the essence of declaratory relief is that when an actual controversy exists a party may bring an action seeking an authoritative determination and declaration of "the jural relationships between parties to a controversy" before the occurrence of actual breach or harm. Comment, *Developments in the Law, Declaratory Judgments—1941–1949*, 62 HARV L REV 787 (1949). The availability of declaratory relief represents an accommodation between the rigid requirement of actual harm before an action is permissible and the futile expenditure of judicial resources on a purely advisory opinion.

Thus, although courts have said that the purposes of declaratory relief are "to quiet and stabilize an uncertain or disputed jural relationship . . . and to make the courts more serviceable to the people" (*Manchel v Los Angeles* (1966) 245 CA2d 501, 509, 54 CR 53, 58), they have warned that declaratory relief is not available for determining hypothetical or abstract questions or mere differences of opinion (*Wilson v Transit Authority* (1962)

§24.5 DECLARATORY RELIEF

199 CA2d 716, 19 CR 59; see *Sugarman v Federal Ins. Co.* (1968) 265 CA2d 563, 71 CR 542).

Accordingly, under CCP §1060 (see §24.3) and case law (see *Wilson v Transit Authority* (1962) 199 CA2d 716, 723, 19 CR 59, 63), declaratory relief is available only when there is an actual controversy between the parties involving their legal rights, and when that controversy is subject to judicial resolution. See §§24.9–24.10.

Among the advantages of an action for declaratory relief are the following: (a) to provide a quicker method of adjudicating legal disputes; (b) to clarify and stabilize legal relations before irretrievable acts have been taken; (c) to resolve certain issues on which other rights depend and thus to preclude contests over more complicated issues that would result from a breach of contract or other actions; (d) to save plaintiff from the dilemma of acting on his own interpretation of his rights or to forbear from acting for fear of liability; (e) to remove uncertainty from legal relations; (f) to combine in one action interdependent disputes among several parties; (g) to have a court determine in one action disputes that would normally be involved in successive actions, *e.g.*, when questions of indemnification are involved; (h) to establish legal rights in properties and among parties; and (i) to resolve and clarify the application or validity of statutes and regulations. See generally Borchard, DECLARATORY JUDGMENTS 279–289 (2d ed 1941).

2. Typical Uses

§24.5   a. Oral or Written Contracts

Code of Civil Procedure §1060 authorizes an adjudication of rights, with respect to an oral or written contract. Such adjudications can include questions of the construction, interpretation, effect and validity of a contract. *Ermolieff v R.K.O. Radio Pictures, Inc.* (1942) 19 C2d 543, 122 P2d 3 (territory covered by written motion picture distribution agreement); *Columbia Pictures Corp. v DeToth* (1945) 26 C2d 753, 161 P2d 217 (oral employment agreement and renewal options); *Common Wealth Ins. Sys., Inc. v Kersten* (1974) 40 CA3d 1014, 115 CR 653 (escrow instructions); *Cinmark Inv. Co. v Reichard* (1966) 246 CA2d 498, 54 CR 810 (written contract providing for lease of and option to purchase land); *Karbelnig v Brothwell* (1966) 244 CA2d 333, 53 CR 335 (rights of lessor and lessee under terms of written lease and its assignment, including whether lease had been forfeited); *General Ins. Co. v Whitmore* (1965) 235 CA2d 670, 45 CR 558 (coverage under liability insurance policy; in this regard, see Note, *The Role of Declaratory Relief and Collateral Estoppel in Determining the Insurer's Duty to Defend and Indemnify*, 21 HASTINGS LJ 191 (1969)); *Ralphs Grocery Co. v Amalgamated Meat Cutters, Local No. 439* (1950) 98 CA2d 539, 220 P2d 802 (written labor contract); *Putnam v Putnam* (1942) 51 CA2d 696, 125 P2d 525 (written separation agreement).

Declaratory relief is not available when the contract in question has not yet come into existence. *Escondido Mut. Water Co. v George A. Hillebrecht, Inc.* (1966) 241 CA2d 410, 50 CR 495. In a declaratory relief action the court may, however, determine whether or not the contract exists. See *Howard v Howard* (1955) 131 CA2d 308, 280 P2d 802.

In summary, "questions relating to the formation of a contract, its validity, its construction and effect, excuses for nonperformance, and termination are proper subjects for declaratory relief." *Foster v Masters Pontiac Co.* (1958) 158 CA2d 481, 486, 322 P2d 592, 594.

§24.6   b. Other Instruments

Code of Civil Procedure §1060 specifically provides for a declaration of rights by any person "interested under a deed, will or other written instrument." Reported cases cover declaration of rights in connection with a number of different types of instruments.

Holt v College of Osteopathic Physicians & Surgeons (1964) 61 C2d 750, 40 CR 244 (charitable purposes of trust and whether certain conduct by trustees would be a breach of trust);

Lomanto v Bank of America (1972) 22 CA3d 663, 99 CR 442 (rights under trust deed);

Ross v Harootunian (1967) 257 CA2d 292, 64 CR 537 (enforceability of covenants or servitudes asserted against property);

Thompson v Boyd (1963) 217 CA2d 365, 32 CR 513 (whether spouses had entered into agreement not to revoke joint and mutual will);

Marden v Bailard (1954) 124 CA2d 458, 268 P2d 809 (deed and building restrictions);

Sullivan v San Francisco Art Ass'n (1950) 101 CA2d 449, 225 P2d 993 (rights under decree of distribution);

§24.7 DECLARATORY RELIEF

Chase v Leiter (1950) 96 CA2d 439, 215 P2d 756 (whether in a joint will and agreement, property was transformed into community property);

Talcott v Talcott (1942) 54 CA2d 743, 129 P2d 946 (rights under decree of distribution);

Chaplin v Chaplin (1935) 9 CA2d 182, 49 P2d 296 (interpretation of property settlement agreement incorporated into final divorce decree).

Compare *McCaughna v Bilhorn* (1935) 10 CA2d 674, 52 P2d 1025 (holding that it is proper for superior court sitting in equity to take jurisdiction of declaratory relief action when plaintiff had filed claim rejected in probate court, and plaintiff was uncertain of his rights under the will, and probate court could not settle the entire controversy) with *Howard v Bennett* (1942) 53 CA2d 546, 127 P2d 1012 (holding that superior court sitting in probate, which can give full relief, has exclusive jurisdiction to construe terms of will in estate it is administering so as to preclude a declaratory relief action for that purpose) and *Colden v Costello* (1942) 50 CA2d 363, 122 P2d 959 (holding that because probate court has jurisdiction to determine, as between a decedent's widow and other claimants, what part of an estate is community property and what part is separate property, it is improper to grant her the right to bring separate declaratory relief action).

§24.7   c. Other Uses Under CCP §1060 and Govt C §11440

Code of Civil Procedure §1060 provides for a declaration of rights or duties "with respect to another, or in respect to, in, over or upon property, or with respect to the location of the natural channel of a watercourse." Under this broad language, and Govt C §11440 covering declarations as to the validity of administrative regulations, declaratory relief is available in a variety of situations, *e.g.*,

(1) To determine constitutionality and validity of statutes and ordinances. *Carmel-By-The-Sea v Young* (1970) 2 C3d 259, 85 CR 1; *Walker v Los Angeles* (1961) 55 C2d 626, 12 CR 671; *Abbott v Los Angeles* (1960) 53 C2d 674, 678 n2, 3 CR 158, 161 n2; *Lord v Garland* (1946) 27 C2d 840, 168 P2d 5; see Note, *Declaratory Relief in the Criminal Law*, 80 HARV L REV 1490 (1967).

(2) To construe statutes, ordinances, and charters. *LePage v Oakland* (1970) 13 CA3d 689, 91 CR 806; *Squire v San Francisco*

(1970) 12 CA3d 974, 91 CR 347; *San Joaquin v State Bd. of Equalization* (1970) 9 CA3d 365, 88 CR 12.

(3) To determine validity of administrative regulations. *Chas. L. Harney, Inc. v Contractors' State License Bd.* (1952) 39 C2d 561, 247 P2d 913; see *Santa Barbara School Dist. v Superior Court* (1975) 13 C3d 315, 118 CR 637 (validity of school desegregation plan). But see *Imperial Mut. Life Ins. Co. v Caminetti* (1943) 59 CA2d 501, 139 P2d 691, requiring exhaustion of administrative remedies before declaratory relief action will lie, and *Honeywell, Inc. v State Bd. of Equalization* (1975) 48 CA3d 907, 122 CR 243 to the same effect.

(4) To determine power of regulatory agencies to resolve rights among various water users (*Orange County Water Dist. v Riverside* (1959) 173 CA2d 137, 343 P2d 450), and to determine the rights of various parties in water (*Tehachapi-Cummings County Water Dist. v Armstrong* (1975) 49 CA3d 992, 122 CR 918).

(5) To determine certain tax questions. *Maxwell v Santa Rosa* (1959) 53 C2d 274, 1 CR 334 (fraudulent local property tax assessment); *Valley Fair Fashions, Inc. v Valley Fair* (1966) 245 CA2d 614, 54 CR 306 (ultimate liability as between lessor and lessee for tax increase for improvements to property); *Whittell v Franchise Tax Bd.* (1964) 231 CA2d 278, 41 CR 673 (under CCP §1060.5, an individual claiming to be a nonresident of California may bring an action against the Franchise Tax Board to determine the fact of residency for income tax purposes); *Pacific Motor Transp. Co. v State Bd. of Equalization* (1972) 28 CA3d 230, 236, 104 CR 558, 562 (to test validity of administrative tax regulation even if statute bars injunctive relief or mandamus to prevent collection of a tax). But see *Faix, Ltd. v Los Angeles* (1976) 54 CA3d 992, 1002, 127 CR 182, 189 (plaintiff which had not paid tax in full could not challenge validity of assessment); *Honeywell, Inc. v State Bd. of Equalization, supra* (declaratory relief will not lie to ascertain whether a transaction is taxable after transaction has been completed or when a statute bars an injunction or mandamus to prevent collection of a tax (Rev & T C §6931)).

(6) To test validity of labor union constitution. *Weber v Marine Cooks' & Stewards' Ass'n* (1949) 93 CA2d 327, 208 P2d 1009.

(7) To determine rights of labor union members. *Miller v International Union of Operating Eng'rs* (1953) 118 CA2d 66, 257 P2d 85; *Taylor v Marine Cooks' & Stewards' Ass'n* (1953) 117 CA2d 556, 256 P2d 595.

(8) To determine rights of shareholders in a corporation. *Maguire v Hibernia Sav. & Loan Soc'y* (1944) 23 C2d 719, 146 P2d 673.

(9) To determine ownership of stock. *East Coalinga Oil Fields Corp. v Robinson* (1948) 86 CA2d 153, 194 P2d 554.

(10) To determine rights of civil service employees. *Hoyt v Board of Civil Serv. Comm'rs* (1942) 21 C2d 399, 132 P2d 804.

(11) To determine whether individual was properly excluded from membership in an association. *Kronen v Pacific Coast Soc'y of Orthodontists* (1965) 237 CA2d 289, 46 CR 808.

(12) To determine validity of divorce decree and rights and duties under it. *Klinker v Klinker* (1955) 132 CA2d 687, 283 P2d 83.

(13) To determine parental relationship. *Tomasello v Tomasello* (1952) 113 CA2d, 247 P2d 612; *Smith v Bank of Cal.* (1937) 19 CA2d 579, 65 P2d 1361 (relationships and rights under a trust).

(14) To determine in cross-complaint that cross-defendant is liable or that cross-defendant must indemnify cross-complainant if latter held liable in action brought by third party. *Brokate v Hehr Mfg. Co.* (1966) 243 CA2d 133, 52 CR 672 (slander action); *J. C. Penney Co. v Westinghouse Elec. Corp.* (1963) 217 CA2d 834, 32 CR 172 (personal injury action); *Indenco, Inc. v Evans* (1962) 201 CA2d 369, 20 CR 90 (personal injury action). See also *Sattinger v Newbauer* (1954) 123 CA2d 365, 266 P2d 586; *Common Wealth Ins. Sys., Inc. v Kersten* (1974) 40 CA3d 1014, 115 CR 653.

(15) To determine boundaries of electoral district. *Girth v Thompson* (1970) 11 CA3d 325, 89 CR 823.

(16) To determine a person's right to vote. *Ferreira v Keller* (1970) 4 CA3d 292, 84 CR 253.

(17) To determine whether a redevelopment plan violated residents' statutory and constitutional rights to enjoy free access to the ocean. *Lane v Redondo Beach* (1975) 49 CA3d 251, 122 CR 189.

II. DETERMINING AVAILABILITY OF DECLARATORY RELIEF

§24.8 A. Who May Obtain Relief

Under CCP §1060, those who can obtain declaratory relief include "any person interested under a deed, will or other written instrument, or under a contract, or who desires a declaration of his rights or duties with respect to another, or in respect to, in, over or upon property, or with respect to the location of the natural channel of a watercourse." Perhaps because of the breadth of this language, there have been few reported appellate cases in which the issue of which persons are entitled to obtain a declaratory relief has been raised. See *Wollenberg v Tonningsen* (1935) 8 CA2d 722, 48 P2d 738.

The word "person" includes corporations and other entities (CCP §17; *Oil Workers Int'l Union v Superior Court* (1951) 103 CA2d 512, 230 P2d 71), and the word "property" includes both real and personal property (CCP §17(1)).

Whether a party qualifies as a person who is "interested under" a contract or other instrument as specified in CCP §1060 has been often resolved by a determination that the requirement of an "actual controversy relating to the legal rights and duties of the respective parties" (see CCP §1060; §§24.9–24.10) has been met. See *California Water & Tel. Co. v Los Angeles* (1967) 253 CA2d, 16, 22, 61 CR 618, 623, in which the court stated, "the concept of justiciability involves the intertwined criteria of ripeness and standing." In a case under Govt C §11440, which provides for declaratory relief in connection with administrative regulations, the court defined "interested person" as "a person having a direct and not merely consequential interest in the litigation" and held that an incorporated trade association does not fall within that definition in an action with respect to a regulation affecting its members. *Associated Boat Indus. v Marshall* (1951) 104 CA2d 21, 230 P2d 379. In *Zetterberg v State Dep't of Pub. Health* (1974) 43 CA3d 657, 662, 118 CR 100, 103, the court stated that "plaintiffs' allegation that they are taxpayers does nothing to establish their standing to seek the relief sought and their complaint fails to set forth any circumstances indicating that as citizens of the state they have any greater or different interest in the subject than any other member of the body politic." See also *Rowland School Dist. v State Bd. of Educ.* (1968) 264 CA2d 589, 593, 70 CR 504, 507 (plaintiff must have "an interest affected by the invalidity of the provisions it attacks").

In *Residents of Beverly Glen, Inc. v Los Angeles* (1973) 34 CA3d 117, 125, 109 CR 724, 730, however, the court said that it is too narrow to focus on the word "interested" alone, and that the inquiry should rather be whether a plaintiff purporting to represent a group can fairly protect its rights; it then held that a homeowners' corporation had standing to seek a declaration with respect to the validity of a city ordinance. See also *Chas. L. Harney, Inc. v Contractors' State License Bd.* (1952) 39 C2d 561, 247 P2d 913 (licensed engineering contractor is an interested person with standing to seek a declaration on the validity of an administrative regulation prohibiting engaging in a certain type of work without obtaining a specific license); *Sperry & Hutchinson Co. v State Bd. of Pharmacy* (1966) 241 CA2d 229, 50 CR 489 (trading stamp company is an "interested person" to obtain declaratory relief with regard to validity of regulation prohibiting pharmacists from giving trading stamps).

A person who has rights flowing from a contract has an interest in the contract, and should, in the trial court's discretion (see §24.19), be permitted to secure a declaration of the character and extent of those rights when an actual controversy exists. *Gardiner v Gaither* (1958) 162 CA2d 607, 621, 329 P2d 22, 31 (creditors of one party to contract can seek declaration construing contract as creating partnership). In *Siciliano v Fireman's Fund Ins. Co.* (1976) 62 CA3d 745, 753, 133 CR 376, 380, the court stated, in connection with a declaratory relief action by discharged attorney against insurance company which had settled directly with the attorney's client, knowing he had a contingent fee contract with his client, that "section 1060 does not require the existence of a legal instrument between parties as a predicate for declaratory relief."

Declaratory relief actions may be brought on behalf of a class. *Serrano v Priest* (1971) 5 C3d 584, 96 CR 601; *Los Angeles County Democratic Cent. Comm. v Los Angeles* (1976) 61 CA3d 335, 132 CR 43; *LePage v Oakland* (1970) 13 CA3d 689, 91 CR 806; see *Residents of Beverly Glen, Inc. v Los Angeles, supra; Romero v Weakley* (SD Cal 1955) 131 F Supp 818, rev'd on other grounds (9th Cir 1955) 226 F2d 399.

B. Requirement of Existence of Actual Controversy

§24.9   1. Definition

Declaratory relief is available only "in cases of actual controversy relating to the legal rights and duties of the respective parties." CCP §1060. In *Selby Realty Co. v San Buenaventura* (1973) 10 C3d 110, 117, 109 CR 799, 803, the court stated that "the 'actual controversy' referred to in this statute is one which admits of definitive and conclusive relief by judgment within the field of judicial administration, as distinguished from an advisory opinion on a particular or hypothetical state of facts."

While it is usually said that there is a requirement of an "actual, present controversy over a proper subject" (3 Witkin, CALIFORNIA PROCEDURE Pleading §716 (2d ed 1971)), Witkin adds that it "seems desirable to allow the action even in the absence of a showing of present controversy, where the likelihood of future controversy clearly appears in the complaint" (3 Witkin, PROCEDURE, Pleading §717. See *Chas. L. Harney, Inc. v Contractors' State License Bd.* (1952) 39 C2d 561, 247 P2d 913 (licensed contractor entitled to declaratory relief under Govt C §11440 with respect to a regulation requiring specialty license even though it did not allege it had bid or intended to bid on particular job). Some courts have developed an even more flexible test by stating that requirement of an actual controversy is met when the controversy "has reached, but has not passed, the point that the facts have sufficiently congealed to permit an intelligent and useful decision to be made." *California Water & Tel. Co. v Los Angeles* (1967) 253 CA2d 16, 22, 61 CR 618, 623 (private water utility can seek declaration of validity of application of a county water ordinance, even though it had complied with such ordinances because to plan for the future it needs to know if it must comply with specifications of ordinance). See *Cook v Craig* (1976) 55 CA3d 773, 380 127 CR 712, 716, in which the court stated that "while it has been said that the declaratory judgment acts necessarily deal with present rights, the 'present right' contemplated is the right to have immediate judicial assurance that advantages will be enjoyed or liabilities escaped in the future."

There are numerous opinions applying the general language of CCP §1060 to determine the existence of the required "actual controversy ." See 3 Witkin, PROCEDURE, Pleading §716. In *California Water & Tel Co.* (1967) 253 CA2d 16, 22 n9, 61 CR 618, 623 n9, the court stated it "is easier to illustrate ripeness [which the court equated with "actual controversy "] than it is to define it." See 253 CA2d at 22 n9, 61 CR 623 n9.

§24.10   a. Examples of Actual Controversy

Courts have found actual controversies in the following cases: *Southern Counties Gas Co. v Ventura Pipeline Constr. Co.* (1971) 19 CA3d 372, 381, 96 CR 825, 829 (declaration of rights under the indemnification sections of a series of contracts when there was the "prospect, if not likelihood," that future disputes would arise as a result of gas leaks due to corrosion in improperly wrapped pipes);

Schafer v Wholesale Frozen Foods, Inc. (1959) 171 CA2d 232, 340 P2d 308 (dispute over whether landlord, tenant, or subtenant responsible for damage to property);

Western Motors Corp. v Land Dev. & Inv. Co. (1957) 152 CA2d 509, 313 P2d 927 (dispute over lessor's duty to replace certain worn out elevator parts under provisions of a written lease);

Talcott v Talcott (1942) 54 CA2d 743, 129 P2d 946 (dispute over a testator's widow's right to sell certain property without the son's widow's consent despite an agreement and decree of distribution conditioning such sale on the deceased son's consent).

§24.11 b. Examples of No Actual Controversy

The following are examples of cases holding that no actual controversy existed:

State v Superior Court (1974) 12 C3d 237, 115 CR 497 (real parties-in-interest's contention that they had a right to develop land without a permit from the Coastal Zone Conservation Commission did not create an actual controversy because they had made no effort to obtain a vested right determination from the commission).

Selby Realty Co. v San Buenaventura (1973) 10 C3d 110, 109 CR 799 (declaration with respect to validity of a general plan adopted by a county; such relief could be obtained only if and when the plan was implemented so as to affect plaintiff's free use of its property); *Fracasse v Brent* (1972) 6 C3d 784, 100 CR 385 (no present controversy with respect to discharged attorney's claim for compensation for services rendered under contingent fee contract when contingency of recovery had not yet occurred).

Burke v San Francisco (1968) 258 CA2d 32, 65 CR 539 (no present actual controversy with respect to future tax assessments because it was only conjecture that such assessments would be improperly made);

Wilson v Transit Authority (1962) 199 CA2d 716, 19 CR 59 (union officers' claim that a public agency could legally include a compulsory arbitration clause in a collective bargaining agreement does not create actual controversy because there was no allegation of any dispute under the existing agreement and no claim that defendant transit authority had to include such a clause in the ensuing contract);

Taliaferro v Taliaferro (1959) 171 CA2d 1, 339 P2d 594 (no actual controversy when no allegation that defendant controverted a claim made by plaintiff);

Pittenger v Home Sav. & Loan Ass'n (1958) 166 CA2d 32, 332 P2d 399 (when defendant's assignee had voluntarily agreed to plaintiff's request the matter was moot);

Young v Young (1950) 100 CA2d 85, 223 P2d 25 (no actual controversy when action to declare validity of a foreign divorce decree did not show that anyone had claimed it was invalid);

Silva v San Francisco (1948) 87 CA2d 784, 198 P2d 78 (no actual controversy shown in action to determine value of land when condemnation proceedings had not been commenced).

C. Effect of Availability of Other Remedies on Availability of Declaratory Relief

§24.12 1. Remedies Cumulative

Code of Civil Procedure §1062 provides that the remedies set forth in the declaratory relief sections are "cumulative, and shall not be construed as restricting any remedy, provisional or otherwise, provided by law for the benefit of any party to such action," and that no declaratory judgment "shall preclude any party from obtaining relief based upon the same facts."

In addition, CCP §1060 provides that a plaintiff "may ask for a declaration of rights or duties, either alone or with other relief."

§24.13 2. Availability of Other Forums or Procedures May Preclude Relief

Notwithstanding the cases in which it has been held that the availability of other remedies does not preclude declaratory relief (see §24.12), courts have denied declaratory relief when other forums or procedures are available.

Communist Party v Peek (1942) 20 C2d 536, 127 P2d 889 (not an abuse of discretion for trial court to deny declaratory relief with respect to constitutionality of Election Code provisions because sections of that code provided speedy and adequate remedy);

Holden v Arnebergh (1968) 265 CA2d 87, 71 CR 401 (affirmed sustaining of demurrer because other remedies were available in criminal proceedings);

Barber v Irving (1964) 226 CA2d 560, 38 CR 142 (declaratory relief action not proper to decree nonexistence of corporation, which can be done only in a quo warranto action);

Rapaport v Forer (1937) 20 CA2d 271, 66 P2d 1242 (trial court properly exercised discretion in sustaining demurrer to declaratory relief action because plaintiff had right under CCP §689 to speedy hearing to determine ownership of subject matter of purported levy);

Fritz v Superior Court (1936) 18 CA2d 232, 63 P2d 872 (declaratory relief not necessary to determine claims of plaintiffs that they are directors because another statutory remedy available under Corp C §709 (former CC §315);

Stenzel v Kronick (1929) 102 CA 507, 283 P 93 (plaintiff, a judgment creditor, not entitled to declaratory relief with respect to rights in certain property because remedy of levying in execution available which would result in proceeding testing lien's validity if question arose).

Although CCP §1060 provides for a declaration of rights by any person interested under a will, rights under a will are usually adjudicated in the course of the proceedings of the probate court. When this is not possible, CCP §1060 provides another remedy. See §24.6 for discussion of cases such as *Howard v Bennett* (1942) 53 CA2d 546, 127 P2d 1012, and *Colden v Costello* (1942) 50 CA2d 363, 122 P2d 959. In both cases, the court held that declaratory relief did not lie because the probate court could give complete relief and therefore had exclusive jurisdiction.

§24.14 D. Effect of Accrued Cause of Action on Availability of Declaratory Relief

By virtue of CCP §1062 (see §24.3), the existence of an accrued cause of action does not necessarily preclude declaratory relief. In *Ermolieff v R.K.O. Radio Pictures, Inc.* (1942) 19 C2d 543, 547, 122 P2d 3, the court stated that a court may make a binding declaration of rights whether other relief is or could be claimed or obtained and that the remedy is cumulative. See also *Warren v Kaiser Foundation Health Plan, Inc.* (1975) 47 CA3d 678, 121 CR 19.

The fact that a cause of action has accrued and that other adequate relief may be available to plaintiff does not preclude declaratory relief, although such a situation may lead a court to exercise its discretion under CCP §1061 (see §24.19) not to grant declaratory relief (*Columbia Pictures Corp. v DeToth* (1945) 26 C2d 753, 161 P2d 217). This is also true if another action is already pending. See cases cited in §24.19.

It has been stated, however, by one court, quoting from Borchard, DECLARATORY JUDGMENTS 302 (2d ed 1941), that:

[I]t is wrong for courts to decline a declaration on the mere ground that another remedy was available . . . . It is only where the court believes that *more* effective relief can and should be obtained by another procedure, and that for that reason a declaration will not serve a useful purpose, that it is justified in refusing a declaration because of the availability of another remedy.

Jones v Robertson (1947) 79 CA2d 813, 819, 180 P2d 929, 933. See, however, the discussion in §§24.13, 24.23–24.25.

§24.15 E. Effect of Declaration That Party Has No Rights on Availability of Other Relief

Code of Civil Procedure §1062 provides that the remedy of declaratory relief is cumulative and does not restrict a party from seeking additional relief. Plaintiff in a declaratory relief action who has been determined in a declaratory relief action to have no rights, cannot obtain different relief. *Dills v Delira Corp.* (1956) 145 CA2d 124, 130, 302 P2d 397, 401. In *Dills*, the court held that after such a determination, plaintiff could not obtain relief under a common counts allegation.

III. GROUNDS FOR DENIAL
§24.16 A. Lack of Jurisdiction

The declaratory relief statutes do not enlarge the courts' jurisdiction to decide a particular matter, but rather are intended to provide an additional procedure for utilizing the existing jurisdiction of the courts. *Hoyt v Board of Civil Serv. Comm'rs* (1942) 21 C2d 399, 403, 132 P2d 804, 806. See also *Harmon v Pacific Tel. & Tel. Co.* (1960) 183 CA2d 1, 6 CR 542. Thus, challenges to lack of subject matter and party jurisdiction may be sustained in declaratory relief actions as in other types of actions. On jurisdiction generally, see 1 CALIFORNIA CIVIL PROCEDURE BEFORE TRIAL chap 2 (Cal CEB 1977). See also §24.27.

§24.17 B. Lack of Actual Controversy

Lack of an actual controversy is ground for denial of declaratory relief. Actual controversy is defined in §24.9. Examples of fact situations in which courts found no actual controversy existed are set forth in §24.11.

§24.18 C. Lack of Standing

The doctrine of standing to bring an action applies to declaratory relief actions to the same extent it does to other types of actions because CCP §1060 in effect provides a standing requirement by limiting declaratory relief to "any person interested" under a contract or other instruments, or "who desires a declaration of his rights or duties with respect to another, or in respect to, in, over or upon property," or with respect to a watercourse. See *Rowland School Dist. v State Bd. of Educ.* (1968) 264 CA2d 589, 593, 70 CR 504, 507, in which the court said that plaintiff had not stated a cause of action for declaratory relief unless plaintiff had alleged facts showing that plaintiff had an interest affected by the invalidity of the provisions plaintiff had attacked.

Standing can also be considered as an element of a justiciable controversy . It has been noted that "the concept of justiciability involves both ripeness and standing." *California Water & Tel. Co. v Los Angeles* (1967) 253 CA2d 16, 22, 61 CR 618, 623. See §§24.9–24.10 on actual controversy.

D. Judicial Discretion to Deny Relief
§24.19 1. When Not Necessary or Proper

Under CCP §1061 "[t]he court may refuse to exercise the power granted by [the declaratory relief provisions] in any case where its declaration or determination is not necessary or proper at the time under all the circumstances." As this section is interpreted in some decisions, a court may deny declaratory relief even though plaintiff pleads and proves the required facts that could permit a declaratory relief action to be brought. See §§24.8–24.11. The California Supreme Court stated in *Orloff v Metropolitan Trust Co.* (1941) 17 C2d 484, 489, 110 P2d 396, 399, that the lower court's refusal to entertain the complaint for declaratory relief was not reviewable except for an abuse of discretion. See also *Travers v Louden* (1967) 254 CA2d 926, 62 CR 654.

As Witkin has pointed out, however, "The sweeping dicta asserting unlimited discretion are usually found in cases in which there are distinct grounds for denial." 3 Witkin, CALIFORNIA PROCEDURE, Pleading §720 (2d ed 1971). This view seems to be borne out in cases decided after *Orloff, supra*. For example, in *Columbia Pictures Corp. v DeToth* (1945) 26 C2d 753, 762, 161 P2d 217, 221, the court said that "Declaratory relief must be granted when the facts justifying that course are sufficiently alleged." See also *International Ass'n of Fire Fighters v Palo Alto* (1963) 60 C2d 295, 301, 32 CR 842, 845; *Kessloff v Pearson* (1951) 37 C2d 609, 233 P2d 899. Witkin has also stated that, "in some of the cases the court, for good measure, refers to the broad discretion under CCP §1061, but this only confuses the issue. When these decisions are properly classified and the real reasons for denial made clear, the list of discretionary refusal cases is considerably reduced." 3 Witkin, CALIFORNIA PROCEDURE, Pleading §729 (2d ed 1971). See also Stern, *The Availability of Declaratory Relief in California* 39 BEV HILLS BJ (1972):

Although it may be argued that lack of clearer guidance from appellate courts has been largely the result of Section 1061, allowing broad discretion in the denial of relief, the appellate cases have nevertheless failed to develop satisfactory standards for the availability of declaratory relief under the existing statute.

Courts have invoked CCP §1061 in denying declaratory relief when the issues have already been or can be disposed of in other proceedings which are pending (*Allstate Ins. Co. v Fisher* (1973) 31 CA3d 391, 107 CR 251); see *Fagerstedt v Continental Ins. Co.* (1968) 266 CA2d 370, 72 CR 126; *Baker v Commeford* (1956) 140 CA2d 599, 295 P2d 522) and when another remedy is available (see *Alturas v Gloster* (1940) 16 C2d 46, 104 P2d 810; *General of America Ins. Co. v Lilly* (1968) 258 CA2d 465, 65 CR 750; *Girard v Miller* (1963) 214 CA2d 266, 29 CR 359.

In some instances the courts have apparently viewed the merits (see §24.20) or equitable defenses in determining whether to refuse to entertain a declaratory relief action (see *Moss v Moss* (1942) 20 C2d 640, 128 P2d 526, in which the court held that the trial court did not abuse its discretion in denying declaratory relief when the parties were in pari delicto; *Fay Sec. Co. v Mort-*

gage Guar. Co. (1940) 37 CA2d 637, 100 P2d 344, indicating that laches might support refusal to grant declaratory relief).

In *California Water & Tel. Co. v Los Angeles* (1967) 253 CA2d 16, 61 CR 618, dealing with the validity of an ordinance, the court set forth the following factors as affecting the exercise of judicial discretion; (1) the penal nature of the ordinance or statute concerned; (2) the present need for a declaration; (3) the character of the parties' and the public's interest in the subject matter; (4) the existence of alternative remedies; and (5) the character of the challenged ordinance or statute. The court added that declaratory relief "is properly denied, for example, if the factual matrix is insufficiently set to permit a useful and intelligent adjudication to be made." 253 CA2d at 24, 61 CR at 624.

Although the precise application of CCP §1061 is unclear, it seems that when plaintiff adequately pleads a cause of action for declaratory relief and states facts showing that other remedies would not be as speedy or adequate as declaratory relief, a refusal to entertain an action under CCP §1061 will be considered an abuse of discretion.

In *Warren v Kaiser Foundation Health Plan, Inc.* (1975) 47 CA3d 678, 683, 121 CR 19, 22, after referring to *Columbia Pictures Corp. v DeToth, supra,* the court stated that any doubt should be resolved in favor of granting declaratory relief and that while the trial court may refuse to grant declaratory relief when the complaining party has a cause of action for past wrongs, and all relationship between the parties has ended, it may not deny relief when a suit on the matured breach is not as speedy and adequate or as well suited to plaintiff's needs as declaratory relief. The court held that dismissal of the complaint in *Warren* was error when plaintiff sought a declaration construing a health care contract because, even though there had been an alleged breach, the contract created a continuing relationship. *Warren v Kaiser Foundation Health Plan, Inc.* (1975) 47 CA3d 678, 121 CR 19. See also *Lomanto v Bank of America* (1972) 22 CA3d 663, 667, 99 CR 442, 444.

§24.20 2. When Complaint Does Not State a Cause of Action

An area of seeming conflict arises from the fact that some courts have denied declaratory relief on the basis that the complaint shows that plaintiff does not have a meritorious claim.

People v Ray (1960) 181 CA2d 64, 67, 5 CR 113 ("declaratory relief does not lie on a case in which a complaint makes no case on the merits and would merely produce a useless trial"). See also *Silver v Los Angeles* (1963) 217 CA2d 134, 31 CR 545 (denial seems also to be based on the trial court's discretion (see §24.19)); *Konecko v Konecko* (1955) 164 CA2d 249, 330 P2d 393.

Other courts have said that if a complaint sets forth facts showing the existence of an actual controversy relating to the parties' legal rights and duties (see §§24.9–24.10), the trial court must declare their rights regardless of whether the alleged facts establish that plaintiff is entitled to a favorable declaration. *Bennett v Hibernia Bank* (1956) 47 C2d 540, 549, 305 P2d 20, 26; see *Los Angeles County Democratic Cent. Comm. v Los Angeles* (1976) 61 CA3d 335, 338, 132 CR 43, 44. See also *Loupias v Rosen* (1951) 102 CA2d 781, 784, 228 P2d 611, 613, which stated that a party may seek a declaratory judgment as distinguished from declaratory relief even though his pleading shows affirmatively that he is not entitled to any relief.

In *Western Homes v Herbert Ketell, Inc.* (1965) 236 CA2d 142, 146, 45 CR 856, 859, the court attempted to reconcile the apparent conflict by stating that the declaratory relief remedy is subject to the trial judge's informed and sensible discretion under CCP §1061 (see §24.19). It held that an order sustaining a general demurrer by the trial court should not be reversed when the allegations of the complaint showed that plaintiff had no cause of action because the appellate court's declaration accomplished declaratory relief. See also *Los Angeles County Democratic Cent. Comm. v Los Angeles* (1976) 61 CA3d 335, 338, 132 CR 43, 44.

§24.21 E. Failure to Exhaust Administrative Remedies

Before a party may obtain judicial review of an administrative agency's decision he must exhaust the remedies before that agency. This principle applies also to the right to seek declaratory relief. *Louis Eckert Brewing Co. v Unemployment Reserves Comm'n* (1941) 47 CA2d 844, 119 P2d 227 (plaintiff that failed to appeal to a commission as provided by its rule had not exhausted administrative remedies and thus was not entitled to a declaration regarding its rights). Compare *Honeywell, Inc. v State Bd. of Equalization* (1975) 48 CA3d 907, 122 CR 243 and *Imperial Mut. Life Ins. Co. v Caminetti* (1943) 59 CA2d 501, 139 P2d 691 (declaratory relief not available when administrative remedies

§24.22   DECLARATORY RELIEF   84

have not been exhausted) with *Environmental Law Fund, Inc. v Corte Madera* (1975) 49 CA3d 105, 114, 122 CR 282, 287 ("the failure of a private person to exhaust an administrative remedy, against governmental action taken in an administrative proceeding to which he was not a party, does not bar him from seeking judicial relief from such action by way of enforcing rights which he holds as a member of the affected public").

In *Walker v Munro* (1960) 178 CA2d 67, 77, 2 CR 737, 744, the court stated that it would be an anomaly if a party facing punitive or disciplinary proceedings before an administrative body, could bypass them by bringing a declaratory relief action based on the very questions before the administrative body in its quasi-judicial capacity. It declared that the trial court had not abused its discretion in requiring the matter to be determined first by the administrative agency. *Walker* illustrates that it is not always clear whether the denial of relief is based on the jurisdictional ground of failure to exhaust an administrative remedy or on an exercise of the court's discretion to deny declaratory relief (see §24.19).

A principle related to the exhaustion of administrative remedies doctrine is that judicial relief, including declaratory relief, is not available if the subject matter of the action is, at least initially, within the primary or exclusive jurisdiction of an executive, administrative, or legislative body (see §24.23).

§24.22   F. Underlying Claim Barred by Statutes of Limitation or Laches

There is no statute of limitations specifically applicable to declaratory relief actions. The courts determine whether a statute of limitations bars a declaratory relief action by ascertaining whether the underlying controversy is barred.

The periods of limitations applicable to ordinary actions at law and suits in equity are applicable to actions for declaratory relief. Thus if a party seeks declaratory relief on an obligation that has been breached and the right to commence an action for coercive relief on the cause of action is barred, the right to declaratory relief is also barred. If, however, a party seeks declaratory relief *before* there has been a breach of the obligation, the right to relief is not barred by any period of limitations. *Maguire v Hibernia Sav. & Loan Soc'y* (1944) 23 C2d 719, 734, 146 P2d

673, 681. See also *Pena v Los Angeles* (1970) 8 CA3d 257, 87 CR 326; *Liberty Mut. Ins. Co. v Colonial Ins. Co.* (1970) 8 CA3d 427, 87 CR 348; *Tostevin v Douglas* (1958) 160 CA2d 321, 325 P2d 130; *Leahey v Dep't of Water & Power* (1946) 76 CA2d 281, 173 P2d 69.

If the underlying claim is equitable in nature, the doctrine of laches can be applied under appropriate circumstances. See *Empire W. Side Irr. Dist. v Stratford Irr. Dist.* (1937) 10 C2d 376, 74 P2d 248 (held laches applicable, although unclear if there was any underlying equitable claim); *Rivieccio v Bothan* (1946) 27 C2d 621, 165 P2d 677 (upholding trial court's decision that the facts in the particular case did not support the application of laches).

§24.23 G. Mandatory Use of Other Forums or Procedures; Matters Within Exclusive Province of Another Government Branch or Agency May Preclude Relief

Courts have denied declaratory relief on the ground that relief must be sought in another forum, or in a different manner, or that declaratory relief would include matters within the exclusive province of another government branch or agency. See *State v Superior Court* (1974) 12 C3d 237, 115 CR 497 (declaratory relief not appropriate to review administrative decision such as, in the particular case, a refusal by the Coastal Zone Conservation Commission to grant a land development permit); *Selby Realty Co. v San Buenaventura* (1973) 10 C3d 110, 118, 109 CR 799, 804 (a landowner may not maintain a declaratory relief action to challenge the merits of the adoption of a general plan, which is a legislative act, absent an allegation of a defect in the proceedings leading to its enactment); *Subriar v Bakersfield* (1976) 59 CA3d 175, 194, 130 CR 853, 864 (challenge to the validity of an ordinance involving administrative action as it applies to plaintiff's situation should be by judicial review under CCP §§1094–1095, and not by a declaratory relief action); *Zetterberg v State Dep't of Pub. Health* (1974) 43 CA3d 657, 118 CR 100 (declaratory relief not available to test administrative discretion); *Valley Fair Fashions, Inc. v Valley Fair* (1966) 245 CA2d 614, 54 CR 306 (declaratory relief cannot be used to circumvent statutory provisions prohibiting injunctive or mandamus relief to prevent collection of tax); *West Coast Poultry Co. v Glasner* (1965) 231 CA2d 747, 42

§24.24   DECLARATORY RELIEF

CR 297 (declaratory relief not available to determine whether government inspector not legally qualified to hold position; matter should be resolved by civil service or personnel boards, or perhaps by taxpayer's suit); *Harmon v Pacific Tel. & Tel. Co.* (1960) 183 CA2d 1, 6 CR 542; *Independent Laundry v Railroad Comm'n* (1945) 70 CA2d 816, 161 P2d 827 (orders and regulations of Public Utilities Commission reviewable only in Supreme Court); *Monahan v Department of Water & Power* (1941) 48 CA2d 746, 120 P2d 730 (declaratory relief not available with respect to matter within exclusive province of executive branch).

§24.24   H. Generally Not Available With Respect to Criminal Statutes; Exception

Declaratory relief should not be granted when its only effect would be to decide a matter that is more appropriately decided in the criminal courts. *Manchel v Los Angeles* (1966) 245 CA2d 501, 507, 54 CR 53, 57 (court refused declaration that specified cardgame is not a game of chance and thus that gambling ordinance could not be enforced against those who play the game for money). Although an action for declaratory relief lies to determine the alleged obscenity of a book or other material under applicable statutes, the court may exercise its discretion (see §24.19) to deny relief because other adequate remedies are available to test the seizure of allegedly obscene material. *Holden v Arnebergh* (1968) 265 CA2d 87, 71 CR 401. Declaratory relief, however, will be granted with respect to criminal statutes when constitutional rights are concerned. *Zeitlin v Arnebergh* (1963) 59 C2d 901, 31 CR 800; *Abbott v Los Angeles* (1960) 53 C2d 674, 3 CR 158. See also *Tiburon v Northwestern Pac. R.R.* (1970) 4 CA3d 160, 84 CR 469 (right to impose penal sanctions for violation of subdivision requirements did not justify refusal to exercise power to grant declaratory relief on whether land had been properly divided under state and local law).

§24.25   I. No Declaration Regarding Future Conduct Sought

Courts have denied declaratory relief when all the acts complained of were concluded before commencement of the declaratory relief action, and plaintiff, in effect, sought a declaration that he was entitled to a monetary judgment. *Orloff v Metropolitan*

Trust Co. (1941) 17 C2d 484, 110 P2d 396. See also *Watson v Sansoe* (1971) 19 CA3d 1, 96 CR 387 (plaintiff who received a medical bill could not maintain a declaratory relief action to determine that he did not owe the money because the doctor had not filed an action to collect the bill). Cases stating that the availability of another remedy does not preclude declaratory relief (see §24.13) do not stand "for the proposition that a declaration with respect to past wrongs would be proper when there was no occasion to define respective rights which would govern the future conduct of the parties." *Travers v Louden* (1967) 254 CA2d 926, 932, 62 CR 654, 658. The court also noted that it could find no authority supporting declaratory relief when the plaintiff's rights had "crystallized" into a cause of action for past wrongs, all relationship between the parties had ended, and there was no conduct of the parties subject to the court's regulation. 254 CA2d at 929, 62 CR at 656. See also *Watson v Sansoe, supra; Bachis v State Farm Mut. Auto. Ins. Co.* (1968) 265 CA2d 722, 71 CR 486.

§24.26 J. Other Grounds for Denial

In addition to the grounds set forth in §§24.16–24.25, declaratory relief may be denied on other grounds which preclude relief in ordinary legal or equitable actions. See *Dawson v Los Altos Hills* (1976) 16 C3d 676, 687, 129 CR 97, 104; *Burke v San Francisco* (1968) 258 CA2d 32, 65 CR 539 (when matter is moot); *Taliaferro v Taliaferro* (1959) 171 CA2d 1, 339 P2d 594 (defendant not served with process); *Monahan v Department of Water & Power* (1941) 48 CA2d 746, 753, 120 P2d 730, 734 (essential allegations set forth by way of conclusions rather than by ultimate facts). Moreover, declaratory relief cannot be utilized to circumvent other prohibitions against the maintenance of actions. See, e.g., *Cooper v Leslie Salt Co.* (1969) 70 C2d 627, 634, 75 CR 766, 770 (cannot use declaratory relief to challenge existence of municipal entity when quo warranto not available); see *Honeywell, Inc. v State Bd. of Equalization* (1975) 48 CA3d 907, 122 CR 243 (cannot use declaratory relief to circumvent statute precluding injunctive relief or mandamus to prevent the collection of a tax); *Faix, Ltd. v Los Angeles* (1976) 54 CA3d 992, 127 CR 182 (landowner not entitled to sue for declaratory relief respecting validity of tax assessment when statutory condition precedent of payment in full not satisfied).

IV. PROCEDURE

A. Commencing the Action

1. Court in Which Action May Be Brought

§24.27 a. Jurisdiction

Actions for declaratory relief "are not intended in any way to enlarge the jurisdiction of the courts over parties and subject matter." *Hoyt v Board of Civil Serv. Comm'rs* (1942) 21 C2d 399, 403, 132 P2d 804, 806. See also *Harmon v Pacific Tel. & Tel. Co.* (1960) 183 CA2d 1, 6 CR 542. Superior courts have exclusive original jurisdiction over complaints for declaratory relief without regard to the amount in controversy; superior, municipal, and justice courts have jurisdiction over cross-complaints for declaratory relief in pending actions. CCP §1060. However, CCP §86(a)(7) appears to limit municipal and justice court jurisdiction solely to cross-complaints for declaratory relief "as to a right of indemnity with respect to the relief demanded in the complaint or a cross-complaint in an action or proceeding otherwise within the jurisdiction of the municipal or justice court."

Jurisdictional requirements with regard to the amount in controversy may not be circumvented by labeling a fully matured cause of action as a declaratory relief action, when no future rights or duties are concerned. Thus, in an action for money damages of $5000 or less when nothing remained to be done but the payment of money, the court transferred the action to the municipal court even though plaintiff purported to seek declaratory relief. *Bachis v State Farm Mut. Auto Ins. Co.* (1968) 265 CA2d 722, 71 CR 486. See also *Watson v Sansoe* (1971) 19 CA3d 1, 96 CR 387. When, however, a complaint for declaratory relief is bona fide and not a vehicle for forum shopping or calendar preference, the superior court has jurisdiction regardless of the amount in question. CCP §1060; *Southern Counties Gas Co. v Ventura Pipeline Constr. Co.* (1971) 19 CA3d 372, 377, 96 CR 825, 826.

There have been few cases in California on jurisdiction relating specifically to jurisdiction in declaratory relief actions. When a California court has jurisdiction over the parties a declaratory relief action may be brought for a declaration of the parties' rights with respect to real property outside the state. The action is considered transitory and properly brought. *Mills v Mills* (1956) 147 CA2d 107, 118, 305 P2d 61, 68.

In *Alpha Beta Food Mkts., Inc. v Amalgamated Meat Cutters* (1956) 147 CA2d 343, 305 P2d 163, the court held that it had jurisdiction to render a declaration whether a contract executed and to be performed in California violated federal (as well as California) law even though federal jurisdiction was exclusive with regard to actions under the federal laws involved. See also *Patel v Athow* (1973) 34 CA3d 727, 110 CR 460, in which the court held that it had jurisdiction over a declaratory relief action to determine that a lease option was impossible of performance by virtue of wage and price control laws because the cause of action did not arise under the federal Economic Stabilization Act of 1970 which vested exclusive jurisdiction in the federal courts.

On occasion, in considering whether there is a justiciable controversy (see §§24.9–24.11), or in determining whether to exercise discretion to entertain a declaratory relief action (see §24.19), courts will discuss whether they have "jurisdiction," but the term "jurisdiction" is not used in such cases in the traditional sense. See, e.g., *Columbia Pictures Corp. v DeToth* (1945) 26 C2d 753, 762, 161 P2d 217, 221; *Monahan v Department of Water & Power* (1941) 48 CA2d 746, 749, 120 P2d 730, 731. On jurisdiction generally, see 1 CALIFORNIA CIVIL PROCEDURE BEFORE TRIAL chap 2 (Cal CEB 1977).

§24.28   b. Venue

Venue of an action for declaratory relief is governed by the same statutes as those affecting any other action. *Tomasello v Tomasello* (1952) 113 CA2d 23, 247 P2d 612; *Dallman Supply Co. v Sweet* (1948) 86 CA2d 780, 195 P2d 864. In both these cases, traditional venue requirements were applied in declaratory relief actions. On venue generally, see 1 CALIFORNIA CIVIL PROCEDURE BEFORE TRIAL chap 3 (Cal CEB 1977).

Venue or jurisdictional requirements (see §24.27) may restrict the scope of relief that a court grants in a declaratory relief action. Compare *Davis v Stulman* (1945) 72 CA2d 255, 164 P2d 787 (scope of judgment restricted because the real estate concerned was located in another county and thus within exclusive jurisdiction of another court) with *Mills v Mills* (1956) 147 CA2d 107, 305 P2d 61 (full declaratory relief available with respect to rights in realty in another state because court had in personam jurisdiction).

§24.29 2. Necessary, Indispensable, and Proper Parties; Governmental Entities

Declaratory relief actions are governed by the same rules regarding necessary, indispensable, and proper parties that apply to civil actions generally. The California Supreme Court stated in *Hoyt v Board of Civil Serv. Comm'rs* (1942) 21 C2d 399, 403, 132 P2d 804, 806, that "[i]t has been held repeatedly that actions for declaratory relief involve matters of practice and procedure only and are not intended in any way to enlarge the jurisdiction of courts over *parties* and subject-matter." [Emphasis added.]

A person whose absence from the proceeding will cause substantial prejudice is an indispensable party and thus must be joined as a jurisdictional matter; a person whose joinder would be desirable is a necessary party and such joinder will often be compelled, but is not essential to the court's jurisdiction. See §§25.2–25.6.

In addition, parties may be joined in the action if they have certain connections with the action. *Vanoni v Sonoma* (1974) 40 CA3d 743, 746, 115 CR 485, 487; *Martin v Corning* (1972) 25 CA3d 165, 170, 101 CR 678, 681; see generally 1 CALIFORNIA CIVIL PROCEDURE BEFORE TRIAL §§7.14–7.15 (Cal CEB 1977).

Questions about parties depend on the facts of the particular case. Most of the cases concerning parties in declaratory relief actions were decided before certain statutes on parties, *i.e.*, CCP §§378–379, 379.5, 382 (see §25.13; 1 CIV PROC BEFORE TRIAL 3.12, 7.13–7.15, 12.13, 20.24) were amended operative 1972, but these cases may be relevant. See *San Joaquin v State Bd. of Equalization* (1970) 9 CA3d 365, 88 CR 12 (in action against an agency concerning the interpretation of a statute, plaintiff need not join everyone who may ultimately be affected by the court's decision); *General of America Ins. Co. v Whitmore* (1965) 235 CA2d 670, 45 CR 556 (in action by an insurer whether it is obligated under a public liability policy to parties injured by its insured, the injured parties, while not indispensable, are proper parties); *Leonard Corp. v San Diego* (1962) 210 CA2d 547, 26 CR 730 (in action by a property owner to determine validity of zoning ordinance with respect to subdivision property, owners in adjacent subdivision are not indispensable parties); *Lushing v Riviera Estates Ass'n* (1961) 196 CA2d 687, 16 CR 763 (in action by a lot owner against a developer regarding the scope of a restrictive covenant, other lot owners are not necessary parties because such a declaration will not prejudice their interests; the court noting, however, that if the action had been to obtain an order violative of the restrictions that would prejudice other lot owners, they would be necessary parties); *Jones v Feichtmeir* (1949) 95 CA2d 341, 212 P2d 933 (in action by a sublessee against a sublessor for a declaration of rights under the sublease, the lessor is not an indispensable party when permission to sublease is not in issue); *Pasadena v Alhambra* (1949) 33 C2d 908, 207 P2d 17 (in action to determine rights to underground water, no error not to join certain users of small amounts of the water because of the impracticality of joining all such users).

Declaratory relief may be sought against any "person" who can otherwise be sued. Thus, in *Hoyt v Board of Civil Serv. Comm'rs* (1942) 21 C2d 399, 403, 132 P2d 804, 806, the court stated that the right to bring an action for declaratory relief against a governmental agency exists "if an acceptance of liability and subjection to suit on the part of a sovereign body is found elsewhere in the statutes of the state and the declaratory judgment procedure is not barred by the provisions of the waiver of immunity." See also *Cooper v Leslie Salt Co.* (1969) 70 C2d 627, 75 CR 766; *San Ysidro Irr. Dist. v Superior Court* (1961) 56 C2d 708, 16 CR 609. Generally, declaratory relief is available against governmental entities. See *Lord v Garland* (1946) 27 C2d 840, 852, 168 P2d 5.

3. Drafting the Complaint

§24.30 a. Requisite Contents

General pleading requirements are applicable to actions for declaratory relief. See *Mackay v Whitaker* (1953) 116 CA2d 504, 510, 253 P2d 1021, 1025. Courts have repeatedly stated that declaratory relief is a broad remedy and the rule that a complaint is to be liberally construed is particularly applicable to a complaint for declaratory relief. *Burke v San Francisco* (1968) 258 CA2d 32, 33, 65 CR 539, 540. See also *Tiburon v Northwestern Pac. R.R.* (1970) 4 CA3d 160, 84 CR 469.

To state a cause of action for declaratory relief under CCP §1060, it is, however, necessary to plead facts showing a real controversy between the parties involving justiciable questions relating to their rights and obligations and a proper subject within the scope of that section. See §§24.9–24.10. The complaint must set forth the claims of the parties; merely alleging a conclusion that there is a controversy is insufficient. See *Alturas v Gloster* (1940) 16 C2d 46, 104 P2d 810; *E. M. Cotton Appliances, Inc. v Felton Aluminum Co.* (1954) 124 CA2d 546, 269 P2d 64; *Loupias v Rosen* (1951) 102 CA2d 781, 784, 228 P2d 611, 613 (plaintiff should plead facts showing that "the controversy is real and not merely illusory"); *Hagan v Fairfield* (1965) 238 CA2d 197, 202, 47 CR 600, 604 ("must plead facts rather than conclusions of law"). *Appliance, Inc. v Felton Aluminum Co.* (1954) 124 CA2d 546, 548, 269 P2d 64 (plaintiff's failure to set forth defendant's claim with particularity precluded declaratory relief).

In asking for declaratory relief, the pleader need not specify the relief sought. The court will make the appropriate declaration. *California Canning Peach Growers v Corcoran* (1936) 14 CA2d 264, 267, 57 P2d 1360. It is better practice, however, to set forth the desired declaration. See §§24.32–24.33.

Because an action for declaratory relief usually involves an adjudication of rights before they have been invaded (see, however, §§24.13–24.14), a plaintiff need not allege facts showing a breach of an instrument or violation of an ordinance. See *Chas. L. Harney, Inc. v Contractors' State License Bd.* (1952) 39 C2d 561, 247 P2d 913; *Pacific States Corp. v Pan-American Bank* (1931) 213 C 58, 1 P2d 4.

§24.31 b. Joinder of Causes of Action

Declaratory relief actions may be brought either alone or in combination with causes of action for other types of relief. CCP §1062. Thus, plaintiff may seek coercive relief and declaratory relief in the same complaint. Plaintiff is not required to set forth claims for coercive and declaratory relief in separate counts when both claims arise out of the same transaction, because a single cause of action may call for more than one remedy. *Marden v Bailard* (1954) 124 CA2d 458, 268 P2d 809. Nevertheless, for clarity it is advisable to set forth the claims for coercive relief and declaratory relief in different counts.

Usually, a declaratory relief cause of action is joined with a cause of action seeking other relief. Joinder of a claim for declaratory relief with a claim for other relief has certain advantages for plaintiff. For example, if plaintiff cannot establish an immediate right to coercive relief, a declaration may establish future rights so that a subsequent action will not be necessary. An action for coercive relief alone may not resolve the entire controversy between the parties.

When the other causes of action are found insufficient, adding a declaratory relief cause of action containing the same facts as in defective causes of action does not necessarily preclude a dismissal of the entire action. See *Girard v Miller* (1963) 214 CA2d 266, 29 CR 359. The failure to include a claim for coercive relief does not preclude a party from seeking such relief in a new action. *Lortz v Connell* (1969) 273 CA2d 286, 300, 78 CR 6, 15.

When an inappropriate cause of action for declaratory relief is added to gain trial-calendar precedence under CCP §1062a (see §24.39), a court may exercise its discretion to sustain a demurrer to such a cause of action. See *Travers v Louden* (1967) 254 CA2d 926, 932, 62 CR 654, 658, in which the court said "the courts should not temporize with the improper use of the declaratory procedure to gain a preferred position on the trial calendar [citation]. Undeserving cases should be disposed of in a summary manner, as upon demurrer."

§24.32   4. Form: Complaint for Declaratory Relief on Contract

Copies: Original (filed with court clerk); copies for service (one for each defendant who is to be served); office copies.

[Caption. See §§23.18–23.19]

No. _____

COMPLAINT FOR DECLARATORY RELIEF ON ____[WRITTEN / ORAL]____ CONTRACT

Plaintiff alleges:

1. **Plaintiff is, and at all times mentioned was** ____[e.g., a corporation duly organized and existing under the laws of the State of California]____.

2. **Defendant** ____[name]____ **is, and at all times mentioned was** ____[e.g., a resident of _____ County, California]____.

3. **Plaintiff does not know the true names of defendants sued as Doe 1 through Doe** ____[number of fictitiously named defendants]____.

4. **On or about** _____, 19____, **plaintiff and defendant entered into a** ____[written / oral]____ **contract which provided** ____[state essential provisions of contract between parties]____.

[When written contract]

A copy of this contract is attached as Exhibit A and is incorporated by reference.

5. ____[*State ultimate facts that show the existence of an actual controversy, e.g., defendant's position with regard to the contract or refusal to perform in accordance with plaintiff's interpretation of the contract*]____.

6. **An actual controversy has arisen and now exists between plaintiff and defendant concerning their respective rights and duties under the contract** ____[*state plaintiff's contentions concerning the dispute*]____. **Defendant disputes plaintiff's contentions and contends that** _____.

7. **Plaintiff desires a judicial determination and declaration of plaintiff's and defendant's respective rights and duties under the contract and specifically whether under the contract** ____[*state the declaration requested, e.g., that plaintiff's interpretation of the contract is correct and that defendant is obligated to perform the disputed acts under the contract*]____.

8. **The declaration is necessary and appropriate at this time so that plaintiff can determine** ____[*his / her / its*]____ **obligations and duties with respect to the subject matter of the contract and specifically** ____[*state facts showing the need for the declaration and, in particular, any financial or other burdens that are being caused by the unsettled state of affairs resulting from the different interpretations of the contract and, when appropriate, that other remedies are inadequate*]____.

WHEREFORE, plaintiff demands judgment as follows:

1. **That the Court declare plaintiff's and defendant's respective rights and duties under the** ____[*written / oral*]____ **contract; that defendant is obligated to** ____[*state defendant's obligation(s)*]____;

2. ____[*For attorneys' fees, if provided for in the contract or by statute*]____;

3. **For costs and all other just relief.**

Dated: _____

_____
[*Signature of attorney or party*]

[*Typed name*]
____[*Attorney for plaintiff*]____

Comment: Plaintiff may add specific declaration that he would prefer, *e.g.*, that the court render a declaration in conformity with plaintiff's contentions and that defendant is obligated to perform the acts in question. Note that plaintiff may seek declaratory relief under either a written or oral contract, but that other instruments under which relief is sought must be written. See §§24.5–24.6.

A complaint for declaratory relief may also claim damages or other forms of relief. Any additional relief claimed should be specified in the title of the complaint (*e.g.*, by adding "AND DAMAGES" or other designation), supported by factual allegations (preferably stated in a separate cause of action; see §24.31) and demanded in the prayer. If damages are sought in addition to declaratory relief, the amount of damages sought should be stated.

On preparation of complaints generally, see 1 CALIFORNIA CIVIL PROCEDURE BEFORE TRIAL chap 7 (Cal CEB 1977). See §29.73 on obtaining attorneys' fees as part of costs.

§24.33 5. Form: Complaint for Declaratory Relief on Statute or Ordinance

Copies: Original (filed with court clerk); copies for service (one for each defendant who is to be served); office copies.

[Caption. See §§23.18–23.19]

No. _____

COMPLAINT FOR DECLARATORY RELIEF ON ____[STATUTE / ORDINANCE]____

Plaintiff alleges:
1. Plaintiff is, and at all times mentioned was ____[e.g., a corporation duly organized and existing under the laws of the State of California]____.
2. Defendant ____[name]____ is, and at all times mentioned was, a governmental entity organized and existing under

[Choose appropriate statement]

____[Constitution / laws]____ of the State of California.

[Or]

____an ordinance of the ____[e.g., County of _____]____.

[Continue]

Defendant ____[name]____ is ____[title]____ and the person charged with ____[describe responsibility for administering statute or ordinance]____.
3. Plaintiff does not know the true names of defendants sued as Doe 1 through Doe ____[number of fictitiously named defendants]____.
4. On or about _____, 19____, a ____[statute / ordinance]____ described as _____ was enacted by ____[the California State Legislature / City Council of _____ / (Etc.)]____. A copy of this ____[statute / ordinance]____ is attached as Exhibit A and is incorporated by reference. This ____[statute / ordinance]____ is in full force and effect.
5. ____[State facts showing that statute or ordinance is being applied or could be applied to plaintiff and that application of the statute or ordinance interferes with or impairs plaintiff's rights and privileges]____.
6. ____[State facts showing that plaintiff has exhausted all administrative remedies]____.
7. An actual controversy now exists between plaintiff and defendants concerning their respective rights and duties. Plaintiff contends that the

§24.34   DECLARATORY RELIEF

____[statute / ordinance]____ **is invalid and unenforceable on its face and as applied to plaintiff in that** ____[state facts and contentions regarding statute's or ordinance's invalidity or unenforceability]____. **Defendants dispute plaintiff's contentions and contend that the** ____[statute / ordinance]____ **is valid and enforceable and applies to plaintiff.**

8. Plaintiff desires a judicial determination and declaration of plaintiff's and defendants' respective rights and duties whether plaintiff's activities violate the ____[statute / ordinance]____ and with respect to the validity and enforceability of the ____[statute / ordinance]____ as applied to plaintiff. Such a declaration is necessary and appropriate at this time so that plaintiff may ascertain ____[his / her / its]____ rights and duties without being subjected to liability for violation of the ____[statute / ordinance]____. ____[State any facts showing harm that may result to plaintiff if declaratory relief is not obtained]____.

WHEREFORE, plaintiff demands judgment as follows:

1. That the Court declare plaintiff's and defendants' respective rights and duties under the ____[statute / ordinance]____ and declare the ____[statute / ordinance]____ is not valid and enforceable against plaintiff.

2. For costs and all other just relief.

Dated: _____

[Signature of attorney]

[Typed name]
____[Attorney for plaintiff]____

Comment: If appropriate or necessary a cause of action for mandamus, injunctive, or other relief should be added, preferably in a separate cause of action (see §24.31) and demanded in the prayer. If such additional relief is claimed, it should be specified in the title of the complaint by adding, *e.g.,* "AND MANDAMUS."

On preparation of complaints generally, see 1 CALIFORNIA CIVIL PROCEDURE BEFORE TRIAL §§7.16–7.41 (Cal CEB 1977).

B. Responsive and Other Pleadings

1. Methods of Responding

§24.34   a. Answer

The general rules of pleading in civil actions apply to the answer in declaratory relief actions. See *Mackay v Whitaker* (1953) 116 CA2d 504, 510, 253 P2d 1021, 1025, in which the court held that the declaratory judgment statutes do not abrogate the ordinary rules of pleading, practice procedure, and evidence. On answers generally see 1 CALIFORNIA CIVIL PROCEDURE BEFORE TRIAL chap 11 (Cal CEB 1977).

If plaintiff has stated a cause of action for declaratory relief and defendant desires a favorable declaration, he should not deny the allegation that there is a justiciable controversy and should not pray that the complaint be dismissed or that plaintiff take nothing. Instead, defendant should pray for specific relief. It is improper for the trial court simply to hold that plaintiff take nothing by the complaint for declaratory relief when plaintiff has prayed for a declaration of rights. See *Kroff v Kroff* (1954) 127 CA2d 404, 274 P2d 45. But see *Boyar v Krech* (1937) 10 C2d 207, 73 P2d 1218, holding that a judgment that plaintiff take nothing is not reversible error when the findings and conclusions amount to a declaration.

The defendant can, by denial, put in issue whether there is a justiciable controversy or a controversy at all. Moreover, if plaintiff incorrectly sets forth or omits some or all of defendant's contentions, defendant can deny plaintiff's allegations in connection with those contentions. For clarity, however, it is good practice for defendant to set forth accurately his actual contentions, at least in general terms, although there is no requirement to do so. See *California Canning Peach Growers v Corcoran* (1936) 14 CA2d 264, 267, 57 P2d 1360, 1361, in which the court said that the court's declaration "will be in response to the allegations contained in the complaint, some in response to the new matter contained in the answers and some, perhaps, in response to the new matters, if any, introduced by the plaintiff in avoidance of new matter set forth in the answer, that is, matter introduced in the nature of a replication to the defendants' plea."

It is not clear whether defendant must set forth in his answer affirmative defenses in support of his position with respect to the controversy. It is safer, however, to set forth such affirmative defenses (*e.g.*, the statute of limitations), in defendant's answer to plaintiff's allegations concerning defendant's contentions. With regard to the statute of limitations defense, see 2 Witkin, CALIFORNIA PROCEDURE, Actions §360 (2d ed 1970); Note, *Declaratory Judgments-Procedure—Use of Demurrer—Applicability of Statutes of Limitations*, 18 S CAL L REV 54 (1944); §24.22. On the form for an answer, see 1 CIV PROC BEFORE TRIAL §§11.5–11.9.

§24.35 b. Cross-Complaint

Cross-complaints for declaratory relief are governed by the same rules of pleading that are applicable to complaints. See

Mackay v Whitaker (1953) 116 CA2d 504, 510, 253 P2d 1021, 1025. On the form for a cross-complaint, see 1 CALIFORNIA CIVIL PROCEDURE BEFORE TRIAL §§12.22–12.28 (Cal CEB 1977). Frequently, a defendant cross-complains for a declaration that if he is found liable in an action against him he should be reimbursed or indemnified by another person. See, e.g., *Lewis Ave. Parent Teachers' Ass'n v Hussey* (1967) 250 CA2d 232, 58 CR 499 (cross-complaint for declaration for indemnification in personal injury action is proper); *Brokate v Hehr Mfg. Co.* (1966) 243 CA2d 133, 52 CR 672 (cross-complaint for declaration of corporation's duty to indemnify defendant director is proper); *J. C. Penney Co. v Westinghouse Elec. Corp.* (1963) 217 CA2d 834, 32 CR 172 (store being sued by person injured on escalator entitled to declaratory relief on cross-complaint that it is entitled to indemnification, if found liable to the injured party, by the party that installed escalator and warranted the product).

A court may exercise its discretion to deny declaratory relief (see §24.19) sought in a cross-complaint if "the issues and evidence produced in the main case are substantially the same as would be produced under the cross-complaint [citations]." *International Ass'n of Fire Fighters, Local 1319 v Palo Alto* (1963) 60 C2d 295, 301, 32 CR 842, 845 (declaration on validity of statute sought in cross-complaint denied because the issue would be resolved in the main action.

The compulsory cross-complaint provisions (CCP §§426.10–426.50) do not apply "where the only relief sought is a declaration of the rights and duties of the respective parties in an action for declaratory relief [under CCP §1060]." CCP §426.60(c). *Russo v Scrambler Motorcycles* (1976) 56 CA3d 112, 127 CR 913.

§24.36 c. Demurrers

A court may sustain a general demurrer to a declaratory relief complaint if plaintiff has failed to plead the necessary requisites to state a cause of action for declaratory relief. See §§24.9–24.10. Thus, if plaintiff does not set forth a present, justiciable controversy (see *Zetterberg v State Dept of Pub. Health* (1974) 43 CA3d 657, 665, 118 CR 100, 105; *Ephraim v Metropolitan Trust Co.* (1946) 28 C2d 824, 172 P2d 501; see also §24.11) or pleads facts showing that the court does not have jurisdiction (see §24.16) or the power to grant declaratory relief (*Igna v Baldwin*

Park (1970) 9 CA3d 909, 88 CR 581; *Carrier v Robbins* (1952) 112 CA2d 32, 245 P2d 676), the court may sustain a general demurrer to the complaint.

If plaintiff has pleaded facts sufficient to state a cause of action for declaratory relief, the court should not sustain a general demurrer "on a theory that assumes any declaration would necessarily be unfavorable to plaintiff." *Safeway Stores, Inc. v Royal Indem. Co.* (1971) 21 CA3d 44, 47, 98 CR 234, 235. See generally 3 Witkin, CALIFORNIA PROCEDURE, Pleading §732 (2d ed 1971). On the other hand, in *Jefferson Inc. v Torrance* (1968) 266 CA2d 300, 303, 72 CR 85, 86 the court stated that "where a complaint sets forth a good cause of action for declaratory relief regarding only a disputed question of law, declarations on the merits unfavorable to a plaintiff have been upheld although such determinations were made in the form of a judgment sustaining a demurrer." See also *Wilson v Civil Serv. Comm'n* (1964) 224 CA2d 340, 36 CR 559.

The court may exercise its discretion to deny declaratory relief under CCP §1061 (see §24.19) by sustaining a general demurrer without leave to amend. *Lord v Garland* (1946) 27 C2d 840, 168 P2d 5; *Moss v Moss* (1942) 20 C2d 640, 128 P2d 526; *General of America Ins. Co. v Lilly* (1968) 258 CA2d 465, 65 CR 750. In *Auberry Union School Dist. v Rafferty* (1964) 226 CA2d 599, 602, 38 CR 223, 225, the court said "it is better procedure for the court to exercise its discretion by granting a motion to dismiss or by some other procedure." In *Whipple v Haberle* (1963) 223 CA2d 477, 484, 36 CR 9, 14, the court stated that a conclusion that there is no proper ground for declaratory relief "is normally made by a trial judge, if at all, at the beginning of litigation by means of a ruling on a general demurrer to the complaint, or by granting a motion to dismiss [Citation], and it is most unusual to carry a case through a lengthy trial and then to conclude on a discretionary basis that it is not a proper suit for declaratory relief."

In some instances, when the courts have found that nondeclaratory relief causes of action failed to set forth sufficient facts to constitute a cause of action, they have also sustained a general demurrer to the declaratory relief cause of action. *Monolith Portland Cement Co. v Tendler* (1962) 206 CA2d 800, 808, 24 CR 38, 43. See also *Bos v United States Rubber Co.* (1950) 100 CA2d 565, 224 P2d 386. Sustaining a demurrer to a declaratory relief

§24.37   DECLARATORY RELIEF

cause of action because other causes of action are defective may be based, under CCP §1061, on the court's exercise of discretion. See §24.19; *Girard v Miller* (1963) 214 CA2d 266, 29 CR 359. However, such a ruling would seemingly conflict with the principle that a court should not sustain a general demurrer merely because the declaration would have to be unfavorable to plaintiff. See *Anderson v Stansbury* (1952) 38 C2d 707, 242 P2d 305 (nonsuit proper with respect to causes of action for accounting and declaration of resulting trust but trial court erred in granting a nonsuit on declaratory relief cause of action on which it should have rendered an unfavorable declaration; however the error was not prejudicial).

Courts have resisted efforts by plaintiffs to avoid general demurrers by labeling a cause of action as one for declaratory relief, when, in fact, declaratory relief was inappropriate. See *Irwin v Blythe* (1945) 72 CA2d 161, 163 P2d 900.

In *Columbia Pictures Corp. v DeToth* (1945) 26 C2d 753, 762, 161 P2d 217, 221, however, the court suggested that complaints for declaratory relief are subject to special demurrers.

§24.37   d. Motion for Judgment on the Pleadings or Summary Judgment

When there is no factual dispute, it is preferable for the court to grant judgment on the pleadings rather than to sustain a general demurrer. See §24.36. Such a judgment, in effect, constitutes a declaration. *Dohrmann Co. v Security Sav. & Loan Ass'n* (1970) 8 CA3d 655, 87 CR 792; *Silver v Beverly Hills Nat'l Bank* (1967) 253 CA2d 1000, 61 CR 751; *Wilson v Board of Retirement* (1957) 156 CA2d 195, 319 P2d 426.

If the complaint sets forth facts showing that declaratory relief is proper (see §24.30), the trial court may not refuse to provide a declaration by entering a judgment on the pleadings. *Chas. L. Harney, Inc. v Contractors' State License Bd.* (1952) 39 C2d 561, 247 P2d 913.

Summary judgment under CCP §437c (see generally chap 29) provides another means for obtaining a declaratory judgment by motion when there are no factual issues in dispute. *National Exhibition Co. v San Francisco* (1972) 24 CA3d 1, 100 CR 757; *Spencer v Hibernia Bank* (1960) 186 CA2d 702, 9 CR 867.

§24.38 e. Form of Demurrer and Pretrial Motions

The forms used for demurrers and the motions in declaratory relief actions discussed in §§24.36–24.37 do not differ from those used in other actions. Other pretrial motions, *e.g.*, special demurrers, motions to strike, motions to amend the pleadings or to file supplementary pleadings, and discovery motions, in declaratory relief actions are not different from those in other types of actions. See *Mackay v Whitaker* (1953) 116 CA2d 504, 510, 253 P2d 1021, 1025.

C. Trial Aspects
§24.39 1. Precedence on Calendar

Code of Civil Procedure §1062a was amended in 1976 to provide that, except as provided in subdivision (b), actions brought under CCP §§1060–1062 "shall be set for trial at the earliest possible date and shall take precedence of all other cases, except older matters of the same character and matters to which special precedence may be given by law." CCP §1062a(a). Subsection (b) provides that any action in which "the plaintiff seeks any relief, in addition to a declaration of rights and duties, shall take precedence only upon noticed motion and a showing that the action requires a speedy trial." Thus, the previous automatic precedence for all declaratory relief actions has been abolished. Even though the subdivision refers only to a "plaintiff," presumably it also applies to a cross-complaint for declaratory relief.

It has been stated that "courts should not temporize with the improper use of the declaratory procedure to gain a preferred position on the trial calendar." *Travers v Louden* (1967) 254 CA2d 926, 932, 62 CR 654, 658. If plaintiff improperly casts his action as one for declaratory relief solely to obtain precedence on the court calendar, the court should not dismiss the action, but should rather prevent his obtaining precedence by an appropriate order or procedure. *Kessloff v Pearson* (1951) 37 C2d 609, 614, 233 P2d 899, 902. Code of Civil Procedure §1062a does not override the court's discretion to refuse to grant declaratory relief. *State Farm Mut. Auto. Ins. Co. v Superior Court* (1956) 47 C2d 428, 304 P2d 13. See §24.19 on trial court's discretion to grant declaratory relief.

§24.40 DECLARATORY RELIEF

§24.40 2. Right to Jury Trial

It has long been established that disputed questions of fact may be resolved in declaratory relief actions. *R. G. Hamilton Corp. v Corum* (1933) 218 C 92, 21 P2d 413. A party may not be denied a jury trial because the action is for declaratory relief. *State Farm Mut. Auto. Ins. Co. v Superior Court* (1956) 47 C2d 428, 304 P2d 13; *Veale v Piercy* (1962) 206 CA2d 557, 24 CR 91. A party to a declaratory relief action is entitled to a jury trial of those issues in the action which would normally be triable to a jury. 4 Witkin, CALIFORNIA PROCEDURE, Trial §77 (2d ed 1971). See Comment, *Jury Trials in Declaratory Relief Actions: The Right Exists, But Under What Circumstances?* 6 UCLA L REV 678, 687 (1959).

If there are legal and equitable issues, the equitable issues are generally tried first (*Raedeke v Gibraltar Sav. & Loan Ass'n* (1974) 10 C3d 665, 111 CR 693; *Veale v Piercy, supra*) although the order rests in the discretion of the court (*Jaffe v Albertson Co.* (1966) 243 CA2d 592, 53 CR 25; 4 Witkin, PROCEDURE, Trial §123). It has been stated that the better practice is for the trial court first to determine the equitable issues before submitting the legal ones to the jury. See, *e.g.*, *Bate v Marsteller* (1965) 232 CA2d 605, 43 CR 149.

If plaintiff wishes to avoid a jury trial, he may attempt to assert equitable issues that will probably be tried first and may dispose of the legal issues. If plaintiff wants a jury trial, he should avoid inserting any equitable issues in the complaint. A defendant desiring a jury trial should be careful about defenses or cross-complaints raising equitable issues. See generally 6 UCLA L REV 678 at 690.

§24.41 3. Burden of Proof

Plaintiff has the burden of proof to establish facts justifying the court in exercising its discretion to grant declaratory relief. *Boosman v United Bldg. Co.* (1952) 109 CA2d 486, 241 P2d 58.

In *Roadside Rest, Inc. v Lankershim Estate* (1946) 76 CA2d 525, 173 P2d 554, the court relied on former CCP §1981 (now Evid C §§500, 550) in stating that the burden of proof on any issue lies on the party who would be defeated if no evidence were given on either side.

In another case, the court quoted with approval the following from Borchard, DECLARATORY JUDGMENTS 407 (2d ed 1941): "the burden of proof . . . is not automatically on the plaintiff, . . . but on him who without evidence would be compelled to submit to an adverse judgment before the introduction of any evidence, or who asserts the affirmative of any issue." *American Home Assur. Co. v Essy* (1960) 179 CA2d 19, 23, 3 CR 586, 589 (in declaratory relief action by insurance companies to determine their liability under fire policies issued to defendant, insured must prove coverage and breach, but insurers have burden of proving arson). See also *Pacific Portland Cement Co. v Food Mach. & Chem. Corp.* (9th Cir 1949) 178 F2d 541, 546, *State Farm Mut. Auto. Ins. Co. v Spann* (1973) 31 CA3d 97, 106 CR 923. See also Comment, *Developments in the Law, Declaratory Judgments— 1941–1949*, 62 HARV L REV 787, 836 (1949).

§24.42 4. Trial Court's Duty To Render Full and Complete Declaration

As with demurrers, judgments on the pleadings in actions that allege facts warranting declaratory relief and summary judgments (see §§24.36–24.38), nonsuits or equivalent resolutions should not be granted unless the court renders a declaration. *Essick v Los Angeles* (1950) 34 C2d 614, 213 P2d 492; see *Anderson v Stansbury* (1952) 38 C2d 707, 242 P2d 305; *Kessloff v Pearson* (1951) 37 C2d 609, 233 P2d 899; *San Francisco v Budde* (1956) 139 CA2d 101, 292 P2d 955.

In an action for declaratory relief, the court should make a full and complete declaration, "disposing of all questions of rights, status or other legal relations encountered in construing the instrument before it" (*American Enterprise, Inc. v Van Winkle* (1952) 39 C2d 210, 219, 246 P2d 935, 939), including all legal and equitable issues (*Anderson v Southern Pac. Co.* (1968) 264 CA2d 230, 70 CR 389). It is the duty of a court hearing a declaratory relief action to make a complete determination and disposition of the controversy. *Amerson v Christman* (1968) 261 CA2d 811, 68 CR 378. In *Amerson* the court added that the parties' rights should be determined on the facts found and not be limited by the issues joined or by counsels' claims. 261 CA2d at 824, 68 CR at 387. The requirements in declaratory relief actions with respect to findings of fact and conclusions of law are identical to the requirements in other types of actions. See *Anderson v Southern Pac. Co.* (1968) 264 CA2d 230, 234, 70 CR 389. The findings can serve as the declaration. *Boyar v Krech* (1937) 10 C2d 207, 73 P2d 1218.

D. Judgment
§24.43   1. Content and Effect

The declaratory judgment is intended to constitute a judicial resolution of disputes between the parties. Although the court should dispose of the entire controversy between the parties (see §24.42), it has "discretion as to the extent of the relief to be afforded in a proceeding for declaratory relief [citation omitted], but where a case is made for such relief the court should not deny it." *Record Mach. & Tool Co. v Pageman Holding Corp.* (1954) 42 C2d 227, 234, 266 P2d 1, 5. The declaration may be either affirmative or negative, declaring that a party is or is not under a duty. CCP §1060; see *Record Mach. & Tool Co. v Pageman Holding Corp.*, supra.

The declaratory judgment "must decree, not suggest, what the parties may or may not do." *Selby Realty Co. v San Buenaventura* (1973) 10 C3d 110, 117, 109 CR 799, 803; *Monahan v Department of Water & Power* (1941) 48 CA2d 746, 751, 120 P2d 730, 732.

As with any judgment, a declaratory judgment "should not rest upon probabilities, conjecture or vague inferences" (*Roadside Rest, Inc. v Lankershim Estate* (1946) 76 CA2d 525, 535, 173 P2d 554, 560), but should be in conformity with the evidence and on the merits (*Phelps v Loop* (1942) 53 CA2d 541, 128 P2d 63). The court should make "a complete determination of the controversy between the parties to [a declaratory relief] action in accord with the facts as they exist at the time of its decree." *Munson v Linnick* (1967) 255 CA2d 589, 595, 63 CR 340, 343.

Even though the declaratory judgment does not decree any coercive relief, it has a binding effect on the parties that will support the application of the doctrines of collateral estoppel and res judicata in any subsequent litigation involving the issues resolved by the declaratory judgment. See *Lortz v Connell* (1969) 273 CA2d 286, 78 CR 6; *Dills v Delira Corp.* (1956) 145 CA2d 124, 302 P2d 397. But see *Los Angeles v San Fernando* (1975) 14 C3d 199, 123 CR 1 (in which the court stated that the res judicata or collateral estoppel effect of a prior determination between the parties of a question of law may differ from a prior determination of a question of fact, especially when the public interest is involved). See also *Louis Eckert Brewing Co. v Unemployment Reserves Comm'r* (1941) 47 CA2d 844, 846, 119 P2d 227, 228 ("An obvious frailty of such a declaratory judgment lies in the fact that such relationship [between the parties] need not remain unchanged. It is conceivable that immediately after judgment that relationship might be modified so that a subsequent consideration by a trial court would result in a totally different conclusion.")

The court has the power to award coercive relief in addition to a declaratory judgment. If such relief is indicated in a declaratory relief action, it is error to deny it. *Lortz v Connell* (1969) 273 CA2d 286, 299, 78 CR 6, 14. Thus, in an action in which declaratory relief is sought, a court may award money damages (*Lortz v Connell, supra*; *Bertero v National General Corp.* (1967) 254 CA2d 126, 62 CR 714; order specific performance (*Beeler v Plastic Stamping, Inc.* (1956) 144 CA2d 306, 300 P2d 852); order an accounting (*Steeve v Yaeger* (1956) 145 CA2d 455, 302 P2d 704); issue injunctive relief (*Knox v Wolfe* (1946) 73 CA2d 494, 167 P2d 3, holding that the court could grant injunctive relief necessary to a complete determination of the controversy, even though not prayed for). But see *California Water & Tel. Co. v Los Angeles* (1967) 253 CA2d 16, 32, 61 CR 618, 629, in which the court stated, "[a]n ancillary injunction should not issue as a concomitant to a declaratory judgment unless the pleading and proof demonstrate that the traditional requisites of injunctive relief have been met."

In appropriate cases, the court may retain jurisdiction to make such orders in the future that may be necessary (*Bertero v National General Corp.* (1967) 254 CA2d 126, 62 CR 714) because "[i]n giving declaratory relief a court has the powers of a court of equity." *Los Angeles v Glendale* (1943) 23 C2d 68, 81, 142 P2d 289, 297. The failure to seek coercive relief in a declaratory relief action does not preclude another action to enforce the rights obtained by the declaratory judgment. *Lortz v Connell, supra*.

§24.44 2. Form: Judgment for Declaratory Relief

Copies: Original (presented to judge for signature, and filed); copies for service (one for each attorney of record and unrepresented party); office copies.

[Caption. See §§23.18–23.19]

No. _____

JUDGMENT FOR DECLARATORY RELIEF

§24.44 DECLARATORY RELIEF

This action came on regularly for trial on _____, 19____, in Department _____ of this Court, the Honorable _____, Judge, presiding ____ [with / without]____ a jury. _____ appeared as attorney for plaintiff and _____ appeared as attorney for defendant. ____[Both]_____[oral / documentary]____ evidence was presented and the matter argued and submitted for decision. ____[The Court has made and caused to be filed its written findings of fact and conclusions of law / The parties have waived findings of fact and conclusions of law]____. Good cause appearing,

IT IS ORDERED that:

[When action is based on contract]

1. Under the ____[oral / written]____ contract dated _____, 19____, between plaintiff and defendant, ____[plaintiff / defendant]____ is obligated to _____.

[When action based on a written instrument other than a contract]

1. Under the ____[e.g., will dated _____, 19____, of ____[name]____, of which ____[e.g., plaintiff is the beneficiary]____, ____[plaintiff / defendant]____ is obligated to _____.

[When declaration sought with respect to statute or ordinance]

1. ____[Code of _____ section _____ / Ordinance No. ____]____ of the ____[e.g., County of _____]____.

[Choose appropriate statement]

does ____[not]____ apply to plaintiff and therefore plaintiff is ____[not]____ required to _____.

[Or]

violates California Constitution Article _____, section ____ on its face and as applied to plaintiff and, therefore, is unenforceable against plaintiff. Plaintiff is therefore not required to ____[e.g., obtain a permit under the statute or ordinance]____.

[Continue when applicable]

2. Plaintiff shall have and recover judgment against defendant in the amount of $_____.

[Continue]

3. ____[Plaintiff / Defendant]____ shall recover costs from ____[defendant / plaintiff]____ in the sum of $_____.

[*Continue, if provided for by statute or contract*]

4. ____[*Plaintiff / Defendant*]____ **shall recover attorney's fees against** ____[*defendant / plaintiff*]____ **in the amount of** $_____.

Dated: _____

_____
Judge

Comment: On preparation of form and format of court papers generally, see 1 CALIFORNIA CIVIL PROCEDURE BEFORE TRIAL chap 22 (Cal CEB 1977).

Attorney's fees may be obtained as part of costs under the circumstances described in §29.73.

If the prevailing party wishes to obtain injunctive relief in the judgment, he may request the court to include a statement specifically describing the act or threatened acts to be enjoined.

§24.45 V. APPELLATE REVIEW

If an action has been dismissed by the trial court or the question on appeal concerns legal issues resolved at trial, rather than procedural, evidentiary, or factual matters, the appellate court's decision constitutes a declaration of the parties' rights and duties. *Taschner v City Council* (1973) 31 CA3d 48, 107 CR 214; *Cherry v Home Sav. & Loan Ass'n* (1969) 276 CA2d 574, 81 CR 135; *Western Homes, Inc. V Herbert Ketell, Inc.* (1965) 236 CA2d 142, 45 CR 856. Moreover, a declaratory judgment that fails to determine all of the rights between the parties, may be modified on appeal to add what the trial court should have determined. *Cinmark Inv. Co. v Reichard* (1966) 246 CA2d 498, 502, 54 CR 810, 812.

PART II
BRINGING CASE TO TRIAL; DETERMINING SCOPE OF ACTION

MICHAEL HOLTZMAN

Chapter 25
Intervention

I. NATURE OF PROCEEDING
   A. Intervention Under CCP§387   §25.1
   B. Intervention Under Special Statutes   §25.2
   C. Other Procedures Compared With Intervention Under CCP §387
      1. Application by Indispensable Party   §25.3
      2. Application by Person Claiming Interest in Real or Personal Property   §25.4
      3. Judgment Creditor's Lien on Judgment Debtor's Cause of Action and Judgment   §25.5
      4. Third Party Claims to Personal Property Levied on, Attached, or Subjected to Claim and Delivery Actions   §25.6
      5. Class Actions   §25.7
      6. Coordination of Actions Sharing Common Question of Fact or Law   §25.8
      7. Appearance as Amicus Curiae   §25.9
II. WHO MAY INTERVENE
   A. Statutory Criteria   §25.10
   B. Examples of Categories of Persons Permitted To Intervene Under Pre-1978 Law
      1. Real Parties in Interest   §25.11
      2. Successors in Interest   §25.12
      3. Insurers and Sureties   §25.13
      4. Judgment Creditors   §25.14
      5. Owners of Property Levied on, Attached, or Subjected to Claim and Delivery Actions   §25.15
      6. Limited Partners   §25.16
      7. Husband and Wife   §25.17
      8. Owners of Adjoining Property in Zoning Law Enforcement Actions   §25.18
      9. Voters   §25.19
   C. Examples of Categories of Persons Generally Not Permitted To Intervene Under Pre-1978 Law
      1. Shareholders   §25.20
      2. Attorneys   §25.21

MICHAEL HOLTZMAN, LL.B., 1967, Washington University, St. Louis, Mo. Mr. Holtzman is a member of the firm of Mitchell, Silberberg & Knupp of Los Angeles. CEB attorney-editor was ISADORE ROSENBLATT.

3. Taxpayers and Persons Interested in Legal Precedent §25.22
4. Owners of Adjoining Property in Actions Other Than Zoning Actions §25.23
5. General Creditors §25.24

III. EXAMPLES OF PROCEEDINGS IN WHICH INTERVENTION PERMITTED UNDER PRE-1978 LAW
   A. Foreclosure §25.25
   B. Quiet Title Action §25.26
   C. Actions for Possession of Property §25.27
   D. Condemnation Proceedings §25.28
   E. Actions for Impression of Trust §25.29
   F. Will Contests and Heirship Proceedings §25.30
   G. Marriage Dissolution Proceedings §25.31

IV. TIMING OF APPLICATION TO INTERVENE
   A. Application Must Be "Timely" §25.32
      1. Motions Under CCP §473 §25.33
      2. No Intervention After Dismissal of Action §25.34
      3. Before New Trial or Retrial §25.35
   B. Effect of Intervenor's Delay After Learning of Action §25.36
   C. Statute of Limitations §25.37

V. APPLYING FOR LEAVE TO INTERVENE
   A. Available Procedures
      1. Ex Parte Application §25.38
         a. Form: Declaration for Order Granting Leave To Intervene §25.39
         b. Form: Order Granting Leave To Intervene §25.40
      2. Order To Show Cause §25.41
         a. Form: Declaration for Order and Order To Show Cause re Intervention §25.42
         b. Form: Order To Show Cause Why Leave To Intervene Should Not Be Granted §25.43
      3. Noticed Motion §25.44
         a. Form: Notice of Motion for Leave To Intervene §25.45
         b. Form: Order Granting Leave To Intervene §25.46
   B. Burden of Proof on Intervenor §25.47
   C. Opposition to Intervention
      1. Procedure for Presenting Opposition §25.48
      2. Grounds for Opposition §25.49
      3. Waiver of Objections §25.50
   D. Appellate Review
      1. When Leave To Intervene Denied §25.51
      2. When Leave To Intervene Granted §25.52

VI. COMPLAINT IN INTERVENTION
   A. Requirements §25.53
   B. Form: Complaint in Intervention §25.54
   C. Service: Payment of Fees §25.55

VII. RESPONSES TO COMPLAINT IN INTERVENTION
   A. Available Responses; Timing §25.56

B. Cross-Complaint Against Intervenor §25.57
VIII. PARTIES' RIGHTS AND REMEDIES AFTER INTERVENTION
A. Intervenor's Rights and Remedies §25.58
B. Dismissal of Action After Intervention
1. By Original Plaintiff §25.59
2. By Intervenor §25.60

I. NATURE OF PROCEEDING
§25.1 A. Intervention Under CCP §387

Intervention is a process by which a person becomes a party in a pending action or proceeding between other parties. CCP §387. Code of Civil Procedure §387 is the fundamental and most frequently invoked basis for intervention, but other statutes provide similar remedies in particular situations. See §§25.3–25.9.

Code of Civil Procedure §387 was amended, effective January 1, 1978, to add new criteria for intervention. Under former CCP §387, which was retained as subdivision (a) of the section, the trial court had discretion to determine whether to permit a party to intervene. *In re Yokohama Specie Bank* (1948) 86 CA2d 545, 555, 195 P2d 555, 560. Under newly added subdivision (b), the trial court appears to be required to permit a party to intervene if (1) any other provision of law confers an unconditional right to intervene (see §25.2), or (2) the court finds that specified criteria have been met. See §25.10 for a discussion of criteria for intervention. Subdivision (b) is a nearly verbatim adoption of Fed R Civ P 24(a). Code of Civil Procedure §387(a) differs substantially from its counterpart Fed R Civ P 24(b).

In addition to adding the federal mandatory intervention rule (subdivision (b)), the 1978 amendment of CCP §387 substituted the federal criterion that an application to intervene must be "timely" for the prior requirement that it be made "before trial." See §25.32. Some legislative proponents of the amendment that added subdivision (b) to CCP §387 appear to have believed that it would require trial courts to permit intervention by parties whose own status or position would be affected by the outcome of a pending action (*e.g.*, as the status of minority group professional school applicants was affected by a lawsuit challenging the constitutionality of "affirmative action" admissions programs). See *Review of Selected 1977 California Legislation*, 9 PAC L J 356 (1978). There is a question whether adoption of the federal mandatory intervention criteria will reduce the importance of the discretionary criteria of the former law still embodied in CCP §387(a). See §25.10.

Many appellate opinions predating January 1, 1978, state that one cannot intervene to broaden the issues in the action or enlarge its scope. See, *e.g., Faus v Pacific Elec. Ry.* (1955) 134 CA2d 352, 285 P2d 1017, and cases cited. However, it is clear that an intervenor may seek affirmative relief; the fact that the intervenor seeks equitable relief in an action which is legal in nature, or legal relief in an equitable action, will not prevent intervention. *Belt Cas. Co. v Furman* (1933) 218 C 359, 23 P2d 293. Similarly, the intervenor's ability to protect his rights in an independent proceeding is not controlling. See *Dennis v Kolm* (1900) 131 C 91, 63 P 141.

§25.2   B.   Intervention Under Special Statutes

Several narrowly defined statutes provide that in certain situations the court must allow particular persons to intervene. For example:

(1) All persons claiming legal or equitable interests in real property subject to condemnation proceedings may intervene. CCP §1250.230. See also §25.4.

(2) Any shareholder or creditor may intervene at any time before trial in proceedings for involuntary dissolution of a corporation. Corp C §1800(c).

(3) Any creditor of a corporation may intervene in an action against a shareholder based on an unpaid subscription for its shares. Corp C §414.

(4) Any dissenting shareholder demanding the purchase of his shares as a result of a corporate reorganization or any interested corporation may intervene in an action to determine whether the shareholder's shares are dissenting shares or to determine the fair market value of dissenting shares. Corp C §1304(a).

(5) Either an employer or an employee may intervene in an action commenced by the other against a third party who causes damages cognizable under the worker's compensation statutes. Lab C §3853. See discussion in CALIFORNIA WORKMEN'S COMPENSATION PRACTICE 1973 §§17.15, 18.16–18.23 (Cal CEB 1973).

See §25.7 on class actions.

C. Other Procedures Compared With Intervention Under CCP §387

§25.3   1. Application by Indispensable Party

Code of Civil Procedure §389(a) provides that:

[a] person who is subject to service of process and whose joinder will not deprive the court of jurisdiction over the subject matter of the action shall be joined as a party in the action if (1) in his absence complete relief cannot be accorded among those already parties or he (2) claims an interest relating to the subject of the action and is so situated that the disposition of the action in his absence may (i) as a practical matter impair or impede his ability to protect that interest or (ii) leave any of the persons already parties subject to a substantial risk of incurring double, multiple, or otherwise inconsistent obligations . . . .

See 1 CALIFORNIA CIVIL PROCEDURE BEFORE TRIAL §§7.12–7.13 (Cal CEB 1977) for discussion of CCP §389.

Under CCP §389(b), if a person described in CCP §389(a) cannot be made a party, the court must determine whether the action should proceed or be dismissed without prejudice, "the absent person being thus regarded as indispensable." Under CCP §389(b) the factors to be considered by the court in so determining include the extent to which the judgment, if the person is not joined, might be prejudicial to him or the existing parties; the extent to which by protective provisions in the judgment, by the shaping of relief, or other measures, the prejudice can be lessened or avoided; whether a judgment in his absence will be adequate; and whether plaintiff or cross-complainant will have an adequate remedy if the action is dismissed.

Although CCP §389 is most frequently invoked by an existing party, the omitted person may apply to the court for an order joining him as a party. See *Cuneo v Superior Court* (1963) 213 CA2d 452, 28 CR 791; *Muller v Robinson* (1959) 174 CA2d 511, 345 P2d 25.

Any person who must be made a party under CCP §389 also has a sufficient interest in the matter in litigation to justify his intervention under CCP §387 and such a person may base his application to become a party on both statutes. *Crofton v Young* (1941) 48 CA2d 452, 119 P2d 1003. Under CCP §389, the court orders the nonparty to be joined as a party within the existing pleadings, while CCP §387 offers the omitted person an opportunity to set forth his position in his own ways in his complaint in intervention. In *Crofton v Young, supra,* the omitted person was permitted to become a party under both statutes and to file both an answer and a cross-complaint setting forth his interest. Thus there might be an advantage to proceeding under both statutes simultaneously if the more rigorous requirements of CCP §389 can be satisfied.

In limited circumstances, CCP §389 may be available when CCP §387 is not. One may not be able to intervene under CCP §387 after trial has commenced (see §25.32), but an indispensable person can seek an order under CCP §389 joining him as a party at any time. In *Abbot Kinney Co. v Los Angeles* (1959) 53 C2d 52, 346 P2d 385, the state first asserted its indispensability in a brief filed after the rendering of an opinion by the court of appeal. The Supreme Court held that the state was indispensable and should be joined as a party for the purposes of a new trial.

§25.4   2. Application by Person Claiming Interest in Real or Personal Property

A person who claims an interest in real or personal property may apply to the court to be made a party to an action for the recovery of or to determine conflicting claims to that property. CCP §389.5. See *Allen v Pitchess* (1973) 36 CA3d 321, 111 CR 658. The court, in its discretion, may order the parties to bring such a claimant into the action by proper amendment of the pleadings. This statute and CCP §387(a) both call for an exercise of the court's discretion, and it appears that any person whose interest is such that the court would order him made a party under CCP §389.5 would also be permitted to intervene under CCP §387(a).

As in the case of CCP §389 (see §25.3) under CCP §389.5, the nonparty is brought in by means of an amendment to the existing pleadings. An intervenor enters the action by filing his own complaint in intervention, in which he can state the issues and causes of action in his own language, which may explain why CCP §389.5 is infrequently used.

§25.5   3. Judgment Creditor's Lien on Judgment Debtor's Cause of Action and Judgment

A judgment creditor of a party to an action may, in the court's discretion, be granted a lien on that party's cause of action and on any judgment subsequently obtained. CCP §688.1. After the granting of such a lien, the judgment debtor may not agree to any compromise or settlement of his cause of action, or any satisfaction of his judgment, without the judgment creditor's consent.

In addition, a judgment creditor may be permitted to intervene in the action, although such intervention is not required and, in most instances, the judgment creditor's lien will be adequate to his needs. See *McClearen v Superior Court* (1955) 45 C2d 852, 219 P2d 449. The granting of a lien does not itself make the lienor a party to the action; to accomplish this, the judgment creditor must specifically seek and be granted leave to intervene. *Apostolos v Estrada* (1958) 163 CA2d 8, 328 P2d 805.

A judgment creditor may obtain a lien and permission to intervene if appropriate or necessary, by making a motion, on written notice to all parties, in the court in which the action is pending. Making a motion does not itself create a lien or make the judgment creditor a party to the action. Accordingly, the parties to the action may, without the judgment creditor's consent, settle and dismiss the case before the hearing on the motion. See *Egly v Superior Court* (1970) 6 CA3d 476, 86 CR 18. However, the judgment debtor cannot defeat the judgment creditor's rights during pendency of the motion merely by granting a third party a lien on the cause of action. See *Del Conte Masonry Co. v Lewis* (1971) 16 CA3d 678, 94 CR 439.

§25.6 4. Third Party Claims to Personal Property Levied on, Attached, or Subjected to Claim and Delivery Actions

A nonparty who claims an interest in personal property levied on may assert his claim and try the question of title. CCP §689. Code of Civil Procedure §488.090 provides identical procedures for nonparty claimants to property attached, while CCP §514.050 is the counterpart statute in claim and delivery proceedings. Nonparty claimants may also intervene. See §25.15.

§25.7 5. Class Actions

Any member of a consumer class on learning of the existence of a consumer class action affecting his class may enter his appearance as a party to the action. CC §1781(e)(3). See also Fed R Civ P 23(c)(2) governing intervention in certain class actions.

§25.8 6. Coordination of Actions Sharing Common Question of Fact or Law

Code of Civil Procedure §§404–404.8 and Cal Rules of Ct 1501–1550 set up elaborate procedures whereby any party to an action that shares a common question of fact or law with any other civil action pending in California may seek to have those actions coordinated. See generally chap 29.

§25.9 7. Appearance as Amicus Curiae

Persons interested in an action solely because of its potential consequences as a legal precedent have not been considered to have an interest sufficient to permit them to intervene, at least before the 1978 addition of CCP §387(b). See §25.22. However, such persons may frequently accomplish their objectives by obtaining permission to file amicus curiae briefs. See *Jersey Maid Milk Prods. Co. v Brock* (1939) 13 C2d 661, 91 P2d 599; Cal Rules of Ct 14(b). An amicus is not a party and must limit himself to arguing questions of law; he cannot plead or offer evidence. 3 Witkin, CALIFORNIA PROCEDURE, Pleading §215 (2d ed 1971).

II. WHO MAY INTERVENE

§25.10 A. Statutory Criteria

A person trying to persuade a judge to permit intervention in a pending action under the discretionary provisions of CCP §387(a) should show (by allegations in the pleading in intervention and supporting declarations) that:

(1) The application is timely (see §25.32);

(2) The person seeking to intervene has an interest in the matter in litigation or in the success of either of the parties, or has an interest against both.

The person seeking to intervene may also have to frame his pleading to allege or show that he (a) joins plaintiff in claiming what is sought by the complaint; (b) unites with defendant in resisting plaintiff's claims; or (c) demands something adverse to both plaintiff and defendant. See CCP §387(a).

Cases decided before 1978, interpreting what is now CCP §387(a), indicated that, in determining whether to allow intervention, the courts would try to balance the objectives of intervention, such as the avoidance of delay or multiplicity of actions, or prejudice to the intervenor against the likelihood of delay, inconvenience, or prejudice to the original parties if intervention is permitted. See generally *Continental Vinyl Prods. Corp. v Mead Corp.* (1972) 27 CA3d 543, 103 CR 806, and the cases cited at 27 CA3d at 552, 103 CR at 182.

It was said that the intervenor's interest must be "direct and immediate" (see *Olson v Hopkins* (1969) 269 CA2d 638, 641, 75 CR 33, 35), rather than "remote and consequential" (*Burlingame v San Mateo* (1951) 103 CA2d 885, 230 P2d 375) and properly determinable in the action *(Continental Vinyl Prods. v Mead, supra)*. The intervenor should be in a position to gain or lose by the direct operation of the judgment in the action as it exists, without reference to issues not involved in the action. See, *e.g.*, *Olson v Hopkins, supra*.

A person trying to persuade a judge that he must grant leave to intervene under the mandatory provisions of CCP §387(b), in a situation in which no other provision of law conferred an unconditional right to intervene (see §25.2), should show (by allegations in the pleading in intervention and supporting declarations) that:

(1) The application is timely (see §25.32);

(2) The person seeking to intervene claims an interest relating to the property or transaction which is the subject of the action;

(3) That person is so situated that the disposition of the action may as a practical matter impair or impede that person's ability to protect that interest;

(4) That person's interest is not adequately represented by existing parties.

The 1978 addition of subdivision (b) to CCP §387 leaves unanswered such questions as whether, in practice, most intervention applications will be decided under the criteria of CCP §387(b), or whether the addition of subdivision (b) expands the classes of cases in which courts will grant leave to intervene. A judge who decides that one of the elements listed in CCP §387(b) is absent (or has not been shown by the applicant) appears to be both free and required, to exercise the discretion traditionally held to reside in what is now subdivision (a) of CCP §387. Until there are California cases on the amended statute, guidance on interpreting CCP §387(b) should be sought from cases decided under Fed R Civ P 24(a) and the statutes or rules of states that have previously adopted the federal rule.

B. Examples of Categories of Persons Permitted To Intervene Under Pre-1978 Law

§25.11   1. Real Parties in Interest

One who is or has become the real party in interest in an action may intervene. *Robinson v Crescent City Mill & Transp. Co.* (1892) 93 C 316, 28 P 950; *Cohn v County Bd. of Supervisors* (1955) 135 CA2d 180, 286 P2d 836. (These cases were decided under CCP §387 before it was amended, effective January 1, 1978.)

§25.12   2. Successors in Interest

On any party's death or disability or the transfer of his interest there may be a substitution of parties on motion under CCP §385. Under this statute, executors, administrators, heirs, transferees, and other such successors in interest may become substitute parties. In addition, such successors in interest may intervene under CCP §387(a). *Marc Bellaire, Inc. v Fleischman* (1960) 185 CA2d 591, 8 CR 650; *Keyes v Hurlbert* (1941) 43 CA2d 497, 111 P2d 447. Availability of intervention may be of particular significance to successors, such as assignees of fractional interests. See *Dabney v Philleo* (1951) 38 C2d 60, 237 P2d 648.

§25.13   3. Insurers and Sureties

An insurer or surety may intervene in an action involving the insured or the principal debtor, respectively, if the latter is not defending in good faith or has defaulted. *Johnson v Hayes Cal Builders, Inc.* (1963) 60 C2d 572, 35 CR 618; *Coburn v Smart* (1879) 53 C 742. For an insurer, availability of statutory intervention may be superfluous because of an insurer's usual contractual right to defend its insured. See *Cradduck v Financial Indem. Co.* (1966) 242 CA2d 850, 52 CR 90.

However, an insurer who denies coverage, or has offered to defend on the basis of a reservation of rights concerning coverage, was not permitted to intervene under CCP §387 before its amendment, at least in part because the courts resist interjection of insurance issues into actions for damages. *Corridan v Rose* (1955) 137 CA2d 524, 290 P2d 939. Similarly, an insurer which is a prospective subrogee of a party to an action was not permitted to intervene. *Hausmann v Farmers Ins. Exch.* (1963) 213 CA2d 611, 29 CR 75.

§25.14   4. Judgment Creditors

Judgment creditors may intervene under CCP §387(a) in actions by their judgment debtor's insurers against the judgment debtors to rescind the insurance policies or declare them cancelled. *Fireman's Fund Ins. Co. v Gerlach* (1976) 56 CA3d 299, 128 CR 396; *Belt Cas. Co. v Furman* (1933) 218 C 359, 23 P2d 293 (decided under former CCP §387).

A judgment creditor may also proceed under CCP §688.1 to obtain a lien on his debtor's claim and ultimate judgment in an unrelated action against a third party and to intervene if necessary. See §25.5.

§25.15   5. Owners of Property Levied on, Attached, or Subjected to Claim and Delivery Actions

There are specific statutory procedures to enable the persons claiming ownership of personal property levied on, attached, or subjected to claim and delivery proceedings to assert their claims to the property. See discussion in §25.6 of CCP §§689, 488.090, 514.050. In addition, such persons may intervene under CCP §387. *Berghauser v Golden State Orchards* (1929) 208 C 550, 282 P 950; *Hi-Valley Dev. Corp. v Walters* (1963) 223 CA2d 778, 36 CR 140. Similarly, an attaching creditor may intervene to litigate priority of attachment in an action in which the property has been attached by another creditor. *Kimball v Richardson-Kimball Co.* (1896) 111 C 386, 43 P 1111.

The third party claim procedure discussed in §25.6 is not available to persons claiming to be the owners of real property levied on or attached; such persons must seek leave to intervene under CCP §387. *Beshara v Goldberg* (1963) 221 CA2d 392, 34 CR 501.

§25.16   6. Limited Partners

In *Linder v Vogue Invs., Inc.* (1966) 239 CA2d 338, 48 CR 633, a limited partner was permitted to intervene in an action against the limited partnership when the general partner failed to provide a defense and permitted entry of a default. The court analogized to *Eggers v National Radio Co.* (1929) 208 C 308, 281 P 58 (see §25.20) and other cases in which shareholders were allowed to intervene in actions against corporations, and noted that the limited partner in *Linder* had withdrawn its contribution to the limited partnership and might have been subject to individual liability to the plaintiff.

§25.17   7. Husband and Wife

A husband or wife, like any other person, may intervene to protect his or her interest in property which is the subject matter of the action or has been attached. *Bonfiglio v Bonfiglio* (1928) 203 C 409, 264 P 747; *Carter v Garetson* (1922) 56 CA 238, 204 P 1090. However, in *Bechtel v Axelrod* (1942) 20 C2d 390, 125 P2d 836, defendant's wife sought to intervene on the theory that plaintiff might attempt to subject community property to payment of defendant husband's obligation. The wife's interest in the action was termed "remote and contingent," and she was denied leave to intervene because plaintiff had not as yet threatened to seize the community property.

§25.18   8. Owners of Adjoining Property in Zoning Law Enforcement Actions

Neighboring property owners may intervene in actions involving the enforcement of zoning laws. *Weiner v Los Angeles* (1968) 68 C2d 697, 68 CR 733. In the case of *Alphonzo E. Bell Corp. v Bell View Oil Syndicate* (1938) 24 CA2d 587, 76 P2d 167, adjoining landowners who claimed that their property had also been trespassed on by the slant-drilling of oil wells were permitted to intervene in an action for subsurface trespass.

§25.19   9. Voters

In *Baroldi v Denni* (1961) 197 CA2d 472, 17 CR 647, a voter who had signed a petition to recall certain members of a city council was permitted to intervene in an action by them to restrain the council from conducting a recall election. The council had adopted a position of neutrality. In permitting intervention the court referred to the necessity of resolving election questions promptly.

C. Examples of Categories of Persons Generally Not Permitted To Intervene Under Pre-1978 Law

Note: The cases cited in §§25.20–25.24 were decided before amendment of CCP §387, effective January 1, 1978, and denial of leave to intervene to persons in these categories will probably be reexamined in light of criteria in new CCP §387(b).

§25.20   1. Shareholders

A shareholder generally may not intervene in an action by or against the corporation; his interest in the corporation's success is considered consequential and indirect. *Continental Vinyl Prods. Corp. v Mead Corp.* (1972) 27 CA3d 543, 103 CR 806. However, if the corporation is not defending or prosecuting in good faith, a shareholder may intervene. *Eggers v National Radio Co.* (1929) 208 C 308, 281 P 58; *Thorman v Dome Producing & Developing Co.* (1942) 50 CA2d 201, 122 P2d 927.

§25.21   2. Attorneys

Attorneys have not been permitted to intervene in an action in order to collect fees or protect fee arrangements. *Meadow v Superior Court* (1963) 59 C2d 610, 30 CR 824. In *Fields v Potts* (1956) 140 CA2d 697, 295 P2d 965, an attorney with a contingent fee arrangement with respect to the "amount collected" was denied leave to intervene. In *Kelly v Smith* (1928) 204 C 496, 268 P 1057, an attorney who was to receive an interest in land which was the subject of a quiet title action was not permitted to intervene, because he had no "present" interest.

§25.22   3. Taxpayers and Persons Interested in Legal Precedent

Taxpayers, property owners, and other persons interested in the potential precedential effect of a judgment have been denied leave to intervene in actions involving validity or interpretation of legislation or validity of bond issues. See *Jersey Maid Milk Prods. Co. v Brock* (1939) 13 C2d 661, 91 P2d 599; *La Mesa Lemon Grove & Spring Valley Irr. Dist. v Halley* (1925) 195 C 739, 235 P 999; *Squire v San Francisco* (1970) 12 CA3d 974, 91 CR 347; *Kenney v Wolff* (1948) 88 CA2d 163, 198 P2d 582.

Note, however, that the 1978 addition of subdivision (b) to CCP §387 was believed by some proponents to authorize intervention in certain cases, *e.g.*, when the judgment might affect professional school admission programs. See §25.1.

§25.23 4. Owners of Adjoining Property in Actions Other Than Zoning Actions

The California courts have refused to permit the owners of adjoining or neighboring property to intervene in condemnation proceedings (*Alhambra v Jacob Bean Realty Co.* (1934) 138 CA 251, 31 P2d 1052); in actions to quiet title (*People ex rel State Lands Comm'n v Long Beach* (1960) 183 CA2d 271, 6 CR 658); in proceedings for incorporation of cities (*Burlingame v San Mateo* (1951) 103 CA2d 885, 230 P2d 375). Similarly, owners of and claimants to riparian rights other than those in suit have also not been allowed to intervene. *San Joaquin & Kings River Canal & Irr. Co. v Stevinson* (1912) 164 C 221, 128 P 924; *Lindsay-Strathmore Irr. Dist. v Wutchumna Water Co.* (1931) 111 CA 707, 296 P 942. But see *Alphonzo E. Bell Corp. v Bell View Oil Syndicate* (1938) 24 CA2d 587, 76 P2d 167, discussed in §25.18.

§25.24 5. General Creditors

General creditors of a plaintiff or a defendant have been denied leave to intervene even though the outcome of the action may cause the debtor to become insolvent. See *Continental Vinyl Prods. Corp. v Mead Corp.* (1972) 27 CA3d 543, 103 CR 806; *Olson v Hopkins* (1969) 269 CA2d 638, 75 CR 33.

III. EXAMPLES OF PROCEEDINGS IN WHICH INTERVENTION PERMITTED UNDER PRE-1978 LAW

§25.25 A. Foreclosure

One claiming an interest in property subject to foreclosure proceedings may intervene. *Mabury v Ruiz* (1881) 58 C 11 (wife claiming homestead right); *Stich v Dickinson* (1869) 38 C 608 (claimant to note and mortgage).

§25.26 B. Quiet Title Action

Claimants to property which is the subject of a quiet title action may intervene. *Townsend v Driver* (1907) 5 CA 581, 90 P 1071 (claimants to ownership of portions of property). However, in *Stockwell v McAlvay* (1929) 97 CA 609, 275 P 960, a former owner of property sought to intervene claiming that she was defrauded when she conveyed the property to a third party who, she alleged, was the undisclosed agent of plaintiff's husband. In denying intervention, the court emphasized that the would-be intervenor was not in a position to return the consideration she received in the transaction of which she complained. See also *Muller v Robinson* (1959) 174 CA2d 511, 345 P2d 25 (intervention denied when title as between intervenor and plaintiff had been previously litigated to conclusion).

§25.27   C. Actions for Possession of Property

In actions to recover possession of property, claimants to interests in the property may intervene. *Goes v Perry* (1941) 18 C2d 373, 115 P2d 441 (person seeking to impose trust on property based on claim that funds with which property purchased belonged to her); *Bogue v Roeth* (1929) 98 CA 257, 276 P 1071 (holder of contract to purchase property).

§25.28   D. Condemnation Proceedings

Persons not named in the complaint may intervene to assert their interests in property which is the subject of condemnation proceedings. CCP §1250.230; *San Bernardino Valley Munic. Water Dist. v Gage Canal Co.* (1964) 226 CA2d 206, 209, 37 CR 856, 858; see *Stratford Irr. Dist. v Empire Water Co.* (1941) 44 CA2d 61, 70, 111 P2d 957, 962.

§25.29   E. Actions for Impression of Trust

Claimants to interests in property subject to an action for the impression of a trust may intervene. *Dabney v Philleo* (1951) 38 C2d 60, 237 P2d 648 (assignees of interests in property); *Coffey v Greenfield* (1880) 55 C 382 (purchaser at foreclosure sale).

§25.30   F. Will Contests and Heirship Proceedings

Any interested person may intervene in a will contest initiated by another interested person, and he may do so at any time before trial, so long as the original contest was timely commenced. *Estate of Harootenian* (1951) 38 C2d 242, 238 P2d 992; *Voyce v Superior Court* (1942) 20 C2d 479, 127 P2d 536; see *Estate of Collins* (1968) 268 CA2d 86, 90, 73 CR 599, 602. Similarly, interested persons may intervene in heirship proceedings initiated by an appropriate person. *Estate of Quinn* (1955) 43 C2d 785, 278 P2d 692.

§25.31   G. Marriage Dissolution Proceedings

A person claiming an interest in specific property in marriage dissolution proceedings may intervene (*Elms v Elms* (1935) 4 C2d 681, 52 P2d 223), but that person may not be heard with respect to the dissolution itself or any matter other than the claimed interest in the specific property (*Bernheimer v Bernheimer* (1948) 87 CA2d 242, 196 P2d 813).

Intervention in marriage dissolution proceedings is governed by CC §§4363–4363.3 and Cal Rules of Ct 1250–1255.

IV. TIMING OF APPLICATION TO INTERVENE
§25.32   A. Application Must Be "Timely"

Amendment of CCP §387, effective January 1, 1978, substituted the requirement that application to intervene must be "timely" for the former provision that application could be made "at any time before trial." Thus it appears that some applications may be denied as untimely even though made before trial commences (see §§25.36–25.37), while some applications made after commencement of trial will be granted. See generally cases decided under Fed R Civ p 24, which also calls for timely application, and similar state statutes.

Even under the pre-1978 law, it was argued that intervention might be permitted while a trial is in progress if the resultant delay and inconvenience to the original parties can be kept to a minimum. See 3 Witkin, CALIFORNIA PROCEDURE, Pleading §201 (2d ed 1971). In *People ex rel State Lands Comm'n v Long Beach* (1960) 183 CA2d 271, 6 CR 658, a nonparty tried to intervene after commencement of trial, receipt of evidence, and a recess, but before the date set for the continuation of the trial. This intervention was held untimely; the opinion emphasized the delay and enlargement of the scope of the action which would have resulted had intervention been permitted.

Note that a person who qualifies as "indispensable" under CCP §389 may apply to be made a party under that statute, which contains no time limitation (see §25.3).

§25.33   1. Motions Under CCP §473

Under CCP §473, a party may move to set aside a default within six months after its entry, and an appropriate nonparty may intervene to do so. *Linder v Vogue Invs., Inc.* (1966) 239 CA2d 338, 48 CR 633; see *Fireman's Fund Ins. Co. v Gerlach* (1976) 56 CA3d 299, 128 CR 396. However, if the intervenor does not attack the validity of the default under CCP §473 with diligence, intervention should not be allowed. *Drinnon v Oliver* (1972) 24 CA3d 571, 101 CR 120. Several cases suggest that one who is merely the successor in interest of a party who defaulted should not be permitted to intervene under such circumstances. *Stern & Goodman Inv. Co. v Danziger* (1929) 206 C 456, 274 P 748; *Martin v Lawrence* (1909) 156 C 191, 103 P 913. But see *Linder v Vogue Invs., Inc., supra.* Even after the expiration of six months, a nonparty may intervene to set aside a default judgment if the judgment is void on its face. *Johnson v Hayes Cal Builders, Inc.* (1963) 60 C2d 572, 35 CR 618.

Under pre-1978 law, intervention was not generally available under CCP §387 after entry of judgment. *Allen v California Water & Tel. Co.* (1947) 31 C2d 104, 187 P2d 393; *Leonard Corp. v San Diego* (1962) 210 CA2d 547, 26 CR 730. However, in *Gardner v Trevaskis* (1958) 158 CA2d 410, 322 P2d 545, nonparties who claimed interests in the fund which was the subject of the action were permitted to move to set aside a judgment decreeing that the fund belonged to plaintiff. The motions were made under CCP §473 within six months after entry of judgment, apparently on the theory that, while defendant did not default, he made no effort to defend. In affirming, the court stated that a "motion to set aside the judgment is the recognized method for one not a party to the action to become such in order to assert his rights." 158 CA2d at 413, 322 P2d at 547. The opinion also relied on a court's inherent power to vacate a judgment obtained through extrinsic fraud.

§25.34   2. No Intervention After Dismissal of Action

Intervention cannot take place after an action has been dismissed. Pendency of an application for leave to intervene cannot defeat the original parties' right to dismiss. *Burlingame v San Mateo* (1951) 103 CA2d 885, 230 P2d 375. Even after leave to intervene has been granted, the original parties are free to dismiss the action at any time before filing of the complaint in intervention. *Klinghoffer v Barasch* (1970) 4 CA3d 258, 84 CR 350.

§25.35   3. Before New Trial or Retrial

When intervention was permitted at any time before trial (*i.e.*, before 1978), if a motion for a new trial has been granted, application by a nonparty to intervene before the commencement of the new trial was considered timely. *Eggers v National Radio Co.* (1929) 208 C 308, 281 P 58. Similarly, it appears that after a general reversal on appeal and before commencement of the retrial, intervention could properly have been sought. However, this was not the case if the appellate court had merely modified the judgment, permitting a further hearing in the trial court limited to specific issues. *Allen v California Water & Tel. Co.* (1947) 31 C2d 104, 187 P2d 393.

§25.36   B. Effect of Intervenor's Delay After Learning of Action

Even before CCP §387 was amended in 1978, an application to intervene was denied if the would-be intervenor delays unreasonably in applying for leave to intervene after learning of the pendency of the action. *Allen v California Water & Tel. Co.* (1947) 31 C2d 104, 187 P2d 393; *In re Yokohama Specie Bank* (1948) 86 CA2d 545, 195 P2d 555. It was, however, suggested that mere delay or lack of diligence in the absence of some form of prejudice to the original parties should not prevent an otherwise proper intervention. 3 Witkin, CALIFORNIA PROCEDURE, Pleading §205 (2d ed 1971). As a practical matter, it is difficult to imagine a situation in which the original parties cannot demonstrate that an unreasonably delayed intervention is prejudicial if any new issues are presented.

§25.37   C. Statute of Limitations

A complaint in intervention, like any other complaint, is subject to an affirmative defense based on an applicable statute of limitations and, if it asserts a new cause of action, the application for leave to intervene must be filed within the pertinent limitations period. *Alphonzo E. Bell Corp. v Bell View Oil Syndicate* (1938) 24 CA2d 587, 76 P2d 167. If the complaint in intervention raises no new issues, it is timely whenever filed if the original action was commenced in a timely manner. *State Com-*

pensation Ins. Fund v Matulich (1942) 55 CA2d 528, 131 P2d 21; *State Compensation Ins. Fund v Allen* (1930) 104 CA 400, 285 P2d 105 3. See also cases cited in CALIFORNIA WORKMEN'S COMPENSATION PRACTICE 1973, §§17.15, 18.17 (Cal CEB 1973). Similarly, an "interested" person (see §25.10) may intervene in a will contest if the contest was originally commenced within the statutory period. *Voyce v Superior Court* (1942) 20 C2d 479, 127 P2d 536; *Estate of Harootenian* (1951) 38 C2d 242, 238 P2d 992.

V. APPLYING FOR LEAVE TO INTERVENE

A. Available Procedures

§25.38   1. Ex Parte Application

A nonparty may proceed ex parte to obtain the court's permission to intervene. See *Allen v California Water & Tel. Co.* (1947) 31 C2d 104, 187 P2d 393; *Marc Bellaire, Inc. v Fleischman* (1960) 185 CA2d 591, 8 CR 650. To do so, the better practice is to submit a written application for leave to intervene, setting forth the facts showing the applicant's interest, in a properly verified proposed complaint in intervention or in an affidavit or declaration under penalty of perjury (see §25.39). See LA SUPER CT EX PARTE MAN §473.

For a general discussion of ex parte applications, including the need, under Cal Rules of Ct Appendix, Div 1, §15, that notice be given to other parties, see §§23.64–23.66.

If the intervenor is concerned that the existing parties might dismiss the action during the pendency of a noticed motion for leave to intervene (see §25.44), an ex parte application is clearly preferable, and specific facts supporting that concern should be set forth in an affidavit, declaration, or verified pleading. If the court is in doubt whether to grant an ex parte application to intervene, and believes that a fuller exposition of the issues would be helpful, it can order a hearing. See *In re Yokohama Specie Bank* (1948) 86 CA2d 545, 195 P2d 555. In that event, the intervenor should ask the court to stay all proceedings in the action, including any attempts to dismiss, pending the hearing.

§25.39   a. Form: Declaration for Order Granting Leave To Intervene

Copies: Original (presented to the judge and filed with court clerk); copies for service (one for each attorney of record and unrepresented party); office copies.

§25.40 INTERVENTION

[Caption. See §§23.18–23.19]

No. _____

DECLARATION FOR ORDER ____[AND ORDER GRANTING LEAVE TO INTERVENE]____

____[Name]____ **declares:**

1. I am the ____[intervenor / attorney for intervenor]____. **I have personal knowledge of all facts stated in this declaration, and if called as a witness I could and would testify competently to them.**

2. Under Code of Civil Procedure section 387, ____[name of intervenor]____ **applies to the Court for an order granting** ____[him / her / it]____ **leave to intervene in this action and file the attached complaint in intervention which is by this reference incorporated in this application. Trial of this action has not yet begun.**

3. ____[In successively numbered paragraphs, set forth facts showing nature of applicant's interest in the matter in litigation, or relating to the property or transaction that is the subject of the action, and conformance to the other criteria for intervention specified in either CCP §387(a) or (b). See §25.10]____.

4. I have notified all other parties that this application would be made by ____[describe method]____.

I declare under penalty of perjury that the foregoing is true and correct and that this declaration was executed on _____, 19____, **at** _____, **California.**

[Signature of declarant]

[Typed name]

Comment: Such a declaration may not be necessary; a properly verified complaint in intervention, setting forth the requisite facts, may be sufficient. However, use of a declaration enables the intervenor to make a more detailed, and therefore persuasive, evidentiary showing.

§25.40 b. Form: Order Granting Leave To Intervene

Copies: Original (presented to judge for signature, then filed); copies for service (one for each attorney of record and unrepresented party); office copies.

[Caption. See §§23.18–23.19]

No. _____

ORDER GRANTING LEAVE TO INTERVENE

Good cause appearing as shown by the declaration of _____, **and the proposed complaint in intervention attached to the declaration,**

IT IS ORDERED that ____[name]____ is granted leave to intervene in this action and to file the complaint in intervention.

Dated: _____

                                                  Judge

Comment: This form may be attached to a declaration or application for it (see §25.39) or it may be a separate document.

§25.41   2. Order To Show Cause

The intervenor may appear ex parte and seek an order directed to the existing parties requiring them to show cause why the intervenor should not be granted leave to file the complaint in intervention. On the order to show cause procedure generally, see §§23.67–23.69. *Thorman v Dome Producing & Developing Co.* (1942) 50 CA2d 201, 122 P2d 927. If the order to show cause provides that all proceedings in the action are stayed and that the action may not be dismissed until determination of the application for leave to intervene, the intervenor will be protected, and the court will have the benefit of a thorough briefing of all questions.

§25.42   a. Form: Declaration for Order and Order To Show Cause Re Intervention

Copies: Original (presented to judge for signature, then filed); copies for service (one for each attorney of record and unrepresented party); office copies.

[*Caption. See §§23.18–23.19*]	No. _____ **DECLARATION FOR ORDER ____[AND ORDER]____ TO SHOW CAUSE RE INTERVENTION**

____[Name]____ declares:

   1. I am the ____[*intervenor / attorney for intervenor*]____.

   2. Under Code of Civil Procedure section 387, ____[*name of intervenor*]____ applies for an order directing the parties to this action to show cause why ____[*he / she / it*]____ should not be granted leave to intervene and file the attached proposed complaint in intervention which is by this reference incorporated in this application. Trial of this action has not yet begun.

   3. ____[*Continue as paragraphs 3 and 4 in §25.39*]____.

I declare under penalty of perjury that the foregoing is true and correct and that this declaration was executed on _____, 19____ at _____, California.

> _____
> [Signature of declarant]
>
> [Typed name]

Comment: See Comment to §25.39.

§25.43   b. Form: Order To Show Cause Why Leave To Intervene Should Not Be Granted

Copies: Original (presented to judge for signature, then filed); copies for service (one for each attorney of record and unrepresented party); office copies.

[Caption. See §§23.18– 23.19]

No. _____

ORDER TO SHOW CAUSE WHY LEAVE TO INTERVENE SHOULD NOT BE GRANTED

Good cause appearing, as shown by the declaration of ____[name]____ ____[and the proposed complaint in intervention attached to the declaration]____, IT IS ORDERED that on _____, 19____, at ____ __.m., or as soon thereafter as the matter can be heard, in Department No. _____ of the above Court, at ____[address]____, California, plaintiff _____ and defendant _____ shall show cause, if any, they have, why leave to intervene in this action should not be granted to ____[name of intervenor]____.

[When appropriate]

IT IS FURTHER ORDERED that, until the determination of this order to show cause, all proceedings in this action, including all efforts to dismiss this action, are stayed.

[Continue]

IT IS FURTHER ORDERED that copies of this order, the declaration of _____, the proposed complaint in intervention, and the accompanying memorandum of points and authorities shall be served on all parties no later than _____, 19____.

Dated: _____

> **Judge**

Comment: This form may be attached to the declaration in application for it (if one is used) or to the proposed complaint in intervention, or it may be a separate document.

§25.44   3. Noticed Motion

If the intervenor is not concerned that the action may be dismissed by the original parties before a noticed motion may be heard, he may give each of the existing parties written notice of a motion for leave to intervene. See *Muller v Robinson* (1959) 174 CA2d 511, 345 P2d 25. See generally, on noticed motion procedures, §§23.8–23.63.

§25.45   a. Form: Notice of Motion for Leave To Intervene

Copies: Original (filed with court clerk with proof of service); copies for service (one for each attorney of record and unrepresented party); office copies.

[*Caption. See §§23.18–23.19*]

No. _____

NOTICE OF MOTION FOR LEAVE TO INTERVENE; POINTS AND AUTHORITIES; DECLARATION

To each party and attorney of record:
   PLEASE TAKE NOTICE that on _____, 19____, **at** _____.m., **or as soon thereafter as the matter can be heard, in Department No.** ____ **of the above Court, located at** ____*[address]*____, **California,** ____*[name of intervenor]*____ **will move the Court for an order granting** ____*[him / her / it]*____ **leave to intervene by filing** ____*[his / her / its]*____ **complaint in intervention.**
   The motion will be made under Code of Civil Procedure section 387 on the ground that ____*[name of intervenor]*____ **has an interest** ____*[in the matter in litigation / in the success of* ____*[name of party]*____ */ against both parties to this action / relating to the property or transaction which is the subject of this action]*____. **The motion is based on this notice, the attached proposed complaint in intervention, memorandum of points and authorities, declaration of** _____, **and all pleadings, papers, and records filed in this action,** ____*[and on such evidence as may be presented at the hearing]*____.

Dated: _____

[*Signature of attorney*]

[*Typed name*]
Attorney for _____

Comment: The form of declaration in §25.39 may be adapted for use with this motion.

§25.46 b. Form: Order Granting Leave To Intervene

Copies: Original (presented to judge for signature, then filed); copies for service (one for each attorney of record and unrepresented party); office copies.

[Caption. See §§23.18– 23.19]

No. _____

ORDER GRANTING LEAVE TO INTERVENE

_____[The order to show cause why ____[name of intervenor]____ should not be granted leave to intervene in this action / The motion of ____[name of intervenor]____ for leave to intervene in this action]____ **was regularly heard on** _____, 19____, **in Department No.** ____ **of the above Court.** _____ **appeared as attorney for the intervenor,** _____ **appeared as attorney for plaintiff, and** _____ **appeared as attorney for defendant.**

The Court having considered the documents submitted in support of and in opposition to the proposed intervention, and the arguments of counsel, and good cause appearing,

IT IS ORDERED that ____[name of intervenor]____ **is granted leave to intervene in this action and to file the complaint in intervention.**

Dated: _____

Judge

§25.47 B. Burden of Proof on Intervenor

The intervenor has the burden of demonstrating that he satisfies the requirements of either CCP §387 (a) or (b) and that leave to intervene should be granted. If an insufficient showing is made, the court may deny the application to intervene even in the absence of objections by existing parties. *Fields v Potts* (1956) 140 CA2d 697, 295 P2d 965. Thus, to obtain leave to intervene under the discretionary provisions of CCP §387(a) the intervenor's papers should set forth his interest in the matter in litigation, his interest in the success of either of the parties, or his interest against both parties. Further, the intervenor must take a position with respect to the pleadings as contemplated by the statute, *i.e.*, the intervenor must state explicitly that he joins plaintiff in claiming what is sought by the complaint, that he unites with defendant in resisting plaintiff's claims, or that he demands something adversely to both plaintiff and defendant. On the showing required under CCP §387-(b), see §25.10.

C. Opposition to Intervention

§25.48 1. Procedure for Presenting Opposition

If the intervenor has used a noticed motion for leave to intervene (see §25.44–25.46) or an order to show cause why leave to intervene should not be granted (see §25.41–25.43), any party to the action may submit an affidavit or declaration (see CCP §2015.5) and a memorandum of points and authorities in opposition to the proposed intervention.

If the intervenor has obtained leave to intervene by an ex parte application (see §25.38–25.40), the existing parties' first opportunity to object to the intervention will occur after the filing and service of the complaint in intervention. At that time, any party may:

(1) move to strike the complaint in intervention on the ground that intervention is improper under the circumstances. (*Jersey Maid Milk Prods. Co. v Brock* (1939) 13 C2d 661, 91 P2d 599);

(2) demur to the complaint in intervention on the ground that it fails to state facts sufficient to constitute a ground for intervention (see *People v Brophy* (1942) 49 CA2d 15, 120 P2d 946); or

(3) move to strike and demur;

(4) "otherwise plead to the complaint [in intervention] in the same manner as to an original complaint." CCP §387(a).

§25.49 2. Grounds for Opposition

The most common ground for objection to an application for intervention made under what is now CCP §387(a) is that the intervenor lacks the requisite interest in the action, *i.e.*, that the intervenor's interest is "remote" or "consequential." See §25.10. A party may submit an affidavit or declaration to show that the inconvenience or prejudice to the existing parties, or either of them, which would result if intervention were permitted far outweighs the intervenor's interest in the action. See §25.10.

An existing party may also argue that the application to intervene was untimely, and show, *e.g.*, that the intervenor delayed unreasonably in seeking intervention after learning of the existence of the action thereby prejudicing the objecting party. See §§25.32, 25.36.

The words of CCP §387(b) suggest several grounds for opposing an application made under subdivision (b). For example, an opposing party could argue, or show that (1) the applicant's claimed interest does not in fact relate to the property or transaction that is the subject of the action; (2) the applicant has adequate means other than intervention to protect his claimed interest; (3) the applicant's interest is adequately represented by existing parties; or (4) the application was not timely made (see §25.32). See generally §25.10.

§25.50   3. Waiver of Objections

If a party fails to object to the intervention at his first opportunity (using one of the appropriate methods discussed in §25.48), he has effectively waived any objections he might have had and may not raise such objections on appeal. *Watson v Collins* (1962) 204 CA2d 27, 21 CR 832; *Bloom v Waxman* (1941) 48 CA2d 646, 120 P2d 509. Thus if a party answers the complaint in intervention, or demurs to it on the ground that it fails to state a cause of action (as distinguished from a failure to state grounds for intervention; see §25.48), all objections to the intervention are waived. *Traweek v Draper* (1956) 143 CA2d 119, 299 P2d 391.

D. Appellate Review
§25.51   1. When Leave To Intervene Denied

An unsuccessful intervenor may appeal immediately if his application for leave to intervene is denied, because denial operates as a final determination of the action with respect to him. *Bowles v Superior Court* (1955) 44 C2d 574, 283 P2d 704. Similarly, if the intervenor obtains leave ex parte to file a complaint in intervention, and the complaint in intervention is later stricken, the intervenor may appeal immediately. *Jersey Maid Milk Prods. Co. v Brock* (1939) 13 C2d 661, 91 P2d 599. Appeal at this time is the only relief available to the unsuccessful intervenor; he has no right to appeal from the judgment ultimately rendered in the action in which he sought to intervene. *Braun v Brown* (1939) 13 C2d 130, 87 P2d 1009. If intervention is erroneously denied on the ground that the intervenor has no interest in the subject matter of the action, the intervenor must appeal from this determination or a subsequent independent action based on the same theory will be barred by the doctrine of res judicata. *Berman v Aetna Cas. & Sur. Co.* (1974) 40 CA3d 908, 115 CR 566.

The pendency of an appeal from the denial of leave to intervene has no effect on the progress of the action, which may continue to trial and judgment. *Olson v Hopkins* (1969) 269 CA2d 638, 75 CR 33; *Lindsay Strathmore Irr. Dist. v Superior Court* (1932) 121 CA 606, 9 P2d 579.

§25.52   2. When Leave To Intervene Granted

An order permitting intervention is not itself appealable. *Taylor v Western States Land & Mortgage Co.* (1944) 63 CA2d 401, 147 P2d 36. After intervention, any party, including the intervenor, may appeal after judgment from any order, including the order permitting intervention, which aggrieves that party. *Corridan v Rose* (1955) 137 CA2d 524, 290 P2d 939.

VI. COMPLAINT IN INTERVENTION
§25.53   A. Requirements

A complaint in intervention must set forth facts sufficient to constitute a cause of action or, if the intervenor resists plaintiff's claims, facts sufficient to constitute a defense. *People v Brophy* (1942) 49 CA2d 15, 34, 120 P2d 946, 956. In addition, however, the complaint in intervention must set forth the intervenor's interest in the matter in litigation or relating to the property or transaction that is the subject of the action, his interest in the success of either of the parties, or his interest against both parties. At least in an intervention sought under CCP §387(a), the complaint must expressly state that the intervenor joins plaintiff in claiming what is sought by the complaint, that the intervenor unites with defendant in resisting plaintiff's claims, or that the intervenor demands something adversely to both plaintiff and defendant. *Bowles v Superior Court* (1955) 44 C2d 574, 589, 283 P2d 704, 714. While the nature of the action and the circumstances of the intervention should be alleged, the complaint in intervention should be a fully independent pleading and should not incorporate any other pleadings by reference.

§25.54   B. Form: Complaint in Intervention

Copies: Original (filed with court clerk with proof of service); copies for service (one for each attorney of record and unrepresented party); office copies.

§25.55 INTERVENTION

[Caption. See §§23.18-23.19]

No. _____

COMPLAINT IN INTERVENTION

Intervenor _____, by leave of Court, alleges:

1. On or about _____, 19____, ____[plaintiff commenced this action against defendant for _____ / defendant cross-claimed against plaintiff for _____]____. ____[Trial of this action has not yet begun]____.

2. In this action, intervenor ____[joins plaintiff in claiming what is sought by the complaint / unites with defendant in resisting plaintiff's claims / demands relief adversely to both plaintiff and defendant]____.

[When application under CCP §387(a)]

3. Intervenor has an interest in the matter in litigation in this action ____ [and]____ ____[in the success of plaintiff / in the success of defendant / against both plaintiff and defendant]____ **as more particularly set forth below.**

[When application under CCP §387(b)]

3. **Intervenor has an interest in the matter in litigation in this action** ____[and]____ ____[in the success of plaintiff / in the success of defendant / against both plaintiff and defendant]____ **as more particularly set forth below.**

4. ____[Set out intervenor's claims in successively numbered paragraphs, as in any other pleading]____.

WHEREFORE, intervenor demands:

1. ____[Set out relief desired]____; and
2. Costs and all other just relief.

_____
[Signature of attorney or party]

[Typed name]
____[Attorney for intervenor]____

Comment: There is a question whether the allegation in paragraph 2 must be used when intervention is sought under CCP §387(b).

§25.55   C. Service: Payment of Fees

After leave to intervene is granted by the court, whether ex parte (see §§25.38–25.40), or after an order to show cause (see §§25.41–25.43), after a noticed motion (see §§25.44–25.46), the complaint in intervention may be filed on payment of the required appearance fee. At that time, the summons on the complaint in intervention will be issued.

Copies of the summons, the complaint in intervention, the court's order permitting intervention, and all the papers filed by the intervenor in application for leave to intervene must then be served on the attorneys of record for the parties who have appeared (or on a party himself, if he has appeared without an attorney), by mail or by hand, in the same manner as a summons or responsive pleading is served. Copies of these documents must be served on any party who has not yet appeared in the same manner as on a party at the commencement of an action. CCP §387. See 1 CALIFORNIA CIVIL PROCEDURE BEFORE TRIAL chap 8 (Cal CEB 1977) on service and CCP §§1010–1020 for manner of service.

VII. RESPONSES TO COMPLAINT IN INTERVENTION
§25.56 A. Available Responses; Timing

The original parties may respond within 30 days of service to the complaint in intervention by answer, demurrer, or motion just as a party may respond to an original complaint. CCP §387. If the intervenor has intervened solely as a defendant, joining the original defendant in resisting plaintiff's claims, the complaint in intervention is, in effect, considered an answer and its allegations are considered controverted; the original parties need not file any pleading in response. *Drinkhouse v Van Ness* (1927) 202 C 359, 371, 260 P 869, 874; *People v Perris Irr. Dist.* (1901) 132 C 289, 64 P 399. If a responsive pleading is required, it must be filed and served within 30 days after service of the complaint in intervention. CCP §387.

§25.57 B. Cross-Complaint Against Intervenor

If the intervenor asserts any claim adverse to an existing party, that party may file a cross-complaint against the intervenor. See CCP §§428.10–428.80. See *Wall v Mines* (1900) 130 C 27, 62 P 386. (Accordingly, it appears that any cross-complaint against the intervenor which is "compulsory" under CCP §§426.10–426.70 must be asserted or it will be deemed waived.)

No cross-claim may be asserted against an intervenor who has intervened solely as a defendant, joining the original defendant in resisting plaintiff's claims. *Drinkhouse v Van Ness* (1927) 202 C 359, 372, 260 P 869, 873. See 1 CALIFORNIA CIVIL PROCEDURE BEFORE TRIAL chap 12 (Cal CEB 1977)).

VIII. PARTIES' RIGHTS AND REMEDIES AFTER INTERVENTION

§25.58   A. Intervenor's Rights and Remedies

Generally, an intervenor has all the rights and remedies afforded an original party to an action. *People v Perris Irr.Dist.* (1901) 132 C 289, 64 P 399. An intervenor may seek any form of affirmative relief, legal or equitable (*Belt Cas. Co. v Furman* (1933) 218 C 359, 23 P2d 293; *Marc Bellaire, Inc. v Fleischman* (1960) 185 CA2d 591, 8 CR 650); object to the court's jurisdiction (*Maguire v Cunningham* (1923) 64 CA 536, 222 P 838); move for a change of venue (see *San Diego v Andrews* (1924) 195 C 111, 231 P 726); and may assert that the original complaint fails to state a cause of action (*Maguire v Cunningham, supra*) or, presumably, assert that the original answer fails to state a defense. It has been suggested that an intervenor may demand a jury trial in an appropriate action even if the original parties have waived a jury trial. See *McNeil v Morgan* (1910) 157 C 373, 377, 108 P 69, 70. An intervenor may move to disqualify a judge. *San Diego v Andrews, supra.*

It is frequently stated that an intervenor takes the action as he finds it and is bound by the record at the time intervention is sought. *Allen v California Water & Tel. Co.* (1947) 31 C2d 104, 187 P2d 393. This generality is not entirely accurate and has many exceptions (see *Hausmann v Farmers Ins. Exch.* (1963) 213 CA2d 611, 617, 29 CR 75, 79); 3 Witkin, CALIFORNIA PROCEDURE, Pleading §207 (2d ed 1971), and means merely that an intervenor cannot rely on irregularities that were waived by the original parties. See *Maguire v Cunningham* (1923) 64 CA 536, 541, 222 P 838, 840. It has been suggested that an intervenor may be "bound by" depositions taken before his intervention. See *McNeil v Morgan* (1910) 157 C 373, 377, 108 P 69, 70.

An intervening plaintiff's position is subordinate to that of the original plaintiff (and the latter's attorney), who has an absolute right to control the action, unless the original plaintiff consents or the court orders otherwise. In *Mann v Superior Court* (1942) 53 CA2d 272, 127 P2d 970, a shareholder's derivative suit, the court pointed out that the general rule that the original plaintiff has the absolute right to control the action does not apply when it is shown that the action is not being prosecuted in the best interests of the shareholders in whose behalf it was instituted.

An intervenor may not bring a new party into the action in his complaint in intervention. CCP §387; see *Cobe v Crane* (1916) 173 C 116. However, it would seem that the compulsory joinder provisions of CCP §389 are applicable to a complaint in intervention, and that the court must order that a nonparty be made a party when the statutory requirements are met. However, the necessity for such a joinder might convince the court not to permit intervention in the first place. It would seem that the original plaintiff or defendant, in responding to a complaint in intervention, may cross-claim against a nonparty.

B. Dismissal of Action After Intervention

§25.59 **1. By Original Plaintiff**

If neither the defendant nor the intervenor seeks any form of affirmative relief, the original plaintiff is free to dismiss the action at any time. *Henry v Vineland Irr. Dist.* (1903) 140 C 376, 73 P 1061. However, plaintiff may not dismiss solely as to the intervenor and purport to proceed against the other parties. *Townsend v Driver* (1907) 5 CA 581, 90 P 1071. If the intervenor asserts a claim for relief, he is entitled to proceed on it regardless of the dismissal of any other claims in the action. *Voyce v Superior Court* (1942) 20 C2d 479, 127 P2d 536; *Poehlmann v Kennedy* (1874) 48 C 201.

§25.60 **2. By Intervenor**

If no relief is sought against the intervenor, he may dismiss his intervention at any time. *Sheldon v Gunn* (1880) 56 C 582. However, if the intervenor has intervened as a defendant, joining the original defendant in resisting plaintiff's claims, the intervenor has presumably brought about a situation in which claims are asserted against him and he may not withdraw.

RICHARD P. BYRNE

Chapter 26
Setting Case For Trial

I. INTRODUCTION
A. Superior Court Settings
 1. Basic Steps §26.1
 2. Special Situations
  a. Short Causes §26.2
  b. Counties Having Ten or Fewer Judges §26.3
  c. Statutory Priority §26.4
B. Municipal and Justice Court Settings §26.5
C. Small Claims Court Settings §26.6
D. Local Variations and Changes in Setting Procedures §26.7

II. INITIAL PAPERS FOR SETTING
A. At-Issue Memorandum
 1. Nature and Function §26.8
 2. Effect of Filing; Civil Active List §26.9
 3. Procedures for Filing Party
  a. Severing Unanswered Cross-Complaint Before Filing §26.10
  b. Content of Memorandum §26.11
  c. Effect of Failure To Demand Jury in At-Issue Memorandum §26.12
  d. Form: At-Issue Memorandum §26.13
 4. Responses of Nonfiling Party
  a. Countermemoranda; Motion To Strike §26.14
  b. Opposing Jury Trial Request §26.15
B. Certificate of Readiness
 1. Nature and Purpose §26.16
 2. Counties in Which Certificate Required §26.17
 3. Time for Filing §26.18
 4. Effect of Filing §26.19
 5. Effect of Failure To File §26.20

RICHARD P. BYRNE, B.A., 1955, University of California (Los Angeles); J.D., 1958, University of Southern California Law School. Judge Byrne is a judge of the Superior Court of Los Angeles County.
 The material in this chapter on demand for jury trial is based in part on portions of chap 5, Selection of a Jury, CALIFORNIA CIVIL PROCEDURE DURING TRIAL (1960), by CARL J. SCHUCK of the Los Angeles Bar.
 CEB attorney-editor was JON A. RANTZMAN.

SETTING CASE FOR TRIAL

    6. Procedures
      a. Who May Prepare §26.21
      b. Content of Certificate §26.22
      c. Form: Certificate of Readiness §26.23
      d. Filing and Service §26.24
    7. Changing Setting or Vacating Certificate
      a. Authority; Grounds §26.25
      b. Court's Discretion §26.26
      c. Procedure §26.27
 III. DEMAND FOR JURY TRIAL
  A. Right to Jury §26.28
  B. Court's Discretion When No Right to Jury Exists; Procedures §26.29
  C. Deciding Whether To Demand or Retain Jury; Factors §26.30
  D. Procedures
    1. Necessity and Time for Demand; Effect §26.31
    2. Form of Jury Demand §26.32
    3. Deposit of Fees and Expenses; Refunds §26.33
  E. Reliance on Other Party's Demand §26.34
  F. Waiver of Jury Trial
    1. Acts Resulting in Waiver §26.35
    2. Relief from Waiver
      a. Authority §26.36
      b. Procedures §26.37
 IV. CONFERENCES PREREQUISITE TO TRIAL
  A. Trial Setting Conference
    1. Nature and Purpose; When Required §26.38
    2. Relationship to Pretrial Conference §26.39
    3. Attendance by Counsel; Knowledge of Case §26.40
      a. Local Variations; Los Angeles Policy §26.41
      b. Deciding Whether To Attend §26.42
    4. Matters Considered at Conference §26.43
    5. Matters Precluded From Consideration §26.44
    6. Sanctions
      a. Power of Court To Impose; Types §26.45
      b. Local Variations; Los Angeles Policy §26.46
    7. Procedures §26.47
      a. Setting Conference Date §26.48
      b. Notice §26.49
      c. Continuances; Motions To Advance, Specially Set, or Reset §26.50
      d. Setting for Trial §26.51
      e. Trial Setting Conference Order
        (1) When Used; Content §26.52
        (2) Form of Order; Who Prepares §26.53
        (3) Service §26.54
      f. Notice of Trial §26.55
  B. Pretrial Conference
    1. Introduction
      a. Nature and Purpose §26.56
      b. Statutory Authority; When Used §26.57
      c. Duties of Counsel; Sanctions §26.58

2. Selecting Cases for Pretrial Conference
     a. Conference Ordered on Court's Own Motion §26.59
     b. Conference on Request of Counsel
        (1) Deciding Whether To Request §26.60
        (2) Procedures for Requesting
           (a) In At-Issue Memorandum §26.61
           (b) After Filing At-Issue Memorandum §26.62
  3. Setting for Pretrial Conference §26.63
  4. Notice §26.64
  5. Conduct of Conference
     a. Location; Use of Court Reporter §26.65
     b. Matters Considered §26.66
     c. Continuances §26.67
  6. Pretrial Conference Order
     a. Who Must Prepare; Time §26.68
     b. Content §26.69
     c. Service; Corrections or Modifications; Filing §26.70
     d. Effect of Failure To Comply §26.71
     e. Appellate Review §26.72
  7. Effect of Order and Conference §26.73
  8. Setting for Trial After Pretrial Conference §26.74
C. Settlement Conference §26.75
V. MOTIONS TO ADVANCE, SPECIALLY SET, AND RESET
 A. Authority §26.76
 B. When To Use
  1. Motions To Advance or Specially Set §26.77
  2. Motions To Reset §26.78
 C. Court's Discretion §26.79
 D. Procedures
  1. To Whom Motion Is Made §26.80
  2. Form: Notice of Motion To Advance, Specially Set, or Reset §26.81
  3. Form: Declaration in Support of Motion To Advance, Specially Set, or Reset §26.82
VI. TRIAL CONTINUANCES
 A. Introduction; Scope of Discussion §26.83
 B. Policy Against Continuances §26.84
 C. Grounds; Effect of Appellate Decisions §26.85
  1. Basic Requirement of Good Cause §26.86
     a. Examples of Good Cause
        (1) Death of Attorney or Witness §26.87
        (2) Illness of Party, Attorney, or Witness §26.88
        (3) Unavailability of Trial Attorney, Party, or Witness §26.89
        (4) Substitution of Trial attorney §26.90
        (5) Significant Change in Status of Case §26.91
     b. Local Variations; Los Angeles Policy §26.92
  2. Statutory Grounds §26.93
  3. Inherent Power of Court To Continue §26.94
 D. Court Discretion; Factors Considered §26.95
 E. Procedures
  1. Noticed Motion and Declaration §26.96

§26.1   SETTING CASE FOR TRIAL

> 2. Form: Notice of Motion for Continuance §26.97
> 3. Form: Declaration in Support of Motion for Continuance §26.98
> 4. Payment of Costs as Condition for Granting Motion §26.99
> 5. Procedures When Motion Denied
>   a. Trailing Cases §26.100
>   b. Severance §26.101
> 6. Appellate Review §26.102

I. INTRODUCTION
A. Superior Court Settings
§26.1   1. Basic Steps

The basic steps for setting a case for trial in California superior courts are set forth in Cal Rules of Ct 206–221. The first step in the trial setting process is for the party who desires setting (usually the plaintiff) to file and serve an at-issue memorandum (and any locally required certificate of readiness). Unless these papers have been filed and served, no civil case may be placed on the civil active list, set for pretrial conference, trial setting conference, or trial. Cal Rules of Ct 206(a), 221(a), (c). See generally §§26.8–26.27; for forms, see §§26.18, 26.23.

The certificate of readiness, when required, may be filed with the at-issue memorandum or later. In courts with calendars so congested that the case cannot be brought to trial within six months from the date the certificate was filed, the certificate may be filed only after court notification. Cal Rules of Ct 221(d). For discussion, see §26.18. In either event, many plaintiffs' attorneys file the certificate as soon as possible to maintain pressure on the defense by establishing a position on the civil active list.

After an at-issue memorandum (and, when required, a certificate of readiness) is filed and the case placed on the civil active list, a pretrial conference is held only if either party requests or the court orders it (Cal Rules of Ct 208) and a trial date is assigned in the pretrial order or by notification from the court clerk (Cal Rules of Ct 219(b)). See §26.57 for discussion of the extent to which pretrial conferences currently are in use. If a pretrial conference is neither requested nor ordered, the case usually is set for a trial setting conference (Cal Rules of Ct 220(a), 220.4), at which a trial date is assigned (Cal Rules of Ct 220.1). See §§26.38–26.55 for discussion of trial setting conferences.

Short causes set for trial under Cal Rules of Ct 207.1 are exempt from both pretrial and trial setting conferences. For discussion, see §26.2. Regardless of whether a pretrial or trial setting conference is held, courts in many counties require that a settlement conference be held in each superior court case, except possibly a short cause. For discussion, see §26.75.

2. Special Situations

§26.2 a. Short Causes

Short causes (*i.e.*, those cases which all parties estimate can be tried in one day or less (five hours trial time)) are exempt from pretrial, settlement, or trial setting conferences, and are set for trial by the clerk, under judicial supervision, as soon as feasible after the at-issue memorandum and any required certificate of readiness, is filed. Cal Rules of Ct 207.1. If trial of the case is not completed within that time, the court may complete the trial, or in the interests of justice, declare a mistrial. If a mistrial is declared, the case will not be replaced on the civil active list until a party serves and files a new at-issue memorandum that estimates trial time at more than one day. Cal Rules of Ct 207.1.

When the parties have agreed in their at-issue memorandum that a case is entitled to setting as a short cause, and one of them subsequently learns that the case may take more than one day to try, counsel should file an amended at-issue memorandum or write to the court clerk explaining that because of unforeseen developments the case should not be set as a short cause. Content, service, and filing of the amended memorandum are governed by the same procedures as in the original. See generally, §§26.8–26.15.

§26.3 b. Counties Having Ten or Fewer Judges

In counties having ten or fewer superior court judges, the trial setting conference rules discussed in §§26.38–26.55 apply unless dispensed with by local rule. Cal Rules of Ct 220.4. See, *e.g.*, Mendocino Super Ct R II, §1; Solano Super Ct R 2.2. The rationale for rule 220.4 is that smaller counties may be able to calendar efficiently through the mail, telephone discussions with counsel, or other informal methods. Short causes and cases subject to pretrial conference are set for trial in the same manner as in counties having more than ten judges. Cal Rules of Ct 220.4.

In counties having a local rule dispensing with the trial setting conference, the court, at least once a month, sets for trial as many cases on the civil active list (other than short causes and cases subject to pretrial conference) as may reasonably be tried during the period to be calendared. Cal Rules of Ct 220.4. If local rules require a certificate of readiness, only those cases in which a certificate has been filed are eligible for trial setting. Cal Rules of Ct 221(a). The cases are assigned a trial date by the judge, or under judicial supervision, in the sequence in which they appear on the civil active list, subject to statutory priority. Cal Rules of Ct 220.4. See §26.4 for discussion of statutory priority.

The clerk must give at least 90 days' notice of the trial date by mail to all parties appearing in the case, except when the time is shortened (1) by stipulation, (2) by the court to prevent a dismissal under CCP §583, or (3) for other good cause shown on noticed motion. Cal Rules of Ct 220.4. The 90-day period is designed to afford the parties ample opportunity to complete discovery and other trial preparations. Discovery in superior court may be pursued as a matter of right up to 30 days before trial, and is a matter of trial court discretion within 30 days of trial. Cal Rules of Ct 222.

It is not certain whether the clerk's notice of trial under Cal Rules of Ct 220.4 obviates the need for counsel also to serve notice as required by CCP §594(a) to preserve the right to proceed to trial in the absence of an adverse party. It is thus good practice for counsel to serve written notice of trial at least 15 days before trial. See CCP §594.

§26.4   c. Statutory Priority

The usual practice of setting cases for trial in the order in which the at-issue memoranda are filed (see §26.9) is subject to priorities created by statute. Cases in which priority in trial setting is recognized include (1) actions seeking a preliminary injunction (CCP §527), (2) taxpayer's actions to enjoin a waste of public funds (CCP §526a), (3) actions seeking declaratory relief only (CCP §1062a), (4) unlawful detainer proceedings (CCP §1179a), (5) eminent domain proceedings (CCP §1260.010), and (6) defamation actions when the likelihood of continuous publication is shown (CCP §460.5). For further examples, see 4 Witkin, CALIFORNIA PROCEDURE, Trial §47 (2d ed 1971).

Code of Civil Procedure §1062a states that actions seeking only declaratory relief are entitled to priority in trial setting. In 1976, the legislature added CCP §1062a(b), which provides that whenever plaintiff's action seeks any additional relief, the action is entitled to priority only on noticed motion and a showing that the action requires a speedy trial. This provision should eliminate the practice of some plaintiffs' counsel of adding to the complaint an action for declaratory relief solely to obtain an early trial date. For discussion, see *Review of Selected 1976 California Legislation* 8 PAC LJ 239 (1977).

§26.5 B. Municipal and Justice Court Settings

The first step in setting a municipal or justice court case for trial is filing and serving a memorandum to set the case for trial, which is similar to the at-issue memorandum required in superior court. Compare Cal Rules of Ct 206(a) with Cal Rules of Ct 507(a). (Preprinted forms similar to the one shown in §26.13 for an at-issue memorandum are usually available from the court clerk.) When a civil active list is required by local rule or by the presiding judge, filing the memorandum to set places the case on the list. Cal Rules of Ct 508(a). California Rules of Court references in this discussion are to Rules 501–534 (municipal court rules), which under Rule 701 apply equally to justice courts.

At least once a month, cases are chosen from the civil active list or the memoranda, in the order in which they appear or were filed, and are set for trial during the succeeding month. Cal Rules of Ct 509(a). Special settings, *e.g.*, for cases entitled to setting priority, are set out in Cal Rules of Ct 510. Notice of the time and place of trial must be given under CCP §594.

There are no procedures for pretrial, trial setting, or settlement conferences in municipal or justice courts. Nor does Cal Rules of Ct 222 (which provides that discovery may be pursued as a matter of right up to 30 days before trial, and as a matter of trial court discretion within 30 days of trial) apply to municipal or justice courts. For further discussion of municipal and justice court trial settings, see Cal Rules of Ct 506–515.

§26.6 C. Small Claims Court Settings

Cases in small claims court are set for trial by the judge or court clerk on receipt of plaintiff's claim. (No attorney can prosecute or defend against unless a small claims case is brought by or against the attorney personally. CCP §117.4.) The judge or clerk signs an order directing defendant to appear on a date not more than 40 days nor less than ten days from the date of the order (not more than 70 days nor less than 30 days if defendant resides outside the county in which the action is filed), and serves it on defendant by mail (using a return receipt) or in person. CCP §116.4. For discussion of personal service and service by mail, see 1 CALIFORNIA CIVIL PROCEDURE BEFORE TRIAL §§8.31–8.33, 8.36–8.39 (Cal CEB 1977). When there are two or more defendants and one or more of them resides outside the county of filing, the date for appearance of all defendants cannot be more than 70 nor less than 30 days from the date of the order to appear. CCP §117.3.

When service of plaintiff's claim and order has not been completed at least five days before the hearing date (15 days if defendant resides outside the county of filing), the court must, unless defendant personally appears and does not request a continuance, continue the hearing for at least ten days, and must so notify by first class mail any served defendant who did not personally appear. CCP §116.4.

§26.7 D. Local Variations and Changes in Setting Procedures

The rules and procedures discussed in this chapter for setting a case for trial, whether in superior, municipal, or justice court, frequently vary from county to county. For example, pretrial conferences are widely used in some rural counties, and hardly ever used in urban counties. See §26.57. Some smaller counties have dispensed with the need for a trial setting conference. See §26.3. Court clerks sometimes will not accept setting papers for filing unless their own preprinted forms are used. See Caveat to the form in §26.13.

Keeping up with local practice has been made more difficult by the fact that often local rules and procedures are not published but rather are the result of unpublished "court policy." Even when a policy has been published, courts have been known to contradict that policy when necessary, often on short notice. See, e.g., the discussion in §26.92 on Los Angeles superior court policy regarding trial continuances. Thus, the attorney should always contact the clerk of a particular court to determine current local practice if he or she has any doubt as to what is required.

II. INITIAL PAPERS FOR SETTING

A. At-Issue Memorandum

§26.8   1. Nature and Function

The at-issue memorandum is required in all California superior court cases, and is the first step in bringing a superior court case to trial. Cal Rules of Ct 206(a); see §26.9 on the effect of filing. Its primary purpose is to inform the court that all essential parties have been served or have appeared in the action, and that the case is at issue as to those parties. The memorandum also states whether the case is entitled to setting priority, whether a pretrial conference or a jury is demanded, and the estimated time for trial.

§26.9   2. Effect of Filing; Civil Active List

When an at-issue memorandum has been served and filed, the case is placed on the civil active list, which is a list of all cases in which an at-issue memorandum has been filed, but for which no trial date has been assigned. Cal Rules of Ct 206(a), 207(a). The court clerk prepares the list at least once a month (Rule 207(a)), based on the order in which the memoranda have been filed. Cal Rules of Ct 207(b). Subject to statutory priority and to the court's authority to shorten time, the civil active list determines the priority of cases for further calendaring proceedings. See Cal Rules of Ct 209(a)(ii), 220(a)(ii), 220.4. However, in counties that also require filing a certificate of readiness, that filing date may govern priority. Cal Rules of Ct 221(e)–(f). For discussion, see §26.19.

3. Procedures for Filing Party

§26.10   a. Severing Unanswered Cross-Complaint Before Filing

Occasionally, the party who desires to file an at-issue memorandum (usually plaintiff) finds that because a cross-complaint has been filed against a third party who has not yet filed an answer, the case is not at issue as to all essential parties as required by Cal Rules of Ct 206(a). If, in this situation, plaintiff's attorney is unable to resolve the matter informally (*e.g.*, by a telephone call to defense counsel and counsel for cross-complainant), he might consider filing a motion to sever the cross-complaint from the main action. See generally chap 27. However, the propriety of this procedure is in doubt, at least in a personal injury case when the cross-complaint seeks to join a third party for the purpose of comparing the third party's negligence to that of the other parties, thus avoiding piecemeal litigation. See *American Motorcycle Ass'n v Superior Court* (1977) 65 CA3d 694, 706, 135 CR 497, 504.

§26.11   b. Content of Memorandum

The at-issue memorandum must state (Cal Rules of Ct 206(a));

(1) The title, number, and nature of the case, and the names, addresses, and telephone numbers of the parties appearing personally or attorneys for the parties (some counties, *e.g.*, Los Angeles, also require attorneys' state bar numbers);

(2) That all essential parties have been served with process or have appeared, and that the case is at issue as to them;

(3) Whether the case is entitled to statutory preference and, if so, citation of the relevant code or statute;

(4) Whether a pretrial conference is requested;

(5) The estimated trial time (one day or less is classified as short cause) and;

(6) Whether a jury trial is demanded.

When a jury is a matter of right, the demand is made in the at-issue memorandum and no motion is required. On the effect of failure to so demand, see §26.12. When a jury trial is not a matter of right, the demanding party must, after the case is at issue and before or at the time of filing the at-issue memorandum, or within five days after service of the memorandum by any other party, file a notice of motion for jury trial. Cal Rules of Ct 231. See §26.29. For discussion of demanding and waiving a jury trial generally, see §§26.28–26.37.

§26.12   c. Effect of Failure To Demand Jury in At-Issue Memorandum

It has been said that a party's failure to demand a jury trial in its at-issue memorandum does not result in a waiver of the right to jury trial. See §26.31. However, in *March v Pettis* (1977) 66 CA3d 473, 136 CR 3, the court held that a party who has answered "No" in an at-issue memorandum in response to the question whether a jury is demanded has consented in writing to a waiver of the right to jury trial under CCP §631(2). See §§26.35–26.37 for discussion of waiver. In *March*, plaintiff initially stated in her at-issue memorandum that she did not demand a jury, and defendants filed a countermemorandum in which a jury was demanded. Later, when the case was assigned to a specific department for trial, defendants waived their right to jury, and plaintiff immediately demanded a jury and offered to tender jury fees. The court held that relief from a waiver by written consent under CCP §631(2) is not an absolute right, and that the trial court did not abuse its discretion by denying plaintiff a jury trial. See also *Taylor v Union Pac. R.R.* (1976) 16 C3d 893, 130 CR 23.

The holding in *March v Pettis, supra,* should end the practice by some plaintiffs' attorneys of failing to demand a jury in their at-issue memorandum, even though one is desired, on the assumption that (1) defendant will probably demand one (and therefore will be responsible for depositing jury fees), or (2) if defendant does not or if, as in *March,* defendant demands a jury but later waives, the court will always entertain plaintiff's demand for a jury at that time. In light of *March,* a party who wishes a jury trial is well advised to demand one in his at-issue memorandum.

§26.13   d. Form: At-Issue Memorandum

Copies: Original (filed with court clerk with proof of service); copies for service (one for each attorney of record and unrepresented party); office copies.

Caveat: Many counties have their own printed forms for at-issue memoranda, and the attorney should use those forms whenever possible. These counties frequently will not accept an at-issue memorandum for filing unless a court-approved form is used. See, *e.g.*, San Mateo Super Ct R IX. The following form may be used in counties that have no printed forms, or when those forms are unavailable, but should be modified to include any additional information (*e.g.*, attorneys' state bar numbers) required by that county.

§26.13 SETTING CASE FOR TRIAL 154

NAME, ADDRESS, AND TELEPHONE NUMBER
OF ATTORNEY(S)

ATTORNEY(S) FOR _____

SUPERIOR COURT OF CALIFORNIA, COUNTY OF ....

	CASE NUMBER
PLAINTIFF(S)	
vs	MEMORANDUM THAT CIVIL CASE IS AT ISSUE
	Rule 206 of California Rules of Court
DEFENDANT(S)	

Nature of case (state fully) ....

.... Do you request a pretrial conference? ....
(Yes or No)

Do you demand a jury? .... Time estimated for trial ....
(Yes or No)

Is this case entitled to legal preference in setting? ....

....
(If Yes, state reasons citing section of the code or statute granting such preference)

    I hereby represent to the court that all essential parties have been served with process or have appeared herein and that this case is at issue as to all such parties; that no amended or supplemental complaint or cross-complaint or other affirmative pleading remains unanswered; that to my knowledge no other parties will be served with a summons prior to the time of trial, and I know of no further pleading to be filed.

Dated ....
                                                                      Attorney(s) for ....

Any party not in agreement with the information or estimates given in an at-issue memorandum shall within ten days after service thereof serve and file a memorandum in his behalf.

Names, Address, and Telephone Numbers of all Attorneys in Action.
    (For Additional Attorneys Use Reverse Side)

.... Attorney for ....
(Address)
.... Tel. No. ....
.... Attorney for ....
(Address)
.... Tel. No. ....
.... Attorney for ....
(Address)
.... Tel. No. ....
.... Attorney for ....
(Address)
.... Tel. No. ....

Comment: On the content of the at-issue memorandum, see Cal Rules of Ct 206(a), discussed in §26.11. Many courts will not accept an at-issue memorandum that does not comply with the requirements of rule 206(a).

    The memorandum must be served on all parties before the case will be placed on the civil active list and set for pretrial conference, trial setting conference, or trial. Cal Rules of Ct 206(a). Service may be by mail under CCP §§1010–1020. For discussion, see 1 CALIFORNIA CIVIL PROCEDURE BEFORE TRIAL §§8.59–8.69 (Cal CEB 1977).

4. Responses of Nonfiling Party

§26.14   a. Countermemoranda; Motion To Strike

Counsel who has been served with an at-issue memorandum should immediately scrutinize it, and, if he disagrees with any part, must within ten days file and serve a countermemorandum. Cal Rules of Ct 206(b). A countermemorandum may be used, for example, to request a pretrial conference if opposing counsel has not done so, to demand a jury trial, or to correct an inaccurate estimate of trial time. The printed form used for the at-issue memorandum (see §26.13) may be used for a countermemorandum. Conflicts between the original memorandum and the countermemorandum are usually resolved by the court at the pretrial or trial setting conference. On procedures when the conflict involves the right to a jury trial, see §26.15.

When counsel disagrees with the statement in the at-issue memorandum that the case is at issue as to all essential parties or that the case is entitled to setting priority, he should consider filing, in addition to a countermemorandum, a motion to strike the at-issue memorandum. Although no statute or court rule authorizes such a motion, a court may entertain it in the exercise of its inherent power to control its proceedings. The motion, if granted, removes the case from the civil active list and has the effect of postponing the trial date. The party seeking to set the case for trial must then file and serve a new at-issue memorandum, and the case will, unless a motion to advance is granted, be placed at the bottom of the civil active list. See §26.9.

In Los Angeles, unless counsel stipulate to the contrary, the at-issue memorandum and certificate of readiness must be stricken whenever a party files an amended or new pleading (e.g., a cross-complaint) that requires a responsive pleading. LA & SF LAW & MOTION MANUALS §121.

§26.15   b. Opposing Jury Trial Request

Unless a jury trial is a matter of right (in which case the demand should be made in the at-issue memorandum; see §26.11),

Cal Rules of Ct 231 requires that a noticed motion for jury trial be filed and served. See §26.29 for discussion. Opposition to the motion can be asserted at the hearing on the motion; a countermemorandum need not be filed. A problem may arise when the at-issue memorandum demands a jury but no notice of motion under Rule 231 is filed and served, and counsel on whom the memorandum is served believes a jury is not a matter of right. If counsel objects to the case being set for jury trial, he should obtain a ruling on the point before the case is set for trial. Although the rules do not establish a procedure to accomplish this, it should be done by filing a countermemorandum (see §26.14), and by raising the issue at the pretrial or trial setting conference.

If objection is not made before pretrial or trial setting and the case is set for jury trial, a motion to vacate setting for jury trial may be filed no later than five days after receiving notice of setting from the clerk. Cal Rules of Ct 231. However, the motion is proper only if setting was made by the court "without opportunity for the party to oppose it." Rule 231. The "opportunity" referred to is not explained, but undoubtedly refers to opposition at the pretrial or trial-setting conference, or by noticed motion for jury trial. Because some smaller counties do not normally hold such conferences (see §26.3), the recommended practice in those counties is to proceed by noticed motion to vacate promptly after being notified that a jury trial is demanded.

B. Certificate of Readiness

§26.16   1. Nature and Purpose

A certificate of readiness is a paper that asks the court to set the case for pretrial conference, trial setting conference, or trial, and that advises the court of the filing party's readiness in terms of what discovery has been completed and what remains to be done. If a certificate is required by local rule, the certificate must be filed before a superior court case will be set for pretrial conference, trial setting conference, or trial. Cal Rules of Ct 221(a). See §26.17. No case on the civil active list, including a short cause, is exempt from this requirement. On procedures, see §§26.21–26.24. The filing of a certificate of readiness is designed to ensure that cases placed on the trial calendar will be ready for trial when called. The certificate accomplishes this by assuring the court that the party or parties signing the certificate are prepared to proceed. On whether all parties must sign the certificate, see §26.21.

§26.17 2. Counties in Which Certificate Required

The certificate-of-readiness procedure provided by Cal Rules of Ct 221 operates only in counties that, by local rule, require the filing of a certificate. Cal Rules of Ct 221(a). Although most counties do not have such a rule, some do, especially the larger counties (*e.g.*, Alameda, San Francisco, Los Angeles). The attorney should consult local rules to determine whether a certificate of readiness is required in the particular county where the cause of action is pending.

§26.18 3. Time for Filing

Counties Issuing Notice of Eligibility: In counties where, due to calendar congestion, the case cannot be brought to trial within six months after a certificate of readiness is filed (*e.g.*, Los Angeles, San Francisco, Alameda), the certificate may be filed only after the parties receive a notice of eligibility from the court. Cal Rules of Ct 221(e). This notification procedure enables the court to keep the backlog of cases on the trial ready list (see §26.19) within manageable proportions.

Counties Not Issuing Notice of Eligibility: In most counties a certificate of readiness may be filed with or after the filing of the at-issue memorandum. Cal Rules of Ct 221(d). Many counties (*e.g.*, Santa Clara, San Mateo) that require a certificate of readiness, but do not serve a notice of eligibility to file, have adopted a combined at-issue memorandum and certificate of readiness, which simplifies filing.

In such counties, at least once a month the court (or clerk, under judicial supervision) selects cases on the civil active list (*i.e.*, those in which an at-issue memorandum has been served and filed) for notification of eligibility to file a certificate of readiness. Cal Rules of Ct 221(e). The cases are selected in their order of placement on the civil active list, subject to statutory priority. As many cases as can be brought to trial during the next six months are chosen. The clerk notifies the parties by mail that

§26.19   SETTING CASE FOR TRIAL

they may file a certificate of readiness if they are prepared to proceed to trial. Within 20 days from mailing of the clerk's notice, any party may file a certificate. Rule 221(e). On the effect of failure to file, see §26.20.

§26.19   4. Effect of Filing

Filing a certificate of readiness in counties where the court does not issue a notice of eligibility (see §26.18) ensures that the case will be set for pretrial conference (if required), trial setting conference, or trial. It does not ensure priority over cases in which a certificate has not been filed, because priority is based on the order of cases on the civil active list, which in turn is based on the order of filing the at-issue memorandum. For discussion, see §26.9. However, in setting cases on the civil active list for trial setting or pretrial conference, the court will not select a case in which no certificate of readiness has been filed.

The priority is different in counties that issue a notice of eligibility to file a certificate of readiness. The clerk, after the certificate is filed, places the case on a trial-ready list in the order of filing. The trial-ready list supersedes the civil active list in establishing priority (subject to statutory priority) for setting for pretrial conference, trial setting conference, or trial. Cal Rules of Ct 221(f).

In Los Angeles, after the time provided by Cal Rules of Ct 221(c) to object to the certificate of readiness has expired, filing the certificate has the additional effect of cutting off the time to file a cross-complaint or other pleading. The court will deny a request to file a late pleading unless the requesting party would be precluded by the doctrine of res judicata from bringing a new action, in which event the court in ruling on the request will apply the rules set out in CCP §473 for relief from default (see §§30.56–30.61). LA CT LAW & MOTION MANUALS §122.

§26.20   5. Effect of Failure To File

In counties that do not issue a notice of eligibility (see §26.18), failure to file a certificate of readiness temporarily precludes a case from being set for pretrial conference, trial setting conference, or trial. Cal Rules of Ct 221(a). Although the case retains its priority on the civil active list, the court will not select it for setting until a certificate has been filed.

In counties that issue a notice of eligibility before permitting a party to file a certificate of readiness, the effect of failure to file a certificate is different. Failure to respond to the first notification of eligibility does not alter the position of a case on the civil active list; the case usually is selected in the next monthly listing of eligible cases and a second (or final) notification is sent. Any party may file a certificate within 20 days from the date this second notice is mailed. However, when notice is given in each of two months and no certificate is filed within 20 days, the case is removed from the civil active list and may be restored, at the bottom of the list, only if counsel files and serves a new at-issue memorandum. Cal Rules of Ct 221(e).

Failure timely to respond to a second notice of eligibility may result not only in protracted delay in bringing the case to trial, but also in dismissal. In some counties (*e.g.*, Los Angeles, San Francisco), if plaintiff does not file a certificate of readiness within 20 days after the second notice of eligibility is mailed, the court will automatically set a hearing on an order to show cause at which plaintiff must show cause why the court should not enter its order dismissing the case.

6. Procedures

§26.21   a. Who May Prepare

A certificate of readiness may be prepared and filed by any party, and may be joined in by any other party to the action. Cal Rules of Ct 221(b). It is not necessary for each party to sign the certificate before filing, although it may be appropriate to do so in a particular (*e.g.*, a complex) case. Moreover, some counties (*e.g.*, Los Angeles) encourage all parties to sign by providing that a special declaration be completed when all parties have not signed (see form in §26.23). For further discussion, see §26.24.

§26.22   b. Content of Certificate

The certificate of readiness must state (Cal Rules of Ct 221(b)):
(1) That the party or parties signing the certificate are prepared

§26.23   SETTING CASE FOR TRIAL

to have the case set for pretrial conference or trial setting conference (if required), or for trial (if a pretrial conference is desired, and no previous request has been filed, the request may be made in the certificate);

(2) What discovery has been commenced or completed at the time of signing the certificate, and, to the extent known, what discovery remains to be done; and

(3) That all discovery will be completed at least 30 days before trial except as may be allowed by court order for good cause or as may be had by stipulation, or through voluntary exchanges of information in preparation for trial.

Compliance with requirements (2) and (3) is achieved if a party generally describes the number and kinds of discovery initiated, completed, or remaining to be done, without identifying names of persons or other details of such discovery. Cal Rules of Ct 221(b).

Because minor variations in the content of the certificate are permissible (Cal Rules of Ct 221(a) requires only substantial compliance with Rule 221), the attorney should consult local rules and forms to determine the content required in a particular county.

§26.23   c. Form: Certificate of Readiness

Copies: Original (filed with court clerk with proof of service); copies for service (one for each attorney of record and unrepresented party); office copies.

Caveat: Many counties have their own printed forms for certificates of readiness, and the attorney should use those forms whenever possible. These counties frequently will not accept a certificate of readiness for filing unless a court-approved form is used. See, *e.g.,* San Mateo Super Ct R IX. Other counties (*e.g.,* Santa Clara) have forms that combine the certificate of readiness and at-issue memorandum in a single document. The following form may be used in counties that have no preprinted forms, or when those forms are unavailable, but should be modified to include any additional information required by that county (*e.g.,* attorneys' state bar numbers), and to delete information that may not be required (*e.g.,* the declaration re service at the conclusion of the form).

161 SETTING CASE FOR TRIAL §26.23

Name, Address and Telephone Number of Attorney(s)

ATTORNEY(S) FOR

SUPERIOR COURT OF CALIFORNIA, COUNTY OF

	CASE NUMBER
PLAINTIFF(S)	
VS	
DEFENDANT(S)	CERTIFICATE OF READINESS

We certify that the following information is true and that this case is ready to be set for trial setting conference, pretrial conference or for trial as indicated hereon.

1. Specify one of the following: ☐ Pretrial requested (Rule 208)
   ☐ Case Exempt, as Short Cause Matter (Rule 207.1)
   ☐ Trial Setting Conference Required (Rule 220 (A)

2. ....
   (Nature of case. State fully)

3. Time estimated for trial: .... hrs. .... days

4. Case entitled to preference: Yes ☐ No ☐ Code Section ....

5. All attorneys of record or parties appearing in person are listed below:
   (Indicate whether attorney for plaintiff or defendant)

                                                                Request Jury

Plaintiff
   Trial Attorney
   Name of Firm   Telephone   ☐
   Address

Defendant
   Trial Attorney
   Name of Firm   Telephone   ☐
   Address

Attorney For:
   Trial Attorney
   Name of Firm   Telephone   ☐
   Address

Attorney For:
   Trial Attorney
   Name of Firm   Telephone   ☐
   Address

Attorney For:
   Trial Attorney
   Name of Firm   Telephone   ☐
   Address

CERTIFICATE OF READINESS

FOR USE OF COURT ONLY
Preference claim verified
By .... Date: ....

§26.24   SETTING CASE FOR TRIAL

6. The case is at issue and no further pleadings will be filed and no additional parties will be served:
   All law and discovery matters are now completed and no further pleadings will be filed;
   That the default has been entered as to any remaining party served with process who has not answered;
   That unless good cause be shown, each unserved party may be dismissed at the pretrial or trial setting conference.

7. Substantially all discovery proceedings have now been completed, to wit:
   Party   Kind of Discovery

8. The following discovery remains to be done: (If none, state none)
   Party   Kind of Discovery

9. All discovery can be and will be completed at least 30 days prior to trial date.
   Exceptions: (Rule 222) (List exceptions and reasons therefor. If none, state none)
   Party   Exception   Reason

10. Each of the undersigned certifies that the foregoing is true and correct:

    Executed by .... on .... at ....
                  Signature of Declarant   *Date*   *Place*

    Executed by .... on .... at ....
                  Signature of Declarant   *Date*   *Place*

    Executed by .... on .... at ....
                  Signature of Declarant   *Date*   *Place*

    Executed by .... on .... at ....
                  Signature of Declarant   *Date*   *Place*

    Executed by .... on .... at ....
                  Signature of Declarant   *Date*   *Place*

NOTE: THE FOLLOWING TO BE COMPLETED UPON FAILURE OR REFUSAL OF ALL PARTIES TO SIGN CERTIFICATE OF READINESS. [Rule 221 (c)]

DECLARATION

11. The undersigned declares and certifies that the parties listed in 5 above have been mailed or served with a copy of the Certificate of Readiness on _____ at the address shown and that their signed Certificate is attached or that more than 10 days has elapsed from such service or mailing and that they have failed or refused to sign same and that a copy of this certificate and declaration is concurrently being mailed said parties.

    Executed by_____ on_____ at _____
                Signature of Declarant   *Date*   *Place*

                    Attorney for_____

Comment: On who may prepare a certificate of readiness, see §26.21. For discussion of content, see §26.22.

§26.24   d. Filing and Service

The certificate of readiness is filed with the court clerk in the usual manner, *i.e.*, by mail or in person by using attorney's messenger service. See §26.18 on the time for filing. A copy of the certificate must be served on all parties who have not signed the certificate. (Cal Rules of Ct 221(c).

Some counties (*e.g.*, Los Angeles) require that the party who prepares the certificate must, before filing, mail a copy to all other parties for their signature. If, after ten days, all parties have not signed, the party filing the certificate must complete a special declaration (see form in §26.23) and serve it on the parties with the certificate.

7. Changing Setting or Vacating Certificate

§26.25   a. Authority; Grounds

After the certificate of readiness is filed, the case is assigned a time and place for pretrial conference, trial setting conference, or trial, "in regular order" (Cal Rules of Ct 221(c)), *i.e.*, in the order of priority on the civil active list, or, in counties issuing a notice of eligibility, on the trial-ready list, subject to cases having statutory priority. Cal Rules of Ct 221 (f). The court however may change the setting on noticed motion (*e.g.*, to advance a setting or to vacate a certificate) and a showing of good cause. Cal Rules of Ct 221 (c). Although Rule 221(c) does not directly state the grounds for the motion, it appears that proper grounds would be, (*e.g.*, a cross-complaint) that requires a responsive pleading. LA LAW & MOTION MANUALS §121.
case is entitled to statutory priority, despite a contrary statement in the at-issue memorandum.

In Los Angeles, unless counsel stipulate to the contrary, the at-issue memorandum and certificate of readiness must be stricken whenever a party files an amended or new pleading (*e.g.*, a cross-complaint) that requires a responsive pleading. LA LAW & MOTION MANUALS §121.

§26.26   b. Court's Discretion

The court's authority to act on a motion to change a setting or to vacate a certificate of readiness under Cal Rules of Ct 221(c) appears to be discretionary. If the deficiencies of an allegedly prematurely filed certificate can be cured with only a slight delay, the court may continue the hearing on the motion; but a showing that the case will not be ready for setting in the foreseeable future may justify an order vacating the certificate. In some cases the court may vacate the certificate on its own motion, *e.g.*, when the parties represent that all discovery will be concluded 30 days before trial, but appear to be on the threshold of extensive discovery proceedings; in this situation, the court might decline to set the case until a more realistic certificate is filed.

§26.27 c. Procedure

A notice of motion to change a setting or to vacate certificate must be served and filed within ten days after service of the certificate of readiness. The motion must be supported by affidavits or declarations showing good cause, and must be noticed for hearing within ten days after service of the notice of motion on opposing counsel. Cal Rules of Ct 221(c).

III. DEMAND FOR JURY TRIAL
§26.28 A. Right to Jury

The right to a jury trial in California civil actions is set forth in Cal Const art I, §16 and CCP §592, which in effect provide that in certain classes of cases a jury trial on factual issues is a matter of right unless waived. See §§26.35–26.37 for discussion of waiver. Actions in which a jury trial is a matter of right under the constitution are those that were triable by jury at common law, *i.e.*, legal as distinguished from equitable actions. *People v One 1941 Chevrolet Coupe* (1951) 37 C2d 283, 231 P2d 832. It has been said that whether an action is legal or equitable depends on the "gist of the action" as framed by the pleadings and facts and on the type of relief sought (*Paularena v Superior Court* (1965) 231 CA2d 906, 911, 42 CR 366, 369, cited with approval in *Southern Pac. Transp. Co. v Superior Court* (1976) 58 CA3d 433, 129 CR 912); that determination is not always simple, as the following categories show:

Legal Actions. Under CCP §592, legal actions include actions for:

(1) Recovery of real or personal property, with or without damages;

(2) Money due under contract or as damages for breach of contract;

(3) Damages for injuries to person or property.

Legal actions also include cases that appear superficially to be equitable but are more similar to common law actions, *e.g.*, an action to compel a fiduciary to account for money owed (*Ripling v Superior Court* (1952) 112 CA2d 399, 247 P2d 117).

For further discussion, see 4 Witkin, CALIFORNIA PROCEDURE, Trial §§75–76 (2d ed 1971).

Equitable Actions. These include:

(1) Actions for specific performance (*Connell v Bowes* (1942) 19 C2d 870, 123 P2d 456);

(2) Actions for rescission (*Bank of America v Greenbach* (1950) 98 CA2d 220, 219 P2d 814);

(3) Quiet title actions (*Peterson v Peterson* (1946) 74 CA2d 312, 168 P2d 474);

(4) Actions for cancellation (*Clyne v Brock* (1947) 82 CA2d 958, 188 P2d 263);

(5) Actions to declare a constructive trust (*Bodley v Ferguson* (1866) 30 C 511); and

(6) Shareholders' derivative actions (*Rankin v Frebank Co.* (1975) 47 CA3d 75, 121 CR 348).

Equitable actions also include those in which monetary recovery is sought on a right cognizable only in equity, *e.g.*, an action for a commission based on an estoppel theory (*Ford v Palisades Corp.* (1950) 101 Ca2d 491, 225 P2d 545).

Hybrid Actions. In hybrid actions, *i.e.*, those raising both legal and equitable issues, jury trial is a right only on the severable legal issues. *Robinson v Puls* (1946) 28 C2d 664, 171 P2d 430. For example, the equitable issue of estoppel to raise a statute of limitations defense is triable by the court. *Moss v Bluemm* (1964) 229 CA2d 70, 40 CR 50. When an action seeks equitable relief to protect a common law right (*e.g.*, an injunction against injury to land) and there is an issue as to the existence or violation of the common law right, that issue must first be litigated (before a jury, if demanded) before the court determines whether to grant the equitable relief. *Pacific W. Oil Co. v Bern Oil Co.* (1939) 13 C2d 60, 87 P2d 1045. However, a party may ensure a full jury trial by dropping the claim for equitable relief and seeking only damages. *Raedeke v Gibraltar Sav. & Loan Ass'n* (1974) 10 C3d 665, 111 CR 693.

For further discussion, see 4 Witkin, CALIFORNIA PROCEDURE, Trial §§73–79 (2d ed 1971).

§26.29   B. Court's Discretion When No Right to Jury Exists; Procedures

In actions in which a jury trial is not a matter of right, the factual issues must be tried before the court "subject to its power to order any such issue tried by a jury." CCP §592. See also CCP

§1090 (court may order jury trial in mandamus or prohibition proceeding). However, the jury's verdict is advisory only, and does not bind the court. *Cutter Labs. v R. W. Ogle & Co.* (1957) 151 CA2d 410, 311 P2d 627. Because the verdict is simply advisory, there are no grounds for appeal if the jury is instructed erroneously (*Richardson v Eureka* (1895) 110 C 441, 42 P 965), or if counsel's misconduct prejudically affects the jury (*Cutter Labs. v R. W. Ogle & Co., supra*). The court may dismiss the jury at any time. See *Constantine v Sunnyvale* (1949) 91 CA2d 278, 204 P2d 922.

Procedures to obtain a jury trial when it is not a matter of right are governed by Cal Rules of Ct 231, which provides that the party desiring a jury trial must, after the issue is joined and before or at the time of filing the at-issue memorandum, or within five days of being served with the memorandum by any other party, give notice of motion that the entire issue, or any specific issues of fact, be tried by jury. A copy of the issues proposed to be tried by jury must be served with the motion. The motion must be noticed for hearing on the eighth court day after giving notice, but if the law and motion calendar is not regularly heard on that day, then on the next calendar day. The court may, for good cause shown, order the hearing on an earlier or later date. Cal Rules of Ct 231.

§26.30 C. Deciding Whether To Demand or Retain Jury; Factors

Whether to demand a jury in a particular case, or to retain a jury already demanded, can have important consequences on the outcome of the litigation. Although many attorneys routinely demand a jury early in all cases (*e.g.*, in the at-issue memorandum), a decision must be made later (*e.g.*, at the trial setting conference) whether a jury is really desired.

In deciding whether to demand or retain a jury, the attorney should consider whether:

(1) The judge assigned to the case has shown fairness in past similar cases or has tended to be "proplaintiff" or "prodefendant," and the extent of his judicial competence and temperament;

(2) The case, as a whole, has "jury appeal," *i.e.*, whether the strength of the case on the law and facts, the credibility of parties and witnesses, the relative impressions the parties will make,

and the nature and extent of damages or injuries make a jury desirable;

(3) The size of the probable recovery warrants a jury trial. Many lawyers prefer juries in cases in which the probable recovery is substantial, so that the decision will not reflect the judgment of one person (who, even though a capable judge, may occasionally err) but the collective judgment of twelve or fewer jurors (CCP §194). The judge, as the "thirteenth juror," provides some insurance to correct jury errors by his authority to set aside a grossly erroneous or excessive verdict on a motion for new trial (CCP §§655–663.2);

(4) The case is weak on the law. Many attorneys prefer to submit a weak case (or defense) to a jury on the assumption that the weakness will not be as readily detected by them. The hazard in this reasoning is that juries frequently demonstrate remarkable insight and ability to detect weaknesses, distortions, and exaggerations, which can affect their verdict;

(5) The primary defense is technical, *e.g.*, a statute of limitations defense. Many defense lawyers prefer a court trial in this situation, on the assumption that jurors are less likely than judges to respond to this type of defense, even if clearly presented;

(6) The case is unusually complex or involves primarily issues of law, in which case a court trial may be indicated. Cases involving many technical details (*e.g.*, antitrust litigation or a suit on a construction contract) frequently are considered not well suited for jury evaluation; and

(7) The nature of the jury panel and of the economic and sociological region from which the panel was drawn would make it favorable, *i.e.*, whether the panel is composed mostly of blue collar workers (often preferred by plaintiffs' attorneys) or of elderly or retired professional persons (often preferred by defense counsel).

D. Procedures

§26.31   1. Necessity and Time for Demand; Effect

A jury trial is obtained by making a demand for it; failure to make a timely demand for a jury results in a waiver. CCP §631(4); *Glogau v Hagan* (1951) 107 CA2d 313, 237 P2d 329. A jury trial in superior and municipal courts must be demanded

§26.32   SETTING CASE FOR TRIAL

when the case is first set for trial (if set on notice or stipulation), or within five days after notice of setting (if, as is usually the case, the matter is set without notice or stipulation). CCP §631(4); *Mutual Bldg. & Loan Ass'n v Corum* (1934) 220 C 282, 30 P2d 509. In justice courts a demand must be made within two days after service of the notice of trial date provided for in CCP §594. CCP §631(4). Failure to make a timely demand results in a waiver of the right to jury trial. See §§26.35–26.37 for further discussion.

The California Rules of Court 206(a) requires that parties indicate in the at-issue memorandum whether a jury is demanded or not. See §26.11. A party who disputes the demanding party's right to a jury trial or who himself wishes to demand a jury after being served with an at-issue memorandum stating that a jury is not demanded, normally serves and files a countermemorandum. See §26.14–26.15. It has been said that a party's failure to demand a jury in the at-issue memorandum is not a waiver because a waiver is governed by the provisions of CCP §631. *Mutual Bldg. & Loan Ass'n v Corum, supra.* But see *March v Pettis* (1977) 66 CA3d 473, 136 CR 3, discussed in §26.12.

The effect of a demand for jury trial made under CCP §631(4) is continuing, and it is not necessary to repeat it in subsequent proceedings, *e.g,* when the case is set for a second trial after reversal and granting a new trial on appeal. *Hoffman v Southern Pac. Co.* (1929) 101 CA 218, 281 P 681.

§26.32   2. Form of Jury Demand

No particular form for a demand for jury trial is prescribed by statute or court rule; an oral demand on the record when the case is first set for trial (*e.g.*, at the trial setting conference) is sufficient. *Union Oil Co. v Hane* (1938) 27 CA2d 106, 80 P2d 516. A written demand is also acceptable, for example:

[Caption. See §§23.18–23.19]

JURY DEMAND

____[Plaintiff / Defendant]____ ____[name]____ **demands a jury trial.**

[Signature of attorney

[Typed name]

Attorney for ____

If the case has inadvertently been placed on the nonjury calendar, or if a party wishes to demand a jury after having previously waived it, the party should file a noticed motion for jury trial. On the court's discretion and procedures to excuse a waiver under CCP §631, see §§26.36–26.37.

§26.33 3. Deposit of Fees and Expenses; Refunds

In addition to a demand, a party who desires a jury trial must deposit with the clerk or judge one day's jury fees at least 14 days before the trial date in superior and municipal court or two days before the trial date in justice court. CCP §631(5). Parties suing in forma pauperis are excused from payment. See 1 CALIFORNIA CIVIL PROCEDURE BEFORE TRIAL §6.8 (Cal CEB 1977). The amount of jury fees is set at $5 per day per juror, unless a higher fee is provided for by law. CCP §§196, 233; Govt C §§76000–76058. Failure to make the required deposit is a waiver of the party's right to jury trial. CCP §631(5). See §§26.35–26.37 on waiver. However, the county in which the action is pending may pay the jury fees out of the general fund and recover them from the responsible party. CCP §631.1.

Promptly after the jury has been impaneled, the demanding party also must deposit the accrued mileage or transportation charges ($0.15 per mile, one way, unless a higher rate is provided by law (CCP §§196, 233)). At the beginning of the second and each succeeding day's session, the demanding party must deposit the jury fees and mileage or transportation charges for that day. Failure to make any of these deposits also results in a waiver of the party's right to jury trial. CCP §631(6)–(7). On the deposit of jury fees and mileage in eminent domain cases, see CCP §631.5.

When a party demands a jury and then waives it during trial after having deposited fees, the adverse party may "pick up" the jury and continue to pay fees. If, however, the adverse party also waives a jury later in the trial, the first party cannot withdraw his waiver as a matter of right, but must make a motion to seek relief from it. See *Taylor v Union Pac. R. R.* (1976) 16 C3d 893, 130 CR 23. On the court's discretion to relieve a waiver, see §26.36.

When jury fees have been deposited, but the case is settled or a continuance is granted on motion of depositing party, none of the deposit will be refunded if the court finds there has been insufficient time to notify the jurors that the trial will not proceed. CCP §631.3. In addition, local rules frequently prescribe the time and manner in which the clerk must be given notice to avoid a forfeiture of fees. See, *e.g.*, San Mateo Super Ct R XIX (written notice at least two court days before trial).

For further discussion, see 4 Witkin, CALIFORNIA PROCEDURE, Trial §§81–83 (2d ed 1971).

§26.34   E. Reliance on Other Party's Demand

In superior court, when a party demands a jury in his at-issue memorandum, other parties are entitled to rely on that demand and need not make another demand unless a waiver occurs. See §§26.35–26.37 for discussion of waiver. If the demanding party later waives a jury trial, either by announcement or by operation of law, the court clerk must give all adverse parties ten days' written notice of the waiver. If, by reason of the trial date, the clerk cannot give ten days' notice, or if in any case notice is not given, the trial must be continued for a sufficient time to enable the clerk to give proper notice. CCP §631(4). See also *Leslie v Roe* (1975) 52 CA3d 686, 125 CR 157. The adverse parties then have not more than five days following receipt of the clerk's notice of waiver within which to file and serve a demand for jury trial and, when required by court rule, to deposit advance jury fees. CCP §631(4).

The purpose of the above provisions of CCP §631(4) is to protect a party who, in reliance on another party's jury demand, fails to demand a jury, and not a party who expressly waives a jury and who later changes his mind. *March v Pettis* (1977) 66 CA3d 473, 136 CR 3 (see discussion in §26.12). In *March*, the court appeared impressed by the fact that plaintiff's only reason for the later demand was a change of mind based on trial tactics, and that three other parties, who neither desired nor requested a jury, would have been at a disadvantage if the trial court had granted relief from the waiver. 66 CA3d at 480, 136 CR at 7.

The provisions in CCP §631(4) that entitle a party to rely on another party's jury demand apply only to superior court actions. In municipal and justice court actions, a party who wishes a jury trial should file a memorandum to set the case for trial (see §26.5) and in it make a jury demand regardless of whether other parties also have demanded a jury.

For discussion of waiver of jury trial (a) on or after assignment for trial to a specific court department, (b) on or after commencement of trial, or (c) by failure to deposit jury fees or mileage and transportation charges, see CCP §631(8), cited in §26.35.

F. Waiver of Jury Trial

§26.35   1. Acts Resulting in Waiver

Under CCP §631 a party waives a jury trial by:
(a) Failing to appear at trial (CCP §631(1));
(b) Written consent filed with the clerk or judge (CCP §631(2); see also *March v Pettis* (1977) 66 CA3d 473, 136 CR 3, discussed in §26.12, on a party's failure to demand a jury in the at-issue memorandum as waiver by written consent);
(c) Oral consent, in open court, entered in the minutes or docket (CCP §631(3));
(d) Failing to make a timely demand for a jury (CCP §631(4); see discussion in §26.31);
(e) Failing to deposit with the clerk or judge the jury fees or mileage charges (CCP §631(5)–(7); see §26.33); and
(f) Failing, when a nondemanding party, promptly to demand a jury trial before the judge in whose department a waiver was made, or promptly to deposit the required fees when the demanding party either waives a jury trial on or after assignment to a specific trial department or on or after commencement of trial, or fails to deposit jury fees as required by CCP §631(6)–(7) (CCP §631(8)).

A party may also waive a jury trial by entering into an agreement that provides that any dispute will be resolved by arbitration, even though the arbitration provision does not expressly waive the right to jury trial. *Madden v Kaiser Foundation Hosp.* (1976) 17 C3d 699, 131 CR 882.

For further discussion, see 4 Witkin, CALIFORNIA PROCEDURE, Trial §§85–88 (2d ed 1971).

2. Relief From Waiver

§26.36   a. Authority

The trial court has discretion to allow a jury trial, on such terms as may be just, even though a party previously has waived a jury trial. CCP §631(4), (8). Because of the constitutional guarantee of a jury, doubt about whether to relieve a jury trial waiver should be resolved in favor of granting a jury trial. *Cowlin v Pringle* (1941) 46 CA2d 472, 116 P2d 109. However, relief will usually be denied when there is no sufficient basis for the exercise of the court's discretionary power, *e.g.*, when the only reason for seeking relief from a waiver appears to be a party's change of mind (*Cloud v Market St. Ry.* (1946) 74 CA2d 92, 168 P2d 191), or when granting the motion will prejudice other parties (see *March v Pettis* (1977) 66 CA3d 473, 136 CR 3, discussed in §26.12). On procedures, see §26.37.

§26.37   b. Procedures

A party who wishes to be relieved of a jury waiver must do so by motion. CCP §631. See also *Taylor v Union Pac. R.R.* (1976) 16 C3d 893, 130 CR 23 (waiver cannot be withdrawn as matter of right, and counsel objecting to denial of jury trial after waiver must seek relief from it). Although no statute or rule requires that the motion be noticed, the motion should be written and noticed if time permits. The motion should state why a jury trial was initially waived (*e.g.*, through mistake, inadvertence, or excusable neglect), and why the interests of justice would be served by a jury trial. See CCP §631. Counsel should remember that the court ordinarily will not grant the motion simply because a party has changed his mind or if granting the motion will prejudice other parties to the litigation. See §26.36.

IV. CONFERENCES PREREQUISITE TO TRIAL

A. Trial Setting Conference
§26.38   1. Nature and Purpose; When Required

A trial setting conference is essentially a calendar-control device that determines when the case will be ready for trial, and, based on that determination, sets a time and place for trial. Cal Rules of Ct 220.3. The court's function at the conference is to screen cases either by setting a firm trial date for each ready case or by dropping the case from the civil active list. Cal Rules of Ct Appendix, Div I §9(a).

A trial setting conference is mandatory in all cases in which a pretrial conference is not required, except in courts with ten or fewer judges, when it may be dispensed with by local rule (Cal Rules of Ct 220(a), 220.4), and in short causes, which are always exempt from trial setting conferences, regardless of where they are pending. See §§26.2–26.3.

§26.39 2. Relationship to Pretrial Conference

Although the function of pretrial and trial setting conferences overlap (both are calendar-control devices and both set a time and place for trial), the trial setting conference is not a substitute for the pretrial conference, and specific limitations have been imposed by the California Judicial Council in order to foreclose that possibility. See §26.44. Trial setting conferences are held to determine when a case will be ready for trial, and either to set an appropriate date for trial (Cal Rules of Ct 220.3), or to drop the case from the civil active list (Cal Rules of Ct Appendix, Div I, §9(a)). At the pretrial conference, on the other hand, issues to be resolved are defined and parties' agreements and stipulations recorded. The results are set out in a pretrial order, which becomes part of the court record, and controls, unless modified by court order, subsequent inconsistencies in the pleadings. See §26.73.

Either at or before the trial setting conference the court may order a pretrial conference, and such an order is within the court's discretion. See §26.59.

§26.40 3. Attendance by Counsel; Knowledge of Case

Under Cal Rules of Ct 220.2, each party appearing in a case must, unless excused by local rule, attend the trial setting conference either in person or by counsel. In practice, the conference is routinely attended by the attorney, unless he determines (in a county where attendance is not required) that attendance is not necessary. See §26.42 on deciding whether to attend. The attorney must be sufficiently familiar with the case to state whether it is ready for setting, and to furnish information to enable the court to make a decision on setting. Cal Rules of Ct 220.2(a). Counsel must also be prepared to tell the court what discovery has been completed, what further discovery may be required, and when it can be completed. Cal Rules of Ct 220.2(b). See §26.45–26.46 for discussion of sanctions.

The California Judicial Council Standards of Judicial Administration go further, and recommend that each superior court require attorneys to attend the trial setting conference with full

§26.41   SETTING CASE FOR TRIAL

authority to act in all matters pertaining to the case. Cal Rules of Ct Appendix, Div I, §9(c). Failure to attend, unless excused under local rule, or fully to participate is grounds for removal of the case from the civil active list when the failure is the plaintiff's; and when it is the defendant's, for setting an early trial date. Cal Rules of Ct Appendix, Div I, §9(c). On matters discussed at the trial setting conference, see §26.43.

§26.41   a. Local Variations; Los Angeles Policy

The requirement of personal appearance at the trial setting conference discussed in §26.40 may be changed by local rule or policy. Cal Rules of Ct 220.2 and Cal Rules of Ct Appendix, Div I, §9(c). Los Angeles County, for example, has adopted a policy that an attorney of record may, instead of appearing personally, file with the clerk of the appropriate department, at least 48 hours before the trial setting conference date, a document entitled "Stipulation/Declaration in Lieu of Personal Appearance at Trial Setting Conference," which is available from the county clerk. The stipulation (or declaration) may be used only when each attorney signing it is prepared to try the case within 90 days of the conference date, *i.e.*, that his client and all essential witnesses will be available at that time. Otherwise, counsel must personally appear at the conference, so that the court may determine whether the testimony of the client or witness is necessary or may be presented by deposition. See LA SUPER CT CIV TRIALS MAN §§5–6. On the factors in determining whether to attend a trial setting conference, see §26.42.

§26.42   b. Deciding Whether To Attend

In practice, whether to attend a trial setting conference in counties where attendance is not required is a matter of balancing the cost and time required for attendance and preparation against the value of attending. Many attorneys feel that in the ordinary case attendance is a waste of time. Others feel that it is important to attend, if only to signal to the opposition that the attorney considers the case sufficiently important to warrant attendance. There is always the possibility of also conducting informal but fruitful settlement negotiations when all sides are present. Whenever the proximity of the trial date is important, *e.g.*, when it is vital for plaintiff to obtain an early date, attendance by plaintiff's attorney is crucial. Finally, many attorneys prefer to attend the conference whenever further discovery is contemplated to ensure that an order for further discovery is included in the trial setting order. See §26.43 on matters considered at the conference.

§26.43   4. Matters Considered at Conference

In determining whether the case is ready for trial, and either setting a trial date for those that are ready, or dropping from the civil active list those that are not, the court at the trial setting conference considers, as far as practicable (Cal Rules of Ct Appendix Div I, §9(c)):

(1) The number of sides and peremptory challenges allocated to each side if a jury is demanded;
(2) Whether the case is at issue and whether all parties necessary to its disposition have been served or have appeared;
(3) The fictitiously named defendants to be dismissed or severed;
(4) The name of the attorney or attorneys who actually will try the case;
(5) Whether a pretrial conference or bifurcated trial should be held;
(6) Whether a settlement conference is ordered; and
(7) A firm trial date and estimated time for trial.

In some counties the court considers additional matters, *e.g*, jurisdictional objections, amendments to pleadings, and scheduling further discovery. Such deliberations are limited, however, by the restriction against considering at trial setting matters normally considered at a pretrial conference. See §26.44.

When a settlement conference is ordered at the trial setting conference, the court should set the settlement conference about 20 days before the trial date. Cal Rules of Ct Appendix, Div I, §9(a). Many counties follow this practice (see, *e.g.*, LA SUPER CT CIV TRIALS MAN §4, which provides for a mandatory settlement conference in each case about 15 court days before trial). For further discussion of mandatory settlement conferences, see §26.75.

§26.44   5. Matters Precluded From Consideration

Under Cal Rules of Ct 220.3, the court at a trial setting conference may not (a) require any written preconference statement; (b) redetermine or restate issues made by the pleadings; (c) dismiss fictitious defendants or condition the setting of a trial date on dismissal of such defendants without the consent of all parties; or (d) require the parties to disclose evidence or exhibits.

6. Sanctions

§26.45   a. Power of Court To Impose; Types

Judicial authority to impose sanctions for disregard of its rules, including trial setting conference procedures and requirements, is both explicit (see Cal Rules of Ct 217) and inherent (see CCP §128(3); *Santandrea v Siltec Corp.* (1976) 56 CA3d 525, 128 CR 629; *Cantillon v Superior Court* (1957) 150 CA2d 184, 309 P2d 890). Under Rule 217, the failure of any person to appear at, prepare reasonably for, or participate in good faith in a trial setting conference, as required by the California Rules of Court, local rule, or court order, unless good cause is shown, is an unlawful interference with court proceedings, for which the court may order the person at fault to pay the opposing party's reasonable expenses and attorney's fees. The court also may order a change in calendar status by, *e.g.*, dropping the case from the civil active list when such failure is the plaintiff's and setting the case for an early trial when it is the defendant's. Cal Rules of Ct Appendix, Div I, §9(c). If the court orders the case dropped from the civil active list, it usually requires counsel to file a new at-issue memorandum (in effect beginning the setting process anew) or orders the memorandum reinstated as of a date after it was filed. Either procedure results in substantial delay in obtaining a trial date.

§26.46   b. Local Variations; Los Angeles Policy

Notwithstanding the recommendations of the California Judicial Council Standards of Judicial Administration discussed in §26.45, local courts may enforce trial setting conference procedures and requirements in their own way. In Los Angeles, for example, when plaintiff fails to appear at the trial setting conference and has not filed a Stipulation/Declaration in Lieu of Personal Appearance (see §26.41), the court may issue a show cause order re dismissal, or may order the case off calendar and the at-issue memorandum reinstated as of a later date. At the hearing on the show cause order the court may, in lieu of dismissal, impose conditions for proceeding, *e.g.*, payment of costs. Trial Setting Conferences §2, Policy of Los Angeles Super Ct.

§26.47   7. Procedures

The trial setting conference procedures discussed in §§26.48–26.56 are governed primarily by Cal Rules of Ct 220.1–220.3, and by Cal Rules of Ct Appendix, Div I, §9(c) (Recommended Standards of Judicial Administration), but may be varied by local rule or policy. For example, in Los Angeles the trial setting conference is conducted by a court clerk who assigns dates for both the mandatory settlement conference and trials based on agreements between counsel. A judge is not present but is available to resolve disputes. The attorney should always consult and follow the appropriate local procedure.

§26.48   a. Setting Conference Date

Once an at-issue memorandum and any required certificate of readiness have been filed, the attorney need not take further steps to obtain a trial setting conference date. In counties in which a trial setting conference is required, the presiding judge must provide for a trial setting conference calendar. Cal Rules of Ct 220(a), 220.4. At least once a month, the presiding judge, or someone under his supervision, assigns a date for trial setting conference to cases on the civil active list in which no pretrial conference is required. The cases are assigned conference dates as closely as possible to their order of appearance on the civil active list (Rule 220(a)) or, when a certificate of readiness is required, the trial-ready list (Cal Rules of Ct 221(f), subject to statutory priority. As many cases are selected as can be set for trial within 12 weeks of the conference (the maximum time allowed by Rule 220.1 between conference and trial). Whenever feasible, the same conference date is assigned to cases in which the same attorney appears. Rule 220(a). For discussion of continuances and motions to advance, reset, or specially set a trial setting conference, see §26.50.

§26.49   b. Notice

Unless the parties agree to a shorter time, or the court orders time shortened for good cause shown on noticed motion, the clerk must give each party at least 60 days' notice by mail of the time and place of the trial setting conference. No other notice need be given by any party. Cal Rules of Ct 220(b).

In some counties, the notice of trial setting conference may be combined with an invitation to attend a settlement conference under Cal Rules of Ct 207.5. If counsel wishes to accept the invitation, he should file a written acceptance with the clerk not later than 20 days before the trial setting conference date. Cal Rules of Ct 207.5.

A party may request a pretrial conference even after receiving notice of the trial setting conference. If the request is granted, the trial setting conference is placed off calendar.

§26.50 c. Continuances; Motions To Advance, Specially Set, or Reset

A motion to continue the trial setting conference must be made before the conference judge, or, if he is not available, before the presiding judge. Cal Rules of Ct 220(a). For discussion, and a form that may be adapted for motion, see §26.97.

Although the rules do not expressly so state, a continuance may be ordered during a trial setting conference. The court's inherent power to control its proceedings constitutes ample authority for such an order. See §26.91. A continuance might be prompted by (1) the need for substantial further discovery before the case will be ready for trial setting, (2) the existence of substantial unresolved law and motion matters, (3) the failure of counsel to provide the setting judge with sufficient information to evaluate the case for setting purposes, or (4) the need for time for the parties to consummate a settlement agreement.

Motions to advance, specially set, or reset a case for trial setting conference must be made on notice to all other parties, and presented to the judge supervising the master calendar, or, in counties where there is no master calendar, to the judge in whose department the case is pending. Cal Rules of Ct 220(a), 225; for discussion, and form for motion, see §§26.76–26.82.

§26.51 d. Setting for Trial

If, at the trial setting conference, the court is satisfied that the case is ready for trial, it must set a trial date at least 30 days and not more than 12 weeks after the conference. Cal Rules of Ct

220.1. Within these restrictions, the court endeavors to set a date that is both reasonably convenient to counsel and consistent with the court's calendar. The 30-day minimum may, in the court's discretion, be shortened to prevent dismissal under CCP §583(b) for failure to bring the case to trial within five years (see generally §§31.18–31.31), or for other good cause shown on noticed motion. Cal Rules of Ct 220.1.

e. Trial Setting Conference Order
§26.52 (1) When Used; Content

Although it is not required by the California Rules of Court, the Judicial Council has recommended and most courts follow a procedure in which the court, at or after a trial setting conference, prepares an order specifying a trial date, and delineating the matters considered at the conference. Cal Rules of Ct Appendix Div I §9(c). The order should include a date for a settlement conference, if required or requested under Cal Rules of Ct 207.5, which should be approximately 20 days before trial. Cal Rules of Ct Appendix, Div I, §9(a). For discussion of the form of order, see §26.53.

If a party has questioned another party's demand for a jury trial, the order may properly include the court's determination of this issue, *e.g.*, on a stipulation made by the parties before the conference to submit the matter to the trial setting judge. However, because of calendar pressures, most courts defer consideration of the matter at the conference, and set the case for jury trial without prejudice to a later motion to vacate the jury trial setting under Cal Rules of Ct 231.

§26.53 (2) Form of Order; Who Prepares

Local practice varies widely in the forms used for trial setting conference orders, and even regarding whether to make an order. Los Angeles, for example, uses a document entitled "Trial Setting Conference Memorandum." Counsel should consult the court clerk in the county in which the action is pending to ascertain whether that court has a preprinted form.

Practice varies also regarding who prepares the order. In some counties (*e.g.*, Alameda), counsel receives from the clerk, before the conference, a preprinted form which is then filled in and presented to the court at the conference for signature. In others (*e.g.*, San Francisco, Los Angeles), the order or memorandum is prepared by the court commissioner or court clerk after the conference. The order is always filed, but need not be served. See §26.54 on service.

§26.54 (3) Service

The court clerk need not serve a copy of the trial setting order on the parties, and ordinarily the order is not served. An exception is Los Angeles, where the trial setting conference memorandum (see §26.53) and notice of trial (see §26.55) are combined in a single document and served on each party. In any event, the attorney should obtain a copy of the trial setting conference order, so that he can prepare for trial based on the content of the order. See §26.43 for discussion of content.

§26.55 f. Notice of Trial

The court clerk need not serve a copy of the trial setting conference order on the parties (see §26.54), and no court rule requires him to give notice of the time and place of trial after the conference. However, under CCP §594(a), the party seeking a dismissal, verdict, or judgment may not proceed at trial on an issue of fact when the adverse party is absent, unless the adverse party had at least 15 days' notice of trial (five days in an unlawful detainer proceeding). The clerk must serve such notice by mail on all parties not less than 20 days before trial, and if he does not, notice may be served by any party on the adverse party not less than 15 days before trial (ten days in an unlawful detainer proceeding when notice is served by mail). CCP §594(b).

The notice of trial requirement does not apply when the adverse party has given notice at least five days before trial (CCP §594(a)), and may be waived, *e.g.*, by stipulation or by service of a trial setting conference order that states the trial date. See 4 Witkin, CALIFORNIA PROCEDURE, Trial §51 (2d ed 1971).

If the trial date is set at a trial setting conference with all counsel present, the court will usually obtain and include in the order a stipulation from all parties waiving notice of trial date. When not all parties are present, or when notice has not been waived, the court usually requires counsel to serve written notice of the trial date on all parties. Even when the court does not so require, it is good practice to file and serve a notice of time and place of trial. See CCP §594(a).

B. Pretrial Conference

1. Introduction

§26.56   a. Nature and Purpose

A pretrial conference may be required before trial of a civil case pending in superior court. See §26.57. Its primary purpose is to simplify and define the issues, and to expedite trial. *Trickey v Superior Court* (1967) 252 CA2d 650, 60 CR 761. When used, it replicates the trial setting conference as a calendar-control device but has a broader impact than the trial setting conference. On matters discussed at the pretrial conference, see §26.66. The pretrial conference judge prepares and signs a pretrial order, which states the nature of the case, incorporates the agreements and stipulations of all parties, and specifies the issues to be resolved. Cal Rules of Ct 214(a)(1). When filed, the order becomes part of the record in the case and, when inconsistent with the pleadings, controls the subsequent proceedings unless modified by court order. Cal Rules of Ct 216. See §26.73.

§26.57   b. Statutory Authority; When Used

Code of Civil Procedure §575 provides that the California Judicial Council may, in superior, municipal, and justice court cases that are at issue, or in one or more classes of such cases, promulgate rules governing pretrial conferences. Acting under this authority, the Judicial Council has promulgated Cal Rules of Ct 208–219, which apply only to superior courts; pretrial conferences are not held in municipal or justice court cases.

A pretrial conference must be held when requested by a party, or ordered by the court on its own motion. Cal Rules of Ct 208. Short causes are exempt from this requirement under Cal Rules of Ct 208, 207.1. No local rule or general court order can require pretrial conferences in all cases or certain classes of cases. Rule 208.

Since 1967, when the last major amendments to Cal Rules of Ct 208–219 were made, pretrial conferences in larger counties have become the exception rather than the rule. Although some smaller counties continue to use pretrial conferences in most cases, the pretrial conference in many counties has been superseded by the mandatory settlement conference, as provided by local rule, or by settlement conferences in general, as provided by Cal Rules of Ct 207.5. See §26.75 for discussion of settlement conferences. On whether to request a pretrial conference, see §26.60.

§26.58 c. Duties of Counsel; Sanctions

Before the pretrial conference, counsel for each party (or the party, when there is no counsel) must attempt to reach agreement on as many matters as possible, either in person or by correspondence. Cal Rules of Ct 210(b). Counsel (or the parties) must make reasonable efforts to complete discovery proceedings before the conference, and to be prepared to inform the court what discovery has been completed, what discovery remains to be completed, and when it can be accomplished. Cal Rules of Ct 210(d).

At or before the conference, counsel must prepare and submit to the pretrial conference judge a joint written statement of the matters agreed on, and separately written statements of factual and legal contentions as to remaining issues. Cal Rules of Ct 210(c). Local rules may require additional matters in the statement, *e.g.*, the completion or reservation of law and motion matters, settlement efforts, pendency of related cases, summary of damages, jury demand, and estimated trial time.

Under Cal Rules of Ct 210(a), each party must either personally attend the pretrial conference or be represented by counsel, must have a thorough knowledge of the case, be prepared to discuss it and to make stipulations or admissions when appropriate. Unless good cause is shown, the failure of any person to reasonably prepare for, appear at, or participate in good faith in the pretrial conference is an unlawful interference with court proceedings, for which the court may impose the same sanctions as may be applied with respect to trial setting conferences. Cal Rules of Ct 217. For discussion, see §§26.45–26.46.

2. Selecting Cases for Pretrial Conference

§26.59 a. Conference Ordered on Court's Own Motion

The court's power to order a pretrial conference on its own motion is limited by Cal Rules of Ct 208, which provides that the court may order a pretrial conference in a case only after considering the necessities of that particular case, and which expressly prohibits local rules or general court orders that prescribe pretrial conferences in all cases or certain classes of cases. Therefore, the court's decision whether to select a case for pretrial is usually based on: (1) the complexity of the issues as stated in the pleadings; (2) the amount in controversy, interests at stake, and public significance; (3) the probability that estimated trial time may be substantially shortened; (4) whether there are any special problem areas; and (5) the effectiveness of pretrial in similar cases in the past.

Although Cal Rules of Ct 208 provides that the court may not on its own motion order a pretrial conference unless it first examines individual cases on the civil active list to determine which merit pretrial, this procedure is practical only in smaller counties, which partially explains the greater use of pretrial in those counties. Because large metropolitan courts are unable to commit the necessary judicial time to screening individual cases, pretrial conferences in larger counties ordinarily are ordered by the court on its own motion only when a particular case in which pretrial might be beneficial comes to the court's attention, *e.g.*, during law and motion proceedings or the trial setting conference.

b. Conference On Request of Counsel
§26.60 (1) Deciding Whether To Request

Because there may be practical or tactical advantages to be derived from a pretrial conference, counsel should screen each case to decide whether to request one. However, these potential advantages (such as learning more about the adverse party's case) often prove to be more illusory than real. More effective procedures than pretrial are available to clarify and simplify the issues, *e.g.*, discovery, summary judgment motions, and, to cure pleading deficiencies, motions to amend.

A pretrial conference may occasionally be advantageous, *e.g.*, in a lengthy, complex case with many parties or issues or in which the attorneys anticipate that many documents will be introduced into evidence. In these situations, the pretrial function of narrowing and clarifying the issues, or of obtaining stipulations on which documents will be admissible, can result in a smoother, shorter trial.

A pretrial conference may be valuable when counsel believes his opponent has a weak case but has not yet examined it closely enough to ascertain that fact. By requiring that each party file a pretrial statement, the pretrial conference gives the judge a tool with which to expose weaknesses and to open the door to realistic settlement negotiations. Although this process often occurs at the mandatory settlement conference, that conference typically is held about 20 days before trial and by that time much trial preparation already has occurred. See §26.75.

(2) Procedures for Requesting

§26.61   (a) In At-Issue Memorandum

Counsel who wants a pretrial conference must request it in the at-issue memorandum. Cal Rules of Ct 206(a)(5); see form in §26.13. When pretrial has not been requested in the original memorandum, the nonfiling party may request it in a counter-memorandum. Cal Rules of Ct 206 (b). See §26.14. If any party requests a pretrial conference, no further request is necessary, but if no party so requests, a pretrial conference still may be requested at a later date. See §26.62.

§26.62   (b) After Filing At-Issue Memorandum

The court must grant any party's request for pretrial made after the at-issue memorandum has been filed, unless to do so would unreasonably interfere with bringing the case to trial or would otherwise result in unfair advantage to any party. Cal Rules of Ct 206(c).

The rules do not indicate the procedure for requesting pretrial after the at-issue memorandum has been filed, and local practice varies. Some counties may include the request in the certificate of readiness; others may permit a simple request to be filed; still others may require a noticed motion. A recommended practice is to file a noticed motion, supported by declarations showing that pretrial is necessary to clarify the issues or to otherwise expedite trial.

§26.63   3. Setting for Pretrial Conference

The presiding judge, or someone under his supervision, at least once a month assigns a time and place for pretrial conference to as many cases on the civil active list that require a pretrial conference as may be set for trial within 12 weeks after the conference. Cal Rules of Ct 209(a), 219(a). Cases must be selected as closely as possible to their order of appearance on the civil active list (subject to statutory priority), and cases in which the same attorney appears, should, if possible, be assigned the same pretrial conference date.

The court must provide for a pretrial conference calendar or for one or more departments to hear pretrial conferences. Cal Rules of Ct 209(a). For discussion of continuances and motions to advance, reset, or specially set a pretrial conference, see §§26.67, 26.76–26.82.

§26.64 4. Notice

Unless the parties agree to a shorter time or the court orders the time shortened for good cause shown on noticed motion, the clerk must give each party at least 60 days' notice by mail of the time and place of the pretrial conference. No further notice need be given by any party. Cal Rules of Ct 209(b).

5. Conduct of Conference
§26.65 a. Location; Use of Court Reporter

The pretrial conference may, in the court's discretion, be held in the courtroom or in chambers. Cal Rules of Ct 211(a). Most judges prefer to hold the conference in chambers, to encourage greater informality and candor.

Because the pretrial conference is not designed to produce a formal record of its proceedings, but instead a pretrial order embodying its results, the conference normally is not reported by a court reporter. However, a court reporter may be requested by court order, in which case any reporter's fee is divided between the parties, or by either party, who must advance the fee when the demand is made. Local rules can require that the party must request that the conference be reported at least 48 hours before the scheduled date. Cal Rules of Ct 211(b).

§26.66 b. Matters Considered

At the pretrial conference the judge may, without adjudicating controverted facts, consider and rule on (Cal Rules of Ct 212(a)):

(1) The parties written pretrial statements admitted under Cal Rules of Ct 210 (see §26.58) of the matters agreed on and of contentions made as to remaining issues;

(2) Any proposed amendments to the pleadings not previously

§26.67   SETTING CASE FOR TRIAL

ruled on by any court, and the time within which amended pleadings must be filed;

(3) Simplification of the factual and legal issues involved;

(4) Admissions of fact and authentication of documents, to avoid unnecessary proof;

(5) References to a referee, commissioner, or other person, as provided by law;

(6) Whether the court has jurisdiction to act in the case and, if not, to transfer or to dismiss the case;

(7) Whether discovery proceedings have been completed under Cal Rules of Ct 210 and, if not, fix time limits for further discovery, subject to Cal Rules of Ct 222;

(8) Whether to require a trial brief or a memorandum of points and authorities and, if so, fix the time of service and filing;

(9) Estimated time for trial after inquiring whether a jury trial is to be had; and

(10) Assignment of the date and place of trial in accordance with Cal Rules of Ct 219 (see §26.74).

In addition, under Cal Rules of Ct 211 (f), the court determines whether any party remains in the case who has neither been served with process nor appeared, and whether any law and motion matter is pending or is likely to arise. If so, the judge may either continue the conference or order the case off the civil active list. The court may (and usually does) inquire into the possibility of settlement (Cal Rules of Ct 213), especially in smaller counties, where the court's schedule is more likely to permit it.

The parties also may stipulate to submit, and the judge may rule on, any other matter that aids in disposition of the case. Cal Rules of Ct 212(b).

A party cannot be required to disclose his witnesses at the pretrial conference, because such disclosure is governed by discovery proceedings. Cal Rules of Ct 211(e).

§26.67   c. Continuances

The pretrial conference judge may continue the conference (Cal Rules of Ct 211(c)), e.g., when a party who has neither appeared nor been served with process (Cal Rules of Ct 211 (f) remains in the case. For discussion of additional grounds and procedures for continuing the conference, see §§26.83–26.102.

6. Pretrial Conference Order

§26.68   **a. Who Must Prepare; Time**

The pretrial conference judge must prepare and sign a pretrial conference order at, or within five days of, the conference. Cal Rules of Ct 214(a). If, at the conclusion of the conference, the order is dictated and transcribed to the satisfaction of all parties, it may be signed and filed at once.

After the order is prepared by the judge, it is given to the court reporter, secretary, or court stenographer for typing, and copies are available to any party without charge. Cal Rules of Ct 214(c). For discussion of filing and service, see §26.70.

§26.69   **b. Content**

The pretrial conference order must contain a concise and descriptive statement of the nature of the case and the matters agreed on or admitted to, a list of exhibits marked in evidence, for identification, or as authenticated by consent of the parties, the factual and legal contentions made by each party as to the remaining issues, and a concise and descriptive statement of every ruling and order of the judge at the conference. Cal Rules of Ct 214(a). The order also may state the time and place of trial. See Cal Rules of Ct 219(b).

The pretrial order shall not contain any reference to settlement of the case. Cal Rules of Ct 214(b).

§26.70   **c. Service; Corrections or Modifications; Filing**

The court clerk must serve a copy of the pretrial conference order by mail on each attorney in the case, and must file a certificate of mailing. Cal Rules of Ct 215(a). Within five days after service, any attorney may file and serve on all other attorneys in the case a request for correction or modification of the order. The pretrial judge may deny, grant, or provide for a hearing on the request, and cause notice of his action to be given to each attorney. Cal Rules of Ct 215(b). If the court denies the request for correction or modification of the order, the clerk must notify all parties by mail of the denial and of the date the order was filed. If the request is granted, the clerk must mail to all parties a copy of the corrected or modified order, with an endorsement by the clerk showing the date of filing. Cal Rules of Ct 215(b).

The pretrial order is filed after expiration of the five-day period or, when applicable, after the ruling on a request for correction or modification. Cal Rules of Ct 215(b).

After filing, the court may, in furtherance of justice, modify the order at any time before or after commencement of trial on such terms as may be proper. CCP §576. See also Cal Rules of Ct 216 (modification proper "to prevent manifest injustice"). A motion under Rule 216 should be made as soon as possible after grounds for it are discovered. The court may consider unreasonable delay in ruling on the motion, and may deny it if granting it would prejudice the opposing party. See *Feykert v Hardy* (1963) 213 CA2d 67, 28 CR 510. If made before trial, the motion must be heard by the pretrial judge or, if unavailable, the presiding judge or, if none, by any judge of the court. Rule 216.

§26.71 d. Effect of Failure To Comply

There are no express sanctions for a party's failure to comply with the pretrial order, as distinguished from failure to attend or participate in the pretrial conference (see §26.58). However, if the order requires affirmative action by the parties, or imposes time limits on trial preparation (*e.g.*, discovery), the court has inherent power to implement these requirements by appropriate sanctions that accord with the purposes of pretrial. See *Mellone v Lewis* (1965) 233 CA2d 4, 43 CR 412 (trial court properly excluded plaintiff's evidence of claimed special damages that had not been submitted to defendant within the time prescribed by pretrial order).

§26.72 e. Appellate Review

Although the pretrial conference order is not directly appealable, the order, and any proceeding to correct or modify it, may be reviewed on appeal from a final judgment in the case. Cal Rules of Ct 218. Interlocutory review is also available by means of mandamus and prohibition. See *Dowell v Superior Court* (1956) 47 C2d 483, 304 P2d 1009 (mandamus granted because no other speedy or adequate remedy available).

Because granting or denying a motion to modify a pretrial order rests in the court's discretion, a party appealing the court's ruling must show an abuse of discretion resulting in prejudice to the aggrieved party.

§26.73   7. Effect of Order and Conference

The pretrial conference order crucially affects subsequent proceedings in the case. When filed, it becomes part of the record in the case and, when inconsistent with the pleadings, supersedes them. The order controls the subsequent course of the case, unless it is modified as discussed in §26.70. Cal Rules of Ct 216. See also *Feykert v Hardy* (1963) 213 CA2d 67, 28 CR 510 (trial judge may rely on posture of case as defined by pretrial order); *Fitzsimmons v Jones* (1960) 179 CA2d 5, 8, 3 CR 373, 374 (purpose of pretrial is "to place the case in focus"). Therefore, the content and language of the order is extremely important.

It has been held that the pretrial order should be liberally construed to cover any theory of recovery inherent in the issues (*Frasca v Warner* (1967) 249 CA2d 593, 57 CR 683), and to permit amendments to conform to proof, even when the order has not been modified (*Atkins v Atkins* (1960) 177 CA2d 207, 2 CR 104). For example, in *Frasca*, the court admitted defendant's testimony, which did not conform to her pretrial statement, about the location of her automobile just before colliding with plaintiff's automobile, thereby permitting defendant to raise the issue of contributory negligence. But see *Spence v State* (1961) 198 CA2d 332, 18 CR 302 (defendant cannot raise for first time at trial issue of plaintiff's failure to file claim with state as required by former Govt C §643, when issue not raised in pleadings and not referred to in pretrial order).

For further discussion, see 4 Witkin CALIFORNIA PROCEDURE, Trial §§66–70 (2d ed 1971).

No part of the pretrial conference, other than the pretrial order as filed, may be referred to at trial, or used other than in proceedings to correct, modify, or interpret the order, or on appeal under Cal Rules of Ct 218. Cal Rules of Ct 211(d).

§26.74   8. Setting for Trial After Pretrial Conference

Every case in which a pretrial conference is held must be set for trial not earlier than 30 days after filing the pretrial order, and within 12 weeks after the conference, giving priority to those cases entitled to it by law. See §26.4 on statutory priority. The

30-day minimum may, in the court's discretion, be shortened if there is a danger of dismissal under CCP §583, or for other good cause shown on noticed motion. Cal Rules of Ct 219(a).

If the time and place of trial is fixed in the pretrial order, no further notice need be given. If not, the clerk must give to all parties at least 30 days' notice by mail, unless the court shortens time to prevent a dismissal under CCP §583, or for other good cause shown on noticed motion. Cal Rules of Ct 219(b). See also CCP §594, discussed in §26.55.

Although it is not necessary for counsel to give notice, it is good practice to do so to ensure compliance with CCP §594(a), which provides that when an issue of fact exists, no dismissal, verdict, or judgment may be taken unless the adverse party had notice of trial. See §26.55.

§26.75 C. Settlement Conference

The settlement conference has become the most important of all pretrial conferences, and plays a major role in keeping superior court trial calendars within manageable limits. See generally §§33.16–33.27. The conference derives its authority from Cal Rules of Ct 207.5, which provides that as part of its pretrial facilities the superior court in each county shall establish and maintain a settlement calendar. Procedures are set forth in Rule 207.5 for the timing and conduct of voluntary settlement conferences. For discussion, see §33.16. However, Rule 207.5 states that these procedures are not intended to be exclusive and expressly authorizes local settlement procedures after the completion of pretrial proceedings. See also *Wisniewski v Clary* (1975) 46 CA3d 499, 120 CR 176. Moreover, Cal Rules of Ct Appendix, Div I §9(d) (Recommended Standards of Judicial Administration) recommends that a mandatory settlement conference be held in all ready cases pending in superior court.

Acting under this authorization and recommendation, many courts, especially those in large counties, have established rules and procedures for mandatory settlement conference in all except short causes or nonjury trials. See, *e.g.*, San Francisco Super Ct R §2.6(B). Under these rules, mandatory settlement conferences are usually scheduled at the trial setting conference and are held approximately three weeks before trial (see, *e.g.*, LA SUPER CT CIV TRIALS MAN §4. Attendance normally is required by all persons whose consent is required to effect a binding settlement and sanctions are provided for a party's failure to attend, to be prepared, or to participate in good faith. See §§33.22–33.23.

For further discussion of voluntary and mandatory settlement conferences, see §§33.16–33.17.

V. MOTIONS TO ADVANCE, SPECIALLY SET, AND RESET
§26.76   A. Authority

The authority for motions to specially set, advance, or reset a pretrial or a trial setting conference is found in Cal Rules of Ct 209(a), 220(a), 220.4. See also *Swartzman v Superior Court* (1964) 231 CA2d 195, 41 CR 721, and Cal Rules of Ct 209(b), 220(b), which state that the court may, for good cause, shorten the time for notice of the conference.

Motions to specially set, advance, or reset the trial itself, as distinguished from the pretrial or trial setting conference, are authorized by Cal Rules of Ct 225. For example, the attorney might want to move to advance the trial date, rather than the trial setting conference date, to avoid a five-year mandatory dismissal under CCP §583(b), or when a client is elderly or in poor health. For further discussion, see §26.77.

B. When To Use
§26.77   1. Motions To Advance or Specially Set

Because a motion to advance or specially set asks the court to depart from normal setting practices, a strong showing ordinarily is necessary before the motion will be granted. An exception is a motion that seeks to avoid an impending mandatory dismissal under CCP §583(b) for failure to bring the case to trial within five years. For discussion, see §26.79. Counsel should adhere to the court's normal scheduling practice whenever possible, and seek special treatment only in unusual cases when the courts will ordinarily be sympathetic to the motion. For example, an unavoidable scheduling conflict might justify unusual treatment. A pretrial conference in a related case scheduled for another date would also support a motion to set the second conference at the same time before the same judge.

Personal hardship of a party or material witness (*e.g.*, old age, poor health) is usually accepted by courts as a valid reason for granting the motion. On the other hand, economic hardship is not usually sufficient justification, unless the evidence shows that it is serious and will be aggravated unless the trial date is advanced.

The distinction between a motion to advance and a motion to specially set is unclear, and in practice attorneys use them interchangeably. Technically, a motion to advance is proper when a party already has a date for pretrial, trial setting, or trial, and seeks to advance it. A motion to specially set is proper when no date has been set. See, *e.g.*, *Swartzman v Superior Court* (1964) 231 CA2d 195, 41 CR 721, in which a case entitled to statutory priority (eminent domain) was specially set for pretrial conference and for trial.

§26.78 2. Motions To Reset

Motions to reset ordinarily are made when a case previously set for pretrial, trial setting, or trial is ordered off calendar. The court usually will deny the motion unless the circumstances that resulted in the case's being dropped have changed. If the case was dropped without fault of the party seeking to reset (*e.g.*, because of a reasonable but mistaken belief that settlement had been reached), the court usually grants the motion and assigns an early date for trial. If the case was ordered off calendar because the party seeking to reset was at fault (*e.g.*, because of failure to attend trial setting conference), the court may (a) deny the motion and require the party to file a new at-issue memorandum; (b) grant the motion, but set the case for trial later than the date requested (*e.g.*, by assigning a definite date or by considering the at-issue memorandum as filed on a later date, thus reestablishing civil active list priority as of that date); or (c) take other remedial action.

§26.79 C. Court's Discretion

Motions to advance, specially set, or reset a pretrial conference, trial setting conference, or trial date are subject to the court's discretion. The court's ruling will not be reversed on appeal unless abuse of discretion is shown. However, the court does not have discretion to deny a motion made to avoid mandatory dismissal under CCP §583(b) for failure to bring the case to trial within five years. In 1967, Cal Rules of Ct 219(a) and 220.1 were amended to authorize expressly an early trial setting to avoid dismissal under CCP §583(b), and recent cases have held that the court must comply. See, *e.g.*, *Weeks v Roberts* (1968) 68 C2d 802, 69 CR 305; *Vogelsang v Owl Trucking Co.* (1974) 40 CA3d 1068, 115 CR 666. For further discussion, see §31.20.

A motion to advance or specially set does not affect the court's discretion to dismiss the case under CCP §583(a) for failure to prosecute if not brought to trial within two years after filing. Dismissal in that situation may be ordered after a separate noticed motion by counsel opposing the motion to advance or specially set has been heard or by the court on its own motion. See Cal Rules of Ct 203.5 for procedures.

D. Procedures
§26.80   1. To Whom Motion Is Made

Motions to advance, specially set, or reset cases for pretrial conference, trial setting conference, or trial must be made on notice to all parties, and presented to the judge supervising the master calendar or, when there is no master calendar, to the judge in whose department the case is pending. Cal Rules of Ct 209(a), 220(a), 225. Local rules (see *e.g.*, LA Super Ct Rule 6, §3) should also be consulted.

§26.81   2. Form: Notice of Motion To Advance, Specially Set, or Reset

Copies: Original (filed with court clerk with proof of service); copies for service (one for each attorney of record and unrepresented party); office copies.

[Caption. See §§23.18–23.19]

No. _____

NOTICE OF MOTION TO
____[ADVANCE / SPECIALLY SET / RESET]____ **CASE FOR**
____[PRETRIAL CONFERENCE / TRIAL SETTING CONFERENCE / TRIAL]____;
POINTS AND AUTHORITIES; DECLARATION

To each party and attorney of record:
  PLEASE TAKE NOTICE that on _____, 19____, **at** _____.m., **or as soon thereafter as the matter can be heard, in** ____[e.g., Department No. ____]____ **at** ____[address]____, **California,** ____[name of moving party]____ **will move the**

§26.82   SETTING CASE FOR TRIAL   194

Court for an order ____[advancing / specially setting / resetting]____ the ____[pretrial conference / trial setting conference / trial]____ in this case to _____ trial conference / trial setting conference / trial]____ because _____.

   This motion is made on the grounds that ____[e.g., that this action will not otherwise be brought to trial within five years after the complaint was filed, as required by Code of Civil Procedure section 583(b)]____, as more particularly set forth in the declaration of ____[name]____ filed with this notice.

   This motion is based on this notice, the pleadings, records, and files in this action, the attached memorandum of points and authorities and the attached declaration of ____[name]____, ____[and oral and documentary evidence to be presented at the hearing of the motion]____.

Dated: _____
                              _____
                              [Signature of attorney]
                              [Typed name]
                              Attorney for ____[name]____

Comment: As with all pretrial motions, a memorandum of points and authorities must accompany the motion. Cal Rules of Ct 203(a), 503(a).

   In counties having more than ten judges, in which the trial date ordinarily is assigned after a pretrial conference or at a trial setting conference and the motion should request an early date for the conference. Regardless of what the motion requests, however, the court may set the case directly for trial if circumstances warrant it (*e.g.*, when expiration of the five-year period for bringing the case to trial under CCP §583(b) is imminent). In counties having ten or fewer judges, and which dispense with the trial setting conference (see §26.3), a motion to advance or specially set should simply request the court to set an early trial date.

§26.82   3. Form: Declaration in Support of Motion To Advance, Specially Set, or Reset

   Copies: Original (filed with court clerk with proof of service); copies for service (one for each attorney of record and unrepresented party); office copies.

[Caption. See §§23.18–23.19]

No. _____

DECLARATION IN SUPPORT OF MOTION TO ____[ADVANCE / SPECIALLY SET / RESET]____ **CASE FOR** ____[PRETRIAL CONFERENCE / TRIAL SETTING CONFERENCE / TRIAL]____

1. I am ____[e.g., the attorney for _____]____.

[When advancement sought]

2. A ____[pretrial conference / trial setting conference / trial]____ **date of** _____, **19**____, **has been assigned to this case, but this date is not satisfactory and assignment of an earlier date is necessary because** ____[state reasons]____.

[When special setting is sought]

2. This case involved ____[describe nature of case]____. **An at-issue memorandum** ____[and certificate of readiness]____ ____[was / were]____ **filed on** ____[date or dates]____, **but no date for** ____[pretrial conference / trial setting conference / trial]____ **has been set. It is necessary to specially set this case for** ____[pretrial conference / trial setting conference / trial]____ **because** _____.

[When resetting sought]

2. A ____[pretrial conference / trial setting conference / trial]____ **date was set by the Court for** _____, **19**____, **but** ____[the conference was not concluded / the matter was dropped from the calendar]____ **because** ____[state reason]____. **This case** ____[should / is now ready to]____ **be reset for** ____[pretrial conference / trial setting conference / trial]____ **because** _____.

[Continue]

I declare under penalty of perjury that the foregoing is true and correct and that this declaration was executed on _____, **19**____, **at** _____, **California.**

[Signature of declarant]

[Typed name]

Comment: On grounds for a motion to advance, specially set, or reset, see §26.50.

VI. TRIAL CONTINUANCES

§26.83   A. Introduction; Scope of Discussion

A continuance is a postponement of trial to a later time and may be granted for good cause shown before or during trial. See §§26.89–26.92 on what constitutes good cause. A continuance differs from an order removing a case from the calendar in that a case placed off calendar must be reset for trial (*e.g.*, by reinstatement on the civil active list after filing a new at-issue memorandum), while a continuance remains on calendar and the matter is heard at a later date.

The following discussion applies primarily to trial continuances. Motions to continue a trial setting conference or a pretrial conference are discussed in §§26.50, 26.67. The discussion in §§26.84–26.102 is appropriate as a guide in those situations, but it should be remembered that courts are usually more liberal in granting conference continuances than trial continuances.

§26.84 B. Policy Against Continuances

Many California courts, especially those in metropolitan counties, have become concerned with the increasing number of untried civil cases, and have adopted a firm no-continuance policy as a means of reducing the backlog. This policy is reflected in the California Judicial Council Standards of Judicial Administration, and discussion of the grounds for a continuance in §§26.85–26.94 must be considered in light of those standards. See *San Bernardino v Doria Min. & Eng'r Corp.* (1977) 72 CA3d 776, 140 CR 383; *Young v Redman* (1976) 55 CA3d 827, 128 CR 86.

California Rules of Court, Appendix, Div I, §9(a) recommends that the court, at the trial setting or pretrial conference, set a firm trial date for each ready case, and that all cases proceed to trial on the date set or within two court days afterwards. Cases that cannot proceed to trial within that time should be reset for a date certain, and have priority over all other cases set for the same day, except those entitled to precedence by statute. See §26.4 on statutory priority.

California Rules of Court Appendix, Div I, §9(b) states that the court should adopt a firm policy regarding continuances, emphasize that counsel must regard the dates assigned for trial as a definite court appointment, and that a continuance will be granted only on an affirmative showing of good cause. Ordinarily, the continuance motion should have resulted from an unavoidable and unforeseen emergency occurring after the trial setting conference, which can be properly remedied only by granting a continuance. Cal Rules of Ct Appendix, Div I, §9(b) (Recommended Standards of Judicial Administration). See also *Young v Redman, supra.*

§26.85 C. Grounds; Effects of Appellate Decisions

There is no comprehensive statutory scheme relating to trial continuances. The basic grounds for granting continuances are set out in the California Rules of Court (see §26.86), the Standards of Judicial Administration (see §§26.87–26.91), local rules or policy (see §26.92) and, in a few situations, by statute (see §26.93).

California Rules of Court Appendix, Div I, §9(b) (Recommended Standards of Judicial Administration) relating to trial continuances, was adopted by the California Judicial Council on January 1, 1972. Although these standards are only recommendations, and consequently not binding on a court, they constitute a policy statement by an influential body against the general granting of continuances (see §26.84), and earlier appellate decisions that express a more liberal view in granting continuances (see, e.g., *Whalen v Superior Court* (1960) 184 CA2d 598, 7 CR 610; *Capital Nat'l Bank of Sacramento v Smith* (1944) 62 CA2d 328, 339, 144 P2d 665, 671) must be viewed in this light. See also *San Bernardino v Doria Min. & Eng'r Corp.* (1977) 72 CA3d 776, 140 CR 383 (California has no rule or philosophy that courts should be indulgent and liberal in granting continuances).

§26.86   1. Basic Requirement of Good Cause

The basic requirement for allowing a continuance of a civil case before or during trial is expressed in Cal Rules of Ct 224 (superior court), 512 and 701 (municipal and justice courts), which provide that no such continuance may be granted, except on an affirmative showing of good cause. See also Cal Rules of Ct Appendix, Div I, §9(b) (Recommended Standards of Judicial Administration), discussed in §26.84. This rule, however, does not prevent cases from being dropped from the calendar by stipulation or order. Cal Rules of Ct 224, 512.

Courts will not accept a perfunctory showing as good cause for a continuance. *San Bernardino v Doria Min. & Eng'r Corp.* (1977) 72 CA3d 776, 140 CR 383. For discussion of what constitutes good cause, see §§26.87–26.91. On the effect of local rules or policy, see §26.92.

Sometimes the good cause requirement is implied by statute. See, e.g., CCP §594a, discussed in §26.93.

a. Examples of Good Cause
§26.87   (1) Death of Attorney or Witness

According to Cal Rules of Ct Appendix, Div I, §9(b)(1), the death of the trial attorney, or an essential or expert witness, any of whom cannot be replaced because of the proximity of their death to the trial date, is good cause for a continuance. The death of any other witness is good cause for granting a continuance when no one else can testify to the same facts, or, again because of the proximity of death to the trial date, there has been no reasonable opportunity to obtain a substitute.

§26.88 (2) Illness of Party, Attorney, or Witness

Good cause for continuing a trial normally exists on a showing of illness of a party or an essential witness. Cal Rules of Ct Appendix, Div I, §9(b)(2). See also *Young v Redman* (1976) 55 CA3d 827, 128 CR 86. Allegations of illness must be supported, whenever possible, by a physician's declaration stating the nature of the illness and anticipated period of incapacity. When incapacity of a party or essential witness is expected to continue for an extended period, the continuance should be granted, but a deposition should be taken so that trial may proceed on the next date set. Similarly, the court will usually grant a continuance for a properly documented illness of the trial attorney or of an expert witness. However, instead of granting a continuance, the court may recommend substituting another attorney or expert, depending on the proximity of illness to the trial date, the anticipated duration of incapacity, the complexity of the case, and the availability of a substitute attorney or expert. Cal Rules of Ct Appendix, Div I, §9(b)(2)(ii).

Illness of any witness other than a party, an essential witness, or an expert is considered good cause only when no other witness can testify to the same facts, either because there is none, or the constraints of time preclude obtaining a substitute. Cal Rules of Ct Appendix, Div I, §9(b)(2)(iii).

§26.89 (3) Unavailability of Trial Attorney, Party, or Witness

Good cause for continuing a trial date normally exists on a showing that the trial attorney is unavailable because he is engaged in another trial, provided that the attorney could not have reasonably anticipated the trial date conflict when he accepted the trial date in the present case, and the court was informed and made a finding at the pretrial or trial setting conference, or an order on motion made at least 30 days before the date set for trial, that the case was assigned for trial to an attorney in a particular law firm and that no other attorney in that firm was both available and capable of trying the case. Cal Rules of Ct Appendix, Div I, §9(b)(3)(i).

Good cause for a trial continuance exists when a party, or a witness who has been subpenaed (or who was beyond subpena but has consented to appear), is unavailable because of an unavoidable and unforeseen emergency. *Young v Redman* (1976) 55 CA3d 827, 128 CR 86; Cal Rules of Ct Appendix Div 1 §9(b)(3)(ii). However, even in this situation, the court has discretion to deny a continuance when the parties or witness' testimony has been adequately preserved in a deposition. *Young v Redman, supra*. On the exercise of trial court discretion in ruling on a motion for continuance, see §26.95.

§26.90 (4) Substitution of Trial Attorney

The substitution of the trial attorney is considered good cause for a trial continuance only when there is an affirmative showing that the substitution is required in the interests of justice. Cal Rules of Ct Appendix, Div I, §9(b)(4). Courts usually determine whether substitution is required "in the interests of justice" by examining various factors, including counsel's diligence in preparing for trial, the party's ability to secure other representation, and whether any continuances were granted earlier. For discussion, see 4 Witkin, CALIFORNIA PROCEDURE, Trial §10 (2d ed 1971).

Notwithstanding the Judicial Council's policy against granting continuances, it is an abuse of discretion for the court to deny a party's motion for continuance, even though made on the day of trial, when the party's attorney has withdrawn from the case too soon before trial for the party to procure another attorney. *Vann v Shilleh* (1975) 54 CA3d 192, 126 CR 401 (attorney withdrew on Friday and case called to trial the following Monday).

§26.91 (5) Significant Change in Status of Case

A significant change in the status of a case is considered good cause for a trial continuance only when, due to a change in parties or pleadings ordered by the court, the case is not ready for trial. Cal Rules of Ct Appendix, Div I, §9(b)(5). See also CCP §§473, 594a, discussed in §26.93.

§26.92 b. Local Variations; Los Angeles Policy

Because the California Judicial Council recommendations on trial continuances as set forth in Cal Rules of Ct Appendix, Div I, §9(b) (see §§26.87–26.91) are not binding on California trial courts, counsel must ascertain whether court policy in a particular county conforms with those recommendations. In smaller counties, where court business is less voluminous and more informal, courts may adopt a more liberal attitude regarding continuances than that expressed by the Judicial Council. But see §26.84. Conversely, courts in larger counties may follow the Judicial Council recommendations or may adopt an even more restrictive policy. Los Angeles County, for example, has followed a policy requiring that all unsettled cases go to trial on the date scheduled, unless a continuance predicated on good cause is granted. The policy in effect states that good cause exists only in emergencies, or the unavailability of a court, and that it is the duty of counsel to manage his calendar to avoid conflicts. If, on the date a case is scheduled for trial, counsel is engaged in the trial of another case and a replacement is unavailable, the case will trail from day to day until counsel is available, except when doing so imposes an unreasonable burden on others. Stipulations to continue are not binding on the court and are not considered good cause. Further, counsel may not stipulate that any trial go off calendar unless the case is settled. Continuances §§1–3, Policy of Los Angeles Super Ct. But see CCP §595.2, discussed in §26.93.

The extent to which Los Angeles superior courts apply their own policy varies, depending on the exigencies of the civil case workload in relation to the number of judges who are available to process it. Due to a shortage of judges for civil trials, Los Angeles courts recently have liberally granted requests or stipulations for continuance. This situation underscores the importance of the attorney contacting the court clerk to determine current local policy. See §26.7.

§26.93 2. Statutory Grounds

The more common statutory grounds for granting trial continuances are:

(a) *Amendment of pleadings:* The court may, on its own motion, grant a continuance when allowance of an amendment of a pleading, or of time to plead, makes a continuance necessary. As a condition for granting the continuance, the court may require payment of costs to the adverse party. CCP §§473, 594a.

(b) *Membership in legislature:* Code of Civil Procedure §595 provides that a trial or proceeding in a court "shall be postponed" when any party, attorney, or principal witness to such trial or proceeding is a member of the California legislature, and the legislature is in session or in recess (not exceeding a recess of 40 days). The language of CCP §595 has, however, been construed as directory and not mandatory. See *Thurmond v Superior Court* (1967) 66 C2d 836, 59 CR 273. On the definition of "proceeding in a court," see CCP §595.1.

(c) *Party in armed forces:* The Soldiers' and Sailors' Civil Relief Act of 1940 (50 USC App §§501–548, 560–590) provides that in any action or proceeding in which a plaintiff or defendant (not a witness) is in military service, the court may, on its own motion, and must on motion of the party, grant a continuance, unless the party's ability to prosecute or defend the action is not materially affected by his military service. 50 USC App §521.

(d) *Court convenience:* The court may, on its own motion, order a continuance when it is engaged in another trial (CCP §594a) or when, in a jury trial, no jury is available (CCP §214). In such instances, the court may order that the case trail until the judge or jury is available. See §26.100.

(e) *Stipulation:* Code of Civil Procedure §595.2 provides that the court in all cases "shall" postpone a trial (or hearing of any motion or demurrer) for up to 30 days when all attorneys of record for parties who have appeared stipulate in writing to the postponement. The apparently mandatory language of the statute, however, has been held to be directory only (see *San Bernardino v Doria Min. & Eng'r Corp.* (1977) 72 CA3d 776, 140 CR 383; *Lorraine v McComb* (1934) 220 C 753, 32 P2d 960, in which the court construed the same language in former CCP §595), and some courts have adopted rules or policies that contradict it. See, e.g., Continuances §2(a)–(b), Policy of Los Angeles Super Ct. (stipulations to continue trial are not binding on court and are not considered good cause). See discussion of Los Angeles policy in §26.92.

(f) *Absence of evidence:* Code of Civil Procedure §595.4 provides for a trial postponement on the ground of absence of evidence on a showing by affidavit (or declaration) that the expected evidence is material and that due diligence has been used to procure it. When the motion is due to the absence of a material witness, the court may require the moving party to state by affidavit what the expected testimony will be; and if the adverse party admits that the evidence would be given, and that it may be considered as having been actually given at trial, or offered and overruled as improper, trial cannot be postponed. CCP §595.4.

§26.94   3. Inherent Power of Court To Continue

In addition to the grounds for trial continuances set forth in Cal Rules of Ct 224 (see §26.86), the Standards of Judicial Administration (see §§26.87–26.91), local rules or policy (see §26.92), or particular statutes (see §26.93), the court may exercise its inherent powers to continue a case on its own motion, provided neither party is prejudiced by the continuance. *Santandrea v Siltec Corp.* (1976) 56 CA3d 525, 529, 128 CR 629, 632 ("[e]very court has the inherent power to regulate the proceedings of matters before it and to effect an orderly disposition of the issues presented."). See *e.g., People v Hernon* (1951) 106 CA2d 638, 235 P2d 614 (court may order continuance to hear testimony from material and necessary witness although neither party so requests).

§26.95   D. Court Discretion; Factors Considered

The court has broad discretion to determine whether good cause exists for granting a motion for trial continuance; its decision will be reversed on appeal only when there is a clear abuse of discretion. *Eastwood v Froehlich* (1976) 60 CA3d 523, 131 CR 577; *People ex rel Dep't of Pub. Works v Busick* (1968) 259 CA2d 744, 66 CR 532.

In ruling on a motion for continuance, the court will consider all relevant matters, including the declarations concerning the motion, the diligence and promptness of counsel in bringing the emergency to the court's and opposing counsel's attention, and the proximity of the trial date. The court will also take into consideration any previous continuances, extensions of time or other delays, the condition of the court's calendar and the availability of an earlier trial date if the matter is ready for trial; also whether a continuance may be avoided by substitution of attorneys or witnesses, use of depositions instead of oral testimony, or trailing the matter for trial, and whether the interests of justice are best served by granting a continuance or by granting it subject to conditions. Any other fact or circumstance relevant to a fair determination of the motion will also be considered, *e.g.*, the merits of an asserted defense (*Schwartz v Magyar House, Inc.* (1959) 168 CA2d 182, 335 P2d 487); Cal Rules of Ct Appendix, Div I, §9(b).

E. Procedures

§26.96   1. Noticed Motion and Declaration

Except for good cause, a motion for continuance made before trial must be made on written notice to all parties. Cal Rules of Ct 224. See also Cal Rules of Ct Appendix, Div I, §9(b) (oral motions for continuance are proper only in emergencies). A noticed motion is required even when the continuance is uncontested or stipulated to by the parties. Cal Rules of Ct Appendix, Div I, §9(b). But see CCP §595.2 discussed in §26.93 (court must grant continuance of up to 30 days on written stipulation signed by all parties).

The moving party must proceed promptly on ascertaining the necessity for the continuance (see *Allstate Ins. Co. v King* (1967) 252 CA2d 698, 60 CR 892; Cal Rules of Ct 224), and must show good cause for the continuance (see §§26.86–26.92). The motion must be made to the judge supervising the master calendar or, when there is no master calendar, the judge in whose department the action is pending. Cal Rules of Ct 224.

Although a supporting affidavit (or declaration; see CCP §2015.5) is not mandatory, it is preferred as a means of encouraging prompt trial of lawsuits. *Cade v Mid-City Hosp.* (1975) 45 CA3d 589, 119 CR 571. Moreover, CCP §595.4 requires that a motion for continuance on the ground of absence of evidence must be supported by an affidavit showing the materiality of the evidence and that due diligence has been used to procure it. When the motion is grounded on absence of a material witness, the court may require an affidavit that states the expected evidence; and the motion must be denied when the adverse party stipulates that the evidence be considered as having been given at trial.

By implication, Rule 224 apparently authorizes the making of an oral motion for continuance during trial. But see *Cade v Mid-City Hosp. supra.*

§26.97   SETTING CASE FOR TRIAL

§26.97   2. Form: Notice of Motion for Continuance

Copies: Original (filed with court clerk with proof of service); copies for service (one for each attorney of record and unrepresented party); office copies.

[*Caption. See §§23.18 – 23.19*]

No. _____

NOTICE OF MOTION FOR CONTINUANCE; POINTS AND AUTHORITIES; DECLARATION

To each party and attorney of record:
PLEASE TAKE NOTICE that on _____, 19____, at _____.m., or as soon thereafter as the matter can be heard, in ____[*e.g., Department No.* _____]____ at ____[*address*]____, **California,** ____[*name of moving party*]____ will move the Court for a continuance of the trial of this case.

This motion is made on the ground that good cause exists, in that ____[*specify facts showing good cause, e.g., trial of this case has been set for* ____[*date*]____, *and that* ____[*name of witness*]____ *whose testimony on behalf of plaintiff in this case is essential, will be outside the State of California from* ____[*date*]____ *until* ____[*date*]____, *due to an unavoidable emergency, as more fully appears in the attached declaration of* ____[*name*]____].

This motion is based on this notice, the pleadings, records, and files in this action, the attached memorandum of points and authorities and the attached supporting declaration of ____[*name*]____, and ____[*and on such evidence as may be presented at the hearing of this motion*]____.

Dated: _____

[*Signature of attorney*]

[*Typed name*]

Attorney for ____[*name*]____

Comment: The notice of motion should be made as soon as possible after the need for a continuance has been ascertained. Cal Rules of Ct 224. If necessary, an order shortening time for service of the motion can be obtained. On the grounds for continuance, see §§26.86–26.92.

§26.98   3. Form: Declaration in Support of Motion for Continuance

Copies: Original (filed with court clerk with proof of service); copies for service (one for each attorney of record and unrepresented party); office copies.

[Caption. See §§23.18–23.19]

No. _____

DECLARATION OF ____[NAME]____ IN SUPPORT OF MOTION FOR CONTINUANCE

____[Name]____ declares:

1. I am ____[e.g., the attorney for _____]____ in this action for ____[state nature of action]____.

   [State facts showing good cause, e.g., when witness is unavailable]

2. ____[Name]____ is a material and essential witness to the ____[describe event or transaction witnessed]____. Plaintiff expects that this witness will testify substantially as follows: ____[briefly summarize testimony]____.

3. This witness was subpenaed on _____[date]_____, to appear on ____[date]____, but will be outside the State of California from ____[date]____, until ____[date]____, due to the following unavoidable emergency: _____.

4. Plaintiff first learned of the unavailability of this witness on ____[date]____, and cannot safely proceed to trial without the testimony of this witness.

5. ____[Plaintiff / Defendant]____ will be ready for trial on any date after _____, 19____.

[Continue]

I declare under penalty of perjury that the foregoing is true and correct and that this declaration was executed on _____, 19____, at _____, California.

[Signature of declarant]

[Typed name]

Comment: On the need for a declaration in support of a motion for continuance, see §26.96.

The declaration should clearly indicate why the facts supporting the motion were not and could not have been known when the case was set for trial, or at the trial setting or pretrial conference, and that the motion was made promptly after the moving party learned of them. See Cal Rules of Ct Appendix, Div I, §9(b) and Cal Rules of Ct 224, discussed in §26.84. Some cases also hold, with respect to the absence of a material witness, that the declaration must give reasonable assurance that the witness would be present at trial on a future specified date. See, *e.g.*, *Allstate Ins. Co. v King* (1967) 252 CA2d 698, 60 CR 892. See also §26.89.

§26.99 4. Payment of Costs as Condition for Granting Motion

When a motion for trial continuance is made, the court may, as a condition of granting the motion, require the moving party to pay to the adverse party any just costs resulting from the continuance. CCP §§473, 1024. Such costs may include, *e.g.*, jury fees, mileage costs for witnesses, and other court costs and expenses incurred in preparing for trial. *Williams v Myer* (1907) 150 C 714, 89 P 972; *Wilkin v Tadlock* (1952) 110 CA2d 156, 241 P2d 1066. A plaintiff's failure to pay such costs or, alternatively, to proceed with trial, may result in a judgment of dismissal. *Fraser v Fraser* (1919) 39 CA 467, 179 P 427.

5. Procedures When Motion Denied

§26.100 a. Trailing Cases

When trial cannot begin for some reason that may be cured within a day or two, the court may deny a motion for continuance but trail the case from day to day. For example, a case may be trailed if an attorney is engaged in trial of another matter, and no replacement is available (see, *e.g.*, LA SUPER CT CIV TRIALS MAN §3), or for lack of an available trial department (Cal Rules of Ct 223(c)).

California Rules of Court Appendix, Div I, §9(a) provides that the court should trail cases only in extraordinary circumstances, and recommends that all cases proceed to trial on the date set or within two court days afterwards. For discussion, see §26.84.

§26.101 b. Severance

When a motion for continuance has been denied, and the moving party must either proceed to trial or face dismissal for failure to prosecute, counsel should consider moving to sever (or bifurcate, see generally chap 27) as an alternative. When certain issues can be severed from others, and a continuance is not necessary as to trial of those issues, the trial can proceed as to them. See §27.3. For a form for motion to sever, see §27.18.

§26.102 6. Appellate Review

An order granting or denying a motion for continuance is not directly appealable; it is reviewable on appeal only from a final judgment or order in the case. *Haraszthy v Horton* (1873) 46 C 545. See also *Estate of McCarthy* (1937) 23 CA2d 389, 73 P2d 910. Although it is practically impossible to show reversible error in the granting of a continuance (see 4 Witkin, CALIFORNIA PROCEDURE, Trial §7 (2d ed 1971)), it may be possible for a party to seek to obtain relief from an order denying a continuance, *e.g.*, by writ of prohibition.

On appeal, the appellate court will not disturb a ruling on a motion for continuance unless there is a clear showing that the trial court abused its discretion. See §26.95.

RICHARD P. BYRNE

Chapter 27
Consolidation and Severance

    I. INTRODUCTION
    A. Nature and Purpose
        1. Consolidation §27.1
        2. Severance §27.2
    B. Statutory Authority
        1. Basic Statute §27.3
        2. When Other Statutes Apply
            a. Consolidation §27.4
            b. Severance §27.5
    C. Consolidation of Actions or Issues Under CCP §1048(a) §27.6
    D. Severance of Actions or Issues Under CCP §1048(b) §27.7
    II. DECIDING WHETHER TO SEEK CONSOLIDATION OR SEVERANCE
    A. Judicial Attitude
        1. Consolidation §27.8
        2. Severance §27.9
    B. Other Consolidation Procedures Compared §27.10
    C. Court's Discretion; Factors Considered
        1. Consolidation §27.11
        2. Severance §27.12
    III. PROCEDURES
    A. For Consolidation
        1. Noticed Motion §27.13
        2. Form: Notice of Motion To Consolidate Actions or Issues §27.14
        3. Form: Declaration in Support of Motion To Consolidate §27.15
        4. Form: Order For Consolidation §27.16
    B. For Severance
        1. Noticed Motion §27.17
        2. Form: Notice of Motion To Sever Actions or Issues §27.18
        3. Form: Order Severing Actions or Issues §27.19
        4. Procedure After Trial of Severed Issues §27.20
    C. Review of Orders §27.21

See footnote to chap 26. CEB attorney-editor was JON A. RANTZMAN.

I. INTRODUCTION

A. Nature and Purpose

§27.1   1. Consolidation

Consolidation is a procedure by which, when actions involving common questions of law or fact are pending in the same court, the court orders a joint trial of those particular questions, or orders all such actions consolidated for trial. CCP §1048(a). The actions may have been brought by one party (who has elected not to join his causes of action in the same complaint) or by different parties.

The purpose of consolidation is to promote trial convenience and economy by avoiding duplication in proof of common issues. See *McClure v Donovan* (1949) 33 C2d 717, 205 P2d 17. On the types of consolidation, see §27.6. For discussion of statutory authority for consolidation in particular situations, see §27.4.

The court's authority to consolidate under CCP §1048(a) is limited to actions pending in that court. *Cochrane v Superior Court* (1968) 261 CA2d 201, 67 CR 675; *Caballero v Richardson* (1959) 173 CA2d 459, 343 P2d 302. Actions pending in different courts may be consolidated through the coordination procedures of CCP §§404–404.8. See §27.10; see generally chap 28.

§27.2   2. Severance

Severance is a procedure by which the court may, when convenient, order a separate trial of any action or any issue in an action pending before it to avoid prejudice, or when conducive to expedition and economy. CCP §1048(b). This procedure counterbalances the joinder provisions of CCP §§378–379 (see §27.10), and the consolidation provisions of CCP §1048(a), by giving the court discretion to try actions and issues in the manner most fair, convenient, and economical. On statutory authority for severance in particular situations, see §27.5.

B. Statutory Authority

§27.3   1. Basic Statute

The basic consolidation and severance statute is CCP §1048, which provides that whenever actions involving common questions of law of fact are pending before the court, it may order a joint hearing or trial of any or all issues, or order all the actions consolidated and make such orders concerning the proceedings that may avoid unnecessary costs or delay. CCP §1048(a). For convenience, to avoid prejudice, or when separate trials will be conducive to expedition and economy, the court may order a separate trial of any action, including one asserted in a cross-complaint, any separate issue, or any number of actions or issues, while preserving the right of jury trial required by the federal or state constitutions or by statute. CCP §1048(b). Code of Civil Procedure §1048 was amended effective July 1, 1972, to permit consolidation or severance of issues as well as actions, and to make it coextensive with Fed R Civ P 42. For discussion, see Comment to CCP §1048.

The provisions of CCP §1048 do not affect other statutes that authorize or require consolidation or severance in specific situations. See §§27.4–27.5. However, in exercising its discretion to order consolidation or severance under another statute, the court also will consider the standards and purposes of CCP §1048.

2. When Other Statutes Apply

§27.4   a. Consolidation

Although CCP §1048(a) confers on the court discretionary power to consolidate (see §27.11), that power does not affect other statutes that permit or require consolidation of particular actions or proceedings. See Comment to CCP §1048.

Consolidation Required. On motion of any party, the court must consolidate:

(1) A wrongful death action and a survival action under Prob C §573 arising from the same wrongful act or neglect (CCP §377; see also *General Motors Corp. v Superior Court* (1966) 65 C2d 88, 52 CR 460); and

(2) An action by parents to recover out-of-pocket damages for personal injuries sustained by their child and an action for wrongful death of the child arising from the same wrongful act or neglect (CCP §376).

When both an injured employee and his employer bring separate actions against a third party tortfeasor under workers' compensation laws, the actions must be consolidated. Lab C §3853.

Consolidation in Court's Discretion. The court may order consolidation in actions or proceedings:

(a) For suspension or revocation of a contractor's license in any action involving performance of his legal obligation as a contractor (Bus & P C §7106);

(b) To foreclose loggers' liens (CC §3065a);

(c) By different claimants to foreclose mechanics' liens on the same property (CC §3149);

(d) By persons who have given stop notices on private works of improvement (CC §3175);

(e) To condemn under eminent domain separate parcels of land lying in the same county and required for the same project (CC §1250.24);

(f) By two or more dissenting shareholders against a corporation (Corp C §4307);

(g) By producers against processors to foreclose liens on farm products (Food & A C §55653);

(h) To quiet title to all realty sold to the state for taxes in any county in the same year (Rev & T C §3596);

(i) To recover assessments levied under the Improvement Act of 1911 (Str & H C §5414).

§27.5   b. Severance

Although CCP §1048(b) permits the court to sever actions or issues in its discretion (see §27.3), that authority does not affect other statutes that authorize severance in particular situations. See Comment to CCP §1048. For example, the court may order severance:

(1) In actions against several defendants the court may, whenever a several judgment is proper, render judgment against one or more of them, and allow the action to proceed against the others (CCP §579);

(2) When a defendant, in his answer, raises a statute of limitations defense or other special defense not addressed to the merits, the court may, on motion, order trial of those issues before any other issue (CCP §597). See also CCP §597.5, which requires the court, on motion of either party, to sever special defenses raised in medical malpractice cases; and

(3) To promote convenience of witnesses or the ends of justice, the court may, on motion, order that any issue precede trial of any other issue except special defenses (CCP §598; effective

January 1, 1978. Formerly this provision authorized severance only of the liability issue). But it is an abuse of discretion to sever liability from damages when damages must be proved in order to establish liability. *Cohn v Bugas* (1974) 42 CA3d 381, 116 CR 810. Motions under CCP §598 are frequently made by defendants whenever there is the possibility of plaintiff bootstrapping his way to a favorable verdict (*e.g.*, a personal injury case with weak liability but severe injuries).

On the judicial attitude towards motions for severance generally, see §27.9.

§27.6   C. Consolidation of Actions or Issues Under CCP §1048(a)

Under CCP §1048(a), a court may consolidate for trial entire causes of action or particular issues. The court may order a complete consolidation when parties to two or more actions are the same, or substantially the same, and the causes of action could have been joined. The separate actions then become a single action with one action number (the earlier one), separate pleadings are treated as one set, and a single verdict or judgment is given. *Bank of Cal. v Connolly* (1973) 36 CA3d 350, 111 CR 468. The actions are viewed as if the same plaintiff or plaintiffs had in a single complaint joined all causes of action against the same defendant or defendants. See 3 Witkin, CALIFORNIA PROCEDURE, Pleading §260 (2d ed 1971).

When issues are similar, and the evidence would be substantially the same in two or more actions, the court may consolidate the actions for trial or order a joint hearing of the common issues, even though the parties are not the same and the causes of action could not have been joined. In either situation, the cases maintain their separate identities and case numbers, evidence particular to each case will be restricted to that case, the pleadings will be considered separately, and the verdicts, findings, and judgments will be separate. 3 Witkin, *Procedure,* Pleading §261. On consolidation procedures, see §§27.13–27.16.

§27.7   D. Severance of Actions or Issues Under CCP §1048(b)

Under CCP §1048(b), a court may sever for trial causes of action, including those asserted by cross-complaint, or issues. When causes of action are severed, it is immaterial whether they were joined in the complaint by one or more plaintiffs or were originally separate actions that were ordered consolidated by the court (see *Seidell v Tuxedo Land Co.* (1934) 1 CA2d 406, 36 P2d 1102).

Severance of a cause of action results in division of the action into two or more actions that are then prosecuted separately. The court may even order one action transferred to a different court, while retaining jurisdiction over the other. *Omni Aviation Managers, Inc. v Municipal Court* (1976) 60 CA3d 682, 131 CR 758.

Unlike the effect of severing causes of action, severed issues are tried separately, but the action remains essentially intact. See, *e.g.*, CCP §598, discussed in §27.5. On procedures, see §§27.17–27.20.

II. DECIDING WHETHER TO SEEK CONSOLIDATION OR SEVERANCE
A. Judicial Attitude

§27.8   1. Consolidation

Most courts, especially those with extremely full calendars, ordinarily favor consolidation or a joint trial of issues, provided that consolidation will serve the statutory ends of avoiding unnecessary costs or delay in the trial of cases having common questions of law or fact (see CCP §1048(a)), by promoting trial convenience and economy by eliminating duplication in proof of common issues (*McClure v Donovan* (1949) 33 C3d 717, 205 P2d 17). However, a court will not automatically order consolidation simply because common questions of law or fact are present. See §27.11 for discussion of factors the court will consider.

§27.9   2. Severance

Because courts do not favor the piecemeal trial of issues and actions, they frequently are reluctant to order severance. Most courts will not do so unless the motion clearly demonstrates that the purposes of CCP §1048(b) (see §27.3) will be promoted by granting the motion. For examples, and discussion of factors the court will consider, see §27.12.

§27.10   B. Other Consolidation Procedures Compared

In deciding whether to seek consolidation or severance in a particular case, the attorney should consider, in addition to the judicial attitude discussed in §27.8, whether consolidation can best be achieved by other means. Other statutorily authorized procedures that achieve the same result as consolidation, *i.e.*, a joint trial of similar issues or causes of action, include:

(1) *Cross-complaint* under CCP §§428.10–428.80, which is in effect a consolidation of defendant's cause of action with that of plaintiff (under CCP §§426.10–426.40, a cross-complaint usually is compulsory when defendant's action is founded on the same transaction or occurrence as plaintiff's action). See generally 1 CALIFORNIA CIVIL PROCEDURE BEFORE TRIAL chap 12 (Cal CEB 1977);

(2) *Interpleader* under CCP §386, which permits a party defendant in effect to consolidate any conflicting multiple actions that might be brought against him. See generally 1 CIV PROC BEFORE TRIAL chap 20.

(3) *Permissive joinder of parties* under CCP §§378–379, which permits joinder in a single action of all persons asserting or defending against (a) a joint, several, or alternative right to relief arising out of the same transaction or occurrence, and presenting a common question of law or fact, or (b) a claim, right, or interest adverse to them in the subject property or controversy (in such situations the court may, under either CCP §379.5 or CCP §1048(b), order separate trials or make other orders to prevent injustice);

(4) *Abatement,* under which a court may abate, dismiss, or transfer an action involving the same subject matter as another action filed earlier in the same or a different court (see 1 Witkin, CALIFORNIA PROCEDURE, Jurisdiction §§290–291 (2d ed 1970)); and

(5) *Coordination* under CCP §§404–404.8 and Cal Rules of Ct 1501–1550, which although similar to abatement, is designed to handle multiple conflicting or overlapping claims sharing common questions of law or fact efficiently and at less expense to the court and parties (see CCP §404.1). Unlike consolidation (see §27.1), coordination is not limited to actions pending in the same court. CCP §404. On coordination procedures, see generally chap 28.

C. Court's Discretion; Factors Considered
§27.11   1. Consolidation

The trial court has broad discretion to decide whether consolidation under CCP §1048(a) is desirable (but see §27.4 for statutes providing for mandatory consolidation), and the appellate courts will usually uphold the trial court's decision. See *National Elec. Supply Co. v Mount Diablo Unified School Dist.* (1960) 187 CA2d 418, 9 CR 864. The trial court may even vacate a prior order severing the cases for trial, and may order consolidation, if, based on the facts after the pleadings have closed, consolidation seems appropriate. *Vegetable Oil Prods. Co. v Superior Court* (1963) 213 CA2d 252, 28 CR 555.

Although courts generally favor consolidation (see §27.8), the presence of common questions of law or fact alone will not always result in consolidation. In making its decision, the court weighs the factors favoring consolidation against those opposing it. Factors favoring consolidation include (a) the number of common questions of law and fact at issue (generally, the greater the number, the greater the likelihood of consolidation), (b) whether consolidation would save trial time and expense, (c) the general convenience to the parties and the court in avoiding repetition of procedures and duplication of evidence, and (d) the unfairness to the parties that might result from requiring the defense of multiple actions. Factors opposing consolidation include (i) inconvenience, (ii) prejudice to a party, (iii) whether consolidation would consume additional trial time and expense, (iv) the complexity of the issues, (v) the possible likelihood of confusing the jury, and (vi) the right of each party to a jury trial.

Because a decision to consolidate made near the time of trial probably would require the court to continue the case, the court would also have to weigh the continuance factors (see §26.95) as well as consolidation factors before making its decision.

§27.12   2. Severance

As with a motion to consolidate (see §27.11), a trial court's decision to sever ordinarily is discretionary, and the decision of the trial court is normally upheld. *Carpenson v Najarian* (1967) 254 CA2d 856, 62 CR 687. The trial court also has discretion to vacate a prior consolidation order and to order severance. *Seidell v Tuxedo Land Co.* (1934) 1 CA2d 406, 36 P2d 1102. An exception to the general rule of court discretion occurs when severance is required by statute. See, *e.g.*, CCP §597.5, discussed in §27.5.

Because the courts do not favor piecemeal trial of issues and actions, most will order severance only when they believe it will achieve the purposes of the statute on which the motion is based.

In deciding whether to sever, the court weighs the factors set forth in that statute, *e.g.*, whether separate trials will best serve the convenience of parties and the court, avoid prejudice, and minimize expense and delay (CCP §1048(b)). When trial of a relatively simple issue could be dispositive of the case, *e.g.*, a statute of limitations defense under CCP §597, a separate trial of that issue is usually desirable. However, when trial of the action or issue sought to be severed will involve extensive proof, and substantially the same facts as the other issues, or if savings in time and expense are speculative, a separate trial usually will be denied. Many courts, for example, feel that granting a motion by defendant under CCP §598 to try the issue of liability before all other issues except special defenses (see §27.5) results in little savings of time, and will grant the motion only when it appears that plaintiff's case on liability is very weak.

Another factor courts consider is whether, when severance is requested in a jury trial, the remaining issues or actions can be tried with minimal delay. If tried before the same jury, there will be a lag in use of court time between submission of the first issue or action and trial of the remaining issues or actions. The jury might deliberate for several days, and the parties may need additional time after a verdict to discuss settlement or to subpena witnesses. Use of a different jury eliminates this lag, because the court can hear another matter while the jury is deliberating, and, when a verdict is reached, can set the rest of the case for trial on a later date.

III. PROCEDURES

A. For Consolidation

§27.13   1. Noticed Motion

The procedure for obtaining an order of consolidation is not specified in CCP §1048(a) or any other statute. Although consolidation may be effected by stipulation between the parties, or on the court's own motion (see *McClure v Donovan* (1949) 33 C2d 717, 205 P2d 17), the commonly accepted method is by noticed motion, which should be made as soon as practicable after the cases are at issue.

The motion should be supported by points and authorities and by a declaration under penalty of perjury setting forth the facts in support of the grounds for consolidation, *e.g.*, that different actions involving a common question of law or fact are pending before the court or, in specific statutes (see §27.4), that the facts of each case bring them within the statute. For a form of motion, see §27.14. On the effect of failure to include a memorandum of points and authorities, see §23.26.

§27.14   2. Form: Notice of Motion To Consolidate Actions or Issues

Copies: Original (filed with court clerk with proof of service); duplicate original for filing in each action to be consolidated; copies for service (one for each attorney of record and unrepresented party); office copies.

[Caption. See §§23.18–23.19. Add case title and number for each case to be consolidated]

No. _____
NOTICE OF MOTION TO CONSOLIDATE ____[ACTIONS / ISSUES]____ FOR TRIAL (CCP §1048(a)); POINTS AND AUTHORITIES; DECLARATION

To each party and attorney of record:
   PLEASE TAKE NOTICE that on _____, 19____, at _____.m., or as soon thereafter as the matter can be heard, in ____[e.g., Department No. ____]____ at ____[address]____, **California,** ____[name of moving party]____ **will move the Court for an order that the above-captioned actions be consolidated** ____[for trial of following issue(s):_ _____]____.
   This motion is made under Code of Civil Procedure section 1048(a) on the grounds that ____[both / all]____ actions are pending before this Court, and involve common questions of law or fact in that ____[specify]____, and that consolidation will avoid unnecessary costs or delay.
   This motion is based on this notice, the pleadings, records, and files in this action, the attached memorandum of points and authorities, the attached supporting declaration of _____, and on such evidence as may be presented at the hearing.
   Dated: _____

[Signature of attorney]

[Typed name]
Attorney for ____[name]____

Comment: This form may be adapted for use when consolidation is based on a statute other than CCP §1048(a) (see §27.4). On the content and time for motion, see §27.13. For discussion of form and format for points and authorities, see §§23.26–23.35.

§27.15 3. Form: Declaration in Support of Motion To Consolidate

Copies: Original (filed with court clerk with proof of service); duplicate original for filing in each action consolidated; copies for service (one for each attorney of record and unrepresented party); office copies.

[Caption. See §§23.18–23.19. Add case title and number for each case to be consolidated]

No. _____

DECLARATION IN SUPPORT OF MOTION TO CONSOLIDATE ____[ACTIONS / ISSUES]____ FOR TRIAL

____[Name]____ **declares:**
　1. **I am** ____[e.g., attorney for _____]____.
　　　[Set forth facts showing that consolidation is proper, e.g.]
　2. **Plaintiffs in actions numbered _____ and _____ were passengers in the automobile that collided with defendant's automobile on _____, 19____, in _____, California, and the primary issue in each action is the liability for the collision.**
　3. **Defendant in each action is the same person, and consolidation will avoid unnecessary delay and costs in that the same witnesses will be called in each action to testify on the issue of liability.**

[Continue]

I declare under penalty of perjury that the foregoing is true and correct, and that this declaration was executed on _____, 19____, at _____, California.

[Signature of declarant]

[Typed name]

§27.16 4. Form: Order for Consolidation

Copies: Original (filed with court clerk with proof of service); duplicate original for filing in each action to be consolidated; copies for service (one for each attorney of record and unrepresented party); office copies.

[Caption. See §§23.18–23.19. Add case title and number for each case to be consolidated]

No _____

ORDER FOR CONSOLIDATION OF ____[ACTIONS / ISSUES]____

The motion of ____[name]____ for an order consolidating ____[issues in]____ the above-captioned actions was regularly heard on _____, 19____. ____[Name]____ appeared as attorney for moving party and ____[name]____ appeared as attorney for responding party. On proof being made to the satis-

faction of the Court that the above-captioned actions pending in this Court involve a common question of ____[law / fact / law and fact]____, and that consolidation will avoid unnecessary ____[costs / delay / costs and delay]____, and good cause appearing
IT IS ORDERED that:

[*When actions are consolidated*]

1. Action No. _____ is consolidated with Action No. _____ for all purposes.

[*When issues of law or fact consolidated for trial*]

1. Action No. _____ is consolidated with Action No. _____ for the purpose of trying the issue(s) of ____[specify]____.

[*Continue with additional orders to implement consolidation, e.g.*]

2. A copy of this order shall be filed in both actions but all further pleadings and papers shall be filed only in Action No. _____, which shall be entitled _____ v _____.

3. In lieu of filing an answer to the complaint in Action No. _____, each allegation of that complaint is considered denied by defendant.

Dated: _____

                          Judge

Comment: The order should set forth each ruling made to implement the order of consolidation. See CCP §1048(a) ("and it may make such orders concerning proceedings therein as may tend to avoid unnecessary costs or delay"). To aid the parties, the order should specify what is to be done procedurally to effect consolidation.

B. For Severance

§27.17   1. Noticed Motion

Although CCP §1048(b) contains no specific procedures for making a motion to sever and by implication permits a court to order severance on its own motion, the general practice is to file a noticed motion. See also CCP §§597, 597.5, 598, discussed in §27.5, which authorize or require severance "on motion." Most courts do not favor informal severance motions, *e.g.*, by request at the pretrial or trial setting conference, and this procedure is not recommended. The motion may be set for hearing in the usual manner (see CCP §§1005, 1010–1013a, discussed in §§23.9–23.10, which generally require that notice be given at least ten days before the hearing, with additional time if the notice is served by mailing), or it may be heard at the pretrial or trial setting conference.

Other statutes authorizing severance in particular situations may establish a particular procedure for making a motion. See statutes discussed in §27.5. For example, under CCP §598, which authorizes severance and trial of any issue or part of an issue before trial of any other issue, severance is initiated on noticed motion made no later than the close of the pretrial conference, or, in cases that are not pretried, no later than 30 days before the trial date.

For a form for notice of motion, see §27.18.

§27.18   2. Form: Notice of Motion To Sever Actions or Issues

Copies: Original (filed with court clerk with proof of service); copies for service (one for each attorney of record and unrepresented party); office copies.

[*Caption. See §§23.18 – 23.19*]

No. _____

NOTICE OF MOTION TO SEVER AND TRY SEPARATELY THE ____*[e.g., CAUSE OF ACTION FOR DECLARATORY RELIEF STATED IN THE CROSS-COMPLAINT FROM ALL OTHER CAUSES OF ACTION (CCP §1048(b) / DEFENSE OF STATUTE OF LIMITATIONS (CCP §597) / ISSUE OF LIABILITY (CCP §598)]*____; **POINTS AND AUTHORITIES; DECLARATION**

To each party and attorney of record:
      PLEASE TAKE NOTICE that on _____, **19**____, **at** _____.**m., or as soon thereafter as the matter can be heard, in** ____*[e.g., Department No.* ____]____ **at** ____*[address]*____, **California,** ____*[name of moving party]*____ **will move the Court for an order that** ____*[e.g., the first cause of action of the cross-complaint for declaratory relief be severed from and tried before all other causes of action / the special defense of statute of limitations be severed from and tried before all other issues / the issue of liability be severed from and tried before the issue of damages]*____.
      This motion is made under ____*[e.g., Code of Civil Procedure section 1048(b) / Code of Civil Procedure section 597 / Code of Civil Procedure section 598]*____ **on the grounds that**

[When severance from cross-complaint]

trial on the declaratory relief action will be conducive to expedition and economy, since findings in the declaratory relief action will substantially resolve all issues in the other causes of action.

[When severance of statute of limitations]

the statute of limitations defense may be tried on facts totally different from the merits; trial of this defense will be relatively short as compared to trial on the merits; and if trial on the statute of limitations defense is resolved in favor of defendant, will save time and money.

[When severance of liability issue]

the convenience of witnesses and the ends of justice will be promoted by severance, in that the liability issue can be tried in substantially less time than the more complex damages issue, and probably will be resolved against plaintiff.

[Continue]

This motion is based on this notice, the pleadings, records, and files in this action, the attached memorandum of points and authorities, the attached supporting declaration of _____, and on such evidence as may be presented at the hearing.

Dated: _____

[Signature of attorney]

[Typed name]
Attorney for ____*[name]*____

Comment: The motion for severance should set forth facts that bring it within the particular statute on which it is based (see §§27.3, 27.5), and should be accompanied by a supporting declaration under penalty of perjury and by a memorandum of points and authorities. See §23.26 on the effect of failure to include points and authorities. The supporting declaration usually is made by the attorney. The content of the declaration varies depending on the grounds for the motion, but should generally contain facts showing that severance will be expeditious and economical, and in the interest of justice. For a form that may be adapted, see §27.15.

§27.19   3. Form: Order Severing Actions or Issues

Copies: Original (filed with court clerk with proof of service); copies for service (one for each attorney of record and unrepresented party); office copies.

[Caption. See §§23.18–23.19]

No. _____

ORDER OF SEVERANCE

The motion of ____[name]____ **for an order that** ____[e.g., the first cause of action of the cross-complaint for declaratory relief be severed from and tried before all other causes of action / the special defense of statute of limitations be severed from and tried before all other issues / the issue of liability be severed from and tried before the issue of damages]____ **was regularly heard on** _____, 19____. ____[Name]____ **appeared as attorney for moving party, and** ____ [name]____ **appeared as attorney for responding party. On proof being made to the satisfaction of the Court, the Court finds that severance will** ____[e.g., be in furtherance of convenience / avoid prejudice / be conducive to expedition and economy / promote the convenience of witnesses and the ends of justice]____.
Good cause appearing

IT IS ORDERED that ____[e.g., the first cause of action of the cross-complaint for declaratory relief be severed from and tried before all other causes of action / the special defense of statute of limitations be severed from and tried before all other issues / the issue of liability be severed from and tried before the issue of damages]____.

IT IS FURTHER ORDERED that ____[specify additional orders that implement severance order]____.

Dated: _____

Judge

Comment: The order of severance should provide for how the case is to be handled after severance. For example, when the issue of liability is tried first in a jury trial, the order should state whether the remaining issues should be tried before the same jury. See §27.20.

§27.20 4. Procedure After Trial of Severed Issues

If, after severance, the court's decision or the jury verdict on the severed issue is in favor of the party on whom liability is sought to be imposed (*e.g.*, a finding in favor of defendant on the issue of liability), judgment in favor of such party is entered, and the remaining issues will not be tried against that party unless judgment is reversed or otherwise set aside. CCP §598. When the court's decision or a jury verdict is against a party on whom liability is sought to be imposed, trial of the other issues must take place at the time ordered by the court on its own motion, or on motion of any party. Judgment is not entered until after a verdict or decision is rendered on the last issue. CCP §598. See also Cal Rules of Ct 232.5. A similar procedure is established by CCP §597 when the severed issue is a special defense.

A motion for a new trial following a severed trial must be made after all issues are tried. If the issues were tried before different judges, each judge must hear and determine the motion as to the issues tried before him. Cal Rules of Ct 232.5. Although rule 232.5 governs only nonjury trials, courts follow the same practice in jury trials.

§27.21   C. Review of Orders

An order granting or denying a motion to consolidate or sever is not directly appealable (CCP §§904.1–904.2), but is reviewable only on appeal from a subsequent judgment. A more effective remedy is a petition for writ of mandate. *State Farm Mut. Auto. Ins. Co. v Superior Court* (1956) 47 C2d 428, 304 P2d 13.

On review, the appellate court will not reverse the order unless the trial court clearly abused its discretion. On the discretionary nature of court orders regarding consolidation and severance, see §§27.11–27.12.

WILLIAM H. LEVIT
ALEXANDER B. YAKUTIS

Chapter 28
Coordination

I. INTRODUCTION
   A. Scope of Chapter §28.1
   B. Applicable Statutes and California Rules of Court §28.2
   C. Applicable Local Rules §28.3
   D. Nature of Proceeding; Definitions §28.4
   E. When Coordination Is Appropriate §28.5
   F. Types of Actions Coordinated §28.6

II. TRANSMITTAL AND SERVICE OF PAPERS DURING PENDENCY OF COORDINATION PROCEEDING
   A. Papers To Be Sent to Assigned Judge; Preparation §28.7
   B. Papers To Be Sent to Chairperson of Judicial Council §28.8
   C. Preparation of Papers; Service on Parties §28.9

III. MOTION TO COMMENCE COORDINATION
   A. When Motion to Presiding Judge Required §28.10
   B. Moving Papers; Content §28.11
   C. Authority of Presiding Judge at Hearing §28.12
   D. Forms
      1. Notice of Motion for Order That Petition for Coordination Be Transmitted §28.13
      2. Order That Petition for Coordination Be Transmitted §28.14

IV. PETITION FOR COORDINATION
   A. Petitioning Papers
      1. Petition and Supporting Documents §28.15
      2. Proof of Filing and Service §28.16
   B. Notice of Submission of Petition for Coordination §28.17
   C. Timing and Transmittal of Petition §28.18
   D. Forms
      1. Petition for Coordination §28.19
      2. Notice of Submission of Petition for Coordination §28.20

WILLIAM H. LEVIT, A.B., 1928, Stanford University; J.D., 1930, Stanford Law School. Mr. Levit was Judge of the Superior Court (1962–1976, retired).

ALEXANDER B. YAKUTIS, J.D., 1956, Hastings College of the Law. Mr. Yakutis is the attorney for the Judicial Council, Administrative Office of the Courts, San Francisco.

CEB attorney-editor was CAROL C. BROSNAHAN.

- E. Procedures After Petition Filed
    1. Coordination Motion Judge Assigned; Proceeding Given Special Title and Number §28.21
    2. Service of Assignment Order; Stay of Trials §28.22
    3. Review by Coordination Motion Judge of Notice to Parties §28.23
    4. Application for Stay Order
        a. Timing and Contents of Application §28.24
        b. Timing and Contents of Opposition Papers §28.25
        c. Authority of Coordination Motion Judge §28.26
        d. Effect and Duration of Stay Order §28.27
        e. Form: Order Staying Action §28.28
    5. Response to Petition
        a. Party Opposition or Support §28.29
        b. Forms
            (1) Statement in Opposition to Petition for Coordination §28.30
            (2) Statement in Support of Petition for Coordination §28.31
    6. Hearing on Petition
        a. When Hearing Required; Who May Appear §28.32
        b. Coordination Motion Judge Sets Hearing and Determines Issues To Be Heard §28.33
        c. Presentation of Evidence at Hearing §28.34
        d. Orders After Hearing
            (1) Order Granting Petition and Selecting Reviewing Court §28.35
            (2) Order Granting Coordination in Part §28.36
            (3) Order Denying Coordination §28.37
    7. Report When Coordination Determination Delayed §28.38

V. PRETRIAL PROCEDURES AFTER COORDINATION ORDERED

- A. Service and Filing of Coordination Order; Automatic Stay of Proceedings §28.39
- B. Assignment of Coordination Trial Judge; Designation of Service Address
    1. Assignment Order. Contents, Filing, and Service of Papers §28.40
    2. Challenges to Assignment §28.41
    3. Powers of Coordination Trial Judge §28.42
- C. Preliminary Trial Conference
    1. Timing; Role of Counsel §28.43
    2. Matters for Discussion and Determination at Conference
        a. Appointment and Role of Liaison Counsel §28.44
        b. Establishment of Pretrial Proceedings Schedule §28.45
    3. Forms
        a. Proposed Order Setting Preliminary Trial Conference §28.46
        b. Preliminary Trial Conference Order §28.47

- D. Motion for Transfer of Action
  1. Transfer on Motion of Party or Court's Own Motion §28.48
  2. Objections and Hearing §28.49
  3. Contents of Transfer Order §28.50
  4. Form: Order of Transfer on Motion of Party §28.51
- VI. PETITION TO COORDINATE AN ADD-ON CASE
  - A. Who Petitions; Grounds §28.52
  - B. Procedure
    1. Petition and Opposition §28.53
    2. Hearing and Order §28.54
- VII. EFFECT OF DENIAL OF COORDINATION §28.55
- VIII. REVIEW OF COORDINATION ORDERS §28.56

I. INTRODUCTION

§28.1　A. Scope of Chapter

Coordination of civil actions sharing a common question of fact or law and pending in different California courts has been possible in California since January 1, 1974, the operative date of CCP §§404–404.8 (the coordination statute) and Cal Rules of Ct 1501–1550 adopted under the authority of CCP §404.7. Although the California statute, unlike the federal statute (28 USC §1407) sets forth a coordination procedure for both pretrial and trial, this chapter deals only with the procedures for initiating coordination of the actions and pretrial procedures after coordination has been ordered.

§28.2　B. Applicable Statutes and California Rules of Court

Code of Civil Procedure §§404–404.8 provide general authority for coordination and establish the broad parameters of the procedure to be followed. California Rules of Court 1501–1550 set forth the specific practice and procedures.

The California constitution empowers the Judicial Council to adopt rules for court administration, practice and procedure, not inconsistent with statute. Cal Const art VI, §6. The coordination statute authorizes the Judicial Council to provide by rule the practice and procedure for coordination of civil actions "not withstanding any other provision of law." CCP §404.7. This is the same plenary grant of power extended to the Judicial Council in the formulation of rules under the Family Law Act (CC §§4000–5174), the practical effect of which is to remove any restraints of statutory consistency on the Judicial Council's rules of practice and procedures. CC §4001. *Marriage of McKim* (1972) 6 C3d 673, 678 n4, 100 CR 140, 142 n4. The coordination rules state expressly that to the extent they conflict with provisions of law applicable to civil actions generally, the coordination rules prevail. Cal Rules of Ct 1504(a).

If the prescribed manner of proceeding cannot, with reasonable diligence, be followed in a particular proceeding, the assigned judge may establish any manner of proceeding that appears to conform best to the statutes and rules. Cal Rules of Ct 1504(a), (b).

§28.3 C. Applicable Local Rules

When a judge is assigned by the chairperson of the Judicial Council to handle a coordination proceeding, that judge must specify any local rules to be followed. The local rules of the court designated in the order appointing the assigned judge apply unless the assigned judge specifies differently or Cal Rules of Ct 1501–1550 provide otherwise. Cal Rules of Ct 1504(c).

§28.4 D. Nature of Proceeding; Definitions

On petition, the Chief Justice, acting as chairperson of the Judicial Council, will assign a judge to determine whether coordination is appropriate and, if that judge orders coordination, the chairperson will assign a judge to exercise all the powers over each coordinated action that could be exercised by a judge of the court in which that action is pending. Cal Const art VI, §6; CCP §404; Cal Rules of Ct 1540. A "coordinated action" means any action ordered coordinated with one or more other actions after petition. Cal Rules of Ct 1501(e). "Included action" means any action or proceeding included in the petition. Cal Rules of Ct 1501(k). The judge assigned to determine whether coordination is appropriate is denominated the "coordination motion judge." Cal Rules of Ct 1501(g). If the coordination motion judge decides that coordination is appropriate, a judge is assigned to hear and determine the coordinated actions. That judge is denominated the "coordination trial judge." Cal Rules of Ct 1501(i). Each is denominated "assigned judge." Cal Rules of Ct 1501(c).

§28.5 E. When Coordination Is Appropriate

A petition for coordination requests a determination whether coordination of civil actions sharing a common question of fact or law and pending in different California courts is appropriate. CCP §404; see Cal Rules of Ct 1501(n), 1521(a). Coordination of civil actions sharing a common question of fact or law is appropriate if the ends of justice will be promoted by one judge hearing all the actions for all purposes in a selected site or sites. The decision on appropriateness must take into account (1) whether the common question of fact or law predominates and is significant to the litigation; (2) convenience of parties, witnesses, and counsel; (3) relative development of the actions and the work product of counsel; (4) efficient utilization of judicial facilities and manpower; (5) court calendars; (6) disadvantages of duplicative and inconsistent rulings, orders, or judgments; and (7) the likelihood of settlement without further litigation if coordination is denied. CCP §404.1.

§28.6 F. Types of Actions Coordinated

According to statistics published in the 1976 and 1977 Annual Reports of the Administrative Office of the Courts, during the first three years that the coordination statute and rules of court have been in effect, 280 petitions for coordination were received by the chairperson of the Judicial Council. Analysis by subject matter, described in a general way, indicates that the largest number of petitions arose from personal injury litigation, *e.g.*, airplane crashes (134 petitions) followed in frequency by commercial disputes (42), real property actions (38), multiparty claims in construction and subdivision projects (33), public law questions (12), fire casualties (11), miscellaneous torts (8), and family law applications (2). A total of 983 actions were included in the petitions, of which 227 included actions pending in a municipal court.

II. TRANSMITTAL AND SERVICE OF PAPERS DURING PENDENCY OF COORDINATION PROCEEDING

§28.7 A. Papers To Be Sent to Assigned Judge; Preparation

Unless the assigned judge orders otherwise, routine filings in cases that have been made the subject of coordination proceedings continue to be made as if no such proceeding were pending, except that copies of all filings are sent to the assigned judge at the address specified in the assignment order. See Cal Rules of Ct 1501(q), 1524, 1529; see 1504(a), 1510. Until there is an assigned judge, these filings are transmitted to the chairperson of the Judicial Council. Cal Rules of Ct 1501(q).

For a discussion of who prepares the papers, see §28.9.

§28.8   B. Papers To Be Sent to Chairperson of Judicial Council

A copy of the following papers must be transmitted in duplicate to the chairperson of the Judicial Council when they are filed unless one copy is transmitted together with proof that the original or a copy has been submitted to the assigned judge (Cal Rules of Ct 1511).

(1) Petition for coordination;
(2) Notice of submission of petition for coordination;
(3) Notice of opposition;
(4) Application for stay order;
(5) Stay order;
(6) Notice of hearing on petition;
(7) Order granting or denying coordination;
(8) Order of remand;
(9) Order of transfer; and
(10) Orders terminating a coordination proceeding in whole or in part.

All papers submitted to the chairperson of the Judicial Council are sent to (Cal Rules of Ct 1511):

Administrative Office of the Courts,
c/o Coordination Attorney,
4200 State Building,
San Francisco, California 94102

For a discussion of who prepares the papers, see §28.9.

§28.9   C. Preparation of Papers; Service on Parties

Certain filings are always prepared by counsel, and counsel are responsible for filing and service, *e.g.*, petition, notice of submission. See §§28.15–28.19. Orders of the court (*e.g.*, order setting preliminary trial conference (see §28.48), order of transfer (see §28.52)), may be served by the court clerk. In the case of other orders (*e.g.*, order granting coordination), the court may issue a minute order and instruct counsel to prepare the formal order and effect service.

Unless the coordination rules otherwise provide, all filed papers must be accompanied by proof of prior service on all other parties to the coordination proceeding, including all parties appearing in all included actions and coordinated actions. Service and proof of service is made as required for civil actions generally. Cal Rules of Ct 1510.

If any defendant is not served with a copy of the summons and of the complaint, or if any party is not served with any other paper or order as required by these rules, coordination of the actions is not precluded, but that defendant or party may assert the failure of service as a basis for appropriate relief. Cal Rules of Ct 1510.

III. MOTION TO COMMENCE COORDINATION

§28.10   A. When Motion to Presiding Judge Required

In most cases, the coordination proceeding can be begun by petition directly to the Chairperson of the Judicial Council. See §28.15. Only rarely, when there are multiple parties plaintiff or parties defendant in the action that is the vehicle for coordination, and disagreement among coparties plaintiff or defendant in any one case on whether a petition for coordination should be filed, must the party seeking coordination first move the presiding judge for an order commencing the coordination proceeding. Code of Civil Procedure §404 provides that "the presiding judge . . . on his own motion or the motion of any party or all the parties plaintiff or defendant . . ." may request a coordination determination. See Cal Rules of Ct 1520. This motion may also contain a request to the court to stay all related actions pending in that court for a reasonable time (not exceeding 30 days) to allow any party to petition for coordination. Cal Rules of Ct 1520.

§28.11   B. Moving Papers; Content

A motion for commencement of a coordination proceeding directed to the presiding judge is made in the manner provided for motions in civil actions generally. Cal Rules of Ct 1520. On motion practice generally, see chap 23. The motion must state by affidavit the matters required in a petition for coordination. Cal Rules of Ct 1520(u). Code of Civil Procedure §2015.5 permits a declaration under penalty of perjury to be used in California whenever an affidavit is called for. This requirement is usually met by attaching a petition and affidavit to the motion. A supporting memorandum of points and authorities must also be presented. Cal Rules of Ct 1521(a).

If a stay is requested, the affidavits must show that the stay will promote the ends of justice, with the court considering the imminence of any trial or other proceeding that might materially affect the status of the action to be stayed, and whether a final judgment in that action would have a res judicata or collateral estoppel effect with regard to any common issue of the included actions. Cal Rules of Ct 1514(e).

§28.12 C. Authority of Presiding Judge at Hearing

The presiding judge who hears the motion to commence coordination does not determine the appropriateness of coordination, because that power is expressly conferred on the coordination motion judge. CCP §§404, 404.3; Cal Rules of Ct 1521(a), 1527–1529. For a definition of "coordination motion judge," see §28.4. In ruling on the motion to commence coordination proceedings, the judge may consider only preliminary matters, e. g., whether the motion is made for improper purposes such as oppression or delay and whether the papers are technically sufficient. The court, however, may stay all related actions pending in that court for up to 30 days to allow a party to petition for a coordination, if it determines that the ends of justice will be promoted by the stay. Cal Rules of Ct 1514(e), 1520.

D. Forms

§28.13 1. Notice of Motion for Order That Petition for Coordination Be Transmitted

Copies: Original (filed with court clerk with proof of service); copies for filing (one to be filed in each court in which an action sought to be included in the coordination proceeding is pending (not mandatory, but advisable)); copies for service (one for each attorney of record and unrepresented party in action used as vehicle for coordination); office copies.

[Title of Court Where
Moving Party's Case Pending]

[Title of moving
party's case]

No. _____

NOTICE OF MOTION FOR ORDER THAT PETITION FOR COORDINATION BE TRANSMITTED TO CHAIRPERSON OF JUDICIAL COUNCIL ____[AND FOR ORDER STAYING RELATED ACTION(S)]____; **POINTS AND AUTHORITIES; DECLARATIONS**

To all parties and their attorneys:

[List all actions sought to be included in coordination proceeding]

    PLEASE TAKE NOTICE that on ____ 19____, at or after _____.m., in ____[e.g., Department No. _____]____ at ____[address]____, **California,** ____[plaintiff / defendant]____ ____[name]____ **will move the Presiding Judge for an order that a petition be transmitted to the Chairperson of the Judicial Council that a judge be assigned to determine whether the coordination of this action with certain other actions included in the petition for coordination is appropriate** ____[and for an order staying this and all such actions for ____[e.g., 30]____ days]____.

This motion will be made under Code of Civil Procedure section 404 and on the grounds set forth in Code of Civil Procedure section 404.1,

[When stay requested]

and on the ground that a stay of ____[list proceedings]____ will promote the ends of justice because _____.

This motion will be based on all pleadings, papers, and records in this action, on the attached petition for coordination, declaration, and memorandum of points and authorities.

Dated: _____

    [Signature of attorney]
    _____
    [Typed name]
    Attorney for _____

§28.14   COORDINATION

§28.14   2. Order That Petition for Coordination Be Transmitted

Copies: Original (filed with court clerk with proof of service); copies for filing (one to be filed in each court in which an action sought to be included in the coordination proceeding is pending (not mandatory, but advisable)); copies for service (one for each attorney of record and unrepresented party in the action used as vehicle for coordination); office copies.

[Title of Court Where Moving
Party's Case Pending]

[Title of moving
party's case]

No. _____

ORDER THAT PETITION FOR COORDINATION BE TRANSMITTED TO CHAIRPERSON OF JUDICIAL COUNCIL ____[AND THAT RELATED ACTION(S) BE STAYED]____; POINTS AND AUTHORITIES; DECLARATION

The motion of ____[name]____ for an order that a petition for coordination be transmitted to the Chairperson of Judicial Council ____[and that certain actions be stayed until a determination is made on that petition]____ came on regularly for hearing on ____[date]____.

Appearing as attorneys were _____.

Satisfactory proof having been made, and good cause appearing, ____[and this court finding that, e.g., a stay of proceedings will promote the ends of justice]____,

IT IS ORDERED that:

1. On compliance by moving party with California Rules of Court 1521(b), 1522, and 1523, the moving party may transmit an original and a duplicate copy of the petition for coordination, accompanied by proof of filing and service to the Chairperson of the Judicial Council.

[When stay is issued]

2. The following proceedings are stayed for a period of _____ days: ____[List stayed proceedings]____.

Dated: _____

_____
Presiding Judge

Comment: See §§28.15–28.20 for discussion of what constitutes compliance with Cal Rules of Ct 1521(b), 1522–1523. See also Cal Rules of Ct 1514(e), 1520 on the duration and criteria for issuance of stay orders.

IV. PETITION FOR COORDINATION

A. Petitioning Papers

§28.15   1. Petition and Supporting Documents

A petition for coordination must be submitted to the chairperson of the Judicial Council, supported by an affidavit or declaration under penalty of perjury stating facts showing that the actions meet the standards specified for coordination. CCP §§404–404.1; see §28.5. The petition must state whether a hearing is requested and be supported by points and authorities and an affidavit or affidavits or declaration under penalty of perjury showing (Cal Rules of Ct 1521(a)):

(1) Name of each petitioner, or, when the petition is submitted by a presiding or sole judge, the name of each real party in interest, and the name and address of his attorney of record, if any;

(2) Names of the parties to all included actions, and the name and address of each party's attorney of record, if any;

(3) Complete title of each included action together with the title of the court in which the action is pending and the action number;

(4) Complete title of any other action known to petitioner to be pending in a court of this state that shares a common question of fact or law with the included actions but which is not included in the petition and a statement of the reasons for not including that other action in the petition;

(5) Status of each included action, including the status of any pretrial or discovery motions or orders, if known to petitioner;

(6) Facts relied on to show that each included action meets the coordination standards specified in CCP §404.1;

(7) Any facts relied on in support of a request that a particular site or sites be selected for a hearing on the petition.

A certified or endorsed copy of pleadings may be attached to the petition, as a substitute for factual support by affidavit of items (2), (3), (6) and (7), if petitioner specifies with particularity the portions of the pleading relied on. Cal Rules of Ct 1521(c).

The petition may also contain a request that any action being considered for, or affecting an action being considered for coordination be stayed pending determination of the petition. If petitioner wants actions stayed, the request may be included in the petition. However, it may be necessary to make a separate request to the court for a stay if one is wanted at a different time.

§28.16 2. Proof of Filing and Service

When the petition for coordination is submitted to the chairperson of the Judicial Council, it must be accompanied by proof that a notice of submission of petition for coordination and copy of the petition have been filed with the court in which each included action is pending. Cal Rules of Ct 1521(b), 1522. See §28.17 for discussion of contents of notice.

A petition must also be accompanied by proof of prior service of the notice, petition, and supporting papers on each party appearing in the included actions unless the notice contains a statement that a copy of the petition will be made available on request. See §28.20 for form of notice. Cal Rules of Ct 1521(b), 1523(a)(b).

§28.17 B. Notice of Submission of Petition for Coordination

Each notice of submission of petition for coordination must carry the title of the court in which the notice is to be filed and the title and number of the included action that is pending in that court, and set forth:

(1) The date that the petition for coordination was submitted;

(2) The name and address of the petitioner's attorney of record;

(3) The title and number of the included action to which the petitioner is a party;

(4) The title of the court in which that action is pending; and

(5) A notice that if a party intends to oppose the petition for coordination, he must submit and serve written opposition not later than 45 days after notice is served on him. Cal Rules of Ct 1522, 1523(b).

This notice must be filed with each court in which an included action is pending, and a copy of the notice of submission, together with a copy of the petition and the supporting papers must be served on each party appearing in that included action. Cal Rules of Ct 1521(b), 1523(a).

To avoid having to serve copies of the petition and supporting papers on all parties, the petitioning party may include in the notice of submission a statement advising the party served that, within five days after service, he may request, in writing, the petitioner to furnish him with copies of the petition and supporting documents. If a party makes a timely written request, copies of the petition and supporting documents must immediately be furnished. Cal Rules of Ct 1523(b).

§28.18   C. Timing and Transmittal of Petition

A petition for coordination may be made at any time after filing of the complaint. Cal Rules of Ct 1521(a). However, if trial is imminent in an action otherwise appropriate for coordination, that imminence may be a ground for summarily denying a petition, either in whole or in part. Cal Rules of Ct 1521(d). Therefore, it may be unwise to delay petitioning.

The original and a copy of the petition for coordination, the supporting papers, proofs of filing and service, are transmitted to the chairperson of the Judicial Council at the address shown in §28.8. Cal Rules of Ct 1511.

D. Forms

§28.19   1. Petition for Coordination

Copies: Original and one copy (filed with chairperson of judicial council together with proof of service of notice of submission and petition (see §28.16); copies for filing (one for filing in each court in which an included action is pending); copies for service (one for each attorney of record and unrepresented party in each included action); office copies.

[*Titles of Courts in Which Each Included Action Pending*]

[*Title of moving party's case*]   No. _____

PETITION FOR COORDINATION
____[AND APPLICATION FOR STAY ORDER]____

1. Petitioner(s) _____, petition(s) the Chairperson of the Judicial Council for assignment of a judge to determine whether the coordination of this action with the actions listed in the declaration(s) attached to this petition, is appropriate.

2. This petition is brought under Code of Civil Procedure section 404 on the following grounds: ____[set forth appropriate grounds as stated in CCP §404.1; see §28.5]____.

[When stay sought]

3. Pending determination of whether coordination is appropriate, petitioner requests that the coordination motion judge order a stay of the proceedings in the following named action(s) that are ____*[being considered for coordination / affecting an action being considered for coordination]*____ : ____*[list by title, number, and court]*____ . **All known related actions pending in any California court are set forth in the declaration attached to this petition.**

[Optional]

4. The request for stay of the pending action(s) is made on the ground that the stay order is necessary and appropriate to effectuate the purposes of coordination listed above.

[Continue]

____*[5]*____ . **This petition is based on all pleadings, papers, and records in these actions, as specified with particularity in the attached declaration(s) and on the attached memorandum of points and authorities; proof(s) of filing in each included action of a notice of submission of petition for coordination and a copy of this petition as required by California Rules of Court 1522; and proof(s) of service on each party appearing in each included action of a notice of submission of petition for coordination and a copy of petition as required in California Rules of Court 1523.**

A hearing on this petition ____*[is / is not]*____ **requested.**

Dated: _____

_____
[Signature of attorney]

[Typed name]
Attorney for petitioner

Comment: Declarations attached to the petition may be used to list the names of each petitioner and the name and address of each attorney of record, or to state the facts relied on to show that each included action meets the standards specified in CCP §404.1. See §28.5.

§28.20 2. Notice of Submission of Petition for Coordination

Copies: Original (filed with court clerk in which included action is pending, together with copy of petition); copies for filing (two for filing with chairperson of Judicial Council, one for filing in each court in which an included action is pending, together with copy of petition); copies for service (one for each attorney of record and unrepresented party in each included action); office copies.

[Titles of Courts in Which Each Included Action Pending]

[Title and number of all included actions]

NOTICE OF SUBMISSION OF PETITION FOR COORDINATION 1522 (CAL RULES OF COURT)

To the Clerk of the above-named Courts and to each party:

PLEASE TAKE NOTICE That on ____[date]____, a petition for coordination was submitted by ____[name of party]____ through his attorney ____[name and address]____ to the Chairperson of the Judicial Council, requesting assignment of a judge to determine whether coordination of ____[title, number, and court of petitioner's action]____ **with above action(s) is appropriate.**

[When notice is filed with court or when petitioner chooses to provide party with petition]

A copy of the petition for coordination is attached.

[When petition is not attached]

A copy of the petition for coordination is not attached. Under California Rules of Court 1523(b) any party who desires a copy of the petition and the supporting documents may request petitioner in writing within five days after service of this notice.

[Continue]

Any party intending to oppose the petition for coordination must serve and submit written opposition to it not later than 45 days after service of this notice. California Rules of Court 1523(b).

Dated: _____

[Signature of attorney]

[Typed name]
Attorney for petitioner

E. Procedures After Petition Filed

§28.21 1. Coordination Motion Judge Assigned; Proceeding Given Special Title and Number

On receipt of a petition for coordination, the chairperson of the Judicial Council assigns a coordination motion judge to determine whether coordination is appropriate. CCP §404; Cal Rules of Ct 1501(g), 1524.

The order bears a special title and number assigned to the coordination proceeding by the coordination attorney in the Administrative Office of the Courts. All future papers in that proceeding will bear that title and number. Cal Rules of Ct 1501(f), 1524, 1550(b). See Cal Rules of Ct 1501(f) for definition of "coordination attorney." The special title indicates in a general way the nature of the included actions, *e.g.*, "Landscaped Freeway Advertising Cases," "Palo Alto Fire Cases."

§28.22   2. Service of Assignment Order; Stay of Trials

A copy of the order assigning a coordination motion judge is served by the Judicial Council's coordination attorney on each party appearing in an included action and is sent to each court in which an included action is pending with directions to the clerk to file the order in the included action. The order specifies a court address to which all documents submitted to the coordination motion judge in the future must be sent. Cal Rules of Ct 1524.

Even without a stay order (see §§28.24–28.28), a court receiving an order assigning a coordination motion judge must not commence trial of an action included in the assignment and no judgment can be entered in such action unless trial of the action began before the coordination motion judge was assigned, although pretrial and discovery proceedings may continue. Cal Rules of Ct 1514(d).

§28.23   3. Review by Coordination Motion Judge of Notice to Parties

The coordination motion judge determines whether the petitioner has served appropriate notice on all parties who should receive notice of the coordination proceeding. See §§28.7–28.9 for discussion of who must receive notice. If he finds that any party has not been appropriately served, he must order petitioner to serve that party promptly. Cal Rules of Ct 1527(b). See §28.9 on effect of failure of service.

4. Application for Stay Order
§28.24   a. Timing and Contents of Application

An application for an order staying any action being considered for, or affecting an action being considered for, coordination may be included with a petition for coordination or may be served and submitted by any party at any time before the petition is determined. If it is a separate document it is entitled application for order staying pending action(s), and is made to the assigned judge. Cal Rules of Ct 1514(a).

If the action to be stayed was not included in the petition for coordination, copies of the application for stay and of all supporting documents must be served on each party to the action to be stayed and any such party may serve and submit opposition to the application for stay order. Cal Rules of Ct 1514(a).

An application for a stay order lists all known related cases pending in any California court and states whether the stay order should extend to any of these related cases. It is supported by a memorandum of points and authorities and by affidavits establishing the facts relied on to show that a stay order will promote the interests of justice. Cal Rules of Ct 1514(a), (e). See §28.28 for form of stay order.

§28.25   b. Timing and Contents of Opposition Papers

Points and authorities and affidavits opposing an application for a stay order must be served on all parties and submitted within ten days after service of the application. Cal Rules of Ct 1514(a).

The opposition papers must also list all known related cases pending in any California court and set forth reasons why the stay order should not be issued. Cal Rules of Ct 1514(a).

§28.26   c. Authority of Coordination Motion Judge

Pending any determination of whether coordination is appropriate, the coordination motion judge may, on application, stay any action being considered for, or affecting an action being considered for, coordination. CCP §404.5. After application is made, if there is opposition, the coordination motion judge may schedule a hearing to determine whether a stay order will issue, or be extended. Cal Rules of Ct 1514(b).

Notice of the hearing to determine whether a stay order should be granted or terminated is prepared and served at the direction of the coordination motion judge.

In ruling on an application for a stay order the assigned judge determines whether good cause has been shown that the stay will promote the ends of justice, considering the imminence of any trial or other proceeding that might materially affect the status of the action to be stayed, and whether a final judgment in that

§28.27   COORDINATION

action would have a res judicata or collateral estoppel effect with regard to any common issue of the included actions. Cal Rules of Ct 1514(b), (e).

§28.27   d. Effect and Duration of Stay Order

Unless it otherwise specifies, a stay order suspends all proceedings in the action to which it applies. It may, however, by its terms be limited to specified proceedings, orders, motions, or other phases of the action to which the stay order applies. Cal Rules of Ct 1514(c).

Any stay order issued without a hearing over prior written objection of a party to the action stayed by the order terminates on the 30th day after filing. A stay order issued without any timely written objection and without a hearing terminates on the 30th day after any party to the stayed action submits a written request for a hearing on whether the stay order should remain in effect. Cal Rules of Ct 1514(b).

The time during which any stay order is in effect under the coordination rules is not included in determining whether the action stayed should be dismissed for lack of prosecution under CCP §583. Cal Rules of Ct 1514(f).

§28.28   e. Form: Order Staying Action

Copies: Prepared and served by clerk.

[Title of Court of Coordination Motion Judge]

[Coordination proceeding special title (Cal Rules of Ct 1550(b))]

**JUDICIAL COUNCIL COORDINATION PROCEEDING NO. _____;
ORDER STAYING ACTION**

The application of _____ for an order that proceedings be stayed in the following **action(s):** ____[List name, number, and court in which action is pending]____, **came on regularly for hearing on** ____[date]____. **Appearing as attorneys were** _____ **and** _____.

Satisfactory proof having been made, and good cause appearing, the Court finds that: ____[state findings on need an appropriateness of stay]____.
  IT IS ORDERED That:
  1. **Proceedings in the above action(s) are stayed** ____[in the following particulars: _____]____ **pending determination of whether coordination is appropriate.**
  2. **The clerks of** ____[name courts in which action is pending]____ **shall file a copy of this order in the Court file.**
  3. **Counsel for the moving party shall serve notice of this order on**

____[names of designated parties]____ **immediately and submit proof of that service to this Court.**

Dated: _____

Coordination Motion Judge

5. Response to Petition

§28.29 **a. Party Opposition or Support**

Any party may serve and submit points and authorities and affidavits opposing the petition within 45 days after being served with a copy of a notice of submission of petition for coordination. Cal Rules of Ct 1525. See Cal Rules of Ct 1501(m) for definition of "party." Any party to an included action may serve and submit a written statement supporting the petition. This statement, however, must be submitted within 30 days after service of the notice of submission. Cal Rules of Ct 1526. All memoranda of points and authorities and affidavits in support or opposition must be served and submitted not later than five days before any hearing on the matter at issue unless the coordination motion judge directs otherwise. Cal Rules of Ct 1512.

b. Forms

§28.30 **(1) Statement in Opposition to Petition for Coordination**

Copies: Original (filed with coordination motion judge at court address designated in assignment order with proof of service on each party to an included action) (Cal Rules of Ct 1501(g)); copy (transmitted to Chairperson of Judicial Council) (Cal Rules of Ct 1511); copy (filed with court in which included action is pending); copies for service (one for each attorney of record and unrepresented party to an included action); office copies.

[Title of Court of Coordination Motion Judge]

[Coordination proceeding special title (Cal Rules of Ct 1550(b))]	**JUDICIAL COUNCIL COORDINATION PROCEEDING NO.** _____ **STATEMENT IN OPPOSITION TO PETITION FOR COORDINATION** ____[AND STAY OF ACTION]____

_____, **a party to the included action, opposes the petition for coordination made by** _____, **a party to the included action on the ground(s) that:**

____[*e.g., the actions do not share a common question of fact or law / the actions are not pending in different courts / one judge hearing all of the actions for all pur-*

§28.31   COORDINATION   244

poses in a selected site will not promote the ends of justice because ____ [select appropriate reasons as set forth in CCP §404.1; see §28.5] ____] ____ .

[When stay of action is opposed]

____ [Name] ____ also opposes a stay of action No. ____ on the grounds that such a stay will not promote the interests of justice and is not necessary and appropriate to effectuate the purposes, if any, of coordination.

[Continue]

All known related actions pending in any California court are set forth in declaration(s) _____, attached to this statement in opposition.

This statement in opposition is based on the attached declaration(s) of _____, and on the attached memorandum of points and authorities.

Dated: _____

[Signature of attorney]

[Typed name]
Attorney for _____

§28.31   (2) Statement in Support of Petition for Coordination

Copies: Original (filed with coordination motion judge at court address designated in assignment order with proof of service on each party to an included action) copy (transmitted to chairperson of Judicial Council) (Cal Rules of Ct 1511); copies for service (one for each attorney of record and unrepresented party to an included action); office copies.

[Title of Court of Coordination Motion Judge]

| [Coordination proceeding special title (Cal Rules of Ct 1550 (b))] | JUDICIAL COUNCIL COORDINATION PROCEEDING NO. _____ STATEMENT IN SUPPORT OF PETITION FOR COORDINATION |

_____, a party to an included action, supports the petition for coordination on the grounds stated in the petition for coordination.

[Add when applicable]

and on the additional ground(s) that: _____.

This support is based on the attached declaration(s) of _____, and the attached memorandum of points and authorities.

[Signature of attorney]

[Typed name]
Attorney for _____

6. Hearing on Petition

§28.32 a. When Hearing Required; Who May Appear

An action cannot be ordered coordinated over the objection of any party, nor a petition for coordination denied, without a hearing on the petition. Cal Rules of Ct 1527(a).

However, the imminence of a trial in any action otherwise appropriate for coordination may be a ground for summary denial of a petition for coordination in whole or in part. Cal Rules of Ct 1521(d).

Unless, on a showing of good cause, the coordination motion judge permits appearance, only parties who have submitted a petition, or a written response or opposition to the petition, are permitted to appear at the hearing. Cal Rules of Ct 1513.

§28.33 b. Coordination Motion Judge Sets Hearing and Determines Issues To Be Heard

The coordination motion judge makes the determination that a hearing is required and determines the time, place, and matters or issues to be heard, and serves a notice of hearing on each party appearing in an included action. Cal Rules of Ct 1527 (b).

When it appears that a petition for coordination may be disposed of by determining a specified issue or issues, without the necessity of conducting a hearing on all issues, the coordination motion judge may order that issue or issues heard and determined before a hearing on other issues. Cal Rules of Ct 1528.

§28.34 c. Presentation of Evidence at Hearing

For factual matters to be heard, they must be presented by declarations, answers to interrogatories, or requests for admissions, depositions, or they may be judicially noticed. Cal Rules of Ct 1513. Oral testimony is not permitted at a hearing unless factual issues are put in dispute by conflicting affidavits, in which case the court may, but is not required, to hear testimony. Cal Rules of Ct 1513.

d. Orders After Hearing

§28.35 (1) Order Granting Petition and Selecting Reviewing Court

If the coordination motion judge determines that coordination is appropriate, he orders the included actions coordinated and reports that fact to the Chairperson of the Judicial Council. CCP §404.3. The coordination motion judge also selects the reviewing court having appellate jurisdiction if the actions are within the jurisdiction of more than one reviewing court, giving consideration to which court will promote the ends of justice under the standards set forth in CCP §401.1. CCP §404.2; see §28.5. The order also specifies the court in which any petition for a writ relating to any subsequent order in the coordination proceeding must be filed. Cal Rules of Ct 1505.

§28.36 (2) Order Granting Coordination in Part

A petition for coordination may be granted or denied as to any action included in the petition for coordination or of any severable claim in any included action. The original trial court continues to exercise jurisdiction over any severable claim that has not been ordered coordinated. Cal Rules of Ct 1529.

§28.37 (3) Order Denying Coordination

An order denying coordination will not prejudice a party from applying again if a stronger showing can be made. See CCP §1008. Written notice of entry of an order denying coordination should be served on each party to begin the running of the time for review. A party may petition for writ of mandate within 10 days after service of such notice. CCP §404.6. See §28.57. Sometimes the judge's order will instruct the prevailing party to serve the notice, but even if it does not, the prevailing party should undertake service.

§28.38 7. Report When Coordination Determination Delayed

If appropriateness of coordination has not been determined within 90 days after the coordination motion judge's assignment, he must promptly submit a written report to the Chairperson of the Judicial Council. This report describes: (a) the present status of the coordination proceeding; (b) any factors or circumstances that may have caused undue or unanticipated delay in the determination of the issue of appropriateness; and (c) any stay orders that are in effect. Cal Rules of Ct 1527(c).

V. PRETRIAL PROCEDURES AFTER COORDINATION ORDERED

§28.39 A. Service and Filing of Coordination Order; Automatic Stay of Proceedings

A copy of the order granting coordination is served on each party appearing in that action and on each party appearing in an included action. Another copy is filed in each action. As soon as it is filed, the order automatically stays all further proceedings except filing of papers in an action or unless the coordination trial judge directs otherwise. Severable claims not ordered coordinated are not stayed. Cal Rules of Ct 1529.

B. Assignment of Coordination Trial Judge; Designation of Service Address

§28.40 1. Assignment Order: Contents, Filing, and Service of Papers

After coordination is ordered by the coordination motion judge, the Chairperson of the Judicial Council assigns a coordination trial judge to hear and determine the actions at the site or sites which the judge finds appropriate. CCP §404.3; Cal Rules of Ct 1501(i), 1540.

The assignment order designates a single address to which all papers to be submitted to that judge must be transmitted. Thereafter, every paper filed in coordinated actions must be accompanied by proof that a copy was sent to the coordination trial judge at the designated address. Cal Rules of Ct 1540.

A copy of the assignment order is sent to each party appearing in a coordinated action and filed in each such action. Cal Rules of Ct 1540.

§28.41 2. Challenges to Assignment

Any motion or affidavit of prejudice regarding the judge assigned as coordination trial judge must be submitted in writing to the Chairperson of the Judicial Council within 20 days after service of the assignment order. Cal Rules of Ct 1515. For purposes of CCP §170.6, which governs challenges for prejudice generally, all parties plaintiff in the included or coordinated actions constitute one side and all parties defendant in such actions constitute the other side unless the Chairperson of the Judicial Council orders otherwise. Cal Rules of Ct 1515.

§28.42   3. Powers of Coordination Trial Judge

Immediately on assignment, the coordination trial judge may exercise all the powers over each coordinated action of a judge of the court in which the action is pending. Cal Rules of Ct 1540. The coordination trial judge assumes an active role in managing all steps of the pretrial, discovery, and trial proceedings to expedite determination of the coordinated actions. Cal Rules of Ct 1541. The coordination trial judge may, for the purpose of coordination and to serve the ends of justice: (a) order any coordinated action transferred to another court; (b) schedule and conduct hearings, conferences, and trial or trials at any site in California, considering convenience of parties, witnesses, and counsel, relative development of the actions and work product of counsel, efficient utilization of judicial facilities and manpower and court calendars; and (c) order any issue or defense tried separately and before trial of the remaining issues when it appears that doing so might expedite disposition. Cal Rules of Ct 1541(b)(1)(3).

C. Preliminary Trial Conference

§28.43   1. Timing; Role of Counsel

A preliminary trial conference must be held, preferably within 30 days after the assignment order is issued. Cal Rules of Ct 1541(a).

Although the coordination trial judge issues the order setting the conference (see form in §28.47), counsel may, at any time following assignment of the coordination trial judge, serve and submit a proposed agenda for the conference and a proposed form of order covering appropriate matters of procedure and discovery. Counsel, and all persons appearing without counsel, must attend the conference prepared to discuss all matters specified in the conference order. Cal Rules of Ct 1541(a).

2. Matters for Discussion and Determination at Conference

§28.44   a. Appointment and Role of Liaison Counsel

At the conference, the coordination trial judge may appoint one liaison counsel for each side. Cal Rules of Ct 1541(a)(1). The appointment is usually made by the coordination trial judge after requesting that parties on each side of the coordinated actions designate one or more of the attorneys of record on that side to be appointed. The judge may appoint liaison counsel if parties are unable to agree. Cal Rules of Ct 1506(a).

Liaison counsel serves as representative of all parties on a side, and has the following powers and duties (Cal Rules of Ct 1501(b)):

(1) To receive on behalf of and promptly distribute to the parties for whom he acts notices and other court documents;

(2) To act as spokesman for the side which he represents at all noticed pretrial proceedings, subject to the right of each party to present individual or divergent positions;

(3) To call meetings of counsel to propose joint action.

§28.45 b. Establishment of Pretrial Proceedings Schedule

The coordination trial judge may establish a timetable for filing motions other than discovery motions, establish a discovery schedule, provide a method and schedule for preliminary legal questions to be submitted that might expedite disposition of the coordinated actions, and schedule further pretrial conferences if appropriate. In class actions, he may establish a schedule, if practicable, for prompt determination of matters pertinent to the class action issue.

The coordination trial judge may also establish a central depository or depositories to receive, and maintain for inspection by the parties, evidentiary material and specified documents that are not required by the coordination rules to be served on all parties. Cal Rules of Ct 1541(a)(2)(7).

4. Forms

§28.46 a. Proposed Order Setting Preliminary Trial Conference

Copies: The actual order is served by the clerk of the court of the coordination trial judge.

[*Title of Court of Coordination Trial Judge*]

[*Coordination proceeding special title (Cal Rules of Ct 1550(b))*]

JUDICIAL COUNCIL COORDINATION PROCEEDING NO. _____
ORDER SETTING PRELIMINARY TRIAL CONFERENCE

IT IS ORDERED that:

1. A preliminary trial conference will be held in this coordination proceeding at _____.m. on _____, 19____ in Department No. ____ of the _____ County Superior Court located at _____, California.

2. Counsel and all persons appearing without counsel shall come to the conference prepared to discuss all matters specified in this order, as applicable. Additional matters may be considered on suggestion of the parties as hereafter provided, or as the Court deems appropriate.

3. The items on the agenda under California Rules of Court 1541(a) are:

a. Appointment of liaison counsel in accordance with California Rules of Court 1506;

b. Establishment of a timetable for filing motions other than discovery motions;

c. Establishment of a schedule for discovery;

d. Provision for a method and schedule for the submission of preliminary legal questions that might serve to expedite the disposition of the coordinated actions;

e. Establishment of a central depository or depositories to receive and maintain for inspection by the parties evidentiary material and specified documents that are not required by these rules to be served on all parties; and

f. Scheduling of further pretrial conferences if appropriate.

[Add when class action]

g. Establishment of a schedule, if practicable, for the prompt determination of matters pertinent to the class action issue;

[Continue]

4. Not later than _____, 19____, each party must serve on all other parties, and file with the coordination trial judge, a memorandum setting forth that party's views and suggestions as to each item on the agenda, or proposals and views on additional items which might appropriately be added to the agenda, including proposed stipulations with respect to issues of fact and law and other matters.

Dated: _____

Coordination Trial Judge

Comment: Although Cal Rules of Ct 1541(a) relates specifically to actions the coordination trial judge may take at the preliminary trial conference, if the judge determines that the purpose of coordination will be furthered and the interests of justice served, he may also take the actions specified in Cal Rules of Ct 1541(b), *i.e.*, he may also consider whether to:

(1) Order any coordinated action transferred to another court;

(2) Schedule and conduct hearings, conferences, and a trial or trials at any site in California he deems appropriate considering convenience to parties, witnesses, and counsel; relative development of actions and the work product of counsel; efficient utilization of judicial facilities and manpower; and the courts' calendars;

(3) Order any issue or defense to be tried separately and before trial of the remaining issues when disposition of any of the coordinated actions might be expedited.

If transfer of an action is considered, Cal Rules of Ct 1543 must be complied with. See §28.48.

§28.47 b. Preliminary Trial Conference Order

Copies: This order is served by the clerk of the court of the coordination trial judge.

[Title of Court of Coordination Trial Judge]

[Coordination proceeding special title (Cal Rules of Ct 1550(b))]

No. _____

JUDICIAL COUNCIL COORDINATION PRELIMINARY TRIAL CONFERENCE ORDER

The preliminary trial conference in this coordinated proceeding was held on _____, 19____. Appearing as attorneys were _____, and _____. Appearing without counsel were _____, and _____.

Satisfactory proof having been made, and good cause appearing,
IT IS ORDERED that:

As to the agenda specified in the order setting preliminary trial conference order under California Rules of Court 1541(a):

1. _____, and _____, are appointed as liaison counsel;
2. ____[State timetable for filing motions other than discovery motions]____;
3. ____[State schedule for discovery]____;
4. ____[State method and schedule for the submission of preliminary legal questions that might serve to expedite the disposition of the coordinated actions]____;
5. ____[If class actions, set out a schedule, if practicable, for the prompt determination of matters pertinent to the class action issue]____;
6. ____[Designate, when applicable, a central depository or depositories to receive and maintain for inspection by the parties evidentiary material and specified documents that are not required by court rules to be served on all parties]____; **and**
7. ____[State schedule of further pretrial conferences if any]____.

Dated: _____

Coordination Trial Judge

D. Motion for Transfer of Action

§28.48   1. Transfer on Motion of Party or Court's Own Motion

"Transfer" means to remove a coordinated action or severable claim in that action from the court in which it is pending to any other court, without removing such action or claim from the coordination proceedings, and includes "retransfer." Cal Rules of Ct 1501(s). The coordination trial judge, on his own motion or on motion of any party to a coordinated action, may order the coordinated action or a severable claim in that action transferred from the court in which it is pending to another court for a specified purpose or for all purposes. Cal Rules of Ct 1543(a). See form in §28.51.

§28.49   2. Objections and Hearing

Transfer of an action cannot take place over the objection of any party unless a hearing has been held on ten days' written notice served on all parties to the action. At the hearing, the court must consider convenience of parties, witnesses, and counsel; relative development of actions and work product of counsel; efficient utilization of judicial facilities and manpower, the court calendars and any other relevant matter. Cal Rules of Ct 1543(a).

§28.50   3. Contents of Transfer Order

The order transferring the action or claim designates the court to which the action is transferred and directs that a copy of the transfer order be filed in each coordinated action. See form in §28.51. It also orders the clerk of the court in which the action was pending immediately to prepare and send to the transferee court a certified copy of the transfer order and of the pleadings and proceedings in that action. If it is necessary to have any of the original pleadings or other papers before the coordination trial judge, the clerk of the court in which the action was pending must on written request of a party to that action or of the coordination trial judge, send original papers or pleadings to the transferee court, retaining a certified copy. Cal Rules of Ct 1543(b).

The clerk of the court in which the action was pending must also serve a copy of the transfer order on each party appearing in that action.

The court to which the action is transferred is to file the action as if the action had been begun in that court (Cal Rules of Ct

1543(b)), and, on receipt of an order of transfer, may exercise jurisdiction over the action in accordance with orders and directions of the coordination trial judge. No other court exercises jurisdiction over that action except as provided in the coordination rules. Cal Rules of Ct 1543(b).

§28.51 4. Form: Order of Transfer on Motion of Party

Copies: This order is served by the clerk of the court of the coordination trial judge.

[*Title of Court of Coordination Trial Judge*]

[Coordination proceeding special title (Cal Rules of Ct 1550(c))]

No. _____

JUDICIAL COUNCIL COORDINATION PROCEEDING ORDER OF TRANSFER (Cal Rules of Ct 1543)

The motion of ____[name of party]____ for an order transferring this action from _____ County Superior Court to _____ County Superior Court, came on regularly for hearing on _____, 19____.
  Appearing as attorneys were _____.
Satisfactory proof having been made, and good cause appearing,
IT IS ORDERED that:
1. The clerk of the transferring County ____[Superior / Municipal]____ Court immediately prepare and transmit to the clerk of the receiving County ____[Superior / Municipal]____ Court a certified copy of the pleadings and proceedings in this action together with a certified copy of this order of transfer.
2. The clerk of the transferring County ____[Superior / Municipal]____ Court serve a copy of this order of transfer on each party appearing in this action and file a copy of this order of transfer.
3. The clerk of each of the courts in which the coordinated actions listed below are pending file a copy of this order of transfer in those actions.

[*List included actions*]

4. The clerk of the receiving County ____[Superior / Municipal]____ Court, on receipt of a certified copy of the pleadings and proceedings in this action along with a certified copy of this order of transfer, file the action as if the action had been commenced in the receiving County ____[Superior / Municipal]____ Court.
  No fees shall be required for this transfer.
5. This action is transferred from the transferring County ____[Superior / Municipal]____ Court to the receiving County ____[Superior / Municipal]____ Court for all purposes, and jurisdiction may be exercised in accordance with the orders and directions of the Court to which action is transferred.

6. **No other court may exercise jurisdiction over this action except as provided by this Court.**

Dated: _____

_____

Coordination Trial Judge

VI. PETITION TO COORDINATE AN ADD-ON CASE

§28.52   A. Who Petitions; Grounds

A petition to coordinate an add-on case is a request made to the coordination trial judge for an order coordinating an action with actions previously ordered coordinated. CCP §404.4; Cal Rules of Ct 1501(b), 1521, 1544.

The presiding or sole judge of any court in which an action is pending that shares a common question of fact or law with coordinated actions, on his own motion or the motion of any party supported by a declaration stating facts showing that the action meets the standards of CCP §404.1 (see §28.5), or all parties plaintiff or defendant in any such action, supported by the same type of declaration, may request that the coordination trial judge order coordination of that action. CCP §404.4. Appropriateness of coordination of add-on cases is determined by applying the same standards as those used in determining appropriateness of coordination in the first instance. CCP §§404.1, 404.4.

B. Procedure

§28.53   1. Petition and Opposition

The procedure for securing coordination of an add-on case is the same as that for coordination in the first instance (see §§28.15–28.20) except in the following aspects:

(a) The request is submitted to the coordination trial judge with proof of mailing of one copy to the Chairperson of the Judicial Council and with proof of service on all other parties to the coordination proceeding, including all parties appearing in all coordinated actions.

(b) Within ten days after such service any party may serve and submit a notice of opposition to such request and thereafter, within 15 days after submitting his notice of opposition, the party must serve and submit points and authorities and declarations in opposition to the request. Cal Rules of Ct 1544.

Any application for an order staying the add-on case is made to the coordination trial judge in the manner provided for stay orders generally. Cal Rules of Ct 1514, 1544. See §§28.24–28.28.

§28.54 2. Hearing and Order

The coordination trial judge may order a hearing to be held on the request to coordinate an add-on case in the same manner as provided in hearing an original petition for coordination and may allow the parties to serve and submit additional written materials in support of, or in opposition to, the request. At the hearing, the court considers the relative development of the actions and the work product of counsel, in addition to any other relevant matters. Cal Rules of Ct 1544. See §28.35 on contents of coordination order; see §§28.7–28.9 on preparation and service.

§28.55 VII. EFFECT OF DENIAL OF COORDINATION

When an order denying a petition for coordination of that action is filed and served, authority of the coordination motion judge over an action terminates. Any stay that has been ordered in that action terminates on the tenth day after filing. Cal Rules of Ct 1529. A petition may be made again after having been denied, if the facts have changed. See CCP §1008.

§28.56 VIII. REVIEW OF COORDINATION ORDERS

Within ten days after service of a written notice of entry of any order relating to coordination under CCP §§404–404.8 and the related rules of court, any party may petition the appropriate reviewing court for a writ of mandate to require the court to make whatever order the reviewing court finds appropriate. CCP §404.6; Cal Rules of Ct 1505. Mandate, rather than appeal, is the method of review of orders made in connection with coordination proceedings. *Lautrup, Inc. v Trans-West Discount Corp.* (1976) 64 CA3d 316, 134 CR 348. If coordination has been granted, the coordination order will include a designation of the court to which petitions for writs relating to subsequent orders must be directed. See §28.35.

§28.56 COORDINATION

A petition for a writ relating to an order granting or denying coordination may be filed in any reviewing court that has jurisdiction under the rules applicable to civil actions generally. Cal Rules of Ct 1505. Except as the coordination statutes or rules provide differently, all provisions for review of civil actions generally apply to coordination proceedings. Cal Rules of Ct 1504(a).

PART III
TERMINATION WITHOUT TRIAL

ROBERT FAINER
JAN T. CHILTON

Chapter 29
Summary Judgment

I. INTRODUCTION
   A. Scope of Chapter §29.1
   B. Statutory Nature of Procedure §29.2
   C. Purposes of Motion §29.3
   D. Constitutionality §29.4
   E. Alternative Methods of Resolving and Narrowing Issues §29.5
II. SIGNIFICANT ELEMENTS OF CURRENT CCP §437c
   A. No Triable Issue of Any Material Fact §29.6
   B. Certain Issues Are "Without Substantial Controversy" §29.7
   C. "Admissible Evidence" Standard; Sanctions for Bad Faith Declarations §29.8
   D. Effect of Disputes About Immaterial Facts §29.9
   E. Court To Draw Reasonable Inferences §29.10
   F. Lack of Credibility as Ground for Denial §29.11
   G. When Motion May Be Made §29.12
   H. Continuance on Certain Conditions §29.13
III. OTHER PROCEEDINGS COMPARED
   A. Pretrial Motions
      1. Motion To Dismiss Action as Sham §29.14
      2. Motion To Strike Answer §29.15
      3. Motion for Judgment on the Pleadings §29.16
   B. Motions at Trial
      1. Objection to Introduction of All Evidence §29.17
      2. Motions for Nonsuit, Directed Verdict, and Judgment Notwithstanding Verdict §29.18
      3. Motion for Judgment Under CCP §631.8 §29.19
      4. Motion for Trial Under CCP §597 §29.20
IV. DECIDING TO MAKE OR TO OPPOSE MOTION
   A. Moving Party's Objectives §29.21
   B. Moving Party's Substantive Burden §29.22
      1. Plaintiff's Burden §29.23
      2. Defendant's Burden §29.24

ROBERT FAINER, B.A., 1945, University of California (Los Angeles); J.D., 1949, University of Southern California Law School. Judge Fainer is a Superior Court Judge for the County of Los Angeles.

JAN T. CHILTON, B.A., 1967, University of California (Berkeley); J.D., 1970, University of Chicago. Mr. Chilton practices in San Francisco with the firm of Severson, Werson, Berke & Melchoir. CEB attorney-editor was ISADORE ROSENBLATT.

- C. Opposing Party's Substantive Burden
  1. When Moving Party Has Not Met Burden §29.25
  2. When Moving Party Has Met Burden §29.26
  3. When Opposing Party Files Cross-Motion §29.27
  4. When Opposing Party Wants Delay or Amendment of Pleadings §29.28
- V. PREPARING TO MAKE OR OPPOSE MOTION
  - A. Reviewing and Amending the Pleadings §29.29
  - B. Gathering the Facts §29.30
  - C. Timing the Motion §29.31
- VI. DRAFTING THE MOTION
  - A. Checklist: Common Drafting Defects That Prevent Consideration of Merits
    1. Defects in Notice of Motion §29.32
    2. Defects in Supporting Papers §29.33
  - B. Notice of Motion and Motion
    1. Contents §29.34
       a. Designation of Opposing Party §29.35
       b. Statement of Grounds §29.36
       c. Nature of Order Sought §29.37
       d. Description of Documents Relied On §29.38
    2. Forms
       a. Notice of Motion for Summary Judgment or for Summary Adjudication of Issues §29.39
       b. Notice of Motion for Summary Adjudication of Issues §29.40
  - C. Memorandum of Points and Authorities §29.41
  - D. Summary of Issues and Evidence
    1. Need for Summary §29.42
    2. Sample: Summary of Issues and Evidence: Contract Case §29.43
  - E. Supporting Papers
    1. Types of Supporting Papers §29.44
    2. Stipulations and Admissions §29.45
    3. Judicially Noticed Matters
       a. Matters for Mandatory and Permissible Judicial Notice §29.46
       b. Form: Request for Judicial Notice §29.47
    4. Affidavits and Declarations
       a. Formal Requirements §29.48
       b. Competence and Personal Knowledge Requirements §29.49
       c. Admissible Evidence Requirement §29.50
          (1) Inadmissible Conclusions and Opinions; Examples §29.51
          (2) Inadmissible Hearsay §29.52
    5. Documents §29.53
       a. Incorporation of Document by Reference in Declaration §29.54
       b. Authentication of Documents
          (1) Methods of Authentication §29.55

                (2) Examples: Statements Used To Authenticate Documents §29.56
            c. Best Evidence Rule
                (1) Compliance With Best Evidence Rule Required §29.57
                (2) Examples: Statements Supporting Introduction of Secondary Evidence §29.58
                (3) Form: Notice To Produce Books, Documents, Records, or Other Physical Evidence §29.59
            d. Business Records
                (1) Business Record as Exception to Hearsay Rule §29.60
                (2) Examples: Statements Laying Foundation for Introduction of Business Records §29.61
        6. Discovery Documents §29.62
            a. Depositions §29.63
            b. Interrogatories and Requests for Admissions §29.64
            c. Documents Produced on CCP §2031 Request §29.65
            d. Other Discovery Documents §29.66
VII. SERVING AND FILING THE MOTION §29.67
VIII. PREHEARING AND HEARING PROCEDURES
  A. Moving for Continuance §29.68
  B. Filing Supplemental Declarations and Late Papers §29.69
  C. Oral Argument Generally Permitted; Testimony Generally Not Permitted §29.70
IX. ORDERS AND JUDGMENTS
  A. Who Prepares; Contents §29.71
  B. Types of Judgments §29.72
  C. Costs and Attorneys' Fees §29.73
  D. Sanctions §29.74
  E. Forms
    1. Order for Entry of Summary Judgment §29.75
    2. Order Denying Summary Judgment and Granting Summary Adjudication of Issues §29.76
    3. Order Granting Summary Adjudication of Issues §29.77
    4. Judgment by Court Under CCP §437c §29.78

X. POSTJUDGMENT PROCEDURES
  A. Review of Summary Judgment in Trial Court
    1. By Motion Under CCP §657 for New Trial §29.79
    2. By Application Under CCP §473 for Relief From Judgment §29.80
    3. By Motion or Separate Action To Set Aside Judgment for Extrinsic Fraud or Mistake §29.81
    4. Improper Use of Nonstatutory Motions §29.82
  B. Review by Appeal From Judgment
    1. Final Judgment Rule
        a. Final Judgment Required §29.83

   b. Examples: Final and Nonfinal Summary Judgments §29.84
  2. Scope of Appellate Review
   a. Applicability of General Rules §29.85
   b. Exception for Evidentiary Objections §29.86
  3. No Judgment for Nonmoving Party §29.87
 C. Review of Order Adjudicating Issues To Be Without Substantial Controversy §29.88
 D. Review of Order Denying Summary Judgment
  1. By Extraordinary Writ §29.89
  2. By Renewal of Motion §29.90

I. INTRODUCTION

§29.1 A. Scope of Chapter

 This chapter discusses California's basic summary judgment law, analyzing both tactical and procedural aspects of preparation and use of the important pretrial strategic tool, and considers common defects in the papers supporting or opposing the motion (see §§29.32–29.33).

 For discussion of California summary judgment, see Zack, *California Summary Judgment: The Need for Legislative Reform*, 59 CALIF L REV 439 (1971); Zack, *The 1973 Summary Judgment Act—New Teeth for an Old Tiger*, 48 CAL SBJ 654 (1973).

§29.2 B. Statutory Nature of Procedure

 A motion for summary judgment is a valuable pretrial procedure permitting resolution of meritless lawsuits or uncontested issues in a lawsuit, saving both the court and counsel "a great deal of time and unnecessary work." *Martens v Winder* (1961) 191 CA2d 143, 149, 12 CR 413, 416. See also *Northwestern Nat'l Ins. Co. v Corley* (7th Cir 1974) 503 F2d 224, 230.

 The summary judgment procedure is entirely statutory. See *Werner v Sargeant* (1953) 121 CA2d 833, 837, 264 P2d 217, 219. But see Zack, *California Summary Judgment: The Need for Legislative Reform*, 59 CALIF L REV 439, 440 (1971). Summary judgment motions have become particularly useful since enactment of new CCP §437c, effective January 1, 1974. This section (further amended, effective January 1, 1977), is referred to as "current CCP §437c" whenever necessary to distinguish it from "former" CCP §437c (repealed by Stats 1973, ch 366, §1). Significant elements of current CCP §437c are discussed in §§29.6–29.13.

§29.3 C. Purposes of Motion

A motion for summary judgment may be made by either party "in any action or proceeding if it is contended that the action has no merit or that there is no defense thereto." CCP §437c.

The motion is not a device for trying disputed issues of fact. *Joslin v Marin Munic. Water Dist.* (1967) 67 C2d 132, 147, 60 CR 377, 387. See also Zack, *California Summary Judgment: The Need for Legislative Reform*, 59 CALIF L REV 439, 440 (1971). Summary judgment must be denied if any issue of material fact must be decided in order to render judgment. See *Walsh v Glendale Fed. Sav. & Loan Ass'n* (1969) 1 CA3d 578, 583, 81 CR 804, 807 (disapproved on other grounds in *Garrett v Coast & Southern Fed. Sav. & Loan Ass'n* (1973) 9 C3d 731, 108 CR 845).

Motions for summary judgment may be used to resolve cases in which:

(1) There is no triable issue of fact. *Pettis v General Tel. Co.* (1967) 66 C2d 503, 58 CR 316.

(2) The issue is one of law. *Loma Portal Civic Club v American Airlines* (1964) 61 C2d 582, 588, 39 CR 708, 712; see 59 CALIF LAW REV at 473.

(3) The pleadings conceal a factual defect in one party's position which the motion will expose. *Weir v Snow* (1962) 210 CA2d 283, 289, 26 CR 868, 871.

The motion may also be used to resolve specific issues about which there is no substantial controversy. CCP §437c. There is no provision for a "partial" summary judgment under CCP §437c, but on proper notice the court must determine whether specific issues are without substantial controversy and are to be deemed established, permitting only the remaining issues to be resolved at the time of trial. See §29.7. A court may, on its own motion, order that specific issues are without substantial controversy and deemed established on denial of full summary judgment. See §29.7 on certain court rules relating to requirement of motion for such an order.

Courts have the inherent power to dismiss a sham action (see §29.14) or to strike a sham defense (CCP §453; see *Neal v Bank of America* (1949) 93 CA2d 678, 209 P2d 825; see §29.15). However, as a practical matter a sham often cannot be exposed unless the court can be shown that the claimed contentions or defenses are without factual basis. See 4 Witkin, CALIFORNIA PROCEDURE, Proceedings Without Trial §173 (2d ed 1971). The statutory summary judgment procedure provides a pretrial method of rooting out the sham action or defense, and disposing of the action on affidavits, declarations, admissions, answers to interrogatories, depositions, and judicially noticed matters. See §§29.44–29.66. These various means of proof are referred to in this chapter by the term "supporting papers," except when the context requires otherwise.

Summary judgment motions have replaced the "speaking demurrer," the "speaking motion to strike," the "speaking motion for judgment on the pleadings," and motions to dismiss by which a party could attack the factual sufficiency of pleadings. See *Vesely v Sager* (1971) 5 C3d 153, 167, 95 CR 623, 633, referred to in §29.14.

§29.4 D. Constitutionality

Code of Civil Procedure §831d, from which former CCP §437c was derived, was held constitutional when attacked on the ground that it deprived the opposing party of a jury trial and the right of cross-examination. *Cowan Oil & Refining Co. v Miley Petroleum Corp.* (1931) 112 CA Supp 773, 777, 295 P 504, 505, and subsequent cases. The rationale of these cases was that the motion could be granted only when there was no issue of fact to be tried, and that the right to jury trial and the right to cross-examination do not arise except for triable issues of fact. Because this rationale is equally applicable to current CCP §437c, it appears to be constitutionally valid, although some lawyers believe that elimination of the right to deny a motion for summary judgment on the ground of credibility (see §29.11) may raise a constitutional question.

§29.5 E. Alternative Methods of Resolving and Narrowing Issues

Because defective or improperly prepared motions for summary judgment may adversely affect the case, the following other methods for relief should be explored, *i.e.*, (1) stipulations based on settlement discussions; (2) requests for admissions under CCP §2033; (3) other discovery; and (4) a demand for a bill of particulars under CCP §454. See generally California Civil Discovery Practice (Cal CEB 1975). Settlement and pretrial conferences may also be used to resolve uncontested facts and issues.

II. SIGNIFICANT ELEMENTS OF CURRENT CCP §437c

§29.6   A. No Triable Issue of Any Material Fact

Code of Civil Procedure §437c provides that a motion for summary judgment "*shall* be granted if all the papers submitted show that there is no triable issue as to any material fact and that the moving party is entitled to a judgment as a matter of law." [Emphasis added.] See *Thierfeldt v Marin Hosp. Dist.* (1973) 35 CA3d 186, 110 CR 791; Zack, *California Summary Judgment: The Need for Legislative Reform*, 59 CALIF LAW REV 439, 441 (1971). If no triable issue of material fact exists, the motion must be granted. The decision is no longer discretionary with the trial court.

Summary judgment may not be entered for the party opposing the motion unless he has countermoved for summary judgment. A summary judgment granted to a nonmoving party denies the moving party the opportunity to present additional facts that may justify a trial of the factual issues. Such a judgment cannot be saved by the curative provisions of Cal Const art VI, §13. *Dvorin v Appellate Dep't* (1975) 15 C3d 648, 125 CR 771.

§29.7   B. Certain Issues Are "Without Substantial Controversy"

Code of Civil Procedure §437c, as adapted from Fed R Civ P 56(d), permits the court to make an order that certain issues are "without substantial controversy," *i.e.*, the court may make a summary adjudication of issues, which may be of fact or law. At trial, the issues so specified are deemed established and the trial proceeds on the remaining issues. *Beech Aircraft Corp. v Superior Court* (1976) 61 CA3d 501, 514, 132 CR 541, 548. The summarily adjudicated issues may be incorporated into the court's findings of fact, conclusions of law, and judgment; or into jury instructions when appropriate. Summary adjudications may also limit the scope of evidence presented at trial. See, *e.g.*, *Kiernan v Union Bank* (1976) 55 CA3d 111, 127 CR 441.

Under CCP §437c, it appears that the court must make an order limiting the trial to issues other than those it determines to be without substantial controversy, while under Fed R Civ P 56(d) the court can decline to make such an order if the federal judge determines that it will not materially expedite disposition of the case. See 10 Wright & Miller, FEDERAL PRACTICE AND

PROCEDURE: CIVIL §2737 (1973); Zack, *The 1973 Summary Judgment Act—New Teeth for an Old Tiger*, 48 CAL SBJ 654 (1973).

A motion for summary adjudication of issues may be made separately (*e.g., Kirtland & Packard v Superior Court* (1976) 59 CA3d 140, 143, 131 CR 418) or alternatively to a contemporaneous summary judgment motion (see, *e.g., Beaumont-Gribin-Von Dyl Mgmt. Co. v California Union Ins. Co.* (1976) 63 CA3d 617, 621, 134 CR 25, 26. Certain California courts have indicated that they will not deem specific issues to be established as an alternative to awarding full summary judgment unless that relief is requested in the notice of motion. See LA & SF Super Ct Law & Motion Manuals §77.

The procedure for declaring issues "without substantial controversy" may be the most significant change from former law, because it empowers the court to simplify and expedite the trial by eliminating uncontroverted issues. See *C-Thru Prods., Inc. v Uniflex, Inc.* (2d Cir 1968) 397 F2d 952; *E. I. duPont de Nemours & Co. v United States Camo Corp.* (WD Mo 1956) 19 FRD 495.

However, in actual practice, the motion for a summary adjudication of issues has been time consuming for both courts and counsel. Most of the difficulty arises from poorly organized and presented motions. In addition, the motion for summary adjudication of issues may be undesirable, even if successful, because it may remove from the jury's consideration important evidence by eliminating the issue to which the evidence relates. *Fuentes v Tucker* (1947) 31 C2d 1, 4, 187 P2d 752, 754.

§29.8 C. "Admissible Evidence" Standard; Sanctions for Bad Faith Declarations

Code of Civil Procedure §437c requires that opposing, as well as supporting, affidavits and declarations show that they are made on personal knowledge and based on admissible evidence (see §§29.49–29.52). The trend of California cases was in this direction even before enactment of current CCP §437c. See, *e.g., Parker v Twentieth Century-Fox Film Corp.* (1970) 3 C3d 176, 89 CR 737. Codifying this trend, current CCP §437c reverses an older line of California summary judgment decisions that permitted conclusions of law and other inadmissible evidence in counterdeclarations to defeat motions for summary judgments. See *Craig Corp. v Los Angeles* (1975) 51 CA3d 909,

915, 124 CR 621, 624; Zack, *California Summary Judgment: The Need for Legislative Reform*, 59 CALIF L REV 439, 446 (1971).

Personal knowledge must be shown factually and not by conclusion. See §29.49. The requirements for admissibility of evidence offered in a summary judgment declaration are the same as those prescribed for oral testimony. *Kramer v Barnes* (1963) 212 CA2d 440, 446, 27 CR 895, 899. Inadmissible evidence will not be considered by the court even when there is no objection. *Larsen v Johannes* (1970) 7 CA3d 491, 86 CR 744.

Under CCP §437c counterdeclarations are insufficient to prevent summary judgment if they merely (1) suggest evidence that may be adduced at trial (see *Whitney's at the Beach v Superior Court* (1970) 3 CA3d 258, 83 CR 237), (2) restate the pleadings (*Whitney's at the Beach v Superior Court, supra,* and cases cited), (3) present evidence outside the issues framed (*Keniston v American Nat'l Ins. Co.* (1973) 31 CA3d 803, 812, 107 CR 583, 589; but see *Varco-Pruden Inc. v Hampshire Constr. Co.* (1975) 50 CA3d 654, 123 CR 606, in which the court reversed a summary judgment after considering nonpleaded issues), or (4) set forth inadmissible evidence (see *Aguirre v Southern Pac. Co.* (1965) 232 CA2d 636, 43 CR 73).

However, declarations "of the moving party are strictly construed and those of his opponent liberally construed, and doubts as to the propriety of granting the motion should be resolved in favor of the party opposing the motion." *Stationers Corp. v Dun & Bradstreet, Inc.* (1965) 62 C2d 412, 417, 42 CR 449, 452. See also *Empire West v Southern Calif. Gas Co.* (1974) 12 C3d 805, 117 CR 423; *Tool Research & Eng'r Corp. v Henigson* (1975) 46 CA3d 675, 120 CR 291.

Former CCP §437c required that declarations state facts "with particularity." *Residents of Beverly Glen, Inc. v Los Angeles* (1973) 34 CA3d 117, 109 CR 724; *Jack v Wood* (1968) 258 CA2d 639, 65 CR 856. See also Zack, *The 1973 Summary Judgment Act—New Teeth for an Old Tiger*, 48 CAL SBJ 654 (1973). This requirement is no longer part of the statutory language; the only standard is the requirement of "admissible evidence."

Opinion evidence is only acceptable under CCP §437c if the declarations lay a proper foundation. 48 CAL SBJ at 654; see Jefferson, CALIFORNIA EVIDENCE BENCHBOOK chap 29 (CCJ-CEB 1972); Witkin, CALIFORNIA EVIDENCE chap 6 (2d ed 1966); see §29.51.

Code of Civil Procedure §437c goes further than merely providing that the motion will only be determined on the basis of admissible evidence. It affirmatively provides that a declaration presented in bad faith or for purposes of delay will result in sanctions being imposed on the party acting in bad faith. See §29.74.

§29.9   D. Effect of Disputes About Immaterial Facts

If there appears to be a dispute on the facts, the court must initially determine whether the disputed facts are material. A dispute about an immaterial fact does not preclude a summary judgment. Although "any material fact" was added in the current CCP §437c, the same result was reached under prior law. *Walsh v Glendale Fed. Sav. & Loan Ass'n* (1969) 1 CA3d 578, 583, 81 CR 804, 807, overruled on other grounds in 9 C3d at 737.

Current CCP §437c is similar to Fed R Civ P 56(c), which refers to "no genuine issue as to any material fact." Under federal cases, a fact is material if it tends to resolve any of the issues properly raised by the parties and within the range of allowable controversy in a particular lawsuit. 10 Wright & Miller, FEDERAL PRACTICE AND PROCEDURE: CIVIL §2725 (1973).

In California, two cases under former CCP §437c help in defining "triable issue as to any material fact." In *Oxford v Signal Oil & Gas Co.* (1970) 12 CA3d 403, 410, 90 CR 700, 704, material facts were defined as those "which are material to the lawsuit and could change the result one way or the other if resolved in favor of one side or the other." In *Coyne v Krempels* (1950) 36 C2d 257, 261, 223 P2d 244, 246, the court defined the phrase as those "facts [which] if proved, would be sufficient to sustain judgment . . . ." See also *Vesely v Sager* (1971) 5 C3d 153, 169, 95 CR 623, 635.

§29.10   E. Court To Draw Reasonable Inferences

In ruling on a summary judgment motion, the court must "consider all of the admissible evidence set forth in the papers and all inferences reasonably deducible from such evidence, except summary judgment shall not be granted by the court based on inferences reasonably deducible from such evidence, if contradicted by other inferences or evidence, which raise a triable issue as to any material fact." CCP §437c. The court must now consider presumptions and must draw an inference when it is the only inference to be drawn. See *Hale v George A. Hormel & Co.*

(1975) 48 CA3d 73, 121 CR 144; see cases cited in Zack, *The 1973 Summary Judgment Act—New Teeth for an Old Tiger*, 48 CAL SBJ 654 (1973). However, the court has no power under CCP §437c to weigh one inference against another or against other evidence. For definitions and use of inferences and presumptions, see Jefferson, CALIFORNIA EVIDENCE BENCHBOOK ch 46 (CCJ-CEB 1972); Witkin, CALIFORNIA EVIDENCE §§1132–1135 (2d ed 1966).

A party opposing a motion for summary judgment must file counteraffidavits when the moving papers establish facts that in themselves, or through inferences drawn from them, eliminate any triable issue of fact. In addition, the nonmoving party should point out any opposing inferences that can be drawn from the moving party's facts. See, *e.g.*, *Western Contracting Corp. v Southwest Steel Rolling Mills, Inc.* (1976) 58 CA3d 532, 129 CR 782; *Robinson v San Francisco* (1974) 41 CA3d 334, 116 CR 125; *De Angeles v Roos Bros., Inc.* (1966) 244 CA2d 434, 52 CR 783. See §§29.22–29.28 on moving and opposing parties' burdens.

§29.11 F. Lack of Credibility as Ground for Denial

Under former CCP §437c, even when the moving party's supporting declarations demonstrated that no triable issue of material fact existed, the courts in their discretion often refused to grant the motion because they felt the declarant's credibility was an issue. See Zack, *California Summary Judgment: The Need for Legislative Reform*, 59 CALIF LAW REV 439, 461 (1971). Under prior law, it was also held that if an issue concerning a material fact could not be resolved without observation of the demeanor of a witness, summary judgment could be denied. This is no longer so. See Zack, *The 1973 Summary Judgment Act—New Teeth for an Old Tiger*, 48 CAL SBJ 654, 658 (1973).

Although current law generally holds that summary judgment cannot be denied "on grounds of credibility or for want of cross-examination" of declarants (*Lerner v Superior Court* (1977) 70 CA3d 656, 139 CR 51) CCP §437c provides that summary judgment can be denied on these grounds, in the discretion of the court,

[1] where the only proof of a material fact offered in support of the summary judgment is an affidavit or declaration made by an individual

who was the *sole witness* to such fact; or [2] where a material fact is an individual's state of mind, or lack thereof, and such fact is sought to be established solely by the individual's affirmation thereof. [Emphasis added.]

Although CCP §437c does not define "sole witness," it seems to mean "sole available witness." If all other witnesses who have knowledge of the facts are unavailable within the meaning of Evid C §240, the declarant should be considered a "sole witness."

Although CCP §437c does not explicitly so provide, the court does have discretion to deny a motion for summary judgment when credibility of a witness is appropriately challenged by impeachment evidence supplied by the opposing party or by inherent contradictions in the witness' own statements. The California Supreme Court has held that a witness' declaration contradicting his previous admission in pretrial discovery must be disregarded because of the great credibility given to admissions. The court stated that such an inconsistent declaration made to oppose a motion for summary judgment is insufficient to raise a triable issue of material fact. *D'Amico v Board of Medical Examiners* (1974) 11 C3d 1, 21, 112 CR 786, 801. See also *Leasman v Beech Aircraft Corp.* (1975) 48 CA3d 376, 382, 121 CR 768, 771. Both cases were based on former CCP §437c before its amendment (see §29.2) but appear even more applicable under current CCP §437c.

§29.12   G. When Motion May Be Made

When CCP §437c was enacted in 1973, it provided only that the motion could be made at any time after 60 days had elapsed from the general appearance of the party against whom the motion was made. (For definition of "general appearance" see CCP §1014. See also 1 Witkin, CALIFORNIA PROCEDURE, Jurisdiction §§118–131 (2d ed 1970).) Because the motion is "made" when filed (CCP §1005.5) the motion must be filed more than 60 days after the general appearance. Scheduling the hearing more than 60 days after the general appearance is not sufficient compliance with CCP §437c.

In 1976, CCP §437c was amended to allow the 60-day period to be shortened. It now provides:

[t]he motion may be made at any time after 60 days have elapsed since the general appearance in the action or proceeding of each party

against whom the motion is directed *or at such earlier time after such general appearance as the court, with or without notice and upon good cause shown, may direct. Notice of the motion and supporting papers shall be served on the other party to the action at least 10 days before the time fixed for the hearing.* [Emphasis added.]

See §23.10 on whether notice served by mail under CCP §1013(a) must be mailed 15, 20, or 30 days before the hearing.

Even under this language, summary judgment probably cannot be entered against a defendant who still has time to answer. The answer defines the issues that must be addressed by a summary judgment motion. *Orange County Air Pollution Control Dist. v Superior Court* (1972) 27 CA3d 109, 113, 103 CR 410, 413. The same reasoning applies to motions for summary judgment on cross-complaints unless the cross-complaint reiterates the issues raised by the cross-complainant's answer. *Nationwide Inv. Corp. v California Funeral Serv., Inc.* (1974) 40 CA3d 494, 504, 114 CR 77, 83.

A defendant can move for summary judgment before filing an answer, but not until 60 days after filing of the complaint, unless time is shortened. The filing of a motion for summary judgment does not extend the time within which a responsive pleading must be filed. CCP §437c.

§29.13   H. Continuance on Certain Conditions

Under CCP §437c, the court is specifically given the power to deny the motion, to order a continuance to permit filing of further opposition papers or the pursuit of further discovery, or to make "such other order as may be just," if the opposing party shows by affidavit "that facts essential to justify opposition may exist but cannot, for reasons stated, then be presented." This language safeguards against a premature grant of summary judgment. This provision is adapted from Fed R Civ P 56(f), and the applicable federal cases (see 10 Wright & Miller, FEDERAL PRACTICE AND PROCEDURES: CIVIL §§2740–2741 (1973)) will be persuasive authority for the California courts.

The opposing affidavit need not contain evidentiary facts going to the merits of the case, but must state facts showing why opposing facts on the merits cannot yet be presented. A court will usually not be receptive to vague and general declarations, or declarations that do not refer to the statutory factors. For example, in *Coast-United Advertising v Long Beach* (1975) 51 CA3d

766, 124 CR 487, a continuance was properly denied when the facts sought to be presented later were not relevant to the litigation, and therefore were not facts "essential to justify opposition." Similarly, a request for time to conduct discovery will be denied when there was ample time previously to have obtained the desired information, and the opposition has been dilatory. *King v National Indus., Inc.* (6th Cir 1975) 512 F2d 29, 34 (interpreting Fed R Civ P 56(f)); *Windiate v Moore* (1962) 201 CA2d 509, 517, 19 CR 860, 866.

Counsel who are not diligent in presenting specific justification risk having summary judgment granted against them, although some federal courts have occasionally allowed parties who did not state the specific facts to obtain a short continuance under Fed R Civ P 56(f). See *Toebelman v Missouri-Kansas Pipe Line Co.* (3d Cir 1942) 130 F2d 1016; *La Cotonniere de Moislains v H. & B. Am. Mach. Co.* (D Mass 1956) 19 FRD 6. But see *Adickes v S. H. Kress & Co.* (1970) 398 US 144.

A moving party may be granted a continuance in certain circumstances to avoid what some judges believe would be denial of due process, *e.g.*, when the opposing party has filed late opposition papers that require a reply. Although not a statutory ground for continuance, it appears to be a sound exercise of discretion. On reasons for granting or denying a continuance generally, see *Wright & Miller, §2741*.

III. OTHER PROCEEDINGS COMPARED

A. Pretrial Motions

§29.14   1. Motion To Dismiss Action as Sham

A motion to dismiss an action as sham, based on matters outside the pleadings, is difficult to distinguish from a motion for summary judgment. Use of a sham motion caused considerable confusion until the California Supreme Court held that the judicially developed "speaking motion" to dismiss had been superseded by the statutory summary judgment motion under CCP §437c. See *Vesely v Sager* (1971) 5 C3d 153, 167, 95 CR 623, 633 (disapproving *Lincoln v Didak* (1958) 162 CA2d 625, 328 P2d 498); *Pianka v State* (1956) 46 C2d 208, 293 P2d 458.

§29.15   2. Motion To Strike Answer

Code of Civil Procedure §453 provides for a statutory motion to strike sham answers or affirmative defenses. In *Ford Motor Co. v Superior Court* (1971) 16 CA3d 442, 446, 94 CR 127, 129, the court differentiated between the procedures of motion to strike and motion for partial summary judgment (no longer permitted under current CCP §437c) noting that the purpose of the motion to strike is to determine whether issues raised by the pleadings are offered in good faith, and not to decide those issues. The court implied that a motion to strike under CCP §453 will reach only the issue of good faith of defendant's pleading, and a showing in support of this motion must necessarily be limited to facts related to that issue.

If a plaintiff or cross-complainant believes an answer or affirmative defense has been tendered in bad faith, he may move to strike. The motion must be filed within the time permitted for demurring to the answer (CCP §435), and the supporting facts must be limited to the issue of bad faith. If a plaintiff or cross-complainant wishes to show that no triable issue of fact exists concerning an answer or affirmative defense, he should move for summary judgment. See generally 1 CALIFORNIA CIVIL PROCEDURE BEFORE TRIAL ch 10 (Cal CEB 1977).

§29.16   3. Motion for Judgment on the Pleadings

A motion for summary judgment assumes that the pleadings are sufficient and requires evidentiary affidavits to permit the court to determine whether there are actually contested factual issues. A motion for judgment on the pleadings attacks fundamental defects in the pleadings.

A motion for a judgment on the pleadings may be made at any time after time to demur has expired. As a pretrial motion, it must be noticed. See generally chap 23. After trial commences, and the jury is sworn in a jury trial, or the first witness is sworn in a jury trial, a motion to exclude evidence because the pleadings are insufficient (*e.g.*, because the complaint fails to allege facts sufficient to state a cause of action) has the same effect as a pretrial motion for judgment on the pleadings and may even be more effective. See §29.17. At that point the trial court may be less likely to grant leave to amend the complaint. See §29.29 on amendment of pleadings. See generally 1 CALIFORNIA CIVIL PROCEDURE BEFORE TRIAL ch 13 (Cal CEB 1977).

A judgment on the pleadings will be entered on plaintiff's motion if the complaint states a cause of action and the answer raises no valid defense by denial or an affirmative allegation.

Adjustment Corp. v Hollywood Hardware & Paint Co. (1939) 35 CA2d 566, 96 P2d 161.

In some cases, a litigant has successfully moved for summary judgment under CCP §437c on the ground that the complaint fails to state a cause of action. However, appellate courts have treated the trial court judgment as if it had been made under a motion for judgment on the pleadings. See *Franklin v Municipal Court* (1972) 26 CA3d 884, 103 CR 354; *Pylon, Inc. v Olympic Ins. Co.* (1969) 271 CA2d 643, 655, 77 CR 72, 80; *Maxon v Security Ins. Co.* (1963) 214 CA2d 603, 29 CR 586. In *Magna Dev. Co. v Reed* (1964) 228 CA2d 230, 234, 39 CR 284, 287, the court affirmed a summary judgment, treating it as a judgment on the pleadings, on the basis that essential allegations were absent from the complaint.

Other appellate courts, however, have held that if the pleadings are insufficient, the defect must be raised by demurrer, or motion to strike or motion for judgment on the pleadings, and *not* by a motion for summary judgment. *Polin v Chung Cho* (1970) 8 CA3d 673, 680, 87 CR 591, 596.

B. Motions at Trial

§29.17 1. Objection to Introduction of All Evidence

Either party may object to the introduction of all evidence at the time of trial on the ground that the pleadings of the other party are fatally defective. *Miller v McLaglen* (1947) 82 CA2d 219, 223, 186 P2d 48, 50; 4 Witkin, CALIFORNIA PROCEDURE, Proceedings Without Trial §171 (2d ed 1971). This objection is similar to a motion for judgment on the pleadings, in which "the objecting party seeks to end the trial and obtain a favorable judgment, on the pleadings, without any evidence" on the ground "that if the allegations were proved they still would not state a cause of action or defense." 4 Witkin, PROCEDURE, Proceedings Without Trial §171; see §29.16.

§29.18 2. Motions for Nonsuit, Directed Verdict, and Judgment Notwithstanding Verdict

Motions for nonsuit (CCP §581c), directed verdict (see 4 Witkin, CALIFORNIA PROCEDURE, Trial §§352–353 (2d ed 1971), and judgment notwithstanding verdict (CCP §629; 4 Witkin, PROCEDURE, Trial §374), are jury trial motions. A motion for nonsuit is made after plaintiff has completed his opening statement or presentation of his evidence, a motion for directed verdict is usually made after all the evidence has been presented, and a motion for judgment notwithstanding verdict is made in the trial court after the jury has rendered its verdict. The court may direct a verdict only when there is no substantial conflict in the evidence. The trial court does not weigh evidence in these motions but "gives to the evidence of the party against whom it [the motion] is directed all of its legal value, indulges every legitimate inference from such evidence in favor of that party, and disregards conflicting evidence." 4 Witkin, PROCEDURE, Trial §353. See also 4 Witkin, PROCEDURE, Trial §§350–352, 366, 374. A judgment notwithstanding verdict is rendered "whenever a motion for a directed verdict for the aggrieved party should have been granted had a previous motion been made." CCP §629.

These trial motions entail many of the same decision-making problems for a lawyer or a judge as a motion for summary judgment. See Zack, *California Summary Judgment: The Need for Legislative Reform,* 59 CALIF L REV 439 (1971); Wright & Miller, 10 FEDERAL PRACTICE AND PROCEDURE: CIVIL §2713 (1973). These authorities point out that some California and federal appellate courts have denied summary judgment motions under former CCP §437c or Fed R Civ P 56 absent a showing that, if the case had been tried, a verdict would have been directed in favor of the party making the motion. These cases should be considered questionable authority under current CCP §437c, which permits the court to draw inferences. See §29.10.

A motion for summary judgment is not the equivalent of a motion for a nonsuit. A motion for nonsuit can be premised on plaintiff's failure to produce evidence at the time of trial to prove essential elements of his case. The party moving for summary judgment, however, must affirmatively prove beyond controversy each fact necessary to judgment in his favor, even on issues on which his opponent would bear the burden of proof at trial. He cannot rely simply on his opponent's failure or inability to present evidence. See *Barnes v Blue Haven Pools* (1969) 1 CA3d 123, 81 CR 444.

§29.19   3. Motion for Judgment Under CCP §631.8

A motion for judgment under CCP §631.8 may be made in a nonjury trial after one party has completed his presentation of evidence. The court, as the trier of fact, weighs the evidence and may render a judgment. In a motion for summary judgment the court determines whether triable issues of material facts exist (*Coyne v Krempels* (1950) 36 C2d 257, 223 P2d 244); in a motion under CCP §631.8 the court makes a fact determination (*Greening v General Air-Conditioning Corp.* (1965) 233 CA2d 545, 43 CR 662).

§29.20   4. Motion for Trial Under CCP §597

A motion may be made under CCP §597 at trial that special defenses, not related to the merits (*e.g.*, statute of limitations or res judicata) be tried first. Decision on these issues may make a trial on the merits unnecessary.

Defenses such as statute of limitations or res judicata are determined at trial when testimony and other evidence must be received to resolve a controverted issue of fact. However, if an adequate and undisputed factual showing can be made, these special defenses can be determined by a motion for summary judgment. See *Kaiser Foundation Hosp. v Superior Court* (1967) 254 CA2d 327, 62 CR 330. On the distinction between a motion under CCP §597 and a motion for summary judgment, see *Gardner v Shreve* (1949) 89 CA2d 804, 202 P2d 322.

IV. DECIDING TO MAKE OR TO OPPOSE MOTION

§29.21   A. Moving Party's Objectives

The moving party's objective in a motion for summary judgment is to demonstrate, by admissible evidence, admissions, and stipulations, either that there are no triable issues of any material fact and that judgment should therefore be entered in his favor or that there is no actual controversy over certain issues and they may be eliminated from the case.

§29.22   B. Moving Party's Substantive Burden

A party moving for summary judgment bears the substantive burden of setting forth admissible evidence sufficient to establish all legal elements for judgment. *Beech Aircraft Corp. v Superior Court* (1976) 61 CA3d 501, 520, 132 CR 541, 551; Zack, *California Summary Judgment: The Need for Legislative Reform*, 59 CALIF L REV 439, 444 (1971). This is true even though at trial the opposing party might bear the burden of proof on one or more of these elements. *Barnes v Blue Haven Pools* (1969) 1 CA3d 123, 127, 81 CR 444, 447.

If the moving party is a plaintiff, he must bear the burden of proof on all theories of recovery, and also negate all theories of defense raised by the pleadings, even if they are not immediately apparent. *Residents of Beverly Glen, Inc. v Los Angeles* (1973) 34 CA3d 117, 127, 109 CR 724, 731. If the moving party is a defendant, he must take the same role with respect to an affirmative defense. In *Chakmak v H. J. Lucas Masonry, Inc.* (1976) 55 CA3d 124, 127 CR 404, a motion for summary judgment on an affirmative defense that the contract sued on had been entered into as a result of mutual mistake was denied because it failed to negate the possibility that defendant had been so negligent in its communications with plaintiff that plaintiff could reasonably have believed a contract existed. See also *Pasadena City Fire Fighters Ass'n v Board of Directors* (1974) 36 CA3d 901, 112 CR 56; *Coyne v Krempels* (1950) 36 C2d 257, 223 P2d 244.

A party seeking summary adjudication of issues bears a lighter burden than the party seeking summary judgment. To secure an order deeming an issue to be without substantial controversy, the party need only present sufficient admissible evidence to establish each element necessary to a determination in his favor on that issue. Although the issue that the party seeks to have summarily adjudicated often involves only one element, the issue may involve many elements. See, *e.g.*, *Beech Aircraft Corp. v Superior Court* (1976) 61 CA3d 501, 132 CR 541.

§29.23 1. Plaintiff's Burden

When plaintiff moves for summary judgment, he must prove every element of his cause of action and also that the defenses raised are "sham." *Hayward Union High School Dist. v Madrid* (1965) 234 CA2d 100, 120, 44 CR 268, 280. The plaintiff's motion for summary judgment should be denied whenever the moving or opposing papers raise a triable issue of material fact concerning any element of plaintiff's affirmative case or all elements of any affirmative defense.

§29.24 2. Defendant's Burden

A defendant moving for summary judgment must disprove at least one material allegation of the complaint. See *Swaffield v*

Universal Ecsco Corp. (1969) 271 CA2d 147, 76 CR 680; *Fuller v Goodyear Tire & Rubber Co.* (1970) 7 CA3d 690, 86 CR 705, or prove all elements of an affirmative defense. *Chakmak v H. J. Lucas Masonry, Inc.* (1976) 55 CA3d 124, 127 CR 404. Any defense, whether an affirmative defense or denial, may be the basis of a motion for summary judgment, although some defenses, e.g., statute of limitations, release, and res judicata, are more often appropriate for summary judgment than others.

C. Opposing Party's Substantive Burden

§29.25 1. When Moving Party Has Not Met Burden

The moving party must present sufficient admissible evidence to establish each element necessary for summary judgment. See §§29.22–29.24. Until the moving party's burden is met the opposing party need not file counteraffidavits and may base his opposition solely on the inadequacy of the showing supporting the motion. *Beech Aircraft Corp. v Superior Court* (1976) 61 CA3d 501, 520, 132 CR 541, 551; *Vesely v Sager* (1971) 5 C3d 153, 169, 95 CR 623, 635.

Nevertheless, even when the moving party does not appear to have carried his initial burden, it may be advisable for the opposing party to file counteraffidavits. Absent counteraffidavits, the court may accept as true any facts properly set forth in the moving party's affidavits. See *Beech Aircraft Corp. v Superior Court, supra; Truslow v Woodruff* (1967) 252 CA2d 158, 164, 60 CR 304, 308. If no counteraffidavits are filed, the court may conclude that the opposing party has no serious opposition to the motion. In courts that do not require a specific notice within the summary judgment motion of an intent to move alternatively for summary adjudication of issues (see §29.7), counteraffidavits should be filed to preclude the possibility that particular issues may be summarily adjudicated even though summary judgment is denied.

§29.26 2. When Moving Party Has Met Burden

When the papers filed by the moving party meet his initial burden, the opposing party then has the substantive burden of presenting sufficient admissible evidence to establish that there is at least one triable issue of material fact on at least one of the elements necessary for judgment for the moving party. See §§29.22–29.24 on moving party's burden.

A plaintiff opposing a defendant's motion for summary judgment must show a triable issue of fact on each element of plaintiff's case which defendant's motion has properly attacked and on at least one element of each affirmative defense established by defendant's motion. See §29.24 on moving defendant's burden.

A defendant opposing a plaintiff's motion for summary judgment must show a triable issue of fact on each of the elements of each affirmative defense attacked by plaintiff's motion or on at least one element of plaintiff's affirmative case. See §29.23 on moving plaintiff's burden.

When the motion is for summary adjudication of issues (see §29.7), the opposing party must satisfy the court that at least one triable issue of material fact exists as to each issue for which the moving party seeks summary adjudication.

§29.27 3. When Opposing Party Files Cross-Motion

When the party opposing a motion for summary judgment desires a favorable summary judgment or adjudication of issues, he must file a cross-motion for summary judgment or adjudication of issues, thereby becoming a moving party. *Dvorin v Appellate Dep't* (1975) 15 C3d 648, 125 CR 771. Even when a cross-motion is filed, the court need not grant summary judgment, unless either the moving or cross-moving party has met his burden. *Coast Elevator Co. v State Bd. of Equalization* (1975) 44 CA3d 576, 583, 118 CR 818, 823, overruled on other grounds in 17 C3d at 93 n4.

§29.28 4. When Opposing Party Wants Delay or Amendment of Pleadings

If the opposing party has not developed the facts he needs to oppose the summary judgment motion, his objective will be to have the motion denied or continued by filing declarations showing that "facts essential to justify opposition may exist but cannot, for reasons stated, then be presented . . . ." CCP §437c. See §29.13 on conditions for continuance.

V. PREPARING TO MAKE OR OPPOSE MOTION
§29.29 A. Reviewing and Amending the Pleadings

The pleadings define the scope of the issues on a motion for summary judgment. *Warfield v McGraw-Hill, Inc.* (1973) 32

CA3d 1041, 108 CR 652. Affidavits must be directed to issues raised by the pleadings. *Keniston v American Nat'l Ins. Co.* (1973) 31 CA3d 803, 107 CR 583. But see *Varco-Pruden, Inc. v Hampshire Constr. Co.* (1975) 50 CA3d 654, 123 CR 606. Review of the pleadings will reveal the elements of each cause of action or defense, including affirmative defense, that must be proved in order for the moving party to obtain judgment. *Coyne v Krempels* (1950) 36 C2d 257, 223 P2d 244. The pleadings also show whether a party has made a judicial admission that may be used in the motion. See §29.45 on admissions.

Defects in the moving party's pleadings, which might render the pleadings vulnerable to a general demurrer or a motion for judgment on the pleadings do not preclude a summary judgment in his favor if the supporting affidavits are factually within the general scope of the causes of actions in the pleadings. *Varco-Pruden, Inc. v Hampshire Constr. Co., supra; Ramos v Santa Clara* (1973) 35 CA3d 93, 110 CR 485; *State Medical Ed. Bd. v Roberson* (1970) 6 CA3d 493, 501, 86 CR 258, 263. *Rodes v Shannon* (1961) 194 CA2d 743, 15 CR 349. However, because amendments are liberally granted as long as they are in the "general area of the cause set up in the pleadings" (*Residents of Beverly Glen, Inc. v Los Angeles* (1973) 34 CA3d 117, 128, 109 CR 724, 731), if a moving party finds his pleadings are inadequate it is better practice to move to amend.

An opposing party may also wish to reframe his complaint or answer to defeat or soften the impact of a summary judgment motion. If the defect in the opposing party's pleading is one of uncertainty or omission that might render the pleading subject to demurrer, that defect may be corrected by declaration, without necessity of amendment. *U.S. Fidelity & Guar. Co. v Sullivan* (1949) 93 CA2d 559, 209 P2d 429. If, however, the opposing party wishes to base opposition on a defense or claim not previously pleaded, an amendment is generally required, because a counterdeclaration would be restricted to issues raised by the pleadings. *Keniston v American Nat'l Ins. Co.* (1973) 31 CA3d 803, 812, 107 CR 583, 589.

If an amendment is needed to oppose a motion for summary judgment, the opposing party should serve, file, and set for hearing a formal motion to amend before the hearing on the summary judgment motion. The two motions should not be heard on the same day because the amendment may make the summary judgment motion moot. If the defect is not discovered until the time of the hearing on the motion for summary judgment, an oral motion may be made at the time of hearing, accompanied by a declaration to preserve the record.

The burden is on the party opposing the motion for summary judgment to put the request for amendment properly before the court. *Cullincini v Deming* (1975) 53 CA3d 908, 915 n5, 126 CR 427, 431 n5. If no effort to amend is made, or if a motion is not diligently pursued, the court does not abuse its discretion by failing to permit an amendment. *Alameda Conservation Ass'n v Alameda* (1968) 264 CA2d 284, 289, 70 CR 264, 266. No inquiry need be made by the court if the issue is not raised. *Krupp v Mullen* (1953) 120 CA2d 53, 260 P2d 629, 632. However, once a proper application is made, a rule of great liberality applies. *Residents of Beverly Glen, Inc. v Los Angeles* (1973) 34 CA3d 117, 128, 109 CR 724, 731.

As a practical matter, a defect in pleadings is usually called to the attention of the erring party, and, in most cases, the court will grant a continuance and permit an amendment to correct the defect before proceeding with a motion for summary judgment. See CCP §594a.

§29.30   B. Gathering the Facts

Factual preparation for a pretrial summary judgment motion and for trial are essentially the same. Each requires investigation, discovery, and fact gathering (*e.g.*, (1) acquiring originals of necessary documents or, alternatively, foundational proof for admission of secondary evidence; (2) interviewing to determine which persons can identify documents).

One beneficial side effect of preparing for a motion for summary judgment, even if the motion is denied, is that both parties are better prepared for trial. Because CCP §437c provides sanctions when the court determines that one or more of the affidavits was presented in bad faith or solely for purposes of delay, both sides are likely to exercise care in fact gathering so that affidavits are factual and made by persons having personal knowledge of the facts.

§29.31   C. Timing the Motion

A summary judgment motion usually may not be made until after 60 days have elapsed from the general appearance of the party against whom the motion is directed. However, for good cause shown, the court may shorten this time, but the opposing party must still be given at least ten days' notice of the hearing. CCP §437c. See §29.12.

As a tactical matter, a motion for summary judgment usually should not be filed until the issues are joined by the pleadings (*Keniston v American Nat'l Ins. Co.* (1973) 31 CA3d 803, 107 CR 583) and the moving party has completed all discovery, formal and informal (*Whitney's at the Beach v Superior Court* (1970) 3 CA3d 258, 271, 83 CR 237, 246; *Cox v State* (1970) 3 CA3d 301, 311, 82 CR 896, 902). The trial court may choose to continue a motion for summary judgment brought before the issues of the case have been defined by responsive pleadings. A continuance is particularly likely if a demurrer, motion to strike, or motion to amend is pending.

Delaying the motion until after all discovery has been completed is also usually advisable because (1) discovery helps the moving party determine whether triable issues of fact exist, (2) admissions and answers and other information gained in discovery may provide unrebuttable proof of elements of the moving party's case (*D'Amico v Board of Medical Examiners* (1974) 11 C3d 1, 21, 112 CR 786, 801); (3) discovery preserves evidence for later use should a witness become unavailable for any reason (see Zack, *A Primer for Summary Judgment*, 2 UWLA L REV 1 (1970)); and (4) information gained by discovery is usable at trial if the motion is denied.

In some unusual cases, it may be advisable to bring a summary judgment motion early, before all discovery has been completed and perhaps even before the pleading stage has been completed. An early motion may (1) avoid expensive and unnecessary discovery, (2) result in a quick disposition of a case in which delay would prejudice the moving party, and (3) dispose of a case before an opposing party has time to prepare fully and learn facts that would strengthen his case.

VI. DRAFTING THE MOTION

A. Checklist: Common Drafting Defects That Prevent Consideration of Merits

§29.32   1. Defects in Notice of Motion

(a) Failure to state date, time, place of hearing, or any of these. *Bohn v Bohn* (1913) 164 C 532, 129 P 981.

(b) Failure to state nature of relief sought. CP §1010; Cal Rules of Ct 201(c)(6); 501(c)(6).

(c) Failure to state grounds of motion. CCP §1010.

(d) Failure to specify papers or documents relied on. CCP §1010.

§29.33   2. Defects in Supporting Papers

(a) Failure to comply with CCP §2015.5 relating to declarations under penalty or perjury by: (1) omission of signature; (2) omission of date, place of execution, or both; (3) failure to assert the truth of the matter stated. *Baron v Mare* (1975) 47 CA3d 304, 120 CR 675. A mere jurat, without vouching for the truth of the contents of the document, will not suffice. *Hoffman v Palm Springs* (1959) 169 CA2d 645, 337 P2d 521. But see *People v Pacific Land Research Co.* (1976) 63 CA3d 873, 134 CR 114, which questions *Baron* on the ground that form should not be exalted over substance when there is substantial compliance with CCP §2015.5, and *Pacific Air Lines, Inc. v Superior Court* (1965) 231 CA2d 587, 42 CR 68 (statement declared to be made "under penalty of perjury" sufficient even without saying "true and correct"); (4) failure to use an affidavit form when the witness makes his statement out of state, unless it is a state that permits declarations under penalty of perjury.

(b) Failure to comply with the requirement of CCP §2003 that an affidavit show the witness has been sworn. See *Pacific Air Lines, Inc. v Superior Court* (1965) 231 CA2d 587, 42 CR 68. (However, unless required by a particular statute, an affidavit need not be subscribed or dated. See *Dodge v Free* (1973) 32 CA3d 436, 108 CR 311.)

(c) Failure to comply with the requirement of CCP §437c that "[s]upporting and opposing affidavits or declarations shall be made by any person on personal knowledge, shall set forth admissible evidence, and shall show affirmatively that the affiant is competent to testify to the matters stated therein," by (1) reciting legal conclusions or ultimate fact instead of statements of evidentiary facts (*Baron v Mare* (1975) 47 CA3d 304, 120 CR 765; *Jack v Wood* (1968) 258 CA2d 639, 65 CR 856; see §29.51); (2) reciting matters that would be excluded under the rules of evidence (see 4 Witkin, CALIFORNIA PROCEDURE, Proceedings Without Trial §§184–185 (2d ed 1971); Zack, *California Summary Judgment: The Need for Legislative Reform*, 59 CALIF L REV 439, 448); (3) failure to authenticate a necessary writing (see §§29.55–29.56); (4) failure to meet foundational requirements of Evid C §1271 for introduction of business records (see §§29.60–

29.61); (5) failure to meet foundational requirements of Evid C §1272 to introduce fact of absence of business records (see *People v Torres* (1962) 201 CA2d 290, 20 CR 315 (decided under former CCP §1953e–1953h, now Evid C §1272)); (6) failure to comply with the best evidence rule (Evid C §§1500–1510) or to show the applicability of an exception to the rule by preliminary or foundational facts (see Jefferson, CALIFORNIA EVIDENCE BENCHBOOK chap 31 (CCJ-CEB 1972); Witkin, CALIFORNIA EVIDENCE §§688–702 (2d ed 1966); see §§29.57–29.58); (7) failure to lay a proper foundation for introduction of expert opinion testimony (see Evid C §801); (8) failure to comply with Evid C §435, when judicial notice is sought.

B. Notice of Motion and Motion

§29.34 1. Contents

The notice of motion for summary judgment must meet all the requirements of CCP §1010 for motions generally, *i.e.*, it must state nature of relief sought, grounds on which the motion is made, date, time, and place of hearing and papers or documents relied on. *Bohn v Bohn* (1913) 164 C 532, 129 P 981; see generally §§23.18–23.25.

§29.35 a. Designation of Opposing Party

The moving party should specifically identify in the body of the notice the party against whom the motion is directed rather than designating "all parties and their attorneys of record." This is particularly important in a complicated case in which there are multiple parties.

§29.36 b. Statement of Grounds

Although the statement of the grounds can be made in general terms, it is better practice to specify the particular ground or grounds on which the motion is based.

A defendant moving party can usually be more specific than a plaintiff in stating grounds for a motion because he attacks only one or two elements of the cause of action or relies on an affirmative defense. If defendant's motion is based on denial of a fact that is a necessary element of plaintiff's case, the motion should set forth the fact denied. When a moving defendant relies on an affirmative defense, he should state the defense and the facts showing its applicability, *e.g.*, that the action is barred by a designated judgment or that the obligation sued on is barred because of a specific statute of limitations, citing the statute and stating the facts that bring the case with it.

§29.37   c. Nature of Order Sought

It is advisable in most motions for summary judgment to characterize that the motion is one for summary judgment and also request summary adjudication of specific issues. Some courts refuse to adjudicate issues to be without substantial controversy unless the notice of motion specifically requests such relief. See §29.7.

§29.38   d. Description of Documents Relied On

Although reference to the pleadings, records, and files in the action is sufficient to put all matters in the file before the court (*Larsen v Johannes* (1970) 7 CA3d 491, 86 CR 744), it is better practice specifically to identify in the notice of motion each document that is the basis for or supports the motion, *e.g.*, specific depositions and interrogatories. See, *e.g.*, *Howe v Pioneer Mfg. Co.* (1968) 262 CA2d 330, 336, 68 CR 617, 621, in which the record did not show that depositions referred to in the papers filed in connection with a motion for summary judgment had been filed with the court before hearing or that the depositions or their contents (other than abstracts contained in the supporting affidavits) were offered in evidence at the hearing. The appellate court held that references to "pleadings, records and files" in the notice of motion and to "the papers or records on file or lodged with the clerk" were not sufficient to show that entire depositions were received as exhibits or evidence at the hearing and that therefore its review was limited only to those portions of the depositions placed before the trial court in the affidavit filed in connection with the motion. See generally §23.24.

2. Forms

§29.39   a. Notice of Motion for Summary Judgment or for Summary Adjudication of Issues

Copies: Original (filed with court clerk with proof of service); copies for service (one for each attorney of record and unrepresented party); office copies.

§29.39 SUMMARY JUDGMENT 286

[Caption. See §§23.18–23.19]

No. ----------

NOTICE OF MOTION FOR SUMMARY JUDGMENT FOR ----[PLAINTIFF / DEFENDANT]---- OR FOR ADJUDICATION OF ISSUES WITHOUT SUBSTANTIAL CONTROVERSY; POINTS AND AUTHORITIES; DECLARATIONS

To ----[name of each party against whom relief is sought]---- and his attorney(s) of record:

PLEASE TAKE NOTICE that on ----[date of hearing; see §29.12]---- at ----.m., in ----[e.g., Department No. ----]-- at ----[address]----, ----[name of moving party]---- **will move the Court for**

[If plaintiff is moving party and only a complaint
and answer are on file]

entry of summary judgment in favor of plaintiff and against defendant as prayed for in the complaint in this action.

This motion is made on the grounds that no triable issue of material fact exists and that there is no defense to the action.

[When plaintiff is moving party and a
cross-complaint also is on file]

an order for entry of summary judgment on the complaint in favor of plaintiff and against defendant as prayed for in the complaint, and on the cross-complaint in favor of cross-defendant and against cross-complainant.

This motion is made on the ground that no triable issue of material fact exists, there is no defense to the action, and the cross-complaint is without merit in that _____.

[When defendant is moving party and only a complaint
and an answer are on file]

entry of summary judgment in favor of defendant and against plaintiff.

This motion is made on the ground that no triable issue of material fact exists and the action has no merit in that _____.

[When defendant is moving party and no answer is on file]

an order for entry of summary judgment that plaintiff take nothing and that defendant recover his costs incurred in this action.

This motion is made on the ground that no triable issue of material fact exists and the action has no merit in that _____.

[When defendant is moving party and a
cross-complaint is on file]

an order for entry of summary judgment against plaintiff and in favor of de-

fendant and in favor of cross-complainant and against cross-defendant on the cross-complaint as prayed for in the cross-complaint.

This motion is made on the ground that no triable issue of material fact exists, the action has no merit in that _____, and there is no defense to the cross-complaint in that _____.

[When order adjudicating issues sought]

In the event summary judgment is not granted, ____[plaintiff / defendant]____ will move the Court for an order adjudicating the following issues as without substantial controversy and deemed established against ____[defendant / plaintiff]____: ____[list issues] _____.

This motion is made on the ground that there is no triable issue of material fact on these issues.

[Continue]

This motion is based on this notice, the pleadings, records, and files in this action, the attached memorandum of points and authorities and supporting declaration of ____[name]____, ____[and on such evidence as may be presented at the hearing]____.

Dated: _____

[Signature of attorney]

[Typed name]
Attorney for ____[name]____

§29.40   b. Notice of Motion for Summary Adjudication of Issues

Copies: Original (filed with court clerk with proof of service); copies for service (one for each attorney of record and unrepresented party); office copies.

[Caption. See §§23.18–23.19]

No. _____

NOTICE OF MOTION FOR SUMMARY ADJUDICATION OF ISSUES UNDER CCP §437c; POINTS AND AUTHORITIES: DECLARATION

To ____[name each party against whom relief is sought]____ and ____[his]____ attorney(s) of record:

PLEASE TAKE NOTICE that on ____[date of hearing; see §29.12]____ at ____ __.m., or as soon thereafter as the matter can be heard, at the courtroom of ____[Department No. ____]____ at ____[address]____, **California,** ____[name of moving party]____ will move the Court for an order adjudicating the following issues as without substantial controversy and deemed established against ____[plaintiff / defendant]____: ____[list issues] _____.

This motion is made on the ground that there is no triable issue of material fact on these issues in that _____.

This motion is based on this notice, the pleadings, records, and files in this action, the attached memorandum of points and authorities and declaration of ____[name]____ ____[and on such evidence as may be presented at the hearing] _____.

Dated: _____

[Signature of attorney]

[Typed name]
Attorney for ____[name]____

§29.41 C. Memorandum of Points and Authorities

California Rules of Court 203(a) and 503(a) require a memorandum of points and authorities to be filed with a motion for summary judgment. While reference to CCP §437c may be sufficient to satisfy these rules (*Taliaferro v Coakley* (1960) 186 CA2d 258, 9 CR 529), and permit a judge, in the exercise of his discretion, to consider the motion, that reference may not be sufficient to satisfy local rules. See §23.26. Reference to cases restating general principles of summary judgment law is usually not necessary, but the memorandum should clearly list the issues confronting the court, and the authorities supporting the moving party's position on those issues.

Local rules in Los Angeles and San Francisco require a memorandum in support of a motion for summary adjudication of issues to show the evidence which establishes that each issue is without substantial controversy. LA & SF LAW & MOTION MANUALS §77.

Reference to cases supporting sufficiency of evidentiary foundations or sufficiency of evidence to sustain a judgment is also helpful.

D. Summary of Issues and Evidence
§29.42 1. Need for Summary

Usually, the judge who rules on a summary judgment motion has no background knowledge of the facts and issues involved. Therefore, the moving party should summarize for the court the facts and issues involved in the motion within the context of the entire case so that the court will not have to glean the information from the entire file.

One effective method of presenting facts and issues is by a detailed statement of facts, with references to the record, made part of the memorandum of points and authorities; another is by a table of contents or appendix to the memorandum. (By local rule, some federal courts require a separate listing of contested or uncontested facts containing appropriate reference to the affidavits.)

§29.43 2. Sample: Summary of Issues and Evidence: Contract Case

Elements of Case

Issue	Location of Evidence
Making of contract	Declaration of _____, p 2, lines 18, 23
Delivery of contract	Declaration of _____, p 2, line 26
Consideration for contract	Deposition of _____, p 36, lines 2–5
Performance of conditions precedent	Contract, see Exhibit "A"
Breach of contract	Deposition of _____, p 18, lines 7–10 p 29, lines 14–28
Damages suffered by breach	Declaration of _____, p 3, lines 1–27

Documents: Authentication

Contract, Exhibit "A"	Declaration of _____, p 4, lines 6–14
Letter, Exhibit "B"	Deposition of _____, p 12, lines 15–17
Bill, Exhibit "C"	Response to request for admission #3

Hearsay: Foundations

Bill, Exhibit "C"	Response to interrogatories 5–9, declaration of _____, p 2, line 5–19

Secondary Evidence Foundation

Letter, Exhibit "B"	Notice to produce, served and filed _____

§29.44 SUMMARY JUDGMENT 290

E. Supporting Papers

§29.44 1. Types of Supporting Papers

Code of Civil Procedure §437c permits the moving or opposing party to prove the facts necessary to carry his substantive burden by the following methods:

(a) Stipulations or admissions in the opposite party's pleadings or other papers. *Parker v Twentieth Century-Fox Film Corp.* (1970) 3 C3d 176, 89 CR 737; *Joslin v Marin Munic. Water Dist.* (1967) 67 C2d 132, 60 CR 377; *Residents of Beverly Glen, Inc. v Los Angeles* (1973) 34 CA3d 117, 109 CR 724; *Larsen v Johannes* (1970) 7 CA3d 491, 86 CR 744. See §29.45.

(b) Judicially noticed matters. See §29.46.

(c) Affidavits or declarations if these affidavits or declarations set forth admissible factual evidence. See §§29.49–29.52.

(d) Evidence derived from discovery procedures, *e.g.*, depositions, answers to interrogatories or requests for admissions, documents produced in response to requests for production of documents, or reports of physical or mental examinations. *Craig Corp. v Los Angeles* (1975) 51 CA3d 909, 124 CR 621; *Leasman v Beech Aircraft Corp.* (1975) 48 CA3d 376, 121 CR 768; *Dixon v Grace Lines, Inc.* (1972) 27 CA3d 278, 103 CR 595; *Bank of America v Baker* (1965) 238 CA2d 778, 48 CR 165. See §§29.62–29.66.

(e) Inferences that may be drawn from undisputed facts. See §29.10.

A party may not rely on the following methods to prove any fact needed to support or oppose a summary judgment motion.

(1) His own pleadings. *Slobojan v Western Travelers Life Ins. Co.* (1969) 70 C2d 432, 437, 74 CR 895, 898.

(2) Inconsistent theories or facts pleaded by an opposing party. See 3 Witkin, CALIFORNIA PROCEDURE, Pleading §§290–299 (2d ed 1971). (However, a triable issue of fact may be raised if the moving party submits mutually contradictory or inconsistent declarations in support of the motion. *Spencer v Hibernia Bank* (1960) 186 CA2d 702, 718, 9 CR 867, 877.)

(3) Admissions or answers to interrogatories made by a party other than the party opposing or moving for summary judgment. *People v One 1950 Mercury Sedan* (1953) 116 CA2d 746, 254 P2d 666. See Evid C §1220.

(4) Oral testimony. *Spencer v Hibernia Bank* (1960) 186 CA2d 702, 717, 9 CR 867, 876.

§29.45 2. Stipulations and Admissions

Stipulations may be used to demonstrate that material facts are not in issue. *Parker v Twentieth Century-Fox Film Corp.* (1970) 3 C3d 176, 181, 89 CR 737, 740. For a stipulation to be binding, it must be in writing and filed with the court clerk, or made orally and entered in the court minutes. CCP §283(1). Exceptions may exist to these requirements, but they should not be relied on. See 1 Witkin, CALIFORNIA PROCEDURE, Attorneys §§129–130 (2d ed 1970). An endorsed copy of the stipulation or the court minutes should accompany the motion papers if a stipulation is relied on.

Admissions in the other party's pleadings may be used to show that facts are not in dispute. See *Residents of Beverly Glen, Inc. v Los Angeles* (1973) 34 CA3d 117, 127, 109 CR 724, 731. The other party's pleadings need not be verified in order to be used in this manner. See generally Witkin, CALIFORNIA EVIDENCE, §§501–506 (2d ed 1966).

Judicial admissions by an affirmative allegation or failure to deny an allegation will support a motion for summary judgment. CCP §437c; *Reich v Yow* (1967) 249 CA2d 12, 57 CR 117.

A judicial admission also results:

(a) If an unverified answer is filed to a verified complaint. *Patterson v Blackburn* (1920) 47 CA 362, 190 P 483. When this occurs a summary motion may be combined with a motion for a judgment on the pleadings. See *Hearst v Hart* (1900) 128 C 327, 60 P 846;

(b) When a denial of matter peculiarly within defendant's knowledge is made on information and belief (*Dobbins v Hardister* (1966) 242 CA2d 787, 791, 51 CR 866, 869), or

(c) When denial of a matter of public record is made on information and belief (*Oliver v Swiss Club Tell* (1963) 222 CA2d 528, 539, 35 CR 324, 329).

Judicial admissions need not be referred to in a declaration (*Rooney v Vermont Inv. Corp.* (1973) 10 C3d 351, 370, n15, 110 CR 353, 366, n15) but rather should be listed or referred to in the points and authorities.

As a practical matter, however, judicial admissions are usually eliminated by amendment of the pleadings. *Board of Educ. v Mulcahy* (1942) 50 CA2d 418, 423, 123 P2d 114, 118 (failure to verify); *Jenssen v R.K.O. Studios, Inc.* (1937) 20 CA2d 705, 67 P2d 757.

The moving party may not rely on his own pleadings, admissions in the pleadings of a party not the opposing party, or properly pleaded inconsistent allegations. See §29.44.

3. Judicially Noticed Matters

§29.46   a. Matters for Mandatory and Permissible Judicial Notice

The court may consider facts that are properly the subject of judicial notice. CCP §437c; *Parker v Twentieth Century-Fox Film Corp.* (1970) 3 C3d 176, 181, 89 CR 737, 740. Evidence Code §451 states those facts that are the subject of mandatory judicial notice; Evid C §452 lists the facts that are permissibly the subject of judicial notice.

Often a party will find useful facts within public records. "[W]hile the courts take judicial notice of public records, they do not take notice of the truth of matters stated therein." *People v Long* (1970) 7 CA3d 586, 591, 86 CR 590, 593. The official character of a document does not make inadmissible material in it admissible. *People v Long, supra; Marocco v Ford Motor Co.* (1970) 7 CA3d 84, 89, 86 CR 526, 528; Witkin, CALIFORNIA EVIDENCE §167 (2d ed 1966). These authorities specifically apply to court records. *Day v Sharp* (1975) 50 CA3d 904, 914, 123 CR 918, 924. However, if the matters stated in the records are themselves independently appropriate for judicial notice, they may be so noticed. If they are admissible as evidence, the court may consider them. For example, if the document is a pleading or declaration by the adverse party, its contents may be admissible as an admission. See §29.45. Similarly, an evidentiarily sufficient declaration made by a person with personal knowledge of matters stated may be used even though it was filed in a different action. *R. D. Reeder Lathing Co. v Allen* (1967) 66 C2d 373, 380, 57 CR 841, 845.

Facts personally observed by the court are not properly considered on summary judgment (*Stewart v Whitmyre* (1961) 192 CA2d 327, 13 CR 235) and are generally not subject to judicial notice. Witkin, CALIFORNIA EVIDENCE §151 (2d ed 1966).

For notice to be taken of matters of mandatory judicial notice under Evid C §451, reference to the matter usually need only be made in the memorandum of points and authorities or in the summary of facts. For notice to be taken of matters of permissive judicial notice under Evid C §452 however, the following three steps must be taken:

(1) The party must request judicial notice;

(2) the adverse party must be given sufficient notice of the request to prepare to meet it, and

(3) the court must be given sufficient information to enable it to take judicial notice. Evid C §453.

Although there is no specific time set for "sufficient notice" to the adverse party, it is good practice to make the request, thereby giving notice together with the motion papers. See §29.47 for form of request.

Although the requirements of Evid C §453 may be met by appropriate language in the notice of motion, the memorandum of points and authorities, or the summary of the evidence, it is usually preferable to file a separate request for judicial notice. The request should specify each matter of which judicial notice is requested, citing the subdivision of Evid C §452 under which notice may be taken, and applying sufficient information to permit notice to be taken. If judicial notice of a document is requested, the document should be appended.

§29.47   b. Form: Request for Judicial Notice

[Caption. See §§23.18– 23.19]

No. _____

REQUEST FOR JUDICIAL NOTICE

____[Name of party]____ requests this Court, under Evidence Code sections 452 and 453, to take judicial notice of the following matters:

[For example]

1. The fictitious deed of trust recorded _____, 19____, at Book _____, page _____, of the official records of the County of _____, California, and specifically paragraph _____, which reads as follows: _____. A true copy of this Fictitious Deed of Trust is attached as Exhibit _____. Judicial notice of this matter may be taken under Evid C section 452(h).

2. The records of the _____ Court of the State of California, for the County of _____, in the action entitled _____ Action No. ____, and specifically the findings of fact and conclusions of law in that action. A copy of the findings of fact and conclusions of law is attached as Exhibit No. _____. Judicial notice of this matter may be taken under Evidence Code section 452(d).

Dated: _____

[Signature of attorney]

[Typed name]
Attorney for ____[name]____

§29.48   SUMMARY JUDGMENT

4. Affidavits and Declarations

§29.48   a. Formal Requirements

Affidavits are written declarations under oath. CCP §2003. The affidavit must recite the fact that it was made under oath or the fact that the affiant was sworn. An affidavit must be sworn to and signed before a suitable official. In California, any officer authorized to administer oaths may accept the oath (CCP §2012), although normally only notaries public will take affidavits. Special provisions govern out-of-state and foreign affidavits. CCP §§2013–2015. The officer taking the affidavit should certify on the affidavit that it was subscribed and sworn to before him, stating the date of execution. See *People v McDaniels* (1903) 141 C 113, 74 P 773.

To meet these requirements, the affidavit normally begins with the words:

I,____[name of affiant]____, **being first duly sworn, say:**

It ends with a signature of the affiant and the jurat of the notary public in the following form:

Subscribed to and sworn before me,_____, 19____.

after which the notary signs and impresses his stamp. The jurat of an out-of-state declaration should also show the state and county of notarization.

Declarations are used much more often than affidavits to support motions for summary judgment in California. They may be used instead of affidavits whenever the declarant signs the declaration in California or in a state that permits declarations under penalty of perjury. CCP §2015.5. For this reason, the term "declaration" is used in this book to include the term "affidavit" except when the context requires the use of both terms to distinguish one from the other. The place of signature governs, not the declarant's place of residence.

A declaration must show the date and place of its execution. The place of execution must be in California or another state allowing declarations under penalty of perjury. CCP §2015.5. The declaration must also state that the declarant certifies or declares the contents of the declaration to be true under penalty of perjury.

These requirements are normally met by including the following language at the end of the declaration immediately preceding the declarant's signature:

I certify under penalty of perjury that the foregoing is true and correct and that this declaration was executed on_____, 19____, at_____, California.

See generally §23.42.

Although the formal requirements of affidavits and declarations are not complicated, many motions for summary judgment (or other relief) are denied because these requirements have not been met. See, *e.g.*, *Dodge v Free* (1973) 32 CA3d 436, 441, 108 CR 311, 315, and authorities cited; §29.33.

§29.49 b. Competence and Personal Knowledge Requirements

Declarations must be made "on personal knowledge" and affirmatively show that the declarant is competent to testify to the matters stated. CCP §437c.

Every person is qualified to be a witness unless otherwise provided by statute. Evid C §700. See exceptions in Evid C §701; Veh C §40804. However, courts have read the "competency" requirement, either expressly or implicitly, as encompassing a requirement of personal knowledge rather than "competency" in the traditional sense. See, *e.g.*, *Fisher v Cheeseman* (1968) 260 CA2d 503, 506, 67 CR 258, 260. To the extent traditional competence is intended by CCP §437c, the filing of the declaration itself is probably a sufficient prima facie showing under the liberal language of Evid C §700. Nevertheless, both San Francisco and Los Angeles local rules require declarations to recite the conclusion that the declarant could and would competently testify if called as a witness. LA & SF Law & Motion Manuals §72(b). Because affirmation that a declarant could competently testify is a legal conclusion, it is of no legal effect and probably need not be set forth except when specifically required, *e.g.*, by the rule cited above. A mere statement that the declarant has personal knowledge of the stated facts is probably insufficient to meet the CCP §437c requirement that the declaration demonstrate that the facts stated are "on personal knowledge." LA & SF Law & Motion Manuals §2(c). Code of Civil Procedure §437c appears to override the usual presumption that declarations are deemed to be made on personal knowledge unless otherwise indicated (*Foraker v O'Brien* (1975) 50 CA3d 856, 863, 124 CR 110, 114); see §23.40. Averments made "to the best of my knowledge" or "to the best of my knowledge and recollection" are insufficient. They are treated as allegations on information and belief and considered not to show the requisite personal knowledge. *Bowden v Robinson* (1977) 67 CA3d 705, 719, 136 CR 871, 881. Properly qualified experts may, however, submit declarations based on expert opinion rather than personal knowledge. See Evid C §801.

Only rarely will attorneys have sufficient personal knowledge to allow them to file sufficient declarations in a summary judgment motion. See, *e.g.*, *Cullincini v Deming* (1975) 53 CA3d 908, 914, 126 CR 427, 430; *Craig Corp. v Los Angeles* (1975) 51 CA3d 909, 915, 124 CR 621, 624; *Dixon v Grace Lines, Inc.* (1972) 27 CA3d 278, 290, 103 CR 595, 604.

Personal knowledge of facts is shown by statement of the particular facts that show such knowledge, *e.g.*, presence at an oral conversation, receipt of a document, observation of an event, or status as custodian of records. See §23.40. Foundational facts must be set forth with the same particularity as all other facts sought to be established. See Evid C §702; LA & SF LAW & MOTION MANUALS §72(d).

§29.50   c. Admissible Evidence Requirement

Code of Civil Procedure §437c specifically requires that declarations "set forth admissible evidence." This language was added to overrule a line of cases that had denied summary judgment motions when opposing declarations were filed that set out "popular conclusions" or similarly inadmissible matters. See Zack, *California Summary Judgment: The Need for Legislative Reform*, 59 CALIF L REV 439, 466 (1971); Zack, *The 1973 Summary Judgment Act—New Teeth for an Old Tiger*, 48 CAL SBJ 654, 656 (1973); see §29.8.

Under CCP §437c all declarations are judged by the rules of evidence codified in the Evidence Code. Some of the more common evidentiary defects are set forth in §29.33.

§29.51   (1) Inadmissible Conclusions and Opinions; Examples

Conclusions, "popular conclusions" and ultimate facts are usually not admissible evidence and must be disregarded when they appear.

The following are examples of improper conclusions that often appear in declarations:

(1) "These are business records."
(2) "She was served with a three-day notice."
(3) "The defendant has no defense."
(4) "The action is a sham." See *de Echeguren v de Echeguren* (1962) 210 CA2d 141, 148, 26 CR 562, 565.
(5) "The defendant is indebted for goods, wares, and merchandise sold and delivered."
(6) "I have a good cause of action." See *Whitney's at the Beach v Superior Court* (1970) 3 CA3d 258, 270, 83 CR 237, 245.
(7) Employment was not "different from or inferior to" that under a different contract of employment. *Parker v Twentieth Century-Fox Film Corp.* (1970) 3 C3d 176, 184, 89 CR 737, 742.
(8) Employee was not acting in "course of scope" of employment. *McIvor v Savage* (1963) 220 CA2d 128, 134, 33 CR 740, 743; *Johnson v Banducci* (1963) 212 CA2d 254, 263, 27 CR 764, 768.
(9) There was fraudulent "concealment." *Weir v Snow* (1962) 210 CA2d 283, 293, 26 CR 868, 873.
(10) Employee was "doing nothing" for employer or was engaged in "personal pursuit." *Johnson v Banducci* (1963) 212 CA2d 254, 263, 27 CR 764, 768.
(11) Action was "sham," "frivolous," "brought solely for vindictive purposes." *de Echeguren v de Echeguren* (1962) 210 CA2d 141, 148, 26 CR 562, 565.
(12) "Each acting for themselves and . . .," or "as agents for," or "acting for and on behalf of," or the corporation "did participate in negotiations, discussions or proceedings." *Dashew v Dashew Business Mach., Inc.* (1963) 218 CA2d 711, 714, 32 CR 682, 684.
(13) Administrative action was "wholly" the result of independent investigation. *Miley v Harper* (1967) 248 CA2d 463, 465, 56 CR 536, 537.

The line between admissible facts and inadmissible conclusions is frequently narrow, but the problems can be avoided by stating underlying facts with specificity whenever possible.

Generally, an opinion is inadmissible. A nonexpert witness, however, may properly state an opinion if the declaration sets forth foundational facts that show that the opinion is (a) rationally based on the witness' perception and (b) helpful in understanding other facts in the document. Evid C §800.

Expert witnesses may give opinions if the declaration establishes the foundational facts, *e.g.*, qualification as an expert, enumerated in Evid C §720. Zack, *The 1973 Summary Judgment Act—New Teeth for an Old Tiger*, 48 CAL SBJ 654, 657 (1973).

§29.52 (2) Inadmissible Hearsay

The hearsay rule excludes testimony concerning statements made by a person other than the declarant when such statements are used to prove the truth of the matters stated. Evid C §1200. A common example of this type of violation occurs when the supervisor of an organization attempts to testify about the business carried on by his subordinates. See, *e.g.*, *People v Pacific Land Research Co.* (1976) 63 CA3d 873, 889, 134 CR 114, 123. There are numerous exceptions to the rule, particularly as it relates to statements in documents. See, *e.g.*, §§29.60–29.61 on business records. See Evid C §§1220–1341; Witkin, CALIFORNIA EVIDENCE, §§448–628 (2d ed 1966); Jefferson, EVIDENCE BENCHBOOK §§1.1–18.8 (CCJ-CEB 1972).

§29.53 5. Documents

Many types of documents may be used in connection with a summary judgment motion. However, the use of documents raises a number of problems including failure properly to attach them to the moving papers (see §29.54), to authenticate (see §§29.55–29.56), to comply with the best evidence rule (see §§29.57–29.59) and to prove that the documents fall within the business records exception to the hearsay rule (see §§29.60–29.61).

§29.54 a. Incorporation of Document by Reference in Declaration

Portions of a pleading or document or any paper on file in the action or any other document may be incorporated by reference in a declaration. *Newport v Los Angeles* (1960) 184 CA2d 229, 234, 7 CR 497, 501; *Union Trust Co. v Superior Court* (1938) 11 C2d 449, 455, 81 P2d 150, 153; *Woodward v Brown* (1897) 119 C 283, 300, 51 P 2, 7.

Because facts in a declaration must conform to requirements for oral testimony, incorporation of documents that contain statements or testimony of one other than the declarant may be improper because the statements are hearsay. *Kramer v Barnes* (1963) 212 CA2d 440, 446, 27 CR 895, 898. See §§29.50–29.52. The declarant must have personal knowledge of the incorporated facts before he may adopt them as his own testimony. Pleadings rarely set forth admissible evidence, because they are usually phrased in terms of conclusions or ultimate facts. See §§29.50–29.51.

If pleadings or documents are incorporated by reference, copies of the incorporated material should be directly attached to the declaration or the packet of motion papers and the specific pertinent portions should be referred to in the notice of motion, declaration, or points and authorities, as appropriate for the court's convenience.

It is especially important to identify documents specifically when a supplemental or reply affidavit (*Johnson v Banducci* (1963) 212 CA2d 254, 260, 27 CR 764, 767) is filed after the motion but before the hearing. See, *e.g.*, *Oliver v Swiss Club Tell* (1963) 222 CA2d 528, 546, 35 CR 324, 334.

Failure to attach to a declaration exhibits referred to in it can preclude entry of summary judgment. Subsequent attempts to undo the damage may only compound the error. *Dugar v Happy Tiger Records, Inc.* (1974) 41 CA3d 811, 815, 116 CR 412, 414. Therefore, before motion papers are filed, they should routinely be reviewed to assure that all documents are properly attached. If a declaration is filed without attaching the exhibits incorporated within it by reference, a new declaration by the same declarant should be filed, properly authenticating and attaching the omitted exhibits.

b. Authentication of Documents

§29.55 (1) Methods of Authentication

Before a document or its contents may be introduced or considered, sufficient facts must be shown to sustain a finding that the document is the writing the proponent claims it is. Evid C §§1400–1401.

The Evidence Code sets forth several methods for authenticating documents: (a) by the testimony of anyone who saw the writing made or executed (Evid C §1413); (b) by evidence that the opposing party has admitted its authenticity or acted on it as if it were genuine (Evid C §1414); (c) by testimony confirming the genuineness of the signature or handwriting by a witness personally familiar with the handwriting; by a handwriting expert or by the trier of fact (Evid C §§1415–1418); (d) by evidence that the writing was received in response to a communication sent to the claimed author (Evid C §1420); or, (e) by evidence that it states matters unlikely to be known by anyone other than the purported author (Evid C §1421). Special rules apply to the introduction of official records. See Evid C §§1530–1532. Authentication may also be accomplished by appropriate use of discovery devices, *e.g.*, requests for admissions, interrogatories, depositions.

Counsel may request the court to compare and take judicial notice of similarity of signature on a promissory note or contract with signature on verification to the answer or complaint. Evid C §1417.

A statement that an exhibit is a true and correct copy of a document is not sufficient authentication, unless the declaration in which the statement is made also shows why the declarant has personal knowledge of the original. *U.S. v Dibble* (9th Cir 1970) 429 F2d 598, 602.

§29.56 (2) Examples: Statements Used To Authenticate Documents

The following are examples of statements that may be used in declarations of competent witnesses to provide proper authentication of documents.

(a) The following statement reports an admission by the adverse party. Evid C §1414.

When defendant came to my office on April 2, 1972, he asked me if I had received the letter he had sent me. I showed him the letter, and he stated that the letter was in fact the one he had sent. A true copy is attached as Exhibit A.

(b) The following statement presents a proper handwriting identification by a nonexpert familiar with the handwriting. Evid C §1416.

I have known the defendant since we went to high school together, a period of over 11 years. We have often corresponded and I recognize the signature on the note as being his signature.

(c) The following statement refers to a written reply received in response to a communication. Evid C §1420.

On March 1, 1968, I sent a letter to the defendant, a true copy of which is attached and incorporated as Exhibit A. On March 14, 1968, I received in reply the letter, a true copy of which is attached and incorporated as Exhibit B.

(d) The following statement provides evidence that the writing states matters unlikely to be known to one other than the statement's author. Evid C §1421.

The defendant states in the letter, which is attached and incorporated as Exhibit A, that he would take off from work on the 16th so that he could go to his bank and discuss the Spring Street loan. The court's attention is directed to the declaration of Mr. John Jones in which he states that on the 16th, the defendant was at the bank and did discuss the Spring Street loan.

c. Best Evidence Rule

§29.57 (1) Compliance With Best Evidence Rule Required

Evidence Code §1500 states "[N]o evidence other than the original of a writing is admissible to prove the content of a writing." The "best evidence" rule creates particular problems in summary judgment motions because parties are understandably reluctant to attach original documents to declarations that may be lost, or may be needed for other purposes.

Despite these concerns, declarations in summary judgment motions must comply with the best evidence rule; attaching copies is insufficient. Documents filed in connection with the motion or on the record of the hearing must affirmatively show compliance with the best evidence rule. *Dugar v Happy Tiger Records, Inc.* (1974) 41 CA3d 811, 815, 116 CR 412, 415.

If the originals are in the possession of the party relying on them, he should attach copies to the declarations and state that the originals will be produced at the hearing on the motion. At the hearing, the party should state on the record that he has the originals with him and allow the judge and opposing party to inspect them. All originals should be tagged for identification at the hearing with the same designation as the filed and served copy. This facilitates comparison by the court and the opposing party.

If originals are in the possession of the opposing party, the party relying on them should attach copies to his declarations and serve a notice under CCP §1987(c) on the opposing party, requesting him to produce the originals at the hearing. Evid C §1503(a). If the opposing party does not produce the originals at the hearing, the copies attached to the declaration are admissible secondary evidence. Evid C §1503(a). Counsel should, however, be aware that such a notice must be given at least 20 days before the required appearance with the materials, and should set the time of hearing to permit 20 days to elapse, even though the hearing on the motion can be held on ten days' notice. CCP §1987(c). For form of notice, see §29.59.

If the originals are in the possession of a third person, a subpena duces tecum should be served on that person requiring production of the originals at the hearing. Secondary evidence may be introduced if the originals are not produced under subpena. Evid C §1502.

The best evidence rule may also be overcome by admissions of the party against whom the document is sought to be used or by reliance on one of the exceptions to the rule set forth in Evid C §§1501–1505.

For purposes of the best evidence rule, a carbon copy is considered a duplicate original, but photographs, photostats, photocopies, or similar copies are all considered secondary evidence. *Dugar v Happy Tiger Records, Inc.* (1974) 41 CA3d 811, 817, 116 CR 412, 415; Witkin, CALIFORNIA EVIDENCE, §690 (2d ed 1966); See Evid C §§1550–1551.

§29.58 (2) Examples: Statements Supporting Introduction of Secondary Evidence

(a) The following statement explains that a writing was lost or destroyed without fraudulent intent. Evid C §1501.

I normally kept my receipts loose in my desk drawer. I cleaned out the desk drawer several times after the date when I first received the bill. I recall seeing the receipt each time I cleaned out the desk. When I looked for it to produce it for this motion, the receipt was gone. I had a photocopy of the receipt made, which I gave to my attorney when I first consulted him. The photocopy, which is attached and incorporated as Exhibit A, is the copy I had made.

(b) The following statement explains that the writing is not reasonably procurable through the court's process. Evid C §1502.

The written contract in question is an exhibit, as People's Exhibit 15, in an action now pending in _____ County Superior Court, entitled *People v Jones*, Case No. 137802. The trial is in progress and this exhibit has been admitted into evidence. Judicial notice of the trial record of the above case is requested pursuant to sections 452 and 453 of the Evidence Code.

(c) The following statement explains that the writing is under the control of the opponent. See Evid C §1503.

Twenty-five days ago, the defendant, ____[name]____, met me at work. He stated that he had the check, which is the document in question, but would not make it available for this motion. I served a notice under CCP §1987(e) on _____ to produce the check.

(d) The following statement explains that a record is in the custody of a public entity. Evid C §§1506, 1508, 1532.

Attached and incorporated as Exhibit A, is a certified copy of the Health Department Inspection Report. The original record is in the custody of the County Health Department in Room 202 of the Health Building.

(e) The following statement explains that the writing is a matter of public record. Evid C §§1507–1508, 1530–1532.

Attached and incorporated as Exhibit A, is a certified copy of the chattel mortgage. This mortgage is recorded in Book X, Page 561, Document No. 1326, of the Book of Records for the County of Los Angeles.

(f) The following statement explains the use of a summary and excerpts. Evid C §1509.

The agreement in question consists of 436 pages. Pages 85 through 196 of the agreement contain rates and conditions on which the employees' fringe benefits, the subject matter of this lawsuit, are to be paid. These pages of the agreement, setting forth the applicable rates, and the employer's time records, attached and incorporated as Exhibits B and C, show that each of the employees admittedly hired by the defendant was entitled to fringe benefits during the period in question, in the total amount of $1362.58, in accordance with the employer's time records. The agreement, the employment records, and the time records cannot be examined in detail in less than eight hours. Preparation of the summary of the agreement and records took twelve hours and was prepared by employee ____[name]____ under the direction and supervision of declarant.

§29.59 (3) Form: Notice To Produce Books, Documents, Records, or Other Physical Evidence

Copies: Original for court clerk; one copy for service on the attorney of record of each party (or party if he has no attorney); office copies.

[Caption. See §§23.18–23.19]

No. _____

NOTICE TO PRODUCE

To ____[name of opponent in possession or control of evidence]____ **and to** ____[his / her]____ **attorney of record.**

PLEASE TAKE NOTICE that you are required by Code of Civil Procedure section 1987(c) to produce at the hearing on ____[plaintiff's / defendant's]____ **motion for summary judgment or order adjudicating issues without substantial**

controversy, to be held on _____, 19____, at ____ ____.m., at ____[address]____, California, the following: ____[describe each book, document, record, or other item of physical evidence]____ which are in your possession or under your control.

Failure to produce these original ____[e.g., documents]____ at the time of hearing will permit ____[plaintiff / defendant]____ to introduce secondary evidence of the contents under Evidence Code section 1503(a).

Dated: _____

[Signature of attorney]

[Typed name]
Attorney for ____[name]____

Comment: The notice to produce is an alternative to service of a subpena duces tecum. See CCP §1985. Twenty days' notice must be given. See §29.57.

d. Business Records

§29.60 (1) Business Record as Exception to Hearsay Rule

If the mere existence of a document (*e.g.*, a contract), and not the truth of its contents, is the essential fact to be shown in a summary judgment motion, no hearsay problem arises. See Evid C §1200. See also Evid C §622 on the conclusive presumption of truth of certain recitals in written instruments.

However, when a document is used in a summary judgment motion to prove the truth of the matters stated, the hearsay problem must be overcome, usually by use of the business records exception to the hearsay rule. Evid C §§1270–1272.

For a document to fall within the business records exception, an appropriate foundation must be laid. Evid C §1271. It must be shown that (a) the writing was made in the regular course of business, (b) at or near the time of the act, condition, or event recorded, (c) the custodian or other qualified witness attests to the record's identity and mode of preparation, and (d) the sources of information and method and time of preparation indicate the record's trustworthiness.

§29.61 (2) Examples: Statements Laying Foundation for Introduction of Business Records

The following are examples of statements in declarations that may be used to lay foundation for consideration of a business record.

(a) The following statement is used to establish that a record showing assignment and nonpayment was made in the regular course of business (Evid C §§1271–1272).

I am an employee of plaintiff and it is one of my duties to receive assignments of accounts, to make and to maintain accurate records of payments received on these assigned accounts. I am required to, and do, receive all payments on these accounts and make all entries relating to them.

On August 14, 1972, I received an assignment of the account of defendant in this action from ____[name of assignor]____ attached and incorporated as Exhibit C. Immediately after receipt of this assignment, I set up a ledger card with defendant's name on it for the purpose of recording all payments made by defendant after the assignment. If I had received any payments, I would have recorded them on this card within a day or so after receiving them. I have searched the defendant's ledger card, and it appears from it that no entries have been made reflecting, or with regard to, the payment of any sums by defendant on this account since the date the card was made up. This ledger card is attached and incorporated as Exhibit ____.

(b) The following statement by a custodian of a record identifies the record, its mode of preparation, timeliness, and trustworthiness (Evid C §1271).

I, _____, declare as follows: I am the credit manager of ____ [name of company]____ and have been so employed since January, 1972. My duties include supervision and control over the employees of, and the bookkeeping procedures in, the receivables department. I am required to know, and in fact do know the responsibilities of the employees I supervise, and the methods they use in making bookkeeping entries and maintaining other records for which I am responsible.

The receivables department records incoming payments directly from the checks or drafts used to make such payments. These entries are made on cards. For each account, a stiff cardboard card is maintained which contains all the transactions respecting that account in ink. The card is kept in a regular file which contains similar cards. As supervisor, I require that entries be made on the card of each account within two days of the date a payment is received or a charge is incurred. I am sure that the ledger sheets and other records are audited semi-annually to preserve their accuracy.

§29.62   6. Discovery Documents

All methods of discovery may be used to support a summary judgment motion. See generally CALIFORNIA CIVIL DISCOVERY

PRACTICE (Cal CEB 1975). However, some methods are more easily adaptable to the summary judgment procedure than others. See §§29.63–29.66.

§29.63   a. Depositions

Depositions of any person, whether or not a party to the action, can be used to support a summary judgment motion. Although some lawyers have expressed doubts about the propriety of a party using his own deposition, in fact the deposition allows an opponent who has participated in the deposition a greater opportunity for cross-examination than would a declaration.

If a deposition has been signed and filed with the court, there is no need to authenticate it beyond establishing the signing and filing. The court may take judicial notice of its own file. Evid C §452(d); *Stepan v Garcia* (1974) 43 CA3d 497, 500, 117 CR 919. However, if the deposition has not been filed at the time of the summary judgment motion hearing, a declaration, preferably by a lawyer who attended the deposition, should identify the transcript as a correct rendition of the testimony given.

The portions of the deposition relied on should be attached to the motion papers. Because depositions are not usually filed with the rest of the papers in the case, the judge may not have the deposition before him if a copy is not attached to the motion papers.

§29.64   b. Interrogatories and Requests for Admissions

Only the answers to interrogatories and admissions to requests for admission of the party making or opposing the motion may be used against that party. The specific questions or requests and responses relied on should be included in the motion papers, because they may not otherwise be filed with the court. See CCP §2030.

§29.65   c. Documents Produced on CCP §2031 Request

Documents produced on a request for production of documents under CCP §2031 may be used to support a summary judgment motion. However, the mere fact that these documents have been produced will not overcome the problems discussed in §§29.51–29.52, 29.55, 29.57, 29.60. To use these documents, the moving party must authenticate them (see §§29.55–29.56), comply with the best evidence rule (see §§29.57–29.59), and, when appropriate, establish that they are within the business records exception to the hearsay rule (see §§29.60–29.61).

§29.66 d. Other Discovery Documents

A bill of particulars may be used to support a summary judgment motion. However, it cannot be used by the party filing the bill because it is only an amplification of that party's pleadings. See 3 Witkin, CALIFORNIA PROCEDURE Pleading §378 (2d ed 1971).

The results of an order for examination by a physician under CCP §2032 may also be used. Normally, these results will be presented in a declaration by the examining physician.

§29.67 VII. SERVING AND FILING THE MOTION

The notice of motion must be served at least ten days before the time fixed for the hearing. CCP §437c; CCP §1005. See 1 CALIFORNIA CIVIL PROCEDURE BEFORE TRIAL §§8.61–8.63 (Cal CEB 1977) on personal or substituted service. Service is ordinarily made on the attorney of record by mail under CCP §1011(1). See §23.10 for discussion of service by mail.

Many courts have local rules requiring filing with the court at least nine days before the scheduled hearing unless an order shortening time has been granted. See, *e.g.,* LA & SF LAW & MOTION MANUALS §16(A). Proof of service should be filed with the motion. See §23.47. Because statutes permitting service by mail are strictly construed (*Valley Vista Land Co. v Nipomo Water & Sewer Co.* (1967) 255 CA2d 172, 63 CR 78), counsel should carefully review the proof of service before the motion is filed.

VIII. PREHEARING AND HEARING PROCEDURES
§29.68 A. Moving for Continuance

By the time of the hearing on the motion for summary judgment, the issues should be well defined by the pleadings (see §29.29) and the evidentiary support for each party's position should be apparent. Occasionally, however, defects in pleadings or the moving or opposing papers come to light at or immediately before the hearing. In such cases, motion for a continuance may be made to allow sufficient time to cure the defect by amendment of the pleadings or submission of supplemental declarations.

A continuance may be granted for the purpose of obtaining additional evidence on a showing that the additional evidence may exist, but cannot, for reasons stated, then be presented. CCP §437c. See §29.13. In addition, the court retains its inherent discretionary power to permit either party to file supplemental declarations or amend his pleadings and to grant continuances for those purposes.

If possible, a formal motion should be made under CCP §594a, supported by declarations stating the grounds and necessity for the proposed continuance. If the motion cannot be scheduled for hearing before the date on which the summary judgment motion is to be heard, it should be set on the same day as the hearing on the motion for summary judgment by order shortening time for good cause shown (see CCP §1005). See §§23.12–23.13.

If the problem came to light only at the time of hearing, an oral motion for continuance may be made under CCP §437c or §594a. Even if the motion is oral, a declaration in support of the motion for continuance should be filed to make a record in case a petition for writ of mandate or for other review is necessary because the motion is denied.

§29.69   B. Filing Supplemental Declarations and Late Papers

Under former CCP §437c, the courts permitted parties to file supplemental declarations at any time before the summary judgment motion was submitted. *Johnson v Banducci* (1963) 212 CA2d 254, 27 CR 764. It was an abuse of discretion for the court to refuse to accept declarations submitted by the opposing party at the hearing of the motion. A local rule of court that prohibited such late filings was held improper. *Albermont Petroleum, Ltd. v Cunningham* (1960) 186 CA2d 84, 93, 9 CR 405, 410.

At the present time, most courts have local rules limiting the time when papers other than those initiating a proceeding must be filed and served. The rules usually require these papers to be filed at least two days before the scheduled hearing. See, *e.g.*, LA & SF Law & Motion Manuals §16(B). The opposing party may be exempted from these rules, but it is better practice to follow them anyway. *Albermont Petroleum, Ltd. v Cunningham, supra.*

Even under former CCP §437c some courts refused to consider a moving party's supplemental declarations if they were submitted without the court's permission after the motion was set for hearing and not mentioned in the notice of motion. *Oliver v Swiss Club Tell* (1963) 222 CA2d 528, 546, 35 CR 324, 334. This ruling appears to lack logic, because the moving party should have the right (with a short continuance, if necessary) to file supplemental declarations and additional points and authorities in reply to papers filed by the opposing party, especially if unanticipated legal or factual matters are raised. Granting the moving party these rights does not prejudice the opposing party because, if such a filing is not permitted, the moving party can merely renew the motion later and at that time present any additional evidence and arguments.

Late papers may not be filed with the court after the matter has been submitted, except on a noticed motion to reopen the submitted matter. *Alvak Enterprises v Phillips* (1959) 167 CA2d 69, 334 P2d 148.

§29.70 C. Oral Argument Generally Permitted; Testimony Generally Not Permitted

Most judges permit oral argument, and some supply tentative rulings to aid counsel in directing their remarks to the points that the court wants discussed. Counsel should be prepared at oral argument to assist the court in examining the entire case and identifying the evidence supporting or opposing each element necessary for a judgment on each issue sought to be adjudicated as without substantial controversy.

The right to argue is, however, a matter within the court's discretion (see generally cases cited in 4 Witkin, CALIFORNIA PROCEDURE, Trial, §134 (2d ed 1971)) unless the court decides the motion on a ground not discussed in the motion paper, in which case it becomes a matter of constitutional right. *Moore v California Mineral Prods. Corp.* (1953) 115 CA2d 834, 252 P2d 1005.

Testimony may not be taken in summary judgment proceedings (*Spencer v Hibernia Bank* (1960) 186 CA2d 702, 717, 9 CR 867, 876), even though the court has discretion to hear such testimony in hearings on other types of motions (*Ascherman v Superior Court* (1967) 254 CA2d 506, 62 CR 547).

IX. ORDERS AND JUDGMENTS

§29.71   A. Who Prepares; Contents

Ordinarily, the court enters a minute order either granting or denying a motion for summary judgment. If the motion is granted, the minute order directs that judgment be entered for the designated party. If affirmative relief is awarded, the order specifies the relief. The order may recite that the necessary showing has been made by declaration or other proof, *i.e.*, that there is no defense to the action or that the action has no merit and that there is no triable issue of a material fact.

No findings of fact are made because no factual trial has taken place. CCP §437c; see *Business Title Corp. v Division of Labor Law Enforcement* (1976) 17 C3d 878, 882 n3, 132 CR 454, 456 n3; *Perry v Farley Bros. Moving & Storage, Inc.* (1970) 6 CA3d 884, 889, 86 CR 397, 400.

In some courts, in uncomplicated summary judgment matters, the clerk prepares the judgment. Other courts require, and some lawyers prefer, counsel for the prevailing party to prepare the order and judgment. If the attorney for the prevailing party wishes to prepare the order and judgment or is directed to do so, no judgment will be entered until the judge approves the form of the order and judgment and signs them.

Because summary judgments are often appealed and most summary judgment motion proceedings are not reported, both moving party and opposing party have a definite interest in determining precisely what the court has ordered. If the motion is granted after strong opposition, the opponent should respectfully request the court's reasons for not accepting his argument. If the opposing party believes the court has committed an error of law, he will want that error reflected in the minute order.

When the court adjudicates certain issues to be without substantial controversy, it is essential that the minute order properly identify those issues. If the court requests the prevailing attorney to prepare an order, care should be used to recite those issues with great specificity.

§29.72   B. Types of Judgments

Code of Civil Procedure §437c permits judgments to be entered in many types of proceedings, not only proceedings seeking money judgments or judgments of dismissal. See, *e.g.*, *Stanton v Dumke* (1966) 64 C2d 199, 207, 49 CR 380, 386 (mandamus); *National Exhibition Co. v San Francisco* (1972) 24 CA3d 1, 11, 100 CR 757, 763 (declaratory relief); *Adoption of Backhaus* (1962) 209 CA2d 13, 20, 25, CR 581, 585; *MCA, Inc. v Universal Diversified Enterprises Corp.* (1972) 27 CA3d 170, 103 CR 522 (unlawful detainer); *Estate of Kerner* (1969) 275 CA2d 785, 80 CR 289 (will contest); *Eagle Elec. Mfg. Co. v Keener* (1966) 247 CA2d 246, 253, 55 CR 444, 449 (action to vacate judgment); *People ex rel Mosk v Lynam* (1967) 253 CA2d 959, 968, 61 CR 800, 807 (injunction); *Williams v Williams* (1967) 255 CA2d 648, 63 CR 354 (partition); *Ahmanson Bank & Trust Co. v Tepper* (1969) 269 CA2d 333, 345, 74 CR 774, 783 (interpleader); *Greenwald v U.S.* (1963) 223 CA2d 434, 441, 35 CR 772, 776 (quiet title); *People v One 1964 Chevrolet Corvette Convertible* (1969) 274 CA2d 720, 724, 79 CR 447, 449 (forfeiture).

Counsel should request a judgment appropriate to the requirements of his case. See *e.g., Siemon v Russell* (1961) 194 CA2d 592, 15 CR 218 (declaratory relief).

§29.73   C. Costs and Attorneys' Fees

Costs are properly included in any judgment. A memorandum of costs and disbursements must be filed within ten days after entry of the judgment. CCP §1033.

If the judgment is on a contract authorizing an award of attorneys' fees to either party, the prevailing party may recover his attorneys' fees as costs. CC §1717; *T. E. D. Bearing Co. v Walter E. Heller & Co.* (1974) 38 CA3d 59, 64, 112 CR 910, 914. Attorneys' fees need not be pleaded or proved, and no trial is necessary to establish them. They may be included in the memorandum of costs and disbursements and adjusted in the trial court's discretion if challenged by the party against whom they were granted by a motion to tax costs. CCP §1033; *Beneficial Standard Prop. Inc. v Scharps* (1977) 67 CA3d 227, 232, 136 CR 549, 552.

§29.74   D. Sanctions

Adapting a sanction provision from Fed R Civ P 56(g), CCP §437c provides that the court "shall" order a party presenting summary judgment declarations in bad faith or for the purpose of delay "to pay the other party the amount of the reasonable expenses which the filing . . . caused such other party to incur." Applying the same provision, federal courts have awarded such expenses without a motion by the opposing party. See, *e.g.*, *Alart Assocs., Inc. v Aptaker* (SD NY 1968) 279 F Supp 268. It appears that under CCP §437c a party can, but need not, make a formal motion for reasonable expenses.

Whether declarations are presented in bad faith cannot usually be determined by the court until after the motion has been denied and a trial is conducted in which (1) the evidence reveals the bad faith of the party presenting them and (2) the other party has incurred expenses in preparing and proceeding to the trial. Intentional delay may, however, in some instances be revealed at the summary judgment motion stage, giving grounds for a motion for sanctions at that time. The apparent purpose of the provision is to prevent use of tactics that delay an inevitable judgment against a meritless claim or defense. Federal courts have not been easy to convince of bad faith (see *Sonobond Corp. v Uthe Technology, Inc.* (ND Cal 1970) 314 F Supp 878), and it is likely that California courts will also be difficult to convince.

It is not clear if the legislature intended "reasonable expenses" in CCP §437c to include attorneys' fees. Although attorneys' fees will normally be awarded only if there is an express statutory authorization (see, *e.g.*, CCP §2034(d)), some attorneys believe the better interpretation of the term "reasonable expenses" in this action includes attorneys' fees.

E. Forms

§29.75   1. Order for Entry of Summary Judgment

Copies: Original (filed with court clerk with proof of service); copies for service (one for each attorney of record and unrepresented party); office copies.

[*Caption. See §§23.18–23.19*]

No. _____

ORDER FOR ENTRY OF SUMMARY JUDGMENT IN FAVOR OF
____[NAME]____ ____[AND AGAINST _____]____

The motion of ____[plaintiff / defendant]____ for ____[summary judgment / specify order sought]____ was regularly heard on _____, 19____. Appearing as attorneys were _____. After full consideration of moving and responding papers, all supporting papers, and oral arguments of counsel, it appears and the Court finds that ____[plaintiff / defendant]____ has shown by admissible evidence and reasonable inferences from that evidence that ____[there is no defense to the action / the action has no merit]____, and that ____[name of responding party]____ has presented no triable issue of fact.

IT IS ORDERED that judgment be entered in accordance with this order in favor of ____[plaintiff / defendant]____ and against ____[plaintiff / defendant]____ as prayed for in the ____[complaint / answer]____.

Dated: _____

Judge

Comment: This order should be used when the court does not make a minute order. It should be submitted together with a proposed judgment. The judgment may even be set forth on the same form as the order. See §29.78.

§29.76   2. Order Denying Summary Judgment and Granting Summary Adjudication of Issues

Copies: Original (filed with court clerk with proof of service); copies for service (one for each attorney of record and unrepresented party); office copies.

[Caption. See §§23.18–23.19]

No. _____

ORDER DENYING SUMMARY JUDGMENT AND GRANTING SUMMARY ADJUDICATION OF ISSUES IN FAVOR OF ____[NAME]____ ____[AND AGAINST _____]____

The motion of ____[plaintiff / defendant]____ for an order granting summary judgment or adjudicating issues without substantial controversy in this action was regularly heard on _____, 19____. Appearing as attorneys were _____. After full consideration of moving and responding papers, all supporting papers, and oral arguments of counsel, it appears and the Court finds that certain triable issues of fact exist and that summary judgment should therefore be denied. The Court further finds that the issues stated below are without substantial controversy, and that ____[plaintiff / defendant]____ has shown such issues to be without substantial controversy by admissible evidence and reasonable inferences from the evidence.

IT IS ORDERED that ____[plaintiff's / defendant's]____ motion for summary judgment be denied.

§29.77   SUMMARY JUDGMENT

IT IS FURTHER ORDERED that the following issues be deemed established in favor of ____[plaintiff / defendant]____ **and against** ____[defendant / plaintiff]____**, at the trial of this action, or on final disposition of the action by the Court:** ____[State issues]____

Dated: _____

Judge

§29.77   3. Order Granting Summary Adjudication of Issues

Copies: Original (filed with court clerk with proof of service); copies for service (one for each attorney of record and unrepresented party); office copies.

[Caption. See §§23.18–23.19]

No. _____

ORDER GRANTING SUMMARY ADJUDICATION OF ISSUES IN FAVOR OF ____[PLAINTIFF / DEFENDANT]____ **AND AGAINST** ____[DEFENDANT / PLAINTIFF]____

The motion of ____[plaintiff / defendant]____ for an order granting summary adjudication of issues without substantial controversy in this action was regularly heard on _____, 19____. Appearing as attorneys were _____. After full consideration of moving and responding papers, all supporting papers, and oral argument of counsel, it appears and the Court finds that the issues stated below are without substantial controversy, and that ____[plaintiff / defendant]____ has shown such issues to be without substantial controversy by admissible evidence and reasonable inferences from that evidence.

IT IS ORDERED that the following issues be deemed established in favor of ____[plaintiff / defendant]____ **and against** ____[defendant / plaintiff]____**, at the trial of this action, or on final disposition of the action by this Court:** ____[State issues]____.

Dated: _____

Judge

§29.78   4. Judgment by Court Under CCP §437c

Copies: Original (filed with court clerk with proof of service); copies for service (one for each attorney of record and unrepresented party); office copies.

[Caption. See §§23.18–23.19]

No. _____

JUDGMENT BY COURT UNDER CCP §437c

On _____, 19____, the Court granted the motion of ____[plaintiff / defendant]____ under CCP §437c to enter judgment for ____[plaintiff / defendant]____. In accordance with that order,

IT IS ORDERED that plaintiff

[When plaintiff is moving party]

recover from defendant the sum of $_____, together with his costs in the sum of $_____.

[When defendant is moving party]

take nothing, and that defendant recover from plaintiff his costs in the sum of $_____.

Dated: _____

_____
Judge

Comment: This judgment may be set forth following the order in §29.75.

X. POSTJUDGMENT PROCEDURES

A. Review of Summary Judgment in Trial Court

§29.79 1. By Motion Under CCP §657 for New Trial

A summary judgment is a judgment made on a question of law (*Kindt v Kauffman* (1976) 57 CA3d 845, 862, 129 CR 603, 614; *Poochigian v Layne* (1953) 120 CA2d 757, 765, 261 P2d 738, 742) and may be vacated by the granting of a motion for new trial. *Jacuzzi v Jacuzzi Bros., Inc.* (1966) 243 CA2d 1, 22, 52 CR 147, 162; *Green v Del-Camp Inv. Inc.* (1961) 193 CA2d 479, 14 CR 420. A new trial motion may be made after the court's "decision" and before entry of judgment (CCP §659(1); *Olson v Sacramento* (1969) 274 CA2d 316, 323, 79 CR 140, 144) or within 15 days after the date of mailing of notice of entry of judgment. CCP §659(2). A motion for new trial automatically extends the time for appeal from the summary judgment. Cal Rules of Ct 3(a).

If the new trial motion is based on newly discovered evidence, counsel must show that the evidence could not have been discovered with reasonable diligence and produced at or before the hearing on the summary judgment motion, or the new trial motion will properly be denied. When it is properly denied, newly discovered evidence raised by that motion cannot be considered on appeal to defeat the judgment. See *Jacobs v Retail Clerk's Union, Local 1222* (1975) 49 CA3d 959, 966, 123 CR 309, 314 (appellate court will not consider newly discovered evidence not presented to trial court). If a motion is improperly denied, this error must be raised on appeal from the judgment.

If a new trial is granted, counsel should be sure that the order stating the reasons for the court's decision meets the specificity requirements of CCP §657 and the cases interpreting it.

§29.80 2. By Application Under CCP §473 for Relief From Judgment

A party may seek relief from any judgment or order, in the absence of contrary authority, within a reasonable time, not to exceed six months from its entry, on the grounds specified in CCP §473, *i.e.*, mistake, inadvertence, surprise, or excusable neglect.

The remedy of CCP §473 may be resorted to when, for legally acceptable reasons, the party seeking relief failed to make as strong a showing as he might otherwise have made. See, *e.g.*, *Coyne v Krempels* (1950) 36 C2d 257, 263, 223 P2d 244, 248 (claimed failure to prepare opposition to summary judgment based on opposing counsel's representation about a continuance).

§29.81 3. By Motion or Separate Action To Set Aside Judgment for Extrinsic Fraud or Mistake

Any judgment or order may be set aside on a showing of extrinsic fraud or mistake that prevented a party from having a fair hearing, if diligence and the existence of a meritorious case are also established. See *Westphal v Westphal* (1942) 20 C2d 393, 397, 126 P2d 105, 106; see generally 5 Witkin, CALIFORNIA PROCEDURE Attack on Judgment in Trial Court §§175–198 (2d ed 1971). The relief may be had on motion or by a separate action.

§29.82 4. Improper Use of Nonstatutory Motions

Occasionally, counsel will file a motion denominated a "motion to vacate" or a "motion to reconsider." No established statutory basis for such motions exists. *Santandrea v Siltec Corp.* (1976) 56 CA3d 525, 529, 128 CR 629, 631 (granting sanctions for "frivolous" "motion to reconsider"). Courts that have considered a "motion to reconsider" have generally treated it as "in the nature of" a motion under CCP §473. See, *e.g.*, *Los Angeles v Gleneagle Dev. Co.* (1976) 62 CA3d 543, 553, 133 CR 212, 218, and cases cited; *San Francisco Lathing, Inc. v Superior Court* (1969) 271 CA2d 78, 81, 76 CR 304, 306. But see references to "motion for reconsideration" in *R. D. Reeder Lathing Co. v Allen* (1967) 66 C2d 373, 381, 57 CR 841, 845; *State Medical Educ. Bd. v Roberson* (1970) 6 CA3d 493, 499, 86 CR 258, 261. Cases that have considered "a motion to vacate" have generally treated it as a motion for a new trial. *Poochigian v Layne* (1953) 120 CA2d 757, 765, 261 P2d 738, 742. Because "[a] judgment may be reviewed and changed only by one of the established methods of direct attack" (*Santandrea v Siltec Corp.* (1976) 56 CA3d 525, 529, 128 CR 629, 631), counsel should follow the procedures set forth in §§29.79–29.81, and motions to "vacate" or "reconsider" should not be made.

B. Review by Appeal From Judgment

1. Final Judgment Rule

§29.83   a. Final Judgment Required

No appeal may be taken from an order granting summary judgment. The appeal lies from the judgment itself. CCP §437c; see *Fraser-Yamor Agency, Inc. v Del Norte* (1977) 68 CA3d 201, 207, 137 CR 118, 122. A notice of appeal from the order may, however, be construed by an appellate court to refer to the judgment. *Artucovich v Arizmendiz* (1967) 256 CA2d 130, 63 CR 810.

Code of Civil Procedure §437c provides that judgments rendered under that section are appealable as in other cases, *i.e.*, when final judgment has been entered, stating that:

Except where a separate judgment may properly be awarded in the action, no final judgment shall be entered on a motion for summary judgment prior to the termination of such action, but the final judgment in such action shall, in addition to any matters determined in such action, award judgment as established by the summary proceeding herein provided for.

A summary judgment is generally final if it determines all of the claims actually pled in the action between at least two parties, even if there are other parties to the action. CCP §§578–579; see *Walker v Stauffer Chem. Corp.* (1971) 19 CA3d 669, 671, 96 CR 803, 804. See also 6 Witkin, CALIFORNIA PROCEDURE Appeal §48 (2d ed 1971). If unresolved claims remain between the parties to the summary judgment (*i.e.*, if the judgment resolves less than all the causes of action asserted against one party), it is not final or appealable. *Fraser-Yamor Agency, Inc. v Del Norte* (1977) 68 CA3d 201, 207, 137 CR 118, 122; *Trani v R. G. Hohman Enterprises* (1975) 52 CA3d 314, 125 CR 34; 6 Witkin, PROCEDURE Appeal §§46–47.

A judgment may be final even though less than all the causes of action have been resolved, if there has been (1) a previous order for severance under CCP §1048 (*Schonfeld v Vallejo* (1975) 50 CA3d 401, 417, 123 CR 669, 680), (2) an abandonment of unresolved issues; (3) a dismissal of undetermined causes of action, (4) a stipulation disposing of all remaining issues between the two parties (see, *e.g.*, *Marsh v Home Fed. Sav. & Loan Ass'n* (1977) 66 CA3d 674, 676, n1, 136 CR 180, 181 n1; *Jacobs v Retail Clerk's Union, Local 1222* (1975) 49 CA3d 959, 960, 123 CR 309, 310); or (5) an amendment of the judgment by the appellate court in the interests of justice to provide a final and appealable disposition of all the contentions of the parties involved. See *Fraser-Yamor Agency, Inc. v Del Norte* (1977) 68 CA3d 201, 208, 137 CR 118, 122.

§29.84 b. Examples: Final and Nonfinal Summary Judgments

The following are examples of final, and therefore appealable, summary judgments:

(1) In a two-party action, a summary judgment against plaintiff on all causes of action or against defendant for all relief demanded.

(2) In a three-party (plaintiff, defendant-cross-complainant, and cross-defendant) action, a summary judgment against defendant-cross-complainant (in favor of the cross-defendant) or against the cross-defendant for all relief demanded in the cross-complaint. See 6 Witkin, CALIFORNIA PROCEDURE Appeal §44 (2d ed 1971).

(3) In a three-party action (plaintiff and two defendants named in different causes of action), a summary judgment against plaintiff on either cause of action or against one of the defendants for the relief demanded against him. *Wilson v Sharp* (1954) 42 C2d

675, 677, 268 P2d 1062; 1064; 6 Witkin, PROCEDURE Appeal §48.

The following summary judgments are nonfinal and therefore not appealable:

(a) A summary judgment in favor of plaintiff-cross-defendant only on the cross-complaint, because the claims raised by the complaint against the defendant-cross-complainant are unresolved. See 6 Witkin, PROCEDURE Appeal §45.

(b) A summary judgment against plaintiff on less than all causes of action against one defendant. *Lopes v Capital Co.* (1961) 192 CA2d 759, 763, 13 CR 787, 790; 6 Witkin, PROCEDURE Appeal §47. An appeal erroneously taken from such a judgment may, however, in certain circumstances be "saved" by the appellate court amending the judgment. See *Gombos v Ashe* (1958) 158 CA2d 517, 524, 322 P2d 933, 937; 6 Witkin, PROCEDURE Appeal §§49–51.

2. Scope of Appellate Review

§29.85   a. Applicability of General Rules

General rules relating to the scope of appellate review apply to appellate review of summary judgment, with two major exceptions. See §§29.86–29.87. An argument or theory will generally not be considered if it is raised for the first time on appeal (*G & D Holland Constr. Co. v Marysville* (1970) 12 CA3d 989, 91 CR 227) unless the question is one of the law to be applied to undisputed facts. *Roberts v Roberts* (1966) 241 CA2d 93, 98, 50 CR 408, 411. Thus, possible theories that were not fully developed or factually presented to the trial court cannot create a "triable issue" on appeal. See *National Indem. Co. v Manley* (1975) 53 CA3d 126, 133, 125 CR 513, 518; *Cullincini v Deming* (1975) 53 CA3d 908, 914, 126 CR 427, 430. Issues raised and then abandoned in the trial court also cannot be considered on appeal. *Chesney v Gresham* (1976) 64 CA3d 120, 131, 134 CR 238, 244.

§29.86   b. Exception for Evidentiary Objections

The ordinary appellate rule that evidentiary objections are waived if not raised at the trial level does not apply on review of summary judgments. Such objections may be asserted for the first time on appeal, at least by the opposing party. *Dugar v Happy Tiger Records, Inc.* (1974) 41 CA3d 811, 817, 116 CR 412, 416; *Rodes v Shannon* (1961) 194 CA2d 743, 749, 15 CR 349, 353. It is unclear whether the principle applies to the moving party, because the rationale for the rule is that the right to summary judgment rests on adequacy of the moving party's factual showing, not on deficiencies in the opposing papers. See *Family Service Agency v Ames* (1958) 166 CA2d 344, 351, 333 P2d 142, 146; *Southern Pac. Co. v Fish* (1958) 166 CA2d 353, 365, 333 P2d 133, 141. Nevertheless, in *Larsen v Johannes* (1970) 7 CA3d 491, 500, 86 CR 744, 749, the court applied the same rule to a moving party without discussion. It is arguable that the exception is unfair because most evidentiary problems can be corrected at the trial level if objection is made.

This exception may create a trap for the lawyer who does not closely scrutinize the supporting papers to be sure they meet all evidentiary requirements (see §29.33 for common defects), because evidentiary failures give the opposing party two opportunities to defeat the motion (1) on the merits in the trial court, and (2) on evidentiary issues in the appellate court.

The exception is subject to two qualifications. First, evidentiary objections may be waived by failure to raise them in the appellate court. *Residents of Beverly Glen, Inc. v Los Angeles* (1973) 34 CA3d 117, 128 n12, 109 CR 724, 732 n12. Second, objections to declarations based on their failure to comply with the formal requisites of CCP §2015.5 are waived by failure to object in the trial court. *Rader v Thrasher* (1972) 22 CA3d 883, 889, 99 CR 670, 674; *Fuller v Goodyear Tire & Rubber Co.* (1970) 7 CA3d 690, 86 CR 705; *People v United Bonding Ins. Co.* (1966) 240 CA2d 895, 896 n2, 50 CR 198, 199 n2.

§29.87 3. No Judgment for Nonmoving Party

Another important exception to ordinary appellate rules is that an appellate court may not reverse a summary judgment with directions to enter judgment for the other party absent a cross-motion and appeal by that party. To permit such a judgment would deny the original moving party the right to allege or produce additional facts justifying a trial of factual issues. *Dvorin v Appellate Dep't.* (1975) 15 C3d 648, 125 CR 771; see §29.6.

§29.88 C. Review of Order Adjudicating Issues To Be Without Substantial Controversy

A summary adjudication that issues are without substantial controversy is not a judgment and is not appealable. *Beech Aircraft Corp. v Superior Court* (1976) 61 CA3d 501, 517, 132 CR 541,

549; *Travelers Indem. Co. v Erickson's, Inc.* (5th Cir 1968) 396 F2d 134. Such an adjudication may be attacked by extraordinary writ in an appellate court (*Beech Aircraft Corp. v Superior Court, supra;* see also *Field Research Corp. v Superior Court* (1969) 71 C2d 110, 77 CR 243) or, presumably, in the trial court by a motion under CCP §473 (see §29.80) or by a motion under equitable principles for extrinsic fraud or mistake (see §29.81).

Nothing in the language of CCP §473c compels a drastic limitation on the trial court's power to review a summary adjudication of issues, despite language in *Beech Aircraft Corp. v Superior Court* (1976) 61 CA3d 501, 517, 132 CR 541, 549, which suggests that the trial court is without power to change such an adjudication. Federal cases have held that summary adjudications of issues may be modified by the trial court on a proper showing. See, *e.g., New Amsterdam Cas. Co. v B. L. Jones & Co.* (5th Cir 1958) 254 F2d 917.

If the summary adjudication is not overturned, the issues adjudicated are "deemed established" and the action proceeds only "as to the issues remaining." *Beech Aircraft Corp. v Superior Court, supra.*

D. Review of Order Denying Summary Judgment

§29.89   1. By Extraordinary Writ

An order denying summary judgment is not appealable. *Whitney's at the Beach v Superior Court* (1970) 3 CA3d 258, 261, 83 CR 237, 239. Such an order may be reviewed only on appeal from a final judgment (*Nevada Constr. Inc. v Mariposa Public Util. Dist.* (1952) 114 CA2d 816, 251 P2d 53) or by writ of mandate (*Diamond Bar Dev. Corp. v Superior Court* (1976) 60 CA3d 330, 332, 131 CR 458, 459). *Beech Aircraft Corp. v Superior Court* (1976) 61 CA3d 501, 517, 132 CR 541, 549.

§29.90   2. By Renewal of Motion

A summary judgment motion may be renewed. See *Schulze v Schulze* (1953) 121 CA2d 75, 83, 262 P2d 646, 651; *Muller v Tanner* (1969) 2 CA3d 445, 460, 82 CR 738, 748. A motion may not be renewed without new facts. The renewed motion must indicate the existence and fate of prior motions and the manner in which the renewed motion differs from the earlier one. CCP §1008.

SANDOR T. BOXER

Chapter 30
Default

I. INTRODUCTION
A. Nature and Effect
 1. Default §30.1
 2. Entry of Default §30.2
 3. Default Judgment §30.3
B. Statutory Scheme Under CCP §585
 1. Service by Means Other Than Publication
    a. Actions on Contract or Judgment for Damages Only §30.4
    b. Other Actions §30.5
 2. Service by Publication §30.6
C. Distinctions
 1. Dismissal and Uncontested Action §30.7
 2. Discovery Defaults §30.8
D. Situations in Which Default Judgments Prohibited or Restricted §30.9
E. Ethical Considerations §30.10

II. ENTRY OF DEFAULT
A. Requirements
 1. Service of Process §30.11
 2. Failure To Make Timely Response
    a. When To Respond §30.12
    b. Effect of Plaintiff's Failure To Request Entry of Default §30.13
    c. Effect of Amendment to Complaint §30.14
 3. Failure To File Responsive Paper
    a. Basic Rule; Terminology §30.15
    b. Particular Papers
       (1) Answer or Demurrer §30.16
       (2) Notice of Motion To Strike §30.17
       (3) Notice of Motion To Transfer §30.18
       (4) Notice of Motion To Quash Service or To Stay or Dismiss; Petition §30.19
B. Entry of Default as Prerequisite to Default Judgment §30.20

SANDOR T. BOXER, A.B., 1961, University of California (Los Angeles); J.D., 1964, University of California (Los Angeles). Mr. Boxer is a member of the Los Angeles firm of Coskey, Coskey & Boxer. CEB attorney-editor was JON A. RANTZMAN. Sections 30.67–30.70 are based on materials prepared by the Honorable WARREN H. DEERING, judge of the Los Angeles municipal court.

DEFAULT

    C. Procedures
       1. Moving Papers
          a. Required Papers; Use of Judicial Council Form **§30.21**
          b. Additional Papers **§30.22**
          c. Requirements and Content
             (1) Request for Entry of Default **§30.23**
             (2) Proof of Service of Summons **§30.24**
             (3) Declaration Under CCP §585.5 **§30.25**
             (4) Declaration of Mailing Under CCP §587 **§30.26**
             (5) Memorandum of Costs **§30.27**
             (6) Declaration of Nonmilitary Status **§30.28**
       2. Judicial Council Form: Request To Enter Default, Declaration Under CCP §585.5, Declaration of Mailing, Memorandum of Costs, and Declaration of Nonmilitary Status **§30.29**
       3. Amending Complaint To Conform to Proof of Service
          a. When Amendment Required **§30.30**
          b. Procedures **§30.31**
    D. Clerk's Duties on Application for Entry of Default
       1. Nature of Clerk's Duties **§30.32**
       2. Entry of Default **§30.33**
    E. Effect of Amended Complaint on Default Previously Entered **§30.34**

  III. DEFAULT JUDGMENTS
    A. Introduction
       1. Types of Default Judgments **§30.35**
       2. Extent of Relief Available **§30.36**
    B. Judgment by Clerk Under CCP §585(1)
       1. When Available **§30.37**
          a. Effect of Multiple Causes of Action **§30.38**
          b. Effect of Defendants' Several Liability **§30.39**
       2. Effect of Clerical Error in Entering or Denying Judgment **§30.40**
       3. Procedures
          a. Required Papers **§30.41**
             (1) Judicial Council Form; Instructions **§30.42**
             (2) Written Contract or Judgment **§30.43**
             (3) Request for Dismissal of Unserved Defendants; Judicial Council Form **§30.44**
             (4) Additional Papers **§30.45**
          b. Form: Default Judgment by Clerk **§30.46**
    C. Default Judgment by Court
       1. When Required **§30.47**
       2. Procedures
          a. Judgment and Attorneys' Fees Under CCP §585(1) **§30.48**
          b. Judgment in All Other Actions Under CCP §585(2)
             (1) Required Papers; Use of Judicial Council Form **§30.49**
             (2) Use of Affidavits or Declarations **§30.50**
             (3) Calendaring for Hearing **§30.51**
             (4) Hearing **§30.52**

c. Judgment When Summons Served by Publication Under CCP §585(3)
 (1) Application for Hearing §30.53
 (2) Hearing §30.54
d. Form: Default Judgment by Court §30.55

IV. RELIEF FROM DEFAULT OR DEFAULT JUDGMENT
 A. Introduction §30.56
 B. Relief When Service Affords Defendant Actual Notice
  1. Grounds for Relief §30.57
   a. Relief Sought Within Six Months §30.58
   b. Relief Sought After Six Months §30.59
  2. Judicial Policy in Favor of Hearing on Merits §30.60
  3. Court Discretion To Grant Relief; Power To Impose Conditions §30.61
  4. Procedures
   a. Motion Under CCP §473
    (1) Time for Motion §30.62
    (2) Moving Papers §30.63
    (3) Form: Notice of Motion To Set Aside Default or Default Judgment §30.64
    (4) Form: Declaration in Support of Motion To Set Aside Entry of Default or Default Judgment §30.65
    (5) Form: Declaration of Merits §30.66
    (6) Stay of Execution Pending Hearing §30.67
    (7) Form: Order Staying Execution and Order Shortening Time §30.68
    (8) Opposing Papers §30.69
    (9) Hearing and Ruling §30.70
    (10) Form: Order Setting Aside Entry of Default and Default Judgment §30.71
    (11) Renewal on Denial of Motion §30.72
   b. Equitable Motion in Trial Court §30.73
   c. Independent Action in Equity §30.74
 C. Relief When Service Does Not Afford Defendant Actual Notice
  1. Statutory Authority §30.75
  2. Equitable Authority §30.76
  3. Procedures
   a. Time for Motion §30.77
   b. Moving Papers §30.78
   c. Order; Court's Discretion To Impose Conditions §30.79
 D. Appellate Review §30.80

I. INTRODUCTION

A. Nature and Effect

§30.1   **1. Default**

A default occurs when a defendant (or cross-defendant) who has been served with a complaint (or cross-complaint) or amended complaint in a civil action fails, within the time allowed, to (a) file responsive papers (*i.e.*, an answer, demurrer, or certain defensive motions) or (b) answer an overruled demurrer or certain denied defensive motions. CCP §§585–586. For discussion of what constitutes a responsive paper, see §§30.15–30.19. On the time for filing, see §30.12.

Although defendant is "in default" for failure to file a responsive paper within the time allowed, no legal consequences result until plaintiff has obtained an entry of default (see §30.2). Until plaintiff has had the clerk enter the default, defendant can file a responsive paper even after the time allowed has expired.

§30.2   2. Entry of Default

When defendant (or cross-defendant) is in default, plaintiff (or cross-complainant) may apply to the court clerk (or judge, if there is no clerk) for entry of default in the court records. See §§30.21–30.31 for procedures. Once default has been entered, defendant's opportunity to file an answer, demurrer, or other responsive paper is cut off. Unless the default is set aside, defendant is "out of court," *i.e.*, he cannot oppose or object to the relief to which the complaint shows plaintiff is entitled, and need not be served with notice of subsequent proceedings or other papers. *Heathman v Vant* (1959) 172 CA2d 639, 343 P2d 104. See also CCP §1010. For example, defendant is not entitled to notice of trial, or to request a trial continuance (*Hanson v Hanson* (1960) 178 CA2d 756, 3 CR 179), and cannot raise the issue of whether the judge who granted a default judgment was qualified to hear the matter (*Muller v Muller* (1965) 235 CA2d 341, 45 CR 182). An exception to the rule that a defaulting defendant is out of court occurs when plaintiff materially amends the complaint after having obtained entry of default. For discussion see §30.34.

Entry of default ordinarily is a statutory prerequisite to a default judgment. However, once the court acquires jurisdiction over a defendant, it may enter a default judgment even though no default has been entered or the clerk has erred in entering a default. For discussion, see §30.20.

§30.3   3. Default Judgment

A default judgment may be entered by the court or clerk on plaintiff's application at or after entry of defendant's default. (A default judgment can also be entered against defendant or any other party for failure to obey a discovery request. See §30.8.) Application for default judgment is usually made to the court clerk (especially in contract or debt collection actions), but in some cases is made to the court. See §§30.37, 30.47.

A default judgment is a judgment on the merits in favor of plaintiff, and "is res judicata as to all issues aptly pleaded in the complaint." *Fitzgerald v Herzer* (1947) 78 CA2d 127, 132, 177 P2d 364, 366. By defaulting, defendant either (1) admits the truthfulness of all material allegations of the complaint (*Robinson v Early* (1967) 248 CA2d 19, 56 CR 183; see also *Muller v Muller* (1965) 235 CA2d 341, 344, 45 CR 182, 184), or (2) is treated as though there had been a trial on the material allegations and a judgment rendered in favor of plaintiff (*Martin v General Fin. Co.* (1966) 239 CA2d 438, 48 CR 773 (citing *Fitzgerald v Herzer, supra*)). However, a default judgment is not an admission of matters not raised by the complaint or unnecessary to uphold the judgment (*Mitchell v Jones* (1959) 172 CA2d 580, 342 P2d 503); and admissions of the defaulting party cannot be used against a nondefaulting party (*Taliaferro v Hays* (1961) 188 CA2d 235, 10 CR 429). On the collateral estoppel effect of a default judgment, see 4 Witkin, CALIFORNIA PROCEDURE, Judgment §§218–221 (2d ed 1971).

B. Statutory Scheme Under CCP §585

1. Service by Means Other Than Publication

§30.4   a. Actions on Contract or Judgment for Damages Only

When, in an action arising on a contract or California court judgment for recovery of money or damages only, defendant has been served other than by publication, and has failed to file a responsive paper (see §§30.15–30.19) within the time allowed, the clerk (or judge if there is no clerk) must, on plaintiff's written application and on proof of service of summons, enter defendant's default and must "immediately thereafter" enter judgment. CCP §585(1). Because the clerk's duty under CCP §585(1) is ministerial, he can be compelled to perform it. See §30.32; see §§30.37–30.39 on the application of CCP §585(1) to particular situations.

Under CCP §585(1), a written application or request for entry of default is a prerequisite to a default judgment. However, in a proper case plaintiff can compel entry of a default judgment even though no default has been entered. See §30.20.

§30.5 b. Other Actions

When, in an action other than those arising on a contract or judgment for recovery of damages only, defendant has been served other than by publication and has failed to file a responsive paper (see §§30.15–30.19) within the time allowed, the clerk (or judge if there is no clerk) must, on plaintiff's written application, enter defendant's default. Thereafter, "plaintiff may apply to the court for the relief demanded in the complaint." CCP §585(2). After hearing plaintiff's evidence the court may render judgment for a sum not exceeding the amount demanded in the complaint. See §30.52.

Under CCP §585(2), written application or request for entry of default is a prerequisite to a default judgment in actions and the clerk can be compelled to enter the default. See §30.32. However, unlike default judgments under CCP §585(1), entry of the judgment is not a ministerial duty that the clerk must perform, but is done by the court only after a hearing is held and evidence offered. See §30.49. On procedures, see §§30.49–30.52.

§30.6 2. Service by Publication

In all actions in which defendant has been served with summons by publication and has failed to file a responsive paper (see §§30.15–30.19) within the time allowed, plaintiff may, on proof of publication, make written application to the court for judgment. CCP §585(3). At the hearing, the court requires proof of the allegations of the complaint. CCP §585(3).

Unlike defaults under CCP §§585(1)–(2) (see §§30.4–30.5), a default judgment under CCP §585(3) need not be preceded by an entry of default. For discussion of procedures, see §§30.53–30.55.

C. Distinctions

§30.7 1. Dismissal and Uncontested Action

Regardless of whether a default is entered, the time within which to bring an action to trial is governed by CCP §§581a and 583. When plaintiff takes a default, but fails to obtain a default judgment within the time allowed under those provisions, defendant's remedy is a motion for dismissal. See, e.g., *McKenzie v Thousand Oaks* (1973) 36 CA3d 426, 111 CR 584 (mandatory dismissal for failure to reduce entry of default to judgment within three years of service of summons, as required by CCP §581a(c)). For further discussion, see §§31.15–31.17. However, if a dismissal is ordered "without prejudice," plaintiff may institute a new action based on the same facts, unless the action has been barred by the statute of limitations.

A default judgment is a judgment on the merits for plaintiff, and is res judicata as to issues properly pleaded in the complaint. See §30.3. Unlike a dismissal, a default judgment can be entered only when defendant has failed to answer or file a responsive paper within the time allowed; it may not be entered when an answer is on file, regardless of whether defendant fails to appear at trial. *Wilson v Goldman* (1969) 274 CA2d 573, 79 CR 309; but see *Bill Benson Motors, Inc. v Macmorris Sales Corp.* (1965) 238 CA2d Supp 937, 48 CR 123. See also CCP §2034(b)(2) (iii), discussed in §30.8, which allows the court to enter a default judgment against a party who refuses to comply with certain discovery orders. When defendant has answered but fails to appear at trial after having been given proper notice of trial, plaintiff's remedy is to proceed with trial and introduce testimony, on which the court may render judgment. CCP §594; *Wilson v Goldman, supra.*

§30.8   2. Discovery Defaults

A default judgment usually is entered after plaintiff has obtained an entry of default when defendant has failed to file an answer, demurrer or other responsive paper within the time allowed. CCP §585(1)–(2). However, a default judgment also may be entered against any party, (without the need to obtain entry of default), even though that party has filed a proper pleading, when the party has refused to obey certain discovery orders. CCP §§2034(b)(2)(iii), 2034(d). For discussion, see CALIFORNIA CIVIL DISCOVERY PRACTICE §3.38 (Cal CEB 1975).

On motion under either CCP §473 or CCP §§2033–2034, a party may be relieved from the effects of default judgment for failure or refusal to obey a discovery request. See *Zorro Ins. Co. v Great Pac. Sec. Corp.* (1977) 69 CA3d 907, 917, 138 CR 410, 415 (late and defectively served responses to request for admission); *Kaiser Steel Corp. v Westinghouse Elec. Corp.* (1976) 55 CA3d 737, 127 CR 838 (late and unsworn denials to requests for admission). A motion for relief under CCP §§2033–2034 is independent of a motion for relief under CCP §473, and may be made even after the time for making a CCP §473 motion has expired. *Kaiser Steel Corp. v Westinghouse Elec. Corp., supra.*

§30.9 D. Situations in Which Default Judgments Prohibited or Restricted

Default judgments are prohibited and the court must take evidence in:

(1) Quiet title actions (CCP §751; see also CCP §585(3));

(2) Actions to reestablish destroyed land records (CCP §751.14);

(3) Marital dissolution proceedings (CC §4511; but see Cal Rules of Ct 1237, 1240–1241 on default procedures when respondent fails to file a timely response or motion);

(4) Mandamus proceedings (CCP §1088; but see *Rodriguez v Municipal Court* (1972) 25 CA3d 521, 102 CR 45);

(5) Prohibition proceedings (CCP §§1105, 1088);

(6) Small claims court actions (CCP §117); and

(7) Corporate dissolution proceedings under Corp C §1804 (former Corp C §4657; see *Rosner v Benedict Heights, Inc.* (1963) 219 CA2d 1, 32 CR 764).

In addition, a default judgment cannot be obtained against the following persons, regardless of the nature of the proceeding:

(a) A fictitiously named defendant, unless (i) the copy of the summons served on such defendant notifies him that he is being served as, or on behalf of, a fictitiously named defendant, and (ii) the proof of service states the name under which defendant was served and that the above notice was given (CCP §474; *Armstrong v Superior Court* (1956) 144 CA2d 420, 301 P2d 51; for discussion and forms, see 1 CALIFORNIA CIVIL PROCEDURE BEFORE TRIAL §§8.8, 8.12, 8.55, 8.57 (Cal CEB 1977));

(b) An unwilling plaintiff joined as a nominal defendant under CCP §382 (*Watkins v Nutting* (1941) 17 C2d 490, 110 P2d 384): and

(c) A defendant in military service unless the requirements set forth in Soldiers' and Sailors' Civil Relief Act of 1940 (50 USC App §520 are complied with (see §30.28).

§30.10 E. Ethical Considerations

Although CCP §585 authorizes plaintiff to take a default and default judgment following service of the summons and complaint, whenever defendant has not filed a responsive paper "within the time specified in the summons," case law has provided standards for ethical conduct in using default procedures. For example, plaintiff's attorney should give notice to opposing counsel, if known, before taking a default. Failure to do so is sufficient grounds for setting aside the default under CCP §473. *Smith v Los Angeles Bookbinders Union* (1955) 133 CA2d 486, 500, 284 P2d 194, 201, disapproved on other grounds in 52 C2d at 551 (quiet speed of plaintiff's attorney in seeking default judgment without knowledge of defendant's counsel is not to be commended). See also *Farrar v Steenbergh* (1916) 173 C 94, 159 P 707. In *Robinson v Varela* (1977) 67 CA3d 611, 136 CR 783, plaintiff filed an unlawful detainer action against defendant on Friday, December 19, and served defendant on Monday, December 22. On Wednesday, December 24, defendant's attorney called the law firm representing plaintiff and asked for an extension of time in which to answer, but plaintiff's attorney was not present and no one else would grant the extension. Finally, on Monday, December 29, defendant's attorney again attempted to reach plaintiff's attorney, and discovered that plaintiff had just filed for default. The appellate court upheld a trial court order granting defendant's motion to vacate the ensuing default judgment, either because the conduct of defendant's attorney was "excusable" under CCP §473 (see §30.58) in view of the limited office hours during Christmas week and of the attorney's preoccupation with other litigation, or because "the quiet taking of default on the beginning of the first day on which defendant's answer was delinquent was the sort of professional discourtesy which, under *Smith,* justified vacating the default." 67 CA3d at 616, 136 CR at 785.

In addition to the notification requirement, the attorney taking the default has an obligation to avoid treachery or deceit in misleading defense counsel. *Farrar v Steenbergh, supra* (court affirmed order setting aside default judgment on cross-complaint because cross-complaint was buried obscurely in document labeled "answer," and which gave every appearance of being an answer). See also *Westport Oil Co. v Garrison* (1971) 19 CA3d 974, 97 CR 287.

II. ENTRY OF DEFAULT

A. Requirements

§30.11   1. Service of Process

An entry of default can be taken against defendant only if he has been served with process. CCP §585. A default entered against a defendant who has not been served as required by CCP §585 is void and can be set aside by him at any time. *Westport Oil Co. v Garrison* (1971) 19 CA3d 974, 97 CR 287 (discussing personal service requirement of former CCP §585). On the manner in which process may be served, see 1 CALIFORNIA CIVIL PROCEDURE BEFORE TRIAL §§8.29–8.50 (Cal CEB 1977).

The manner of service controls the necessity of entry of default as a prerequisite to default judgment. When defendant has been served other than by publication, entry of default ordinarily is required under CCP §§585(1)–(2). See §§30.21–30.31 for procedures. When defendant has been served by publication, entry of default is not required under CCP §585(3), but may be desirable. See §30.20.

2. Failure To Make Timely Response

§30.12   a. When To Respond

An entry of default can be taken against defendant only after he has been served with process and has not responded within the time specified in the summons, or such further time as may be allowed. CCP §585. Ordinarily, the summons specifies a 30-day period after service has been completed within which to file a responsive paper. CCP §412.20(a)(3). See also CCP §586(1) (30 days to respond to amended complaint). Service is completed: (1) at the time of delivery in the case of personal service (see 1 CALIFORNIA CIVIL PROCEDURE BEFORE TRIAL §8.31 (Cal CEB 1977)); (2) on the tenth day after mailing in the case of substituted service (see 1 CIV PROC BEFORE TRIAL §8.34); (3) on the date of signing the acknowledgment of receipt in the case of service by mail (see 1 CIV PROC BEFORE TRIAL §8.36) and (4) on the 28th day of publication in the case of service by publication (see 1 CIV PROC BEFORE TRIAL §8.40). An exception to the 30-day period is an action for unlawful detainer or forceable entry and detainer, in which the time to answer the complaint cannot exceed five days. CCP §§1167, 1167.3.

The period within which to respond may be extended by stipulation or by the court on motion for an order extending time. CCP §1054. For discussion and forms, see 1 CIV PROC BEFORE TRIAL §11.32. However, an order extending time for more than 30 days without plaintiff's consent under CCP §1054 is void, and does not prevent entry of default, although defendant's reliance on the order might be grounds for relief from default under CCP §473. *Kennedy v Mulligan* (1902) 136 C 556, 69 P 291.

§30.13   b. Effect of Plaintiff's Failure To Request Entry of Default

A default cannot be entered if defendant files a responsive paper after expiration of the time within which to do so, but before plaintiff obtains entry of his default. Plaintiff's failure to request the entry of default is considered the equivalent of having granted defendant an extension of time to respond. *Reher v Reed* (1913) 166 C 525, 137 P 263; *Goddard v Pollock* (1974) 37 CA3d 137, 112 CR 215.

§30.14   c. Effect of Amendment to Complaint

When plaintiff files an amended complaint or an amendment to the complaint either (1) before expiration of defendant's time to respond to the original complaint, or (2) after defendant's time has expired but before plaintiff has requested entry of default, and the amendment is one of substance rather than simply one of form, the new pleading supersedes the original and the time to respond runs from service of the amendment. See *Legg v Mutual Benefit Health & Acc. of Omaha* (1955) 136 CA2d 887, 289 P2d 550, disapproved on other grounds in 55 C2d at 578. For examples of amendments of substance, as distinguished from those of form, see §30.34.

3. Failure To File Responsive Paper
§30.15   a. Basic Rule; Terminology

An entry of default on a complaint can be taken only against a defendant who has not, within the time permitted, filed a "responsive paper," *i.e.*, an answer, demurrer, or notice of motion to strike, notice of motion to transfer under CCP §396b, notice of motion to quash service of summons or to stay or dismiss the action under CCP §418.10, or a petition for writ of mandate as provided for in CCP §418.10. CCP §585. A default may be entered on an amended complaint when defendant has failed to file an answer, demurrer, or notice of motion to strike of the type discussed in §30.17. CC §586(1). For discussion of particular responsive papers, see §§30.16–30.19.

The term "responsive paper" rather than "pleading" is used in this chapter with reference to the above papers because, although courts and commentators frequently refer to them as pleadings (see, e.g., *Goddard v Pollock* (1974) 37 CA3d 137, 112 CR 215 (notice of motion to quash service of summons under CCP §418.10 is a "pleading" for purposes of CCP §585)), neither CCP §585 nor CCP §586 use that terminology. Technically, the only pleadings permitted in civil actions are complaints, demurrers, answers and cross-complaints. CCP §422.10.

If defendant has filed a responsive paper, it is immaterial that the paper has not been served on plaintiff. *Fletcher v Maginnis* (1902) 136 C 362, 68 P 1015. On filing, the clerk cannot enter defendant's default, and cannot review the paper to determine its legal sufficiency. See §30.32.

b. Particular Papers

§30.16 (1) Answer or Demurrer

A default cannot be entered when defendant has filed an answer or demurrer to a complaint (CCP §585), amended complaint (CCP §586(1)), or cross-complaint within the time allowed. Because a cross-complaint is an independent action and must be answered as if it were a complaint, the default statutes, although they refer only to failure to answer or demur to a complaint or amended complaint, apply equally to failure to answer or demur to cross-complaint. See 1 CALIFORNIA CIVIL PROCEDURE BEFORE TRIAL §12.2 (Cal CEB 1977); 3 Witkin, CALIFORNIA PROCEDURE, Pleading §§990, 1028–1029 (2d ed 1971). Whether the answer or demurrer is legally sufficient is immaterial. See *Stevens v Torregano* (1961) 192 CA2d 105, 112, 13 CR 604, 610. On the time allowed for filing, see §§30.12–30.13.

When defendant has answered the original complaint and plaintiff files an amended complaint that differs from the original in form only, the usual practice is for defendant to request a stipulation that the answer to the original complaint be considered applicable to the amended complaint. Failure to obtain a stipulation, or to answer the amended complaint, can result in a default being entered if the court later decides that the amendment was one of substance rather than form. *Bristol Convalescent Hosp. v Stone* (1968) 258 CA2d 848, 863, 66 CR 404, 413. See 4 Witkin, PROCEDURE, Proc Without Trial §129. On what constitutes an amendment of substance, see §30.34.

A demurrer may be filed alone or with a notice of motion to strike. See CCP §586(2). If the demurrer is sustained with leave to amend, defendant need not plead further until plaintiff serves and files an amended complaint. If the demurrer is overruled and the motion to strike is denied, or if a demurrer filed alone is overruled, and defendant then fails to answer within the time allowed, plaintiff may take his default. CCP §586(2). The time allowed for filing an answer usually is stated in the order overruling the demurrer (see CCP §472a), but is ten days when the order is silent (Cal Rules of Ct 202(d), 502(d)). Time begins to run when defendant is served with notice of the order or decision unless notice is waived in open court and the waiver entered in the minutes or docket. CCP §472b; see also 1 CIV PROC BEFORE TRIAL §9.34.

A default may be taken against defendant when plaintiff's demurrer to the answer is sustained, and defendant fails to amend the answer within the time allowed. CCP §586(5). On demurrers to answers generally, see 1 CIV PROC BEFORE TRIAL §§9.44–9.53.

§30.17   (2) Notice of Motion To Strike

A default cannot be entered when defendant has filed a notice of motion to strike the whole or any part of a complaint (CCP §585), amended complaint (CCP §586(1)), or cross-complaint within the time allowed, provided the notice of motion specifies a hearing date of not more than 15 days from the date of filing the notice, in addition to any further time the moving party is required to give the adverse party (CCP §585(3)). On the time allowed for filing, see §§30.12–30.13.

A notice of motion to strike may be filed alone or with a demurrer. See CCP §586(2). If the motion to strike the entire complaint is granted, defendant need not plead further until plaintiff serves and files an amended complaint. If the motion is granted as to part of the complaint, and a demurrer is not pending or has

§30.18 DEFAULT

not been sustained, defendant must answer the unstricken portion of the complaint within the time allowed or plaintiff may take his default. CCP §586(3). Although there are no California cases directly on point, presumably the entry of default applies only to the unstricken portion of the complaint notwithstanding the first sentence of CCP §586, which states that entry of a default may be had "as if the defendant had failed to answer." An entry of default on the entire complaint leads to the anomalous result of a default judgment having been based in part on allegations in a pleading that have been stricken.

If the motion to strike is denied and the demurrer is overruled, or if a motion to strike filed alone is denied, and defendant then fails to answer the complaint within the time allowed, plaintiff may take his default. CCP §586(2).

§30.18 (3) Notice of Motion To Transfer

Under CCP §396b: A default cannot be entered when defendant has, within the time allowed, filed a notice of motion to transfer a complaint. CCP §585. On the time allowed for filing, see §§30.12–30.13. Under CCP §396b, a motion to transfer or change venue is proper when the complaint is filed in a court having subject matter jurisdiction, but which is not the proper court for trial of the action. For discussion, see 1 CALIFORNIA CIVIL PROCEDURE BEFORE TRIAL §§3.44, 3.50–3.66 (Cal CEB 1977).

If a motion to change venue under CCP §396b is denied, the court will set a time for defendant to answer, and plaintiff may enter a default on expiration of that time. CCP §586(6)(a). If the motion is granted and the action transferred, plaintiff may enter a default unless defendant answers within 15 days of the mailing of notice of filing and case number by the clerk of the transferee court. CCP §586(6)(b). If an order granting or denying the motion is challenged by appeal in municipal or justice court (CCP §904.2), or by mandate proceedings in superior court (CCP §400), and a stay is granted, no default can be entered during the stay. CCP §586(6)(c). The trial court, either on application or on its own motion, after the appeal or mandate proceeding has become final or on earlier termination of a stay, must allow defendant a reasonable time to answer the complaint. Notice of the order allowing time to answer must be given by the party who obtained the order or by the court clerk if the order was made on the court's own motion. CCP §586(6)(c).

Under CCP §396a: In municipal or justice court actions that are subject to the venue provisions of CC §§1812.10, 2984.4 (installment sales contracts and installment purchases of motor vehicles under the Unruh or Rees-Levering acts), plaintiff or his attorney must, by verified complaint or by affidavit, state facts showing that the action is subject to those provisions and was brought in the proper court for trial. For discussion of the proper venue in such actions, see 1 CIVIL PROC BEFORE TRIAL §3.34 (Cal CEB 1977). If the complaint or affidavit does not so state, no further proceedings can be had except to dismiss the action without prejudice. CCP §396a. If it appears from the complaint or affidavit that the court in which the action was brought is not the proper court for trial, the court may transfer the action on its own motion or motion of the defendant and the time to answer or otherwise plead dates from service on defendant of written notice of filing the action in the transferee court. CCP §396a.

Although a motion to transfer under CCP §396a is not a motion specified in CCP §§585–586 as sufficient to prevent entry of a default, CCP §586(6)(c) provides that if review is sought of a court order granting or denying a CCP §396a motion, whether a default may be entered is governed by the same rules pertaining to review of motions to transfer under CCP §396b.

Under CCP §396: A motion to transfer under CCP §396 on grounds that the court lacks subject matter jurisdiction is not a motion specified in CCP §§585–586 as sufficient to prevent entry of default. However, granting such a motion produces the same result because CCP §396 provides that when an order of transfer is entered, the time for filing a responsive pleading does not begin to run until defendant receives notice that the action has been filed in the transferee court. For discussion of subject matter jurisdiction in California courts, see 1 CIV PROC BEFORE TRIAL §§2.3–2.19 (Cal CEB 1977).

§30.19 (4) Notice of Motion To Quash Service or To Stay or Dismiss; Petition

A default cannot be entered when defendant has filed, under CCP §418.10 within the time allowed, a notice of motion to quash service of summons for lack of personal jurisdiction or to stay or dismiss the action on the ground of inconvenient forum, or a notice of petition for writ of mandate. CCP §585. On the time allowed for filing, see CCP §418.10(a). See also §§30.12–30.13. For discussion of lack of personal jurisdiction as a ground for the motions and of procedures, see 1 CALIFORNIA CIVIL PROCEDURE BEFORE TRIAL §§2.78, 2.80–2.81 (Cal CEB 1977). For discussion of inconvenient forum, see 1 CIV PROC BEFORE TRIAL §2.43.

A notice of motion under CCP §418.10 extends defendant's time to plead until 15 days after service on him of written notice of an order denying the motion; however, the court may for good cause extend the time for an additional period not exceeding 20 days. CCP §§418.10(b), 586(4). Within ten days after service of notice of denial of the motion, or within such further time as the court for good cause may allow (not exceeding 20 days), defendant may seek review by petition for writ of mandate. Defendant's filing with the trial court of a notice of petition for writ of mandate precludes entry of a default until ten days after service (unless the court, for good cause, extends the time for an additional period not exceeding 20 days) on him of written notice of final judgment in the mandate proceeding. CCP §§418.10(c), 586(4).

§30.20   B. Entry of Default as Prerequisite to Default Judgment

Entry of default by the court clerk is a statutory prerequisite to both a clerk's default judgment (CCP §585(1)) and a court's default judgment (CCP §585(2)), but not to a court's default judgment in an action in which process has been served by publication (CCP §585(3)). However, even under CCP §§585(1)–(2), it has been said that "the only purpose of a default is to limit the time during which the defendant may file his answer, and that time never extends beyond a trial and judgment." *Drake v Duvenick* (1873) 45 C 455, 463, quoted with approval in *Norman v Berney* (1965) 235 CA2d 424, 429, 45 CR 467, 471. Therefore, once the court acquires jurisdiction over defendant, it may enter a default judgment even though no default has been entered or the clerk has erred in entering a default. *Crouch v H. L. Miller & Co.* (1915) 169 C 341, 146 P 880; *Herman v Santee* (1894) 103 C 519, 37 P 509. The same reasoning applies to a default judgment by the clerk under CCP §585(1). *Norman v Berney, supra*.

Although a request for entry of default is unnecessary under CCP §585(3) when summons has been served by publication, some court clerks will process such a request. A request for entry of default in this situation can be useful when plaintiff is unable to proceed to judgment immediately after service by publication has been completed, *e.g.*, when testimony at the default judgment hearing is to be by affidavit (see §30.50), and the affidavit cannot be executed because the affiant is not immediately available. For discussion of when service by publication is complete, see 1 CALIFORNIA CIVIL PROCEDURE BEFORE TRIAL §8.40 (Cal CEB 1977).

C. Procedures
1. Moving Papers
§30.21　a. Required Papers; Use of Judicial Council Form

The required moving papers for entry of default are:
(1) A request to enter default (CCP §585; see §30.23);
(2) Valid proof of service of summons (see §30.24).
(3) (In every request to enter default under CCP §585(1)) a declaration of facts showing whether the action is subject to the venue provisions of CC §§1812.10, 2984.4, or CCP §395(b) (CCP §585.5; see §30.25); and
(4) A declaration that a copy of the request has been mailed to defendant or his attorney (CCP §587; see §30.26).

For discussion of a memorandum of costs and declaration of nonmilitary status as required papers in a request to enter default, see §§30.27–30.28.

The California Judicial Council has prescribed a printed form for mandatory use when requesting an entry of default (Cal Rules of Ct 982(a)(6), which combines all the required moving papers in one document and is usually available in the offices of the court clerk. See form in §30.29, which has been revised, effective July 1, 1975. When the Judicial Council has adopted a form for mandatory use, no court may use a different form purporting to serve the same function. Govt C §68511. The Judicial Council also has prescribed a form for mandatory use when requesting entry of default in marital dissolution cases. See Cal Rules of Ct 1240, 1286.

§30.22　b. Additional Papers

In addition to the papers required for entry of default (see §30.21), the Judicial Council form in §30.29 includes a memorandum of costs and a declaration of nonmilitary status, which in some situations may be required when requesting entry of default, but which usually are required only before entry of default judgment. See §§30.27–30.28.

When a request for entry of default is made under CCP §585(1) (action on contract or judgment for money or damages only), and either the contract sued on provides for unspecified attorneys' fees or plaintiff is entitled to attorneys' fees by statute, plaintiff's moving papers may include a request to have the fees fixed by the court. CCP §585(1); see §30.48.

c. Requirements and Content

§30.23 (1) Request for Entry of Default

The default statutes require no particular form or content for a request for entry of default, other than that there must be a written application. CCP §585(1)–(2). However, the California Judicial Council has prescribed a form for mandatory use in requesting entry of default. See §30.21. For instructions on completing the form, see Comment to form in §30.29.

§30.24 (2) Proof of Service of Summons

Valid proof of service of summons is required on a request to enter default in actions on a contract or state court judgment for recovery of money or damages only (CCP §585(1)), as well as other actions (*Lewis v LeBaron* (1967) 254 CA2d 270, 61 CR 903; *Woods v Stallworth* (1960) 177 CA2d 517, 2 CR 250). Proof of service normally requires filing the original summons and the proof of service with the court clerk. See CCP §§417.10–417.20. On procedures when the original summons has been lost, see CCP §417.30. For further discussion, see 1 CALIFORNIA CIVIL PROCEDURE BEFORE TRIAL §§8.51–8.54 (Cal CEB 1977).

If defendant was served improperly (*e.g.*, John Jones, Jr., named in the complaint; summons served on John Jones), plaintiff must either (a) obtain a court order that the defect in service was immaterial and directing entry of the default, or (b) ordinarily must serve defendant again before the clerk will enter his default.

Similarly, when defendant's name as shown on the summons and complaint differs in any manner, including typographical errors, from that shown on the return of service, and plaintiff wants the default entered against defendant as named in the complaint, he must first obtain a corrected return of service from the process server. There is a presumption that different names designate different persons (see *Brum v Ivins* (1908) 154 C 17, 96 P 876), and although minor defects in the manner of service do not necessarily invalidate service (see 1 CALIFORNIA CIVIL PROCEDURE BEFORE TRIAL §8.4 (Cal CEB 1977), the clerk has no authority to conclude that said defects are minor. See §§30.32–30.33 for discussion of clerk's duties on a request to enter default.

§30.25 (3) Declaration Under CCP §585.5

Every request for entry of default under CCP §585(1) (action on contract or judgment seeking only money or damages) must include, or be accompanied by, an affidavit (or declaration under penalty of perjury; CCP §2015.5) that states facts showing whether the action is subject to the venue provisions of CC §§1812.10, 2984.4, or CCP §395(b). CCP §585.5. Civil Code §§1812.10 and 2984.4 govern venue in actions on installment sales contracts for consumer goods and automobiles under the Unruh and Rees-Levering acts respectively, while CCP §395(b) governs venue in all other actions based on the sale of goods or services, or on loans or extensions of credit, intended primarily for personal, family, or household use. For discussion, see 1 CALIFORNIA CIVIL PROCEDURE BEFORE TRIAL §3.34 (Cal CEB 1977). The purpose of the CCP §585.5 declaration is to require the disclosure of facts that advise the clerk (and perhaps the defendant) whether the action is subject to these venue requirements. When the declaration discloses that the action is subject to these requirements, and the complaint discloses that the court in which the action has been filed is not the proper court for trial under CC §1812.10, §2984.4, or CCP §395(b), the clerk will refuse to enter the default. Any default or default judgment entered without full compliance with CC §§1812.10, 2984.4, or CCP §395(b) may be set aside by defendant on noticed motion (CCP §585.5(b)), and defendant may recover actual damages and costs, including reasonable attorneys' fees, unless plaintiff shows he used reasonable diligence to avoid filing in the wrong court (CCP §585.5(e)). On defendants' procedures on a motion to set aside, see §§30.62–30.74.

§30.26 (4) Declaration of Mailing Under CCP §587

Every request for entry of default under CCP §§585(1)–(2), 586 or for default judgment under CCP §585(3) when defendant has been served by publication, must include an affidavit (or declaration under penalty of perjury; CCP §2015.5) stating that a copy of the request has been mailed to defendant's attorney of record or, if none, to defendant at his last-known address. CCP §587. No default can be entered and no default judgment rendered unless the declaration has been filed. CCP §587. But see *Marriage of Harris* (1977) 74 CA3d 98, 141 CR 333 (default judgment held proper even though no declaration of mailing had been filed, as required by CCP §587, when respondent had actual notice of petitioner's intent to take default, and no harm resulted from defect).

It has been said that the purpose of the statute is to prevent the taking of a default against an unwary litigant (*Slusher v Durr* (1977) 69 CA3d 747, 138 CR 265), as well as entries of default and default judgments procured through chicanery (*Westport Oil Co. v Garrison* (1971) 19 CA3d 974, 978 n1, 97 CR 287, 290 n1). However, CCP §587 does not specify when the request must be mailed to defendant or his attorney, but only that it "has been mailed." Therefore, it is possible that the request will be received after entry of default, *e.g.*, when it has been mailed the same day. The nonreceipt of notice, moreover, does not constitute grounds for setting aside the judgment. CCP §587; *Flood v Simpson* (1975) 45 CA3d 644, 119 CR 675.

When defendant's address is unknown to plaintiff or his attorney, the declaration must so state, and no mailing is then required. CCP §587. Plaintiff first must make a "reasonably diligent search" to ascertain defendant's address, *e.g.*, by investigating city and county directories, utility companies, friends, acquaintances, and relatives. Failure to make such a search is grounds for setting aside the default and default judgment. *Slusher v Durr, supra*. Therefore, as a practical matter, defendant's address will be unknown only when he has been served with summons by publication.

§30.27 (5) Memorandum of Costs

A memorandum of costs is required for default judgments (but not for entry of default) in superior, municipal, and justice courts. CCP §1033 1/2. Ordinarily, the memorandum is not completed until a default judgment is requested because all costs may not be known when entry of default is requested. However, the memorandum is required on a request to enter default when a clerk's default judgment under CCP §585(1) is sought and plaintiff's attorney requests in the Judicial Council form that the clerk enter judgment immediately after entering the default (see Comment to form in §30.29). Moreover, some court clerks require that the memorandum be completed before they will enter a default, and the attorney should consult the court clerk to determine local practice. If a memorandum of costs is required, any recoverable costs incurred between filing request for the entry of default and the request for entry of default judgment probably can be included in a supplemental memorandum.

Includable in the memorandum as recoverable costs are, *e.g.*, clerk's filing fees, sheriff's fees for service of process (currently $8.50; Govt C §26721), fees for service by publication, attachment fees, and notary fees. For further discussion of allowable pretrial costs, see CALIFORNIA CIVIL PROCEDURE DURING TRIAL §§23.25–23.30 (Cal CEB 1960). Costs are not recoverable on default judgment in a quiet title action. CCP §739.

The memorandum must contain a statement under oath by the party or his attorney or agent that to the best of his knowledge and belief, the cost items are correct and have been necessarily incurred. CCP §1033 1/2. See form in §30.29.

§30.28   (6) Declaration of Nonmilitary Status

A default judgment cannot be obtained against a defendant who is in military service, as defined by the Soldiers' and Sailors' Civil Relief Act of 1940 (50 USC App §511), unless certain requirements are met. See 50 USC App §520. A default judgment rendered without compliance with the provisions of this act is voidable by defendant on a showing of prejudice within 90 days after leaving the service. *People v Vogel* (1956) 46 C2d 798, 299 P2d 850. If defendant is in military service, the court may appoint an attorney or make any order necessary to protect defendant's interest. 50 USC App §520(1); *Allen v Allen* (1947) 30 C2d 433, 182 P2d 551. For further discussion, see CALIFORNIA DEBT COLLECTION PRACTICE §§13.19–13.20 (Cal CEB 1968).

Any person with personal knowledge, including plaintiff or his attorney, may sign the declaration of nonmilitary status. Occasionally, there can be a delay between execution of the declaration and filing the request for default judgment, *e.g.*, when the declaration is obtained from a process server.

The declaration of nonmilitary status need not be filed before

§30.29   DEFAULT

entry of default, but only before entry of judgment. 50 USC App §520. Moreover, each court has its own policy on how current the declaration must be relative to the date of entry of default judgment. The Los Angeles municipal court, *e.g.*, will not accept declarations executed more than 60 days before judgment is entered. Thus, in practice, the declaration usually is not filed when entry of default is requested unless plaintiff's attorney (a) is reasonably certain that default judgment will be entered within the time in which the declaration is considered current by the court in which the action is pending, or (b) is seeking a clerk's default judgment under CCP §585(1), and requests in the Judicial Council form that the clerk enter judgment immediately after entering the default (see form and comment in §30.29). However, some court clerks may refuse to enter the default unless the declaration is executed and submitted with the request, and the attorney should consult the court clerk to determine local practice.

For further discussion of compliance with and waiver of the requirements set forth in the Soldiers' and Sailors' Civil Relief Act of 1940 prerequisite to a default judgment, see DEBT COLLECTION PRACTICE §§13.19–13.23.

§30.29   2. Judicial Council Form: Request To Enter Default, Declaration Under CCP §585.5, Declaration of Mailing, Memorandum of Costs, and Declaration of Nonmilitary Status

Copies: Original (filed with court clerk); copies for service (one for each attorney of record or unrepresented party); office copies.

NAME AND ADDRESS OF ATTORNEY	TELEPHONE NO.	FOR COURT USE ONLY
ATTORNEY FOR		
Insert name of court, judicial district or branch court, if any, and Post Office and Street Address:		
PLAINTIFF		
DEFENDANT		
REQUEST TO ENTER DEFAULT		Case Number

DEFAULT §30.29

1. TO THE CLERK   Please enter the default of the following defendant on the (cross/amended) . . . . . .complaint
   Defendant (Name. See footnote° before completing):

2. Check applicable items and apply credits, if any, below
   a. ☐ Enter default only.
   b. ☐ Enter clerk's judgment under CCP 585(1).
      (1) ☐ When authorized by law include attorneys fees below, per court schedule.
      (2) Complete declaration under CCP 585.5, below.
   c. ☐ I request a court judgment under CCP 585(2), (3), 989, etc. (Testimony required. Apply to clerk for hearing date, unless court will enter judgment on affidavit under CCP 585(4).)

   d. Judgment to be entered Amount Credits Acknowledged Balance
      (1) Demand of Complaint . . . . $ $ $
      (2) Attorney Fees . . . . $ $ $
      (3) Interest . . . . $ $ $
      (4) Costs (see reverse side) . . . . $ $ $
      (5) TOTAL . . . . $ $ $

   Dated: . . . .
       (Type or print name of attorney)   Signature of (Attorney for) Plaintiff

DECLARATION UNDER CCP 585.5

3. This action: (Check applicable box for each of the following items)
   a. ☐ Is   ☐ Is not   on a contract or installment sale for goods or services subject to CC 1801, etc. (Unruh Act).
   b. ☐ Is   ☐ Is not   on a conditional sales contract subject to CC 2981, etc. (Rees-Levering Motor Vehicle Sales and Finance Act).
   c. ☐ Is   ☐ Is not   on an obligation for goods, services, loans or extensions of credit subject to CCP 395(b).

I certify (or declare) under penalty of perjury that the foregoing is true and correct and that this declaration is executed on (Date): . . . ., at (Place): . . . ., California.

  (Type or print name of declarant)   (Signature of declarant)

FOR COURT USE ONLY   Default entered as requested on . . . . ☐ Default NOT entered as requested.
  By . . . . (State reason on reverse side.)

(See reverse side for Declaration of Mailing, Memorandum of Costs, and Declaration of Nonmilitary Status)

The word "plaintiff" includes cross-complainant, "defendant" includes cross-defendant, singular includes the plural, and masculine includes feminine. Declaration must be signed in California (CCP 2015.5). Affidavit required when signed outside California.

Form adopted by the Judicial Council of California   **REQUEST TO ENTER DEFAULT, DECLARATION UNDER CCP 585.5, DECLARATION OF MAILING, MEMORANDUM OF COSTS, AND DECLARATION OF NONMILITARY STATUS**   CCP 585, 585.5, 587, 1033½
Revised Effective July 1, 1975

[Reverse side of form]

DECLARATION OF MAILING (CCP 587)

4. a. ☐ On (Date): . . . ., a copy of this Request To Enter Default was mailed (by first-class mail or airmail, postage prepaid) to each defendant's attorney of record, or if none, to such defendant at his last known address, addressed as follows:

   b. ☐ The address of the following defendant and of his attorney of record is unknown to plaintiff and his attorney
      (Name):

I certify (or declare) under penalty of perjury that the foregoing is true and correct, and that this declaration is executed on (Date): . . . . at (Place): . . . ., California.

  (Type or print name)   (Signature of declarant)

MEMORANDUM OF COSTS

5. Costs and disbursements are listed as follows (CCP 1033½):
   a. Clerk's Filing Fees . . . . $
   b. Process Server's Fees . . . . $
   c. . . . . $
   d. . . . . $
   e. TOTAL . . . . $ *[Part 5 continued on page 346]*

§30.29   DEFAULT   346

I am (the attorney or agent for): . . . . the party who claims these costs. To the best of my knowledge and belief the foregoing items of cost are correct and have been necessarily incurred in this action.

I certify (or declare) under penalty of perjury that the foregoing is true and correct, and that this declaration is executed on (Date): . . . . at (Place): . . . ., California.

_____   _____
(Type or Print Name)   (Signature of declarant)

DECLARATION OF NON MILITARY STATUS

6. Defendant (Name): . . . . is not in the military service or in the military service of the United States as defined in Section 101 of the Soldiers' and Sailors' Relief Act of 1940, as amended, and not entitled to the benefits of the Act.

I certify (or declare) under penalty of perjury that the foregoing is true and correct, and that this declaration is executed on (Date): . . . . at (Place): . . . ., California.

_____   _____
(Type or print name)   (Signature of declarant)

Comment: Items 1 and 2 (Request to enter default): Entry of default against several defendants can be requested in the same form. The names of defendants against whom entry of default is requested should conform to the names as set forth in the caption of the summons and complaint. If entry of default is requested against defendants who have been fictitiously named or named incorrectly, it is necessary to amend the complaint to state their true names. See §§30.30–30.31.

The proper box to be checked in item two depends on the nature and extent of relief sought. When plaintiff seeks only entry of default (*e.g.*, when other defendants remain unserved and plaintiff wishes to defer taking a default judgment against him until all defendants are in default), box "a" should be checked. (Even though CCP §585(1) provides that the clerk must enter judgment "immediately" after entering the default, plaintiff in actions subject to that statute can limit the relief sought to entry of default only by checking box "a".) If a clerk's default judgment under CCP §585(1) is sought, box "b" should be checked, the declaration under CCP §585.5 completed, and item "d" is completed (including attorneys' fees, when applicable).

The Judicial Council form does not cover the situation in which a clerk's default judgment under CCP §585(1) is requested, but either the court has no fee schedule or plaintiff wishes to have attorneys' fees fixed by the court (see §30.48). In this situation, the attorney should check box "c" instead of box "b" and attach to the form a written request for attorneys' fees, because, under CCP §585(1), the judgment must be entered by the court. Under item two, part "d(2)," the words "See attached request" should be typed in. The totals in item "d(5)" should be left blank.

Item 3 (Declaration under CCP §585.5): This item must be completed in every request for entry of default under CCP §585(1). CCP §585.5. For discussion, see §30.25.

Although the Judicial Council form implies under box "b(2)" that a CCP §585.5 declaration need be completed only when box "b" is checked, that declaration must also be completed when box "a" is checked if the action is subject to CCP §585(1) because CCP §585.5 says the declaration must be made in "every declaration" to enter default under CCP §585(1).

Item 4 (Declaration of mailing under CCP §587): The declaration of mailing satisfies the requirement of CCP §587 that (a) defendant either be notified that a request has been made for entry of default under CCP §§585(1)–(2), 586, or for default judgment under CCP §585(3), by mailing a copy to defendant's attorney, to defendant at his last-known address, or (b) the declaration state that defendant's address is unknown. Usually, defendant's address is unknown (box "b" of item 4) only when he has been served with summons by publication. See §30.26.

When defendant has moved from the address where he was served with process, as set forth on the proof of service, many attorneys prefer to mail copies of the request to both addresses and prepare the declaration of mailing accordingly.

Item 5 (Memorandum of costs): Although a memorandum of costs usually is not a prerequisite to entry of default, as distinguished from default judgment, the memorandum may be necessary in some situations. For discussion, and discussion of what costs are allowable, see §30.27.

Item 6 (Declaration of nonmilitary status): Although a declaration of nonmilitary status usually is not a prerequisite to entry of default, as distinguished from default judgment, the declaration may be necessary in some situations. See §30.28.

3. Amending Complaint To Conform to Proof of Service

§30.30   a. When Amendment Required

Defendant sued under fictitious name: When plaintiff is ignorant of defendant's name and the complaint so states, he may state a cause of action and obtain a default judgment against a

§30.31 DEFAULT

defendant sued under a fictitious name. CCP §474. On the requirements for summons and proof of service before a default or default judgment may be entered, see CCP §474; see also 1 CALIFORNIA CIVIL PROCEDURE BEFORE TRIAL §§8.12, 8.55 (Cal CEB 1977). However, when plaintiff ascertains defendant's true name he must amend the complaint accordingly. CCP §474.

The requirements of CCP §474 do not apply to situations in which plaintiff erroneously sues defendant under an incorrect name. CCP §474.

Defendant named incorrectly: When plaintiff has erroneously sued defendant under an incorrect name, but serves him under his correct name (*e.g.*, Samuel B. Jones named in complaint, Samuel D. Jones served with summons and complaint), plaintiff must amend the complaint before a default or default judgment will be entered. The amendment normally may be accomplished by ex parte motion under CCP §473. See §30.31. On procedures when defendant is correctly named in the summons and complaint but incorrectly named on the return of service, see §30.24.

§30.31   b. Procedures

When defendant is sued by a fictitious name under CCP §474 and plaintiff later ascertains his correct name, plaintiff must file and serve an amendment to the complaint substituting the correct name for the fictitious name, before requesting entry of default. CCP §474. Because local practice varies, the attorney should first consult the court clerk in the county in which the action is pending to determine whether a court order is required and whether a printed form is available. See 1 CALIFORNIA CIVIL PROCEDURE BEFORE TRIAL §7.54 (Cal CEB 1977) for a form when no printed form is available. The amendment does not require a notice motion unless new allegations are added to the complaint, and any required order is usually made pro forma and ex parte. See 1 CIV PROC BEFORE TRIAL §7.53.

The procedure for amending a complaint to substitute a party's correct name for an erroneous name is set forth in CCP §473, which requires a court order. Unlike an amendment to substitute defendant's correct name for a fictitious name, the attorney should file and serve a noticed motion for an amendment to correct a party's name under CCP §473. For further discussion, and a form for amendment and order when no printed forms are available from the court clerk, see 1 CIV PROC BEFORE TRIAL §§7.51–7.52.

D. Clerk's Duties on Application for Entry of Default

§30.32 1. Nature of Clerk's Duties

When plaintiff has properly applied for entry of default and conditions for entry of default exist, the clerk "shall enter the default." CCP §585(1)–(2). The clerk determines whether conditions exist for entry of default from the face of the record, and must enter it if the conditions do, and refrain if they do not. See 4 Witkin, CALIFORNIA PROCEDURE Proceedings Without Trial §136 (2d ed 1971).

The clerk's duties are ministerial; he can neither take evidence nor determine disputed matters. See, *e.g.*, *Potts v Whitson* (1942) 52 CA2d 199, 125 P2d 947 (entry of default held void when clerk judicially determined answer was not on behalf of all defendants and entered default against unanswering defendants); *Rose v Lelande* (1912) 20 CA 502, 129 P 599 (clerk properly denied entry of default when answer was on file, and had no authority to determine sufficiency of answer).

The clerk's improper failure or refusal to enter a default does not affect plaintiff's rights, and plaintiff can apply to the court for a default judgment even though no default has been entered. See §30.20. Moreover, the court can be restrained from further proceedings by writ of prohibition and can be compelled to enter the default by writ of mandamus. *W. A. Rose Co. v Municipal Court* (1959) 176 CA2d 67, 1 CR 49.

§30.33 2. Entry of Default

When defendant's default is entered by the clerk under CCP §585(1)–(2), the default is entered in the register of actions. Govt C §§69845–69845.5 (superior court); CCP §1052 (municipal and justice court). In superior, municipal, and justice courts, when the complaint has not been answered by any defendant, the complaint and a memorandum endorsed on it and showing entry of default and request for entry of default become part of the judgment roll, together with the summons, declaration of proof of service, and a copy of any judgment. CCP §670(1).

§30.34 E. Effect of Amended Complaint on Default Previously Entered

If plaintiff obtains entry of default against defendant and subsequently files an amended complaint that varies in substance rather than form from the complaint on which the default was entered, the default has no force and effect and judgment cannot be entered on it. *Cole v Roebling Constr. Co.* (1909) 156 C 443, 105 P 255; *Leo v Dunlap* (1968) 260 CA2d 24, 66 CR 888. Defendant has a right to be served with the amendment, and to answer or demur to it. It is immaterial whether the amendment is called an amendment to a complaint or an amended complaint. *Ford v Superior Court* (1973) 34 CA3d 338, 109 CR 844.

Examples of amendments of substance, as opposed to those of form, include amendments that (1) seek substantially higher damages (*Leo v Dunlap, supra*), (2) add a cause of action based on a different legal theory (*Ford v Superior Court, supra*), and (3) in a marital dissolution proceeding, request that child custody be changed from the defaulting parent to the petitioning parent (*Gerardo v Gerardo* (1952) 114 CA2d 371, 250 P2d 276).

Entry of default is not affected by a later amendment when the change pertains to form only, even though defendant is not served with a copy of the amendment. *Rardin Logging Co. v Bullok* (1953) 120 CA2d 67, 260 P2d 81 (in action for conspiracy to destroy plaintiff's business, amendment stating facts having evidentiary value in proof of conspiracy was one of form only).

III. DEFAULT JUDGMENTS

A. Introduction

§30.35 1. Types of Default Judgments

There are two types of default judgments in California: (a) a default judgment entered by the court clerk, which is governed by CCP §585(1) and is available in actions on a contract or California court judgment in which only money or damages is sought; and (b) a default judgment rendered by the court, which is governed by CCP §585(2) and which applies to all other actions. Default judgments in cases in which summons has been served by publication are governed by CCP §585(3) and are available only from the court. See statutory scheme set forth in §§30.4–

30.6; on situations in which default judgments are prohibited or restricted, see §30.9.

Because a default judgment under CCP §585(1) is processed entirely by the clerk without judicial intervention, courts have strictly limited the situations in which its use is permitted. See §§30.37–30.39.

§30.36 2. Extent of Relief Available

Under CCP §580, the relief granted to plaintiff when defendant has not filed an answer cannot exceed that demanded in the complaint. See also CCP §§585(1) (providing for clerk's default judgment "for the principal amount demanded in the complaint"); §585(2) (providing for court's default judgment "for the relief demanded in the complaint"). The purpose of these provisions is to permit defendant to calculate his exposure in the event of a default judgment by reliance on the demand in the complaint, without the need to examine specific allegations. See *Nemeth v Trumbull* (1963) 220 CA2d 788, 34 CR 127. See also 4 Witkin, CALIFORNIA PROCEDURE Proceedings Without Trial §156 (2d ed 1971). A judgment rendered in excess of the relief demanded is void. *Gudarov v Hadjieff* (1952) 38 C2d 412, 240 P2d 621; *Thorson v Western Dev. Corp.* (1967) 251 CA2d 206, 59 CR 299.

In determining the relief demanded in the complaint, the court or clerk must examine specific claims in the demand. Popularly used requests for "such other and for the relief as to this court may deem proper" (*Gudarov v Hadjieff, supra*), or for "damages according to proof" (*Ludka v Memory Magnetics Int'l* (1972) 25 CA3d 316, 101 CR 615; but see *Thorson v Western Dev. Corp., supra*) will not be considered. For further discussion, see 4 Witkin, PROCEDURE, Proc Without Trial §156.

In superior court actions for personal injury or wrongful death, the amount of damages cannot be stated in the demand (CCP §425.10(b)), but notice of the special and general damages must be given to defendant before a default can be taken. CCP §425.11. For discussion, see 1 CALIFORNIA CIVIL PROCEDURE BEFORE TRIAL §7.30 (Cal CEB 1977). Some attorneys serve this notice with the summons and complaint whenever there is a likelihood that a defendant in such case may default, *e.g.*, an uninsured defendant.

B. Judgment by Clerk Under CCP §585(1)

§30.37 1. When Available

A default judgment by clerk is available to plaintiff "in an action arising upon contract or judgment of a court of this state for the recovery of money or damages only." CCP §585(1). Courts have construed this language strictly, and have held that to come within the statute the contract, as pleaded, must seek a fixed and definite sum, which makes it unnecessary to take evidence to fix damages. *Lynch v Bencini* (1941) 17 C2d 521, 110 P2d 662; *Liberty Loan Corp. v Petersen* (1972) 24 CA3d 915, 101 CR 395. Compare, e.g., *Landwehr v Gillette* (1917) 174 C 654, 163 P 1018 (note calling for "reasonable attorneys' fees" in case of suit not within CCP §585(1)) with *Alexander v McDow* (1895) 108 C 25, 41 P 24 (note calling for ten percent as attorneys' fees computable and therefore within CCP §585(1)). In short, "the clerk may only *compute;* he cannot *adjudicate.*" 4 Witkin, CALIFORNIA PROCEDURE, Proceedings Without Trial §140 (2d ed 1971).

It has been held that the clerk may enter judgment under CCP §585(1) in actions on an open book account (*Diamond Nat'l Corp. v Golden Empire Builders, Inc.* (1963) 213 CA2d 283, 28 CR 616; see CCP §337a for definition of "book account"), or on an account stated (*Fallon & Co. v United States Overseas Airlines, Inc.* (1961) 194 CA2d 546, 15 CR 354), but not in actions that require an accounting (*Crossman v Vivienda Water Co.* (1902) 136 C 571, 69 P 220), or on a secured note unless the verified complaint states that the creditor has not resorted to the collateral (*Liberty Loan Corp. v Petersen, supra*). Nor can the clerk enter judgment under CCP §585(1) in an action to establish "reasonable value" or "net profits" (*Gray v Laufenberger* (1961) 195 CA2d Supp 875, 15 CR 813), or on a secured note in which the complaint alleges that the security has become valueless (*Ford v Superior Court* (1973) 34 CA3d 338, 109 CR 844).

Because of the restrictions imposed on the type of cases in which the clerk may enter a default judgment under CCP §585(1), many cases that appear initially to come within that section do not. A default judgment in those cases may be rendered only by the court under CCP §585(2). However, most collection actions fall within the language of CCP §585(1), and thus the number of default judgments entered by clerk is considerable. For further discussion, see 4 Witkin, PROCEDURE, Proc Without Trial §§140–143.

§30.38 a. Effect of Multiple Causes of Action

When defendant is in default on a complaint that pleads several causes of action, one or more of which justifies a clerk's judgment under CCP §585(1), the clerk can enter a default judgment on that cause of action. *Norman v Berney* (1965) 235 CA2d 424, 45 CR 467 (actions for breach of contract and to foreclose mechanics' lien). *Fallon & Co. v United States Overseas Airlines, Inc.* (1961) 194 CA2d 546, 15 CR 354 (actions on account stated and for money owing and unpaid). However, as in the case of the clerk's authority to enter default judgments generally (see §30.37), this rule is strictly construed, and a clerk's judgment is not permitted when an account stated is pleaded only as a separate theory of recovery, and not as a separate cause of action. *Brown v Superior Court* (1966) 242 CA2d 519, 525, 51 CR 633, 636; *Liberty Loan Corp. v Petersen* (1972) 24 CA3d 915, 101 CR 395.

§30.39 b. Effect of Defendants' Several Liability

The effect of defendants' several liability on a contract has posed a problem for courts in determining whether the clerk can enter a default judgment under CCP §585(1). The problem arises because CCP §579 provides: "In an action against several defendants, the court may, in its discretion, render judgment against one or more of them, leaving the action to proceed against the others, whenever a several judgment is proper."

In construing the effect of CCP §579 on the clerk's authority to enter a default judgment, courts have held in cases in which one defendant has defaulted and others have appeared, that a clerk's judgment against the defaulting defendant is improper because under CCP §579 a court must first exercise discretion to determine whether a several judgment is proper. See *Lynch v Bencini* (1941) 17 C2d 521, 110 P2d 662; *Kooper v King* (1961) 195 CA2d 621, 15 CR 848. However, these cases were discussed and distinguished in *Diamond Nat'l Corp. v Golden Empire Builders, Inc.* (1963) 213 CA2d 283, 28 CR 616, in which the court held that a clerk's default judgment is proper when all defendants are in default, and their liability on a contract for goods sold is presumptively joint and several (see CC §1659), possibly joint, but not exclusively several.

Since *Diamond Nat'l Corp. v Golden Empire Builders, Inc.*,

supra, court clerks have been processing default judgments in contract actions in which liability of multiple defendants clearly is joint, or at least joint and several. However, when the pleadings raise any question of whether defendants' liability is exclusively several, the clerk will usually refuse to process a default judgment. For further discussion on joint and several liability in contract actions, see 4 Witkin, CALIFORNIA PROCEDURE, Judgment §§37–38 (2d ed 1971).

§30.40   2. Effect of Clerical Error in Entering or Denying Judgment

If the court clerk enters a default judgment under CCP §585(1) without authority to do so, judgment is void and may be set aside at any time. *Brown v Superior Court* (1966) 242 CA2d 519, 51 CR 633. The court has a duty to set aside such judgment on its own motion. *Lewis v LeBaron* (1967) 254 CA2d 270, 61 CR 903. On the other hand, when the case falls within CCP §585(1), the clerk must enter judgment (CCP §585(1); *Fallon & Co. v United States Overseas Airlines, Inc.* (1961) 194 CA2d 546, 15 CR 354). Plaintiff may compel performance of this ministerial duty by prohibition and mandamus (*W. A. Rose Co. v Municipal Court* (1959) 176 CA2d 67, 1 CR 49), and defendant acquires no rights if the clerk refuses to perform (*W. H. Marston Co. v Kochritz* (1926) 80 CA 352, 251 P 959).

When the clerk erroneously fails or refuses to enter a default (as opposed to a default judgment), and defendant answers or files some other responsive paper while plaintiff is seeking to compel entry of default, it is uncertain whether defendant's response precludes entry of default. Although it is generally true that the entry of default (and not the request for entry) cuts off defendant's time to respond (see §30.2) in this situation the court should require the clerk to enter the default. Defendant may then pursue his remedy under CCP §473 by moving to have the default set aside. See generally, §§30.62–30.72.

3. Procedures

§30.41   a. Required Papers

The basic papers required for a clerk's default judgment under CCP §585(1) are:

(1) The California Judicial Council form for request to enter default (see §30.42);

(2) The original written contract or a certified copy of the judgment sued on (see §30.43);

(3) (In some courts) a request for dismissal of unserved defendants (see §30.44); and

(4) A form for clerk's default judgment (see §30.46).

In some counties, the clerk requires additional papers, and the attorney should be aware of variations in local requirements and should consult the clerk in the county in which the action is pending for specific requirements. See §30.45.

§30.42 (1) Judicial Council Form; Instructions

Application for clerk's entry of default judgment under CCP §585(1) must be made on the multipurpose form prescribed by the California Judicial Council for use in requesting entry of default. See form in §30.29; see §30.21 for discussion of mandatory use. Application is made at the same time as the request for entry of default and by completing the Judicial Council form as required for entry of default (see §§30.21–30.29), except that the attorney should check box "b" instead of box "a" in item two of the form.

The following instructions are keyed to the Judicial Council form set forth in §30.29; for further instructions, see §30.29.

Item 2, box b(1) (Attorneys' fees): In a clerk's default judgment, the clerk may award attorneys' fees under a court-adopted fee schedule, if one exists, and if fees are provided for either in the contract sued on or by statute. CCP §585(1). Many metropolitan courts have adopted these fee schedules. See, e.g., LA Super Ct R 14 §1. When plaintiff requests attorneys' fees under a court schedule, box "b (1)" should be checked. When plaintiff seeks attorneys' fees in excess of those provided by court fee schedule, or when the court has no fee schedule, plaintiff may submit a written request that the court set the fees. CCP §585(1). If plaintiff elects to make such a request, box "c" rather than "b (1)" should be checked, and a written request for fees should be attached to the form. Under item two, part "d (2)," the words "See attached request" should be typed in. The totals in item two, part "d (5)" should be left blank.

Item two, part "d" (Judgment to be entered): The clerk's default judgment includes judgment for the principal amount demanded in the complaint (or a lesser amount if credit has been acknowledged), interest, as allowed by law or by the contract sued on, costs, and attorneys' fees. CCP §585(1). Item two, part "d" shows these amounts and their totals, with deductions for any credits.

Some courts (*e.g.*, Los Angeles superior and municipal courts) require that a partial satisfaction be filed with the clerk whenever credits are to be acknowledged, and have printed forms for this purpose. However, these courts will sometimes accept the information given under item two, part "d," without requiring a separate form, provided the computations are already set out.

The costs in part "d" are the totals from part five (memorandum of costs) of the Judicial Council form. On allowable costs, see §30.27.

§30.43 (2) Written Contract or Judgment

If the action is on a written contract, the clerk must, at the time of entry of judgment, note across the face of the contract the fact and date of rendition and judgment, and title of the court and cause. Cal Rules of Ct 234, 522. The apparent purpose of this rule is to note the merger of the written contract into the judgment. See *Bill Benson Motors, Inc. v Macmorris Sales Corp.* (1965) 238 CA2d Supp 937, 48 CR 123. When the original writing has been lost or destroyed the clerk may, because of this rule, refuse to process a default judgment and may require that judgment be obtained from the court. However, an ex parte order may sometimes be obtained excusing compliance with Cal Rules of Ct 234 and 522, and ordering the clerk to accept a copy of the contract. The order should be supported by a declaration by a person who can establish compliance with Evid C §§1501 and 1551, which pertain to lost or destroyed records.

When the action is on a California court judgment, plaintiff's moving papers for a clerk's default judgment should include a certified copy of the judgment. Court clerks usually will not accept papers and grant judgment unless a copy is included.

§30.44 (3) Request for Dismissal of Unserved Defendants; Judicial Council Form

Before entry of a clerk's default judgment under CCP §585(1), many court clerks require a dismissal of all named defendants who have not been served, and some (*e.g.*, Los Angeles superior court) have extended this requirement to fictitiously named defendants. See §30.30 for discussion of the need to amend the complaint as to fictitiously named defendants who have been served. Defendants should be dismissed without prejudice, so they can, if necessary, be sued again on the same cause of action.

The California Judicial Council has prescribed a printed form for mandatory use when requesting a dismissal (see Cal Rules of Ct 982(a)(5)), which is usually available from the court clerk. See form in §31.84. When the Judicial Council has adopted a form for mandatory use, no court may use a different form purporting to serve the same function. Govt C §68511.

§30.45 (4) Additional Papers

It is not possible to list all documentation required by various California courts before a clerk's default judgment will be entered under CCP §585(1). First, many judicial districts and counties have established their own local rules. Second, in many instances, the clerk's requirement for additional documentation is attributable to unwritten local policy, rather than to local court rule.

The attorney should contact the clerk's office in the court in which the action is pending to ascertain the documentation required in that court before the clerk will enter a default judgment. The following items are frequently required.

Declaration re open book account: Because a high percentage of default judgments by clerk arises from collection actions (see §30.31), and because the commonly used collection complaint contains generalized allegations in the form of common counts (*see* CALIFORNIA DEBT COLLECTION PRACTICE §§5.9–5.21 (Cal CEB 1968)), courts recently have become concerned with the potential for abuse afforded by these pleadings. For example, plaintiffs may seek to evade the venue provisions of CC §§1812.10 and 2984.4, by pleading common counts; or to evade the rule that the clerk cannot enter a deficiency judgment under CCP §585(1) after plaintiff has resorted to the collateral (*Liberty Loan Corp. v Petersen* (1972) 24 CA3d 915, 101 CR 395), by seizing the collateral, suing for the deficiency, and pleading common counts. (When there is any indication that the underlying debt is based on a secured agreement, clerks frequently require an allegation in a verified complaint that the security has not been resorted to; otherwise the default judgment will have to be by court).

§30.46   DEFAULT

To ensure that the collection complaint has not been used as a subterfuge for an action for breach of a written contract, some courts (*e.g.*, Los Angeles municipal court) require that a declaration re open book account be filed stating there are no written contracts between the parties. The declaration typically is executed by an employee of plaintiff company, and states, *e.g.*:

> **I am employed by plaintiff and have personal knowledge of the facts concerning the transactions with defendants in this action. There are no executed written agreements between the parties to this action.**
> **I declare under penalty of perjury that the foregoing is correct.**

Statements and Invoices: For the reasons set forth above, some courts (*e.g.*, Los Angeles municipal court) require additional documentation to support a default judgment in an action on an open book account, *i.e.*, copies of invoices and a complete statement. From these, the clerk can determine whether the complaint has included any nonrecoverable items, *e.g.*, late charges (see *Garrett v Coast & Southern Fed. Sav. & Loan Ass'n* (1973) 9 C3d 731, 108 CR 845) and unearned finance charges (see 58 Ops Cal Atty Gen 166 (1975); *Mann v Earls* (1964) 226 CA2d 155, 37 CR 877).

§30.46   b.   Form: Default Judgment by Clerk

Copies: Original and (in some courts) copies (presented to court clerk for signature and filing); office copies.

NOTE: Many courts (*e.g.*, Los Angeles superior and municipal courts) have their own printed forms for default judgment by court clerk, and the attorney should use those forms whenever possible.

[*Caption. See §§23.18–23.19*]

No. _____

DEFAULT JUDGMENT BY CLERK

Defendant ____[*name*]____ having been regularly served with process other than by publication, having failed to appear and answer plaintiff's complaint within the time allowed by law, and the default of said defendant having been duly entered; on application of plaintiff to the clerk under Code of Civil Procedure section 585(1):

IT IS ADJUDGED that plaintiff ____[*name*]____ recover from defendant

____[name]____ the sum of $_____ damages, $_____ attorneys' fees, $_____ interest, and $_____ costs.
   Judgment entered on _____, 19____.
                              _____, Clerk
                         by _____, Deputy

Comment: A copy of the judgment may, but need not, be served on the defaulting defendant or on other defendants (see CCP §1010), and in practice the judgment usually is not served.

C. Default Judgment by Court

§30.47   1. When Required

There are three basic situations in which a default judgment must be obtained from the court:

(a) In an action on a contract or judgment seeking money or damages only, and which ordinarily would be subject to a default judgment by clerk, except that plaintiff's attorney is seeking attorney's fees greater than those allowed by a court-adopted fee schedule or else there is no such schedule (CCP §585(1));

(b) In all other actions in which defendant has been served other than by publication (CCP §585(2)); and

(c) In all actions in which defendant has been served by publication (CCP §585(3)).

The most common of the above situations is (b). Procedures for obtaining a default judgment by court vary slightly, depending on which of these situations applies. See §§30.48–30.55.

2. Procedures

§30.48   a. Judgment and Attorneys' Fees Under CCP §585(1)

Attorneys' fees may be awarded in a default judgment in an action on a contract or judgment seeking money or damages only, provided fees are allowed by the contract or plaintiff is entitled to them by statute. CCP §585(1). Ordinarily, a default judgment under CCP §585(1) is entered by the court clerk, who awards attorneys' fees from a court-adopted fee schedule. See instructions for completing Judicial Council form in §30.42. When the court has no such schedule, or when plaintiff seeks a higher fee than that provided by the schedule, plaintiff must, at the time entry of default is requested, file a written request to have the court fix the fees. CCP §585(1); see Comment to form in §30.29 for a suggested procedure. After entry of default by the court clerk, the court hears the application for attorneys' fees and renders judgment for such fees and for the other relief demanded in the complaint (or a lesser amount if credit has been acknowledged), together with costs. CCP §585(1). For a form of default judgment by court that may be adopted for use, see §30.55.

In a hearing on attorneys' fees under CCP §585(1), the use of affidavits or declarations under penalty of perjury instead of oral testimony is not permitted. CCP §585(4).

b. Judgment in All Other Actions Under CCP §585(2)

§30.49   (1) Required Papers; Use of Judicial Council Form

The papers required for a default judgment by the court under CCP §585(2) include the California Judicial Council form set forth in §30.29. In addition, if suit is on a written contract, the original contract must be submitted. See §30.43. As in the case of default judgments by clerk under CCP §585(1), the attorney should consult the clerk of the court in which the action is pending to determine whether other papers are required. See §30.45. For example, Los Angeles superior court requires that in all default judgments by court, counsel must file a statement of facts in narrative form, setting forth in general terms the basis of plaintiff's claim. This statement should be distinguished from the affidavits or declarations authorized by CCP §585(4), in which facts must be stated with particularity. See §30.50.

The Judicial Council form set forth is completed in the same fashion as in a request to enter clerk's default judgment under CCP §585(1) (see §30.42), except that in section two, box "c" is checked and boxes "a" and "b" are left blank, and there is no need to complete section three, the declaration under CCP §585.5. See form in §30.29.

§30.50   (2) Use of Affidavits or Declarations

Except in cases pertaining to marital dissolution or annulment, separate maintenance, or child custody, the court may, in a hearing on default judgment under CCP §585(2) or (3) permit the use of affidavits (or declarations under penalty of perjury; see CCP §2015.5) instead of oral testimony as to all or part of the proof required. CCP §585(4). In practice, such declarations are widely used, and even required in some courts, *e.g.*, Los Angeles municipal court. The facts stated in the declaration must be based on personal knowledge of the declarant and set forth with particularity, and each declaration must show that the declarant, if sworn as a witness, can testify competently to the facts stated. CCP §585(4). This latter requirement is not satisfied by a conclusory statement to that effect, but requires a showing of the declarant's competency to make the statements. CCP §585(4).

Whenever it is uncertain whether the court will accept a declaration instead of oral testimony, plaintiff's counsel may, before the hearing, apply for an ex parte order permitting use of the declaration. This procedure enables counsel to present the case as scheduled, and not have to request a continuance at the hearing.

§30.51   (3) Calendaring for Hearing

When the evidence in a hearing on default judgment under CCP §§585(2)–(3) is to be presented entirely by declaration (see §30.50), the clerk normally sets a hearing date on request. See item two, box "c" of California Judicial Council form in §30.29. In such cases, a formal hearing frequently is not held; the judge (or court commissioner) reviews the declarations in chambers on the hearing date, without the need for counsel to be present. If the judge or commissioner finds that oral testimony is necessary, he will so notify plaintiff and request that plaintiff set the matter for hearing.

When oral testimony will be presented, the matter is usually calendared for hearing by filing the required papers and then telephoning the court clerk for a hearing date.

§30.52   (4) Hearing

Court's duties and powers; limitations: At the hearing on a default judgment, the court, "shall hear the evidence offered by the plaintiff, and shall render judgment in his favor for such sum (not exceeding the amount stated in the complaint), as appears by such evidence to be just." CCP §585(2). The court may order certain matters referred, *e.g.*, to an expert in an action on a complicated account (see *Rosati v Heimann* (1954) 126 CA2d 51, 271

§30.52 DEFAULT

P2d 953 (reference during trial)), and may have damages assessed by a jury. CCP §585(2).

The court may not disregard uncontested credible evidence, whether presented by declaration (see §30.50) or by oral testimony, and must enter judgment in favor of plaintiff when such evidence is presented. *Morehouse v Wanzo* (1968) 266 CA2d 846, 853, 72 CR 607, 611; *Csordas v United Slate Tile and Composition Roofers* (1960) 177 CA2d 184, 2 CR 133.

Extent of evidence needed: It is unclear whether, at the hearing, plaintiff must present evidence on all allegations of his prima facie case, *i.e.*, whether a failure to establish evidence on one or more elements will result in denial of the default judgment. On the one hand, the default is an admission by defendant of the truth of all allegations of the complaint giving rise to liability. *Los Angeles v Los Angeles Farming & Milling Co.* (1907) 150 C 647, 89 P 615; *Bristol Conv. Hosp. v Stone* (1968) 258 CA2d 848, 66 CR 404. For further discussion of the effect of defendant's failure to answer, see §30.3. However, it has been held that plaintiff's failure at the hearing to establish adequately damages in a tort action (*Taliaferro v Hoogs* (1963) 219 CA2d 559, 33 CR 415), or a contract action when the complaint demands an amount different from that specified in the contract or when the contract does not specify the amount of liquidated damages (*Lynch v Bencini* (1941) 17 C2d 521, 110 P2d 662), will result in a denial of judgment.

Use of hearsay testimony: Plaintiff's prima facie case can be supported at the hearing by hearsay testimony offered by a witness who is in court. *City Bank v Ramage* (1968) 266 CA2d 570, 72 CR 273. In view of the requirement of CCP §585(4) that an affidavit or declaration must contain facts that are within the personal knowledge of the declarant and must establish affirmatively that the declarant, if sworn as a witness, could testify competently to those facts (see §30.50), it would seem that hearsay testimony offered by declaration should be excluded. But see *Flood v Simpson* (1975) 45 CA3d 644, 119 CR 675 (court permitted use of declaration containing hearsay statements to support default judgment).

Necessity that complaint state cause of action: A complaint on which a default judgment is sought must state a cause of action against defendant. If it does not, no amount of testimony at the hearing can cure the defect. *Taliaferro v Davis* (1963) 216 CA2d 398, 31 CR 164. But see *Trans-Pacific Trading Co. v Patsy Frock*

& *Romper Co.* (1922) 189 C 509, 209 P 357, quoted with approval in *Thorson v Western Dev. Corp.* (1967) 251 CA2d 206, 59 CR 299 (when court has jurisdiction over parties and subject matter, judgment not void regardless of whether complaint states cause of action, provided it apprises defendant of nature of plaintiff's demand).

Findings and conclusions: Findings of fact and conclusions of law are not required in a hearing on a default judgment because (a) the allegations of the complaint are considered admitted and thus there are no factual issues, and (b) defendant waives findings by his failure to appear (CCP §632). See *Remainders, Inc. v Bartlett* (1963) 215 CA2d 295, 297, 30 CR 191, 192. See also *Hittson v Stanich* (1927) 84 CA 434, 258 P 405.

c. Judgment When Summons Served by Publication Under CCP §585(3)

§30.53 (1) Application for Hearing

The procedure for obtaining a default judgment in all cases in which summons has been served by publication is governed by CCP §585(3), which does not require entry of default as a prerequisite, although it may sometimes be useful (see §30.20). Under CCP §585(3), plaintiff may apply in writing for judgment when defendant's time to respond has expired. See §30.12 on defendant's time to respond when summons has been served by publication. Application is made by completing the California Judicial Council form for request to enter default set forth in §30.29 in the same manner as a request for default judgment by court under CCP §585(2) (see §30.49). Calendaring is handled in the same fashion as an application under CCP §585(2). See §30.51 for discussion.

§30.54 (2) Hearing

Before a default judgment can be entered in an action in which summons has been served by publication, the court must require proof of the allegations of the complaint. CCP §585(3). This requirement has been construed to impose on the court the duty to examine plaintiff under oath. *Winston v Idaho Hardwood Co.* (1913) 23 CA 211, 137 P 601. However, as in the case of default judgments by the court under CCP §585(2), testimony may be presented in whole or in part by declaration. CCP §585(4); see §30.50.

The discussion regarding the hearing on default judgment under CCP §585(2) is applicable to a hearing under CCP §585(3). See §30.52. In addition, if defendant is not a resident of California, the court must examine plaintiff or his agent regarding any payments or other credits that would reduce the amount owed. CCP §585(3).

In a hearing on default judgment in cases affecting title to or possession of real property, plaintiff must prove more than occupancy, unless occupancy is of the type and duration necessary to confer title by prescription. When plaintiff's claim is based on "paper title," evidence establishing plaintiff's equitable right to judgment must be provided; but if plaintiff seeks only possession of real property, and the complaint is verified, and establishes by proper allegations that no other party claims title (either by prescription, accession, transfer, will, or succession), the court can render judgment on proof of occupancy by plaintiff and ouster by defendant. CCP §585(3).

§30.55 d. Form: Default Judgment by Court

Copies: Original and (in some courts) copies (presented to court for signature and filing); office copies.

NOTE: Many courts (*e.g.*, Los Angeles superior court) have their own printed forms for default judgment by court, and some (*e.g.*, Los Angeles municipal court) have a separate form for use when summons has been served by publication. The attorney should use those forms whenever possible.

[Caption. See §§23.18–23.19]

No. _____

DEFAULT JUDGMENT BY COURT
____[AFTER PUBLICATION OF SUMMONS]____

The above matter came on regularly for hearing in Department No. _____, Honorable _____ presiding, and ____[name]____ appearing as attorney for plaintiff.

Defendant ____[name]____ **having been regularly** ____[served with process / served with summons by publication]____, **having failed to appear and answer plaintiff's complaint within the time allowed by law** ____[and the default of said defendant having been duly entered]____; **on** ____[evidence having been introduced by plaintiff / proof of publication and of the allegations of plaintiff's complaint]____,

IT IS ADJUDGED that plaintiff ____[name]____ recover from defendant ____[name]____ the sum of $_____ damages, $_____ attorney's fees, $_____ interest, and $_____ costs.

IT IS FURTHER ADJUDGED ____[e.g., that sole possession of the real property described in the complaint and commonly known as 1001 Keith Avenue, Center, California, be awarded to plaintiff]____.

The clerk is ordered to enter the judgment.

Dated: _____

_____
Judge

Comment: This form may be used for a default judgment by court under CCP §585(2) when summons has been served other than by publication, or CCP §585(3) when summons has been served by publication. It may also be adapted for use in a default judgment by court under CCP §585(1) when plaintiff has requested that the court fix attorneys' fees. See §30.48.

A copy of the judgment may, but need not, be served on the defaulting defendant or on other defendants (see CCP §1010), and in practice the judgment usually is not served.

IV. RELIEF FROM DEFAULT OR DEFAULT JUDGMENT

§30.56 A. Introduction

Most requests for relief from entry of default or default judgment result from one of the following situations. The first situation, and probably the most frequent, is when defendant has received actual notice of the action but has not filed a responsive pleading within the time permitted. See §§30.12–30.14 on the time within which to respond. Relief in this situation is usually conditioned on a showing of mistake, inadvertence, surprise, or excusable neglect (CCP §473), but under certain circumstances is limited to situations in which extrinsic fraud or mistake is shown. For discussion, see §§30.57–30.59. Second, defendant defaulted because he did not receive actual notice of the action in time to defend, either because service was defective or was made by means other than personal service, *i.e.*, by substituted service. Relief in this situation is governed by CCP §473.5. For discussion, see §§30.75–30.79.

The discussion in this chapter of obtaining relief from entry of default or default judgment also applies to the situation in which a party has appeared in the action but has had his answer

§30.57 DEFAULT

stricken under CCP §2034(b) for refusing to obey a discovery order. For discussion, see §30.8. See generally CALIFORNIA CIVIL DISCOVERY PRACTICE chap 3 (Cal CEB 1975).

B. Relief When Service Affords Defendant Actual Notice

§30.57 1. Grounds for Relief

When defendant has been served in a manner that affords him actual notice of the litigation, the grounds for relief from entry of default or default judgment vary depending on whether the motion for relief is made within six months after entry of the default or default judgment. If made within six months, the grounds are governed by CCP §473 (see §30.58); if made later, the grounds are governed by the scope of the court's inherent equity power to grant relief (see §30.59).

In all such motions for relief, regardless of when made, the attorney should keep in mind the stated judicial preference for hearings on the merits rather than for default judgments.

§30.58 a. Relief Sought Within Six Months

A motion for relief from entry of default or default judgment made within six months after entry of default or default judgment is governed by CCP §473, which provides that relief may be granted on a showing of mistake, inadvertence, surprise, or excusable neglect. The superior court also has inherent equity power, independent of CCP §473, to vacate a judgment obtained through extrinsic fraud. *Necessary v Necessary* (1962) 207 CA2d 780, 24 CR 713; *Heathman v Vant* (1959) 172 CA2d 639, 343 P2d 104. See also CCP §86(b)(3) (municipal and justice courts have equity jurisdiction to vacate judgments or orders obtained through extrinsic fraud, mistake, inadvertence, or excusable neglect). See §30.59 for discussion of extrinsic fraud.

"Excusable neglect" under CCP §473 means neglect that might have been committed by a reasonably prudent person in the same or similar circumstances and that was the actual cause of the default. *Transit Ads, Inc. v Tanner Motor Livery, Ltd.* (1969) 270 CA2d 275, 75 CR 848. For example, in *Slusher v Durr* (1977) 69 CA3d 747, 138 CR 265, an alleged assault and battery by defendant on plaintiff resulted in both a civil suit and criminal charges. During the criminal proceedings defendant was served with a summons and complaint in the civil action. Defendant pleaded guilty to a charge of disturbing the peace and asked the judge whether his guilty plea concluded the matter (referring to both the criminal and civil matter). The judge (referring to the criminal matter only) responded that it did. Under these circumstances, defendant's failure to answer the complaint was held to be due to excusable neglect, and a lower court order that the default judgment be set aside was affirmed. On the other hand, in *Cyrus v Haveson* (1976) 65 CA3d 306, 135 CR 246, the court held that defendants did not act reasonably, and therefore were not entitled to have a default judgment taken against them set aside because, when told by plaintiff's counsel that a default would be taken unless an answer was filed, defendants took no action until well after the default was entered. For further examples, see *Transit Ads, Inc. v Tanner Motor Livery, Ltd., supra.*

§30.59   b. Relief Sought After Six Months

For further discussion of what constitutes mistake, inadvertence, surprise, or excusable neglect, see 5 Witkin, CALIFORNIA PROCEDURE, Attack on Judgment in Trial Court §§131–147 (2d ed 1971).

The grounds stated in CCP §473 for relief from entry of default or default judgment (see §30.58) do not apply when a motion for relief is made more than six months after entry of default or default judgment, because a motion under CCP §473 cannot be made after that time. See *Martin v Taylor* (1968) 267 CA2d 112, 72 CR 847. However, the superior court has inherent power to entertain a motion in equity to vacate a judgment obtained through extrinsic fraud or extrinsic mistake. *Weitz v Yankosky* (1966) 63 C2d 849, 48 CR 620. Municipal and justice courts also have equity jurisdiction to vacate judgments or orders obtained through extrinsic fraud, mistake, inadvertence, or excusable neglect. CCP §86(b)(3). However, because municipal and justice courts' jurisdiction to grant equitable relief from default after six months is coextensive with that of superior courts, CCP §86(b)(3) does not permit those courts to entertain motions for equitable relief made after six months from entry of judgment and based on inadvertence or excusable neglect. Therefore, municipal or justice courts may grant equitable relief after six months only on grounds of extrinsic fraud or mistake. *Marianos v Tutunjian* (1977) 70 CA3d 61, 138 CR 529.

To the extent that the courts' equity power to grant relief from default after six months differs from its power under CCP §473, the equity power must be considered narrower, not wider. *Weitz v Yankosky, supra.*

Although what constitutes extrinsic fraud or mistake as a ground for setting aside a default or default judgment is a matter of fact, use of the word "extrinsic" indicates a requirement that parties other than defendant must have caused defendant to permit a default to be taken. Examples of extrinsic fraud include (1) plaintiff's granting to defendant an extension of time to respond and then requesting entry of default before the extension of time has expired (*H&H Inv. Co. v T-J Constr. Co.* (1969) 275 CA2d 58, 79 CR 890), (2) defendant's reliance on a reasonable belief that defendant's employer would respond to the complaint (*Desper v King* (1967) 251 CA2d 659, 59 CR 657), and (3) reliance by a wife on a husband's assurance that he would respond to the complaint (*Higley v Bank of Downey* (1968) 260 CA2d 640, 67 CR 365). However, plaintiff's failure to enforce a judgment until after expiration of the six-month time limit of CCP §473 does not of itself constitute extrinsic fraud. *Ford v Herndon* (1976) 62 CA3d 492, 496, 133 CR 111, 113; *Daher v American Pipe Constr. Co.* (1968) 257 CA2d 816, 65 CR 259.

An attorney's mistaken belief as to the applicable law is not extrinsic fraud or extrinsic mistake, but is intrinsic and as such cannot be a ground for equitable relief. *Westinghouse Credit Corp. v Wolfer* (1970) 10 CA3d 63, 88 CR 654. However, when defendant's failure to answer results from the attorney's mistake of fact (*Hallett v Slaughter* (1943) 22 C2d 552, 140 P2d 3), or from his total failure to represent his client (*Orange Empire Nat'l Bank v Kirk* (1968) 259 CA2d 347, 66 CR 240), equitable relief is available. For further discussion, see 5 Witkin, CALIFORNIA PROCEDURE Attack on Judgment in Trial Court §§183–191 (2d ed 1971).

§30.60 2. Judicial Policy in Favor of Hearing on Merits

Judicial policy on a motion for relief from entry of default or default judgment is to favor hearings on the merits and to disapprove a party who, regardless of the merits, seeks to capitalize on the mistake, surprise, inadvertence, or neglect of his adversary. Appellate courts are more disposed to affirm an order that in effect compels trial on the merits than one that permits a default judgment to stand when it appears a meritorious defense can be made. *Weitz v Yankosky* (1966) 63 C2d 849, 48 CR 620; *Slusher v Durr* (1977) 69 CA3d 747, 138 CR 265. See also *Ford v Herndon* (1976) 62 CA3d 492, 133 CR 111. This judicial policy applies regardless of whether relief is sought by motion under CCP §473 (*Martin v Taylor* (1968) 267 CA2d 112, 72 CR 847), by equitable motion in the trial court (*Weitz v Yankosky, supra*), or by independent action in equity to set aside a default judgment (*Shields v Siegel* (1966) 246 CA2d 334, 54 CR 577).

However, the judicial policy favoring hearings on the merits does not mean that relief from entry of default or default judgment is automatic, and appellate courts have recently reversed trial court orders that have granted relief from default judgments and have reinstated the judgment. See *e.g., Transit Ads, Inc. v Tanner Motor Livery, Ltd.* (1969) 270 CA2d 275, 281, 75 CR 848, 851 (moving party must make substantial showing, and "unusual pressure of business" is not by itself sufficient). See also *Ray Kizer Constr. Co. v Young* (1968) 257 CA2d 766, 65 CR 267. For further discussion, see CALIFORNIA CIVIL APPELLATE PRACTICE, SUPP §37 (Cal CEB 1966). Some attorneys have noted an increased willingness on the part of the trial court to deny relief from default, perhaps because (a) the summons with which defendant is served is more informative and easier to understand, and (b) court calendars have become more crowded.

§30.61   3. Court Discretion To Grant Relief; Power To Impose Conditions

A motion for relief from entry of default or default judgment under CCP §473 is addressed to the court's discretion, and its ruling will be disturbed on appeal only on a clear showing of abuse of discretion. *Lynch v Spilman* (1967) 67 C2d 251, 62 CR 12. The same rule applies when the motion is addressed to the court's equity powers, independent of CCP §473. *Weitz v Yankosky* (1966) 63 C2d 849, 48 CR 620. However, whether a motion is made under CCP §473 or under the court's equity powers, appellate courts are more likely to find abuse of discretion when a motion has been denied than when it has been granted. See §30.60.

Whether the motion for relief is made under CCP §473 or under the court's equity powers, the court can grant relief subject to conditions. This rule is explicit under CCP §473 (court may grant relief "upon such terms as may be just"), and implicit under the court's equity powers. For discussion, see 5 Witkin, CALIFORNIA PROCEDURE Attack on Judgment in Trial Court §§192–196 (2d ed 1971).

Conditions can be fashioned to fit particular circumstances. If, e.g., plaintiff has already incurred costs or attorneys' fees in seeking or enforcing the judgment, relief may be conditioned on payment of those costs or fees. *Reeves v Hutson* (1956) 144 CA2d 445, 301 P2d 264. When the action alleges money due and owing, defendant may be required to post a bond to guarantee payment of the judgment if plaintiff prevails on the merits. *Goodson v The Bogerts, Inc.* (1967) 252 CA2d 32, 60 CR 146. If plaintiff establishes that a key witness has moved out of the jurisdiction, relief can be conditioned on payment of the expenses necessary to take his deposition or to the witness to the trial. However, the conditions must be just, i.e., "reasonably proportionate to the other party's prejudice or expense"; excessive conditions can be attacked by writ of mandamus. *Kirkwood v Superior Court* (1967) 253 CA2d 198, 61 CR 316.

When the court has granted relief from entry of default judgment subject to conditions, judgment will not be vacated until compliance has occurred. *Hartman v Olvera* (1874) 49 C 101.

4. Procedures

a. Motion Under CCP §473

§30.62 (1) Time For Motion

A motion for relief from entry of default or default judgment must be made "within a reasonable time, in no case exceeding six months," after entry of the default or default judgment. CCP §473. (The same limitations apply to a renewed motion, made after the initial motion has been denied. *Northridge Fin. Corp. v Hamblin* (1975) 48 CA3d 819, 122 CR 109.) If the action seeks a determination of ownership or the right to possession of real or personal property, and written notice of entry of judgment (stating that defendant's right to seek relief expires within 90 days of service) is served within California on both party and attorney of record, the motion must be made within 90 days after service on the party or his attorney, whichever occurs later. CCP §473.

Six-months' limitation: The six months' time limitation of CCP §473 is jurisdictional; the court has no power to grant relief under CCP §473 after this time has elapsed. *Johnson v Hayes Cal. Builders, Inc.* (1963) 60 C2d 572, 35 CR 618. The period begins to run when the clerk enters the default (*Koski v U-Haul Co.* (1963) 212 CA2d 640, 28 CR 398), and the motion is considered to have been made when the notice of motion was filed and served (CCP §1005.5; *First Small Bus. Inv. Co. v Sistim, Inc.* (1970) 12 CA3d 645, 90 CR 798). For further discussion, see CALIFORNIA CIVIL APPELLATE PRACTICE §3.11 (Cal CEB 1966).

Reasonable-time limitation: In addition to the six-months' maximum, CCP §473 requires that the motion be made "within a reasonable time." This requirement is independent of the six-months' maximum, and whether it has been met is a matter of trial court discretion, based on the circumstances of a particular case. *Benjamin v Dalmo Mfg. Co.* (1948) 31 C2d 523, 190 P2d 593; *Smith v Pelton Water Wheel Co.* (1907) 151 C 394, 90 P 934. The burden is on the moving party to show not only that the default or default judgment was entered due to his "mistake, inadvertence, surprise, or excusable neglect" (CCP §473; see §30.58), but also that relief was sought diligently and any delay in filing the motion was excusable. *Benjamin v Dalmo Mfg. Co., supra* (no explanation given for three-months' delay); *Martin v Taylor* (1968) 267 CA2d 112, 72 CR 847 (almost six-months' delay held inexcusable). In *Romer, O'Connor & Co. v Huffman* (1959) 171 CA2d 342, 341 P2d 62, delay was held excusable on a showing that defendant's attorney, having discovered the entry of default on February 26, filed a notice of motion for relief on April 12. Defendant's attorney filed the motion himself after unsuccessfully attempting to reach his client, who was out of the country on business, and after promptly contacting plaintiff's attorney and explaining these difficulties. See also *Waite v Southern Pac. Co.* (1923) 192 C 467, 221 P 204 (five-month delay due to mistake of law held excusable when no prejudice to adverse party shown). However, courts have almost uniformly rejected the "busy attorney" reason for a delay in seeking relief. *Martin v Taylor, supra.*

§30.63 (2) Moving Papers

A motion to set aside entry of default or default judgment under CCP §473 must include the following papers:

(a) Notice of motion (see form in §30.64);

(b) Supporting declaration that states facts establishing that the default or default judgment was the result of the moving party's mistake, inadvertence, surprise, or excusable neglect (see form in §30.65);

(c) Affidavit (or declaration) of merits, showing a meritorious defense (*Lynch v Spilman* (1967) 67 C2d 251, 62 CR 12; see form in §30.66.) This requirement can be fulfilled by filing, in lieu of a declaration of merits, a verified answer (*First Small Business Inv. Co. v Sistim, Inc.* (1970) 12 CA3d 645, 90 CR 798) or demurrer showing meritorious issues of law (*Jensen v Allstate Ins. Co.* (1973) 32 CA3d 789, 108 CR 498));

(d) Copy of the proposed answer or other pleading (CCP §473; a verified answer or demurrer showing meritorious issues of law obviates the need for a declaration of merits (see above));

(e) Memorandum of points and authorities (Cal Rules of Ct 203 (a), 503(a)); and

(f) Proof of service or certificate of service, showing service of copies of the above documents on plaintiff's attorney (CCP §1013a).

The motion should also be accompanied by a proposed order setting aside the default or default judgment (see form in §30.71), and may need to be accompanied by a stay of execution pending hearing (see §§30.67–30.68).

§30.64 (3) Form: Notice of Motion To Set Aside Default or Default Judgment

Copies: Original (filed with court clerk); copies for service (one for each attorney of record and unrepresented party); office copies.

[*Caption. See §§23.18–23.19*]

No. _____

NOTICE OF MOTION UNDER CCP §473 TO SET ASIDE ENTRY OF ____[*DEFAULT / DEFAULT JUDGMENT / DEFAULT AND DEFAULT JUDGMENT*]____; **POINTS AND AUTHORITIES; SUPPORTING DECLARATION**

To each party and attorney of record:

PLEASE TAKE NOTICE that on _____, 19____, at or after _____a.m., in ____[*e.g., Department No.* ____]____ at ____[*address*]____, California, defendant ____[*name*]____ will move the court for an order vacating and setting aside the ____[*default / default judgment / default and default judgment*]____ entered in this action on ____[*date or dates*]____, and for leave to file the attached proposed ____[*e.g., answer / verified answer / demurrer*]____.

This motion will be made on the ground that defendant's failure to respond to the complaint within the time allowed is due to the mistake, inadvertence, surprise or excusable neglect of ____[defendant / defendant's attorney]____, as is more fully stated in the declaration filed in support of the motion.

This motion will be based on this notice, all papers and records filed in this action, the declaration of ____[name]____, memorandum of points and authorities, proposed ____[e.g., answer / verified answer / demurrer]____,

[When applicable]

and declaration of merits of ____[name]____,

[Continue]

copies of which are attached, and on such evidence as may be presented at the hearing.

Dated: _____

[Signature of attorney]

[Typed name]
Attorney for ____[name]____

Comment: Some attorneys include in the notice of motion a request, *e.g.*, "for such other and further relief as is just." However, this language is unnecessary because the court has the power under CCP §473 to grant conditional relief whether or not requested. See §30.61.

A memorandum of points and authorities must accompany the notice of motion. The court may consider the failure to file a memorandum as an admission that the motion is not meritorious and may deny the motion. Cal Rules of Ct 203(a), 503(a). On form and format of the memorandum, see §§23.27–23.35.

With minor adaptations, this form may also be used to set aside defaults or default judgments entered as a result of fraud (see §§30.58–30.59) or default judgments entered as a sanction against a party who has filed a timely answer but has refused to obey certain discovery orders (see §30.8).

§30.65 (4) Form: Declaration in Support of Motion To Set Aside Entry of Default or Default Judgment

Copies: See §30.64.

[Caption. See §§23.18–23.19]

No. _____

DECLARATION OF ____[NAME]____ IN SUPPORT OF MOTION TO SET ASIDE ENTRY OF ____[DEFAULT / DEFAULT JUDGMENT / DEFAULT AND DEFAULT JUDGMENT]____

§30.65   DEFAULT

____[Name]____ **declares:**

1. I am the attorney for ____[name]____**, defendant in this action.**

2. The entry of ____[default / default judgment / default and default judgment]____ **against defendant in this action was due to** ____[his / her / my]____ **mistake, inadvertence, surprise, or excusable neglect in that** ____[state facts showing mistake, e.g., on September 14, 1977, I spoke with ____[name]____, plaintiff's attorney, by telephone and obtained an oral extension of time of 30 days, until October 13, 1977, in which to answer. This extension notwithstanding, default was entered on September 22, 1977]____.

[Add when applicable]

3. The entry of ____[default / default judgment / default and default judgment]____ **was discovered by me on** ____[date]____**, and this motion was not filed until** ____[date]____ **because** ____[state facts showing excusable delay, e.g., defendant was out of the country on business on October 10, 1977, when I learned of the default, and my efforts to reach him were unsuccessful until November 29, 1977]____.

[Continue]

I declare under penalty of perjury that the foregoing is true and correct, and was executed on _____, 19____, **at** _____, **California.**

[Signature of attorney]

[Typed name]
Attorney for ____[name]____

Comment: The supporting declaration on a motion to set aside entry of a default or default judgment is usually made by the attorney. However, when the facts justifying relief are within defendant's personal knowledge, the attorneys' declaration will not warrant relief unless accompanied by a declaration executed by defendant. When the motion is addressed to the court's equity powers independently of CCP §473 on the grounds of extrinsic fraud or mistake (see §30.59), the declaration may need to be made by defendant or a third person.

See §30.58 for discussion of what constitutes mistake, inadvertence, surprise, or excusable neglect.

When there has been a significant delay between the time when defendant or his attorney learns of the default or default judgment and the time the motion is filed, the declaration must state facts showing that the delay is excusable and that defendant and his attorney acted diligently in seeking to have it set aside. See §30.62.

§30.66 (5) Form: Declaration of Merits

Copies: Original (filed with court clerk with proof of service); copies for service (one on each attorney of record and unrepresented party); office copies.

[Caption. See §§23.18–23.19]

No. ----------

DECLARATION OF MERITS

----[Name]---- **declares:**

[When declaration made by defendant personally]

1. I am the defendant in this action and have fully and fairly stated the case and all facts to ----[name]----, my attorney, who is duly admitted to practice in California. After such statement I have been advised by my attorney and believe that I have a good and substantial defense on the merits to each and every cause of action alleged in plaintiff's complaint.

[When declaration made by attorney]

1. I am the attorney for ----[name of defendant]----, defendant in this action. Defendant has stated the case and all the facts to me and I have made a personal investigation of those facts, and on the basis of the facts disclosed and my personal knowledge I believe that the statement by defendant was fair and complete. From a consideration of the facts disclosed, I believe and have advised defendant that ----[he / she]---- has a good and substantial defense on the merits to each and every cause of action alleged in the complaint.

2. This declaration is not made by defendant because ----[state reason, e.g., defendant presently is out of the country and will not return until November 29, 1977]----.

[Continue]

I declare under penalty of perjury that the foregoing is true and correct and was executed on ----------, 19----, at ----------, California.

[Signature of declarant]

[Typed name]

Comment: On when a declaration of merits is required, see §30.63.

The declaration may be made by defendant or by his attorney. When made by the attorney, the declaration should state why it is not being made by defendant.

When made by the attorney, the declaration of merits may be included in the supporting declaration in §30.65 by adding the words "AND DECLARATION OF MERITS" to the title and by incorporating the language set forth above in that form.

§30.67   (6) Stay of Execution Pending Hearing

Frequently, levy on a writ of execution is made by plaintiff after entry of a default judgment and before defendant files a motion to vacate the judgment. Thus, defendant may need to obtain a stay of execution until the matter is heard. See generally CALIFORNIA DEBT COLLECTION PRACTICE §§17.65–17.69 (Cal CEB 1968). A stay may be obtained ex parte on filing of a motion and supporting declarations. The declarations in support of the motion to vacate frequently are sufficient for granting the stay.

The court may grant a stay without the adverse party's consent for a period not to exceed 30 days. CCP §681a. Therefore, it is frequently necessary to obtain with the stay an order shortening time for service of the notice of motion to vacate. For a form for order, see §30.68.

§30.68   (7) Form: Order Staying Execution and Order Shortening Time

Copies: Original (filed with court clerk with proof of service); copies for service (one on each attorney of record and unrepresented party); office copies.

[Caption. See §§23.18–23.19]

No. _____

ORDER STAYING EXECUTION AND ORDER SHORTENING TIME

IT IS ORDERED that execution on the judgment in this action be stayed until _____, 19____ at _____, __m., or until decision is rendered on the motion to ____[e.g., set aside entry of default judgment]____, whichever time comes first.

IT IS FURTHER ORDERED that the notice of motion to ____[e.g., set aside entry of default judgment]____ may be heard ____ days after service on plaintiff of the ____[above / attached]____ notice of motion and this order.

Judge

Comment: For further discussion of orders shortening time, and for a form for application for the order, see 1 CALIFORNIA CIVIL PROCEDURE BEFORE TRIAL §22.27 (Cal CEB 1977).

§30.69 (8) Opposing Papers

On a motion to set aside entry of default or default judgment, plaintiff may controvert defendant's moving papers with counterdeclarations. See, *e.g.*, *Elms v Elms* (1946) 72 CA2d 508, 164 P2d 936. However, the motion is not a substitute for a trial on the merits (*Skolsky v Electronovision Prods., Inc.* (1967) 254 CA2d 246, 62 CR 91), and once defendant has made a prima facie showing of a meritorious defense, either by filing a declaration of merits or a proposed verified answer or demurrer (see §30.63), it is improper to permit plaintiff to controvert that showing by declaration. (*First Small Business Inv. Co. v Sistim, Inc.* (1970) 12 CA3d 645, 90 CR 798). For further discussion, see 5 Witkin, CALIFORNIA PROCEDURE Attack on Judgment in Trial Court §157 (2d ed 1971).

§30.70 (9) Hearing and Ruling

Usually, a motion to vacate default or default judgment is heard on declaration and counterdeclaration, but the court has discretion to take oral evidence. See *e.g.*, *Reifler v Superior Court* (1974) 39 CA3d 479, 114 CR 356 (pertaining to certain family law matters). Local practice varies. Some courts (*e.g.*, Los Angeles municipal court) will hear oral testimony or permit a party or witness to be called for cross-examination when there are conflicting declarations on an important issue, *e.g.*, whether defendant was served with summons and complaint. When local practice permits oral testimony, the parties should have the witnesses in court available to testify if the court decides oral testimony is necessary. The court may also continue the hearing to take evidence from witnesses not then available.

After hearing the arguments and considering the evidence, the court may rule on the matter or take it under submission. On making its decision, the court enters an order granting or denying the motion. The court may deny the motion without prejudice if the showing in support of the motion is deficient, but can be cured on a new motion. In some cases, a party may renew the motion even if the original motion is denied on the merits. See §30.72.

Some courts (*e.g.*, Los Angeles municipal court) enter findings of fact, although findings are not required.

§30.71 (10) Form: Order Setting Aside Entry of Default and Default Judgment

Copies: Original (filed with court clerk with proof of service); copies for service (one on each attorney and unrepresented party); office copies.

[Caption. See §§23.18–23.19]

No. _____

ORDER UNDER CCP §473 SETTING ASIDE ENTRY OF ____[DEFAULT / DEFAULT JUDGMENT / DEFAULT AND DEFAULT JUDGMENT]____

The motion of defendant ____[name]____ for an order setting aside entry of ____[default / default judgment / default and default judgment]____ **came on regularly for hearing on** ____[date]____. **Appearing as attorneys were** _____.

On proof being made to the court's satisfaction and good cause appearing:

IT IS ORDERED that said motion is granted, ____[subject to the conditions set forth below]____, that the ____[default / default judgment / default and default judgment]____ previously entered be set aside and vacated, and that the proposed ____[e.g., answer / verified answer / demurrer]____ be considered filed and served as of this date.

[Add when applicable]

IT IS FURTHER ORDERED that the above order take effect only after defendant has complied with the following conditions no later than ____[date]____:

1. ____[State conditions]____.
2. _____.

Dated: _____

_____
Judge

Comment: On the court's discretion and power to impose conditions on a motion to set aside entry of default or default judgment under CCP §473.

§30.72 (11) Renewal on Denial of Motion

Unlike the final judgment in an action or proceeding, the court's decision on an ordinary motion is not res judicata, and the court can reconsider it even though the motion was previously denied on the merits. *O'Brien v Santa Monica* (1963) 220 CA2d 67, 33 CR 770. See also *Northridge Fin. Corp. v Hamblin* (1975)

48 CA3d 819, 122 CR 109. As in the case of the original motion, a renewed motion also must be made within six months from entry of the default or default judgment, as prescribed by CCP §473. *Northridge Fin. Corp. v Hamblin, supra* (motion denied when filed 24 days after six-month period had expired).

A renewed motion should be noticed and supported by declarations in the same manner as the original motion. Additionally, it must be shown by declaration that a prior motion was made, when and before what judge it was made, and what order or decision was made. See CCP §1008.

§30.73   b. Equitable Motion in Trial Court

The procedures for an equitable motion for relief from entry of default or default judgment are similar to those for a motion under CCP §473 (see §§30.62–30.72), except that there is no six-month time limitation (see §30.59). The forms set out in §§30.64–30.66 may be adapted for use on a motion for equitable relief. On the grounds for motion, see §§30.57–30.59.

Although there is no maximum time limitation, a motion for equitable relief is subject to the same requirement as a CCP §473 motion that it be made within a reasonable time, *i.e.*, the moving party must move diligently on learning of the entry of default or default judgment. *Weitz v Yankosky* (1966) 63 C2d 849, 48 CR 620. See discussion in §30.62. In determining what is due diligence, the two major factors are the length of time from notice of the entry of default and whether, in that time, anything has occurred that would prejudice plaintiff if the motion were granted. *Weitz v Yankosky, supra*; *McCreadie v Arques* (1967) 248 CA2d 39, 56 CR 188.

Although a motion for equitable relief from entry of default or default judgment will be granted only when the moving party shows that a different result is probable in a trial on the merits (*Smith v Busniewski* (1952) 115 CA2d 124, 251 P2d 697), this rule is satisfied by including a proposed verified answer with the motion. *Shields v Siegel* (1966) 246 CA2d 334, 342, 54 CR 577, 581.

§30.74   c. Independent Action in Equity

An independent action in equity to set aside entry of a default or default judgment is seldom used because an equitable motion for relief (see §30.73) is quicker and less costly. However, in deciding whether to proceed by independent action or by motion, the attorney should consider that, unlike an equitable motion, filing an independent action permits a party to (1) conduct discovery proceedings and (2) present his case by oral testimony rather than by declaration.

The procedures for filing an independent action in equity are similar to those for filing any other action. The time limits for bringing the action are the same as for bringing an equitable motion for relief. See §30.73. Either the superior court, municipal court, or justice court has jurisdiction to hear the action. See discussion in §§30.58–30.59 on the equity jurisdiction of those courts. A verified answer attached to the complaint and incorporated by reference eliminates the need for a declaration of merits. See *Shields v Siegel* (1966) 246 CA2d 334, 342, 54 CR 577, 581. Because the action is equitable, there is no right to a jury trial. *Holt v Palmer* (1951) 106 CA2d 329, 235 P2d 43.

C. Relief When Service Does Not Afford Defendant Actual Notice

§30.75 1. Statutory Authority

When service of summons has not resulted in actual notice to defendant in time to defend the action and a default or default judgment has been entered against him, he may serve and file a notice of motion to set aside such default or default judgment and for leave to defend the action. CCP §473.5(a). The lack of actual notice in time to defend must not have been caused by defendant's avoidance of service or inexcusable neglect. CCP §473.5(b). On procedures, see §§30.77–30.79.

Lack of actual notice usually results from service of process by means other than personal service, *e.g.*, substituted service. On the methods of service available in California, see 1 CALIFORNIA CIVIL PROCEDURE BEFORE TRIAL §§8.30–8.40 (Cal CEB 1977).

§30.76 2. Equitable Authority

When entry of default or default judgment has resulted from defendant not having had actual notice of the action in time to defend, the court may grant relief under CCP §473.5 (see §30.75), or under its inherent equity power to set aside the default or default judgment. Although the grounds for an equitable motion are limited to extrinsic fraud or mistake, those terms are given a broad meaning and include all circumstances that deprive an adversary of fair notice of hearing regardless of whether they would constitute fraud or mistake in the strict sense. *Bennett v Hibernia Bank* (1956) 47 C2d 540, 305 P2d 20; *Munoz v Lopez* (1969) 275 CA2d 178, 79 CR 563 (decided under former CCP §473a). On procedures, see §§30.77–30.79.

3. Procedures

§30.77   a. Time for Motion

A motion for relief from default or default judgment made under CCP §473.5 must be filed within a reasonable time, and in no event later than (1) two years after entry of default judgment or (2) 180 days after service on defendant of written notice that a default or default judgment has been entered, whichever occurs first. CCP §473.5(a). Thus, as in the case of a motion under CCP §473, CCP §473.5 establishes both an outer time limit which is jurisdictional, and a requirement of a reasonable time. See §30.62. The notice of motion must designate a hearing date of not less than ten nor more than 20 days from the date of filing. CCP §473.5(b).

A motion for relief that is addressed to the court's equity powers must be made within a reasonable time, but is not subject to the time limitations of CCP §473.5. *Munoz v Lopez* (1969) 275 CA2d 178, 79 CR 563 (decided under former CCP §473a).

§30.78   b. Moving Papers

A motion under CCP §473.5 for relief from entry of default or default judgment must be accompanied by (1) an affidavit or declaration under penalty of perjury (CCP §2015.5) establishing that defendant's lack of actual notice in time to defend was not caused by his avoidance of service or inexcusable neglect, and (2) a copy of defendant's proposed answer, motion, or other pleading. CCP §473.5(b). It is good practice also to include these documents when the motion is made under the court's equity powers, independent of CCP §473.5. For forms of motion and a declaration that can be adapted for use, see §§30.64–30.65.

§30.79   c. Order; Court's Discretion To Impose Conditions

The court may grant relief from entry of default or default judgment on a motion made under CCP §473.5, provided it finds

(1) that the motion was made within the time stated in §30.77, and (2) that defendant's lack of actual notice in time to defend was not caused by his avoidance of service or inexcusable neglect. CCP §473.5(c). As in the case of a motion made under CCP §473, the court may condition relief on "such terms as may be just." CCP §473.5(c). But see *Smith v Bratman* (1917) 174 C 518, 163 P 892. See §30.61; for a form of order that may be adapted for use, see §30.71.

§30.80 D. Appellate Review

An order granting or denying relief from a default judgment is appealable as an order after judgment. CCP §§904.1(b) (superior court), 904.2(b) (municipal or justice court). An order setting aside or refusing to set aside a clerk's entry of default is not appealable until after judgment is entered. *Bernards v Grey* (1950) 97 CA2d 679, 218 P2d 597. See also CCP §§904.1–904.2. Review by mandamus is available only in unusual situations. For discussion, see 5 Witkin, CALIFORNIA PROCEDURE Attack on Judgment in Trial Court §161 (2d ed 1971).

Because judicial policy in favor of a trial on the merits (see §30.60) usually takes precedence over the policy of upholding a trial court order denying relief unless abuse of discretion is shown, appellate courts usually are more willing to uphold an order granting relief than one that denies relief. See 5 Witkin, PROCEDURE Attack on Judgment §§162–164. However, this result is not automatic and courts will uphold orders denying relief. *e.g.*, when defendant has not been diligent in seeking it. See §30.60.

PETER ABRAHAMS

Chapter 31
Dismissal

I. INVOLUNTARY DISMISSAL
A. Introduction
   1. Purposes of Dismissal Statutes §31.1
   2. Judicial Attitude; Plaintiff's Duty To Bring Case to Trial §31.2
   3. Types of Dismissal Statutes
       a. Chart: Comparison of General Dismissal Statutes §31.3
       b. Statutes Applicable to Particular Actions §31.4
   4. Applicability of General Dismissal Statutes §31.5
   5. Effect of Dismissal §31.6
B. Situations in Which Dismissal Required or Permitted
   1. Failure To Serve and Return Summons Within Three Years §31.7
       a. Requirement That Summons Be Served and Returned §31.8
       b. When Three-Year Period Begins §31.9
       c. When Three-Year Period Tolled §31.10
       d. Statutory Exceptions to Three-Year Requirement
           (1) Written Stipulation §31.11
           (2) General Appearance §31.12
       e. Implied Exceptions to Three-Year Requirement
           (1) Impossibility, Impracticability, or Futility §31.13
           (2) Estoppel §31.14
   2. Failure to Have Judgment Entered Within Three Years
       a. Basic Rule; Tolling of Statute §31.15
       b. Applicability to Default Judgments §31.16
       c. Exceptions to Three-Year Requirement for Entry of Judgment §31.17
   3. Failure To Bring Action to Trial Within Five Years §31.18
       a. When Action Is Brought to Trial §31.19
       b. Court's Duty To Set Case for Trial Within Five-Year Period §31.20

A.B., 1966, University of California (Los Angeles), J.D., 1969, Loyola University, Los Angeles. Mr. Abrahams practices with the law firm of Dryden, Harrington & Swartz, Los Angeles. CEB attorney-editors were ISADORE ROSENBLATT and JON A. RANTZMAN.

            c. Statutory Exceptions to Five-Year Requirement
                (1) Stipulation §31.21
                (2) Defendant Not Amenable to Process §31.22
                (3) Time During Which Court's Jurisdiction
                     Suspended §31.23
            d. Implied Exceptions to Five-Year Requirement
                (1) Impossibility, Impracticability, or
                     Futility §31.24
                     (a) Examples: Exception
                          Applicable §31.25
                     (b) Examples: Exception
                          Inapplicable §31.26
                     (c) Applicability of Exception to Multiple
                          Defendants §31.27
                     (d) Estoppel to Claim Exception §31.28
                (2) Estoppel §31.29
                (3) No Issue of Fact To Be Tried §31.30
            e. Dismissal of Class Action Before Five-Year Period
                Expires §31.31
        4. Failure To Bring Action to Trial Within Three Years After
            New Trial Granted §31.32
        5. Failure To Bring Action to Trial Within Three Years After
            Reversal or After New Trial Order Affirmed §31.33
        6. Failure To Bring Action to Trial Within Three Years After
            Mistrial §31.34
        7. Failure To Bring Action to Trial Within Two Years §31.35
            a. Court's Discretion; Criteria
                (1) Effect of Judicial Decisions §31.36
                (2) Effect of Cal Rules of Ct 203.5(e) §31.37
            b. Effect of Denial §31.38
            c. Appellate Review §31.39
        8. Failure To Appear for Trial §31.40
        9. Failure To Amend After Demurrer Sustained §31.41
       10. Failure To Pay Transfer Fees and Costs
            a. Basic Rule §31.42
            b. Estoppel To Seek Dismissal §31.43
    C. Court's Inherent Power To Dismiss §31.44
    D. Procedures §31.45
        1. Dismissal Under CCP §§581a, 583(a)–(d)
            a. Motion for Dismissal
                (1) Need for Noticed Motion and
                     Declaration §31.46
                (2) Content §31.47
                (3) Who May Make Motion §31.48
                (4) Form: Notice of Motion To Dismiss Action for
                     Failure To Prosecute §31.49
                (5) Form: Declaration in Support of Motion To
                     Dismiss Action for Failure To
                     Prosecute §31.50
                (6) Opposing Papers §31.51
                (7) Who May Hear Motion §31.52
            b. Defendant's Remedies When Dismissal
                Denied §31.53

              c. Form: Order of Dismissal **§31.54**
              d. Plaintiff's Remedies When Dismissal
                 Granted **§31.55**
       2. Dismissal Under CCP §583(a)
              a. Time for Motion **§31.56**
              b. Moving and Opposing Papers **§31.57**
              c. Ruling on Motion; Conditional Denial **§31.58**
       3. Dismissal Under Court's Inherent Power **§31.59**
       4. Dismissal Under CCP §399
              a. Proper Court in Which To Seek Dismissal **§31.60**
              b. Form: Notice of Motion to Dismiss Action for Failure
                 To Pay Transfer Fees and Costs **§31.61**
              c. Form: Declaration in Support of Motion To
                 Dismiss **§31.62**
              d. Effect of Stipulation To Transfer on Motion for
                 Dismissal **§31.63**
              e. Order of Dismissal **§31.64**

II. VOLUNTARY DISMISSAL

   A. Introduction
       1. Statutory Basis; Actions to Which Applicable **§31.65**
       2. Distinction Between Dismissal With Prejudice and
          Dismissal Without Prejudice **§31.66**
   B. Effect of Dismissal
       1. Without Prejudice
              a. New Action Not Barred **§31.67**
              b. Court Divested of Jurisdiction **§31.68**
              c. Defendant's Right to Costs and Attorneys'
                 Fees **§31.69**
       2. With Prejudice **§31.70**
   C. Dismissal Before Trial Commenced
       1. Dismissal as Matter of Right
              a. Basic Rule **§31.71**
              b. Exceptions
                  (1) Cross-Complaint Seeking Affirmative
                       Relief **§31.72**
                  (2) Plaintiff Not Sole Party in Interest **§31.73**
                  (3) Estoppel **§31.74**
              c. Meaning of When Trial Commenced **§31.75**
              d. Dismissal Against Fewer Than All Defendants;
                 Indispensable Parties **§31.76**
              e. Dismissal of Fewer Than All Causes of
                 Action **§31.77**
       2. Dismissal on Parties' Consent **§31.78**
   D. Dismissal After Trial Commenced
       1. With Prejudice
              a. As Matter of Right **§31.79**
              b. By Court Order After Abandonment **§31.80**
       2. Without Prejudice
              a. By Consent of Parties **§31.81**
              b. By Court Order for Just Cause **§31.82**

§31.1   DISMISSAL

E. Procedures
  1. When Dismissal Is Matter of Right
     a. Request for Dismissal §31.83
     b. Judicial Council Form: Request for Dismissal §31.84
     c. Payment of Clerk's Costs §31.85
     d. Delivery of Undertaking §31.86
  2. When Dismissal Not Matter of Right
     a. By Consent §31.87
     b. By Motion §31.88
  3. Entry of Dismissal; Clerk's Duty To Enter §31.89
  4. Judgment §31.90
F. Setting Aside Dismissal; Procedures §31.91

I. INVOLUNTARY DISMISSAL

A. Introduction

§31.1   1. Purposes of Dismissal Statutes

The statutory rules requiring or permitting dismissal of a civil action establish periodic deadlines that a plaintiff's or cross-complainant's attorney must meet to maintain the action. See chart in §31.3. These deadlines are distinguishable from statutes of limitation (which control the time for commencing an action), and from statutes that set time limits on the performance of conditions precedent to filing suit, *e.g.*, the time limits with regard to a claim against a decedent's estate (Prob C §§700–721) or against a public entity (Govt C §§900–915.4), but have been established for similar purposes. The purposes of the dismissal statutes are: (a) promoting the trial of cases before evidence is lost, destroyed, or witnesses' memory becomes dimmed, and (b) protection of defendants who are being subjected to a continuing unmeritorious action remaining undecided. *Crown Coach Corp. v Superior Court* (1972) 8 C3d 540, 105 CR 339; *General Motors Corp. v Superior Court* (1966) 65 C2d 88, 91, 52 CR 460, 462. By requiring timely service of summons, the dismissal statutes also prevent plaintiff from keeping an obligation alive without defendant's knowledge and lying in wait for defendant to acquire more property, from which plaintiff can satisfy a judgment. See *Davis v Hart* (1899) 123 C 384, 386, 55 P 1060, 1061.

Although CCP §§581a and 583, the basic California dismissal statutes, serve the same basic purpose, they differ in their underlying policies. Code of Civil Procedure §581a deals with detriment to a defendant due to his inability to institute discovery, preserve evidence and locate witnesses when not given timely notice of the institution of an action. Code of Civil Procedure

§583 focuses on detriment to the judicial system as well as defendant due to the tardy litigation of a claim. *Ippolito v Municipal Court* (1977) 67 CA3d 682, 136 CR 795.

§31.2 2. Judicial Attitude; Plaintiff's Duty To Bring Case to Trial

Because courts prefer to decide cases on the merits, they have been reluctant to apply the dismissal statutes mechanically if doing so would produce injustice (see *Brunzell Constr. Co. v Wagner* (1970) 2 C3d 545, 86 CR 297), and have developed well-recognized exceptions to supposedly mandatory dismissal statutes (see §§31.13–31.14, 31.24–31.30). The Supreme Court has emphasized that although the dismissal statutes are similar to statutes of limitation (see §31.1), they "involve policy considerations somewhat less crucial than those safeguarded by statutes of limitation," because a defendant who has been served has knowledge of the lawsuit and may protect his interests, *e.g.*, by initiating discovery to preserve evidence, taking depositions, or moving to dismiss a frivolous or sham action. *General Motors Corp. v Superior Court* (1966) 65 C2d 88, 91, 52 CR 460, 462.

However, despite their reluctance to apply the dismissal statutes mechanically, courts have emphasized plaintiff's duty to use diligence to bring the case to trial, whereas defendant, as an involuntary party, is under no similar duty. See, *e.g.*, *Anderson v Erwyn* (1966) 247 CA2d 503, 55 CR 634; *Oberkotter v Spreckles* (1923) 64 CA 470, 221 P 698. For example, when a statutory dismissal deadline is imminent, plaintiff should bring that fact to the court's attention, and should move for an early trial setting under Cal Rules of Ct 225. *Crown Coach Corp. v Superior Court* (1972) 8 C3d 540, 105 CR 339 (dismissal under former CCP §583(b) for failure to bring case to trial within three years from filing of remittitur); *Boyd v Southern Pac. R.R.* (1921) 185 C 344, 197 P 58 (dismissal under former CCP §583 for failure to bring case to trial within five years). Even if defendant is aware of the fact that a statutory deadline is about to expire, he has no duty to call it to plaintiff's attention. *Lane v Davis* (1964) 227 CA2d 60, 38 CR 425.

3. Types of Dismissal Statutes

§31.3 a. Chart: Comparison of General Dismissal Statutes

The two basic California statutes governing involuntary dismissal are CCP §§581a and 583. The chart below compares these statutes, with cross-references to discussion in the text.   See *Comment* on p 392.

Chart: Comparison of

Code of Civil Procedure	When applicable	Dismissal mandatory or discretionary	Who may make motion
§581a(a)	Failure to serve and return summons on complaint within three years after filing.	Mandatory. See §31.7.	Any interested party (whether or not named) or court on own motion. See §31.7.
§581a(b)	(1) *When summons on cross-complaint is required:* failure to serve and return summons within three years after filing. (2) *When summons on cross-complaint is not required* failure to serve cross-complaint within three years after filing.	Mandatory. See §31.7.	Any interested party (whether or not named) or court on own motion. See §31.7.
§581a(c)	Failure to have judgment entered within three years after filing when no answer on file.	Mandatory. See §31.15.	Any interested party or court on own motion. See §31.15.

388

General Dismissal Statutes

When time begins to run	When time tolled	Exceptions	Procedures governed by
Commencement (filing) of action. See §31.9.	Defendant not amenable to court's process. See §31.10.	(1) Stipulation of parties extending time. See §31.11. (2) General appearance by defendant. See §31.12. (3) Impossible, impracticable, or futile to comply. See §31.13. (4) Estoppel. See §31.14.	Ordinary motion procedure. See §§31.46–31.55.
Filing of cross-complaint. See §31.9.	Same as above. See §31.10.	(1) Stipulation of parties extending time. See §31.11. (2) When service of summons required, general appearance by cross-defendant. See §31.12. (3) Impossible, impracticable, or futile to comply. See §31.13. (4) Estoppel. See §31.14.	Ordinary motion procedure. See §§31.46–31.55.
Service on defendant, or general appearance of defendant. See §31.15.	Same as above. See §31.15.	(1) Stipulation of parties. See §31.17. (2) Impossible, impracticable, or futile to comply. See §31.17. (3) Estoppel. See §31.17.	Ordinary motion procedure. See §§31.46–31.55.

Chart: Comparison of

Code of Civil Procedure	When applicable	Dismissal mandatory or discretionary	Who may make motion
§583(a)	Failure to bring action to trial within two years after filing.	Discretionary. See §§31.35–31.37.	Party seeking dismissal or court on own motion. See §31.56.
§583(b)	Failure to bring action to trial within five years after filing.	Mandatory. See §31.18.	Defendant or court on own motion. See §31.18.
§583(c)	*When new trial granted and no appeal:* failure to bring action to trial within three years after entry of order.	Mandatory. See §31.32.	Defendant or court on own motion. See §31.32.
§583(c)	*When judgment reversed (or order granting new trial affirmed) on appeal:* failure to bring action to trial within three years after filing of remittitur.	Mandatory. See §31.33.	Defendant or court on own motion. See §31.33.
§583(d)	Failure to have retrial commenced within three years after mistrial declared or jury has been unable to reach verdict.	Mandatory. See §31.34.	Defendant or court on own motion. See §31.34.

General Dismissal Statutes

When time begins to run	When time tolled	Exceptions	Procedures governed by
Commencement (filing) of action. See §31.35.	(1) Defendant not amenable to court's process. See §31.35. (2) Court's jurisdiction to try action suspended. See §31.35.	(1) Impossible, impracticable, or futile to comply. See §§31.35, 31.37. (2) Estoppel. See §31.35.	Cal Rules of Ct 203.5. See §§31.56–31.58.
Commencement (filing) of action. See §31.18.	Same as above. See §§31.22–31.23.	(1) Stipulation of parties. See §31.21. (2) Impossible, impracticable, or futile to comply. See §§31.24–31.28. (3) Estoppel. See §31.29.	Ordinary motion procedure. See §§31.46–31.55.
Order granting new trial. See §31.32.	Same as above. See §31.32.	(1) Stipulation of parties. See §31.32. (2) Impossible, impracticable, or futile to comply. See §31.32.	Ordinary motion procedure. See §§31.46–31.55.
Date remittitur filed. See §31.33.	Same as above. See §31.33.	Impossible, impracticable, or futile to comply. See §31.33.	Ordinary motion procedure. See §§31.46–31.55.
Order declaring mistrial or disagreement of jury. See §31.34.	Same as above. See §31.34.	(1) Stipulation of parties. See §31.34. (2) Impossible, impracticable, or futile to comply. See §31.34.	Ordinary motion procedure. See §§31.46–31.55.

§31.4   DISMISSAL

Comment: This chart does not include dismissals under CCP §399 for plaintiff's failure to pay transfer fees on certain orders for change of venue. For discussion, see §§31.42–31.43. Also not included are dismissals under CCP §581(3) for failure to (1) appear at trial (see §31.40), or (2) amend the complaint within the time allowed when a demurrer is sustained with leave to amend (see §31.41). For discussion of statutes applicable to particular actions, see §31.4.

§31.4   b. Statutes Applicable to Particular Actions

In addition to the statutory dismissal provisions applicable to civil actions generally (see chart in §31.3), counsel should be aware of statutes relating to particular actions. For example, in the absence of a written stipulation between the parties, the court must dismiss:

(1) A taxpayer's action to contest the validity of a tax sale or tax deed, if not brought to trial within one year after commencement (Rev & T C §3638, which also provides that the ordinary time limitations of CCP §583 shall not apply to such actions); and

(2) An action for a tax refund, unless summons has been issued and served and the return made within one year after commencement (Rev & T C §5147).

The trial court has discretion to dismiss an action to foreclose a mechanics lien if not brought to trial within two years after commencement. CC §3147. See also CCP §583(a), discussed in §§31.35–31.39.

§31.5   4. Applicability of General Dismissal Statutes

The requirements of CCP §§581a and 583 apply to governmental agencies as well as private parties. *People v Kings County Dev. Co.* (1920) 48 CA 72, 191 P 1004 (CCP §581a); *Superior Oil Co. v Superior Court* (1936) 6 C2d 113, 56 P2d 950; *Bank of America v Superior Court* (1948) 84 CA2d 34, 189 P2d 799 (CCP §583). The provisions of CCP §583 apply to actions begun by complaint as well as cross-complaint (CCP §583(e)), and to all actions and special proceedings that are adversary proceedings and that require trial of issues. 4 Witkin, CALIFORNIA PROCEDURE, Proceedings Without Trial §80 (2d ed 1971).

The provisions of CCP §581a apply to actions and special proceedings generally, including eminent domain proceedings (*Big*

Bear Munic. Water Dist. v Superior Court (1969) 269 CA2d 919, 75 CR 580; *Dresser v Superior Court* (1964) 231 CA2d 68, 41 CR 473), but do not apply to involuntary corporate dissolution proceedings (*Rosner v Benedict Heights, Inc.* (1963) 219 CA2d 1, 32 CR 764), or to will contests (*Horney v Superior Court* (1948) 83 CA2d 262, 188 P2d 552).

The provisions of CCP §581a(b) are specifically directed at cross-complaints (see chart in §31.3), and, although no authority has been found, it appears that CCP §581a(c) (failure to have judgment entered within three years after either service or general appearance) applies to judgment on cross-complaints as well as complaints.

For further discussion, see 4 Witkin, Procedure, Proc Without Trial §§61–62, 80.

§31.6   5. Effect of Dismissal

The dismissal provisions of CCP §581a or §583(b)–(d) are mandatory and jurisdictional. *Bernstein v Superior Court* (1969) 2 CA3d 700, 82 CR 775 (CCP §581a); *Turnbull v Superior Court* (1932) 126 CA 141, 14 P2d 540 (CCP §583(b)). (On whether CCP §581a(c) is jurisdictional, see 4 Witkin, California Procedure, Proceedings Without Trial §77 (2d ed 1971)). Subject to the statutory and implied exceptions discussed in this chapter, the trial court must dismiss an action if the time limits prescribed by those sections (see chart in §31.3) have expired. Relief under CCP §473 when failure to comply is due to mistake, inadvertence, surprise, or excusable neglect (see generally §§30.56–30.58) is not available. See *Kaiser Foundation Hosp. v Superior Court* (1975) 49 CA3d 523, 122 CR 432 (pertaining to dismissal under either CCP §581a). However, a judgment of dismissal rendered under either CCP §581a or §583 is not res judicata, and, provided the action is not barred by the statute of limitations, a new lawsuit can be commenced after dismissal. *Gonsalves v Bank of America* (1940) 16 C2d 169, 172, 105 P2d 118, 120; *Watson v Superior Court* (1972) 24 CA3d 53, 60, 100 CR 684, 689.

Because a judgment of dismissal under CCP §583 is not on the merits, it is not a final judgment within the meaning of CC §1717 and therefore defendant is not entitled to attorneys' fees, even if the action is on a contract that provides for them. *Samuels v Sabih* (1976) 62 CA3d 335, 133 CR 74.

B. Situations in Which Dismissal Required or Permitted

§31.7   1. Failure To Serve and Return Summons Within Three Years

Unless the summons is served and return made within three years after commencement of the action, no action commenced by complaint can be further prosecuted, no further proceedings can be had, and the action must be dismissed by the court in which it was commenced, on its own motion or on motion of any interested party, whether or not named. CCP §581a(a).

When an action is commenced by cross-complaint, and a summons is required, summons must be served and return made within three years after filing of the cross-complaint. On failure to do so, the action must be dismissed by the court in which it was commenced, on its own motion or on motion of any interested party, whether or not named. If summons on the cross-complaint is not required, the action must be dismissed in the same manner unless the cross-complaint is served within three years after filing. CCP §581a(b). For discussion of exceptions to the three-year requirement, see §§31.11–31.14.

§31.8   a. Requirement That Summons Be Served and Returned

Under CCP §581a, summons must be served and returned within three years after filing the complaint. For discussion, see CALIFORNIA CIVIL PROCEDURE BEFORE TRIAL §§8.51–8.57 (Cal CEB 1977). This requirement applies regardless of the manner in which service is made. See, *e.g.*, *Hunt v Superior Court* (1976) 63 CA3d 832, 134 CR 128 (summons served by mail); *Ginns v Shumate* (1977) 65 CA3d 802, 135 CR 604 (summons served by substituted service). However, as long as summons is actually served and returned within three years, CCP §581a is satisfied. It is immaterial that, under the substituted service provisions of CCP §415.20, service is not considered complete until after expiration of the three-year period. *Ginns v Shumate, supra.*

Summons is returned when it is filed in the office of the county clerk with proof of service. See *Highlands Inn, Inc. v Gurries* (1969) 276 CA2d 694, 81 CR 273.

The requirement of both service and return within three years can be a trap for the unwary, particularly when there are several defendants and some defendants answer for themselves alone.

For example, assume that A, who is neither B's employee nor agent, borrows B's car with the latter's permission. B has a policy of automobile liability insurance with $100,000 coverage for injury to or death of any person while his car is being driven by himself or by another with his permission. A has no liability insurance of his own or other assets. While driving B's car, A strikes C, inflicting injuries entitling C to $100,000 in damages. C sues and serves both A and B. B's attorney answers solely on B's behalf, but C's attorney overlooks this fact and fails to return the summons served on A within three years.

After expiration of the three-year period, B's attorney offers $15,000 in full settlement of C's lawsuit. Under Veh C §17151(a), B, as owner of the car, is vicariously responsible for A's conduct, but his liability is limited to $15,000. Because C has not timely returned the summons served on A, he cannot recover more than $15,000 from B. If C's action against A were not barred by CCP §581a(a), C would be able to recover the full $100,000 against A and B's insurer, who had extended permissive user coverage to A, would have to pay the entire judgment.

§31.9   b. When Three-Year Period Begins

The three-year period for service and return of summons begins, in the case of a complaint, when the action is commenced (CCP §581a(a)), *i.e.*, when the complaint has been filed (CCP §411.10), and, in the case of a cross-complaint, when the cross-complaint is filed (CCP §581a(b)). The time of commencement is not extended by filing an amended or supplemental complaint or by issuance of an additional summons (*Perati v Atkinson* (1964) 230 CA2d 251, 40 CR 835), unless the amendment adds new parties. When a plaintiff is added to the action by an amended complaint, the action as to that plaintiff is considered to have been commenced, for the purpose of CCP §581a, on the date the amended complaint is filed. See *J. A. Thompson & Sons, Inc. v Superior Court* (1963) 215 CA2d 719, 30 CR 471 (amended complaint named decedent's minor son as plaintiff in wrongful death action).

When defendants are added to an action as necessary or indispensable parties under CCP §389 (see §25.3), the action is considered to have been commenced with respect to them at the time they are joined, rather than when the action was originally filed. *Warren v Atchison, Topeka & Santa Fe Ry.* (1971) 19 CA3d

24, 39, 96 CR 317, 328. This rule applies even though defendants were originally named as parties, then dismissed, and subsequently ordered joined as necessary or indispensable parties. Nor does it matter that the original dismissal was made under CCP §581a. The original dismissal makes the parties strangers to the action; when they are later ordered joined and are named as defendants in the amended complaint, they come in as new parties and the action commences anew with respect to them. See *Monrovia Hosp. Co. v Superior Court* (1967) 253 CA2d 607, 61 CR 737; *Taliaferro v Riddle* (1959) 167 CA2d 567, 334 P2d 950. However, when defendants are named in the original complaint, the three-year period of CCP §581a begins to run when the action is filed, even though the complaint does not state a cause of action as to those defendants, and is later amended to state a cause of action as to them. *Elling Corp. v Superior Court* (1975) 48 CA3d 89, 123 CR 734.

When a party is named as a fictitious defendant, the three-year requirement of CCP §581a runs from the date the action was commenced, and not from the date defendant is served. *Rios v Torvald Klaveness* (1969) 2 CA3d 1077, 83 CR 150; *Dresser v Superior Court* (1964) 231 CA2d 68, 41 CR 473.

§31.10   c. When Three-Year Period Tolled

The time during which a defendant was not amenable to process is tolled in computing the three-year period of CCP §581a. CCP §581a(d). *Taylor v Hizer* (1973) 30 CA3d 846, 850, 106 CR 603, 605, disapproved on other grounds in 12 C3d at 53. See, e.g., *Polony v White* (1974) 43 CA3d 44, 117 CR 341 (deceased defendant not amenable to court's process, and three-year period tolled during time between defendant's death and appointment of a personal representative). However, the time during which a defendant is absent from the state or secrets himself within the state is included. Because of the expanded methods of out-of-state service, under the Jurisdiction and Service of Process Act (CCP §410.10–418.10), the three-year period is not tolled if defendant is absent from the state, provided it is possible to obtain personal jurisdiction over him. See *Cranston v Bonelli* (1971) 15 CA3d 129, 92 CR 828; 4 Witkin, CALIFORNIA PROCEDURE, Proceedings Without Trial (2d ed 1971).

Unlike the rule with respect to time limitations required by CCP §583, the three-year period for serving and returning summons under CCP §581a is not tolled during the period that the court's jurisdiction to try the action is suspended. See chart in §31.3. Nor is it tolled during the time that a default and default judgment are in effect if the default was taken by filing a false return of service. *Ippolito v Municipal Court* (1977) 67 CA3d 682, 136 CR 795.

d. Statutory Exceptions to Three-Year Requirement
§31.11 (1) Written Stipulation

An action cannot be dismissed for failure to serve and return summons within three years after commencement if the parties stipulate in writing to extend the time for such service and return. CCP §581a(a). The same rule applies to actions brought by cross-complaint. CCP §581a(b).

The stipulation should expressly extend the time for return of summons or expressly waive the right to dismiss; a stipulation extending defendant's time within which to plead is not sufficient as a stipulation (*Highlands Inn, Inc. v Gurries* (1969) 276 CA2d 694, 699, 81 CR 273, 276; *Miles & Sons, Inc. v Superior Court* (1960) 181 CA2d 151, 5 CR 73), although it may be sufficient as a general appearance (*General Ins. Co. v Superior Court* (1975) 15 C3d 449, 124 CR 745). See *Tresway Aero, Inc. v Superior Court* (1971) 5 C3d 431, 96 CR 571 (defendant's request for extension of time to plead until after expiration of three-year period under CCP §581a estops him from moving to dismiss the action). See discussion in §§31.12, 31.14.

A stipulation extending the time to serve and return summons is effective even though it is not signed and filed until after expiration of the three-year period, as long as it is filed before the court's order of dismissal. See *Big Bear Munic. Water Dist. v Superior Court* (1969) 269 CA2d 919, 75 CR 580.

§31.12 (2) General Appearance

A defendant who "has made a general appearance in the action" cannot move to dismiss under CCP §581a for failure to serve and return the summons within three years after commencement of the action. CCP §581a(a). The same rule applies to actions brought by cross-complaint. CCP §581a(b). However, the appearance must be made within three years; a general appearance made after that time does not deprive defendant of his right to dismissal. *Busching v Superior Court* (1974) 12 C3d 44, 115 CR 241, disapproving *Taylor v Hizer* (1973) 30 CA3d 846, 106 CR 603 (1970 amendment to CCP §581a, adding quoted language, did not change prior law that filing answer after expiration of three-year period does not constitute general appearance).

Defendant makes a general appearance in an action when (a) he files an answer, demurrer, notice of motion to strike, notice of motion to transfer under CCP §396b, (b) gives plaintiff written notice of his appearance, or when (c) an attorney gives notice of appearance for him. CCP §1014. Defendant also makes a general appearance when he performs an act that indicates an intent to submit to the court's jurisdiction (see *General Ins. Co. v Superior Court* (1975) 15 C3d 449, 124 CR 745), *e.g.*, when he files answers to interrogatories (*Chitwood v Superior Court* (1971) 14 CA3d 522, 92 CR 441). However, when a plaintiff sues and serves interrogatories on both a corporation and one of its employees, answers to interrogatories filed by the employee do not constitute a general appearance by him in his individual capacity. *Semole v Sansoucie* (1972) 28 CA3d 714, 104 CR 897.

Neither a motion to dismiss under CCP §581a, nor any extension of time to plead after such a motion, nor a stipulation extending the time for service and return of summons, constitute a general appearance. CCP §581a(e).

When a defendant moves to change venue, and a codefendant voluntarily executes a declaration in support of the motion but does not join in it, the declaration does not constitute a general appearance because it is simply testimony as to defendant's knowledge of his own residence and that of a codefendant. *Slaybaugh v Superior Court* (1977) 70 CA3d 216, 138 CR 628.

Any written stipulation between attorneys that recognizes the court's jurisdiction over the parties constitutes a general appearance, *e.g.*, a letter accepting service and confirming an extension of time to plead for an indefinite period, subject to termination on ten days' written notice. *General Ins. Co. v Superior Court, supra.* The court in that case distinguished *Busching v Superior Court, supra,* in that *Busching* involved an extension of time to obtain representation, not to plead. A written but unfiled stipulation extending defendant's time in which to appear to a date within the three-year period amounts to a general appearance (*RCA Corp. v. Superior Court* (1975) 47 CA3d 1007, 121 CR 441), and prevents dismissal, even if not filed within the three-year period, as long as it is entered into before expiration of the period (*General Ins. Co. v Superior Court, supra*). However, an extension of time in which "to plead," as distinguished from one in which "to appear," has been held not to be a general appearance that prevents defendant from moving for dismissal under CCP §581a. *Owen v Niagara Mach. & Tool Works* (1977) 68 CA3d 566, 137 CR 378. See also *Busching v Superior Court* (1974) 12 C3d 44, 115 CR 241. The court in *Owen* distinguished *RCA Corp. v Superior Court, supra*, on the ground that a stipulation to appear lulls plaintiff into believing that a general appearance would be made within the statutory period, while a stipulation to plead does not. But see the dissenting opinion in *Owen*. For discussion of estoppel, see §31.14.

For further discussion of what constitutes a general appearance, see 1 CALIFORNIA CIVIL PROCEDURE BEFORE TRIAL §2.49 (Cal CEB 1977).

e. Implied Exceptions to Three-Year Requirement
§31.13 (1) Impossibility, Impracticability, or Futility

The requirement of CCP §581a that summons be served and returned within three years is subject not only to statutory exceptions (see §§31.11–31.12), but also to implied exceptions created by judicial decision when it is impossible, impracticable, or futile to comply. See, *e.g.*, *Wyoming Pac. Oil v Preston* (1958) 50 C2d 736, 329 P2d 489 (impracticable or futile to comply with CCP §581a when defendant in hiding to avoid service). However, since the enactment of CCP §581a(d) in 1970, the three-year period is tolled when defendant is not amenable to the court's process (see §31.10) and there is no need to apply this exception. Impossibility, impracticability, or futility probably will be applied to CCP §581a far less often in the future. See, *e.g.*, *Lopa v Superior Court* (1975) 46 CA3d 382, 120 CR 445 (not impossible, impracticable, nor futile to serve defendant within three years after commencement of action even though plaintiff did not know he had a cause of action until guest statute ruled unconstitutional by Supreme Court in 1973). For further discussion, see the impossibility, impracticability, or futility exceptions to CCP §583, discussed in §§31.24–31.28. However, although the exceptions to CCP §583 have been held applicable to CCP §581a (*Wyoming Pac. Oil Co. v Preston, supra*), a court will not apply them with rubberstamp symmetry (*Ippolito v Municipal Court* (1977) 67 CA3d 682, 136 CR 795). For instance, when a default judgment has been entered, but is void (*e.g.*, because service of summons was invalid), it has been held that while the judgment is in effect, it is impossible, impracticable, or futile to comply with the five-year requirement of CCP §583(b) for bringing the case to trial (*Maguire v Collier* (1975) 49 CA3d 309, 122 CR 510), but not with the three-year requirement of CCP §581a for serving and returning summons (*Ippolito v Municipal Court, supra*).

§31.14   (2) Estoppel

If defendant's conduct induces plaintiff to delay the return of summons, the period of the delay is not included in determining whether the three-year requirement of CCP §581a has been met. *Tresway Aero, Inc. v Superior Court* (1971) 5 C3d 431, 96 CR 571; *Flamer v Superior Court* (1968) 266 CA2d 907, 72 CR 561. In *Tresway*, the court held that defendant's request for an extension of time to plead until after expiration of three-year period estopped him from seeking dismissal under CCP §581a. Service on defendant was defective and, by obtaining an extension of time to plead, defendant lulled plaintiff into believing that service was properly made, thereby denying plaintiff the opportunity to make correct service within the three-year period. But see *Owen v Niagara Mach. & Tool Works* (1977) 68 CA3d 566, 137 CR 378 (no estoppel from seeking dismissal after a stipulation to plead, when service not defective and *Tresway* facts not present).

Estoppel to seek dismissal under CCP §581a is justified not only when defendant (a) makes a misrepresentation to a plaintiff who is not represented by counsel, or (b) stipulates in open court to an extension of the three-year period, but also whenever necessary to serve "the ends of substantial justice." *Tresway Aero, Inc. v Superior Court*, (1971) 5 C3d 431, 439, 96 CR 571, 577 (dictum).

2. Failure To Have Judgment Entered Within Three Years
§31.15   a. Basic Rule; Tolling of Statute

Unless the parties have filed a written stipulation extending time, an action must be dismissed by the court in which it is pending, on its own motion, or on motion of any interested party, if (1) no answer (or demurrer; *Evans v Superior Court* (1936) 14 CA2d 743, 59 P2d 159) has been filed after defendant has either been served or has made a general appearance, and (2) plaintiff fails to have judgment entered within three years after such service or appearance. CCP §581a(c). The legislative intent behind CCP §581a(c) is to require plaintiff to exercise diligence in obtaining default judgments and the statute applies only to such judgments. See 4 Witkin, CALIFORNIA PROCEDURE, Proceedings Without Trial §76 (2d ed 1971). See §31.16.

As in the case of the three-year service and return of summons requirements of CCP §581a(a)–(b), the three-year requirement for entry of judgment under CCP §581a(c) is tolled during the time when defendant is not amenable to the court's process. CCP §581a(d). For discussion, see §31.10.

§31.16 b. Applicability to Default Judgments

The three-year requirement of CCP §581a(c) for entry of default judgments is not satisfied by the clerk's entry of default, and defendant can obtain a dismissal unless plaintiff also obtains a default judgment within the three-year period. *Jacks v Lewis* (1943) 61 CA2d 148, 142 P2d 358. However, only in purely default cases (*i.e.*, when one defendant has been served and defaulted and no defendant has filed an answer) must the court dismiss the action under CCP §581a if no judgment is entered within three years. In multiple defendant cases, when one defendant has defaulted and another has answered and the liability of the defendants might be joint, or joint and several, CCP §579 permits entry of more than one judgment and CCP §581a(c) is inapplicable. *AMF Pinspotters, Inc. v Peek* (1970) 6 CA3d 443, 86 CR 46.

Courts have construed the decision in *AMF Pinspotters, Inc. supra,* to mean that CCP §581a(c) is inapplicable only when a subsequent judgment with respect to an answering defendant might be in direct conflict with the default judgment. When the default judgment would not be in conflict with any such subsequent judgment, CCP §581a(c) is applicable. *McKenzie v Thousand Oaks* (1973) 36 CA3d 426, 111 CR 584. In *McKenzie*, the action had been dismissed with prejudice with respect to the answering defendants before the defaulting defendant's motion to dismiss was made, and consequently the rights of those defendants could not have been adversely affected by the motion to dismiss.

§31.17   c. Exceptions to Three-Year Requirement for Entry of Judgment

The three-year limit for bringing a case to judgment when defendant has been served or has made a general appearance but has not answered is inapplicable when the parties have filed a written stipulation extending the time (CCP §581a(c)), when it is impossible, impracticable, or futile to comply (*General Ins. Co. v Superior Court* (1975) 15 C3d 449, 458, 124 CR 745, 750 (dissenting opinion)), or when a party is estopped from seeking it (see §31.14). See discussion in §31.13.

The rules on stipulations extending the time under CCP §581a(a)–(b) are therefore equally applicable to CCP §581a(c). See §31.11. A written stipulation extending defendant's time to plead for an indefinite period, but which is terminable on ten days' written notice, reflects a mutual intent to defer proceedings and must be enforced. Because such a stipulation precludes plaintiff from taking a default before expiration of the three-year period, defendant may not obtain dismissal under CCP §581a(c). *General Ins. Co. v Superior Court* (1975) 15 C3d 449, 124 CR 745. However, *General Ins. Co.* was a 4—3 decision, and the dissent argued that (1) plaintiff could have obtained a default simply by giving defendant ten days' written notice, and (2) CCP §581a(c) does not except stipulations that merely extend the time to plead. See further discussion in §§31.11–31.12.

In a marital dissolution proceeding, when a party files a response after expiration of the three-year period, the court cannot dismiss under CCP §581a(c) or on its own motion or on motion of respondent because the proceeding can be reinstituted immediately and no public benefit is served by the dismissal. *Mustalo v Mustalo* (1974) 37 CA3d 580, 112 CR 594.

§31.18   3. Failure To Bring Action to Trial Within Five Years

Unless the parties have filed a written stipulation extending the time, an action must be dismissed by the court in which the action is pending on its own motion or on motion of defendant, if it has not been brought to trial within five years after plaintiff has filed the complaint. CCP §583(b). This provision is mandatory and jurisdictional, but a judgment of dismissal under CCP §583(b) is not on the merits and is not res judicata. See §31.6.

The five-year period for bringing the action to trial begins to run when plaintiff (or cross-complainant) has filed the complaint (or cross-complaint). CCP §§583(b),(e). See also *Tomales Bay Oyster Corp. v Superior Court* (1950) 35 C2d 389, 217 P2d 968 (five-year period for cross-complaint begins to run from filing of cross-complaint (rather than complaint), because cross-complaint is treated as independent action). The five-year period is not extended by filing either an amended complaint (*Douglas v Superior Court* (1949) 94 CA2d 395, 210 P2d 853) or a complaint in intervention that asserts the same cause of action as the original complaint (*Bosworth v Superior Court* (1956) 143 CA2d 775, 300 P2d 155).

§31.19 a. When Action Is Brought to Trial

The requirement in CCP §583(b) that the action be brought to trial within five years is not satisfied simply by setting the action for trial. *Boyd v Southern Pac. R.R.* (1921) 185 C 344, 197 P 58; *Stuart v Hollywood Turf Club* (1956) 146 CA2d 261, 303 P2d 897. On the other hand, the action need not be completely tried; the statute is satisfied if the case is partially tried within the five-year period, *e.g.*, by having one witness sworn and then continuing the case. *Los Angeles v Superior Court* (1940) 15 C2d 16, 98 P2d 207. The empanelment of a jury also constitutes a partial trial and prevents dismissal under CCP §583(b). *Kadota v San Francisco* (1958) 166 CA2d 194, 333 P2d 75; *Vecki v Sorensen* (1959) 171 CA2d 390, 340 P2d 1020.

A hearing (1) to enter a default judgment (*Langan v McCorkle* (1969) 276 CA2d 805, 81 CR 535, disapproved on other grounds in 2 C3d at 555), (2) on a motion to set aside a default judgment (*Meier v Superior Court* (1942) 55 CA2d 675, 131 P2d 554), or (3) on application for a preliminary injunction (*Superior Oil Co. v Superior Court* (1936) 6 C2d 113, 56 P2d 950) is not considered a trial for purposes of satisfying the requirement of CCP §583(b). A hearing on a demurrer is not a trial within the meaning of CCP §583(b) (*California Ammonia Co. v Macco Corp.* (1969) 270 CA2d 429, 432, 75 CR 753, 755), unless the demurrer is sustained without leave to amend and the action is dismissed (*McDonough Power Equip. Co. v Superior Court* (1972) 8 C3d 527, 105 CR 330; *Berri v Superior Court* (1955) 43 C2d 856, 279 P2d 8).

The granting of a motion for summary judgment constitutes a

trial and prevents dismissal under CCP §583(b) (*Southern Pac. Co. v Seaboard Mills* (1962) 207 CA2d 97, 24 CR 236), but neither an order granting a motion for a "partial summary judgment" when no summary judgment is entered (*King v State* (1970) 11 CA3d 307, 89 CR 715), nor a denial of a motion for summary judgment (*Bella Vista Dev. Co. v Superior Court* (1963) 223 CA2d 603, 36 CR 106) constitute a trial because final disposition of the action has not been made.

§31.20   b. Court's Duty To Set Case for Trial Within Five-Year Period

When pretrial proceedings have been completed, it is an abuse of discretion for a trial court to refuse to set the case for trial within the five-year period required by CCP §583(b), or to vacate an order specially setting the case for trial on grounds that counsel has been derelict in prosecuting the case. *Weeks v Roberts* (1968) 68 C2d 802, 69 CR 305 (28 days is reasonable period within which to provide courtroom facilities for trial). Even if no pretrial proceedings have been held, it is an abuse of discretion to deny plaintiff's motion to specially set a case for trial when sufficient time remains before expiration of the statutory period (*e.g.*, 46 days) and pretrial proceedings were neither requested nor ordered. *Vogelsang v Owl Trucking Co.* (1974) 40 CA3d 1068, 115 CR 666. (Although the trial court must set the case for trial within the five-year period required by CCP §583(b), the court retains discretion to dismiss the action under CCP §583(a) for failure to bring the action to trial within two years after filing. See §§31.35–31.37.

If plaintiff moves to set the case for trial well within the five years and requests that the case be set for trial before expiration of that period, failure to do so may be an abuse of discretion and the additional time may be excluded from computation of the five years. *Bank of America v Superior Court* (1948) 84 CA2d 34, 37, 189 P2d 799, 801 (dictum). But see *Stuart v Hollywood Turf Club* (1956) 146 CA2d 261, 303 P2d 897 (dismissal upheld when plaintiff delayed until five court days before expiration of five-year period and then moved for immediate trial). See generally the discussion of impracticability, impossibility, or futility in §§31.24–31.28.

c. Statutory Exceptions to Five-Year Requirement
§31.21 (1) Stipulation

The five-year period within which an action must be brought to trial may be extended by the parties' written stipulation. CCP §583(b). However, an oral stipulation entered in the minutes of the court has the same effect as a written stipulation extending the five-year period. *Govea v Superior Court* (1938) 26 CA2d 27, 78 P2d 433. See also *Wright v Groom Trucking Co.* (1962) 206 CA2d 485, 24 CR 80.

The stipulation is effective if it expressly extends the date of trial to a date beyond the five-year period (*Smith v Bear Valley Milling & Lumber Co.* (1945) 26 C2d 590, 160 P2d 1; *Anderson v Erwyn* (1966) 247 CA2d 503, 507, 55 CR 634, 636), or expressly waives the right to dismiss (*Bank of America v Superior Court* (1937) 22 CA2d 450, 71 P2d 296). However, a stipulation that the trial date "be reset for some convenient date" is not sufficient to extend the five-year period. *Hastings v Superior Court* (1955) 131 CA2d 255, 280 P2d 74.

There is no requirement that the stipulation be entered into during the five-year period, and a stipulation made after that period, *e.g.*, extending the time for trial to a certain date, is enforceable. *Estate of Thatcher* (1953) 120 CA2d 811, 262 P2d 337. However, the stipulation does not constitute a permanent waiver of the right to dismiss, and the action is subject to dismissal if not brought to trial on that day. *Fisher v Superior Court* (1958) 157 CA2d 126, 131, 320 P2d 894, 898.

A stipulation that is technically insufficient to extend the five-year period may be material evidence on the issue of whether it was impossible, impracticable, or futile to bring the action to trial. See *Woley v Turkus* (1958) 51 C2d 402, 334 P2d 12; *Pacific Greyhound Lines v Superior Court* (1946) 28 C2d 61, 168 P2d 665. See generally §§31.24–31.28.

§31.22 (2) Defendant Not Amenable to Process

The time during which defendant is "not amenable to the process of the court" is not included in computing the five-year period specified in CCP §583(b) for bringing the case to trial. CCP §583(f). The quoted language has the same meaning as identical language in CCP §581a(d). *Wills v Williams* (1975) 47

CA3d 941, 121 CR 420. For discussion, see §31.10. Thus, if defendant in a personal injury action dies and the complaint seeks damages in excess of his insurance coverage, the five-year period is tolled until a personal representative is appointed. See *Polony v White* (1974) 43 CA3d 44, 117 CR 341, discussed in §31.10.

Defendant is not unamenable to the court's process within the meaning of CCP §583(f) during the time that plaintiff is seeking an order for service on defendant as a foreign corporation. *Hughes & Ladd, Inc. v Rogue River Paving Co.* (1975) 46 CA3d 311, 119 CR 925.

When plaintiff in a wrongful death action joins an unwilling heir as nominal defendant under CCP §382, but is unable to effect service on him, the unwilling heir is not unamenable to the court's process under CCP §583(f) because the heir is considered a plaintiff who will share in any recovery, even though joined as a defendant. See *Sanders v Fuller* (1975) 45 CA3d 994, 119 CR 902, discussed further in §31.23.

An order permitting substituted service (see CCP §415.20) on a defendant who is concealing himself does not preclude the trial court from later concluding that the order was improper. In this situation, the period during which the court had previously determined that defendant was concealing himself is not excludable from the five-year period and does not prevent dismissal. *Maguire v Collier* (1975) 49 CA3d 309, 122 CR 510.

§31.23 (3) Time During Which Court's Jurisdiction Suspended

The time during which the court's jurisdiction to try the action is suspended is not included in computing the five-year period specified in CCP §583(b) for bringing the action to trial. CCP §583(f). This provision codifies as exceptions to the five-year rule certain situations that courts had formerly excused from compliance under the impossible, impracticable, or futile exceptions, discussed in §§31.24–31.28. See, *e.g.*, *Good v State* (1969) 273 CA2d 587, 78 CR 316 (moratorium statute suspending right to sue constituted an implied exception to the operation of CCP §583). Other such situations are, *e.g.*, the period during which defendant is in default (*Maguire v Collier* (1975) 49 CA3d 309, 122 CR 510) or during which an appeal is pending from judgment on the pleadings (*Kinard v Jordan* (1917) 175 C 13, 164 P 894).

The court's jurisdiction to try a wrongful death action is not suspended under CCP §583(b), even though all heirs have not been joined, because the heirs are not indispensable parties under CCP §389. See 1 California Civil Procedure Before Trial §7.12 (Cal CEB 1977) for discussion of indispensable parties. Plaintiff, in such an action, must join the missing heirs unless it is impossible or impracticable to do so, in which case plaintiff must endeavor to proceed to trial without them. *Sanders v Fuller* (1975) 45 CA3d 994, 119 CR 902. See §§31.24–31.28 for discussion of impossibility, impracticability, or futility.

The granting of a motion for change of venue under CCP §397(1) on grounds that the action was brought in the wrong court does not suspend the court's jurisdiction under CCP §583(f), even though the transferor court's jurisdiction to act in such cases is limited. *Moore v Powell* (1977) 70 CA3d 583, 138 CR 914. On the court's limited jurisdiction after granting a motion for change of venue, see 1 California Civil Procedure Before Trial §3.48 (Cal CEB 1977).

d. Implied Exceptions to Five-Year Requirement

§31.24 (1) Impossibility, Impracticability, or Futility

The five-year period of CCP §583(b) is tolled whenever it is impossible, impracticable, or futile to bring the action to trial. *Crown Coach Corp. v Superior Court* (1972) 8 C3d 540, 105 CR 339; see also *Brunzell Constr. Co. v Wagner* (1970) 2 C3d 545, 86 CR 297. This rule is stated in the disjunctive and not the conjunctive. Thus, *e.g.*, plaintiff may be excused from failure to bring the action to trial within five years when it was impracticable, although not impossible, to do so. See *Brunzell Constr. Co. v Superior Court, supra*.

Whether it is impossible, impracticable, or futile to proceed to trial is determined by the circumstances in each case, including the parties' acts and conduct and the nature of the proceedings. *Woley v Turkus* (1958) 51 C2d 402, 334 P2d 12. For examples, see §§31.25–31.26.

§31.25 (a) Examples: Exception Applicable

The impossibility, impracticability, or futility exception to the five-year period required by CCP §583(b) for bringing an action

§31.25   DISMISSAL   408

to trial applies, for example, when the delay has been caused by:

—Unavailability of a trial department after the action is continued by stipulation to a date beyond the five-year period (*Woley v Turkus* (1958) 51 C2d 402, 334 P2d 12);

—The time spent waiting in the master calendar department for assignment to a trial department, provided plaintiff has diligently secured a trial date before expiration of the five-year period (*Goers v Superior Court* (1976) 57 CA3d 72, 129 CR 29);

—(When the case has been timely set for trial) allowance of a challenge to the trial judge and no other judge is immediately available (*Nail v Osterholm* (1970) 13 CA3d 682, 91 CR 908);

—A related pending action on which the success of the present action depends (*Rose v Knapp* (1951) 38 C2d 114, 237 P2d 981 (quiet title action); see also *Bosworth v Superior Court* (1956) 143 CA2d 775, 300 P2d 155 (validity of will));

—(In a state court action) completion of a federal action arising out of the same event (*McRoberts v Gorham* (1971) 18 CA3d 1040, 96 CR 427);

—A pending appeal from an order changing venue (*Christin v Superior Court* (1937) 9 C2d 526, 71 P2d 205);

—A pending appeal in another case involving the same issues and the same defendant (*Stella v Great W. Sav. & Loan Ass'n* (1970) 13 CA3d 732, 91 CR 771; but see *Reserve Ins. Co. v Universal Underwriters Ins. Co.* (1975) 51 CA3d 57, 123 CR 763, holding that the trial court need not as a matter of law find it impracticable to proceed in this situation, and may in its discretion reject the impracticability argument when trial of the main action during an appeal does not result in unnecessary expense, evidentiary duplication, or legal complexity);

—Prosecution of an appeal by a coplaintiff (*Westphal v Westphal* (1943) 61 CA2d 544, 143 P2d 405);

—Consolidation of a personal injury action with a later accruing wrongful death action (*General Motors v Superior Court* (1966) 65 C2d 88, 52 CR 460);

—A necessary party codefendant being in the armed forces (*Pacific Greyhound Lines v Superior Court* (1946) 28 C2d 61, 168 P2d 665; see also *Sanders v Fuller* (1975) 45 CA3d 994, 119 CR 902); and

—The reference to a hearing officer of a controversy over water rights (*Pasadena v Alhambra* (1949) 33 C2d 908, 207 P2d 17).

§31.26 (b) Examples: Exception Inapplicable

The impossibility, impracticability, or futility exception to the five-year period required by CCP §583(b) for bringing an action to trial does not include, *e.g.*, delay caused by:

—Plaintiff's illness (*Singelyn v Superior Court* (1976) 62 CA3d 972, 133 CR 486);

—Ordinary pretrial proceedings, *e.g.*, demurrers and amendment of pleadings, time normally spent waiting for a place on the court's calendar, or securing a jury trial (*Wright v Groom Trucking Co.* (1962) 206 CA2d 485, 497, 24 CR 80, 89);

—Service of process on a foreign corporation by delivery of the summons and complaint to the secretary of state (*Hughes & Ladd, Inc. v Rogue River Paving Co.* (1975) 46 CA3d 311, 119 CR 925);

—Plaintiff's incarceration in jail, provided he is released in sufficient time to prepare for and bring case to trial within the five-year period and makes no attempt to obtain an early trial date (*Brown v Superior Court* (1976) 62 CA3d 197, 132 CR 916);

—The time between defendant's filing of a demand for security for costs under CCP §1030 and plaintiff's filing of the undertaking, even though the court's power to proceed to trial is stayed until the undertaking has been filed (*Hunot v Superior Court* (1976) 55 CA3d 660, 127 CR 703);

—Trial court inadvertence in setting the case for trial one day after expiration of the five-year period (*Singelyn v Superior Court, supra*);

—When the motion is foreseeable, the time between defendant's motion to change venue under CCP §397(1) on grounds that the action was brought in the wrong court and the date of transfer to the transferee court (*Moore v Powell* (1977) 70 CA3d 583, 589, 138 CR 914, 917); and

—(In a class action) the time between a tentative court order and a final order on the manner in which members of the class are to be notified of the action (*Standard Oil Co. v Superior Court* (1976) 61 CA3d 852, 132 CR 761).

§31.27 (c) Applicability of Exception to Multiple Defendants

Whether it is impossible, impracticable, or futile to bring a case to trial as to some defendants when the action is severable from other defendants as to whom it was not possible to bring the case to trial within five years depends on (1) the relationships between the causes of action; (2) the expense and difficulty likely to be engendered by separate trials, including the possibility of inconsistent judicial determinations; (3) plaintiff's diligence and good faith efforts; (4) the prejudice or hardship to the defendants; and (5) all other relevant matters. *Brunzell Constr. Co. v Wagner* (1970) 2 C3d 545, 86 CR 297. In *Brunzell*, plaintiff brought an action against several defendants on a construction contract. More than five years later, some defendants moved to dismiss the action as to themselves under CCP §583(b), on grounds that the causes of action stated against them were severable from those stated against the nonmoving defendants. Because of various pretrial proceedings, *e.g.*, an injunction and an order quashing service of summons, plaintiff was unable to proceed to trial against the nonmoving defendants within five years. The Supreme Court reversed the trial court's order granting the motion, and held that the fact of severability alone does not preclude application of the impossibility, impracticability, or futility doctrine. 2 C3d at 548, 86 CR at 298 (disapproving *Langan v McCorkle* (1969) 276 CA2d 805, 81 CR 535, and *Ross v George Pepperdine Foundation* (1959) 174 CA2d 135, 344 P2d 368).

§31.28 (d) Estoppel To Claim Exception

The implied exceptions to the requirements of CCP §583(b) when it is impossible, impracticable, or futile to proceed to trial are nonstatutory and therefore are guardedly made. *Sherberne & Assocs. v Vector Mfg. Co.* (1968) 263 CA2d 68, 69 CR 284. Thus, plaintiff may be estopped from claiming the exceptions if, following a period of impossibility, impracticability, or futility, plaintiff is guilty of "indolence or procrastination." *Youngblood v Terra* (1970) 10 CA3d 533, 537, 89 CR 13, 16 (decided under former CCP §583(b), now CCP §583(c)). See also *Sherberne & Assocs. v Vector Mfg. Co., supra* (plaintiff not entitled to subtract six months of impracticability in computing the five-year period, when two and one-half years remained after six months period elapsed); *O'Donnell v San Francisco* (1956) 147 CA2d 63, 304 P2d 852 (plaintiff failed to request that case be specially set for trial in seven months remaining after period of impracticability).

On plaintiff's duty to bring the case to trial, see §31.2.

§31.29 (2) Estoppel

It has been held that defense counsel's conduct does not estop defendant from seeking a dismissal under CCP §583(b) for plaintiff's failure to bring the case to trial within five years in the absence of a written stipulation. *Miller & Lux v Superior Court* (1923) 192 C 333, 219 P 1006. See also *Camille's Corp. v Superior Court* (1969) 270 CA2d 625, 628, 75 CR 868, 870. For discussion of a written stipulation as an exception, see §31.21.

However, this line of decisions was rejected in *Tresway Aero, Inc. v Superior Court* (1971) 5 C3d 431, 96 CR 571. In that case, a majority of the court held that defendant's conduct may estop him from seeking a dismissal under CCP §581a for plaintiff's failure to serve and return summons within three years after commencement of the action. See §31.14 for discussion of CCP §581a. The holding appears equally applicable to the five-year period of CCP §583(b), because the dissent argued that, as in the case of CCP §583(b), only a written stipulation can extend the three-year period under CCP §581a, and relied heavily on the *Miller & Lux* line of decisions.

Conduct that will estop defendant from seeking a dismissal under CCP §583(b) can be anything that lulls plaintiff into a false sense of security, *e.g.*, leading plaintiff to believe that compliance with the notice provisions of former CCP §410 and with certain other statutory provisions would not be required. *Tresway Aero, Inc. v Superior Court, supra*. However, failure of plaintiff's counsel to read and understand a stipulation waiving the two-year discretionary dismissal provisions of CCP §583(a) does not estop defendant from seeking a dismissal under CCP §583(b). *Martin v Cook* (1977) 68 CA3d 799, 137 CR 434.

§31.30 (3) No Issue of Fact To Be Tried

The five-year provision of CCP §583(b) does not apply when defendant has admitted all material allegations of the complaint in his answer because by so doing defendant has in effect agreed that trial is unnecessary. *Martin v Gibson* (1941) 48 CA2d 449, 119 P2d 1012. See also *Smithers v Ederer* (1956) 146 CA2d 227, 303 P2d 771.

The same is true when the case is submitted on an agreed statement of facts. *Ryerson v Riverside Cement Co.* (1968) 266

CA2d 789, 72 CR 595. The statute is satisfied when issues of law leading to final determination of the action have been submitted before the five-year period expires even though technically the action has not been brought to trial. *Berri v Superior Court* (1955) 43 C2d 856, 279 P2d 8.

§31.31 e. Dismissal of Class Action Before Five-Year Period Expires

Occasionally, a court on its own motion may dismiss an action on plaintiff's failure to comply with the five-year period prescribed by CCP §583(b) for bringing an action to trial, even though five years has not yet expired. For example, when, in a class action the court has not been asked to determine either the existence of a class or the form of notice to be given members of the class until less than two months before expiration of the five-year period, and dismissal under CCP §583(b) would be mandatory before completion of any reasonable notice period, the trial court on its own motion can dismiss the class aspect of the litigation. *Massey v Bank of America* (1976) 56 CA3d 29, 128 CR 144.

§31.32 4. Failure To Bring Action to Trial Within Three Years After New Trial Granted

When a motion for new trial has been made and granted, and no appeal has been taken, the action must be brought to trial within three years after entry of the order granting a new trial, unless the parties have filed a written stipulation extending time. Any such action not brought to trial within three years must be dismissed on noticed motion of defendants or on the court's own motion. CCP §583(c). However, dismissal is not required before expiration of the five-year period prescribed by CCP §583(b) for bringing actions to trial. CCP §583(c). This provision was apparently enacted to preclude the possibility that a plaintiff could be penalized for diligence in bringing the case to trial. Thus, whenever a trial court grants a new trial following entry of judgment, CCP §583(c) requires that plaintiff bring the action to trial within the longer of (a) three years from entry of the order granting the new trial, or (b) five years from the date of filing the original complaint. See *Review of Selected 1972 California Legislation*, 4 PAC LJ 315 (1973); 4 Witkin, CALIFORNIA PROCEDURE,

Proceedings Without Trial Supp §114 (2d ed 1971). See §§31.18–31.20 for discussion of the five-year limitation of CCP §583(b) for bringing the case to trial.

The phrase "if no appeal has been taken" in CCP §583(c) means an appeal by the party against whom a new trial has been granted. *McDonald Candy Co. v Lashus* (1962) 200 CA2d 63, 65, 19 CR 137, 139.

As in the case of CCP §583(b) (see §§31.22–31.33), the time during which (1) defendant is not amenable to the court's process, and (2) the court's jurisdiction to try the action is suspended, are not included in computing the three-year period of CCP §583(c). CCP §583(f). Also not included are periods during which it is impossible, impracticable, or futile to bring the action to trial. *Crown Coach Corp. v Superior Court* (1972) 8 C3d 540, 105 CR 339; *Good v State* (1969) 273 CA2d 587, 78 CR 316. For discussion, see §§31.24–31.28.

Although no decisions have considered the issue since the 1972 amendment to §583(c), the time from entry of judgment to entry of the order granting a new trial probably should be excluded in computing the three-year period, because it would be impossible for plaintiff to bring the action to trial during that period. Compare discussion in §31.13, to the effect that the period during which a default judgment is entered is excluded from computation of the five-year period under CCP §583(b).

§31.33   5. Failure To Bring Action to Trial Within Three Years After Reversal or After New Trial Order Affirmed

When a judgment is reversed on appeal and the case is remanded for new trial, or when an order granting a new trial is affirmed on appeal, the trial court must dismiss the action on defendant's motion or on its own motion, unless it is brought to trial within three years from the date on which the remittitur is filed by the court clerk. CCP §583(c). However, dismissal is not required before expiration of the five-year period prescribed by CCP §583(b) for bringing the action to trial. CCP §583(c).

A case is remanded for new trial whenever the appellate decision (a) expressly so provides, (b) is an unqualified reversal, or (c) simply directs the trial court to overrule a demurrer. See *McDonough Power Equip. Co. v Superior Court* (1972) 8 C3d 527, 532, 105 CR 330, 333; *Robertson v Superior Court* (1960)

180 CA2d 372, 375, 4 CR 297, 299. However, when a motion to dismiss under CCP §583(a) for want of prosecution (see §31.35) is granted, and the appellate reversal does not require a new trial but simply directs the trial court to exercise its discretion, the reversal is not a remand for new trial within the meaning of CCP §583(c). Therefore, plaintiff does not have another three years under CCP §583(c) to bring the action to trial, and the case must be dismissed under CCP §583(b) if not brought to trial within five years from the filing of the complaint. *Fannin Corp. v Superior Court* (1974) 36 CA3d 745, 111 CR 920.

A petition for writ of mandate is not an appeal but an original proceeding that may result in issuance of a peremptory writ of mandate, but not a remittitur. Therefore, CCP §583(c) is not applicable and does not require dismissal if the action is not brought to trial within three years of issuance of the writ. *Daum Dev. Corp. v Yuba Plaza, Inc.* (1970) 11 CA3d 65, 89 CR 458.

As in the case of CCP §583(b) (see §§31.22–31.23), the time during which (1) defendant is not amenable to the court's process, and (2) the court's jurisdiction to try the action is suspended are not included in computing the three-year period of CCP §583(c). CCP §583(f). Not included also are periods during which it is impossible, impracticable, or futile to bring the action to trial. *Crown Coach Corp. v Superior Court* (1972) 8 C3d 540, 105 CR 339; *Good v State* (1969) 273 CA2d 587, 78 CR 316. For discussion, see §§31.24–31.28.

Unlike the three-year requirement of CCP §583(c) for bringing the action to trial whenever a new trial has been granted (see §31.32), the three-year requirement for bringing an action to trial after judgment is reversed and the case remanded for new trial, or after a new trial order is affirmed, *cannot* be waived by the parties' written stipulation. See *Legg v United Benefit Life Ins. Co.* (1955) 136 CA2d 894, 896, 289 P2d 553, 555.

§31.34 6. Failure To Bring Action to Trial Within Three Years After Mistrial

When a mistrial is declared after trial has commenced or when a jury is unable to reach a decision, the action must again be brought to trial within three years after entry of the order declaring the mistrial or jury disagreement, unless the parties have filed a written stipulation extending time. Any such action not brought to trial within three years must be dismissed on noticed motion of defendant or on the court's own motion. CCP §583(d). It is immaterial whether the action has been commenced by complaint or by cross-complaint. CCP §583(e).

As in the case of other time limits prescribed by CCP §583, the time during which (a) defendant is not amenable to the court's process, or (b) the court's jurisdiction to try the action is suspended, is not included in computing the three-year period under CCP §583(d). CCP §583(f). See §§31.22–31.23. Nor is any period during which it is impossible, impracticable, or futile to bring the action to trial. *Crown Coach Corp. v Superior Court* (1972) 8 C3d 540, 105 CR 339. For discussion, see §§31.24–31.28.

§31.35 7. Failure To Bring Action to Trial Within Two Years

The court, in its discretion, may dismiss an action for want of prosecution if the action is not brought to trial within two years after it was filed. CCP §583(a).

The procedure for obtaining dismissal is governed by Judicial Council Rule. CCP §583(a). See §§31.56–31.58 on procedures.

The criteria established by Cal Rules of Ct 203.5(e) for the exercise of judicial discretion in ruling on a motion to dismiss under CCP §583(a) are well defined and sufficiently broad to enable plaintiff to argue the impossibility, impracticability, or futility of compliance. See §31.37.

When an action is otherwise subject to dismissal under CCP §583(a) a defendant who indicates his readiness to proceed to trial may be estopped from obtaining dismissal. See, *e.g., Los Angeles v Gleneagle Dev. Co.* (1976) 62 CA3d 543, 133 CR 212 (defendant estopped from relying on plaintiff's delay as basis for dismissal when, after delay, defendant filed an at-issue memorandum in response to plaintiff's at-issue memorandum).

The time during which (a) defendant was not amenable to the court's process, or (b) the court's jurisdiction to try the action is suspended, is not included in computing the two-year period. CCP §583(f). For discussion, see §§31.22–31.23.

a. Court's Discretion; Criteria
§31.36 (1) Effect of Judicial Decisions

Before adoption of Cal Rules of Ct 203.5 in 1970 (see §31.37) there were few criteria to assist in determining when the trial court was within its discretion in ordering dismissal under CCP §583(a). The judicially developed rule that plaintiff had the burden of making an adequate showing of excusable delay, and that a court abused its discretion in denying a motion to dismiss under CCP §583(a) when plaintiff failed to sustain that burden (see, *e.g.*, *Paul W. Speer, Inc. v Superior Court* (1969) 272 CA2d 32, 36, 77 CR 152, 154), was disapproved in *Denham v Superior Court* (1970) 2 C3d 557, 86 CR 65. In that case, plaintiff's law firm had undergone numerous personnel changes, including appointment of one attorney as a municipal court commissioner and another as a municipal court judge. The entire caseload of the firm thereafter fell on a 72-year-old partially disabled attorney, who had no familiarity with plaintiff's case and who erroneously believed that an at-issue memorandum had been filed. The Supreme Court held that the trial court did not abuse its discretion in denying a motion to dismiss under CCP §583(a), and that there is no requirement that the dismissal be granted unless opposed by an "adequate showing" of diligence or excuse for delay. 2 C3d at 563, 86 CR at 69. See also *Woolfson v Personal Travel Serv.* (1971) 3 C3d 909, 92 CR 286; *Applegate Drayage Co. v Municipal Court* (1972) 23 CA3d 628, 100 CR 400.

Although *Denham* excuses plaintiff from the burden of making an *adequate* showing of good cause for delay, it does not remove plaintiff's obligation to make *some* showing of good cause, on which the court may exercise its discretion. *Dunsmuir Masonic Temple v Superior Court* (1970) 12 CA3d 17, 90 CR 405. See also *Charles L. Donohoe, Inc. v Superior Court* (1927) 202 C 15, 258 P 1094, quoted with approval in *Denham v Superior Court* (1970) 2 C3d 557, 564, 86 CR 65, 69 (only when there is an entire absence of good cause can the trial court be compelled to dismiss). On the factors that the court will consider, see §31.37.

§31.37 (2) Effect of Cal Rules of Ct 203.5(e)

In 1970, the California Judicial Council adopted Cal Rules of Ct 203.5(e), which states that in exercising its discretion on a motion to dismiss under CCP §583(a), the trial court may consider all relevant matters, including:

(a) The court's file;

(b) The affidavits and supporting data submitted by the parties;

(c) When applicable, the availability of the moving party and other essential parties for service of process;

(d) The extent to which the parties engaged in any settlement negotiations or discussions;

(e) The parties' diligence in pursuing discovery or other pretrial proceedings, including any extraordinary relief sought;

(f) The nature and complexity of the case;

(g) The applicable case law, and the pendency of other litigation under common facts or determinative of the same legal or factual issues;

(h) The nature of any extensions of time or other delay attributable to either party;

(i) The condition of the court's calendar and the availability of an earlier trial date if the matter was ready for trial;

(j) Whether the interests of justice are best served by dismissal of trial or by imposing condition on dismissal or trial;

(k) Any other fact or circumstance relevant to a fair determination of the issue.

For discussion of plaintiff's duty to show good cause for the delay, see §31.36.

§31.38   b. Effect of Denial

Denial of a motion to dismiss under CCP §583(a) is not a determination that plaintiff's delay was justified as a matter of law, and does not bar future motions to dismiss, especially by persons who were not then parties to the action. The trial court has discretion to grant a second motion to dismiss, after denying an earlier motion. *Feingersh v Lutheran Hosp. Soc'y* (1977) 66 CA3d 406, 136 CR 155. However, when the second motion is made on an alleged different set of facts, the provisions of CCP §1008 must be complied with. For discussion, see §23.63.

§31.39   c. Appellate Review

When the court in its discretion has denied a motion to dismiss for lack of prosecution under CCP §583(a), denial may be reviewed on appeal from a final judgment (see, *e.g.*, *Rickless v Temple* (1970) 4 CA3d 869, 84 CR 828), or by petition for writ of mandate (see, *e.g.*, *Dunsmuir Masonic Temple v Superior Court* (1970) 12 CA3d 17, 90 CR 405). The party seeking review must show a "clear" or "manifest" abuse of discretion by the trial court. *Denham v Superior Court* (1970) 2 C3d 557, 564, 86 CR 65, 69; *Feingersh v Lutheran Hosp. Soc'y* (1977) 66 CA3d 406, 136 CR 155. If there is any basis on which the trial court's ruling can be sustained, the ruling will not be disturbed. *Denham v Superior Court, supra.*

§31.40 8. Failure To Appear for Trial

The court may order an action dismissed when either party fails to appear at trial and the other party appears and requests a dismissal. CCP §581(3). However, it is an abuse of discretion for the court to dismiss under CCP §581(3) when a party fails to appear in reliance on misinformation from either the court clerk (*Lynch v De Boom* (1915) 26 CA 311, 146 P 908) or the trial judge (*Schlothan v Rusalem* (1953) 41 C2d 414, 260 P2d 68) that the case would not be tried on a certain day.

The provisions of CCP §581(3) are subject to those of CCP §594(a), and the court should not dismiss unless the nonappearing party has been given 15 days' notice of trial, as required by that statute. *Estate of Dean* (1906) 149 C 487, 87 P 13 (decided under former CCP §594, which required five days' notice of trial).

Under CCP §581(3), a party seeking dismissal when the other party fails to appear at trial need only appear and request it; the formal procedures discussed in §§31.45–31.64 are inapplicable.

When a party fails to appear at trial after having been given notice as required by CCP §594, the appearing party may either request a dismissal under CCP §581(3) or proceed to trial and judgment in absence of the nonappearing party. CCP §594. See also §26.55; 4 Witkin, CALIFORNIA PROCEDURE, Proceedings Without Trial §118 (2d ed 1971).

The court also may dismiss an action without prejudice when, after 30 days' notice of time and place of trial has been given, no party appears for trial. CCP §581(6).

§31.41 9. Failure To Amend After Demurrer Sustained

The court may order an action dismissed when a demurrer to the complaint is sustained without leave to amend or when, after a demurrer has been sustained with leave to amend, plaintiff fails to amend within the time allowed, and either party moves for a dismissal. CCP §581(3). The reference in CCP §581(3) to "either party" moving for dismissal permits plaintiff to challenge the demurrer by moving to dismiss and then appealing the resulting judgment. See *California Ammonia Co. v Macco Corp.* (1969) 270 CA2d 429, 75 CR 753. See also 4 Witkin, CALIFORNIA PROCEDURE, Proceedings Without Trial §120 (2d ed 1971).

Although CCP §581(3) provides for a dismissal only when either party "moves" for one, a formal noticed motion is not required and an ex parte application is sufficient. See *Oppenheimer v Deutchman* (1955) 132 CA2d Supp 875, 281 P2d 650. But see Cal Rules of Ct Appendix, Div I, §15, adopted July 1, 1976, which discourages the granting of ex parte applications for orders. When a demurrer is sustained without leave to amend and the action dismissed, appeal lies from the order of dismissal and not from the order sustaining the demurrer. *Dollar-A-Day Rent-A-Car Sys. v Pacific Tel. & Tel. Co.* (1972) 26 CA3d 454, 102 CR 651. See generally §31.55.

10. Failure To Pay Transfer Fees and Costs

§31.42   a. Basic Rule

When an action is ordered transferred because it was not commenced in the proper court for trial, the action cannot be further prosecuted until the transfer costs and fees are paid. CCP §399. On what constitutes the proper court for trial, see CCP §§392–395.5. See generally 1 CALIFORNIA CIVIL PROCEDURE BEFORE TRIAL chap 3 (Cal CEB 1977). Unless transfer costs and fees are paid within 30 days after notice of the order is served, the court may on noticed motion dismiss the action without prejudice on condition that the same action may not be brought in another court before payment is made. However, plaintiff may be able to avoid dismissal even though payment is made after 30 days, provided the papers are forwarded to transferee court before defendant's motion to dismiss is filed. See *Moore v Superior Court* (1970) 13 CA3d 869, 92 CR 23, decided under former CCP §581b. On the proper court in which to seek dismissal, see §31.60. On procedures generally, see §§31.60–31.64.

An order transferring venue is reviewable by petition for writ of mandate in a superior court action (CCP §400), and by appeal in a municipal or justice court action (CCP §904.2). If review is sought, the time for payment is extended to within 30 days after notice of finality of the transfer. If proceedings are not stayed pending review, the time for payment is 60 days after service of notice of the order. CCP §399. For further discussion, see 1 CIV PROC BEFORE TRIAL §§3.67–3.70.

Former CCP §581b, which was repealed effective January 1, 1975, and replaced by CCP §399 as amended, provided that the court on its own motion or on motion of any party must dismiss the action when plaintiff failed to pay transfer fees and costs within one year after entry of the transfer order. See, *e.g.*, *Bechtel Corp. v Superior Court* (1973) 33 CA3d 405, 109 CR 138. Under CCP §399, the court "may" dismiss, but only on motion of a party.

§31.43   b. Estoppel To Seek Dismissal

Under former CCP §581b, certain conduct on defendant's part estopped him from seeking dismissal for failure to pay transfer fees and costs, and presumably this rule applies equally to motions made under CCP §399. See, *e.g.*, *Marshall v Benedict* (1958) 161 CA2d 284, 326 P2d 516 (defendant's filing discovery papers with clerk of transferor court after order granting change of venue presented fact question for trial court on existence of estoppel). See also *Davis v Superior Court* (1921) 184 C 691, 195 P 390 (dicta). However, defendant's failure to state in his notice of the court's ruling that plaintiff was required to pay transfer costs did not estop him from seeking dismissal under former CCP §581b. *Grime v Superior Court* (1974) 39 CA3d 46, 113 CR 850.

§31.44   C. Court's Inherent Power To Dismiss

Independent of the court's discretion to dismiss under CCP §583(a) (see §§31.35–31.39), the trial court has inherent power to dismiss an action on defendant's motion when it has not been diligently prosecuted. See *Steen v Los Angeles* (1948) 31 C2d 542, 546, 190 P2d 937, 940; *Feingersh v Lutheran Hosp. Soc'y* (1977) 66 CA3d 406, 136 CR 155. However, the court has no inherent power to dismiss for lack of prosecution when less than two years have elapsed from the date the action was commenced. The fact that under CCP §583(a) a court may dismiss an action for lack of prosecution only after two years have elapsed indicates a legislative determination that in all cases a two-year delay is unavoidable. *General Motors Corp. v Superior Court* (1966) 65 C2d 88, 98, 52 CR 460, 467. See also *McKenzie v Albaeck* (1963) 219

CA2d 97, 32 CR 762; *Rouse v Palmer* (1961) 197 CA2d 666, 17 CR 509.

Although a court does not have inherent power to dismiss an action for lack of diligent prosecution when the time for discretionary dismissal under CCP §583(a) has not elapsed, the court can dismiss even though a time period for mandatory dismissal has not elapsed. See, *e.g.*, *Rice v Arden Farms Co.* (1962) 199 CA2d 349, 18 CR 863. For discussion of procedures, see §31.59.

§31.45   D. Procedures

The discussion in §§31.46–31.55 pertains to procedures for mandatory dismissal under CCP §§581a, 583(b)–(d). Procedures for discretionary dismissal under CCP §583(a) or under the court's inherent power to dismiss for failure to bring an action to trial within two years from filing are discussed in §§31.56–31.58 (CCP §583(a)), 31.59 (inherent). Procedures for dismissal under CCP §399 for failure to pay transfer fees and costs on an order changing venue are discussed in §§31.60–31.64.

1. Dismissal Under CCP §§581a, 583(a)-(d)
a. Motion for Dismissal
§31.46   (1) Need for Noticed Motion and Declaration

A motion to dismiss an action for lack of prosecution should be made in the normal manner applicable to pretrial motions, *i.e.*, by filing and service of a noticed motion, memorandum of points and authorities, and an affidavit (or declaration under penalty of perjury; see CCP §2015.5) in support of the motion.

The California Supreme Court has said that ex parte orders for dismissal under CCP §581a should not be granted "in any but the plainest and most certain of cases" (*Consolidated Constr. Co. v Pacific Elec. Ry.* (1920) 184 C 244, 246, 193 P 238), and Cal Rules of Ct Appendix, Div I, §15 states a general policy against giving ex parte orders. Moreover, CCP §583(b)–(d) provide for dismissal on defendant's motion after due notice to plaintiff, or by the court on its own motion. See *Donner v Superior Court* (1927) 82 CA 165, 169, 255 P 272, 274. For a form for notice of motion, see §31.49. On motion practice generally, see chap 23.

Motions made on a mandatory ground for dismissal (*e.g.*, for failure under CCP §581a to have summons served and returned within three years) need not be accompanied by a declaration because the grounds for dismissal are established by the court file. See, *e.g.*, *Simonini v Jay Dee Leather Prods. Co.* (1948) 85 CA2d 265, 267, 193 P2d 53, 54 (declaration unnecessary when notice said motion would be based on "all the records, files and proceedings . . . and the provisions of section 583 of the Code of Civil Procedure"). However, the better practice is to serve and file a declaration so that the judge need not make a separate examination of the court file.

§31.47 (2) Content

As with all noticed motions, a motion to dismiss for lack of prosecution must state the grounds on which it is based. CCP §1010. Some courts will consider only the grounds stated in the notice of motion (see, *e.g.*, *Maguire v Collier* (1975) 49 CA3d 309, 122 CR 510; *Westphal v Westphal* (1943) 61 CA2d 544, 143 P2d 405), while others will consider grounds not so stated if shown in supporting declarations, points and authorities and referred to in the notice or other papers in the court file (see, *e.g.*, *Tarman v Sherwin* (1961) 189 CA2d 49, 10 CR 787). For discussion, see §23.23. The better practice is to specify all grounds in the notice so that the judge need not search through accompanying papers to confirm or deny the existence of other grounds. See form in §31.49.

The declaration should state facts showing why dismissal is required, and should also demonstrate the nonexistence of any statutory exceptions or periods during which the statute would be tolled. See form in §31.50.

§31.48 (3) Who May Make Motion

A joint defendant may move for dismissal of the action with respect to him, and each joint defendant is entitled to separate consideration of his motion. *Larkin v Superior Court* (1916) 171 C 719, 154 P 841; *Contract Eng'rs, Inc. v Welborn* (1968) 258 CA2d 553, 65 CR 903.

Moreover, the general appearance of other defendants does not deprive a defendant of the right to dismiss under CCP §581a. *Watson v Superior Court* (1972) 24 CA3d 53, 57, 100 CR 684, 687.

§31.49 (4) Form: Notice of Motion To Dismiss Action For Failure To Prosecute

Copies: Original (filed with court clerk with proof of service); copies for service (one for each attorney of record and unrepresented party); office copies.

[Caption. See §§23.18– 23.19]

No. _____

NOTICE OF MOTION TO DISMISS ACTION UNDER ____[E.G., CCP §581a / CCP §583]____ **FOR FAILURE TO PROSECUTE; POINTS AND AUTHORITIES; DECLARATION**

To each party and attorney of record:
 PLEASE TAKE NOTICE that on _____, 19____, at or after _____.m., in ____[e.g., Department No. ____]____ at ____[address]____, California, defendant ____[name]____ will move the Court for an order dismissing the above-entitled action.
 This motion will be made on the grounds that plaintiff has failed to _____[e.g., serve and return the summons on the complaint within three years after commencement of this action, as required by CCP §581a(a) / bring this action to trial within five years after the action was commenced, as required by CCP §583(b)]____.
 This motion will be based on all pleadings, papers, and records filed in this action, and on the attached memorandum of points and authorities and supporting declaration of ____[name]____ ____[and on such evidence as may be presented at the hearing]____.

Dated: _____

[Signature of attorney]

[Typed name]
Attorney for ____[name]____

Comment: A memorandum of points and authorities must accompany the notice of motion. See §§23.23–23.35. This form is designed for use when dismissal for failure to prosecute is mandatory under CCP §581a or CCP §583(b)–(d), or is discretionary under CCP §583(a). See chart in §31.3 for situations in which these statutes apply. The form may also be adapted for use when the motion is based on the court's inherent power to dismiss for plaintiff's failure to prosecute the action with reasonable diligence. See §31.57 for discussion.

§31.50   DISMISSAL

§31.50   (5) Form: Declaration in Support of Motion To Dismiss Action for Failure To Prosecute

Copies: Original (filed with court clerk with proof of service); copies for service (one for each attorney of record and unrepresented party); office copies.

[Caption. See §§23.18–23.19]

No. _____

DECLARATION OF ____[NAME]____ IN SUPPORT OF MOTION TO DISMISS ACTION FOR FAILURE TO PROSECUTE

____[Name]____ declares:

1. I am the ____[defendant / attorney for defendant]____ in this action.
2. This action was filed by plaintiff on _____, 19____.

[When motion based on statutory time period]

3. ____[State facts on which motion for dismissal is based, e.g.: Summons on the complaint has not been served and returned within three years from the date of filing / This action has not been brought to trial within five years from the date of filing]____.

[When motion based on failure to use reasonable diligence]

3. **Plaintiff has not prosecuted this action with reasonable diligence in that** ____[state facts showing lack of reasonable diligence, e.g., plaintiff has conducted no discovery and has made no effort to bring the action to trial since the action was filed over two years ago]____.

[When appropriate, add]

4. **The parties stipulated in writing that the time to** ____[e.g., serve and return the summons on the complaint / bring the action to trial]____ **may be extended to** _____, 19____, **but that stipulation has expired and there is no stipulation now in effect.**

[When appropriate, add]

____[Defendant was not amenable to the process of the Court / The jurisdiction of the Court to try this action was suspended]____ from _____, 19____, to _____, 19____, **because** ____[state reasons]____.

[Continue]

I declare under penalty of perjury that the foregoing is true and correct, and was executed on _____, 19____, at _____, California.

[Signature of declarant]

[Typed name]

Comment: The declaration should state any period during which a stipulation extending time was in effect, and any periods during which the statutory time was tolled, *e.g.*, because defendant was unamenable to service of process, the reasons for the tolling, and when the tolling period ended. See chart in §31.3 on when the dismissal statutes are tolled.

§31.51 (6) Opposing Papers

On a motion to dismiss for failure to prosecute an action, plaintiff ordinarily will file counterdeclarations stating facts showing why the motion should be denied. For example, when it has been impossible, impracticable, or futile to comply with the statutory time limit (see §§31.13, 31.24–31.28), plaintiff should so specify. Facts showing that defendant should be estopped from moving for dismissal (see §31.29) should be stated. On a motion based on the court's inherent power to dismiss for lack of diligence (see §31.44), plaintiff's declaration should state facts showing that the action has been prosecuted with due diligence.

§31.52 (7) Who May Hear Motion

A motion for dismissal ordinarily is heard by the court in which the action is pending. However, in counties having at least 900,000 inhabitants a superior court commissioner who has been ordered by the court to hear and determine uncontested matters may hear an uncontested motion for dismissal. CCP §259a(6). See also *Sarracino v Superior Court* (1974) 13 C3d 1, 118 CR 21; *Rooney v Vermont Inv.* (1973) 10 C3d 351, 110 CR 353; *People v Surety Ins. Co.* (1975) 48 CA3d 123, 121 CR 438. Los Angeles County follows the practice of authorizing a commissioner to hear contested matters, provided the parties so stipulate.

§31.53 b. Defendant's Remedies When Dismissal Denied

When the court denies a motion to dismiss, defendant may (a) renew the motion, (b) seek appellate review by petition for writ of mandamus or prohibition, or (c) proceed with the action and appeal from a final judgment. However, defendant cannot appeal from an order denying a motion to dismiss (CCP §§904.1–904.2), and appeal from a final judgment is neither speedy nor adequate (*Rio Del Mar Country Club v Superior Court* (1948) 84 CA2d 214, 190 P2d 295).

§31.54 DISMISSAL

Although there is no statutory authority for a motion to reconsider an order granting or denying dismissal, a trial court has the power, on a subsequent motion, to reconsider its decision denying the motion. The subsequent motion is considered as a renewal of the previous motion. *San Francisco Lathing, Inc. v Superior Court* (1969) 271 CA2d 78, 80, 76 CR 304, 306. Counsel who has had a motion to dismiss denied may find it worthwhile first to renew the motion before seeking appellate relief, particularly when new matters or additional grounds can be shown. See CCP §1008. For further discussion, see §23.63.

An order denying dismissal when the motion was made under the mandatory provisions of CCP §581a or CCP §§583(b)–(d) may be reviewed by extraordinary writ. See *Bernstein v Superior Court* (1969) 2 CA3d 700, 701, 82 CR 775, 775 (CCP §581a); *Turnbull v Superior Court* (1932) 126 CA 141, 142, 14 P2d 540, 541 (CCP §583(b)); *McDonough Power Equip. Co. v Superior Court* (1972) 8 C3d 527, 105 CR 330 (CCP §583(c), formerly CCP §583(b)). Mandamus may issue to compel dismissal and prohibition may issue to restrain the trial. See *McDonough Power Equip. Co. v Superior Court, supra; Coates Capitol Corp. v Superior Court* (1967) 251 CA2d 125, 59 CR 231. When the motion is based on a mandatory ground, defendant may seek review by writ even though he has filed an answer after the motion has been denied. *Watson v Superior Court* (1972) 24 CA3d 53, 100 CR 684 (motion under CCP §581a).

§31.54   c. Form: Order of Dismissal

Copies: Original (filed with court clerk with proof of service); copies for service (one for each attorney of record and unrepresented party); office copies.

[Caption. See §§23.18–23.19]

No. _____

ORDER OF DISMISSAL

The motion of defendant ____[name]____ for an order of dismissal came on regularly for hearing on _____, 19____. Appearing as attorneys were _____.

Satisfactory proof having been made, and good cause appearing,
IT IS ORDERED that this action is dismissed.

Dated: _____

_____
Judge

Comment: All dismissals ordered by the court must be in the form of a written order, signed by the court and filed in the action. CCP §581d. When filed, such orders constitute judgments and are effective for all purposes (CCP §581d), including appeal (see CCP §§904.1–904.2).

§31.55   d. Plaintiff's Remedies When Dismissal Granted

If the trial court grants defendant's motion to dismiss, plaintiff may, when the facts warrant, move to vacate the order of dismissal under CCP §473, on grounds of "mistake, inadvertence, surprise, or excusable neglect." See generally, §§30.56–30.58. If the motion is denied, the order refusing to vacate the dismissal is independently appealable, together with the original order of dismissal. *Farrar v McCormick* (1972) 25 CA3d 701, 102 CR 190. See also *Daley v Butte* (1964) 227 CA2d 380, 388, 38 CR 693, 698.

Plaintiff also may obtain a writ of mandamus from a reviewing court, directing the trial court to vacate its order of dismissal and reset the action for trial. See *Brown v Superior Court* (1970) 7 CA3d 366, 86 CR 670; *Derry v Superior Court* (1968) 266 CA2d 556, 72 CR 313.

Unlike a defendant whose motion to dismiss has been denied (see §31.53), plaintiff may not ask the trial court to reconsider an order of dismissal (*Farrar v McCormick, supra*), unless the motion to reconsider can be treated as a motion for relief under CCP §473 (*San Francisco Lathing, Inc. v Superior Court* (1969) 271 CA2d 78, 76 CR 304). Plaintiff's remedy in this situation is to appeal. An order of dismissal is equivalent to a final judgment and may be directly appealed. CCP §904.1(a). See also *Daley v Butte* (1964) 227 CA2d 380, 38 CR 693. However, the minute entry granting defendant's motion to dismiss is not appealable; to be appealable, the dismissal must be in the form of a written order, signed by the court and filed in the action. CCP §581d.

2. Dismissal Under CCP §583(a)
§31.56   a. Time for Motion

Dismissal under CCP §583(a) for failure to bring the action to trial within two years after it was filed may be ordered after a motion by a party or on the court's own motion. *Andre v General Dynamics, Inc.* (1974) 43 CA3d 839, 118 CR 95. See also

Maguire v Collier (1975) 49 CA3d 309, 122 CR 510. When made on motion of a party, the procedures are governed by Cal Rules of Ct 203.5. CCP §583(a). Thus, the notice of motion must be served and filed at least 45 days before the date set for hearing (Cal Rules of Ct 203.5(a)), rather than the ten days required by CCP §1005 for motions generally. However, counsel may, notwithstanding Cal Rules of Ct 203.5, request an order shortening time under CCP §1005. *Farrar v McCormick* (1972) 25 CA3d 701, 705, 102 CR 190, 193. Objections that the motion is untimely are waived if plaintiff opposes the motion without questioning its timeliness. *Tate v Superior Court* (1975) 45 CA3d 925, 119 CR 835; *Farrar v McCormick, supra.*

§31.57   b. Moving and Opposing Papers

The party seeking dismissal under CCP §583(a) may, together with his memorandum of points and authorities, serve and file a supporting affidavit or declaration with the notice of motion. Filing the notice of motion does not preclude the opposing party from further efforts to bring the case to trial. Cal Rules of Ct 203.5(a). For a form for notice and supporting declaration that may be adapted, see §§31.49–31.50.

Within 15 days after service, the opposing party may serve and file written opposition to the motion, together with points and authorities and a supporting declaration or affidavit. Failure to serve and file written opposition may be construed by the court as an admission that the motion is meritorious, and the court may grant the motion without a hearing on the merits. Cal Rules of Ct 203.5(b).

Within 15 days after service of written opposition, the moving party may serve and file a response. Cal Rules of Ct 203.5(c). Within five days after service of any response, the opposing party may serve and file a reply. Cal Rules of Ct 203.5(d).

For discussion of factors the court considers in ruling on the motion, see §31.57. On the court's power to impose conditions on the granting or denial of relief, see §31.58.

§31.58   c. Ruling on Motion; Conditional Denial

In exercising its discretion on a motion to dismiss under CCP §583(a), the court may grant or deny the motion or, when the facts warrant, may defer its ruling pending performance by either party of any conditions imposed by the court to effectuate substantial justice. Cal Rules of Ct 203.5(f). This rule provides the trial court with sanctions against a dilatory litigant, short of dismissal. For example, when the damage caused by delay is compensable in money, the court can require the offending party to make redress before ordering dismissal. Thus, rule 203.5(f) not only serves to deter and to remedy unreasonable delay, but also to uphold the judicial policy in favor of disposition of litigation on the merits (see §31.2). *Hansen v Snap-Tite, Inc.* (1972) 23 CA3d 208, 100 CR 51.

In *Hansen*, plaintiffs' complaint claimed that defendants were indebted to them in the amount of $1,075,000. More than three years after the action was filed, one of plaintiffs' attorneys advised defense counsel to discontinue trial preparations because plaintiffs were losing their zeal for prosecuting the case. Settlement negotiations were begun and culminated in an oral agreement to settle the action on payment to plaintiffs of $10,000. Thereafter, plaintiffs' attorney advised defense counsel that plaintiffs would not accept the settlement, and wished to proceed to trial. Defense counsel then moved to dismiss under CCP §583(a), asserting in declarations that they had engaged in intensive preparations for trial, which had been billed to and paid by defendants. Due to settlement negotiations, the work was left uncompleted, was largely unusable, and would have to be almost entirely redone. The trial court granted the motion to dismiss unless plaintiffs reimbursed defendants $10,000 for attorneys' fees incurred in trial preparation. Plaintiffs did not pay the $10,000, the trial court dismissed the action, and the appellate court affirmed, holding that the court's imposition of conditions constituted a proper exercise of its discretion under Cal Rules of Ct 203.5(f).

§31.59 3. Dismissal Under Court's Inherent Power

As in the case of a motion under CCP §583(a) (see §31.57), a motion to dismiss under the court's inherent power should always be made by noticed motion. *Poole v Caulfield* (1872) 45 C 107; *Derry v Superior Court* (1968) 266 CA2d 556, 72 CR 313. The motion should be made under the rules of ordinary motion practice (see generally chap 23); the procedures set forth in Cal Rules of Ct 203.5 apply only to motions made under CCP §583(a), and not to motions directed to the court's inherent power. *Blue Chip Enterprises, Inc. v Brentwood Sav. & Loan*

Ass'n (1977) 71 CA3d 706, 139 CR 651. However, the factors set forth in Cal Rules of Ct 203.5(e) for the court to consider on a CCP §583(a) motion are equally applicable to a motion directed to the court's inherent power. 71 CA3d at 712, 139 CR at 654. For discussion, see §31.37.

4. Dismissal Under CCP §399
§31.60   a. Proper Court in Which To Seek Dismissal

When a change of venue has been ordered because the action was brought in the wrong court, and the moving party fails to pay transfer fees and costs within 30 days, CCP §399 says only that "the court" may dismiss the action. Former CCP §581b provided for dismissal "by the court in which the action or proceeding was originally commenced." See also *Moore v Superior Court* (1970) 13 CA3d 869, 92 CR 23 (transferee court had no jurisdiction to entertain motion for dismissal under former CCP §581b).

Under CCP §399, it is clear that a motion to dismiss for failure to pay transfer fees and costs may be made in the transferor court; it is unclear whether such motion may be made also in the transferee court. Although the broader language in CCP §399 arguably indicates a legislative intent to permit the motion in either court, the safer course is to bring the motion in the transferor court.

§31.61   b. Form: Notice of Motion To Dismiss Action for Failure To Pay Transfer Fees and Costs

Copies: Original (filed with court clerk with proof of service); copies for service (one for each attorney of record and unrepresented party); office copies.

[*Caption. See §§23.18– 23.19*]

No. _____

NOTICE OF MOTION TO DISMISS ACTION FOR FAILURE TO PAY TRANSFER FEES AND COSTS (CCP §399); POINTS AND AUTHORITIES; DECLARATION

To each party and attorney of record:
  PLEASE TAKE NOTICE that on _____, 19____, **at or after** ____ __.m., **in** ____[*e.g., Department* ____]____ **at** ____[*address*]____, **California, defendant**

____[name]____ will move the Court for an order dismissing the above action.

This motion will be made under Code of Civil Procedure section 399 on the grounds that an order transferring the place of trial of this action has been made on the ground that the Court in which the action was commenced is not the proper Court for trial,

[When appropriate, add]

and upheld on ____[appeal / petition for writ of mandate]____,

[Continue]

and that plaintiff has failed to pay the transfer fees and costs within

[When no review of order has been sought]

30 days after service of notice of such order.

[When review has been sought and proceedings stayed]

30 days after notice of finality of the order.

[When review has been sought and proceedings not stayed]

60 days after service of notice of the order.

[Continue]

This motion will be based on all pleadings, papers and records filed in this action and on the attached memorandum of points and authorities and supporting declaration of ____[name]____ ____[and on such evidence as may be presented at the hearing]____.

Dated: _____

_____
[Signature of attorney]

[Typed name]
Attorney for ____[name]____

Comment: A memorandum of points and authorities must accompany the notice of motion. See §§23.23–23.35. The time for payment of transfer fees and costs on an order changing venue under CCP §399 depends on whether review of the order was sought and on whether proceedings were stayed pending review. See §31.42.

§31.62   c. Form: Declaration in Support of Motion To Dismiss

Copies: Original (filed with court clerk with proof of service); copies for service (one for each attorney of record and unrepresented party); office copies.

§31.63   DISMISSAL

[Caption. See §§23.18–23.19]

No. _____

DECLARATION OF ____[NAME]____ IN SUPPORT OF MOTION TO DISMISS ACTION FOR FAILURE TO PAY TRANSFER FEES AND COSTS

____[Name]____ declares:

1. I am the ____[defendant / attorney for defendant]____ in this action.

2. On _____, 19____, this Court ordered the above action transferred to the ____[superior / municipal]____ Court of _____ County, on the ground that the Court in which the action was commenced is not the proper Court to trial. Notice of the order of transfer was served on _____, 19____.

[When no review of order has been sought]

3. Plaintiff has failed to pay transfer fees and costs within 30 days after service of the notice of order of transfer.

[When review has been sought and proceedings stayed]

3. Plaintiff filed ____[an appeal of the above order / a petition for writ of mandate to review the above order]____ on _____, 19____, and this Court stayed further proceedings on _____, 19____, pending appellate review. The ____[appeal / petition]____ was heard on _____, 19____, and on _____, 19____, the appellate Court ____[affirmed this Court's order / denied the petition]_____. The Court's order of transfer became final on _____, 19____, and plaintiff has failed to pay transfer costs and fees within 30 days after that date.

[When review has been sought and proceedings not stayed]

3. Plaintiff filed ____[an appeal of the above order / a petition for writ of mandate to review the above order]____ on _____, 19____, and on _____, 19____, this Court declined to stay further proceedings pending appellate review. Plaintiff has failed to pay transfer fees and costs within 60 days after service of notice of this Court's order of transfer.

[Continue]

I declare under penalty of perjury that the foregoing is true and correct, and was executed on _____, 19____, at _____, California.

[Signature of declarant]

[Typed name]

§31.63   d. Effect of Stipulation To Transfer on Motion for Dismissal

When a motion to transfer is made under CCP §399 on wrong court grounds, and the parties stipulate to a transfer before the court has ruled on the motion, it is unclear whether CCP §399 permits a party to move for dismissal for failure to pay transfer fees and costs within the time allowed. In *La Mirada Community Hosp. v Superior Court* (1967) 249 CA2d 39, 57 CR 42, the court held that a motion to dismiss was not permissible under former CCP §581b because the order for transfer was based on the stipulation, and not on a finding that the action was in fact brought in the wrong court. Moreover, the moving papers filed in support of defendants' motion did not set forth facts sufficient to permit the motion to be granted. 249 CA2d at 43, 57 CR at 44.

However, in *Bechtel Corp. v Superior Court* (1973) 33 CA3d 405, 109 CR 138, also decided under former CCP §581b, the court refused to follow *La Mirada*, and directed the trial court to dismiss the action for plaintiffs' failure to pay transfer fees and costs. The court concluded that, according to the record, the stipulation on which the order for transfer was made showed clearly that the action had been brought in the wrong court. 33 CA3d at 410, 109 CR at 141. Moreover, unlike the transfer order in *La Mirada*, the order in *Bechtel* required plaintiff to pay transfer fees and costs as a condition of transfer. 33 CA3d at 410 n4, 109 CR at 141 n4.

Although the decisions in *Bechtel* and *La Mirada* are somewhat conflicting, it is clear from both of them that a motion to dismiss under CCP §399 for failure to pay transfer fees and costs is not permitted when the parties stipulate to a transfer and nothing in the stipulation or the record suggests a reason for the transfer. In that situation, it cannot be said that the transfer was ordered because the action was brought in the wrong court. On the other hand, when the stipulation expressly states that the action was brought in the wrong court, a motion for dismissal for failure to pay transfer fees and costs under CCP §399 is permissible.

§31.64   e. Order of Dismissal

All dismissals ordered by the court must be in the form of a written order, signed by the court and filed in the action (or, in justice court, in the docket). CCP §581d. When filed, such orders constitute judgments and are effective for all purposes (CCP §581d), including appeal (CCP §904.1–2). For a form for order of dismissal that may be adapted, see §31.54.

II. VOLUNTARY DISMISSAL

A. Introduction

§31.65   1. Statutory Basis; Actions to Which Applicable

The basic code section governing voluntary dismissals is CCP §581, which provides for dismissal by plaintiff, by either party, or by the court in particular situations. See §§31.71–31.82. Dismissals under CCP §581 may be with or without prejudice. See §31.66.

Code of Civil Procedure §581 is applicable to all civil actions or special proceedings, including action seeking injunctive relief (*Simpson v Superior Court* (1945) 68 CA2d 821, 158 P2d 46), actions in interpleader (*Kaufman v Superior Court* (1896) 115 C 152, 155, 46 P 904), intervention proceedings (*Egly v Superior Court* (1970) 6 CA3d 476, 86 CR 18), and eminent domain proceedings (*Whittier Union High School Dist. v Beck* (1941) 45 CA2d 736, 114 P2d 731). Although CCP §581 is applicable to probate proceedings, including will contests (*Voyce v Superior Court* (1942) 20 C2d 479, 127 P2d 536; *Estate of Somers* (1947) 82 CA2d 757, 187 P2d 433), plaintiff may lose his right to dismiss the action when he is not the sole party in interest. See discussion in §31.73.

§31.66   2. Distinction Between Dismissal with Prejudice and Dismissal Without Prejudice

Voluntary dismissals are either with prejudice or without prejudice. A dismissal with prejudice terminates the action, operating as a final judgment on the merits, and barring a later action on the same cause. *Gagnon Co. v Nevada Desert Inn* (1955) 45 C2d 448, 455, 289 P2d 466, 472. See also *Kronkright v Gardner* (1973) 31 CA3d 214, 107 CR 270 (dismissal with prejudice operates as retraxit, barring later action). A dismissal without prejudice does not bar a later action on the same cause, provided the statute of limitations has not run. *Gagnon Co., Inc. v Nevada Desert Inn, supra; Kinley v Alexander* (1955) 137 CA2d 382, 290 P2d 287.

A dismissal ordinarily is considered to be without prejudice unless the dismissal provides that it is with prejudice. *Lewis v Johnson* (1939) 12 C2d 558, 563, 86 P2d 99, 102.

For further discussion of the effect of dismissals with and without prejudice, see §§31.67–31.70.

B. Effect of Dismissal

1. Without Prejudice

§31.67 a. New Action Not Barred

Dismissal without prejudice normally is not res judicata and does not bar plaintiff from bringing a new action, provided the statute of limitations has not run. *Crosswhite v American Ins. Co.* (1964) 61 C2d 300, 38 CR 412; *Neil G. v Superior Court* (1973) 30 CA3d 572, 106 CR 505; *Estate of Katz* (1942) 49 CA2d 82, 120 P2d 896. It is immaterial whether the dismissal is given in return for consideration. *Lewis v Johnson* (1939) 12 C2d 558, 86 P2d 99; *Burke v W. R. Chamberlin & Co.* (1942) 51 CA2d 419, 125 P2d 120.

Even though a dismissal without prejudice normally does not bar a subsequent action, it is a termination in favor of defendant, and will support an action by defendant for malicious prosecution. *Hurgren v Union Mut. Life Ins. Co.* (1904) 141 C 585, 75 P 168; *MacDonald v Joslyn* (1969) 275 CA2d 282, 79 CR 707.

§31.68 b. Court Divested of Jurisdiction

A dismissal without prejudice divests the trial court of jurisdiction to act further (*Parenti v Lifeline Blood Bank* (1975) 49 CA3d 331, 335, 122 CR 709, 711) except to award costs and statutory attorneys' fees (*Associated Convalescent Enterprises v Carl Marks & Co.* (1973) 33 CA3d 116, 108 CR 782; *MacLeod v Tribune Publishing Co.* (1958) 157 CA2d 665, 321 P2d 881). See §31.69 for discussion of costs and fees. In the absence of an exception to plaintiff's right to dismiss (see §§31.72–31.74), the court cannot vacate a voluntary dismissal. See, *e.g., Eddings v White* (1964) 229 CA2d 579, 40 CR 453 (court had no jurisdiction to vacate dismissal and then dismiss action under CCP §583); *Home Real Estate Co. v Winnants* (1919) 39 CA 643, 179 P 534 (court had no jurisdiction to vacate dismissal filed to obtain judgment for defendant after demurrer sustained with leave to amend).

When a voluntary dismissal has been filed, the court can neither permit the filing of a complaint in intervention (*Roski v Superior Court* (1971) 17 CA3d 841, 95 CR 312) nor the bringing in of fictitious defendants (*McIntire v Superior Court* (1975) 52 CA3d 717, 125 CR 379). In *McIntire,* plaintiffs stipulated to the dismissal of all fictitious defendants, brought the named defendants to trial, and settled with those defendants with court approval. The court held that the trial court exceeded its jurisdiction in allowing plaintiffs to amend their complaint and serve two new defendants as fictitious defendants after the time for appeal had expired. 52 CA3d at 720, 125 CR at 381.

After dismissal, defendant is a stranger to the action and can neither appeal from the dismissal (*Cook v Stewart McKee & Co.* (1945) 68 CA2d 758, 157 P2d 868), nor move to have it vacated (*Gherman v Colburn* (1971) 18 CA3d 1046, 96 CR 424).

§31.69   c. Defendant's Right to Costs and Attorneys' Fees

When an action has been dismissed without prejudice, defendant is considered the prevailing party within the meaning of CCP §§1031–1032 and therefore is entitled to costs under those statutes. See *Schubert v Bates* (1947) 30 C2d 785, 789, 185 P2d 793, 796; *Spinks v Superior Court* (1915) 26 CA 793, 148 P 798. Under CCP §1033, defendant has ten days after entry of judgment to file a cost bill. The time for filing the cost bill begins to run from the date of entry of judgment under CCP §581d, and not from the date of entry of dismissal in the clerk's register. *MacLeod v Tribune Publishing Co.* (1958) 157 CA2d 665, 321 P2d 881.

Civil Code §1717 transforms a unilateral contractual right to attorneys' fees into a reciprocal provision giving the right to recover fees to whichever party prevails in a contract action. See *San Luis Obispo Bay Prop., Inc. v PG&E* (1972) 28 CA3d 556, 570, 104 CR 733, 743. The question of whether, when plaintiff voluntarily dismisses an action, defendant is entitled to attorneys' fees as the "prevailing party" within the meaning of CC §1717, is presently before the California Supreme Court (*International Indus., Inc. v Olen* (hearing granted March 31, 1977, LA 30760; former opinion at (1977) 66 CA3d 521 (advance reports), 135 CR 906)). In *Olen*, the court of appeals declined to follow its earlier holding in *Associated Convalescent Enterprises v Carl Marks & Co.* (1973) 33 CA3d 116, 108 CR 782 (see also *Gray v Kay* (1975) 47 CA3d 562, 120 CR 915), that the ministerial act of the clerk in entering dismissal does not make defendant the prevailing party under CC §1717.

On dismissal without prejudice of an action for libel or slander, defendant is entitled to $100 attorneys' fees in addition to other costs, "and judgment shall be entered accordingly." CCP §836. See also *MacLeod v Tribune Publishing Co., supra.*

§31.70 2. With Prejudice

In addition to having all the consequences of a dismissal without prejudice (see §§31.67–31.69), a dismissal with prejudice operates as a retraxit and ends the lawsuit. The dismissal is res judicata and bars a subsequent action on the same claim. See *Goddard v Security Title Ins. & Guar. Co.* (1939) 14 C2d 47, 92 P2d 804; *Ghiringhelli v Riboni* (1950) 95 CA2d 503, 213 P2d 17.

C. Dismissal Before Trial Commenced
1. Dismissal as Matter of Right
§31.71 a. Basic Rule

At any time before commencement of trial, plaintiff can dismiss his action on written request to the clerk or on oral or written request to the judge where there is no clerk, and on payment of costs, provided that (1) defendant has not sought affirmative relief by cross-complaint, and (2) there is no pending motion under CCP §396b to transfer the action to another court. CCP §581(1). For exceptions to this rule, see §§31.72–31.74. On procedures and payment of costs, see §§31.83–31.86.

Plaintiff's right to dismiss under CCP §581(1) is absolute, and neither the clerk nor the court can refuse to accept the dismissal. *Simpson v Superior Court* (1945) 68 CA2d 821, 158 P2d 46 (prohibition granted to prevent court from setting aside dismissal). See also *Roski v Superior Court* (1971) 17 CA3d 841, 95 CR 312.

b. Exceptions
§31.72 (1) Cross-Complaint Seeking Affirmative Relief

Plaintiff does not have the right to dismiss the action under CCP §581 when defendant has sought affirmative relief by cross-complaint. CCP §581(1). The same rule applies to a cross-complainant who seeks to dismiss when the cross-defendant has sought affirmative relief in response to the cross-complaint. *Rodgers v Parker* (1902) 136 C 313, 68 P 975. On what constitutes affirmative relief, see 4 Witkin, CALIFORNIA PROCEDURE, Proceedings Without Trial §48 (2d ed 1971).

A complaint in intervention that seeks affirmative relief has the same effect as a cross-complaint and prevents plaintiff from dismissing under CCP §581(1). *Roski v Superior Court* (1971) 17 CA3d 841, 845, 95 CR 312, 315; *In re Mercantile Guar. Co.*

(1968) 263 CA2d 346, 350, 69 CR 361, 364. If, on the other hand, the complaint in intervention only resists plaintiff's cause of action, plaintiff retains the right to dismiss against the intervenor as well as defendant. *Klinghoffer v Barasch* (1970) 4 CA3d 258, 84 CR 350.

A potential intervenor who seeks affirmative relief must intervene before the dismissal is filed. After that time, there is no pending action within which a complaint in intervention can be filed. *Roski v Superior Court, supra.*

A plaintiff in eminent domain proceedings may abandon those proceedings by serving and filing a written notice of such abandonment. CCP §1268.510(a). (But see discussion in §31.74 on estoppel when defendant would be prejudiced by the abandonment.) In *People ex rel Dep't of Pub. Works v Buellton Dev. Co.* (1943) 58 CA2d 178, 136 P2d 793, the court interpreted former CCP §1255a (on which CCP §1268.510 is based), as constituting an express exception to the prohibition in CCP §581(1) against dismissal when defendant has sought affirmative relief by cross-complaint.

If a general demurrer to a complaint is sustained with leave to amend and plaintiff fails to amend within the time allowed, there is no complaint to which defendant can respond, and a cross-complaint cannot prevent plaintiff from filing a request for dismissal in place of an amended complaint. *Malick v American Sav. & Loan Ass'n* (1969) 273 CA2d 171, 79 CR 499.

§31.73 (2) Plaintiff Not Sole Party in Interest

When an action is considered fundamentally a proceeding in rem, jurisdiction of the court attaches to the res and plaintiff cannot, by filing a request for dismissal, oust the court of jurisdiction. *Voyce v Superior Court* (1942) 20 C2d 479, 127 P2d 536 (will contest). See also *Estate of Raymond* (1940) 38 CA2d 305, 100 P2d 1085 (petition for probate of will is proceeding in rem, and court's jurisdiction cannot be divested by request for dismissal).

Similar reasoning has been used to prevent dismissal by plaintiff as a matter of right in custody or guardianship proceedings (*Ford v Superior Court* (1959) 171 CA2d 228, 340 P2d 296; *Guardianship of Lyle* (1946) 77 CA2d 153, 157, 174 P2d 906, 909), shareholders' derivative suits (*Ensher v Ensher, Alexander & Barsoom, Inc.* (1960) 187 CA2d 407, 410, 9 CR 732, 734), and by the named plaintiff in class actions (*Marcarelli v Cabell* (1976) 58 CA3d 51, 55, 129 CR 509, 511). Moreover, a class action brought under the Consumers Legal Remedies Act (CC §§1750–1784) cannot be dismissed, settled, or compromised without court approval, and notice of the proposed dismissal must be given to members of the class as the court directs. CC §1781(f).

§31.74 (3) Estoppel

Plaintiff's conduct may estop him from voluntarily dismissing an action, *e.g.*, in eminent domain proceedings. See *Times-Mirror Co. v Superior Court* (1935) 3 C2d 309, 44 P2d 547 (plaintiff city estopped from dismissing condemnation proceeding after property owner, believing that city was about to take its property, relocated its plant and constructed a new building). The principle of estoppel in eminent domain proceedings is codified in CCP §1268.510(b), which permits the court, on motion made within 30 days after filing of a notice of abandonment of the proceeding, to set the abandonment aside if the moving party has, in justifiable reliance on the proceeding, substantially changed his position to his detriment, and cannot be restored to substantially the position he was in before the proceeding commenced. For further discussion, see §31.72.

It has been held that plaintiff is estopped from dismissing an action after a motion for dismissal has been made for failure to pay costs and transfer fees and costs on an order for change of venue. *London v Morrison* (1950) 99 CA2d 876, 222 P2d 941. However, that case was decided under former CCP §581b, which provided for mandatory dismissal unless such fees and costs were paid within one year. This provision was repealed in 1974, and at the same time CCP §399 was amended to make dismissal in this situation discretionary with the court. See §31.42. These statutory changes have substantially eroded the authority of *London*.

§31.75 c. Meaning of When Trial Commenced

For purposes of dismissal under CCP §581, trial is commenced at the beginning of plaintiff's opening statement or that of his counsel. If there is no opening statement, trial is commenced when the oath or affirmation is administered to the first witness, or on introduction of any evidence. CCP §581(1). A hearing in the trial court's chambers on a motion for jury trial and to quash a subpena duces tecum does not constitute an opening statement, and trial is not commenced within the meaning of CCP §581(a). *Gherman v Colburn* (1971) 18 CA3d 1046, 96 CR 424.

Although a hearing on a demurrer has been interpreted as a trial on an issue of law for purposes of involuntary dismissal under CCP §583 (see *Berri v Superior Court* (1955) 43 C2d 856, 279 P2d 8; *Smith v Los Angeles* (1948) 84 CA2d 297, 190 P2d 943), the language of CCP §581(1) gives plaintiff the right to dismiss after a demurrer has been sustained without leave to amend, because no opening statement has been made, no witness sworn, and no evidence introduced. *Parenti v Lifeline Blood Bank* (1975) 49 CA3d 331, 122 CR 709. Before CCP §581(1) was amended to its present language in 1947, plaintiff could not dismiss his action after a demurrer had been sustained without leave to amend and before judgment had been entered. See *Goldtree v Spreckels* (1902) 135 C 666, 672, 67 P 1091, 1093.

If a demurrer is sustained with leave to amend, the case is considered reopened for further pleading and trial, and plaintiff can voluntarily dismiss the action rather than amend. See *Provencher v Los Angeles* (1935) 10 CA2d 730, 732, 52 P2d 983, 984. Thereafter, the trial court is without jurisdiction to vacate such a dismissal and enter a judgment for the defendant. *Home Real Estate Co. v Winnants* (1919) 39 CA 643, 179 P 534. But see discussion in §31.77 on the dangers to plaintiff if the clerk does not enter judgment of dismissal before plaintiff files a notice of appeal.

§31.76 d. Dismissal Against Fewer Than All Defendants; Indispensable Parties

The dismissal provisions of CCP §581 have been construed to permit dismissal against some but not all defendants. See, *e.g.*, *Lori, Ltd. v Wolfe* (1948) 85 CA2d 54, 61, 192 P2d 112, 116. However, when plaintiff dismisses a defendant who was joined by the court as an indispensable party, the dismissal renders the action untriable. In this situation, the court can either strike the dismissal or dismiss all causes of action to which that defendant is indispensable. See *Wilson v Frakes* (1960) 178 CA2d 580, 584, 3 CR 434, 437. For discussion of indispensable parties, generally, see 1 CALIFORNIA CIVIL PROCEDURE BEFORE TRIAL §§7.12–7.13 (Cal CEB 1977).

§31.77 e. Dismissal of Fewer Than All Causes of Action

The words "action" and "cause of action" in CCP §581 include a count or counts in a pleading that seeks alternative remedies. See *Steele v Litton Indus., Inc.* (1968) 260 CA2d 157, 68 CR 680 (plaintiff can dismiss equitable action and proceed to trial on legal action for damages predicated on same facts). Dismissal in this situation constitutes an election of remedies by plaintiff, and a judgment on one remedy bars the trial of a subsequent action on the same obligation but a different theory. 260 CA2d at 172, 68 CR at 690. See also *Stevens v Marco* (1956) 147 CA2d 357, 383, 305 P2d 669, 685; *Mackenzie v Voelker* (1954) 123 CA2d 538, 266 P2d 867.

The right to partial dismissal can be utilized by a plaintiff who has had a demurrer sustained without leave to amend to some but not all causes of action, and who wishes to obtain appellate review of the court's ruling. As long as at least one cause of action has survived a demurrer, and no order of dismissal has been filed, the one final judgment rule prohibits an appeal. See *United States Fin. v Sullivan* (1974) 37 CA3d 5, 11, 112 CR 18, 21. However, if plaintiff is willing to forego those causes of action to which a demurrer has not been sustained, he can dismiss them, obtain a judgment of dismissal on the causes of action to which a demurrer has been sustained (CCP §581(3)), and then file an appeal. *Shepard v Alexian Bros. Hosp.* (1973) 33 CA3d 606, 608 n1, 109 CR 132, 133 n1. After the appellate ruling, plaintiff may file the action again, and, provided the statute of limitations was not run, may bring the causes of action that were dismissed. See §31.67.

In using the above procedure, plaintiff must be careful to avoid the dilemma illustrated by *Parenti v Lifeline Blood Bank* (1975) 49 CA3d 331, 122 CR 709, in which plaintiff filed a complaint seeking damages from defendant on theories of strict liability, breach of warranty, and negligence. Defendant demurred to all three causes of action, and the demurrer was sustained without leave to amend to the first two causes of action. Plaintiff then filed a request for dismissal of the "entire action as to all defendants," and on the same day, filed a notice of appeal "from a judgment of dismissal entered on the sustaining of a [d]emurrer. . . ," although in fact no judgment of dismissal had been entered. 49 CA3d at 333, 12 CR at 710.

The court held that filing the request for dismissal precluded plaintiff from seeking review of the trial court's ruling on the demurrer, because plaintiff failed to cause judgment to be entered. Therefore, because there was no judgment to appeal from, and the entry of dismissal was not an appealable order, the appeal was improper. Moreover, plaintiff could not now obtain a judgment because after entry of a voluntary dismissal, the trial court is without jurisdiction to act further. 49 CA3d at 335, 122 CR at 711. On the scope of the court's jurisdiction after filing a dismissal, see §31.68.

§31.78 2. Dismissal On Parties' Consent

In addition to plaintiff's right to dismiss an action before trial commences under CCP §581(1) (see §§31.71–31.77), either party may dismiss an action on written consent of the other, subject to the written consent of the applicant's attorney of record, or to court order after notice to the attorney. CCP §581(2). This provision permits dismissal at any time before final judgment, not only before trial is commenced. See 4 Witkin, CALIFORNIA PROCEDURE, Proceedings Without Trial §59 (2d ed 1971). See §31.81.

D. Dismissal After Trial Commenced
1. With Prejudice
§31.79 a. As Matter of Right

A plaintiff (or cross-complainant) may dismiss with prejudice any cause of action at any time before the court renders a decision. However, dismissal of complaint with prejudice does not affect a pending cross-complaint. CCP §581(5). On procedures, see §§31.83–31.86.

§31.80 b. By Court Order After Abandonment

The court may dismiss an action with prejudice after trial commences, and before final submission of the case, when plaintiff abandons it. CCP §581(4). It has been said that CCP §581(4) provides the basis for voluntary dismissal on motion of plaintiff and court order. *Kaufman & Broad Bldg. Co. v City & Suburban Mortgage Co.* (1970) 10 CA3d 206, 88 CR 858. See also 4 Witkin, CALIFORNIA PROCEDURE, Proceedings Without Trial §57 (2d ed 1971). However, CCP §581(4) overlaps CCP §581(5), which permits dismissals with prejudice at any time before decision is rendered, and ordinarily plaintiff would use that provision because no motion is required. See §31.83. Although plaintiff cannot use CCP §581(4) to obtain a dismissal with prejudice when defendant has sought affirmative relief by cross-complaint (*Kershaw v Hogan* (1932) 127 CA 89, 15 P2d 535), plaintiff can accomplish this result by dismissing under CCP §581(5), because a dismissal with prejudice under that provision does not affect a pending cross-complaint.

If, after commencement of trial, plaintiff moves to dismiss the action without prejudice under CCP §581(5) but fails to establish just cause for dismissal (see §31.82), and if defendant objects and requests that the case proceed, the trial court can find that plaintiff has abandoned the action and can order the action dismissed with prejudice under CCP §581(4). *Burnett v Burnett* (1948) 88 CA2d 805, 199 P2d 685. On what constitutes abandonment, see §31.88.

2. Without Prejudice

§31.81   a. By Consent of Parties

An action may be dismissed by either party, on written consent of the other. CCP §581(2). This provision overlaps CCP §581(5), which provides that dismissals without prejudice may be had after commencement of trial by consent of all the parties, except that dismissal under CCP §581(2) may take place at any time before judgment, not just after commencement of trial. See §31.78.

A dismissal under CCP §581(2) requires the written consent of the attorneys of record of each party, or, if such consent is not obtained, an order of court after notice to the attorney refusing to consent. CCP §581(2).

§31.82   b. By Court Order for Just Cause

A dismissal without prejudice after commencement of trial may be had in either of the manners provided for in CCP §581(1)

§31.83   DISMISSAL

(see §31.87), either by consent of all parties or by court order on a showing of just cause. CCP §581(5). If the court concludes that just cause for dismissal has not been shown, it may treat the motion as an abandonment and dismiss the action with prejudice under CCP §581(4). See discussion in §31.80.

E. Procedures
1. When Dismissal Is Matter of Right
§31.83   a. Request for Dismissal

When dismissal is sought before trial commences as a matter of right (see §§31.71–31.77, 31.79), there must be a "written request to the clerk, filed with the papers in the case," or an oral or written request to the judge when there is no clerk. CCP §581(1). Either the written consent of the attorney of record for the dismissing party, or a court order after notice to the attorney, must be obtained. CCP §581(2). Dismissal by the client alone is insufficient. *Boca & Loyalton R. R. v Superior Court* (1907) 150 C 153, 88 P 718.

The California Judicial Council has prescribed a printed form of request for dismissal for mandatory use in all civil actions, wherever applicable. Cal Rules of Ct 982(a)(5). See form in §31.84. These forms are usually available from the court clerk. When the Judicial Council has adopted a form for mandatory use, no court may use a different form purporting to serve the same function. Govt C §68511.

A dismissal with prejudice may be made at any time before decision is rendered, by written request to the court clerk or by oral or written request to the judge. CCP §581(5). See also *Ghiringhelli v Riboni* (1950) 95 CA2d 503, 213 P2d 17 (statutory method of dismissal dispenses with common law need for renunciation in open court). The Judicial Council form in §31.84 may be used, but often it is more convenient to make an oral request, particularly during trial.

§31.84   b. Judicial Council Form: Request For Dismissal

Copies: Original (filed with court clerk with proof of service); copies for service (one for each attorney of record and unrepresented party); office copies.

DISMISSAL §31.84

Name, Address and Telephone No. of Attorney(s)	Space Below for Use of Court Clerk Only
Attorney(s) for	

.....................COURT OF CALIFORNIA, COUNTY OF...................
(SUPERIOR, MUNICIPAL, or JUSTICE)

....
(Name of Municipal or Justice Court District or of branch court, if any)

Plaintiff(s):

Defendant(s):

(Abbreviated Title)

CASE NUMBER

REQUEST FOR DISMISSAL
TYPE OF ACTION
☐ Personal Injury, Property Damage and Wrongful Death:
  ☐ Motor Vehicle   ☐ Other
  ☐ Domestic Relations   ☐ Eminent Domain
☐ Other: (Specify) ....

TO THE CLERK: Please dismiss this action as follows: (Check applicable boxes.)
1. ☐ With prejudice   ☐ Without prejudice
2. ☐ Entire action   ☐ Complaint only   ☐ Petition only   ☐ Cross-complaint only
   ☐ Other: (Specify)*

Dated: ....

*If dismissal requested is of specified parties only, of specified causes of action only or of specified cross-complaints only, so state and identify the parties, causes of action or cross-complaints to be dismissed.

Attorney(s) for ....

_____
(Type or print attorney(s) name(s))

TO THE CLERK: Consent to the above dismissal is hereby given.**

Dated: ....

**When a cross-complaint (or Response (Marriage) seeking affirmative relief) is on file, the attoreny(s) for the cross-complainant (respondent) must sign this consent when required by CCP 581(1), (2) or (5).

Attorney(s) for ....

_____
(Type or print attorney(s) name(s))

(To be completed by clerk)
☐ Dismissal entered as requested on ....
☐ Dismissal entered on .... as to only ....
☐ Dismissal not entered as requested for the following reason(s), and attorney notified on ....

_____, Clerk

Dated..................................... By_____, Deputy

Form Adopted by Rule 982 of
The Judicial Council of California
Revised Effective July 1, 1972

REQUEST FOR DISMISSAL

CCP 581, etc.;
Cal. Rules of Court,
Rule 1233

Comment: The preparer of this form should type an "X" in the box that describes the type of action, as well as in the boxes that signify whether the dismissal is with or without prejudice, and whether dismissal is of the entire action or of a complaint, cross-complaint, or petition only. If the dismissal is only as to certain parties or certain causes of action or cross-complaints, "X" should be typed in the box marked "Other," and the parties, causes of action or cross-complaints should be identified.

When the dismissal is requested by the consent of the parties under CCP §581(2) or CCP §581(5), this form provides a space for the attorney of record for the consenting party (*e.g.*, a cross-complainant) to consent to the dismissal. Although CCP §581(2) states that the written consent of the attorney of record for the requesting party is required for all dismissals under CCP §581(1)–(2), the attorney need not sign the request and the consent. The attorney's signature on the request itself is sufficient.

§31.85 c. Payment of Clerk's Costs

Under CCP §581(1), a dismissal is entered only on payment of the clerk's costs (or judge's costs, when there is no clerk), *i.e.*, the nominal charges for entering the dismissal. Dismissal cannot be conditioned on plaintiff's payment of defendant's costs, because the clerk cannot tax costs and settle a costs bill. *Hopkins v Superior Court* (1902) 136 C 552, 69 P 299; *Eddings v White* (1964) 229 CA2d 579, 40 CR 453. However, on entry of the dismissal, defendant is entitled to costs as the prevailing party. See §31.69

§31.86 d. Delivery of Undertaking

When a provisional remedy has been allowed in the action, the clerk or judge must, on dismissal, deliver the undertaking to defendant, who may have his action on it. CCP §581(1).

2. When Dismissal Not Matter of Right
§31.87 a. By Consent

The California Judicial Council form in §31.84 may be used to request a dismissal by consent of the parties under either CCP §§581(2) or 581(5). The attorney of record for the requesting party should sign the request, and the attorney of record for the consenting party signs the consent. See Comment to form in §31.84.

Under CCP §581(5), dismissals without prejudice may be made during trial by consent of the parties in either manner provided for in CCP §581(1), *i.e.*, by written request to the court clerk or by oral or written request to the judge when there is no clerk. An oral request to the judge should be made on the record, and if there is no opportunity to do so, the request and consent should be made on the Judicial Council form in §31.84.

§31.88   b. By Motion

When plaintiff seeks to dismiss an action during trial (1) with prejudice on grounds of abandonment (CCP §581(4)), or (2) without prejudice on a showing of just cause (CCP §581(5)), a motion is required. The motion may be made orally, and should be on the record. A motion to dismiss under CCP §581(4) must show a clear, unequivocal and express intent to abandon the action, *e.g.*, by motion to dismiss, stipulation of the parties, or some other form of express intent made on the record. *Kaufman & Broad Bldg. Co. v City & Suburban Mortgage Co.* (1970) 10 CA3d 206, 88 CR 858. A dismissal without prejudice under CCP §581(5) requires a showing of just cause, either by written declaration or by oral testimony.

§31.89   3. Entry of Dismissal; Clerk's Duty To Enter

A written notice of dismissal must be entered in the clerk's register (or, in justice court, in the docket), and is effective for all purposes when so entered. CCP §581d. No court judgment or other judicial act is necessary to make the dismissal effective. *Hopkins v Superior Court* (1902) 136 C 552, 69 P 299 (decided under former CCP §581, on which CCP §581d is based). However, no appeal can be taken from an entry of dismissal, because an entry of dismissal is neither a judgment nor an appealable order under CCP §904.1–2. To be appealable, the entry of dismissal must first be reduced to judgment. See §31.90. See also *Parenti v Lifeline Blood Bank* (1975) 49 CA3d 331, 122 CR 709, discussed in §31.77.

The clerk's duty to enter a properly requested dismissal is ministerial, and he can be compelled by the court, to perform it on motion or by writ of mandate (*Silverton v Free* (1953) 120 CA2d 389, 261 P2d 17). Prohibition is available to restrain further proceedings if the court refuses to order entry of dismissal. *Hopkins v Superior Court, supra.*

Notwithstanding the language of CCP §581d, courts have held

that because the clerk's duty is ministerial, the dismissal is effective when filed, even if the clerk fails to enter it. See, *e.g.*, *Kaufman v Superior Court* (1896) 115 C 152, 46 P 904 (cross-complaint ineffective when filed after plaintiff filed dismissal but before clerk entered dismissal). See also *Long v Superior Court* (1936) 14 CA2d 753, 58 P2d 952. For discussion, see 4 Witkin, CALIFORNIA PROCEDURE, Proceedings Without Trial §53 (2d ed 1971).

§31.90 4. Judgment

All dismissals ordered by the court must be in the form of a written order signed by the court and filed in the action (or, in justice court, in the docket). When filed, such orders constitute judgments and are effective for all purposes. CCP §581d. Under this provision, for example, defendant's cost bill need only be filed within ten days from entry of judgment, not from entry of the dismissal. CCP §1033; *MacLeod v Tribune Publishing Co.* (1958) 157 CA2d 665, 321 P2d 881.

The clerk in superior, municipal, and justice courts must note the judgment in the register. CCP §581d.

§31.91 F. Setting Aside Dismissal; Procedures

A plaintiff may move under CCP §473 to set aside a voluntary dismissal entered by mistake, inadvertence, surprise, or excusable neglect. *Isaacs v Jones* (1933) 135 CA 47, 26 P2d 533. Under CCP §473, the motion must be made within a reasonable time, and not later than six months after entry of dismissal. *Davies v Superior Court* (1964) 228 CA2d 535, 39 CR 693. For discussion of procedures for relief under CCP §473 generally, see §§30.62–30.72. A would-be intervenor does not have standing to initiate a CCP §473 motion because he is not a party (*Roski v Superior Court* (1971) 17 CA3d 841, 95 CR 312), and it seems that defendant also does not have standing, because CCP §473 only relieves parties from a judgment, order or other proceeding "taken against him" (*Smith v Roberts* (1905) 1 CA 148, 81 P 1026, cited with approval in *Roski v Superior Court, supra*), and plaintiff's voluntary dismissal is not taken against defendant within the meaning of the statute.

Although a defendant cannot appeal from a voluntary dismissal (*Cook v Stewart McKee & Co.* (1945) 68 CA2d 758, 157 P2d

868); plaintiff may appeal from a judgment entered following the dismissal (see *King v Superior Court* (1936) 12 CA2d 501, 56 P2d 268).

A dismissal with prejudice cannot be collaterally attacked unless it is void. *Wouldridge v Burns* (1968) 265 CA2d 82, 71 CR 394.

JOHN E. HOFFMAN

Chapter 32
Submitted Case

    I. SUBMISSION WITHOUT FILING ACTION
      A. Statutory Authority   §32.1
      B. Submission Papers
         1. Submission of Agreed Case   §32.2
         2. Declaration of Good Faith   §32.3
      C. Forms
         1. Submission of Agreed Case   §32.4
         2. Declaration in Support of Submission of Agreed Case   §32.5
    II. SUBMISSION AFTER ACTION HAS BEEN FILED
      A. Nonstatutory Nature of Procedure   §32.6
      B. Form: Stipulation to Agreed Facts   §32.7

I. SUBMISSION WITHOUT FILING ACTION

§32.1   A. Statutory Authority

Under a rarely used procedure in CCP §§1138–1140, parties to a "question in difference," which might be the subject of a civil action, may, without filing an action, agree on a case containing the facts on which the controversy depends, and present a submission of that case to a court. The matter must be submitted to the court that would have jurisdiction if an action had been brought. See *White v Clarke* (1896) 111 C 425, 428, 44 P 164, 165, in which relief was denied in part because the question submitted could not be the subject of a civil action in California.

The court in which the matter is filed then hears the case, and renders judgment as if an action were pending (CCP §1138), except that no costs may be assessed for any proceedings before trial (CCP §1139). Judgment is entered as in other cases (CCP

JOHN E. HOFFMAN, BSEE, 1969, University of Southern California; J.D., 1972, University of Southern California. Mr. Hoffman practices with the Abbott Professional Corporation in Los Angeles. CEB attorney-editor was CAROL S. BROSNAHAN.

§1139) and enforcement and appeal rights are the same as those for any judgment (CCP §1140).

Code of Civil Procedure §1138 includes a requirement that the "question in difference" be a "real" controversy. This requirement is analogous to the similar requirement in declaratory relief proceedings. *Colusa v Strain* (1963) 215 CA2d 472, 30 CR 415; see generally chap 24. The requirement of "good faith" means that the case must not be contrived in order to obtain a determination of a matter in advance of a real controversy. A contrived case will be dismissed. In *Collier v Lindley* (1928) 203 C 641, 644, 266 P 526, 527, the court stated that the matter would have been dismissed except for the existence of certain questions of public interest independent of any alleged interests of the parties to the proceeding.

B. Submission Papers
§32.2   1. Submission of Agreed Case

Following the procedure provided by CCP §1138, the parties present a submission of the agreed case to the court having jurisdiction of the matter. The District Court of Appeal has no original jurisdiction under CCP §§1138–1140. However, if otherwise sufficient, the submission may be treated as a petition for writ of mandate. *Northridge Water Dist. v McDonell* (1958) 158 CA2d 123, 125, 322 P2d 25, 27.

The statement of facts should be prepared with care because the court is restricted to considering only those facts. Plaintiff's case must be established by proof of the facts pleaded and no others. The court must render judgment for defendant if plaintiff can only make his case by proving facts not pleaded. *Crandall v Amador County* (1862) 20 C 72, 74. However, in *Division of Labor Law Enforcement v Brooks* (1964) 226 CA2d 631, 633, 38 CR 284, 285, the court of appeal, in dictum, expressed the view that the court should refuse to accept a submission on an inadequate agreed statement, pointing out that, although the issue had not been decided in California, "[T]he rule [in other jurisdictions] seems eminently reasonable. The parties should be required to amplify the record by further stipulation or by evidence."

The submission should also state the questions the parties believe the court must determine. A court is bound only by the parties' agreement on the facts. A court is not bound by an erroneous agreement on a conclusion of law (*People v Singh* (1932) 121 CA 107, 111, 8 P2d 898, 900), nor by a stipulation declaring which questions of law the court will determine under the facts. *San Francisco Lumber Co. v Bibb* (1903) 139 C 325, 326, 73 P 864, 865. If the parties agree, the submission may include an agreement allowing a commissioner or judge pro tem of the court to decide the matter.

§32.3 2. Declaration of Good Faith

The submission must be accompanied by a declaration signed by all parties, stating that the controversy is real and the proceedings are brought in good faith to determine the rights of the parties. CCP §1138. See form in §32.4. The declaration incorporates the statutory language. A declaration which, instead of stating that the controversy was real, stated that the "statement of the case" was a "real controversy", and, instead of stating that the proceedings were in good faith, stated that the "contention" was in good faith, was held to be insufficient. *White v Clarke* (1896) 111 C 425, 428, 44 P 164, 165; see §32.5 for form of declaration. No pleadings need to be filed to initiate this procedure.

C. Forms

§32.4 1. Submission of Agreed Case

[*Title of Court*]

[*Caption. See §§23.18–23.19*]
In the Matter of
the Agreed Case
Between _____ and
_____

No. _____

SUBMISSION OF AGREED CASE

____[*Name of party*]____ **and** ____[*name of party*]____, **parties to the following question in difference which might be the subject of a civil action within the jurisdiction of this Court, agree on the following facts concerning the question to be submitted to this Court for its determination and judgment without action as provided for in Code of Civil Procedure section 1138.**
    1. **The parties agree on the following facts:**
        a. ____[*Jurisdiction and venue*]____
        b. ____[*Identity of parties*]____
        c. ____[*Agreed facts relating to transaction in dispute*]____.

2. **The question(s) in difference submitted for determination are as follows:**
____[state legal contentions of each party]____.

[Add when appropriate]

3. **All parties agree that this matter may be assigned to and judgment may be entered by a Commissioner or Judge Pro Tem of the Superior Court of California, County of** _____.

Dated: _____

Approved:

[Signatures of parties]	[Signatures of parties]
[Typed names]	[Typed names]
	Attorney(s) for _____

Comment: This submission should be signed both by the parties themselves, and the attorneys for the parties to avoid subsequent questions concerning whether the papers submitted conform with the actual agreement of the parties. See, 1 Witkin, CALIFORNIA PROCEDURE §§115, 125–126 (2d ed 1970). Although an attorney has authority to stipulate on behalf of his client on procedural or remedial matters (*Armstrong v Brown* (1936) 12 CA2d 22, 28, 54 P2d 1118, 1121), an attorney may not relinquish a substantial right of the client (*Linsk v Linsk* (1969) 70 C2d 272, 278, 74 CR 544, 548). Specifically, an attorney cannot waive findings so no appeal can be prosecuted (*Wuest v Wuest* (1942) 53 CA2d 339, 345, 127 P2d 934, 936) and when a case is submitted on agreed facts no formal findings are required. *Division of Labor Law Enforcement v Brooks* (1964) 226 CA2d 631, 38 CR 284. Counsel should ascertain from the court clerk the filing fee for such a submission, copies needed, and the local procedure for having the matter calendared for hearing.

§32.5 2. Declaration in Support of Submission of Agreed Case

[Caption. See §32.4]

No. _____

DECLARATION IN SUPPORT OF SUBMISSION OF AGREED CASE

____[name of attorney]____, **and** ____[name of attorney]____, **declare:**

1. We are the attorneys for ____[names]____, **parties of record to the question in difference which is submitted to this Court without action on an agreed statement of facts.**

2. We have read the agreed facts and questions in difference stated in the submission of agreed case and declare that the controversy in this proceed-

ing is real and that this proceeding is instituted in good faith to determine the rights of the parties.

We declare, under penalty of perjury, that the foregoing is true and correct and was executed on 19____, at _____, California.

[*Signatures of attorneys*]

[*Typed names*]

II. SUBMISSION AFTER ACTION HAS BEEN FILED

§32.6   A. Nonstatutory Nature of Procedure

After an action has been filed and the issues framed by pleadings in the usual manner, the parties may stipulate to try the case on an agreed statement of facts covering all or a portion of the facts in controversy. This eliminates the need either wholly, or in part, to present evidence on those facts. *Faust v San Diego* (1931) 115 CA 277, 278, 1 P2d 543. When the case is tried solely on the statement of agreed facts no jury trial is available because the statement makes findings unnecessary. See *Division of Labor Law Enforcement v Brooks* (1964) 226 CA2d 631, 38 CR 284. The statement has the force and effect of an unattacked finding of facts made by the court. *Robinson v El Centro Grain Co.* (1933) 133 CA 567, 24 P2d 554.

This is a nonstatutory procedure. "An agreed statement of facts is but a substitute for evidence of those facts, and in this respect differs from an 'agreed case,' which, under section 1138 . . . may be submitted for decision without any pleadings." *Towle v Sweeney* (1905) 2 CA 29, 31, 83 P 74.

An agreed statement of facts is usually presented to the court at the hearing on a demurrer or motion for summary judgment. However, the agreed statement of facts can be made the basis of a request that the case be brought to trial on the short cause calendar. See chap 26.

§32.7   B. Form: Stipulation to Agreed Facts

[*Caption. See §32.4*]   No. _____

STIPULATION TO AGREED FACTS

The undersigned agree that this action may be tried by this Court or by a Commissioner or Judge Pro Tem of this Court without a jury and that judgment may be rendered on pleadings filed in this action and on the following

§32.7 SUBMITTED CASE 456

statement of agreed facts, which serve as a substitute for evidence of those facts.

[State agreed facts]

Dated: _____

Approved:

<table>
<tr><td>_____
[Signatures of parties]
[Typed names]</td><td>_____
[Signatures of parties]
[Typed names]
Attorney(s) for _____</td></tr>
</table>

KENNETH J. ARAN
MARIO L. CLINCO

Chapter 33
Settlement

I. INTRODUCTION
  A. Terminology; Scope of Chapter §33.1
  B. Reasons To Settle §33.2
  C. Factors That Delay Settlement §33.3
  D. Evaluation for Settlement §33.4
  E. Confidentiality §33.5
  F. Attorney's Authority To Settle §33.6
II. INITIATION AND CONDUCT OF NEGOTIATIONS
  A. By or With Parties §33.7
  B. With Adverse Counsel §33.8
  C. Use of Written Statements and Brochures §33.9
III. CCP §998 OFFER TO ALLOW JUDGMENT
  A. Nature; Use §33.10
  B. Serving and Filing Offers and Acceptances §33.11
  C. Offer by Plaintiff
    1. Benefits; Tactics §33.12
    2. Form: Plaintiff's Offer To Allow Judgment (CCP §998) §33.13
  D. Offer by Defendant
    1. Benefits; Tactics §33.14
    2. Form: Defendant's CCP §998 Offer To Allow Judgment §33.15
IV. SETTLEMENT CONFERENCES
  A. Procedures To Set Conference
    1. Voluntary §33.16
    2. Mandatory §33.17
    3. Continuances §33.18
  B. Attorney's Preparation
    1. Review; Reevaluation §33.19
    2. Use of Written Statement; Checklist §33.20
    3. Required Information and Documents §33.21

KENNETH J. ARAN, B.S., 1962, University of California (Los Angeles); J.D., 1965, University of California (Los Angeles); M.B.A., 1967, University of California (Los Angeles). Mr. Aran is a member of the Los Angeles firm of Aran and Rosenberg.
  MARIO L. CLINCO, LL.B., 1936, Fordham Law School, New York. Judge Clinco is a Superior Court Judge for the County of Los Angeles.
  CEB attorney-editor was PAUL PEYRAT.

§33.1   SETTLEMENT

      C. Attendance and Participation
          1. Attorneys   §33.22
          2. Parties; Representatives of Insurers and Entities   §33.23
      D. Conduct of Conference
          1. Judge's Role   §33.24
          2. Presentation By Plaintiff's Attorney   §33.25
          3. Presentation By Defendant's Attorney   §33.26
      E. Sanctions for Failure To Attend or Participate   §33.27
  V. CONCLUDING SETTLEMENT
      A. Methods   §33.28
      B. Release and Dismissal
          1. Nature of Release, Covenant Not To Sue, and Dismissal With Prejudice   §33.29
          2. Drafting Releases   §33.30
      C. Duty To Notify Court of Settlement   §33.31
      D. Settlement With Fewer Than All Defendants   §33.32

I. INTRODUCTION

§33.1   A. Terminology; Scope of Chapter

A settlement is an agreement to terminate or forestall all or part of a lawsuit. See *Setzer v Moore* (1927) 202 C 333, 338, 260 P 550, 552. The agreement may be oral or embodied in a writing, and may be entered into by parties or by their attorneys (see §33.6 on attorneys' authority). General principles of contract law govern the interpretation and enforcement of settlement agreements.

This chapter discusses settlement as a procedure for terminating a lawsuit, although settlements can also be reached before a lawsuit is filed or after entry of judgment. The settlement of a lawsuit is reached when plaintiff agrees to dismiss or otherwise terminate the action in return for defendant's agreement to pay a specified sum or to give relief in another form. Plaintiff's statement of the amount of money or relief sought is called a "demand." An "offer" is defendant's statement of what he will give to obtain termination of the action. Settlement negotiations often comprise an exchange of several demands and offers before agreement is reached.

Special statutes and rules that govern the settlement of minor's claims are discussed in 1 CALIFORNIA CIVIL PROCEDURE BEFORE TRIAL §§5.19–5.23 (Cal CEB 1977).

For discussion of settlement of actions by injured workers against third parties when an employer or workers' compensation insurer has intervened or noticed a lien, see CALIFORNIA WORKMEN'S COMPENSATION PRACTICE 1973 §§17.16–17.20, 18.5 (Cal CEB 1973).

§33.2   B. Reasons To Settle

The law favors settlements. *Fletcher v A. J. Indus., Inc.* (1968) 266 CA2d 313, 325, 72 CR 146, 153. Judges cannot force parties to settle a lawsuit (see §33.24), but do react favorably to attorneys' efforts to compromise and are included to make rulings that encourage and uphold settlements.

For parties, there are many reasons to settle a lawsuit rather than proceed to trial. For example:

(1) Costs of prosecuting or defending a lawsuit, including attorneys' fees, grow as the action progresses, especially as the trial date approaches, and during trial. The net return from an early settlement may thus exceed the net recovery on the expected judgment.

(2) Verdicts and findings are unpredictable; settlement eliminates the risk of a worse result.

(3) A settlement is normally final; verdicts and judgments are subject to post-trial motions be appeal.

(4) A settlement is a private arrangement, the details of which need not become public. See §33.5.

An attorney's paramount concern in advising a client about settling a case is to achieve the best result for the client. However, settlement can have advantages for the attorney as well as the client, permitting the attorney to close the file, obtain a fee, and move on to other cases. Settlement also reduces the attorney's legal malpractice exposure and lessens the possibility of a dispute with the client over the result or the attorney's fee.

§33.3   C. Factors That Delay Settlement

Despite the advantages of early agreement, there are factors that delay settlements. For example:

(1) The party's emotional involvement. A party who is angry at his adversary may refuse to agree to a reasonable demand or offer. An attorney may sometimes delay asking a client for settlement authority until the attorney feels that the client can give the matter rational consideration.

(2) The client's desire for a day in court or a decision on the

§33.4   SETTLEMENT   460

record. Some clients are not satisfied until told by a judge what they may receive or must give. Sometimes this desire can be met by delaying settlement until a settlement conference and having the judge read the settlement into the minutes. See §33.24. In other cases, the client may be satisfied by entry of a consent judgment. See chap 34.

(3) Need to fully assess detriment. An injured person, for example, should delay making a demand or accepting an offer until his physical condition has stabilized, or from medical reports or opinion, he can predict with reasonable certainty the future course of his injury.

§33.4   D. Evaluation for Settlement

Part of a litigation attorney's function is to assess the level at which settlement would be more beneficial to the client than risking the result of a trial. The attorney may have to gather information by research, investigation, and discovery in order to arrive at a reasonably accurate assessment of settlement value. But the result of a trial can rarely be predicted with certainty and settlement evaluations must be made even though they include a measure of speculation.

It is outside the scope of this chapter to discuss all the factors that determine the settlement value of particular kinds of cases. However, there are some evaluation factors that are independent of the nature of plaintiff's cause of action, the extent of the detriment suffered, and the possible defenses to his claim. For example, an attorney may have to assign a lower than usual settlement value to a case because of plaintiff's financial need. The physical appeal or community reputation of the respective parties and their principal witnesses may play a role in evaluation as will the ability of their respective counsel. The nature and availability of evidence for either side, including the infirmity of a party or key witness, are often factors. Some cases are evaluated primarily on the availability and limits of insurance or the ability of the defendant to give the desired relief.

On personal injury case evaluation, see BASIC CALIFORNIA PRACTICE HANDBOOK chap 8 (Cal CEB 1959); on eminent domain, see CONDEMNATION PRACTICE IN CALIFORNIA chap 7 (Cal CEB 1973); for other discussions of evaluation, see sources listed in 1 Witkin, CALIFORNIA PROCEDURE, Attorneys §13 (2d ed 1970).

§33.5 E. Confidentiality

Evidence of demands, offers, and other aspects of settlement negotiations are normally not admissible in evidence if the case or a related case is later tried. Evid C §1152; see *Moving Picture Mach. Operators Local 162 v Glasgow Theaters, Inc.* (1970) 6 CA3d 395, 401, 86 CR 33, 36. For Law Revision Commission comments and annotations, see TRIAL ATTORNEY'S EVIDENCE CODE NOTEBOOK §1152 (Cal CEB 1974). See generally Witkin, CALIFORNIA EVIDENCE §§378–380 (2d ed 1966); Jefferson, CALIFORNIA EVIDENCE BENCHBOOK §§34.3, 21.1 (CCJ-CEB 1972). The inadmissibility of any reference to settlement negotiations (except in the narrow instances specified in Evid C §1152) permits counsel to negotiate freely without fear that a trier of fact will later view an offer or demand as a floor or ceiling to a verdict.

Parties can settle a case privately, off the court record, except when one of the parties is a minor or incompetent and judicial approval of the settlement is required. See 1 CALIFORNIA CIVIL PROCEDURE BEFORE TRIAL §§5.19–5.23 (Cal CEB 1976). A party who wants the terms of a settlement to be kept confidential should so specify as one of the terms of the agreement. If a lawsuit was filed, all that need appear of record is dismissal of the action.

§33.6 F. Attorney's Authority To Settle

An attorney cannot bind a client to pay or accept a settlement without the client's specific authorization or consent. *Bice v Stevens* (1958) 160 CA2d 222, 325 P2d 244; see *Navrides v Zurich Ins. Co.* (1971) 5 C3d 698, 702 n1, 97 CR 309, 311 n1. A client may repudiate an attorney's agreement to settle on terms not authorized by the client. *Burns v McCain* (1930) 107 CA 291, 290 P 623. The attorney-client relationship is governed by the law of principal and agent, however, and a settlement offer is enforceable if the attorney had express, implied, or ostensible authority to settle, or if the client ratifies the settlement. See *Yanchor v Kagan* (1971) 22 CA3d 544, 549, 99 CR 367, 370. See generally 1 CALIFORNIA CIVIL PROCEDURE BEFORE TRIAL §§1.39–1.45 (Cal CEB 1977).

Attorneys protect their own credibility in settlement negotiations by obtaining their clients' advance authorization to settle on specified terms. Some attorneys ask clients to sign written authorizations to forestall later disputes over the extent of the authority given. The authorization normally specifies the least favorable terms acceptable to the client at that time, although the attorney will try to negotiate a more favorable settlement. The attorney need never reveal to an adversary, or even to a settlement conference judge (see §33.25), the limit of authority obtained from the client.

A party's attorney of record is presumed to have authority to settle the case, but the presumption is rebuttable. *Gagnon Co. v Nevada Desert Inn, Inc.* (1955) 45 C2d 448, 460, 289 P2d 466, 475; *Slack v Slack* (1966) 241 CA2d 530, 539, 50 CR 763, 768. Attorneys, for convenience, often rely on the accuracy of an adverse attorney's statement that a case can be settled on stated terms but care must be taken that this reliance does not prejudice the client's rights. If an adverse attorney's belief that he has authority to settle is incorrect, the fact that he has given his word does not negate his client's right to control the terms on which the lawsuit is settled. See *Burns v McCain, supra*. See also *Navrides v Zurich Ins. Co.* (1971) 5 C3d 698, 97 CR 309 (client's later lawsuit ratified unauthorized settlement by former attorney); *Whittier Union High School Dist. v Superior Court* (1977) 66 CA3d 504, 136 CR 86 (plaintiffs, whose attorney had settled case without authority, were properly relieved of dismissal).

II. INITIATION AND CONDUCT OF NEGOTIATIONS

§33.7   A. By or With Parties

An attorney can sometimes help a client to obtain a greater net recovery by advising the client to try to settle the dispute directly with the other party. This advice can benefit the attorney by gaining client goodwill and avoiding the investment of effort in a case that would generate a meager fee. While the attorney can suggest to the client the amount of a fair recovery or payment, and how to discuss settlement with the other party, the attorney should make it clear that the attorney has no further duty until the client contacts him again. See generally 1 CALIFORNIA CIVIL PROCEDURE BEFORE TRIAL §§1.5–1.6 (Cal CEB 1977).

An attorney may speak to and negotiate with an adverse party on a client's behalf, until the attorney learns that the adverse party has an attorney. The attorney should make it clear that he is negotiating as an attorney and that the party is free to seek his own attorney if he wishes. On communicating with adverse parties, see Cal Rules of Prof Cond 7–103; 1 Civ Proc Before Trial §1.30.

Even after attorneys have negotiated on behalf of their clients, an impasse can sometimes be broken by having the clients meet without their attorneys. A client who feels that adversaries are not negotiating in good faith, or who lacks complete faith in his own attorney, sometimes becomes more reasonable after meeting the other party. To avoid any suggestion that the attorney is improperly communicating with the other party through his client, the attorney should not encourage a meeting of the parties unless adverse counsel agrees.

§33.8   B. With Adverse Counsel

Settlement negotiations between attorneys are usually informal, held outside the presence of clients, and marked by some use of bargaining tactics. Attorneys can usually discuss settlement factors more productively when the clients are absent: there is no need to impress the clients and the discussions are not colored by the parties' antagonism or apprehension.

Settlement negotiation is often the process of testing an adversary to determine his most favorable offer or acceptance level. Most lawyers do not consider it a show of weakness to initiate negotiations or to modify a previous demand or offer; both sides know that settlement at the proper level is mutually beneficial. Statements such as "My client will not take a cent less than $ _____ ," or "My final offer is $ _____ ," are commonly used in negotiation, but it is not uncommon for demands to drop and offers to increase as a lawsuit progresses.

An attorney should consider how much to reveal information to the adversary and how soon. For example, a demand may be accompanied by some information about the client's case in order to encourage an offer. Once that offer is heard, more information may be given in the hope of convincing the adversary to better the offer. See §33.9 on use of a settlement brochure.

§33.9   C. Use of Written Statements and Brochures

The attorney for the party who is seeking relief may find it useful to send to adverse parties a written statement that specifies the legal and factual bases of the client's right to the claimed relief and the amount and items of relief demanded. The written statement is sometimes in the form of a brochure containing text, copies of documents, diagrams, and photographs.

The purpose of the written statement is both to furnish defendants and insurers with information and to persuade them to make an acceptable offer. The statement attempts to convince the defendant that he is exposed to a judgment that is substantially worse than the settlement demanded. Experienced practitioners are often willing to set out all the favorable aspects of the client's position, feeling that little is gained by trying to conceal points in the hope of surprising adversaries if the case reaches trial.

A written statement is more than a negotiating tool when it is used as a "bad faith letter." This is a letter or statement sent by a claimant to defendant and defendant's insurer offering to settle the case for the limits of defendant's insurance coverage and stating the factors that show that the probable judgment would exceed those limits. An insurer who in bad faith refuses to settle for policy limits may become liable for amounts in excess of those limits. See, *e.g.*, *Crisci v Security Ins. Co.* (1967) 66 C2d 425, 58 CR 13. However, there is no liability unless the insurer is specifically given an opportunity to settle within the policy limits. *Merritt v Reserve Ins. Co.* (1973) 34 CA3d 858, 110 CR 511.

III. CCP §998 OFFER TO ALLOW JUDGMENT

§33.10   A. Nature; Use

Code of Civil Procedure §998 provides a procedure by which a party may make a formal written offer to allow judgment to be entered in accordance with specified terms. Acceptance or revocation of a CCP §998 offer is governed by the basic laws of contract. *Ward v Superior Court* (1973) 35 CA3d 67, 110 CR 501.

The CCP §998 offer can be used to encourage an adverse party to accept a settlement on the offeror's terms. A party who does not accept such an offer, and who then fails to achieve a better judgment at trial than that offered, may be denied recovery of certain litigation costs or required to pay additional costs. See §§33.12, 33.14.

A judgment entered under CCP §998 is deemed a "compromise settlement." CCP §998(e). The judgment bars relitigation of the same causes of action between the parties, but does not constitute an admission of liability. Because no issues were adjudicated, there is no collateral estoppel. See 4 Witkin, CALIFORNIA PROCEDURE, Proceedings Without Trial §40 (2d ed 1971). The CCP §998 procedure cannot be used in eminent domain actions. CCP §998 (f).

After a verdict or finding, an offeror who has obtained a judgment more favorable than the offer may present a cost bill that includes the additional costs permitted by CCP §998. A defendant whose offer was not bettered by plaintiff may move to strike plaintiff's request for costs. On costs generally, see CALIFORNIA CIVIL PROCEDURE DURING TRIAL §§23.83–23.103 (Cal CEB 1960).

In determining whether the judgment for a plaintiff is more favorable than an offer, plaintiff may add to the amount of the verdict the amount of taxable costs incurred up to the time of the offer, but not costs incurred after that time. *Bennett v Brown* (1963) 212 CA2d 685, 28 CR 485. See generally 4 Witkin, PROCEDURE, Proc Without Trial §42.

For discussion of CCP §1025, under which a tender and deposit of money in an action for recovery of money may bar a plaintiff from recovering costs and require him to pay costs, see 1 CIV PROC BEFORE TRIAL §19.3.

§33.11   B. Serving and Filing Offers and Acceptances

A Code of Civil Procedure §998 offer (see §§33.13, 33.15 for forms) can be served on an adverse party at any time from commencement of the law suit until ten days before commencement of the trial. See §§33.12, 33.14. If the offer is not accepted within 30 days, or before trial begins if that occurs first, the offer is deemed withdrawn. If the offer is accepted, a copy of the offer with proof of acceptance must be filed and the clerk or judge must then enter judgment accordingly. CCP §998(b).

The attorney for a party making a CCP §998 offer may serve the typed original on the adverse party with a request that it be filed with an acceptance form. A copy of the offer with a proof of service form can be filed at the time the offer is served, after time for acceptance has passed, or even when cost bills are presented after trial.

An attorney who wishes to accept an offer may notify the offeror informally, *e.g.*, by letter or telephone. The attorneys then decide how to make the settlement final, *e.g.*, by means of release and dismissal or entry of a judgment. The offeree may complete the settlement by filing the original CCP §998 offer (or a copy of it if he was served with a copy) along with an acceptance form signed by the attorney, the party, or both. CCP §998(b). After a copy of an acceptance is served on the offeror, the offer cannot be revoked.

An offeror may type an acceptance form as part of the offer to assure that the details of any judgment entered will conform to the offer. See forms in §§33.13, 33.15. Otherwise, the party who accepts an offer can prepare a notice of acceptance, file it with the offer, and serve a copy on the offeror.

C. Offer by Plaintiff
§33.12   1. Benefits; Tactics

A plaintiff (or cross-complainant) who makes a written offer to allow judgment to be taken on specified terms and conditions may recover augmented costs at the court's discretion if defendant does not accept the offer and fails to obtain a more favorable judgment. In addition to the costs allowed by CCP §1031 or §1032, the court may order defendant to pay plaintiff a reasonable sum to cover expert witness' costs, which are actually incurred and reasonably necessary in plaintiff's preparation or trial of the case. CCP §998(d). Police officers are deemed to be expert witnesses. CCP §998(e). The costs for expert testimony at trial shall not exceed those specified in Govt C §68092.5 (experts to receive reasonable fee set by court). CCP §998(g).

A plaintiff may serve a CCP §998 demand on a defendant at any time after an action has begun, but no later than ten days before the trial commences, which, under CCP §581(1), is the day the opening statement is begun, evidence is introduced or the first witness sworn. CCP §998(b). The costs plaintiff may recover under CCP §998(d) are the same whether incurred before or after the date of the offer.

The amount or terms of plaintiff's CCP §998 offer is normally lower than the predicted verdict, but need not be the minimum that plaintiff would accept. An offer below the predicted verdict reflects plaintiff's saving of preparation time and expense that result from immediate settlement and is an inducement to defendant to accept.

Plaintiff's offer may be a round figure (*e.g.*, $5000 rather than $4999.99); if the judgment is equal to the amount offered (*e.g.*, $5000) defendant has failed "to obtain a more favorable judgment." See CCP §998(d).

If there are two or more defendants, plaintiff may serve a joint CCP §998 demand on both, or a separate demand on each. If defendants are held to be jointly and severally liable for the total judgment, it would not matter which form was used by plaintiff. However, if each defendant is severally liable for only part of the total judgment, each might be in a position to argue that he has obtained a more favorable judgment than in a joint demand, even though the combined recovery from both may exceed the amount of the CCP §998 demand.

§33.13 2. Form: Plaintiff's Offer To Allow Judgment (CCP §998)

Copies: See Comment below.

[Caption. See §§23.18–23.19]

No. _____

OFFER TO ALLOW JUDGMENT (CCP §998); ACCEPTANCE; REQUEST TO ENTER JUDGMENT

To ____[name(s) of defendant(s)]____:

Under Code of Civil Procedure section 998, plaintiff ____[name]____ **offers to allow judgment to be taken in this action** ____[as specified below / as follows: _____]____.

If you accept this offer, please date and sign the acceptance form below and file this paper with the Clerk of this Court who will enter judgment accordingly.

Dated: _____

[*Signature of attorney*]

[*Typed name*]
Attorney for ____[name(s)]____

ACCEPTANCE

The undersigned accept plaintiff's offer to allow judgment in this action to be entered as specified ____[below / above]____.

Dated: _____

[*Signature of attorney*]

[*Typed name*]
Attorney for ____[name(s)]____

[*Additional signature lines may be typed on the paper if more than one defendant is an offeree*]

REQUEST FOR ENTRY OF JUDGMENT

To the clerk (or a judge) of this Court:

Under the Code of Civil Procedure section 998 and pursuant to the above signed offer and acceptance, please enter judgment in this action as follows:

  1. ____*[E.g., Defendant ____[name]____ shall pay to plaintiff ____[name]____ the sum of $_____ in satisfaction of all claims, damages, costs, expenses, attorneys' fees and interest claimed in this action]____;*
  2. ____*[Continue with other terms and conditions, if any]____.*

Comment: The above form illustrates a CCP §998 offer that also sets out an acceptance form for the adverse attorney's signature and a request to the clerk to enter judgment. An offeror's attorney who prefers that adverse counsel prepare an acceptance form and request for entry of judgment, should omit the "acceptance" and "request" sections from the form, specify the terms and conditions of the offer at the end of the first paragraph of the form, and reword the second paragraph, for example:

Judgment in accordance with this offer will be entered if, within the time allowed by Code of Civil Procedure section 998, this paper and a written notice of acceptance are filed with the clerk of this Court.

Use of a combined offer-acceptance form permits the offeree's attorney to obtain entry of the offered judgment by dating and signing the acceptance and filing the combined form with the court clerk. Making the acceptance part of the offer also assures that the details of judgment entered will conform to the offer. See generally §33.11.

Customarily, only the attorneys sign offers and acceptances. However, the attorney for the offeror may wish to have the party sign the offer as well to assure that the party will not later claim that authority to settle was not given. See §33.6.

The offeror's attorney may wish to prepare an original and at least four copies of this form. The original, accompanied by two copies, can be served on the offeree's attorney or on the party if he is unrepresented. The offeror's attorney keeps one copy to file if the offer is not accepted and at least one office copy. Adverse counsel may accept by dating, signing, and filing the original and may notify the offeror by conforming a copy and returning it to offeror's attorney.

D. Offer by Defendant

§33.14   1. Benefits; Tactics

If defendant makes a written offer to allow judgment to be taken on specified terms and conditions, a plaintiff who does not accept the offer and fails to obtain a more favorable judgment cannot recover costs from defendant and must pay defendant's costs incurred from the time of the offer. In addition, the court may require plaintiff to pay defendant's costs from the date the complaint was filed including a reasonable sum to cover the services of nonemployee expert witnesses. CCP §998(c). Police officers are deemed to be expert witnesses. CCP §998(e). The costs for expert witness services for trial shall not exceed those specified in Govt C §68092.5 (experts to receive reasonable fee set by court). CCP §998(g).

Early service of a CCP §998 offer assures defendant of recovering a larger portion of costs from a plaintiff who fails to obtain a result better than the offer. Some defense lawyers have been known to serve a CCP §998 offer of $1 on the theory that doing so entitles defendant to augmented costs if there is a defense verdict.

If there are two or more plaintiffs, defendant should normally make a separate CCP §998 offer to each plaintiff because (a) an offer that does not specify the amount offered to each plaintiff will be treated as a nullity even though the total recovery by all is lower than the total offer (*Randles v Lowry* (1970) 4 CA3d 68, 74, 84 CR 321, 325); (b) if the terms of the offer are contingent on acceptance by more than one plaintiff, defendant is not entitled to the benefits of CCP §998, which requires an unconditional offer (*Hutchins v Waters* (1975) 51 CA3d 69, 123 CR 819; see generally, 4 Witkin, CALIFORNIA PROCEDURE, Proceedings Without Trial §§41A, 42 (2d ed 1971)).

§33.15   2. Form: Defendant's CCP §998 Offer To Allow Judgment

Copies: See Comment in §33.13.

[Caption. See §§23.18–23.19]

No. _____

OFFER TO ALLOW JUDGMENT (CCP §998); ACCEPTANCE; REQUEST TO ENTER JUDGMENT

§33.16   SETTLEMENT   470

To ____[name of plaintiff]____:
   Under Code of Civil Procedure section 998, defendant ____[name]____ offers to allow judgment to be taken in this action ____[as specified below / as follows: _____]____.
   If you accept this offer, please date and sign the acceptance form below and file this paper with the Clerk of this Court who will enter judgment accordingly.
   Dated: _____
                                         _____
                                         [Signature of attorney]
                                                [Typed name]
                                         Attorney for ____[name]____

ACCEPTANCE

   The undersigned accepts defendant's offer to allow judgment in this action to be entered as specified ____[below / above]____.
   Dated: _____
                                         _____
                                         [Signature of attorney]
                                                [Typed name]
                                         Attorney for ____[name]____

REQUEST FOR ENTRY OF JUDGMENT

To the Clerk (or a Judge) of this Court:
   Under Code of Civil Procedure section 998 and the above signed offer and acceptance, please enter judgment in this action as follows:
   1. ____[E.g., Defendant ____[name]____ shall pay to plaintiff ____[name]____ the sum of $_____ in satisfaction of all damages, costs, expenses, and interest claimed in this action]____;
   2. ____[Continue with other terms and conditions, if any]____.

Comment: See Comment to form in §33.13.

IV. SETTLEMENT CONFERENCES

A. Procedures To Set Conference

§33.16   **1. Voluntary**

   California Rules of Court 207.5 requires the clerk of each superior court, at a time provided by local rule or after the case has been on the civil active list for 30 days, to send all parties an invitation to attend a settlement conference. If one party, at least 20 days before the date set for a pretrial or trial setting conference, advises the clerk that the party accepts the invitation, the clerk must give notice to all other parties of the acceptance and place the case on the court's settlement calendar. Under Rule 207.5, a case must also be put on the settlement calendar on the joint request of all parties, and a court may order any case to be put on the settlement calendar at any time. Thus, even before an invitation has been received, or after the time has passed during which acceptance of an invitation would require the setting of a settlement conference, any party may request a conference and the court may grant the request. In some municipal courts, a settlement conference conducted by a judge can be obtained by written request.

An attorney who believes that an early settlement is possible and would save time and expense may request a settlement conference before an invitation is received. Similarly, an attorney can accept an invitation to a voluntary settlement conference that will be held at or near the trial setting or pretrial conference date even though the case is one that would be set for a later mandatory settlement conference, or, the case is one that, under local court rules, might not be set for a mandatory conference. (*E.g.*, in San Francisco, only cases scheduled for jury trial are set for mandatory conference. See SF Super Ct R 2.6(B).)

The clerk's form on which the invitation is conveyed usually carries a place for an attorney to indicate acceptance, or the attorney may draft a separate notice of acceptance.

After a court has scheduled a settlement conference, the duties of all attorneys and parties to prepare for, attend, and participate, are the same as if the conference were mandatory. See Cal Rules of Ct 217.

§33.17 2. Mandatory

Most superior courts have adopted local rules for scheduling and holding mandatory settlement conferences. The requirements of these rules have the legal effect of procedural statutes; the court may impose sanctions on a party that does not comply with them. *Wisniewski v Clary* (1975) 46 CA3d 499, 504, 120 CR 176, 180. See Cal Rules of Ct 207.5, which expressly authorizes local settlement procedures. See also Cal Rules of Ct Appendix, Div 1, §9(a),(d) which recommends that all superior courts require settlement conferences to be held in all cases approximately 20 days before the trial date before an experienced judge who will actively participate in the settlement negotiations. See

§33.18 SETTLEMENT

generally 4 Witkin, CALIFORNIA PROCEDURE, Trial §72 (2d ed 1971). A settlement conference date is usually assigned by the court at the trial setting (or pretrial) conference. See §26.75.

A party or attorney who does not appear at, prepare reasonably for, or participate in good faith in, a settlement conference as required by the California Rules of Court, local rules, or court order, may be ordered to pay the opposing party's reasonable expenses and counsel fees and the court may change the calendar status of the action. Cal Rules of Ct 217.

§33.18 3. Continuances

Some local court rules provide that a settlement conference may be reset in the discretion of the judge to whom the conference has been assigned, although a continuance of the conference does not affect the trial date. See *e.g.*, SF Super Ct R 2.6(C). See also LA Super Ct Pol on Continuances, printed daily in the *Los Angeles Daily Journal*, which requires a showing of good cause, not merely a stipulation, for a continuance, and states that counsel may not stipulate to take a mandatory settlement conference off calendar unless the case has settled. See also Cal Rules of Ct Appendix, Div 1, §9(b),(d), which recommends that no continuance be granted, except in an emergency, unless applied for by noticed motion with supporting declarations even if the parties have agreed or stipulated to the continuance, and that attorneys give mandatory settlement conferences reasonable priority over other court engagements.

B. Attorney's Preparation

§33.19 1. Review; Reevaluation

It is good practice to prepare carefully for a settlement conference. Sanctions may be imposed on an attorney who fails to "prepare reasonably" for a conference. Cal Rules of Ct 217. Local court rule or policy may require, *e.g.*, that all counsel attend the conference and "be intimately familiar with the pertinent available evidence involving both liability and damages . . . [and] prepared to discuss the case in depth. . . ." See LA SUPER CT CIV TRIALS MAN ¶11(3).

Preparation for a conference often begins with a careful reevaluation of what should be accepted or offered to settle the case. For example, at a mandatory conference three weeks before trial, a plaintiff's attorney should have resolved any earlier uncertainty about the extent of detriment suffered by the client, what evidence is available, which witnesses will appear at trial, and how effective they are likely to be. The attorney should discuss this evaluation with the client and, if necessary, obtain revised settlement authority. See §33.6 on authority.

An attorney preparing to appear before a judge whose conference procedures are unknown can ask other attorneys and judges such questions as: What information does the judge expect attorneys to supply? What techniques does he use to encourage settlement? Will he ask the attorneys to split the difference between demand and offer? Will he ask to speak privately with the plaintiff?

Some local rules require the parties to discuss settlement before the settlement conference. See, *e.g.*, SF Super Ct R 2.6(E), which requires: parties to "undertake good faith settlement discussions" before the date set for the conference; plaintiff's counsel to convey a settlement demand to defendant's counsel at least five court days before the conference; and defense counsel to return a settlement offer within two court days after the demand.

§33.20   2. Use of Written Statement; Checklist

Superior court judges are encouraged by the Judicial Council to require each party claiming damages to furnish all other parties, at least five days before a settlement conference, an itemized list of the special damages and the amount of general damages claimed, and in a personal injury or wrongful death case, a settlement offer. Cal Rules of Ct, Appendix, Div 1, §9(d). Some courts have adopted local rules or policies that require the service of written statements on other parties before the conference. See, *e.g.*, SF Super Ct R 2.6(F), requiring the parties to exchange and deliver to the settlement conference judge, at least two days before the conference, a written statement describing the case and relevant legal issues and contentions; the names, addresses, and specialties of expert witnesses who will be called; and in personal injury cases, a copy of any recent medical reports and a summary of injuries and residuals including a list of any claimed special damages and earnings loss. LA SUPER CT CIV TRIALS MAN ¶12 provides that a judge may direct the parties to submit to the settlement judge's department five days before the conference a written statement of the material facts, the contentions in dispute, the identities and capacities of all parties, and citations to important legal authorities.

Preparing a concise and forceful settlement statement, even when not required by court rule, helps the attorney to analyze the case, assemble information the judge may request, and formulate an effective conference presentation. For example, in a personal injury accident case, a two to three page statement might contain the following information:

(a) Names and ages of plaintiff(s) and defendant(s);

(b) Date and time of accident;

(c) Exact location of accident;

(d) Nature of case, *e.g.*, auto versus auto; auto versus pedestrian; slip and fall; construction.

(e) Weather, traffic, and visibility;

(f) Type, year, and condition of plaintiff's and defendant's vehicles;

(g) Nature and estimated amount of related property damage;

(h) Brief statement of facts;

(i) Diagram of scene of accident;

(j) Plaintiff's theory of recovery;

(k) Defendant's theory of defense;

(l) Names of independent witnesses;

(m) Brief statement of plaintiff's injuries including complaints at time of accident, summary of injuries, and list of residuals;

(n) Amount of present and future medical expenses, whether such expenses are covered by insurance, and any other special damages;

(o) Prior or subsequent accidents or medical complaints.

(p) Whether there has been a defense medical examination and report;

(q) Loss of wages or income, including a description of the type of employment or business, specific dates and amounts of loss, and possible future losses;

(r) Percentage estimate of comparative fault or likelihood of recovery;

(s) Monetary jury range;

(t) Amount of demand and amount of offer.

Counsel may attach to such a settlement statement copies of reports, photographs, and other documents. See §33.21.

§33.21 3. Required Information and Documents

Some local court rules and policies require an attorney to bring specified information and documents to a settlement conference or to deliver them to the settlement judge before the conference. See, *e.g.*, LA SUPER CT CIV TRIALS MAN ¶12 (discussed in §33.20) and ¶13, which requires counsel for a party claiming damages to bring a list of all special damages claimed with corroborating evidence that may be examined by the judge and adversaries. In a personal injury action, the special damages should be up to date and listed, totaled, and categorized separately as medical and related expenses (including hospitalization, ambulance charges, and drugs), and loss of earnings. The attorney should also organize in a separate file and bring to the conference all medical reports and records, depositions (with key passages marked), photographs, books, records, diagrams, maps, bills, contracts, memoranda, and documents pertinent to settlement of the case. See also SF Super Ct R 2.6(F), discussed in §33.20.

C. Attendance and Participation

§33.22 1. Attorneys

Sanctions may be imposed on an attorney who fails to appear at a settlement conference or to participate in good faith as required by local rule or court order. Cal Rules of Ct 217. Some local court rules add that the settlement conference must be attended by the attorney who will try the case. See, *e.g.*, SF Super Ct R 2.6(D). If the party's attorney has associated another attorney to try the case, both should attend the conference.

Counsel's good faith participation is one of the requisites of a successful settlement conference. The attorney must be there not merely to learn more about the adversary's case, but with a willingness to consider points made by the judge and adverse counsel.

§33.23 2. Parties; Representatives of Insurers and Entities

Many local court rules require parties to an action to attend the settlement conference, and sanctions may be imposed on them if they fail to attend or to participate in good faith. Cal Rules of Ct 217. Some local rules provide that a defendant need not attend if a settlement or judgment will be paid by his insurer, but an authorized representative of the insurer must attend in addition to the party's attorney. See *e.g.*, SF Super Ct R 2.6(D). Other rules require that the insurer's representative have full authority to negotiate and make decisions, as must the representative who attends for a business, corporate, or governmental entity party. See, *e.g.*, LA SUPER CT CIV TRIALS MAN ¶11, under which a party or representative who requests it, at least five days before the conference date and notifies adversaries, may be expressly excused for good cause by the settlement judge, although the excused party or representative must be available to court and counsel by telephone at the time of the conference.

Settlement conferences are usually conducted by the judge and the attorneys in the judge's chambers while the parties wait in the courtroom. Clients can be told to stay in the courtroom because the judge might call them into chambers at any time.

D. Conduct of Conference

§33.24   1. Judge's Role

A settlement judge is not empowered to compel a litigant to settle a case, but can direct attorneys and parties to negotiate personally under reasonable conditions. *Wisniewski v Clary* (1975) 46 CA3d 499, 505, 120 CR 176, 180. See generally, 4 Witkin, CALIFORNIA PROCEDURE, Trial §§182, 186 (2d ed 1971). A patient, skillful, and impartial judge acts as a catalyst for settlement by creating a climate in which productive negotiations can occur.

Settlement judges differ in the manner in which they conduct a conference. Many begin by asking each attorney in turn to summarize key facts and contentions. Some take an active role, asking questions, pointing out strengths and weaknesses, and stating their own estimates of the range within which the case should settle. If there is little progress toward agreement with all attorneys present, a judge often meets separately with the attorneys on each side. The judge may require a series of group and separate discussions until agreement is reached or the judge concludes that the case must be tried.

Sometimes attorneys agree on terms for settling a case, but one or more of the parties balk at the agreement. The settlement judge can be asked to assure the client that the proposed settlement is fair and in the client's best interests. With the attorney's consent, the judge can talk with the party alone.

Some judges conclude a successful conference by calling in the parties and a court reporter (or moving from chambers to the courtroom) and reading the terms of the settlement into the record. The record can also show that the parties have understood and consented to the settlement terms.

§33.25 2. Presentation by Plaintiff's Attorney

Plaintiff's attorney is often asked to begin the conference by summarizing the facts of the case, theories of recovery, and the factual and legal basis for the relief sought. This summary should be short and factually accurate, but can state plaintiff's contentions in a favorable light. Detailed discussion of plaintiff's strengths and defendant's weaknesses can be used later in the conference.

The attorney will be asked to state plaintiff's latest demand. This demand need not be the minimum acceptable offer and can be lowered as the conference progresses in response to concessions by the defense. However, judges sometimes ask a plaintiff's attorney to state the minimum offer his client would accept, or the level of settlement authority given by the client, or whether the attorney "controls" the client (*i.e.*, whether he can persuade the client to accept a reasonable offer). The attorney should be prepared to answer such questions respectfully, but without disclosing confidential information or undermining his ability to bargain for the best possible recovery. See Evid C §§950–962 on lawyer-client privilege.

§33.26 3. Presentation by Defendant's Attorney

A defendant's attorney should be prepared to summarize the facts and contentions that are the basis for pleaded defenses and the defense theory of settlement value. In addition, counsel should point out any unsupported or misleading statements in plaintiff's counsel's opening summary. A defense attorney should anticipate being asked the limits of settlement authority given by the client or insurer, and, like plaintiff's attorney (see §33.25), should formulate a response that protects the client's bargaining position.

When a plaintiff has sued more than one defendant, defense counsel should consider ways to present a united front against the plaintiff, with provision for a separate resolution of differences among defendants. For example, a preliminary agreement that defendant A will pay 60 percent of a settlement and B will pay 40 percent permits defendants to concentrate settlement conference discussion on reducing plaintiff's demand.

§33.27 E. Sanctions for Failure To Attend or Participate

A superior court judge may impose sanctions on an attorney or party who fails to prepare reasonably for, appear at, or participate in good faith in, a settlement conference. Unless good cause is shown for the failure, it is an unlawful interference with the proceedings of the court; the court may order the person at fault to pay the opposing party's reasonable expenses and attorney's fees, and order a change in the calendar status of the action. Cal Rules of Ct 217. The Judicial Council recommends that each superior court establish a uniform policy on sanctions and that an unexcused failure to attend a conference justifies a fine of up to $500. Cal Rules of Ct, Appendix, Div 1 §9(e).

Local rules of court may also specify sanctions for a failure to meet settlement conference obligations. See, *e.g.*, LA SUPER CT CIV TRIALS MAN ¶10 (offending party may be assessed actual costs, expenses, and attorneys' fees incurred by other parties and ordered to show cause why sanctions, including vacating trial date or dismissal should not be imposed). The imposition of such sanctions is within the power of the court, although the sanctions imposed must be within the scope of those permitted by the court's rules. *Wisniewski v Clary* (1975) 46 CA3d 499, 120 CR 176.

V. CONCLUDING SETTLEMENT
§33.28 A. Methods

A settlement agreement, oral or written, should provide a procedure for terminating the pending lawsuit, protecting the parties from future litigation, and assuring payment or performance. The method most commonly used to conclude a settlement when there is to be immediate payment is for plaintiff to execute a release or covenant not to sue, and a request for dismissal of the lawsuit, in exchange for a check, draft, or other form of payment or performance. See §§33.29–33.30.

A settlement agreement that contemplates future payment or performance often provides for entry of a consent judgment. See chap 34. The judgment terminates the lawsuit, bars other litigation on the same causes of action, and is enforceable as a judgment rather than as a contract. See §§34.2–34.5. The CCP §998 procedure (see §§33.10–33.15) may also culminate in the entry of a judgment.

B. Release and Dismissal

§33.29   1. Nature of Release, Covenant Not To Sue, and Dismissal With Prejudice

A release is a contract by which a person abandons or relinquishes a right or claim to the person against whom the right or claim might have been demanded or enforced; it extinguishes the cause of action. *Pellett v Sonotone Corp.* (1945) 26 C2d 705, 711, 160 P2d 783, 787. See generally CC §§1541–1543. A release is subject to recission for the same reasons as are other contracts. *Mathews v Atchison, Topeka & Santa Fe Ry.* (1942) 54 CA2d 549, 557, 129 P2d 435, 441. In addition, a general release obtained from an injured person within 15 days after commencement of first confinement for an injury, as either an inpatient or an outpatient, or before release from confinement, whichever occurs first, is presumed fraudulent. Bus & P C §6152(b).

A covenant not to sue is an agreement not to enforce an existing cause of action, but is not an abandonment or relinquishment of the right or claim. *Pellett v Sonotone Corp., supra.* Covenants not to sue were formerly used instead of releases to conclude settlements with fewer than all defendants under a rule that the release of one joint tortfeasor was a release of all. See *Kincheloe v Retail Credit Co.* (1935) 4 C2d 21, 23, 46 P2d 971, 972. Under current CCP §877, however, a release given to one tortfeasor does not discharge the others. See §33.32.

Dismissasl with prejudice (the modern name for retraxit; *Slack v Slack* (1966) 241 CA2d 530, 539, 50 CR 763, 768) is a claimant's voluntary renunciation of his suit or cause of action, and bars further litigation between the parties on the same subject matter (*Datta v Stabb* (1959) 173 CA2d 613, 621, 343 P2d 977, 982). A voluntary dismissal with prejudice by a plaintiff (or cross-complainant) bars a subsequent action on the same cause of action against the persons released. *Gagnon Co. v Nevada Desert Inn* (1955) 45 C2d 448, 455, 289 P2d 466, 472; *Palmquist v Palmquist* (1963) 212 CA2d 340, 343, 27 CR 756, 757. Filing a dismissal with prejudice amounts to a judgment for the defendants; they are entitled to recover costs (see CCP §§1031–1032), although defendants normally waive costs as part of the settlement agreement. See §§31.66, 31.70 for discussion of voluntary dismissal. The judicial counsel request for dismissal form available from most court clerks contains a line for signature by the attorney for the plaintiff or cross-complainant, but some defense attorneys request that the plaintiff also sign the request to forestall any later dispute over the attorneys' authority to dismiss. See §33.6.

§33.30 2. Drafting Releases

The attorney for the party released (*i.e.*, the releasee) usually drafts or provides a printed form for the release. The releasor's attorney reviews the form to assure that his client is not abandoning broader claims than intended. In some situations, a releasee is satisfied with a simple form. For example:

In consideration of the payment to the undersigned of the sum of $____, receipt of which is hereby acknowledged, I release ____ [names]____ from all claims resulting from ____[e.g., the accident that occurred on or about _____, 19____, at or near _____] ____.

Dated:_____

[Signature of releasor]

[Typed name]

Printed release forms, however, usually contain more detailed provisions that seek to assure protection for the releasee. Clauses commonly used in releases include the following:

Releasors: In an attempt to bar claims by other persons on the named releasor's loss or injury, some release forms add to the name of the releasor a clause such as "for himself, his heirs, executors, administrators, and assigns." Another practice requires other persons (*e.g.*, claimant's spouse) to sign the release as coreleasors. Some releasees also require a release to be given by a person or entity who has a cause of action that derives from the releasor's injury, such as the releasor's employer or worker's compensation insurer. See CALIFORNIA WORKMEN'S COMPEN-

SATION PRACTICE 1973 §§17.17–17.18, 18.3–18.9 (Cal CEB 1973) on an employer's claim against a third party for worker's compensation benefits paid to an injured worker.

Releases: A common release form releases the named defendant and "his insurer, agents, employees, partners, and associates." The releasor's attorney should be sure that broad language in the release does not release persons against whom there are possible claims.

Claims and transactions covered: A general release (*i.e.*, one not restricted by its terms to particular claims or demands) ordinarily covers all claims and demands due at the time of its execution that were within the contemplation of the parties. See *Crow v P.E.G. Constr. Co.* (1957) 156 CA2d 271, 319 P2d 47. See also *Larsen v Johannes* (1970) 7 CA3d 491, 503, 86 CR 744, 751. However, CC §1542 states that a general release does not extend to claims which the releasing party does not know of or suspect at the time the release is signed. Thus, the releasee often adds words designed to assure that the releasor cannot assert a different claim. For example:

____[plaintiff]____ releases ____[defendant]____ from any and all claims, known or unknown, arising out of ____[describe event, transaction, or accident]____.

Some forms prefer to quote CC §1542. For example:

The undersigned agrees, as a further consideration and inducement for this compromise settlement, that it shall apply to all unknown and unanticipated injuries and damages resulting from said accident, casualty or event, as well as to those now disclosed, and hereby expressly waives the provisions of Section 1542 of the Civil Code of the State of California, which reads as follows: "A general release does not extend to claims which the creditor does not know or suspect to exist in his favor at the time of executing the release, which if known by him must have materially affected his settlement with the debtor.

Release not an admission: Release forms often state that:

"This settlement is of a disputed claim, and is not an admission of liability by____[name of releasee]____."

See discussion in §33.5.

Factual statements: Some releases state facts that are part of the inducement for the consideration given by the releasee. For example, wrongful death claimants may be asked to state that they are the sole heirs of the decedent. Or an injured person might be asked to state that the injury did not arise out of or in the course of his employment. If another heir, or an employer, then made a claim against the releasee, there would be grounds for voiding or rescinding the release. See CC §1689.

Indemnification: The party released may ask that the releasor agree to indemnify him against the claims of others arising out of the transaction. For example, wrongful death claimants may agree to indemnify the releasee for any loss incurred by reason of claims later made by other heirs; or an injured person may agree to indemnify the releasee from any claim made by an employer or compensation insurer.

Attorney's authority to dismiss: A release may contain a clause authorizing the releasor's attorney to dismiss the action with prejudice. For example:

____[My / Our]____ attorney, _____, is hereby authorized and directed to file a dismissal with prejudice of action number _____ now pending in the _____ Court of _____.

Some releases omit this clause, but require both the releasor and his attorney to sign the request for dismissal form.

Releasor's understanding: Releases often contain clauses to the effect that the releasor does not rely on any promise or inducement other than those set forth in the release, nor on any statement or representation by the releasee or his representatives, or, in a personal injury case, by any doctor. An additional clause may state that the releasor has read and understood the terms of the release and that they have been explained to him by his attorney.

Subscription: Each releasor is asked to sign a release. Sometimes the attorney for each releasor is also asked to sign, either as a witness of the releasor's signature or under a line such as:

The foregoing release was executed in the presence, and under the direction and advice, of ____[name of attorney]____.

Mutual release: In some cases the attorney for a plaintiff-releasor asks that defendant in the action release plaintiff from any liability arising out of the transaction or event that was the subject of the lawsuit and from liability for malicious prosecution or abuse of process in connection with the lawsuit. If a clause releasing plaintiff is included in a release, it can be entitled "Mutual Release" and should be signed by both parties or their attorneys.

§33.31   C. Duty To Notify Court of Settlement

Whenever a case set for trial is settled, each attorney or unrepresented party has a duty to notify the court of the settlement immediately; failure to do so may be deemed an unlawful interference with court proceedings. Cal Rules of Ct 226. Local rule may place the primary burden for notifying the court on the party seeking affirmative relief. See *e.g.*, LA Super Ct Civ Trials Man ¶17 (specifying that notification be given to the settlement judge if a conference was scheduled, or to the master trial department if no settlement conference but a trial date was set).

§33.32   D. Settlement With Fewer Than All Defendants

A plaintiff may settle a case with one tortfeasor-defendant giving him a release, dismissal, or covenant not to sue or not to enforce judgment, without discharging other defendants. CCP §877(a). See also CC §1543 (the release of one debtor does not release the others unless they are mere guarantors). See generally, 4 Witkin, Summary of California Law, Torts §§38–42.

If the release was given in good faith, the plaintiff's judgment is reduced by the amount received from the settling defendant (CCP §877(a)), but the released tortfeasor is discharged from liability for contribution to the other tortfeasors (CCP §877(b)). However, if the settlement with one tortfeasor was not made in good faith, as when the amount of his payment was unreasonably low under the circumstances, the nonsettling defendants may obtain relief against overpayment. *River Garden Farms Inc. v Superior Court* (1972) 26 CA3d 986, 103 CR 498; *Stambaugh v Superior Court* (1976) 62 CA3d 231, 235, 132 CR 843, 845. See also CCP §877.5 on sliding scale agreements with fewer than all alleged defendant tortfeasors.

JOHN E. HOFFMAN

Chapter 34
Consent Judgment

I. INTRODUCTION
A. Nature; Scope of Chapter §34.1
B. Reasons to Use §34.2
C. Characteristics
   1. Res Judicata §34.3
   2. Appealability §34.4
   3. Bankruptcy Dischargeability §34.5
D. Attorney's Authority To Consent §34.6
E. Conditional or Delayed Entry §34.7

II. PROCEDURE
A. Preparation of Documents §34.8
   1. Terms of Settlement Agreement or Stipulation §34.9
   2. Form: Stipulation For Judgment §34.10
   3. Form: Judgment Pursuant to Stipulation §34.11
B. Entry of Judgment; Function of Judge §34.12

I. INTRODUCTION

§34.1   A. Nature; Scope of Chapter

A consent or stipulated judgment is one entered under agreement of the parties rather than on a jury's verdict or judge's findings and conclusions. When entered, a consent judgment is enforceable as a judgment, rather than as a contract, and has many of the attributes of judgments entered after trials (see §§34.3–34.5).

Consent to entry of a judgment may be given orally in open court, or may be presented to the court in the form of a written stipulation for judgment (see §34.10). See *Holmes v Rogers* (1859) 13 C 191, 201. Part of the bargaining in any settlement negotiation may concern whether to consent to entry of judgment, and on what terms. See §34.2.

See biographical note to chap 32. CEB attorney-editor was PAUL PEYRAT.

§34.2   CONSENT JUDGMENT

The type of consent judgment that is obtained by demands and offers under CCP §998 is discussed in §§33.10–33.15. Consent judgment is also distinct from confession of judgment under CCP §§1132–1134, a procedure used before a lawsuit is filed. On confession of judgment, see generally CALIFORNIA DEBT COLLECTION PRACTICE §§2.46, 14.4–14.7, 16.5 (Cal CEB 1968).

§34.2   B. Reasons To Use

When the terms of a settlement can be performed immediately (*e.g.*, by payment of money), the settlement is usually concluded by dismissal and a release. See §§33.29–33.30. Plaintiff receives a check or draft from a solvent defendant; defendant is dismissed from the pending lawsuit with prejudice, giving him a defense to any subsequent lawsuit on the dismissed cause of action (see §31.70), and obtains a release which can be asserted as a defense to the related causes of action to which it refers.

When, however, settlement calls for future performance, *e.g.*, payment of money in installments, a plaintiff may prefer to have the obligation to pay embodied in a judgment, rather than in a settlement agreement or promissory note. An agreement or note is enforceable as a contract, which may require plaintiff to file a new lawsuit. Plaintiff who dismisses an action in exchange for an agreement to make future payments is trading a present cause of action for a future breach of contract cause of action.

The terms of a consent judgment are interpreted as are the terms of a contract, although a judgment is not subject to rescission, and must be challenged, as would a judgment following a trial. *Stevens v Stevens* (1968) 268 CA2d 426, 435, 74 CR 54, 60. See generally 4 Witkin, CALIFORNIA PROCEDURE, Proceedings Without Trial §158 (2d ed 1971); 5 Witkin, PROCEDURE, Attack on Judgment in Trial Court §§186–187. See CCP §85 on terms of payment of money judgments in municipal and justice courts. A consent judgment is a vehicle for enforcement of the settlement. After the judgment is entered, an abstract of judgment can be obtained and recorded as a lien against specific property to secure payment of the settlement. The judgment lien has priority over other subsequently filed liens. See §34.5. If defendant fails to make payments or perform as required, the settlement can be enforced by levy of execution on the judgment; no separate action for breach of the settlement agreement is necessary.

C. Characteristics

§34.3 1. Res Judicata

A judgment entered under the consent or stipulation of the parties has the same merger and bar effects as if the action had been tried on the merits; matters within the issues of the suit are settled by the judgment which is conclusive and binding on the parties and their privies in all subsequent proceedings involving the same issues. *Avery v Avery* (1970) 10 CA3d 525, 529, 89 CR 195, 198; see CCP §§1908–1917 on the effect of judgments generally. However, a judgment based on a stipulation is binding only as to matters consented to, or as to issues within the stipulation; the judgment does not cover matters not in the stipulation. *Larsen v Beekmann* (1969) 276 CA2d 185, 191, 80 CR 654, 658. In determining what matters or issues are covered by a stipulation, and what claims are discharged by a consent judgment, the court construes the stipulation as it would a contract and may take evidence on the circumstances surrounding the stipulation. *Larsen v Beekmann, supra.*

The principle of collateral estoppel provides that in a second action between the same parties on a different cause of action, the judgment in the first action operates as an estoppel or conclusive adjudication of issues in the second action that were actually and necessarily included in the first action judgment or necessary to it. CCP §1911; *Wood v Herson* (1974) 39 CA3d 737, 746, 114 CR 365, 370. Entry of a consent judgment usually precludes actual adjudication of issues in the first action, and a judgment entered on an agreement of the parties does not have collateral estoppel effect in subsequent actions between the parties. Code of Civil Procedure §998(e) explicitly provides that a judgment is deemed a compromise settlement. See also Evid C §1152 (evidence of payments or offers to compromise not admissible in subsequent proceeding). However, statements of fact recited in a stipulation for judgment may be admissible in a subsequent proceeding, under an exception to the hearsay rule. Evid C §1220.

§34.4 2. Appealability

A party who consents to entry of judgment cannot attack that judgment by appeal; consent constitutes a waiver of errors by a consenting party. *Atchison, Topeka & Santa Fe Ry. v Hildebrand* (1965) 238 CA2d 859, 861, 48 CR 339, 341. See also *In re Carter* (1971) 19 CA3d 479, 488, 97 CR 274, 279; *Morrow v Learned* (1926) 76 CA 538, 540, 245 P 442, 443. See generally 4 Witkin, CALIFORNIA PROCEDURE, Proceedings Without Trial §158 (2d ed 1971). However, if the judgment entered does not conform to the stipulation, it is not a consent judgment and is appealable. See *Jones v World Life Research Inst.* (1976) 60 CA3d 836, 843, 131 CR 674, 679. See generally 6 Witkin, PROCEDURE, Appeal §122.

§34.5 3. Bankruptcy Dischargeability

The terms of a settlement, whether embodied in a settlement agreement or in a stipulation for judgment, may determine whether a consent judgment is dischargeable in bankruptcy. See e.g., *Larsen v Beekmann* (1969) 276 CA2d 185, 80 CR 654, in which (a) plaintiff sued defendant for conversion; (b) the parties stipulated to entry of judgment; (c) plaintiff attempted to levy on the judgment; (d) defendant moved to quash execution on the ground that the judgment had been discharged in bankruptcy; (e) plaintiff countered that the conversion was wilful and thus not dischargeable under 11 USC §35; and the trial court was directed to determine whether the stipulation for judgment was intended as a compromise and waiver of plaintiff's right to assert that the judgment was based on a nondischargeable claim, or whether plaintiff should be permitted to prove wilful and malicious injury. But see 11 USC §35(c) on bankruptcy court's jurisdiction to determine dischargeability.

Bankruptcy does not discharge a debt that is a liability for obtaining money, property, credit, or an extension of credit by a false written statement of financial condition. 11 USC §35(a)(2). Some lawyers therefore require a defendant to warrant his solvency in a settlement agreement or stipulation for judgment, on the theory that the judgment will be nondischargeable if the statement proves false. However, defendant can only warrant his present solvency; the debt is discharged if he becomes insolvent after signing the agreement or stipulation. Further, the warranty may protect plaintiff against discharge of the judgment, without making it any more enforceable against an insolvent defendant who has no nonexempt assets.

A judgment may also become a nonvacatable judicial lien

against certain property through filing an abstract of judgment at least four months before a debtor declares bankruptcy. See 11 USC §107; PERSONAL BANKRUPTCY AND WAGE EARNER PLANS §6.10 (Cal CEB 1971); 4 COLLIER ON BANKRUPTCY §67.08 (14th ed 1974). An abstract of judgment also protects against intervening tax liens. See 26 USC §6323(a).

§34.6   D. Attorney's Authority To Consent

An attorney cannot bind a client by stipulating or consenting to a judgment without express authority from the client. *Preston v Hill* (1875) 50 C 43, 51; see *Bice v Stevens* (1958) 160 CA2d 222, 231, 325 P2d 244, 250 (attorney cannot settle case without client's free and intelligent consent with full knowledge of all facts and circumstances). See §33.6 for a discussion of an attorney's implied and ostensible authority to settle, and the rebuttable presumption of authority. See generally 1 CALIFORNIA CIVIL PROCEDURE BEFORE TRIAL §1.42 (1977); 1 Witkin, CALIFORNIA PROCEDURE, Attorneys §115 (2d ed 1970).

The parties as well as the attorneys should normally sign a stipulation for entry of judgment to avoid dispute over whether an attorney had specific authority to agree to entry of the judgment and whether a party consented to particular terms of the judgment. However, if a client who has given his attorney authority to settle on certain terms is not available to sign a stipulation for entry of judgment within those terms, the signature of the attorney alone should be sufficient. See CCP §283; 1 CIV PROC BEFORE TRIAL §1.43 on attorney's authority to stipulate.

§34.7   E. Conditional or Delayed Entry

A defendant often prefers not to have a judgment against him entered, and thus made public (see §34.2), while the plaintiff often wants his claim embodied in a judgment in case there is a default in payment or performance by defendant. In these cases, the parties can agree that the stipulation for judgment will not be filed, the court will not be asked to render or enter judgment, or execution on the judgment will not be levied until, *e.g.*, defendant defaults on payments he has agreed to make.

The settlement agreement or stipulation for judgment should also provide for the procedure to be followed if the creditor feels that there has been a default. See *Rooney v Vermont Inv. Corp.*

(1973) 10 C3d 351, 368, 110 CR 353, 366. For example, the parties may agree that on default plaintiff must serve a notice of motion for entry of judgment, showing the fact of default by declarations attached to the notice of motion to enter judgment, and a defendant who denies default or seeks to excuse it under some provision of the agreement can serve and file counter-declarations. See §§23.8–23.63 on noticed motion procedure. The court in which the action is pending can then determine whether the conditions for entry of consent judgment have been met. See §34.12.

Sometimes a plaintiff will stipulate to postpone entry of judgment, or execution on an entered judgment, until a later date (*e.g.*, when defendant fails to pay or perform as required in the stipulation) only if defendant will stipulate that judgment then be entered for an amount greater than is necessary to pay the debt. Provisions to this effect may be deemed a forfeiture and unenforceable. See *Chambreau v Coughlan* (1968) 263 CA2d 712, 69 CR 783. However, this device for motivating payment might be upheld if the stipulation recited a factual basis justifying judgment for the larger sum, but also stated that the disputed debt could be satisfied by payment of a smaller sum within prescribed time limits.

II. PROCEDURE

§34.8   A. Preparation of Documents

Parties who have reached agreement on the terms of a settlement may write those terms in a written settlement agreement. See §34.9. Whether such an agreement is prepared, if one of the terms of the settlement is that a consent judgment is to be entered, it is customary to prepare a written stipulation for judgment. See §34.10. The stipulation itself may spell out the terms of the settlement, or, if a settlement agreement was prepared, incorporate that agreement by reference. (A written stipulation would not be necessary if the parties in open court consented to entry of judgment.) In addition to the stipulation, it is good practice to prepare a form of the judgment that is to be entered. See §34.11. Agreement by the parties on the judgment form that is submitted to the judge for signature avoids later dispute over whether the judgment conforms to the stipulation.

§34.9 1. Terms of Settlement Agreement or Stipulation

Settlement negotiations may culminate in preparation of a written agreement signed by the parties, their attorneys, or both (see §34.6). At other times, terms orally arrived at are stated in a stipulation for judgment without a preceding written agreement. The terms of settlement agreements and stipulations for judgment vary according to the nature of the case and on when and under what circumstances the consent judgment will be entered. Some common terms are discussed below.

Actions and claims covered: An agreement should describe the action being settled and any limits placed on further litigation among the parties. A defendant normally wants assurance that the plaintiff will not dismiss, or take judgment in, the present action under the settlement, then file a new action on a related cause of action or one arising out of the same event or transaction. A plaintiff may want assurance that the defendant will not allow judgment, then sue plaintiff for malicious prosecution, abuse of process, or a cause of action relating to the basis of the settled lawsuit. For example, a clause in the agreement might read:

> This agreement settles and concludes all claims between ____[name] ____ and ____[name]____ arising out of ____[describe event or transaction]____ including, but not limited to, Action No. _____ now pending in the _____ Court of _____, County and all claims between them for costs and attorneys' fees, and the parties hereby waive any causes of action arising out of the commencement or conduct of that lawsuit.
>
> The signing of this agreement does not constitute an admission either of liability or that any claim or action is without merit.

Terms of payment: The agreement or judgment should indicate both the amount to be paid and the method of payment. For example:

> ____[Name]____ shall pay ____[name]____ the sum of $_____ in full settlement of all claims between them described in paragraph _____. Payment shall be made as follows: _____.

Future payment procedures can cover such matters as commencement date, interest, amount of each installment, prepayment, and place of payment. Some attorneys specify that payments be made to the attorney in trust for his client so that the attorney can know immediately of any default. Other lawyers avoid this bookkeeping burden and rely on the client to report any default.

Terms of entry of judgment: A settlement agreement that provides for entry of a consent judgment should specify the terms for entry. For example:

The parties shall execute a stipulation for judgment consistent with the terms of this agreement to be entered in the action described in paragraph _____. Judgment under that stipulation shall be entered ____[at _____'s request/ or describe conditions, such as a default in payments, under which judgment may be entered]_____.

Execution on the judgment may be levied immediately on entry and an abstract of judgment may be recorded in any county of this state.

When an agreement provides for entry of judgment only if default or some other event occurs, it should also specify the means to determine whether the conditions for entry have been met. For example, the agreement might provide that plaintiff must proceed by noticed motion to obtain an order for entry of judgment. See *Rooney v Vermont Inv. Corp.* (1973) 10 C3d 351, 369, 110 CR 353, 365; *S.E.P. Assoc., Inc. v Peto* (1975) 49 CA3d 305, 307, 122 CR 514. See also §34.7 on delayed entry of judgment. Other effects of default in payment can also be specified. For example:

In the event of any default of any amount due under this agreement, _____ may, at his option, and on _____ days' notice, declare the entire remaining balance due and payable.

In addition to nonpayment, a default shall be deemed to occur if _____ is adjudicated a bankrupt, or files for any reorganization or other proceeding or seeks any relief of any nature whatsoever under the bankruptcy laws of any jurisdiction, or enters into any arrangement or plan with creditors.

If it is necessary to execute on the judgment provided for in this agreement, or otherwise to enforce _____'s rights against _____, _____ shall be entitled to reasonable attorneys' fees from _____ and all other costs reasonably incurred.

Subscription: A settlement agreement, like a stipulation for judgment, should be signed both by the parties and their attorneys whenever reasonably possible. See §34.6 and form in §34.10.

§34.10 2. Form: Stipulation for Judgment

Copies: Original (submitted to judge); a copy for each other party; office copies.

[Caption. See §§23.18–23.19]

No. _____

STIPULATION FOR JUDGMENT

Plaintiff ____[name]____ and defendant ____[name]____, and their respective attorneys of record, stipulate and agree as follows:

[*For example*]

1. Judgment shall be entered by the Court in this action, pursuant to this stipulation, on request of any party without notice to the other parties as follows:

   a. ____[*E.g., defendant _____ shall pay plaintiff _____ the sum of $_____, plus interest at the rate of _____ percent from _____, 19____, to date of payment*]____.

   b. ____[*State other terms, if any*]____.

2. The judgment so entered shall conclude all claims between the parties described in the settlement agreement executed by them on _____, 19____, a copy of which is attached to and incorporated in this stipulation by this reference, including all costs and attorneys' fees.

3. On entry, this judgment shall become final and execution may be levied on it immediately.

Dated: _____

[*Signature of party*]	[*Signature of party*]
[*Typed name*]	[*Typed name*]
[*Signature of attorney*]	[*Signature of attorney*]
[*Typed name*]	[*Typed name*]
Attorney for ____[*name*]____	**Attorney for** ____[*name*]____

Comment. For discussion of other terms that might be included in a stipulation for judgment, see §34.9. Some lawyers append an order form to the stipulation for judgment. For example:

ORDER

Good cause appearing,

IT IS ORDERED that judgment be entered in favor of ____[name]____ as follows: _____.

Dated: _____

_____

Judge

§34.11   CONSENT JUDGMENT

However, it is normally more convenient to present a separate judgment form (see §34.11) to the judge with the stipulation. When the judge signs the judgment, there is less chance for later dispute over whether the judgment conforms to the stipulation.

§34.11   3. Form: Judgment Pursuant to Stipulation

Copies: Original and copy to submit to judge for signature and to clerk for filing and entry; one copy for each other party; office copies.

[Caption. See §§23.18–23.19]

Case No. _____

JUDGMENT
(Pursuant to Stipulation)

Pursuant to the stipulation for judgment filed in this matter ____ [and after a hearing on _____, 19____ at which _____ appeared as attorney for _____, and _____ for _____]____,

IT IS ORDERED that judgment be entered in favor of ____[name]____ **and against** ____[name]____ **as follows:** _____.

Dated: _____

_____
Judge

Judgment entered on _____, 19____, **in Book No.** _____ **of Judgments, page** _____.

_____, Clerk
By _____, Deputy

Comment: Some courts have standard forms for judgments pursuant stipulation, see *e.g.*, SF Muni Ct Form MCF 47, LA Muni Ct Forms, Civ M–32, Ci 28. An attorney can ascertain from the court clerk whether the court prefers the use of a standard form.

§34.12   B. Entry of Judgment; Function of Judge

The filing of a written stipulation that sets forth all the terms of a judgment agreed to by the parties is normally a sufficient basis for entry of judgment on the ex parte application of either party. See *Rooney v Vermont Inv. Corp.* (1973) 10 C3d 351, 368, 110 CR 353, 365. However, to be effective as a judgment, a consent judgment must be entered in the judgment book by the clerk of the court; merely filing the stipulation is not sufficient. *Old Settlers Inv. Co. v White* (1910) 158 C 236, 245, 110 P 922, 926.

A judge asked to render judgment under a stipulation must do so in exact conformity with the stipulation. The court may, if required, interpret the stipulation as it would a contract, but should not add to its provisions, insert a new term, or otherwise make a new stipulation for the parties. *Jones v World Life Research Institute* (1976) 60 CA3d 836, 840, 131 CR 674, 677. If any term of the stipulation is ambiguous, or if entry depends on an event the occurrence of which must be proved, or if the stipulation fails to specify when or on what proof judgment is to be entered, a judge may order entry of judgment only after a noticed hearing or receipt of a further stipulation. See *Rooney v Vermont Inv. Corp.*, *supra*. Before entering judgment, the court must be fully apprised of the circumstances surrounding occurrence of any condition mentioned in the stipulation, and be satisfied that the condition has in fact occurred. This requires some form of hearing unless the stipulation also contains an express and explicit waiver of the right to a hearing. *SEP Assoc., Inc. v Peto* (1975) 49 CA3d 305, 308, 122 CR 514, 515.

Procedures to obtain entry of a consent judgment can vary in detail from court to court. If there is no ambiguity or condition in the stipulation, the attorney who wants the judgment entered normally files the stipulation for judgment, then presents it ex parte or has the clerk forward it, to a judge of the court in which the action is pending along with a judgment form. (Some local court rules require submission of two copies of the unsigned judgment; see LA SUPER CT EX PARTE MAN §461.) After the judge has signed the judgment, it is returned to the clerk who enters it in the judgment book, noting the date and place of entry on the judgment. If the stipulation is not specific about a particular matter (such as postjudgment interest), or specifies that judgment is to be entered only on occurrence of some event (*e.g.*, defendant's failure to make required payments), the attorney who wants judgment entered normally prepares and serves a notice of motion for entry of judgment with a supporting declaration. See §§23.8–23.63 on noticed motions. The stipulation can specify whether a court commissioner is empowered to authorize entry of judgment. See *Rooney v Vermont Inv. Corp.* (1973) 10 C3d 351, 359, 110 CR 353, 358.

TABLES AND INDEX

Table of Statutes and Rules

CALIFORNIA
Constitution
Art I, §16
  26.28
Art VI, §6
  28.2, 28.4
Art VI, §13
  29.6

Statutes
BUSINESS AND PROFESSIONS CODE
6152(b)
  33.29
7106
  27.4

CIVIL CODE
315 (former)
  24.13
1203
  24.3
1250.24
  27.4
1541–1543
  33.29
1542
  33.30
1543
  33.32
1659
  30.39
1689
  33.30
1717
  29.73, 31.6, 31.69
1750–1784
  31.73
1781(e)(3)
  25.7
1781(f)
  31.73
1812.10
  30.18, 30.21, 30.25, 30.45
2984.4
  30.18, 30.21, 30.25
3065a
  27.4
3147
  31.3
3149
  27.4
3175
  27.4
4000–5174
  28.2
4001
  28.2
4212
  24.3
4363
  25.31
4511
  30.9, 30.18, 30.21, 30.25
7006
  24.3
7015
  24.3

499

CODE OF CIVIL PROCEDURE

10
    29.9
12
    23.9
12a–12b
    23.9
17
    24.8
17(1)
    24.8
85
    34.2
86(a)(7)
    24.27
86(b)(3)
    30.58–30.59
116.4
    26.6
117
    30.9
117.3
    26.6
117.4
    26.6
128(3)
    26.45
166
    23.4
170.6
    28.41
194
    26.30
196
    26.33
214
    26.93
233
    26.33, 34.6
259a(b)
    31.52
283(1)
    29.45
337a
    30.37
376
    27.4
377
    27.4
378–379
    24.29, 27.2, 27.10
379.5
    27.10
382
    30.9, 31.22
385
    25.12
386
    24.3, 27.10
387
    25.1, 25.3, 25.11, 25.13–25.15, 25.32–25.33, 25.36, 25.39, 25.42, 25.45, 25.55–25.56, 25.58
387(a)
    25.1, 25.4, 25.10, 25.12, 25.14, 25.39, 25.47–25.49, 25.53–25.54
387(b)
    25.1, 25.9–25.10, 25.22, 25.39, 25.47, 25.49, 25.54
389
    25.3–25.4, 25.32, 25.58, 31.9, 31.23
389(a)
    25.3
389(b)
    25.3
389.5
    25.4
392–395.5
    31.42
395(b)
    30.21, 30.25
396
    30.18
396a
    30.18

396b
    30.15, 30.18, 31.12, 31.71
397(1)
    31.23, 31.26
399
    31.3, 31.42–31.43, 31.45,
    31.60–31.61, 31.63, 31.74
400
    23.62, 30.18, 31.42
401.1
    28.35
404
    27.10, 28.4–28.5, 28.10,
    28.12–28.13, 28.19, 28.21
404–404.1
    28.15
404–404.8
    25.8, 27.1, 27.10,
    28.1–28.2, 28.56
404.1
    27.10, 28.5, 28.13, 28.15,
    28.19, 28.30, 28.52
404.2
    28.35
404.3
    28.12, 28.35, 28.40
404.4
    28.52
404.5
    28.26
404.6
    28.37, 28.56
404.7
    28.1–28.2
410
    31.29
410.10–418.10
    31.10
411.10
    31.9
412.20(a)(3)
    30.12
415.20
    31.8, 31.22

417.10–417.20
    30.24
417.30
    30.24
418.10
    30.15, 30.19
418.10(a)
    30.19
418.10(b)
    30.19
418.10(c)
    30.19
422.10
    30.15
422.40
    23.39
425.10(b)
    30.36
425.11
    30.36
426.10–426.40
    27.10
426.10–426.50
    24.35
426.10–426.70
    25.57
426.60(c)
    24.35
428.10–428.80
    25.57, 27.10
435
    29.15
437c
    23.9, 23.22, 23.41, 24.37,
    29.2–29.4, 29.6–29.16,
    29.18, 29.28–29.31,
    29.33, 29.40–29.41,
    29.44–29.46, 29.49–
    29.50, 29.67–29.69,
    29.71–29.72, 29.74,
    29.78, 29.83, 29.88
437c (former)
    29.2, 29.4, 29.8–29.9,
    29.11

453
  29.3, 29.15
454
  29.5
460.5
  26.4
472a
  30.16
472b
  30.16
473
  23.62, 25.33, 26.19, 26.91,
  26.93, 26.99, 29.80, 29.82,
  29.88, 30.8–30.9, 30.12,
  30.29–30.31, 30.40,
  30.56–30.65, 30.71–30.73,
  30.77, 30.79, 31.6, 31.55,
  31.91
473a (former)
  30.76–30.77
473.5
  30.56, 30.76–30.79
473.5(a)
  30.75, 30.77
473.5(b)
  30.75, 30.77–30.78
473.5(c)
  30.79
474
  30.9, 30.30–30.31
488.090
  25.6, 25.15
514.050
  25.6, 25.15
526a
  26.4
527
  26.4
575
  26.57
576
  26.70
577
  23.58
578–579
  29.83
579
  27.5, 30.39, 31.16
580
  30.36
581
  31.65–31.66, 31.72,
  31.75–31.77
581 (former)
  31.89
581(1)
  31.71–31.72, 31.75, 31.87,
  33.12
581(1)–(2)
  31.84
581(2)
  31.78, 31.81, 31.83–31.84,
  31.87
581(3)
  31.3, 31.40–31.41, 31.78
581(4)
  31.80, 31.82, 31.88
581(5)
  31.79–31.88
581(6)
  31.40
581a
  23.19, 30.7, 31.1, 31.3,
  31.5–31.6, 31.8–31.10,
  31.13, 31.29, 31.45–31.46,
  31.48–31.49, 31.53
581a(a)
  31.3, 31.7–31.9,
  31.11–31.12, 31.16, 31.29
581a(a)–(b)
  31.15, 31.17
581a(b)
  31.3, 31.5, 31.7, 31.9,
  31.11–31.12
581a(c)
  30.7, 31.3, 31.5–31.6,
  31.15–31.17
581a(d)
  31.10, 31.13, 31.15, 31.22
581a(e)
  31.12

581b
   31.43, 31.60, 31.63, 31.74
581b (former)
   31.42
581c
   29.18
581d
   31.54–31.55, 31.64, 31.69,
   31.89–31.90
583
   26.3, 26.74, 28.27, 30.7,
   31.1, 31.3–31.6, 31.10,
   31.13, 31.23, 31.34, 31.46,
   31.49, 31.68, 31.75
583 (former)
   31.2
583(a)
   23.9, 26.79, 31.3–31.4,
   31.20, 31.33, 31.39,
   31.44–31.45, 31.49,
   31.56–31.59
583(a)–(d)
   31.46
583(b)
   26.51, 26.76–26.77, 26.79,
   26.81, 31.3, 31.6,
   31.13–31.14, 31.18–31.28,
   31.30–31.33, 31.49, 31.60
583(b) (former)
   31.2, 31.28, 31.53
583(b), (e)
   31.18
583(b)–(d)
   31.6, 31.45–31.46,
   31.49–31.53
583(c)
   31.3, 31.29, 31.33, 31.53
583(d)
   31.3, 31.34
583(e)
   31.5, 31.34
583(f)
   31.22–31.23, 31.32–31.35

585
   30.10–30.12, 30.15–30.19,
   30.21
585 (former)
   30.11
585–586
   30.1, 30.18
585(1)
   30.4–30.5, 30.20–30.22,
   30.24–30.25, 30.27–30.29,
   30.35–30.42, 30.44–30.49,
   30.55
585(1)–(2)
   30.6, 30.8, 30.11, 30.20,
   30.23, 30.26, 30.29,
   30.32–30.33
585(2)
   30.5, 30.20, 30.35–30.37,
   30.47, 30.49–30.50,
   30.52–30.55
585(2)–(3)
   30.51
585(3)
   30.6, 30.10–30.11, 30.17,
   30.20, 30.26, 30.29, 30.35,
   30.47, 30.50, 30.53–30.55
585(4)
   30.48–30.50, 30.52, 30.54
585.5
   30.21, 30.25, 30.29, 30.49
585.5(b)
   30.25
585.5(e)
   30.25
586
   30.15, 30.17, 30.26, 30.29
586(1)
   30.12, 30.15–30.17
586(2)
   30.16–30.17
586(3)
   30.17
586(4)
   30.19

CCP

586(5)
30.16
586(6)(a)
30.18
586(6)(b)
30.18
586(6)(c)
30.18
587
30.21, 30.26, 30.29
592
26.28–26.29
594
26.3, 26.74, 30.7, 31.40
594(a)
26.3, 26.55, 26.74, 29.29, 31.40
594(b)
26.55
594a
26.86, 26.91, 26.93, 29.29, 29.68
595
26.93
595.1
26.93
595.2
26.92–26.93, 26.96
595.4
26.93, 26.96
597
27.5, 27.12, 27.17–27.18, 27.21, 29.20
597.5
27.5, 27.12, 27.17
598
27.5, 27.7, 27.12, 27.17–27.18, 27.20
629
29.18
631
26.31–26.32, 26.35, 26.37
631(1)
26.35

631(2)
26.12, 26.35
631(3)
26.35
631(4)
26.31, 26.35–26.36
631(5)
26.33
631(5)–(7)
26.35
631(6)–(7)
26.33, 26.35
631(8)
26.34–26.36
631.1
26.33
631.3
26.33
631.5
26.33
631.8
29.19
632
30.52
655–663.2
26.30
657
29.79
659(1)
29.79
659(2)
29.79
670(1)
30.33
681a
30.67
688.1
25.5, 25.14
689
24.13, 25.6, 25.15
738–751.1
24.3
739
30.27

751
  30.9
751.14
  30.9
801.1
  24.3
803–811
  24.3
831d
  29.4
836
  31.69
860
  24.3
877
  33.29
877(a)
  33.32
877.5
  33.32
904–904.2
  23.62, 27.21
904.1–904.2
  30.80, 31.53–31.54, 31.64, 31.89
904.1(a)
  31.55
904.1(b)
  30.80
904.2
  30.18, 31.42
904.2(b)
  30.80
998
  33.10–33.15, 33.28, 34.1
998(b)
  33.11–33.12
998(c)
  33.14
998(d)
  33.12
998(e)
  33.10, 33.12, 33.14, 34.3

998(f)
  33.10
998(g)
  33.12, 33.14
1003
  23.1, 23.58
1003–1020
  23.2
1004
  23.4
1005
  23.9, 23.12, 23.66, 23.67, 27.17, 29.67–29.68, 31.56
1005.5
  23.1, 23.8, 23.55, 29.12, 30.62
1008
  23.63, 28.37, 28.55, 29.90, 30.72, 31.38, 31.53
1010
  23.17, 23.20, 23.24, 29.31, 29.34, 30.2, 30.46, 30.55, 31.46
1010–1013a
  27.17
1010–1020
  25.55, 26.13
1011(1)
  29.67
1013(a)
  23.10, 29.12, 30.63
1013(b)
  23.25
1014
  29.12, 31.12
1024
  26.99
1025
  33.10
1030
  31.26
1031
  33.12

1031–1032
    31.69, 33.29
1032
    33.12
1033
    29.73, 31.69, 31.90
1033½
    30.27
1046
    23.19, 23.39
1048
    27.3–27.5, 29.83
1048(a)
    27.1–27.4, 27.6, 27.8,
    27.11, 27.13–27.14, 27.16
1048(b)
    27.2–27.3, 27.5, 27.7,
    27.9–27.10, 27.12,
    27.17–27.18
1052
    30.33
1054
    23.14, 30.12
1054.1
    23.14
1060
    24.4–24.9, 24.12–24.13,
    24.18, 24.27, 24.30, 24.35,
    24.43
1060–1062
    24.3, 24.39
1060.5
    24.3, 24.7
1061
    24.14, 24.19–24.20, 24.36
1062
    24.12, 24.14, 24.31
1062a
    24.3, 24.31, 24.39, 26.4
1062a(a)
    24.39
1062a(b)
    24.39, 26.4
1088
    30.9
1090
    26.29
1094–1095
    24.23
1105
    30.9
1132–1134
    34.1
1138
    32.1–32.2, 32.4
1138–1140
    32.1–32.3
1139
    32.1
1140
    32.1
1167
    30.12
1167.3
    30.12
1179a
    26.4
1240.690
    24.3
1240.700
    24.3
1250.230
    25.2, 25.28
1255a
    31.72
1260.010
    26.4
1268.510(a)
    31.72, 31.74
1530–1532
    29.58
1908–1917
    34.3
1911
    34.3
1953e–1953h (former)
    29.33
1981 (former)
    24.41
1985
    29.59

1987(b)-(c)
　　23.44
1987(c)
　　29.57, 29.59
1987(e)
　　29.58
2003
　　23.36, 29.33, 29.48
2012
　　29.48
2012-20.15
　　23.43
2013-2015
　　29.48
2015.5
　　23.36, 23.42, 25.48, 26.96,
　　28.11, 29.33, 29.48, 29.86,
　　30.25-30.26, 30.50, 30.78,
　　31.46
2030
　　29.64
2031
　　29.65
2032
　　29.65
2033
　　29.5
2033-2034
　　30.8
2034(a)
　　23.4
2034(b)
　　30.56
2034(b)(2)(iii)
　　30.7-30.8
2034(d)
　　29.74, 30.8
2097
　　23.43
2984.4
　　30.45

CORPORATIONS CODE
414
　　25.2

709
　　24.3, 24.13
1304(a)
　　25.2
1800(c)
　　25.2
1804
　　30.9
1904
　　24.3
4307
　　27.4
4657 (former)
　　30.9

EDUCATION CODE
21180-21203
　　24.3

ELECTIONS CODE
407
　　24.3
20000-20533
　　24.3

EVIDENCE CODE
135
　　23.36
225
　　23.36
240
　　29.11
435
　　29.33
451
　　23.45, 29.46
452
　　23.45, 29.46-29.47, 29.58
452(d)
　　29.47, 29.63
452(h)
　　29.47
453
　　23.45, 29.46-29.47, 29.58

500	**1415–1418**
24.41	29.55
550	**1416**
24.41	29.56
622	**1417**
29.60	29.55
700	**1420**
23.40, 29.49	29.55–29.56
701	**1421**
23.40, 29.49	29.55–29.56
702	**1500**
23.40–23.41, 29.49	23.44, 29.57
720	**1500–1510**
29.51	29.33
800	**1501**
23.41, 29.51	30.43
801	**1501–1505**
23.41, 29.33, 29.49	29.57, 29.58, 30.43
950–962	**1502**
33.25	23.44, 29.57–29.58
1152	**1503**
33.5, 34.3	29.58
1200	**1503(a)**
23.44, 29.52, 29.60	23.44, 29.57, 29.59
1220	**1506**
29.44, 34.3	29.58
1220–1341	**1507–1508**
23.44, 29.52	29.58
1270–1272	**1509**
29.60	29.58
1271	**1530–1532**
29.33, 29.60–29.61	29.55, 29.58
1271–1272	**1532**
29.61	29.58
1272	**1550–1551**
29.33	29.57
1400	**1551**
23.44	30.43
1400–1401	
29.55	**FOOD AND AGRICULTURAL**
1413	**CODE**
29.55	**55653**
1414	27.4
29.55–29.56	

GOVERNMENT CODE

643
    26.73
900–915.4
    31.1
6700
    23.9
6701
    23.9
8207
    23.43
11440
    24.3, 24.7–24.9
26721
    30.27
68092.5
    33.12, 33.14
68511
    30.21, 30.44, 31.83
69845–69845.5
    30.33
71043
    24.3
76000–76058
    26.33

HEALTH AND SAFETY CODE

10550
    24.3

LABOR CODE

3853
    25.2, 27.4

PROBATE CODE

573
    27.4
588
    24.3
700–721
    31.1
1080–1082
    24.3
1170
    24.3
1516
    24.3

PUBLIC RESOURCES CODE

21167
    24.3
25454
    24.3
30803
    24.3

REVENUE AND TAXATION CODE

3596
    27.4
3638
    31.4
5138
    31.4
5147
    31.4
6931
    24.7

STREETS AND HIGHWAY CODE

741.8
    24.3
5265
    24.3
5414
    27.4

VEHICLE CODE

17151(a)
    31.8
40804
    29.49

WATER CODE

7005
    24.3

30066
    24.3
56090
    24.3
Appendix 8– 42.1
    24.3

Rules
RULES OF COURT
3(a)
    29.79
14(b)
    25.9
201
    23.18–23.19, 23.39, 23.66, 23.69
201(c)(6)
    29.32
202(c)
    23.55
202(d)
    30.16
203
    23.2
203(a)
    23.26, 26.81, 29.41, 30.63–30.64, 31.56
203.5
    26.79, 31.36, 31.56, 31.59
203.5(a)
    31.56–31.57
203.5(b)
    31.57
203.5(c)
    31.57
203.5(d)
    31.57
203.5(e)
    31.35, 31.37, 31.59
203.5(f)
    31.58
204
    23.58
206(a)
    26.1, 26.5, 26.8–26.11, 26.13, 26.31
206(a)(5)
    26.61
206(b)
    26.14, 26.61
206(c)
    26.62
206–221
    26.1
207(a)
    26.9
207(b)
    26.9
207.1
    26.1–26.2, 26.57
207.5
    26.49, 26.52, 26.57, 26.74–26.75, 33.16–33.17
208
    26.1, 26.57, 26.59
208–219
    26.57
209(a)
    26.63, 26.76, 26.80
209(a)(ii)
    26.9
209(b)
    26.64, 26.76
210
    26.64, 26.66
210(a)
    26.58
210(b)
    26.58
210(c)
    26.58
210(d)
    26.58
211(a)
    26.65
211(b)
    26.65
211(c)
    26.67
211(d)
    26.73

211(e)	**220.2**
26.66	26.40–26.41
211(f)	**220.2(a)**
26.66–26.67	26.40
212(a)	**220.2(b)**
26.66	26.39
212(b)	**220.3**
26.66	26.38–26.39, 26.44
213	**220.4**
26.66	26.1, 26.3, 26.9, 26.38, 26.48, 26.76
214(a)	**221**
26.68–26.69	26.17, 26.22
214(a)(1)	**221(a)**
26.56	26.1, 26.3, 26.16–26.17, 26.20, 26.22
214(b)	**221(b)**
26.69	26.21–26.22
214(c)	**221(c)**
26.68	26.1, 26.19, 26.24–26.27
215(a)	**221(d)**
26.70	26.1, 26.18
215(b)	**221(e)**
26.70	26.18, 26.20
216	**221(e)–(f)**
26.56, 26.70, 26.73	26.9
217	**221(f)**
26.45, 26.58, 33.16–33.17, 33.19, 33.22–33.23, 33.27	26.19, 26.25, 26.48
218	**222**
26.72–26.73	26.3, 26.5, 26.66
219	**223(c)**
26.66	26.100
219(a)	**224**
26.63, 26.79	26.86, 26.94, 26.96–26.97
219(b)	**225**
26.1, 26.69, 26.74	26.50, 26.76, 26.80, 31.2
220(a)	**226**
26.1, 26.38, 26.48, 26.50, 26.76, 26.80	33.31
220(a)(ii)	**231**
26.9	26.11, 26.15, 26.29, 26.52
220(b)	**232.5**
26.49, 26.76	27.20
220.1	**234**
26.1, 26.48, 26.51, 26.79	30.43
220.1–220.3	**235**
26.47	23.2, 23.14

249(b)
    23.14
501
    23.18–23.19, 23.39, 23.66,
    23.69
501–534
    26.5
501(c)(6)
    29.32
502(c)
    23.55
502(d)
    30.16
503
    23.2
503(a)
    23.26, 26.81, 29.41,
    30.63–30.64
504
    23.58
506–515
    26.5
507(a)
    26.5
508(a)
    26.5
509(a)
    26.5
510
    26.5
512
    26.86
522
    30.43
523
    23.2, 23.14
534(b)
    23.14
701
    26.5, 26.86
982(a)(5)
    30.44, 31.83
982(a)(6)
    30.21
1225
    23.2, 23.67
1226
    23.67
1237
    30.9
1240
    30.21
1240–1241
    30.9
1250–1255
    25.31
1285.10–1285.40
    23.69
1285.60
    23.69
1286
    30.21
1501–1550
    25.8, 27.10, 28.1–28.3
1501(b)
    28.44, 28.52
1501(c)
    28.4
1501(e)
    28.4
1501(f)
    28.21
1501(g)
    28.4, 28.21, 28.30
1501(h)
    28.5
1501(i)
    28.4, 28.40
1501(k)
    28.4
1501(m)
    28.29
1501(q)
    28.7
1501(s)
    28.48
1504(a)
    28.2, 28.7, 28.56
1504(a)–(b)
    28.2
1504(c)
    28.3

1505
    28.35, 28.56
1506
    28.46
1506(a)
    28.44
1510
    28.7, 28.9
1511
    28.8, 28.18, 28.30–28.31
1512
    28.29
1513
    28.32, 28.34
1514
    28.53
1514(a)
    28.24–28.25
1514(b)
    28.26–28.27
1514(c)
    28.27
1514(d)
    28.22
1514(e)
    28.11–28.12, 28.14, 28.24, 28.26
1514(f)
    28.27
1515
    28.41
1520
    28.10–28.12, 28.14
1520(u)
    28.11
1521
    28.52
1521(a)
    28.5, 28.11–28.12, 28.15, 28.18
1521(b)
    28.14, 28.16–28.17
1521(c)
    28.15
1521(d)
    28.18, 28.32
1522
    28.14, 28.16–28.17, 28.19–28.20
1522–1523
    28.14
1523
    28.14, 28.19
1523(a)
    2816–28.17
1523(b)
    28.16–28.17, 28.20
1524
    28.7, 28.21–28.22
1525
    28.29
1526
    28.29
1527–1529
    28.12
1527(a)
    28.32
1527(b)
    28.23, 28.33
1527(c)
    28.38
1528
    28.33
1529
    28.7, 28.36, 28.39, 28.55
1540
    28.4, 28.40, 28.42
1541
    28.42
1541(a)
    28.43, 28.46–28.47
1541(a)(1)
    28.44
1541(a)(2)(7)
    28.45
1541(b)
    28.46
1541(b)(1)(3)
    28.42
1543
    28.46, 28.51

1543(a)
    28.48–28.49
1543(b)
    28.50
1544
    28.52–28.54
1550(b)
    28.21, 28.28, 28.30–28.31,
    28.46–28.47
1550(c)
    28.51
Appendix, Div I, 9(a)
    26.38–26.39, 26.43, 26.52,
    26.84, 26.100, 33.17
Appendix, Div I, 9(b)
    26.84–26.86, 26.92,
    26.95–26.96, 26.98, 33.18
Appendix, Div I, 9(b)(1)
    26.87
Appendix, Div I, 9(b)(2)
    26.88
Appendix, Div I, 9(b)(2)(ii)
    26.88
Appendix, Div I, 9(b)(2)(iii)
    26.88
Appendix, Div I, 9(b)(3)(i)
    26.89
Appendix, Div I, 9(b)(3)(ii)
    26.89
Appendix, Div I, 9(b)(4)
    26.90
Appendix, Div I, 9(b)(5)
    26.91
Appendix, Div I, 9(c)
    26.40–26.41, 26.43, 26.45,
    26.47, 26.52
Appendix, Div I, 9(d)
    26.75, 33.17–33.18, 33.20
Appendix, Div I, 9(e)
    33.27
Appendix, Div I, 15
    23.2, 23.16, 23.65, 23.68,
    25.38, 31.41, 31.46

LOCAL COURT RULES

Los Angeles County Superior Court

6, §3
    26.80
14, §1
    30.42
7
    23.28, 23.49, 23.50
28
    23.28, 23.49–23.50
28, §7
    23.19, 23.39

Mendocino County Superior Court

II, §1
    26.3

San Mateo County Superior Court

IX
    26.13, 26.23
XIX
    26.34

Solano County Superior Court

2.2
    26.3

San Francisco City and County Superior Court

2.6(B)
    26.75, 33.16
2.6(C)
    33.18
2.6(D)
    33.22–33.23
2.6(E)
    33.19
2.6(F)
    33.20–33.21
6.2
    23.27

RULES OF PROFESSIONAL CONDUCT

7–103
    33.7

ACTS BY POPULAR NAMES

California Coastal Conservation Act
    24.3
California Energy and Conservation Development Act
    24.3
Consumers Legal Remedies Act
    31.73
Family Law Act
    28.2
Improvement Act of 1911
    27.4
Jurisdiction and Service of Process Act
    31.10
Rees-Levering Act
    30.25
Unruh Act
    30.25

Statutes

UNITED STATES CODE

Title 11
35
    34.5
35(c)
    34.5
107
    34.5
Title 26
6323(a)
    34.5
Title 28
1407
    28.1
2201–2202
    24.1
Title 50
App 501–548
    26.93
App 511
    30.28
App 520
    30.9, 30.28
App 520(1)
    30.28
App 521
    26.93
App 560–590
    26.93

ACTS BY POPULAR NAMES

Economic Stabilization Act of 1970
    24.27
Soldiers' and Sailors' Civil Relief Act of 1940
    26.93, 30.28

Rules

FEDERAL RULES OF CIVIL PROCEDURE

23(c)(2)
    25.7
24
    25.32
24(a)
    25.1, 25.10
24(b)
    25.1
42
    27.3
56
    29.18
56(c)
    29.9
56(d)
    29.7
56(f)
    29.13, 29.74
57
    24.1

Table of Cases

A

Abbot Kinney Co. v Los Angeles (1959) 53 C2d 52, 346 P2d 385: §25.3

Abbott v Los Angeles (1960) 53 C2d 674, 3 CR 158: §§24.7, 24.24

Adam v Los Angeles Transit Lines (1957) 154 CA2d 535, 317 P2d 642: §§23.58, 23.62

Adams v Cook (1940) 15 C2d 352, 101 P2d 484: §24.2

Adickes v S. H. Kress & Co. (1970) 398 US 144: §29.13

Adjustment Corp. v Hollywood Hardware & Paint Co. (1939) 35 CA2d 566, 96 P2d 161: §29.16

Adoption of Backhaus (1962) 209 CA2d 13, 25 CR 581: §29.72

Aguirre v Southern Pac. Co. (1965) 232 CA2d 636, 43 CR 73: §29.8

Ahmanson Bank & Trust Co. v Tepper (1969) 269 CA2d 333, 74 CR 774: §29.72

Alameda Conserv. Ass'n v Alameda (1968) 264 CA2d 284, 70 CR 264: §29.29

Alart Assocs., Inc. v Aptaker (SD NY 1968) 279 F Supp 268: §29.74

Albermont Petroleum, Ltd. v Cunningham (1960) 186 CA2d 84, 9 CR 405: §29.69

Albin, People v (1952) 111 CA2d 800, 245 P2d 660: §23.1

Alexander v McDow (1895) 108 C 25, 41 P 24: §30.37

Alhambra v Jacob Bean Realty Co. (1934) 138 CA251, 31 P2d 1052: §25.23

Allen v Allen (1947) 30 C2d 433, 182 P2d 551: §30.28

Allen v California Water & Tel. Co. (1947) 31 C2d 104, 187 P2d 393: §§25.33, 25.35–25.36, 25.38, 25.58

Allen v Pitchess (1973) 36 CA3d 321, 111 CR 658: §25.4

Allstate Ins. Co. v Fisher (1973) 31 CA3d 391, 107 CR 251: §24.19

Allstate Ins. Co. v King (1967) 252 CA2d 698, 60 CR 892: §26.96

Alpha Beta Food Mkts., Inc. v Amalgamated Meat Cutters (1956) 147 CA2d 343, 305 P2d 163: §24.27

Alphonzo E. Bell Corp. v Bell View Oil Syndicate (1938) 24 CA2d 587, 76 P2d 167: §§25.18, 25.23, 25.37

Alturas v Gloster (1940) 16 C2d 46, 104 P2d 810: §§24.19, 24.30
Alvak Enterprises v Phillips (1959) 167 CA2d 69, 334 P2d 148: §29.69
American Enterprise, Inc. v Van Winkle (1952) 39 C2d 210, 246 P2d 935: §24.42
American Home Assur. Co. v Essy (1960) 179 CA2d 19, 3 CR 586: §24.41
American Mission Army, Inc. v Lynwood (1956) 138 CA2d 817, 292 P2d 533: §24.30
American Motorcycle Ass'n v Superior Court (1977) 65 CA3d 694, 135 CR 497: §26.10
Amerson v Christman (1968) 261 CA2d 811, 68 CR 378: §24.42
AMF Pinspotters, Inc. v Peek (1970) 6 CA3d 443, 86 CR 46: §31.16
Anderson v Erwyn (1966) 247 CA2d 503, 55 CR 634: §§31.2, 31.21
Anderson v Southern Pac. Co. (1968) 264 CA2d 230, 70 CR 389: §24.42
Anderson v Stansbury (1952) 38 C2d 707, 242 P2d 305: §§24.36, 24.42
Andre v General Dynamics, Inc. (1974) 43 CA3d 839, 118 CR 95: §31.56
Apostolos v Estrada (1958) 163 CA2d 8, 328 P2d 805: §25.5
Applegate Drayage Co. v Municipal Court (1972) 23 CA3d 628, 100 CR 400: §31.36
Armstrong v Brown (1936) 12 CA2d 22, 54 P2d 1118: §32.4

Armstrong v Superior Court (1956) 144 CA2d 420, 301 P2d 51: §30.9
Artucovich v Arizmendiz (1967) 256 CA2d 130, 63 CR 810: §29.83
Ascherman v Superior Court (1967) 254 CA2d 506, 62 CR 547: §§23.3, 29.70
Associated Boat Indus. v Marshall (1951) 104 CA2d 21, 230 P2d 379: §24.8
Associated Convalescent Enterprises v Carl Marks & Co. (1973) 33 CA3d 116, 108 CR 782: §§31.68–31.69
Atchison, Topeka & Santa Fe Ry. v Hildebrand (1965) 238 CA2d 859, 48 CR 339: §34.4
Atkins v Atkins (1960) 177 CA2d 207, 2 CR 104: §26.73
Avery v Avery (1970) 10 CA3d 525, 89 CR 195: §34.3

B

Bachis v State Farm Mut. Auto. Ins. Co. (1968) 265 CA2d 722, 71 CR 486: §§24.25, 24.27
Backhaus, Adoption of (1962) 209 CA2d 13, 25 CR 581: §29.72
Baker v Commeford (1956) 140 CA2d 599, 295 P2d 522: §24.19
Bank of America v Baker (1965) 238 CA2d 778, 48 CR 165: §29.44
Bank of America v Greenbach (1950) 98 CA2d 220, 219 P2d 814: §26.28
Bank of America v Superior Court (1948) 84 CA2d 34, 189 P2d 799: §§31.5, 31.20

TABLE OF CASES

Bank of America v Superior Court (1937) 22 CA2d 450, 71 P2d 296: §31.21.
Bank of Cal. v Connolly (1973) 36 CA3d 350, 111 CR 468: §27.6
Barber v Irving (1964) 226 CA2d 560, 38 CR 142: §24.13
Barnes v Blue Haven Pools (1969) 1 CA3d 123, 81 CR 444: §§29.18, 29.22
Baroldi v Denni (1961) 197 CA2d 472, 17 CR 647: §25.19
Baron v Mare (1975) 47 CA3d 304, 120 CR 675: §29.33
Bate v Marsteller (1965) 232 CA2d 605, 43 CR 149: §24.40
Beaumont-Gribin-Von Dyl Mgmt. Co. v California Union Ins. Co. (1976) 63 CA3d 617, 134 CR 25: §29.7
Bechtel v Axelrod (1942) 20 C2d 390, 125 P2d 836: §25.17
Bechtel Corp. v Superior Court (1973) 33 CA3d 405, 109 CR 138: §§31.42, 31.63
Beckett v Kaynar Mfg. Co. (1958) 49 C2d 695, 321 P2d 749: §§23.36, 23.57–23.58
Beech Aircraft Corp. v Superior Court (1976) 61 CA3d 501, 132 CR 541: §§29.7, 29.22, 29.25, 29.88–29.89
Beeler v Plastic Stamping, Inc. (1956) 144 CA2d 306, 300 P2d 852: §§24.2, 24.43
Bell, Alphonzo E., Corp. v Bell View Oil Syndicate (1938) 24 CA2d 587, 76 P2d 167: §§25.18, 25.23, 25.37
Bella Vista Dev. Co. v Superior Court (1963) 223 CA2d 603, 36 CR 106: §31.19

Bellaire, Marc, Inc. v Fleischman (1960) 185 CA2d 591, 8 CR 650: §§25.12, 25.38, 25.58
Belt Cas. Co. v Furman (1933) 218 C 359, 23 P2d 293: §§25.1, 25.14, 25.58
Beneficial Standard Prop, Inc. v Scharps (1977) 67 CA3d 227, 136 CR 549: §29.73
Benjamin v Dalmo Mfg. Co. (1948) 31 C2d 523, 190 P2d 593: §§23.11, 30.62
Bennett v Brown (1963) 212 CA2d 685, 28 CR 485: §33.10
Bennett v Hibernia Bank (1956) 47 C2d 540, 305 P2d 20: §§24.20, 30.76
Bill Benson Motors, Inc. v Macmorris Sales Corp. (1965) 238 CA2d Supp 937, 48 CR 123: §§30.7, 30.43
Berghauser v Golden State Orchards (1929) 208 C 550, 282 P 950: §25.15
Berman v Aetna Cas. & Sur. Co. (1974) 40 CA3d 908, 115 CR 566: §25.51
Bernards v Grey (1950) 97 CA2d 679, 218 P2d 597: §30.80
Bernheimer v Bernheimer (1948) 87 CA2d 242, 196 P2d 813: §25.31
Bernstein v Superior Court (1969) 2 CA3d 700, 82 CR 775: §§31.6, 31.53
Berri v Superior Court (1955) 43 C2d 856, 279 P2d 8: §§31.19, 31.30, 31.75
Bertero v National Gen. Corp. (1967) 254 CA2d 126, 62 CR 714: §24.43
Beshara v Goldberg (1963) 221 CA2d 392, 34 CR 501: §§23.3, 25.15

Beverly Glen, Inc., Residents of v Los Angeles (1973) 34 CA3d 117, 109 CR 724: §§29.8, 29.22, 29.29, 29.44–29.45, 29.86

Bice v Stevens (1958) 160 CA2d 222, 325 P2d 244: §§33.6, 34.6

Big Bear Munic. Water Dist. v Superior Court (1969) 269 CA2d 919, 75 CR 580: §§31.5, 31.11

Bill Benson Motors, Inc. v Macmorris Sales Corp. (1965) 238 CA2d Supp 937, 48 CR 123: §§30.7, 30.43

Black Bros. Co. v Superior Court (1968) 265 CA2d 501, 71 CR 344: §23.36

Blakeslee v Wilson (1923) 190 C 479, 213 P 495: §24.1

Bloom v Waxman (1941) 48 CA2d 646, 120 P2d 509: §25.50

Blue Chip Enterprises, Inc. v Brentwood Sav. & Loan Ass'n (1977) 71 CA3d 706, 139 CR 651: §31.59

Board of Educ. v Mulcahy (1942) 50 CA2d 418, 123 P2d 114: §29.45

Boca & Loyalton R.R. v Superior Court (1907) 150 C 153, 88 P 718: §31.83

Bodley v Ferguson (1866) 30 C 511: §26.28

Bogue v Roeth (1929) 98 CA 257, 276 P 1071: §25.27

Bohn v Bohn (1913) 164 C 532, 129 P 981: §§23.20, 23.51, 29.32, 29.34

Bonfiglio v Bonfiglio (1928) 203 C 409, 264 P 747: §25.17

Boosman v United Bldg. Co. (1952) 109 CA2d 486, 241 P2d 58: §24.41

Bos v United States Rubber Co. (1950) 100 CA2d 565, 224 P2d 386: §24.36

Bosworth v Superior Court (1956) 143 CA2d 775, 300 P2d 155: §§31.18, 31.25

Bowden v Robinson (1977) 67 CA3d 705, 136 CR 871: §29.49

Bowles v Superior Court (1955) 44 C2d 574, 283 P2d 704: §§25.51, 25.53

Boyar v Krech (1937) 10 C2d 207, 73 P2d 1218: §§24.34, 24.42

Boyd v Southern Pac. R.R. (1921) 185 C 344, 197 P 58: §§31.2, 31.19

Braun v Brown (1939) 13 C2d 130, 87 P2d 1009: §25.51

Bristol Convalescent Hosp. v Stone (1968) 258 CA2d 848, 66 CR 404: §§30.16, 30.52

Brokate v Hehr Mfg. Co. (1966) 243 CA2d 133, 52 CR 672: §§24.7, 24.35

Brophy, People v (1942) 49 CA2d 15, 120 P2d 946: §§25.48, 25.53

Brown v Happy Valley Fruit Growers, Inc. (1929) 206 C 515, 274 P 977: §23.41

Brown v Rouse (1897) 115 C 619, 47 P 601: §23.10

Brown v Superior Court (1976) 62 CA3d 197, 132 CR 916: §31.26

Brown v Superior Court (1970) 7 CA3d 366, 86 CR 670: §31.55

Brown v Superior Court (1966) 242 CA2d 519, 51 CR 633: §§30.38, 30.40

Brum v Ivins (1908) 154 C 17, 96 P 876: §30.24

Brunzell Constr. Co. v Wagner (1970) 2 C3d 545, 86 CR 297: §§31.2, 31.24, 31.27

Buell v Buell (1891) 92 C 393, 28 P 443: §23.25

Burke v San Francisco (1968) 258 CA2d 32, 65 CR 539: §§24.11, 24.26, 24.30

Burke v W. R. Chamberlin & Co. (1942) 51 CA2d 419, 125 P2d 120: §31.67

Burlingame v San Mateo (1951) 103 CA2d 885, 230 P2d 375: §§25.10, 25.23, 25.34

Burnett v Burnett (1948) 88 CA2d 805, 199 P2d 685: §31.80

Burns v McCain (1930) 107 CA 291, 290 P 623: §33.6

Busching v Superior Court (1974) 12 C3d 44, 115 CR 241: §31.12

Business Title Corp. v Division of Labor Law Enforcement (1976) 17 C3d 878, 132 CR 454: §29.71

C

C-Thru Prods., Inc. v Uniflex, Inc. (2d Cir 1968) 397 F2d 952: §29.7

Caballero v Richardson (1959) 173 CA2d 459, 343 P2d 302: §27.1

Cade v Mid-City Hosp. Corp. (1975) 45 CA3d 589, 119 CR 571: §26.96

Caldwell v Geldreich (1955) 137 CA2d 78, 289 P2d 832: §23.25

Caledonian Ins. Co. v Superior Court (1956) 140 CA2d 458, 295 P2d 49: §23.6

California Accounts, Inc. v Superior Court (1975) 50 CA3d 483, 123 CR 304: §23.10

California Ammonia Co. v Macco Corp. (1969) 270 CA2d 429, 75 CR 753: §§31.19, 31.41

California Canning Peach Growers v Corcoran (1936) 14 CA2d 264, 57 P2d 1360: §§24.30, 24.34

California Water & Tel. Co. v Los Angeles (1967) 253 CA2d 16, 61 CR 618: §§24.8–24.9, 24.18–24.19, 24.43

Camille's Corp. v Superior Court (1969) 270 CA2d 625, 75 CR 868: §31.29

Cantillon v Superior Court (1957) 150 CA2d 184, 309 P2d 890: §§23.2, 26.45

Capital Nat'l Bank v Smith (1944) 62 CA2d 328, 144 P2d 665: §26.85

Carmel-By-The-Sea v Young (1970) 2 C3d 259, 85 CR 1: §24.7

Carpenson v Najarian (1967) 254 CA2d 856, 62 CR 687: §27.12

Carrier v Robbins (1952) 112 CA2d 32, 245 P2d 676: §24.36

Carter v Garetson (1922) 56 CA 238, 204 P 1090: §25.17

Carter, In re (1971) 19 CA3d 479, 97 CR 274: §34.4

Chakmak v H. J. Lucas Masonry, Inc. (1976) 55 CA3d 124, 127 CR 404: §§29.22, 29.24

Chambreau v Coughlan (1968) 263 CA2d 712, 69 CR 783: §34.7
Chaplin v Chaplin (1935) 9 CA2d 182, 49 P2d 296: §24.6
Charles L. Donohoe, Inc. v Superior Court (1927) 202 C 15, 258 P 1094: §31.36
Chas. L. Harney, Inc. v Contractors' State License Bd. (1952) 39 C2d 561, 247 P2d 913: §§24.7–24.9, 24.30, 24.37
Chase v Leiter (1950) 96 CA2d 439, 215 P2d 756: §24.6
Cherry v Home Sav. & Loan Ass'n (1969) 276 CA2d 574, 81 CR 135: §§24.30, 24.45
Chesney v Gresham (1976) 64 CA3d 120, 134 CR 238: §29.85
Chitwood v Superior Court (1971) 14 CA3d 522, 92 CR 441: §31.12
Christin v Superior Court (1937) 9 C2d 526, 71 P2d 205: §31.25
Cinmark Inv. Co. v Reichard (1966) 246 CA2d 498, 54 CR 810: §§24.5, 24.45
City Bank v Ramage (1968) 266 CA2d 570, 72 CR 273: §30.52
Cloud v Market St. Ry. (1946) 74 CA2d 92, 168 P2d 191: §26.36
Clough v Compton-Delevan Irr. Dist. (1938) 12 C2d 385, 85 P2d 126: §24.30
Clyne v Brock (1947) 82 CA2d 958, 188 P2d 263: §26.28
Coast Elevator Co. v State Bd. of Equalization (1975) 44 CA3d 576, 118 CR 818: §29.27

Coast-United Advertising v Long Beach (1975) 51 CA3d 766, 124 CR 487: §29.13
Coates Capitol Corp. v Superior Court (1967) 251 CA2d 125, 59 CR 231: §31.53
Cobe v Crane (1916) 173 C 116: §25.58
Coburn v Smart (1879) 53 C 742: §25.13
Cochrane v Superior Court (1968) 261 CA2d 201, 67 CR 675: §27.1
Coffey v Greenfield (1880) 55 C 382: §25.29
Cohn v Bugas (1974) 42 CA3d 381, 116 CR 810: §27.5
Cohn v County Bd. of Supervisors (1955) 135 CA2d 180, 286 P2d 836: §25.11
Colden v Costello (1942) 50 CA2d 363, 122 P2d 959: §§24.6, 24.13
Cole v Roebling Constr. Co. (1909) 156 C 443, 105 P 255: §30.34
Collier v Lindley (1928) 203 C 641, 266 P 526: §32.1
Collins, Estate of (1968) 268 CA2d 86, 73 CR 599: §25.30
Colthurst v Harris (1929) 97 CA 430, 275 P 868: §23.1
Columbia Pictures Corp. v DeToth (1945) 26 C2d 753, 161 P2d 217: §§24.5, 24.14, 24.19, 24.27, 24.36
Colusa v Strain (1963) 215 CA2d 472, 30 CR 415: §32.1
Common Wealth Ins. Sys., Inc. v Kersten (1974) 40 CA3d 1014, 115 CR 653: §§24.5, 24.7
Communist Party v Peek (1942) 20 C2d 536, 127 P2d 889: §24.13

Connell v Bowes (1942) 19 C2d 870, 123 P2d 456: §26.28

Consolidated Constr. Co. v Pacific Elec. Ry. (1920) 184 C 244, 193 P 238: §31.46

Constantine v Sunnyvale (1949) 91 CA2d 278, 204 P2d 922: §26.29

Continental Baking Co. v Katz (1968) 68 C2d 512, 67 CR 761: §§23.44, 23.57

Continental Pac. Lines v Superior Court (1956) 142 CA2d 744, 299 P2d 417: §31.21

Continental Vinyl Prods. Corp. v Mead Corp. (1972) 27 CA3d 543, 103 CR 806: §§25.10, 25.20, 25.24

Contract Eng'rs, Inc. v Welborn (1968) 258 CA2d 553, 65 CR 903: §31.48

Cook v Craig (1976) 55 CA3d 773, 127 CR 712: §24.9

Cook v Stewart McKee & Co. (1945) 68 CA2d 758, 157 P2d 868: §§31.68, 31.91

Cooper v Board of Medical Examiners (1975) 49 CA3d 931, 123 CR 563: §23.10

Cooper v Leslie Salt Co. (1969) 70 C2d 627, 75 CR 766: §§24.26, 24.29

Corcoran v Los Angeles (1957) 153 CA2d 852, 315 P2d 439: §23.11

Corridan v Rose (1955) 137 CA2d 524, 290 P2d 939: §§25.13, 25.52

Cotton, E. M., Appliances, Inc. v Felton Aluminum Co. (1954) 124 CA2d 546, 269 P2d 64: §24.30

County Bank v Jack (1906) 148 C 437, 83 P 705: §23.39

Cowan Oil & Ref. Co. v Miley Petroleum Corp. (1931) 112 CA Supp 773, 295 P 504: §29.4

Cowlin v Pringle (1941) 46 CA2d 472, 116 P2d 109: §26.36

Cox v State (1970) 3 CA3d 301, 82 CR 896: §29.31

Cox v Tyrone Power Enterprises (1942) 49 CA2d 383, 121 P2d 829: §23.22

Coyne v Krempels (1950) 36 C2d 257, 223 P2d 244: §§29.9, 29.19, 29.22, 29.29, 29.80

Cradduck v Financial Indem. Co. (1966) 242 CA2d 850, 52 CR 90: §25.13

Craig Corp. v Los Angeles (1975) 51 CA3d 909, 124 CR 621: §§29.8, 29.44, 29.49

Crandall v Amador County (1862) 20 C 72: §32.2

Cranston v Bonelli (1971) 15 CA3d 129, 92 CR 828: §31.10

Crisci v Security Ins. Co. (1967) 66 C2d 425, 58 CR 13: §33.9

Crocker Citizens Bank v Knapp (1967) 251 CA2d 875, 60 CR 66: §23.57

Crofton v Young (1941) 48 CA2d 452, 119 P2d 1003: §25.3

Crossman v Vivienda Water Co. (1902) 136 C 571, 69 P 220: §30.37

Crosswhite v American Ins. Co. (1964) 61 C2d 300, 38 CR 412: §31.67

Crouch v H. L. Miller & Co. (1915) 169 C 341, 146 P 880: §30.20

Crow v P.E.G. Constr. Co. (1957) 156 CA2d 271, 319 P2d 47: §33.30

Crown Coach Corp. v Superior Court (1972) 8 C3d 540, 105 CR 339: §§31.1–31.2, 31.24, 31.32–31.34

Csordas v United Slate Tile & Composition Roofers (1960) 177 CA2d 184, 2 CR 133: §30.52

Cullincini v Deming (1975) 53 CA3d 908, 126 CR 427: §§29.29, 29.49, 29.85

Cuneo v Superior Court (1963) 213 CA2d 452, 28 CR 791: §25.3

Cutter Labs. v R. W. Ogle & Co. (1957) 151 CA2d 410, 311 P2d 627: §26.29

Cyrus v Haveson (1976) 65 CA3d 306, 135 CR 246: §30.58

D

Dabney v Philleo (1951) 38 C2d 60, 237 P2d 648: §§24.30, 25.12, 25.29

Daher v American Pipe Constr. Co. (1968) 257 CA2d 816, 65 CR 259: §30.59

Daley v Butte (1964) 227 CA2d 380, 38 CR 693: §31.55

Dallman Supply Co. v Sweet (1948) 86 CA2d 780, 195 P2d 864: §24.28

D'Amico v Board of Medical Examiners (1974) 11 C3d 1, 112 CR 786: §§29.11, 29.31

Dashew v Dashew Business Mach., Inc. (1963) 218 CA2d 711, 32 CR 682: §29.51

Datta v Stabb (1959) 173 CA2d 613, 343 P2d 977: §33.29

Daum Dev. Corp. v Yuba Plaza, Inc. (1970) 11 CA3d 65, 89 CR 458: §31.33

Davies v Superior Court (1964) 228 CA2d 535, 39 CR 693: §31.91

Davis v Hart (1899) 123 C 384, 55 P 1060: §31.1

Davis v Stulman (1945) 72 CA2d 255, 164 P2d 787: §24.28

Davis v Superior Court (1921) 184 C 691, 195 P 390: §31.43

Dawson v Los Altos Hills (1976) 16 C3d 676, 129 CR 97: §24.26

Day v Sharp (1975) 50 CA3d 904, 123 CR 918: §29.46

Dean, Estate of (1906) 149 C 487, 87 P 13: §31.40

De Angeles v Roos Bros., Inc. (1966) 244 CA2d 434, 52 CR 783: §29.10

de Echeguren v de Echeguren (1962) 210 CA2d 141, 26 CR 562: §29.51

Del Conte Masonry Co. v Lewis (1971) 16 CA3d 678, 94 CR 439: §25.5

Denham v Superior Court (1970) 2 C3d 557, 86 CR 65: §§31.36, 31.39

Dennis v Kolm (1900) 131 C 91, 63 P 141: §25.1

Dep't of Pub. Works, People ex rel v Buellton Dev. Co. (1943) 58 CA2d 178, 136 P2d 793: §31.72

Dep't of Pub. Works, People ex rel v Busick (1968) 259 CA2d 744, 66 CR 532: §26.95

Derby, E. M., & Co. v Jackman (1891) 89 C 1, 26 P 610: §23.60

Derry v Superior Court (1968) 266 CA2d 556, 72 CR 313: §§31.55, 31.59

Desper v King (1967) 251 CA2d 659, 59 CR 657: §30.59

Diamond Bar Dev. Corp. v Superior Court (1976) 60 CA3d 330, 131 CR 458: §29.89

Diamond Nat'l Corp. v Golden Empire Builders, Inc. (1963) 213 CA2d 283, 28 CR 616: §§30.37, 30.39

Dibble, U.S. v (9th Cir 1970) 429 F2d 598: §29.55

Difani v Riverside County Oil Co. (1927) 201 C 210, 256 P 210: §§23.3, 23.67

Dills v Delira Corp. (1956) 145 CA2d 124, 302 P2d 397: §§24.2, 24.15, 24.43

Division of Labor Law Enforcement v Brooks (1964) 226 CA2d 631, 38 CR 284: §§32.2, 32.4, 32.6

Dixon v Grace Lines, Inc. (1972) 27 CA3d 278, 103 CR 595: §§29.44, 29.49

Dobbins v Hardister (1966) 242 CA2d 787, 51 CR 866: §29.45

Dodge v Free (1973) 32 CA3d 436, 108 CR 311: §§23.43, 29.33, 29.48

Dohrmann Co. v Security Sav. & Loan Ass'n (1970) 8 CA3d 655, 87 CR 792: §24.37

Dollar-A-Day Rent-A-Car Sys., Inc. v Pacific Tel. & Tel. Co. (1972) 26 CA3d 454, 102 CR 651: §31.41

Donner v Superior Court (1927) 82 CA 165, 255 P 272: §31.46

Donohoe, Charles L., Inc. v Superior Court (1927) 202 C 15, 258 P 1094: §31.36

Doran v Burke (1953) 118 CA2d 806, 258 P2d 1078: §23.60

Douglas v Superior Court (1949) 94 CA2d 395, 210 P2d 853: §31.18

Dowell v Superior Court (1956) 47 C2d 483, 304 P2d 1009: §26.72

Drake v Duvenick (1873) 45 C 455: §30.20

Dresser v Superior Court (1964) 231 CA2d 68, 41 CR 473: §§31.5, 31.9

Drinkhouse v Van Ness (1927) 202 C 359, 260 P 869: §§25.56–25.57

Drinnon v Oliver (1972) 24 CA3d 571, 101 CR 120: §25.33

Dugar v Happy Tiger Records, Inc. (1974) 41 CA3d 811, 116 CR 412: §§23.44, 29.54, 29.57, 29.86

Dunas v Superior Court (1970) 9 CA3d 236, 87 CR 719: §23.62

Dunsmuir Masonic Temple v Superior Court (1970) 12 CA3d 17, 90 CR 405: §§31.36, 31.39

duPont de Nemours, E. I., & Co. v United States Camo Corp. (WD Mo 1956) 19 FRD 495: §29.7

Dvorin v Appellate Dep't (1975) 15 C3d 648, 125 CR 771: §§29.6, 29.27, 29.87

E

E. I. duPont de Nemours & Co. v United States Camo Corp. (WD Mo 1956) 19 FRD 495: §29.7

E. M. Cotton Appliances, Inc. v Felton Aluminum Co. (1954) 124 CA2d 546, 269 P2d 64: §24.30

E. M. Derby & Co. v Jackman (1891) 89 C 1, 26 P 610: §23.60
Eagle Elec. Mfg. Co. v Keener (1966) 247 CA2d 246, 55 CR 444: §29.72
East Coalinga Oil Fields Corp. v Robinson (1948) 86 CA2d 153, 194 P2d 554: §24.7
Eastwood v Froehlich (1976) 60 CA3d 523, 131 CR 577: §26.95
Eckert, Louis, Brewing Co. v Unemployment Reserves Comm'n (1941) 47 CA2d 844, 119 P2d 227: §§24.21, 24.43
Eddings v White (1964) 229 CA2d 579, 40 CR 453: §§31.68, 31.85
Eggers v National Radio Co. (1929) 208 C 308, 281 P 58: §§25.16, 25.20, 25.35
Egly v Superior Court (1970) 6 CA3d 476, 86 CR 18: §§25.5, 31.65
Elling Corp. v Superior Court (1975) 48 CA3d 89, 123 CR 734: §31.9
Elms v Elms (1935) 4 C2d 681, 52 P2d 223: §25.31
Elms v Elms (1946) 72 CA2d 508, 164 P2d 936: §30.69
Empire W. v Southern Cal. Gas Co. (1974) 12 C3d 805, 117 CR 423: §29.8
Empire W. Side Irr. Dist. v Stratford Irr. Dist. (1937) 10 C2d 376, 74 P2d 248: §24.22
Ensher v Ensher, Alexander & Barsoom, Inc. (1960) 187 CA2d 407, 9 CR 732: §31.73
Ensher, Alexander & Barsoom, Inc. v Ensher (1964) 225 CA2d 318, 37 CR 327: §23.55
Environmental Law Fund, Inc. v Corte Madera (1975) 49 CA3d 105, 122 CR 282: §24.21
Ephraim v Metropolitan Trust Co. (1946) 28 C2d 824, 172 P2d 501: §24.36
Ermolieff v R.K.O. Radio Pictures, Inc. (1942) 19 C2d 543, 122 P2d 3: §§24.5, 24.14
Escondido Mut. Water Co. v George A. Hillebrecht, Inc. (1966) 241 CA2d 410, 50 CR 495: §24.5
Essick v Los Angeles (1950) 34 C2d 614, 213 P2d 492: §24.42
Estate of _____ (see name of decedent)
Evans v Superior Court (1936) 14 CA2d 743, 59 P2d 159: §31.15

F

Fagerstedt v Continental Ins. Co. (1968) 266 CA2d 370, 72 CR 126: §24.19
Faix, Ltd. v Los Angeles (1976) 54 CA3d 992, 127 CR 182: §§24.7, 24.26
Fallon & Co. v United States Overseas Airlines, Inc. (1961) 194 CA2d 546, 15 CR 354: §§30.37–30.38, 30.40
Family Serv. Agency v Ames (1958) 166 CA2d 344, 333 P2d 142: §29.86
Fannin Corp. v Superior Court (1974) 36 CA3d 745, 111 CR 920: §31.33

Farrar v McCormick (1972) 25 CA3d 701, 102 CR 190: §§23.62, 31.55–31.56
Farrar v Steenbergh (1916) 173 C 94, 159 P 707: §30.10
Faus v Pacific Elec. Ry. (1955) 34 CA2d 352, 285 P2d 1017: §25.1
Faust v San Diego (1931) 115 CA 277, 1 P2d 543: §32.6
Fay Sec. Co. v Mortgage Guar. Co. (1940) 37 CA2d 637, 100 P2d 344: §24.19
Feingersh v Lutheran Hosp. Soc'y (1977) 66 CA3d 406, 136 CR 155: §§31.38–31.39, 31.44
Ferreira v Keller (1970) 4 CA3d 292, 84 CR 253: §24.7
Feykert v Hardy (1963) 213 CA2d 67, 28 CR 510: §§26.70, 26.73
Field Research Corp. v Superior Court (1969) 71 C2d 110, 77 CR 243: §29.88
Fielder v Superior Court (1963) 213 CA2d 60, 28 CR 597: §23.41
Fields v Potts (1956) 140 CA2d 697, 295 P2d 965: §§25.21, 25.47
Fireman's Fund Ins. Co. v Gerlach (1976) 56 CA3d 299, 128 CR 396: §§25.14, 25.33
First Small Business Inv. Co. v Sistim, Inc. (1970) 12 CA3d 645, 90 CR 798: §§30.62–30.63, 30.69
Fisher v Cheeseman (1968) 260 CA2d 503, 67 CR 258: §§23.40, 29.49
Fisher v Superior Court (1958) 157 CA2d 126, 320 P2d 894: §31.21

Fitzgerald v Herzer (1947) 78 CA2d 127, 177 P2d 364: §30.3
Fitzsimmons v Jones (1960) 179 CA2d 5, 3 CR 373: §26.73
Flamer v Superior Court (1968) 266 CA2d 907, 72 CR 561: §31.14
Fletcher v A. J. Indus., Inc. (1968) 266 CA2d 313, 72 CR 146: §33.2
Fletcher v Maginnis (1902) 136 C 362, 68 P 1015: §30.15
Flood v Simpson (1975) 45 CA3d 644, 119 CR 675: §§30.26, 30.52
Foraker v O'Brien (1975) 50 CA3d 856, 124 CR 110: §29.49
Ford v Herndon (1976) 62 CA3d 492, 133 CR 111: §§30.59–30.60
Ford v Palisades Corp. (1950) 101 CA2d 491, 225 P2d 545: §26.28
Ford v Superior Court (1973) 34 CA3d 338, 109 CR 844: §§30.34, 30.37
Ford v Superior Court (1959) 171 CA2d 228, 340 P2d 296: §31.73
Ford Motor Co. v Superior Court (1971) 16 CA3d 442, 94 CR 127: §29.15
Fosters v Masters Pontiac Co. (1958) 158 CA2d 481, 322 P2d 592: §24.5
Fracasse v Brent (1972) 6 C3d 784, 100 CR 385: §24.11
Franklin v Municipal Court (1972) 26 CA3d 884, 103 CR 354: §29.16
Franklin v Nat C. Goldstone Agency (1949) 33 C2d 628, 204 P2d 37: §23.41

Frasca v Warner (1967) 249 CA2d 593, 57 CR 683: §26.73
Fraser v Fraser (1919) 39 CA 467, 179 P 427: §26.99
Fraser-Yamor Agency, Inc. v Del Norte (1977) 68 CA3d 201, 137 CR 118: §29.83
Fritz v Superior Court (1936) 18 CA2d 232, 63 P2d 872: §24.13
Fuentes v Tucker (1947) 31 C2d 1, 187 P2d 752: §29.7
Fuller v Goodyear Tire & Rubber Co. (1970) 7 CA3d 690, 86 CR 705: §§29.24, 29.86

G

G & D Holland Constr. Co. v Marysville (1970) 12 CA3d 989, 91 CR 227: §29.85
Gagnon Co. v Nevada Desert Inn, Inc. (1955) 45 C2d 448, 289 P2d 466: §§31.66, 33.6, 33.29
Gardiner v Gaither (1958) 162 CA2d 607, 329 P2d 22: §24.8
Gardner v Shreve (1949) 89 CA2d 804, 202 P2d 322: §29.20
Gardner v Trevaskis (1958) 158 CA2d 410, 322 P2d 545: §25.33
Garrett v Coast & S. Fed. Sav. & Loan Ass'n (1973) 9 C3d 731, 108 CR 845: §§29.3, 30.45
General Ins. Co. v Superior Court (1975) 15 C3d 449, 124 CR 745: §§31.11–31.12, 31.17
General Ins. Co. v Whitmore (1965) 235 CA2d 670, 45 CR 558: §24.5

General Motors Corp. v Superior Court (1966) 65 C2d 88, 52 CR 460: §§27.4, 31.1–31.2, 31.25, 31.44
General of America Ins. Co. v Lilly (1968) 258 CA2d 465, 65 CR 750: §§24.19, 24.36
General of America Ins. Co. v Whitmore (1965) 235 CA2d 670, 45 CR 556: §24.29
Gerard v Miller (1963) 214 CA2d 266, 29 CR 359: §24.19
Gerardo v Gerardo (1952) 114 CA2d 371, 250 P2d 276: §30.34
Gherman v Colburn (1971) 18 CA3d 1046, 96 CR 424: §§31.68, 31.75
Ghiringhelli v Riboni (1950) 95 CA2d 503, 213 P2d 17: §31.70, 31.83
Gillette v Gillette (1960) 180 CA2d 777, 4 CR 700: §23.56
Ginns v Shumate (1977) 65 CA3d 802, 135 CR 604: §31.8
Girard v Miller (1963) 214 CA2d 266, 29 CR 359: §§24.31, 24.36
Girth v Thompson (1970) 11 CA3d 325, 89 CR 823: §24.7
Glogau v Hagan (1951) 107 CA2d 313, 237 P2d 329: §26.31
Goddard v Pollock (1974) 37 CA3d 137, 112 CR 215: §§30.13, 30.15
Goddard v Security Title Ins. & Guar. Co. (1939) 14 C2d 47, 92 P2d 804: §31.70
Goers v Superior Court (1976) 57 CA3d 72, 129 CR 29: §31.25

Goes v Perry (1941) 18 C2d 373, 115 P2d 441: §25.27
Golden Gate Bridge Dist. v Felt (1931) 214 C 308, 5 P2d 585: §24.3
Goldtree v Spreckels (1902) 135 C 666, 67 P 1091: §31.75
Gombos v Ashe (1958) 158 CA2d 517, 322 P2d 933: §29.84
Gonsalves v Bank of America (1940) 16 C2d 169, 105 P2d 118: §31.6
Good v State (1969) 273 CA2d 587, 78 CR 316: §§31.23, 31.32–31.33
Goodson v The Bogerts, Inc. (1967) 252 CA2d 32, 60 CR 146: §30.61
Govea v Superior Court (1938) 26 CA2d 27, 78 P2d 433: §31.21
Gray v Kay (1975) 47 CA3d 562, 120 CR 915: §31.69
Gray v Laufenberger (1961) 195 CA2d Supp 875, 15 CR 813: §30.37
Green v Del-Camp Inv. Inc. (1961) 193 CA2d 479, 14 CR 420: §29.79
Green v Gordon (1952) 39 C2d 230, 246 P2d 38: §23.67
Greening v General Air-Conditioning Corp. (1965) 233 CA2d 545, 43 CR 662: §29.19
Greenwald v U.S. (1963) 223 CA2d 434, 35 CR 772: §29.72
Grime v Superior Court (1974) 39 CA3d 46, 113 CR 850: §31.43
Guardianship of Lyle (1946) 77 CA2d 153, 174 P2d 906: §31.73
Gudarov v Hadjieff (1952) 38 C2d 412, 240 P2d 621: §30.36

H

H&H Inv. Co. v T-J Constr. Co. (1969) 275 CA2d 58, 79 CR 890: §30.59
Hagan v Fairfield (1965) 238 CA2d 197, 47 CR 600: §24.30
Haldane v Haldane (1962) 210 CA2d 587, 26 CR 670: §23.57
Hale v George A. Hormel & Co. (1975) 48 CA3d 73, 121 CR 144: §29.10
Hallett v Slaughter (1943) 22 C2d 552, 140 P2d 3: §30.59
Hamilton, R. G., Corp. v Corum (1933) 218 C 92, 21 P2d 413: §24.40
Hansen v Snap-Tite, Inc. (1972) 23 CA3d 208, 100 CR 51: §31.58
Hanson v Hanson (1960) 178 CA2d 756, 3 CR 179: §30.2
Haraszthy v Horton (1873) 46 C 545: §26.102
Harmon v Pacific Tel. & Tel. Co. (1960) 183 CA2d 1, 6 CR 542: §§24.16, 24.23, 24.27
Harney, Chas. L., Inc. v Contractors' State License Bd. (1952) 39 C2d 561, 247 P2d 913: §§24.7–24.9, 24.30, 24.37
Harootenian, Estate of (1951) 38 C2d 242, 238 P2d 992: §§25.30, 25.37
Harris, Marriage of (1977) 74 CA3d 98, 141 CR 333: §30.26

Hartman v Olvera (1874) 49 C 101: §30.61
Hastings v Superior Court (1955) 131 CA2d 255, 280 P2d 74: §31.21
Hausmann v Farmers Ins. Exch. (1963) 213 CA2d 611, 29 CR 75: §§25.13, 25.58
Hayward Union High School Dist. v Madrid (1965) 234 CA2d 100, 44 CR 268: §29.23
Hearst v Hart (1900) 128 C 327, 60 P 846: §29.45
Heathman v Vant (1959) 172 CA2d 639, 343 P2d 104: §§30.2, 30.58
Henry v Vineland Irr. Dist. (1903) 140 C 376, 73 P 1061: §25.59
Herman v Santee (1894) 103 C 519, 37 P 509: §30.20
Hernandez v National Dairy Prods. (1945) 126 CA2d 490, 272 P2d 799: §23.23
Hernon, People v (1951) 106 CA2d 638, 235 P2d 614: §26.94
Hi-Valley Dev. Corp. v Walters (1963) 223 CA2d 778, 36 CR 140: §25.15
Highlands Inn, Inc. v Gurries (1969) 276 CA2d 694, 81 CR 273: §§31.8, 31.11
Higley v Bank of Downey (1968) 260 CA2d 640, 67 CR 365: §30.59
Hittson v Stanich (1927) 84 CA 434, 258 P 405: §30.52
Hoffman v Palm Springs (1959) 169 CA2d 645, 337 P2d 521: §29.33
Hoffman v Southern Pac. Co. (1929) 101 CA 218, 281 P 681: §26.31

Holden v Arnebergh (1968) 265 CA2d 87, 71 CR 401: §§24.13, 24.24
Hollenbeck Lodge v Wilshire Blvd. Temple (1959) 175 CA2d 469, 346 P2d 422: §24.2
Hollister Convalescent Hosp., Inc. v Rico (1975) 15 C3d 660, 125 CR 757: §23.58
Holmes v Rogers (1859) 13 C 191: §34.1
Holt v College of Osteopathic Physicians & Surgeons (1964) 61 C2d 750, 40 CR 244: §24.6
Holt v Palmer (1951) 106 CA2d 329, 235 P2d 43: §30.74
Home Real Estate Co. v Winnants (1919) 39 CA 643, 179 P 534: §§31.68, 31.75
Honeywell, Inc. v State Bd. of Equalization (1975) 48 CA3d 907, 122 CR 243: §§24.7, 24.21, 24.26
Hopkins v Superior Court (1902) 136 C 552, 69 P 299: §§31.85, 31.89
Horney v Superior Court (1948) 83 CA2d 262, 188 P2d 552: §31.5
Hover v MacKenzie (1954) 122 CA2d 852, 266 P2d 60: §23.63
Howard v Bennett (1942) 53 CA2d 546, 127 P2d 1012: §§24.6, 24.13
Howard v Howard (1955) 131 CA2d 308, 280 P2d 802: §24.5
Howe v Pioneer Mfg. Co. (1968) 262 CA2d 330, 68 CR 617: §29.38
Hoyt v Board of Civil Serv. Comm'rs (1942) 21 C2d

399, 132 P2d 804: §§24.7, 24.16, 24.27, 24.29
Hughes & Ladd, Inc. v Rogue River Paving Co. (1975) 46 CA3d 311, 119 CR 925: §§31.22, 31.26
Hunot v Superior Court (1976) 55 CA3d 660, 127 CR 703: §31.26
Hunt v Superior Court (1976) 63 CA3d 832, 134 CR 128: §31.8
Hurgren v Union Mut. Life Ins. Co. (1904) 141 C 585, 75 P 168: §31.67
Hutchins v Waters (1975) 51 CA3d 69, 123 CR 819: §33.14

I

Igna v Baldwin Park (1970) 9 CA3d 909, 88 CR 581: §24.36
Imperial Mut. Life Ins. Co. v Caminetti (1943) 59 CA2d 501, 139 P2d 691: §§24.7, 24.21
In re Carter (1971) 19 CA3d 479, 97 CR 274: §34.4
In re Mercantile Guar. Co. (1968) 263 CA2d 346, 69 CR 361: §31.72
In re Morelli (1970) 11 CA3d 819, 91 CR 72: §23.68
In re Yokohama Specie Bank (1948) 86 CA2d 545, 195 P2d 555: §§25.1, 25.36, 25.38
Indenco, Inc. v Evans (1962) 201 CA2d 369, 20 CR 90: §24.7
Independent Laundry v Railroad Comm'n (1945) 70 CA2d 816, 161 P2d 827: §24.23
International Ass'n of Fire Fighters, Local 1319 v Palo Alto (1963) 60 C2d 295, 32 CR 842: §§24.19, 24.35
International Indus., Inc. v Olen (hearing granted March 31, 1977, LA 30760): §31.69
Ippolito v Municipal Court (1977) 67 CA3d 682, 136 CR 795: §§31.1, 31.10, 31.13
Irwin v Blythe (1945) 72 CA2d 161, 163 P2d 900: §24.36
Isaacs v Jones (1933) 135 CA 47, 26 P2d 533: §31.91

J

J. A. Thompson & Sons, Inc. v Superior Court (1963) 215 CA2d 719, 30 CR 471: §31.9
J. C. Penney Co. v Westinghouse Elec. Corp. (1963) 217 CA2d 834, 32 CR 172: §§24.7, 24.35
Jack v Wood (1968) 258 CA2d 639, 65 CR 856: §29.8
Jacks v Lewis (1943) 61 CA2d 148, 142 P2d 358: §31.16
Jacobs v Retail Clerk's Union, Local 1222 (1975) 49 CA3d 959, 123 CR 309: §§29.79, 29.83
Jacuzzi v Jacuzzi Bros., Inc. (1966) 243 CA2d 1, 52 CR 147: §29.79
Jaffe v Albertson Co. (1966) 243 CA2d 592, 53 CR 25: §24.40
Jansson v National Steamship Co. (1917) 34 CA 483, 168 P 151: §23.25
Jefferson Inc. v Torrance (1968) 266 CA2d 300, 72 CR 85: §24.36

Jensen v Allstate Ins. Co. (1973) 32 CA3d 789, 108 CR 498: §30.63

Jenssen v R.K.O. Studios, Inc. (1937) 20 CA2d 705, 67 P2d 757: §29.45

Jersey Maid Milk Prods. Co. v Brock (1939) 13 C2d 661, 91 P2d 599: §§25.9, 25.22, 25.48, 25.51

Johnson v Banducci (1963) 212 CA2d 254, 27 CR 764: §§29.51, 29.54, 29.69

Johnson v Hayes Cal Builders, Inc. (1963) 60 C2d 572, 35 CR 618: §§25.13, 25.33, 30.62

Jones v Feichtmeir (1949) 95 CA2d 341, 212 P2d 933: §24.29

Jones v Robertson (1947) 79 CA2d 813, 180 P2d 929: §24.14

Jones v World Life Research Inst. (1976) 60 CA3d 836, 131 CR 674: §§34.4, 34.12

Josephson v Superior Court (1963) 219 CA2d 354, 33 CR 196: §§23.23, 23.63

Joslin v Marin Munic. Water Dist. (1967) 67 C2d 132, 60 CR 377: §§29.3, 29.44

Judd v Superior Court (1976) 60 CA3d 38, 131 CR 246: §23.41

K

Kadota v San Francisco (1958) 166 CA2d 194, 333 P2d 75: §31.19

Kaiser Foundation Hosp. v Superior Court (1975) 49 CA3d 523, 122 CR 432: §31.6

Kaiser Foundation Hosp. v Superior Court (1967) 254 CA2d 327, 62 CR 330: §29.20

Kaiser Steel Corp. v Westinghouse Elec. Corp. (1976) 55 CA3d 737, 127 CR 838: §30.8

Karbelnig v Brothwell (1966) 244 CA2d 333, 53 CR 335: §24.5

Katz, Estate of (1942) 49 CA2d 82, 120 P2d 896: §31.67

Kaufman v Superior Court (1896) 115 C 152, 46 P 904: §§31.65, 31.89

Kaufman & Broad Bldg. Co. v City & Suburban Mortgage Co. (1970) 10 CA3d 206, 88 CR 858: §§31.80, 31.88

Kelly v Smith (1928) 204 C 496, 268 P 1057: §25.21

Keniston v American Nat'l Ins. Co. (1973) 31 CA3d 803, 107 CR 583: §§29.8, 29.29, 29.31

Kennedy v Mulligan (1902) 136 C 556, 69 P 291: §30.12

Kenney v Wolff (1948) 88 CA2d 163, 198 P2d 582: §25.22

Kerner, Estate of (1969) 275 CA2d 785, 80 CR 289: §29.72

Kershaw v Hogan (1932) 127 CA 89, 15 P2d 535: §31.80

Kessloff v Pearson (1951) 37 C2d 609, 233 P2d 899: §§24.19, 24.39, 24.42

Keyes v Hurlbert (1941) 43 CA2d 497, 111 P2d 447: §25.12

Kiernan v Union Bank (1976) 55 CA3d 111, 127 CR 441: §29.7

Kimball v Richardson-Kimball Co. (1896) 111 C 386, 43 P 1111: §25.15
Kinard v Jordan (1917) 175 C 13, 164 P 894: §31.23
Kincheloe v Retail Credit Co. (1935) 4 C2d 21, 46 P2d 971: §33.29
Kindt v Kauffman (1976) 57 CA3d 845, 129 CR 603: §29.79
King v Hall (1855) 5 C 82: §24.1
King v National Indus., Inc. (6th Cir 1975) 512 F2d 29: §29.13
King v State (1970) 11 CA3d 307, 89 CR 715: §31.19
King v Superior Court (1936) 12 CA2d 501, 56 P2d 268: §31.91
Kings County Dev. Co., People v (1920) 48 CA 72, 191 P 1004: §31.5
Kinley v Alexander (1955) 137 CA2d 382, 290 P2d 287: §31.66
Kinney, Abbot, Co. v Los Angeles (1959) 53 C2d 52, 346 P2d 385: §25.3
Kirkwood v Superior Court (1967) 253 CA2d 198, 61 CR 316: §30.61
Kirtland & Packard v Superior Court (1976) 59 CA3d 140, 131 CR 418: §29.7
Kizer, Ray, Constr. Co. v Young (1968) 257 CA2d 766, 65 CR 267: §30.60
Klinghoffer v Barasch (1970) 4 CA3d 258, 84 CR 350: §§25.34, 31.72
Klinker v Klinker (1955) 132 CA2d 687, 283 P2d 83: §24.7

Knox v Wolfe (1946) 73 CA2d 494, 167 P2d 3: §24.43
Konecko v Konecko (1955) 164 CA2d 249, 330 P2d 393: §24.20
Kooper v King (1961) 195 CA2d 621, 15 CR 848: §30.39
Koski v U-Haul Co. (1963) 212 CA2d 640, 28 CR 398: §30.62
Kostal v Pullen (1950) 36 C2d 528, 225 P2d 217: §§23.26–23.27
Kramer v Barnes (1963) 212 CA2d 440, 27 CR 895: §§29.8, 29.54
Kroff v Kroff (1954) 127 CA2d 404, 274 P2d 45: §24.34
Kronen v Pacific Coast Soc'y of Orthodontists (1965) 237 CA2d 289, 46 CR 808: §24.7
Kronkright v Gardner (1973) 31 CA3d 214, 107 CR 270: §31.66
Krupp v Mullen (1953) 120 CA2d 53, 260 P2d 629: §29.29

L

La Cotonniere de Moislains v H. & B. Am. Mach. Co. (D Mass 1956) 19 FRD 6: §29.13
La Mesa Lemon Grove & Spring Valley Irr. Dist. v Halley (1925) 195 C 739, 235 P 999: §25.22
La Mirada Community Hosp. v Superior Court (1967) 249 CA2d 39, 57 CR 42: §31.63
Lacey v Bertone (1949) 33 C2d 649, 203 P2d 755: §23.6

Landwehr v Gillette (1917) 174 C 654, 163 P 1018: §30.37
Lane v Davis (1964) 227 CA2d 60, 38 CR 425: §31.2
Lane v Redondo Beach (1975) 49 CA3d 251, 122 CR 189: §24.7
Langan v McCorkle (1969) 276 CA2d 805, 81 CR 535: §§31.19, 31.27
Larkin v Superior Court (1916) 171 C 719, 154 P 841: §31.48
Larsen v Beekmann (1969) 276 CA2d 185, 80 CR 654: §§34.3, 34.5
Larsen v Johannes (1970) 7 CA3d 491, 86 CR 744: §§29.8, 29.38, 29.44, 29.86, 33.30
Lautrup, Inc. v Trans-West Discount Corp. (1976) 64 CA3d 316, 134 CR 348: §28.56
Leahey v Department of Water & Power (1946) 76 CA2d 281, 173 P2d 69: §24.22
Leasman v Beech Aircraft Corp. (1975) 48 CA3d 376, 121 CR 768: §§29.11, 29.44
Legg v Mutual Benefit Health & Acc. of Omaha (1955) 136 CA2d 887, 289 P2d 550: §30.14
Legg v United Benefit Life Ins. Co. (1955) 136 CA2d 894, 289 P2d 553: §31.33
Leo v Dunlap (1968) 260 CA2d 24, 66 CR 888: §30.34
Leonard Corp. v San Diego (1962) 210 CA2d 547, 26 CR 730: §§24.29, 25.33
Leonis v Leffingwell (1899) 126 C 369, 58 P 940: §23.11
LePage v Oakland (1970) 13 CA3d 689, 91 CR 806: §§24.7–24.8

Lerner v Superior Court (1977) 70 CA3d 656, 139 CR 51: §29.11
Leslie v Roe (1975) 52 CA3d 686, 125 CR 157: §26.34
Lewis v Johnson (1939) 12 C2d 558, 86 P2d 99: §§31.66–31.67
Lewis v LeBaron (1967) 254 CA2d 270, 61 CR 903: §§30.24, 30.40
Lewis Ave. Parent Teachers' Ass'n v Hussey (1967) 250 CA2d 232, 58 CR 499: §24.35
Liberty Loan Corp. v Petersen (1972) 24 CA3d 915, 101 CR 395: §§30.37–30.38, 30.45
Liberty Mut. Ins. Co. v Colonial Ins. Co. (1970) 8 CA3d 427, 87 CR 348: §24.22
Lincoln v Didak (1958) 162 CA2d 625, 328 P2d 498: §29.14
Linder v Vogue Invs., Inc. (1966) 239 CA2d 338, 48 CR 633: §§25.16, 25.33
Lindsay Strathmore Irr. Dist. v Superior Court (1932) 121 CA 606, 9 P2d 579: §25.51
Lindsay Strathmore Irr. Dist. v Wutchumna Water Co. (1931) 111 CA 707, 296 P 942: §25.23
Linsk v Linsk (1969) 70 C2d 272, 74 CR 544: §32.4
Loma Portal Civic Club v American Airlines (1964) 61 C2d 582, 39 CR 708: §29.3
Lomanto v Bank of America (1972) 22 CA3d 663, 99 CR 442: §§24.6, 24.19
London v Morrison (1950) 99 CA2d 876, 222 P2d 941: §31.74

Long v Superior Court (1936) 14 CA2d 753, 58 P2d 952: §31.89

Long, People v (1970) 7 CA3d 586, 86 CR 590: §29.46

Lopa v Superior Court (1975) 46 CA3d 382, 120 CR 445: §31.13

Lopes v Capital Co. (1961) 192 CA2d 759, 13 CR 787: §29.84

Lord v Garland (1946) 27 C2d 840, 168 P2d 5: §§24.7, 24.29, 24.36

Lori, Ltd. v Wolfe (1948) 85 CA3d 54, 192 P2d 112: §31.76

Lorraine v McComb (1934) 220 C 753, 32 P2d 960: §26.93

Lortz v Connell (1969) 273 CA2d 286, 78 CR 6: §§24.31, 24.43

Los Angeles v Dannenbrink (1965) 234 CA2d 642, 44 CR 624: §24.3

Los Angeles v Glendale (1943) 23 C2d 68, 142 P2d 289: §§24.2, 24.43

Los Angeles v Gleneagle Dev. Co. (1976) 62 CA3d 543, 133 CR 212: §§23.62, 29.82, 31.35

Los Angeles v Los Angeles Farming & Milling Co. (1907) 150 C 647, 89 P 615: §30.52

Los Angeles v San Fernando (1975) 14 C3d 199, 123 CR 1: §24.43

Los Angeles v Superior Court (1940) 15 C2d 16, 98 P2d 207: §31.19

Los Angeles v Superior Court (1969) 271 CA2d 292, 76 CR 256: §§23.36, 23.50

Los Angeles County Democratic Cent. Comm. v Los Angeles (1976) 61 CA3d 335, 132 CR 43: §§24.8, 24.20

Louis Eckert Brewing Co. v Unemployment Reserves Comm'n (1941) 47 CA2d 844, 119 P2d 227; §§24.21, 24.43

Loupias v Rosen (1951) 102 CA2d 781, 228 P2d 611: §§24.20, 24.30

Ludka v Memory Magnetics Int'l (1972) 25 CA3d 316, 101 CR 615: §30.36

Lushing v Riviera Estates Ass'n (1961) 196 CA2d 687, 16 CR 763: §24.29

Lyle, Guardianship of (1946) 77 CA2d 153, 174 P2d 906: §31.73

Lynch v Bencini (1941) 17 C2d 521, 110 P2d 662: §§30.37, 30.39, 30.52

Lynch v De Boom (1915) 26 CA 311, 146 P 908: §31.40

Lynch v Spilman (1967) 67 C2d 251, 62 CR 12: §§30.61, 30.63

M

Mabury v Ruiz (1881) 58 C 11: §25.25

MacDonald v Joslyn (1969) 275 CA2d 282, 79 CR 707: §31.67

Mack v Superior Court (1968) 259 CA2d 7, 66 CR 280: §23.41

Mackay v Whitaker (1953) 116 CA2d 504, 253 P2d 1021: §§24.30, 24.34–24.35, 24.38

Mackenzie v Voelker (1954) 123 CA2d 538, 226 P2d 867: §31.77

MacLeod v Tribune Publishing Co. (1958) 157 CA2d 665, 321 P2d 881: §§31.68–31.69, 31.90

Madden v Kaiser Foundation Hosp. (1976) 17 C3d 699, 131 CR 882: §26.35

Magrra Dev. Co. v Reed (1964) 228 CA2d 230, 39 CR 284: §29.16

Maguire v Collier (1975) 49 CA3d 309, 122 CR 510: §§31.13, 31.22–31.23, 31.47, 31.56

Maguire v Cunningham (1923) 64 CA 536, 222 P 838: §25.58

Maguire v Hibernia Sav. & Loan Soc'y (1944) 23 C2d 719, 146 P2d 673: §§24.7, 24.22, 24.30

Malick v American Sav. & Loan Ass'n (1969) 273 CA2d 171, 79 CR 499: §31.72

Manchel v Los Angeles (1966) 245 CA2d 501, 54 CR 53: §§24.4, 24.24

Mann v Earls (1964) 226 CA2d 155, 37 CR 877: §30.45

Mann v Superior Court (1942) 53 CA2d 272, 127 P2d 970: §25.58

Marc Bellaire, Inc. v Fleischman (1960) 185 CA2d 591, 8 CR 650: §§25.12, 25.38, 25.58

Marcarelli v Cabell (1976) 58 CA3d 51, 129 CR 509: §31.73

March v Pettis (1977) 66 CA3d 473, 136 CR 3: §§26.12, 26.31, 26.34–26.36

Marden v Bailard (1954) 124 CA2d 458, 268 P2d 809: §§24.6, 24.31

Marianos v Tutunjian (1977) 70 CA3d 61, 138 CR 529: §30.59

Marocco v Ford Motor Co. (1970) 7 CA3d 84, 86 CR 526: §29.46

Marriage of Harris (1977) 74 CA3d 98, 141 CR 333: §30.26

Marriage of McKim (1972) 6 C3d 673, 100 CR 140: §28.2

Marsh v Home Fed. Sav. & Loan Ass'n (1977) 66 CA3d 674, 136 CR 180: §29.83

Marshall v Benedict (1958) 161 CA2d 284, 326 P2d 516: §31.43

Marston, W. H., Co. v Kochritz (1926) 80 CA 352, 251 P 959: §30.40

Martens v Winder (1961) 191 CA2d 143, 12 CR 413: §29.2

Martin v Cook (1977) 68 CA3d 799, 137 CR 434: §31.29

Martin v Corning (1972) 25 CA3d 165, 101 CR 678: §24.29

Martin v General Fin. Co. (1966) 239 CA2d 438, 48 CR 773: §30.3

Martin v Gibson (1941) 48 CA2d 449, 119 P2d 1012: §31.30

Martin v Lawrence (1909) 156 C 191, 103 P 913: §25.33

Martin v Taylor (1968) 267 CA2d 112, 72 CR 847: §§30.59–30.60, 30.62

Massey v Bank of America (1976) 56 CA3d 29, 128 CR 144: §31.31

Mather v Mather (1943) 22 C2d 713, 140 P2d 808: §23.10

Mathews v Atchison, Topeka & Santa Fe Ry. (1942) 54 CA2d 549, 129 P2d 435: §33.29

Maxon v Security Ins. Co. (1963) 214 CA2d 603, 29 CR 586: §29.16

Maxwell v Perkins (1953) 116 CA2d 752, 255 P2d 10: §23.58

Maxwell v Santa Rosa (1959) 53 C2d 274, 1 CR 334: §24.7

Mayo v Beber (1960) 177 CA2d 544, 2 CR 405: §23.41

MCA, Inc. v Universal Diversified Enterprises Corp. (1972) 27 CA3d 170, 103 CR 522: §29.72

McCarthy, Estate of (1937) 23 CA2d 389, 73 P2d 910: §26.102

McCaughna v Bilhorn (1935) 10 CA2d 674, 52 P2d 1025: §24.6

McClearen v Superior Court (1955) 45 C2d 852, 219 P2d 449: §25.5

McClure v Donovan (1949) 33 C2d 717, 205 P2d 17: §§27.1, 27.8, 27.13

McCreadie v Arques (1967) 248 CA2d 39, 56 CR 188: §30.73

McDaniels, People v (1903) 141 C 113, 74 P 773: §29.48

McDonald v Severy (1936) 6 C2d 629, 59 P2d 98: §23.6

McDonald Candy Co. v Lashus (1962) 200 CA2d 63, 19 CR 137: §31.32

McDonough Power Equip. Co. v Superior Court (1972) 8 C3d 527, 105 CR 330: §§31.19, 31.33, 31.53

McIntire v Superior Court (1975) 52 CA3d 717, 125 CR 379: §31.68

McIvor v Savage (1963) 220 CA2d 128, 33 CR 740: §29.51

McKenzie v Albaeck (1963) 219 CA2d 97, 32 CR 762: §31.44

McKenzie v Thousand Oaks (1973) 36 CA3d 426, 111 CR 584: §§30.7, 31.16

McKim, Marriage of (1972) 6 C3d 673, 100 CR 140: §28.2

McLellan v McLellan (1972) 23 CA3d 343, 100 CR 258: §§23.40–23.41.

McNeil v Morgan (1910) 157 C 373, 108 P 69: §25.58

McRoberts v Gorham (1971) 18 CA3d 1040, 96 CR 427: §31.25

Meadow v Superior Court (1963) 59 C2d 610, 30 CR 824: §25.21

Meier v Superior Court (1942) 55 CA2d 675, 131 P2d 554: §31.19

Mellone v Lewis (1965) 233 CA2d 4, 43 CR 412: §26.71

Mercantile Guar. Co., In re (1968) 263 CA2d 346, 69 CR 361: §31.72

Merchants Trust Co. v Hopkins (1930) 103 CA 473, 284 P 1072: §24.30

Merigan v Bauer (1962) 206 CA2d 616, 23 CR 872: §24.2

Merritt v Reserve Ins. Co. (1973) 34 CA3d 858, 110 CR 511: §33.9

Miles & Sons, Inc. v Superior Court (1960) 181 CA2d 151, 5 CR 73: §31.11
Miley v Harper (1967) 248 CA2d 463, 56 CR 536: §29.51
Miller v International Union of Operating Eng'rs (1953) 118 CA2d 66, 257 P2d 85: §24.7
Miller v McLaglen (1947) 82 CA2d 219, 186 P2d 48: §29.17
Miller v Stein (1956) 145 CA2d 381, 302 P2d 403: §23.62
Miller & Lux v Superior Court (1923) 192 C 333, 219 P 1006: §31.29
Mills v Mills (1956) 147 CA2d 107, 305 P2d 61: §§24.27–24.28
Misniewski v Clary (1975) 46 CA3d 499, 120 CR 176: §23.2
Mitchell v Jones (1959) 172 CA2d 580, 342 P2d 5033: §30.3
Monahan v Department of Water & Power (1941) 48 CA2d 746, 120 P2d 730: §§24.23, 24.26–24.27, 24.43
Monolith Portland Cement Co. v Tendler (1962) 206 CA2d 800, 24 CR 38: §24.36
Monrovia Hosp. Co. v Superior Court (1967) 253 CA2d 607, 61 CR 737: §31.9
Moore v California Mineral Prods. Corp. (1953) 115 CA2d 834, 252 P2d 1005: §29.70
Moore v Moore (1955) 133 CA2d 56, 283 P2d 338: §23.63
Moore v Powell (1977) 70 CA3d 583, 138 CR 914: §§31.23, 31.26
Moore v Superior Court (1970) 13 CA3d 869, 92 CR 23: §§31.42, 31.60
Morehouse v Wanzo (1968) 266 CA2d 846, 72 CR 607: §30.52
Morelli, In re (1970) 11 CA3d 819, 91 CR 72: §23.68
Morrow v Learned (1926) 76 CA 538, 245 P 442: §34.4
Mosk, People ex rel v Lynam (1967) 253 CA2d 959, 61 CR 800: §29.72
Moss v Bluemm (1964) 229 CA2d 70, 40 CR 50: §26.28
Moss v Moss (1942) 20 C2d 640, 128 P2d 526: §§24.2, 24.19, 24.36
Moving Picture Mach. Operators Local 162 v Glasgow Theaters, Inc. (1970) 6 CA3d 395, 86 CR 33: §33.5
Muller v Muller (1965) 235 CA2d 341, 45 CR 182: §§30.2–30.3
Muller v Robinson (1959) 174 CA2d 511, 345 P2d 25: §§25.3, 25.26, 25.44
Muller v Tanner (1969) 2 CA3d 445, 82 CR 738: §§23.63, 29.90
Munoz v Lopez (1969) 275 CA2d 178, 79 CR 563: §§30.76–30.77
Munson v Linnick (1967) 255 CA2d 589, 63 CR 340: §§24.2, 24.43
Mustalo v Mustalo (1974) 37 CA3d 580, 112 CR 594: §31.17

Mutual Bldg. & Loan Ass'n v Corum (1934) 220 C 282, 30 P2d 509: §26.31

N

Nail v Osterholm (1970) 13 CA3d 682, 91 CR 908: §31.25
National Elec. Supply Co. v Mount Diablo Unified School Dist. (1960) 187 CA2d 418, 9 CR 864: §27.11
National Exhibition Co. v San Francisco (1972) 24 CA3d 1, 100 CR 757: §§24.37, 29.72
National Indem. Co. v Manley (1975) 53 CA3d 126, 125 CR 513: §29.85
Nationwide Inv. Corp. v California Funeral Serv., Inc. (1974) 40 CA3d 494, 114 CR 77: §29.12
Navrides v Zurich Ins. Co. (1971) 5 C3d 698, 97 CR 309: §33.6
Neal v Bank of America (1949) 93 CA2d 678, 209 CR 825: §29.3
Necessary v Necessary (1962) 207 CA2d 780, 24 CR 713: §30.58
Neil G. v Superior Court (1973) 30 CA3d 572, 106 CR 505: §31.67
Nemeth v Trumbull (1963) 220 CA2d 788, 34 CR 127: §30.36
Nevada Constr. Inc. v Mariposa Pub. Util. Dist. (1952) 114 CA2d 816, 251 P2d 53: §29.89
New Amsterdam Cas. Co. v B. L. Jones & Co. (5th Cir 1958) 254 F2d 917: §29.88
Newport v Los Angeles (1960) 184 CA2d 229, 7 CR 497: §29.54
Norman v Berney (1965) 235 CA2d 424, 45 CR 467: §§30.20, 30.38
Northridge Fin. Corp. v Hamblin (1975) 48 CA3d 819, 122 CR 109: §§30.62, 30.72
Northridge Water Dist. v McDonell (1958) 158 CA2d 123, 322 P2d 25: §32.2
Northwestern Nat'l Ins. Co. v Corley (7th Cir 1974) 503 F2d 224: §29.2

O

Oberkotter v Spreckles (1923) 64 CA 470, 221 P 698: §31.2
O'Brien v Santa Monica (1963) 220 CA2d 67, 33 CR 770: §30.72
O'Donnell v San Francisco (1956) 147 CA2d 63, 304 P2d 852: §31.28
Oil Workers Int'l Union v Superior Court (1951) 103 CA2d 512, 230 P2d 71: §24.8
Old Settlers Ins. Co. v White (1910) 158 C 236, 110 P 922: §34.12
Oliver v Swiss Club Tell (1963) 222 CA2d 528, 35 CR 324: §§29.45, 29.54, 29.69
Olson v Hopkins (1969) 269 CA2d 638, 75 CR 33: §§25.10, 25.24, 25.51

Olson v Sacramento (1969) 274 CA2d 316, 79 CR 140: §29.79

Omni Aviation Managers, Inc. v Municipal Court (1976) 60 CA3d 682, 131 CR 758: §27.7

One 1941 Chevrolet Coupe, People v (1951) 37 C2d 283, 231 P2d 832: §26.28

One 1950 Mercury Sedan, People v (1953) 116 CA2d 746, 254 P2d 666: §29.44

One 1964 Chevrolet Corvette Convertible, People v (1969) 274 CA2d 720, 79 CR 447: §29.72

Oppenheimer v Deutchman (1955) 132 CA2d Supp 875, 281 P2d 650: §31.41

Orange County Air Pollution Control Dist. v Superior Court (1972) 27 CA3d 109, 103 CR 410: §29.12

Orange County Water Dist. v Riverside (1959) 173 CA2d 137, 343 P2d 450: §24.7

Orange Empire Nat'l Bank v Kirk (1968) 259 CA2d 347, 66 CR 240: §30.59

Orloff v Metropolitan Trust Co. (1941) 17 C2d 484, 110 P2d 396: §§24.19, 24.25

Owen v Niagara Mach. & Tool Works (1977) 68 CA3d 566, 137 CR 378: §§31.12, 31.14

Oxford v Signal Oil & Gas Co. (1970) 12 CA3d 403, 90 CR 700: §29.9

P

Pacific Air Lines v Superior Court (1965) 231 CA2d 591, 42 CR 70: §23.41

Pacific Air Lines v Superior Court (1965) 231 CA2d 587, 42 CR 68: §§23.42, 29.33

Pacific Greyhound Lines v Superior Court (1946) 28 C2d 61, 168 P2d 665: §§31.21, 31.25

Pacific Land Research Co., People v (1976) 63 CA3d 873, 134 CR 114: §§29.33, 29.52

Pacific Motor Transp. Co. v State Bd. of Equalization (1972) 28 CA3d 230, 104 CR 558: §24.7

Pacific Portland Cement Co. v Food Mach. & Chem. Corp. (9th Cir 1949) 178 F2d 541: §24.41

Pacific States Corp. v Pan-American Bank (1931) 213 C 58, 1 P2d 4: §24.30

Pacific W. Oil Co. v Bern Oil Co. (1939) 13 C2d 60, 87 P2d 1045: §26.28

Palm Springs Alpine Estates, Inc. v Superior Court (1967) 255 CA2d 883, 63 CR 618: §23.36

Palmquist v Palmquist (1963) 212 CA2d 340, 27 CR 756: §33.29

Parenti v Lifeline Blood Bank (1975) 49 CA3d 331, 122 CR 709: §§31.68, 31.75, 31.77, 31.89

Parker v Twentieth Century-Fox Film Corp. (1970) 3 C3d 176, 89 CR 737: §§23.45, 29.8, 29.44–29.46, 29.51

Pasadena v Alhambra (1949) 33 C2d 908, 207 P2d 17: §§24.29, 31.25

Pasadena City Fire Fighters Ass'n v Board of Directors

(1974) 36 CA3d 901, 112 CR 56: §29.22
Patel v Athow (1973) 34 CA3d 727, 110 CR 460: §24.27
Patterson v Blackburn (1920) 47 CA 362, 190 P 483: §29.45
Paul W. Speer, Inc. v Superior Court (1969) 272 CA2d 32, 77 CR 152: §31.36
Paularena v Superior Court (1965) 231 CA2d 906, 42 CR 366: §26.28
Pellett v Sonotone Corp. (1945) 26 C2d 705, 160 P2d 783: §33.29
Pena v Los Angeles (1970) 8 CA3d 257, 87 CR 326: §24.22
Penney, J. C., Co. v Westinghouse Elec. Corp. (1963) 217 CA3d 834, 32 CR 172: §§24.7, 24.35
People ex rel Dep't of Pub. Works v Buellton Dev. Co. (1943) 58 CA2d 178, 136 P2d 793: §31.72
People ex rel Dep't of Pub. Works v Busick (1968) 259 CA2d 744, 66 CR 532: §26.95
People ex rel Mosk v Lynam (1967) 253 CA2d 959, 61 CR 800: §29.72
People ex rel State Lands Comm'n v Long Beach (1960) 183 CA2d 271, 6 CR 658: §§25.23, 25.32
People v _____ (see name of defendant)
Perati v Atkinson (1964) 230 CA2d 251, 40 CR 835: §31.9
Perris Irr. Dist., People v (1901) 132 C 289, 64 P 399: §§25.56, 25.58
Perry v Farley Bros. Moving & Storage, Inc. (1970) 6 CA3d 884, 86 CR 397: §29.71
Petaluma v White (1907) 152 C 190, 92 P 177: §23.43
Peterson v Peterson (1946) 74 CA2d 312, 168 P2d 474: §26.28
Pettis v General Tel. Co. (1967) 66 C2d 503, 58 CR 316: §29.3
Phelps v Loop (1942) 53 CA2d 541, 128 P2d 63: §24.43
Pianka v State (1956) 46 C2d 208, 293 P2d 458: §29.14
Pierce, People v (1967) 66 C2d 53, 56 CR 817: §23.42
Pittenger v Home Sav. & Loan Ass'n (1958) 166 CA2d 32, 332 P2d 399: §24.11
Poehlmann v Kennedy (1874) 48 C 201: §25.59
Polin v Chung Cho (1970) 8 CA3d 673, 87 CR 591: §29.16
Polony v White (1974) 43 CA3d 44, 117 CR 341: §§31.10, 31.22
Poochigian v Layne (1953) 120 CA2d 757, 261 P2d 738: §§29.79, 29.82
Poole v Caulfield (1872) 45 C 107: §31.59
Potts v Whitson (1942) 52 CA2d 199, 125 P2d 947: §30.32
Preston v Hill (1875) 50 C 43: §34.6
Provencher v Los Angeles (1935) 10 CA2d 730, 52 P2d 983: §31.75
Putnam v Putnam (1942) 51 CA2d 696, 125 P2d 525: §24.5
Pylon, Inc. v Olympic Ins. Co. (1969) 271 CA2d 643, 77 CR 72: §29.16

Q

Quinn, Estate of (1955) 43 C2d 785, 278 P2d 692: §25.30

R

R. D. Reeder Lathing Co. v Allen (1967) 66 C2d 373, 57 CR 841: §§29.46, 29.82
R. G. Hamilton Corp. v Corum (1933) 218 C 92, 21 P2d 413: §24.40
Rader v Thrasher (1972) 22 CA3d 883, 99 CR 670: §29.86
Raedeke v Gibraltar Sav. & Loan Ass'n (1974) 10 C3d 665, 111 CR 693: §§24.40, 26.28
Ralphs Grocery Co. v Amalgamated Meat Cutters, Local No. 439 (1950) 98 CA2d 539, 220 P2d 802: §24.5
Ramos v Santa Clara (1973) 35 CA3d 93, 110 CR 485: §29.29
Randles v Lowry (1970) 4 CA3d 68, 84 CR 321: §33.14
Rankin v Frebank Co. (1975) 47 CA3d 75, 121 CR 348: §26.28
Rapaport v Forer (1937) 20 CA2d 271, 66 P2d 1242: §24.13
Rardin Logging Co. v Bullok (1953) 120 CA2d 67, 260 P2d 81: §30.34
Ray, People v (1960) 181 CA2d 64, 5 CR 113: §24.20
Ray Kizer Constr. Co. v Young (1968) 257 CA2d 766, 65 CR 267: §30.60
Raymond, Estate of (1940) 38 CA2d 305, 100 P2d 0185: §31.73

RCA Corp. v Superior Court (1975) 47 CA3d 1007, 121 CR 441: §31.12
Reclamation Dist. v Snowball (1911) 160 C 695, 118 P 514: §23.43
Record Mach. & Tool Co. v Pageman Holding Corp. (1954) 42 C2d 227, 266 P2d 1: §24.43
Reeder, R. D., Lathing Co. v Allen (1967) 66 C2d 373, 57 CR 841: §§29.46, 29.82
Reeves v Hutson (1956) 144 CA2d 445, 301 P2d 264: §30.61
Reher v Reed (1913) 166 C 525, 137 P 263: §30.13
Reich v Yow (1967) 249 CA2d 12, 57 CR 117: §29.45
Reifler v Superior Court (1974) 39 CA3d 479, 114 CR 356: §§23.57, 30.70
Remainders, Inc. v Bartlett (1963) 215 CA2d 295, 30 CR 191: §30.52
Reserve Ins. Co. v Universal Underwriters Ins. Co. (1975) 51 CA3d 57, 123 CR 763: §31.25
Residents of Beverly Glen, Inc. v Los Angeles (1973) 34 CA3d 117, 109 CR 724: §24.8
Rice v Arden Farms Co. (1962) 199 CA2d 349, 18 CR 863: §31.44
Richardson v Eureka (1895) 110 C 441, 42 P 965: §26.29
Rickless v Temple (1970) 4 CA3d 869, 84 CR 828: §31.39
Rimington v General Acc. Group of Ins. Cos. (1962) 205 CA2d 394, 23 CR 40: §24.4

Rio Del Mar Country Club v Superior Court (1948) 84 CA2d 214, 190 P2d 295: §31.53
Rios v Torvald Klaveness (1969) 2 CA3d 1077, 83 CR 150: §31.9
Ripling v Superior Court (1952) 112 CA2d 399, 247 P2d 117: §26.28
River Garden Farms Inc. v Superior Court (1972) 26 CA3d 986, 103 CR 498: §33.32
Rivieccio v Bothan (1946) 27 C2d 621, 165 P2d 677: §24.22
Roadside Rest, Inc. v Lankershim Estate (1946) 76 CA2d 525, 173 P2d 554: §§24.41, 24.43
Roberts v Roberts (1966) 241 CA2d 93, 50 CR 408: §29.85
Robertson v Superior Court (1960) 180 CA2d 372, 4 CR 297: §31.33
Robinson v Crescent City Mill & Transp. Co. (1892) 93 C 316, 28 P 950: §25.11
Robinson v Early (1967) 248 CA2d 19, 56 CR 183: §30.3
Robinson v El Centro Grain Co. (1933) 133 CA 567, 24 P2d 554: §32.6
Robinson v Puls (1946) 28 C2d 664, 171 P2d 430: §26.28
Robinson v San Francisco (1974) 41 CA3d 334, 116 CR 125: §29.10
Robinson v Varela (1977) 67 CA3d 611, 136 CR 783: §30.10
Rodes v Shannon (1961) 194 CA2d 743, 15 CR 349: §§29.29, 29.86
Rodgers v Parker (1902) 136 C 313, 68 P 975: §31.72
Rodriguez v Municipal Court (1972) 25 CA3d 521, 102 CR 45: §30.9
Romer, O'Connor & Co. v Huffman (1959) 171 CA2d 342, 341 P2d 62: §30.62
Romero v Weakley (SD Cal 1955) 131 F Supp 818: §24.8
Rooney v Vermont Inv. Corp. (1973) 10 C3d 351, 110 CR 353: §§29.45, 31.52, 34.7, 34.9, 34.12
Rosati v Heimann (1954) 126 CA2d 51, 271 P2d 953: §30.52
Rose v Knapp (1951) 38 C2d 114, 237 P2d 981: §31.25
Rose v Lelande (1912) 20 CA 502, 129 P 599: §30.32
Rose, W. A., Co. v Municipal Court (1959) 176 CA2d 67, 1 CR 49: §§30.32, 30.40
Roski v Superior Court (1971) 18 CA3d 1046, 96 CR 424: §31.91
Roski v Superior Court (1971) 17 CA3d 841, 95 CR 312: §§31.68, 31.71–31.72
Rosner v Benedict Heights, Inc. (1963) 219 CA2d 1, 32 CR 764: §§30.9, 31.5
Ross v George Pepperdine Foundation (1959) 174 CA2d 135, 344 P2d 368: §31.27
Ross v Harootunian (1967) 257 CA2d 292, 64 CR 537: §24.6
Rouse v Palmer (1961) 197 CA2d 666, 17 CR 509: §31.44

Rowland School Dist. v State Bd. of Educ. (1968) 264 CA2d 589, 70 CR 504: §§24.8, 24.18

Rubin v Toberman (1964) 226 CA2d 319, 38 CR 32: §24.4

Russo v Scrambler Motorcycles (1976) 56 CA3d 112, 127 CR 913: §24.35

Ryerson v Riverside Cement Co. (1968) 266 CA2d 789, 72 CR 595: §31.30

S

S. E. P. Assoc., Inc. v Peto (1975) 49 CA3d 305, 122 CR 514: §§34.9, 34.12

Safeway Stores, Inc. v Royal Indem. Co. (1971) 21 CA3d 44, 98 CR 234: §24.36

Samuels v Sabih (1976) 62 CA3d 335, 133 CR 74: §31.6

San Bernardino v Doria Min. & Eng'r Corp. (1977) 72 CA3d 776, 140 CR 383: §§26.84–26.86, 26.93

San Bernardino Valley Munic. Water Dist. v Gage Canal Co. (1964) 226 CA2d 206, 37 CR 856: §25.28

San Diego v Andrews (1924) 195 C 111, 231 P 726: §25.58

San Francisco v Budde (1956) 139 CA2d 101, 292 P2d 955: §24.42

San Francisco v Muller (1960) 177 CA2d 600, 2 CR 383: §23.63

San Francisco Lathing, Inc. v Superior Court (1969) 271 CA2d 78, 76 CR 304: §§29.82, 31.53, 31.55

San Francisco Lumber Co. v Bibb (1903) 139 C 325, 73 P 864: §32.2

San Joaquin v State Bd. of Equalization (1970) 9 CA3d 365, 88 CR 12: §§24.7, 24.29

San Joaquin & Kings River Canal & Irr. Co. v Stevinson (1912) 164 C 221, 128 P 924: §25.23

San Luis Obispo Bay Props., Inc. v PG&E (1972) 28 CA3d 556, 104 CR 733: §31.69

San Ysidro Irr. Dist. v Superior Court (1961) 56 C2d 708, 16 CR 609: §24.29

Sanders v Fuller (1975) 45 CA3d 994, 119 CR 902: §§31.22–31.23, 31.25

Santa Barbara School Dist. v Superior Court (1975) 13 C3d 315, 118 CR 637: §24.7

Santandrea v Siltec Corp. (1976) 56 CA3d 525, 128 CR 629: §§23.63, 26.45, 26.94, 29.82

Sarracino v Superior Court (1974) 13 C3d 1, 118 CR 21: §31.52

Sattinger v Newbauer (1954) 123 CA2d 365, 266 P2d 586: §24.7

Schafer v Wholesale Frozen Foods, Inc. (1959) 171 CA2d 232, 340 P2d 308: §24.10

Schlothan v Rusalem (1953) 41 C2d 414, 260 P2d 68: §31.40

Schonfeld v Vallejo (1975) 50 CA3d 401, 123 CR 669: §29.83

Schubert v Bates (1947) 30 C2d 785, 185 P2d 793: §31.69

Schulze v Schulze (1953) 121

CA2d 75, 262 P2d 646: §29.90
Schwartz v Magyar House, Inc. (1959) 168 CA2d 182, 335 P2d 487: §26.95
Seidell v Tuxedo Land Co. (1934) 1 CA2d 406, 36 P2d 1102: §§27.7, 27.12
Selby Realty Co. v San Buenaventura (1973) 10 C3d 110, 109 CR 799; §§24.9, 24.11, 24.23, 24.43
Semole v Sansoucie (1972) 28 CA3d 714, 104 CR 897: §31.12
Serrano v Priest (1971) 5 C3d 584, 96 CR 601: §24.8
Setzer v Moore (1927) 202 C 333, 260 P 550: §33.1
Sheldon v Gunn (1880) 56 C 582: §25.60
Shell Oil Co. v Superior Court (1975) 50 CA3d 489, 123 CR 307: §23.10
Shepard v Alexian Bros. Hosp. (1973) 33 CA3d 606, 109 CR 132: §31.77
Sherberne & Assocs. v Vector Mfg. Co. (1968) 263 CA2d 68, 69 CR 284: §31.28
Shields v Siegel (1966) 246 CA2d 334, 54 CR 577: §§30.60, 30.73–30.74
Siciliano v Fireman's Fund Ins. Co. (1976) 62 CA3d 745, 133 CR 376: §24.8
Siemon v Russell (1961) 194 CA2d 592, 15 CR 218: §29.72
Silva v San Francisco (1948) 87 CA2d 784, 198 P2d 78: §24.11
Silver v Beverly Hills Nat'l Bank (1967) 253 CA2d 1000, 61 CR 751: §24.37

Silver v Los Angeles (1963) 217 CA2d 134, 31 CR 545: §24.20
Silverton v Free (1953) 120 CA2d 389, 261 P2d 17: §31.89
Simonini v Jay Dee Leather Prods. Co. (1948) 85 CA2d 265, 193 P2d 53: §31.46
Simpson v Superior Court (1945) 68 CA2d 821, 158 P2d 46: §§31.65, 31.71
Singelyn v Superior Court (1976) 62 CA3d 972, 133 CR 486: §31.26
Singh, People v (1932) 121 CA 107, 8 P2d 898: §32.2
Skolsky v Electronovision Prods., Inc. (1967) 254 CA2d 246, 62 CR 91: §30.69.
Slack v Slack (1966) 241 CA2d 530, 50 CR 763: §§33.6, 33.29
Slaybaugh v Superior Court (1977) 70 CA3d 216, 138 CR 628: §31.12
Slobojan v Western Travelers Life Ins. Co. (1969) 70 C2d 432, 74 CR 895: §29.44
Slusher v Durr (1977) 69 CA3d 747, 138 CR 265: §§30.26, 30.58, 30.60
Smith v Bank of Cal. (1937) 19 CA2d 579, 65 P2d 1361: §24.7
Smith v Bear Valley Milling & Lumber Co. (1945) 26 C2d 590, 160 P2d 1: §31.21
Smith v Bratman (1917) 174 C 518, 163 P 892: §30.79
Smith v Busniewski (1952) 115 CA2d 124, 251 P2d 697: §30.73

Smith v Los Angeles (1948) 84 CA2d 297, 190 P2d 943: §31.75
Smith v Los Angeles Bookbinders Union (1955) 133 CA2d 486, 284 P2d 194: §30.10
Smith v Pelton Water Wheel Co. (1907) 151 C 394, 90 P 934: §30.62
Smith v Roberts (1905) 1 CA 148, 81 P 1026: §31.91
Smithers v Ederer (1956) 146 CA2d 227, 303 P2d 771: §31.30
Somers, Estate of (1947) 82 CA2d 757, 187 P2d 433: §31.65
Sonobond Corp. v Uthe Technology, Inc. (ND Cal 1970) 314 F Supp 878: §29.74
Southern Counties Gas Co. v Ventura Pipeline Constr. Co. (1971) 19 CA3d 372, 96 CR 825: §§24.10, 24.27
Southern Pac. Co. v Fish (1958) 166 CA2d 353, 333 P2d 133: §29.86
Southern Pac. Co. v Seaboard Mills (1962) 207 CA2d 97, 24 CR 236: §31.19
Southern Pac. Transp. Co. v Superior Court (1976) 58 CA3d 433, 129 CR 912: §26.28
Sparks, People v (1952) 112 CA2d 120, 246 P2d 64: §23.1
Speer, Paul W., Inc. v Superior Court (1969) 272 CA2d 32, 77 CR 152: §31.36
Spence v State (1961) 198 CA2d 332, 18 CR 302: §26.73

Spencer v Hibernia Bank (1960) 186 CA2d 702, 9 CR 867: §§24.37, 29.44, 29.70
Sperry & Hutchinson Co. v State Bd. of Pharmacy (1966) 241 CA2d 229, 50 CR 489: §24.8
Spinks v Superior Court (1915) 26 CA 793, 148 P 798: §31.69
Squire v San Francisco (1970) 12 CA3d 974, 91 CR 347: §§24.7, 25.22
Stambaugh v Superior Court (1976) 62 CA3d 231, 132 CR 843: §33.32
Standard Oil Co. v Superior Court (1976) 61 CA3d 852, 132 CR 761: §31.26
Stanton v Dumke (1966) 64 C2d 199, 49 CR 380: §29.72
State v Superior Court (1974) 12 C3d 237, 115 CR 497: §§24.11, 24.23
State Compensation Ins. Fund v Allen (1930) 104 CA 400, 285 P 1053: §25.37
State Compensation Ins. Fund v Matulich (1942) 55 CA2d 528, 131 P2d 21: §25.37
State Farm Mut. Auto. Ins. Co. v Spann (1973) 31 CA3d 97, 106 CR 923: §24.41
State Farm Mut. Auto. Ins. Co. v Superior Court (1956) 47 C2d 428, 304 P2d 13: §§24.2, 24.39–24.40, 27.21
State Lands Comm'n, People ex rel v Long Beach (1960) 183 CA2d 271, 6 CR 658: §§25.23, 25.32
State Medical Educ. Bd. v Roberson (1970) 6 CA3d

493, 86 CR 258: §§29.29, 29.82
Stationers Corp. v Dun & Bradstreet, Inc. (1965) 62 C2d 412, 42 CR 449: §29.8
Steele v Litton Indus., Inc. (1968) 260 CA2d 157, 68 CR 680: §31.77
Steen v Los Angeles (1948) 31 C2d 542, 190 P2d 937: §31.44
Steeve v Yaeger (1956) 145 CA2d 455, 302 P2d 704: §24.43
Stella v Great W. Sav. & Loan Ass'n (1970) 13 CA3d 732, 91 CR 771: §31.25
Stenzel v Kronick (1929) 102 CA 507, 283 P 93: §24.13
Stepan v Garcia (1974) 43 CA3d 497, 117 CR 919: §29.63
Stern & Goodman Inv. Co. v Danziger (1929) 206 C 456, 274 P 748: §25.33
Stevens v Marco (1956) 147 CA2d 357, 305 P2d 669: §31.77
Stevens v Stevens (1968) 268 CA2d 426, 74 CR 54: §34.2
Stevens v Torregano (1961) 192 CA2d 105, 13 CR 604: §30.16
Stewart v Whitmyre (1961) 192 CA2d 327, 13 CR 235: §29.46
Stich v Dickinson (1869) 38 C 608: §25.25
Stockwell v McAlvay (1929) 97 CA 609, 275 P 960: §25.26
Stratford Irr. Dist. v Empire Water Co. (1941) 44 CA2d 61, 111 P2d 957: §25.28
Stuart v Hollywood Turf Club (1956) 146 CA2d 261, 303 P2d 897: §§31.19–31.20

Subriar v Bakersfield (1976) 59 CA3d 175, 130 CR 853: §24.23
Sugarman v Federal Ins. Co. (1968) 265 CA2d 563, 71 CR 542: §24.4
Sullivan v San Francisco Art Ass'n (1950) 101 CA2d 449, 225 P2d 993: §24.6
Superior Court, State v (1974) 12 C3d 237, 115 CR 497: §§24.11, 24.23
Superior Oil Co. v Superior Court (1936) 6 C2d 113, 56 P2d 950: §§31.5, 31.19
Surety Ins. Co., People v (1975) 48 CA3d 123, 121 CR 438: §31.52
Swaffield v Universal Ecsco Corp. (1969) 271 CA2d 147, 76 CR 680: §29.24
Swartzman v Superior Court (1964) 231 CA2d 195, 41 CR 721: §§26.76–26.77

T

T. E. D. Bearing Co. v Walter E. Heller & Co. (1974) 38 CA3d 59, 112 CR 910: §29.73
Talcott v Talcott (1942) 54 CA2d 743, 129 P2d 946: §§24.6, 24.10
Taliaferro v Coakley (1960) 186 CA2d 258, 9 CR 529: §§23.26, 29.41.
Taliaferro v Davis (1963) 216 CA2d 398, 31 CR 164: §30.52
Taliaferro v Hays (1961) 188 CA2d 235, 10 CR 429: §30.3
Taliaferro v Hoogs (1963) 219 CA2d 559, 33 CR 415: §30.52

Taliaferro v Riddle (1959) 167 CA2d 567, 334 P2d 950: §§23.23, 31.9
Taliaferro v Taliaferro (1959) 171 CA2d 1, 339 P2d 594: §§24.11, 24.26
Tarman v Sherwin (1961) 189 CA2d 49, 10 CR 787: §§23.23, 31.47
Taschner v City Council (1973) 31 CA3d 48, 107 CR 214: §24.45
Tate v Superior Court (1975) 45 CA3d 925, 119 CR 835: §§23.6, 23.51, 31.56
Taylor v Hizer (1973) 30 CA3d 846, 106 CR 603: §§31.10, 31.12
Taylor v Marine Cooks' & Stewards' Ass'n (1953) 117 CA2d 556, 256 P2d 595: §24.7
Taylor v Union Pac. R.R. (1976) 16 C3d 893, 130 CR 23: §§26.12, 26.32, 26.37
Taylor v Western States Land & Mortgage Co. (1944) 63 CA2d 401, 147 P2d 36: §25.52
Tehachapi-Cummings County Water Dist. v Armstrong (1975) 49 CA3d 992, 122 CR 918: §24.7
Thatcher, Estate of (1953) 120 CA2d 811, 262 P2d 337: §31.21
Thierfeldt v Marin Hosp. Dist. (1973) 35 CA3d 186, 110 CR 791: §29.6
Thompson v Boyd (1963) 217 CA2d 365, 32 CR 513: §24.6
Thompson, J. A., & Sons, Inc. v Superior Court (1963) 215 CA2d 719, 30 CR 471: §31.9
Thorman v Dome Producing & Developing Co. (1942) 50 CA2d 201, 122 P2d 927: §§25.20, 25.41
Thorson v Western Dev. Corp. (1967) 251 CA2d 206, 59 CR 299: §§30.36, 30.52
Thurmond v Superior Court (1967) 66 C2d 836, 59 CR 273: §26.93
Tiburon v Northwestern Pac. R.R. (1970) 4 CA3d 160, 84 CR 469: §§24.24, 24.30
Times-Mirror Co. v Superior Court (1935) 3 C2d 309, 44 P2d 547: §31.74
Toebelman v Missouri-Kansas Pipe Line Co. (3d Cir 1942) 130 F2d 1016: §29.13
Tolle v Struve (1932) 124 CA 263, 12 P2d 61: §24.1
Tomales Bay Oyster Corp. v Superior Court (1950) 35 C2d 389, 217 P2d 968: §31.18
Tomasello v Tomasello (1952) 113 CA2d 23, 247 P2d 612: §§24.7, 24.28
Tool Research & Eng'r Corp. v Henigson (1975) 46 CA3d 675, 120 CR 291: §29.8
Torres, People v (1962) 201 CA2d 290, 20 CR 315: §29.33
Tostevin v Douglas (1958) 160 CA2d 321, 325 P2d 130: §24.22
Towle v Sweeney (1905) 2 CA 29, 83 P 74: §32.6
Townsend v Driver (1907) 5 CA 581, 90 P 1071: §§25.26, 25.59

Traders Credit Corp. v Superior Court (1931) 111 CA 663, 296 P 99: §23.23

Trani v R. G. Hohman Enterprises (1975) 52 CA3d 314, 125 CR 34: §29.83

Trans-Pacific Trading Co. v Patsy Frock & Romper Co. (1922) 189 C 509, 209 P 357: §30.52

Transit Ads, Inc. v Tanner Motor Livery, Ltd. (1969) 270 CA2d 275, 75 CR 848: §§30.58, 30.60

Travelers Indem. Co. v Erickson's, Inc. (5th Cir 1968) 396 F2d 134: §29.88

Travers v Louden (1967) 254 CA2d 926, 62 CR 654: §§24.4, 24.19, 24.25, 24.31, 24.39

Traweek v Draper (1956) 143 CA2d 119, 299 P2d 391: §25.50

Tresway Aero, Inc. v Superior Court (1971) 5 C3d 431, 96 CR 571: §§31.11, 31.14, 31.29

Tri-State Mfg. Co. v Superior Court (1964) 224 CA2d 442, 36 CR 750: §23.41

Trickey v Superior Court (1967) 252 CA2d 650, 60 CR 761: §26.56

Truslow v Woodruff (1967) 252 CA2d 158, 60 CR 304: §29.25

Turnbull v Superior Court (1932) 126 CA 141, 14 P2d 540: §§31.6, 31.53

U

Union Oil Co. v Hane (1938) 27 CA2d 106, 80 P2d 516: §26.32

Union Trust Co. v Superior Court (1938) 11 C2d 449, 81 P2d 150: §29.54

United Bonding Ins. Co., People v (1969) 272 CA2d 441, 77 CR 310: §§23.42–23.43

United Bonding Ins. Co., People v (1966) 240 CA2d 895, 50 CR 198: §29.86

U.S. v Dibble (9th Cir 1970) 429 F2d 598: §29.55

United States Fid. & Guar. Co. v Sullivan (1949) 93 CA2d 559, 209 P2d 429: §29.29

United States Fin. v Sullivan (1974) 37 CA3d 5, 112 CR 18: §31.77

V

Valley Fair Fashions, Inc. v Valley Fair (1966) 245 CA2d 614, 54 CR 306: §§24.7, 24.23

Valley Vista Land Co. v Nipomo Water & Sewer Co. (1967) 255 CA2d 172, 63 CR 78: §29.67

Vann v Shilleh (1975) 54 CA3d 192, 126 CR 401: §26.90

Vanoni v Sonoma (1974) 40 CA3d 743, 115 CR 485: §24.29

Varco-Pruden, Inc. v Hampshire Constr. Co. (1975) 50 CA3d 654, 123 CR 606: §§29.8, 29.29

Veale v Piercy (1962) 206 CA2d 557, 24 CR 91: §24.40

Vecki v Sorensen (1959) 171 CA2d 390, 340 P2d 1020: §31.19

Vegetable Oil Prods. Co. v Superior Court (1963) 213 CA2d 252, 28 CR 555: §27.11

Vesely v Sager (1971) 5 C3d 153, 95 CR 623: §§29.3, 29.9, 29.14, 29.25
Vogel, People v (1956) 46 C2d 798, 299 P2d 850: §30.28
Vogelsang v Owl Trucking Co. (1974) 40 CA3d 1068, 115 CR 666: §§26.79, 31.20
Voyce v Superior Court (1942) 20 C2d 479, 127 P2d 536: §§25.30, 25.37, 25.59, 31.65, 31.73

W

W. A. Rose Co. v Municipal Court (1959) 176 CA2d 67, 1 CR 49: §§30.32, 30.40
W. H. Marston Co. v Kochritz (1926) 80 CA 352, 251 P 959: §30.40
Waite v Southern Pac. Co. (1923) 192 C 467, 221 P 204: §30.62
Walker v Los Angeles (1961) 55 C2d 626, 12 CR 671: §24.7
Walker v Munro (1960) 178 CA2d 67, 2 CR 737: §24.21
Walker v Stauffer Chem. Corp. (1971) 19 CA3d 669, 96 CR 803: §29.83
Wall v Mines (1900) 130 C 27, 62 P 386: §25.57
Waller v Waller (1970) 3 CA3d 456, 83 CR 533: §23.41
Walsh v Glendale Fed. Sav. & Loan Ass'n (1969) 1 CA3d 578, 81 CR 804: §§29.3, 29.9
Ward v Superior Court (1973) 35 CA3d 67, 110 CR 501: §33.10
Ware v Stafford (1962) 206 CA2d 232, 24 CR 153: §23.41

Warfield v McGraw-Hill, Inc. (1973) 32 CA3d 1041, 108 CR 652: §29.29
Warren v Atchison, Topeka & Santa Fe Ry. (1971) 19 CA3d 24, 96 CR 317: §31.9
Warren v Kaiser Foundation Health Plan, Inc. (1975) 47 CA3d 678, 121 CR 19: §§24.14, 24.19
Watkins v Nutting (1941) 17 C2d 490, 110 P2d 384: §30.9
Watson v Collins (1962) 204 CA2d 27, 21 CR 832: §25.50
Watson v Sansoe (1971) 19 CA3d 1, 96 CR 387: §§24.25, 24.27
Watson v Superior Court (1972) 24 CA3d 53, 100 CR 684: §§31.8, 31.48, 31.53
Weathers v Kaiser Foundation Hosps. (1971) 5 C3d 98, 95 CR 516: §23.41
Weber v Marine Cooks' & Stewards' Ass'n (1949) 93 CA2d 327, 208 P2d 1009: §24.7
Weeks v Roberts (1968) 68 C2d 802, 69 CR 305: §§26.79, 31.20
Weiner v Los Angeles (1968) 68 C2d 697, 68 CR 733: §25.18
Weir v Snow (1962) 210 CA2d 283, 26 CR 868: §§29.3, 29.51
Weissman v Lakewood Water & Power Co. (1959) 173 CA2d 652, 343 P2d 776: §24.30
Weitz v Yankosky (1966) 63 C2d 849, 48 CR 620: §§30.59–30.61, 30.73

Welden v Davis Auto Exch. (1957) 153 CA2d 515, 315 P2d 33: §23.10
Weldon v Rogers (1907) 151 C 432, 90 P 1062: §23.1
Werner v Sargeant (1953) 121 CA2d 833, 264 P2d 217: §29.2
West Coast Poultry Co. v Glasner (1965) 231 CA2d 747, 42 CR 297: §24.23
Westerholm v Twentieth Century Ins. Co. (1976) 58 CA3d 628, 130 CR 164: §24.2
Western Contracting Corp. v Southwest Steel Rolling Mills, Inc. (1976) 58 CA3d 532, 129 CR 782: §29.10
Western Homes, Inc. v Herbert Ketell, Inc. (1965) 236 CA2d 142, 45 CR 856: §§24.20, §24.45
Western Motors Corp. v Land Dev. & Inv. Co. (1957) 152 CA2d 509, 313 P2d 927: §24.10
Westinghouse Credit Corp. v Wolfer (1970) 10 CA3d 63, 88 CR 654: §30.59
Westphal v Westphal (1942) 20 C2d 393, 126 P2d 105: §29.81
Westphal v Westphal (1943) 61 CA2d 544, 143 P2d 405: §§23.23, 31.25, 31.47
Westport Oil Co. v Garrison (1971) 19 CA3d 974, 97 CR 287: §§30.10–30.11, 30.26
Whalen v Superior Court (1960) 184 CA2d 598, 7 CR 610: §26.85
Whipple v Haberle (1963) 223 CA2d 477, 36 CR 9: §24.36

White v Clarke (1896) 111 C 425, 44 P 164: §§32.1, 32.3
Whitney's at the Beach v Superior Court (1970) 3 CA3d 258, 83 CR 237: §§29.8, 29.31, 29.51, 29.89
Whittell v Franchise Tax Bd. (1964) 231 CA2d 278, 41 CR 673: §24.7
Whittier Union High School Dist. v Beck (1941) 45 CA2d 736, 114 P2d 731: §31.65
Whittier Union High School Dist. v Superior Court (1977) 66 CA3d 504, 136 CR 86: §33.6
Wilkin v Tadlock (1952) 110 CA2d 156, 241 P2d 1066: §26.99
Williams v Myer (1907) 150 C 714, 89 P 972: §26.99
Williams v Williams (1967) 255 CA2d 648, 63 CR 354: §29.72
Wills v Williams (1975) 47 CA3d 941, 121 CR 420: §31.22
Wilson v Board of Retirement (1957) 156 CA2d 195, 319 P2d 426: §24.37
Wilson v Civil Serv. Comm'n (1964) 224 CA2d 340, 36 CR 559: §24.36
Wilson v Frakes (1960) 178 CA2d 580, 3 CR 434: §31.76
Wilson v Goldman (1969) 274 CA2d 573, 79 CR 309: §30.7
Wilson v Sharp (1954) 42 C2d 675, 268 P2d 1062: §29.84
Wilson v Transit Authority (1962) 199 CA2d 716, 19 CR 59: §§24.4, 24.11, 24.30

Windiate v Moore (1962) 201 CA2d 509, 19 CR 860: §29.13
Winston v Idaho Hardwood Co. (1913) 23 CA 211, 137 P 601: §30.54
Wisniewski v Clary (1975) 46 CA3d 499, 120 CR 176: §§26.75, 33.17, 33.24, 33.27
Woley v Turkus (1958) 51 C2d 402, 334 P2d 12: §§31.21, 31.24–31.25
Wollenberg v Tonningsen (1935) 8 CA2d 722, 48 P2d 738: §24.8
Wood v Herson (1974) 39 CA3d 737, 114 CR 365: §34.3
Woods v Stallworth (1960) 177 CA2d 517, 2 CR 250: §30.24
Woodward v Brown (1897) 119 C 283, 51 P 2: §29.54
Woolfson v Personal Travel Serv. (1971) 3 C3d 909, 92 CR 286: §31.36
Wouldridge v Burns (1968) 265 CA2d 82, 71 CR 394: §31.91
Wright v Groom Trucking Co. (1962) 206 CA2d 485, 24 CR 80: §§31.21, 31.26
Wuest v Wuest (1942) 53 CA2d 339, 127 P2d 934: §32.4

Wyoming Pac. Oil v Preston (1958) 50 C2d 736, 329 P2d 489: §31.13

Y

Yanchor v Kagan (1971) 22 CA3d 544, 99 CR 367: §33.6
Yokohama Specie Bank, In re (1948) 86 CA2d 545, 195 P2d 555: §§25.1, 25.36, 25.38
Young v Redman (1976) 55 CA3d 827, 128 CR 86: §§26.84, 26.88–26.89
Young v Young (1950) 100 CA2d 85, 223 P2d 25: §24.11
Youngblood v Terra (1970) 10 CA3d 533, 89 CR 13: §31.28

Z

Zeitlin v Arnebergh (1963) 59 C2d 901, 31 CR 800: §24.24
Zetterberg v State Dep't of Pub. Health (1974) 43 CA3d 657, 118 CR 100: §§24.8, 24.23, 24.36
Zorro Ins. Co. v Great Pac. Sec. Corp. (1977) 69 CA3d 907, 138 CR 410: §30.8

Table of References

BASIC CALIFORNIA PRACTICE HANDBOOK (Cal CEB 1959).
Borchard, Edwin. DECLARATORY JUDGMENTS. Cleveland, Ohio: Baldwin Law Publishing Co., 1941.
CALIFORNIA CIVIL APPELLATE PRACTICE (Cal CEB 1966).
CALIFORNIA CIVIL DISCOVERY PRACTICE (Cal CEB 1975).
CALIFORNIA CIVIL PROCEDURE BEFORE TRIAL (Cal CEB 1977). 2 vols.
CALIFORNIA DEBT COLLECTION PRACTICE (Cal CEB 1968).
CALIFORNIA PERSONAL INJURY PROOF (Cal CEB 1970).
CALIFORNIA TRIAL OBJECTIONS (Cal CEB 1967).
CALIFORNIA WORKMEN'S COMPENSATION PRACTICE 1973 (Cal CEB 1973).
COLLIER ON BANKRUPTCY. James W. Moore, editor-in-chief, 14th ed. New York, Matthew Bender, 1975. 17 vols (pocket supplements).
CONDEMNATION PRACTICE IN CALIFORNIA (Cal CEB 1973).
Formichi, Robert E. CALIFORNIA STYLE MANUAL. 2d rev ed. Sacramento, California: California Supreme Court, 1977.
Jefferson, Bernard S. CALIFORNIA EVIDENCE BENCHBOOK (CCJ-CEB 1972).
Lavine, Richard A. & George D. Horning, Jr. MANUAL OF FEDERAL PRACTICE. New York: McGraw-Hill, 1967.
Los Angeles Superior Court Policy Manuals (available from Los Angeles Daily Journal and Los Angeles Metropolitan News):
  CIVIL TRIALS. Prepared by Judge Richard Schauer. Rev. Jan. 3, 1977.
  EX PARTE. Prepared by Commissioner Clinton Rodda. Rev. Jan. 1, 1975.
  LAW AND MOTION. Prepared by Judge Charles S. Vogel. Rev. Jan. 1, 1977.
  TRIAL SETTING CONFERENCES, MANDATORY SETTLEMENT CONFERENCES AND CONTINUANCES.

PERSONAL BANKRUPTCY AND WAGE EARNER PLANS (Cal CEB 1971).
San Francisco Superior Court Policy Manuals (available from Recorder Publishing Co., San Francisco):
  CONDUCT OF PRETRIAL PROCEEDINGS IN CLASS ACTIONS.
  CONDUCT OF PROCEEDINGS RELATING TO LAW AND MOTION MATTERS.
  DISCOVERY.
TRIAL ATTORNEY'S EVIDENCE CODE NOTEBOOK (Cal CEB 1974).
Witkin, B. E. CALIFORNIA EVIDENCE. 2d ed. San Francisco: Bancroft-Whitney, 1966.
Witkin, B. E. CALIFORNIA PROCEDURE. 2d ed. San Francisco: Bancroft-Whitney, 1970–1971. 6 vols.
Witkin, B. E. SUMMARY OF CALIFORNIA LAW. 8th ed. San Francisco: Bancroft-Whitney, 1973–1974. 8 vols.
Wright, Charles Alan, Arthur R. Miller, & Edward H. Cooper. FEDERAL PRACTICE AND PROCEDURE. St. Paul, Minn.: West Publishing Co., 1969–1976. 15 vols.

Index

ABANDONMENT OF CASE
Dismissal of action, 31.80, 31.82, 31.88

ABATEMENT OF ACTIONS
Consolidation compared, 27.10

ABSENCE FROM STATE
Adverse party, effect of absence from trial, 26.55, 26.74
Indispensable party, dismissal of action for absence of, 25.3
Service of process, time considerations, 31.9

ABSTRACT OF JUDGMENT
Consent judgment, 34.2, 34.5, 34.9

ABUSE OF PROCESS
Mutual release, terms of, 33.30

ACCESS RIGHTS
Declaratory relief action, determining residents' right of access to ocean by, 24.7

ACCOUNTS AND ACCOUNTING
See also Records and Recordings
Books, documents, and records, notice to produce in summary judgment proceedings, 29.57; *form*, 29.59
Business records as exception to hearsay rule, 29.52, 29.60–29.61

Default judgments by clerk, 30.37–30.38, 30.45

ACTUAL CONTROVERSY. *See* Declaratory Relief

ADD-ON-CASE. *See* Coordination of Actions

ADDRESSES
See also Mail
Coordination motion judge, address of, 28.22
Coordination trial judge, address of, 28.40

ADEQUACY OF LEGAL REMEDY
Appeal from final judgment, 31.53
Consolidation of actions, other procedures compared, 27.10
Consolidation or severance of actions, appeal of order granting or denying, 27.21
Coordination proceedings, review of orders in, 28.56
Declaratory relief
  Generally, 24.2
  Other remedies, availability of, 24.12–24.15, 24.19, 24.21, 24.24–24.25
Motions and alternative procedures compared, 23.7
Pretrial conference order, review of, 26.72
Summary judgment motion, alternatives to, 26.60, 29.5, 29.14–29.20

INDEX

ADEQUACY OF LEGAL REMEDY—*cont.*
Summary judgment motion, uses of, 29.3
Trial continuance, alternatives to, 26.100–26.102

ADJOINING LANDOWNERS
Intervention by, 25.18, 25.23

ADMINISTRATIVE REGULATIONS
Declaratory relief action, determining validity by, 24.7–24.8

ADMINISTRATIVE REMEDIES
Declaratory relief, denial for failure to exhaust administrative remedies, 24.21, 24.23

ADMINISTRATORS. *See* Executors and Administrators

ADMISSIONS
Authentication of documents by admissions, 29.55–29.56
Coordination petition, requests for admissions at hearing on, 28.34
Five-year trial requirement, effect of defendant's admissions on, 31.30
Pretrial conference, admissions at, 26.58
Release as not admission, 33.30
Summary judgment. *See* Summary Judgment

ADVANCEMENT OF PROCEEDINGS
Authority for advancing pretrial conference, trial setting conference, or trial, 26.76
Declaration in support of motion, *form*, 26.82
Discretion of court, 26.79
Motions to advance and to specially set distinguished, 26.77
Notice of motion, 26.50, 26.80; *form*, 26.81
Shortening of time generally. *See* Time

ADVERSE PARTIES. *See* Parties

AFFIDAVITS
See also Declarations
Caption and introduction, 23.39
Change in setting case, affidavits in support of motion for, 26.27
Contents, 23.40–23.41
Coordination. *See* Coordination of Actions
Counteraffidavits, use in summary judgment proceedings, 29.10, 29.25
Default and default judgments. *See* Default and Default Judgments
Ex parte orders, opposition to, 23.65
Form, affidavit in support of motion, 23.38
Grounds for motion, affidavits as amplification of, 23.23
Identity and competence of affiant, 23.40
Intervention, affidavit in opposition to, 25.48–25.49
Jurat, 23.39, 23.43
Motion, affidavits in opposition to, 23.50, 23.52
Nature and purpose, 23.36
Notice of motion, affidavits accompanying, 23.17, 23.24
Opposition memorandum of points and authorities, 23.49
Summary judgment. *See* Summary Judgment
Supplemental affidavits and declarations, filing in summary judgment proceedings, 29.54, 29.68–29.69
Trial continuance due to absence of evidence on showing by affidavit, 26.93, 26.96

AFFIDAVITS—cont.
Vacating certificate of readiness, affidavit in support of motion, 26.27

AFFIRMATIVE ACTION
School admission programs, intervention in litigation, 25.1, 25.22

AGE
Advancement of proceedings, age as ground for, 26.76–26.77

AGENCY. See Principal and Agent

AGREED CASE. See Submitted Case

AGREEMENTS
See also Contracts
Covenant not to sue defined, 33.29
Employment agreements. See Employment Agreements
Jury trial, waiver by agreement providing for resolution of dispute by arbitration, 26.35
Pretrial conference, recording parties' agreements at, 26.39, 26.56
Settlement agreement. See Settlement

AMENDED AND SUPPLEMENTAL PLEADINGS
At-issue memorandum and certificate of readiness, effect on, 26.14, 26.25
Complaints. See Complaints
Declaratory relief actions, 24.38
Default and default judgments. See Default and Default Judgments
Examples of amendments of substance, 30.34
Pretrial conference and motion to amend compared, 26.60
Pretrial conference, matters considered at, 26.66

Summary judgment. See Summary Judgment
Trial continuance, amendment of pleadings as ground for, 26.93

AMENDMENTS
At-issue memorandum, amending, 26.2
Pretrial order, correcting or modifying, 26.70, 26.72–26.73
Ruling granting motion, modification of, 23.62
Summary judgment, effect of amendment of, 29.83

AMICUS CURIAE. See Friend of Court

AMOUNT IN CONTROVERSY
Declaratory relief action, 24.27
Pretrial, selecting cases for, 26.59

ANSWERS
Admissions. See Admissions
Coordination petition, answering interrogatories at hearing on, 28.34
Declaratory relief actions, 24.34
Default and default judgments. See Default and Default Judgments
Denial in summary judgment proceedings, 29.45
Dismissal order, review by writ after answer filed, 31.53
General appearance, answer as, 31.12
Intervention complaint, answers to, 25.3, 25.48, 25.50, 25.56, 25.58
Judgment on the pleadings, entry resulting from defective answer, 29.16
Striking sham answers or affirmative defenses, 29.3, 29.15
Summary judgment. See Summary Judgment

INDEX

APPEALS

Advancement or change in setting of conferences or trial, 26.79
Agreed case, 32.1–32.2, 32.4
Consent judgment, 34.4
Consolidation or severance of actions, 27.11, 27.21
Coordination of actions, review of, 28.35, 28.56
Coordination trial judge, challenging assignment of, 28.41
Court opinions, citing in memorandum of points and authorities, 23.33
Declaratory judgment, appeal of, 24.45
Declaratory relief, persons entitled to, 24.8
Default and default judgments. *See* Default and Default Judgments
Dismissal of actions. *See* Dismissal of Actions
Exhaustion of administrative remedies doctrine, applicability to declaratory relief, 24.21, 24.23
Intervention. *See* Intervention of Parties
Judgment on the pleadings, appeal from, 31.23
Jury, effect of erroneous instructions to, 26.29
New trial motion, effect of, 31.32–31.33
Notice of appeal, summary judgment orders, 29.83
Order on granted motion, vacation by appellate court for failure of motion to state grounds, 23.23
Orders generally, 23.62
Pretrial conference order, review of, 26.72–26.73
Remittitur. *See* Remittitur
Summary judgment. *See* Summary Judgment

Trial continuances, 26.85, 26.95, 26.102
Trial delay, appeals as ground for, 31.25
Venue change, appealing, 31.42

APPEARANCES

Coordination proceedings
  Petition, hearing on, 28.32
  Preliminary trial conference, 28.43
Defaulting defendant, 30.7
Dismissal of actions. *See* Dismissal of Actions
General appearance defined, 29.12
Jury trial, waiver for failure to appear, 26.35
Motions, attendance at hearing on, 23.55–23.56
Pretrial conference, attendance at, 26.58, 26.63, 26.66
Settlement conference, effect of nonappearance at, 33.17, 33.22–33.23, 33.27
Settlement conference, invitation to attend, 26.49
Show cause order, use of, 23.67
Small claims courts, 26.6
Special appearance
  Adequacy of notice, challenging, 23.8
  Opposing motion by special appearance, 23.51
Stipulation/Declaration in Lieu of Personal Appearance (at trial setting conference), 26.41, 26.46
Stipulation extending defendant's time to plead, effect of, 31.11–31.12
Summary judgment motion, time for making, 29.12, 29.31
Trial setting conference, 26.40–26.42, 26.45–26.46, 26.48, 26.78
Waiver of notice by appearance, 23.6

APPLICATIONS

See also Motions; Motions, Notice of; Orders

Coordination. *See* Coordination of Actions
Default judgments. *See* Default and Default Judgments
Ex parte. *See* Ex Parte Proceedings
General court rules, 23.2
Intervention of parties. *See* Intervention of Parties
Joinder of parties. *See* Joinder of Parties
Motion defined, 23.1
New application following denial of order, 23.63
Place of hearing, 23.4

ARBITRATION

Jury trial, waiver by agreement providing for resolution of dispute by arbitration, 26.35

ARMED FORCES. *See* Servicemen and Veterans

ASSAULT AND BATTERY

Civil and criminal actions, 30.58

ASSESSMENTS. *See* Taxes and Assessments

ASSIGNMENT

Intervention by assignees of fractional interests, 25.12
Statements in declarations for introduction of business records, 29.61

ASSOCIATIONS

Declaratory relief actions involving members, 24.7–24.8

AT-ISSUE MEMORANDUM. *See* Setting Case for Trial

ATTACHMENT

Intervention by claimants, 25.6, 25.15, 25.17

ATTORNEY-CLIENT RELATIONSHIP

Settlement, law of principal and agent, 33.6, 33.25

ATTORNEYS

"Busy attorney" reason for delays, judicial attitude toward, 30.62, 30.65
Consent judgment, authority of attorney, 34.6
Continuance of trial due to death, illness, unavailability, or substitution of attorney, 26.87–26.90, 26.92–26.93, 26.95
Coordination proceedings
　Convenience of attorneys, ground for coordination, 28.5
　Liaison counsel, appointment of, 28.44
　Papers, preparation of, 28.9
Fees. *See* Attorney's Fees
Pretrial conference, attendance at, 26.58, 26.63
Pretrial conference on request of counsel, 26.60
Settlement
　Advantages to attorney, 33.2
　Adverse party and adverse counsel, communicating with, 33.7–33.9
　Authority of attorney, 33.1, 33.6, 33.19, 34.6
　Presentations at conference, 33.25–33.26
Submission of agreed case, rights of attorney, 32.4
Summary judgment declarations, sufficiency of personal knowledge, 29.49
Trial setting conference, attendance at, 26.40–26.42, 26.45, 26.48

ATTORNEY'S FEES

See also Costs
Declaratory relief action by discharged attorney, 24.8, 24.11

INDEX

ATTORNEY'S FEES—*cont.*
Default and default judgments, 30.22, 30.25, 30.29, 30.37, 30.42, 30.48, 30.61
Dismissal of actions. *See* Dismissal of Actions
Intervention by attorney in action for collection of fees, 25.21
Summary judgment proceedings, 29.73–29.74
Trial setting conference, proceedings relating to nonappearance at, 26.45

AUTOMOBILES
Pretrial conference, admission of testimony at, 26.73
Rees-Levering Act. *See* Rees-Levering Act

BALANCE OF CONVENIENCES DOCTRINE
Intervention, balancing objectives of, 25.10

BANKRUPTCY
See also Insolvency
Consent judgment, dischargeability in bankruptcy, 34.5

BIAS AND PREJUDICE
Coordination trial judge, challenging assignment of, 28.41

BILL OF PARTICULARS
Summary judgment proceedings, 29.5, 29.66

BIRTH
Declaratory relief action to establish facts of birth or death, 24.3

BONDS AND UNDERTAKINGS
Declaratory relief action, 24.3
Default judgment proceedings, posting bond in, 30.61
Dismissal of action, delivery of undertaking, 31.86
Intervention by interested persons in actions involving validity of bond issues, 25.22

BREACH OF CONTRACT. *See* Contracts

BRIEFS
Memorandum of points and authorities in format of appellate brief, 23.27
Pretrial conference, matters considered at, 26.66

BURDEN OF PROOF
Declaratory relief, granting, 24.41
Default or default judgment, motion for relief from, 30.62
Intervention of parties, 25.47
Summary judgment. *See* Summary Judgment

CALENDARS
Consolidation of actions, grounds for, 27.8
Continuance and order removing case from calendar distinguished, 26.83
Coordination of actions, grounds for, 28.5
Declaratory relief actions, trial precedence of, 24.31, 24.39, 26.4
Law and motion calendar, listings on, 23.55
Nonappearance at settlement conference, effect on calendar status of action, 33.17, 33.27
Pretrial conference calendar, provision for, 26.63
Settlement calendar, establishing and maintaining, 26.75
Stipulation that trial go off calendar, settlement as precondition to, 26.92
Transfer of actions, calendar considerations, 28.49
Trial setting conference calendar, provision for, 26.48

CALIFORNIA SUPREME COURT
Admissions, credibility of, 29.11
Attorney's fees, recovery by defendant on plaintiff's voluntary dismissal of action, 31.69
Declaratory relief actions, statement regarding, 24.29
Dismissal statutes, judicial attitude toward, 31.2, 31.36
Ex parte orders for dismissal, ruling on, 31.46
Opinions, citing in memorandum of points and authorities, 23.33
Severability of actions, application of impossibility, impracticability, or futility doctrine, 31.27
Summary judgment motion, rulings on, 29.14

CANCELLATION OF INSTRUMENTS
Equitable action, 26.28

CAPTIONS
Affidavits and declarations, 23.39, 23.50
Ex parte application for order, 23.66
Memorandum of points and authorities, 23.28, 23.49
Motions, notice of, 23.17, 23.19
Show cause order, application for, 23.69

CAUSES OF ACTION
Declaratory relief actions, 24.14, 24.19–24.20, 24.31, 24.36
Dismissal
  Fewer than all causes of action, dismissal of, 31.77
  Indispensable party, effect of dismissal of action against, 31.76
Improper conclusions in declarations, examples, 29.51
Intervention
  Complaint asserting new cause of action, timely filing of, 25.37

Intervention—*cont.*
  Failure to state cause of action in complaint, 25.58
  Language in complaint, 25.4
Joinder
  Consolidation of actions or issues, 27.6, 27.10
  Declaratory relief actions, 24.31, 24.33
Judgment creditor's lien on judgment debtor's cause of action and judgment, 25.5, 25.14
Multiple causes of action, default judgment by clerk, 30.38
Objection to introduction of evidence for insufficiency of pleadings, 29.16–29.17
Severance, 27.7
Stating in complaint, 25.58, 30.52
Summary judgment, effect of unresolved causes of action on finality of, 29.83–29.84

CERTIFICATES
Declarations, certification in, 23.42, 29.48
Default judgment, certifying, 30.43
Jurat of affidavit, 23.39, 23.43
Licenses and permits. *See* Licenses and Permits
Readiness, certificate of. *See* Setting Case for Trial

CHARTS
Dismissal statutes, comparisons, 31.3

CITATIONS
Style, citations in memoranda of points and authorities, 23.32–23.33

CITIES
Declaratory relief action to determine validity of city ordinance, 24.8
Intervention in proceedings for incorporation of cities, 25.23

INDEX

CIVIL ACTIVE LIST. *See* Setting Case for Trial

CIVIL SERVICE
Declaratory relief action, determining rights of employees by, 24.7, 24.29

CLAIM AND DELIVERY
Nonparty claimants, procedure, 25.6, 25.15

CLAIMS
Dismissal statutes, effect of, 31.1
Joint relief, intervention of persons claiming, 25.10
Real or personal property, joinder of parties claiming interest in, 25.4
Small claims courts. *See* Small Claims Courts
Third party claims. *See* Third Parties

CLASS ACTIONS
Consumer, intervention by, 25.7
Coordination trial judge, powers of, 28.45
Declaratory relief, 24.8
Dismissal by plaintiff as matter of right, preventing, 31.73
Dismissal for noncompliance with five-year trial requirement, 31.31

CLERKS OF COURT
Consent judgment, procedure for entry of, 34.12
Default and default judgments. *See* Default and Default Judgments
Dismissal notice and judgment, entry of, 31.89–31.90
Misinformation from clerk, nonappearance resulting from, 31.40

COLLATERAL
Default proceedings, 30.45

COLLATERAL ESTOPPEL. *See* Estoppel

COLLECTION ACTIONS. *See* Debts

COMMON COUNTS
Default judgments, use of common counts, 30.37, 30.45

COMMUNITY PROPERTY
Declaratory relief, 24.6
Intervention in community property action by husband or wife, 25.17

COMPLAINTS
Amended complaint
  Default and default judgments. *See* Default and Default Judgments
  Five-year requirement for bringing action to trial, rule affecting, 31.18
  Joinder of parties. *See* Joinder of Parties
  Service and return, time calculations, 31.9
  Summary judgment proceedings, 29.16, 29.29
Causes of action. *See* Causes of Action
Coordination petition, timing of, 28.17
Declaratory relief. *See* Declaratory Relief
Default and default judgment defined, 30.1, 30.3
Dismissal statutes, applicability, 31.5
Intervention. *See* Intervention of Parties
Striking. *See* Motions to Strike
Summary judgment. *See* Summary Judgment
Supplemental complaint, service and return of, 31.9
Transfer of action, use of verified complaint, 30.18

COMPROMISE. *See* Consent Judgment; Settlement

CONDEMNATION
See also Eminent Domain
Consolidation of actions, 27.4
Intervention of parties, 25.2, 25.23, 25.28

CONFIDENTIALITY
See also Disclosure
Settlement negotiations, 33.5–33.6, 33.25

CONFLICTING CLAIMS. *See* Interpleader

CONSENT
See also Consent Judgment
Dismissal of action on consent of parties, 31.78, 31.81, 31.83–31.84, 31.87
Jury trial, consent to waiver of, 26.12, 26.35
Settlement, requirement of client's specific consent, 33.6

CONSENT JUDGMENT
Appealability, 34.4
Attorney's authority, 34.6
Bankruptcy dischargeability, 34.5
Entry
  Conditional or delayed entry, 34.7
  Function of judge, 34.12
  Notice of motion, 34.7, 34.9, 34.12
  Order, *forms*, 34.10–34.11
  Settlement agreement, terms of entry of judgment in, 34.9
Hearing prior to entry, 34.12
Nature and purpose, 34.1–34.2
Res judicata, effect, 34.3
Settlement agreement, 33.28, 34.2, 34.5, 34.8–34.9
Stipulations
  Appealability of judgment not conforming to stipulation, 34.4

Stipulations—*cont.*
  Default, provisions for, 34.7, 34.9
  Express approval of client, requirement, 34.6
  Filing stipulation as basis for entry of judgment, 34.12
  Judgment pursuant to stipulation, 34.8; *form*, 34.11
  Judgment, stipulation for, 34.7–34.9; *form*, 34.10
  Scope of issues and matters, 34.3
  Signing, 34.6, 34.9

CONSERVATORSHIP. *See* Guardianship and Conservatorship

CONSIDERATION
Dismissal of action without prejudice in return for consideration, 31.67

CONSOLIDATION OF ACTIONS
See also Coordination of Actions; Severance of Actions
Judicial attitude, 27.8
Judicial discretion, 27.3, 27.11, 27.21
Mandatory consolidation, examples, 27.4
Motion for consolidation
  Declaration in support of, 27.13; *form*, 27.15
  Notice of, 27.13; *form*, 27.14
  Order granting motion, 27.13; *form*, 27.16
  Preliminary determinations, 27.11
Nature and purpose, 27.1, 27.8
Orders
  Appealability of order granting or denying, 27.21
  Motion for consolidation, order granting, 27.13; *form*, 27.16
  Vacation of, 27.12
Other procedures compared, 27.10
Personal injury and wrongful death actions, consolidation as ground for trial delay, 31.25
Statutory authority, 27.3–27.4, 27.6

CONSTITUTIONAL LAW
See also Due Process
Oral argument in summary judgment proceedings, 29.70
Summary judgment, constitutionality of, 29.4

CONSTRUCTION AND INTERPRETATION
Competency of witnesses, 29.49
Consent judgment, 34.2–34.3, 34.12
Continuances of conferences and trial, granting, 26.83, 26.85, 26.92–26.93
Declaratory relief. See Declaratory Relief
Default and default judgments
  Clerk, default judgment by, 30.37–30.39
  Service of summons by publication, 30.54
  Setting aside by equitable motion, 30.76
  Setting aside, effect of failure to file points and authorities, 30.64
Dismissal of actions
  Defendant seeking affirmative relief by cross-complaint, 31.72
  Effectiveness of dismissal, 31.89
  Fewer than all defendants, dismissal against, 31.76
  Opposition papers, failure to serve and file, 31.57
Health care contract, action for construction of, 24.19
Hearing on demurrer, 31.75
Intent. See Intent
Intervention by interested persons in actions involving interpretation of legislation, 25.22
Intervention statutes, 25.10
Memorandum of points and authorities, failure to file, 23.26
Nonattendance of attorney at hearing on motion, 23.55
Pretrial conference order, 26.73
Reasonable expenses, 29.74
Service by mail, statutory construction, 29.67
Settlement agreements, 33.1
Summary judgment
  Amendment of pleadings, application for, 29.29
  Declarations, 29.8
  Notice of appeal from order, construction of, 29.83

CONSUMER ACTIONS
Dismissal of class action, 31.73
Installment sales. See Installment Sales
Intervention by consumer in class action, 25.7

CONTEMPT
Applications for orders, effect of noncompliance with requirements, 23.63
Findings, rule affecting, 23.58
Show cause order, application for, 23.67

CONTEST OF WILLS. See Wills

CONTINUANCE
Change in setting case for trial, hearing on, 26.26
Consolidation of actions, continuance resulting from, 27.11
Default or default judgment, continuance of hearing to set aside, 30.70
Deposited jury fees, refund of, 26.33
Extension of time generally. See Time
Pretrial conferences, 26.66–26.67
Settlement conferences, 33.18
Small claims hearings, 26.6
Summary judgment. See Summary Judgment
Trial setting conference, continuance of, 26.50
Trials. See Trial

CONTRACTS
  See also Agreements
  Breach
    Collection action as subterfuge for breach of contract action, 30.45
    Consent judgment, effect of, 34.2
    Damages, right to jury trial, 26.28
    Health care contract, action for construction of, 24.19
  Consent judgment, interpretation of terms of, 34.2–34.3, 34.12
  Declaratory relief. *See* Declaratory Relief
  Default and default judgments. *See* Default and Default Judgments
  Health care contracts. *See* Health Care Contracts
  Joint and several liability in contract actions, 30.39
  Public works. *See* Public Works
  Release defined, 33.29
  Signatures, judicial notice of, 29.55
  Summary judgment proceedings, statement of facts in, 29.43

CONTRIBUTORY NEGLIGENCE
  Pretrial conference, admission of testimony at, 26.73

COORDINATION OF ACTIONS
  See also Consolidation of Actions; Severance of Actions
  Add-on case, petition to coordinate
    Defined, 28.52
    Hearing and order, 28.52, 28.54
    Procedure generally, 28.53
  Affidavits and declarations
    Add-on case, declarations supporting and opposing coordination of, 28.52–28.53
    Petition, affidavits supporting and opposing, 28.11, 28.15, 28.29, 28.34
    Stay order, affidavits supporting and opposing, 28.11, 28.24–28.26

  Application for stay order. *See* Stay order, below
  Appropriateness, decision on, 28.5, 28.12, 28.52
  Common questions of law and fact, 25.8, 27.10, 28.1, 28.5, 28.15, 28.52
  Consolidation compared, 27.10
  Declarations. *See* Affidavits and declarations, above
  Definitions, 28.4
  Hearings
    Add-on case, hearing on order for coordination of, 28.52, 28.54
    Petition. *See* Hearings on petition, below
    Stay order, hearing on issuance or extension of, 28.26
    Stay order issued without hearing, termination of, 28.27
  Hearings on petition
    Determinations by coordination motion judge, 28.33
    Evidence, manner of presenting, 28.34
    General rules, 28.32
    Notice, 28.8, 28.33
    Orders after hearing. *See* Orders, below
    Reporting delay in determination, 28.38
    Request, 28.15
  Judges, assignment of
    Generally, 28.2–28.3
    Coordination motion judge, assignment of, 28.4, 28.21–28.22
    Coordination motion judge, powers and duties of, 28.23, 28.26, 28.33, 28.35–28.38, 28.55
    Coordination trial judge, assignment of, 28.4, 28.40–28.41
    Coordination trial judge, powers and duties of, 28.39, 28.42, 28.44–28.45, 28.48, 28.52–28.54
    Motion directed to presiding judge, 28.10–28.12

INDEX

COORDINATION—*cont.*
Judges—*cont.*
  Papers, transmittal to assigned judge, 28.7
  Liaison counsel, appointment of, 28.44
  Local rules, 28.3
  Motion to commence. *See* Petition, below
  Notice of submission of petition
    Essential elements, 28.17
    Filing and service, 28.8–28.9, 28.16–28.17
    Form, 28.20
  Notices
    Add-on case, notice of opposition to coordination of, 28.53–28.54
    Denial of coordination, notice of, 28.37
    Evidence at hearing on petition, judicial notice of, 28.34
    Filing and service, 28.7–28.9, 28.16–28.18, 28.23, 28.26, 28.33, 28.37
    Opposition to petition, notice of, 28.8, 28.17
    Review by judge of notice to parties, 28.23
    Stay order, notice of hearing on, 28.26
    Submission of petition. *See* Notice of submission of petition
  Orders
    Add-on case, order for coordination of, 28.52, 28.54
    Coordination motion judge, order assigning, 28.21–28.22
    Coordination trial judge, order assigning, 28.40–28.41
    Coordination trial judge, powers of, 28.42
    Denial of coordination, 28.18, 28.37, 28.39, 28.55
    Duplicate and inconsistent orders, avoiding by coordination of actions, 28.5
    Filing and service, 28.7–28.9, 28.22, 28.39–28.41

Orders—*cont.*
  Granting coordination, 28.35, 28.39, 28.56
  Granting coordination in part, 28.36, 28.39
  Judge, order assigning, 28.7, 28.21–28.22
  Preliminary trial conference. *See* Preliminary trial conference, below
  Review, 28.35, 28.37, 28.56
  Specified issues, order to hear, 28.33
  Stay order. *See* Stay order, below
Petition
  Generally, 28.4
  Add-on case. *See* Add-on case, petition to coordinate, above
  Affidavit or declaration, requirement, 28.11, 28.15, 28.29, 28.34
  Essential elements, 28.15
  Filing and service, 28.7–28.9, 28.16–28.18
  Form, 28.19
  Hearings. *See* Hearings on petition, above
  Motion directed to presiding judge, 28.10–28.12
  New petition after denial, 28.55
  Notice of motion for order that petition be transmitted and for order staying related actions, *form,* 28.13
  Notice of submission. *See* Notice of submission of petition, above
  Order transmitting petition and staying related actions, *form,* 28.14
  Orders granting or denying. *See* Orders, above
  Purpose, 28.5
  Statement in opposition, *form,* 28.30
  Statement in support, *form,* 28.31
  Timing and transmittal, 28.18
  Types of actions, 28.6

COORDINATION—*cont.*
Preliminary trial conference
General rules, 28.43
Liaison counsel, appointment of, 28.44
Order, *form*, 28.47
Order setting conference, 28.43; *form*, 28.46
Pretrial proceedings schedule, establishment of, 28.45
Statutory and other authority, 28.2
Stay order
Add-on case, application for order staying, 28.53
Affidavits supporting and opposing application, 28.11, 28.24–28.26
Authority of assigned judge, 28.26
Automatic stay, effect of filing order granting coordination, 28.39
Delay in coordination determination, reporting stay orders in effect, 28.38
Duration, 28.10, 28.12, 28.27
Filing and service, 28.7–28.9, 28.55
Form, 28.28
Notice of motion for order that petition be transmitted and for order staying related actions, *form*, 28.13
Order transmitting petition and staying related actions, *form*, 28.14
Request, 28.10–28.11, 28.15
Termination on denial of petition, 28.55
Timing and contents of application, 28.24
Subject matter, analysis of, 28.6
Transfer of actions. See Transfer of Actions

CORPORATIONS
Dissolution
Declaratory relief action, 24.3
Default judgment, prohibition of, 30.9

Dissolution—*cont.*
Dismissal statutes, applicability, 31.5
Intervention of shareholders and creditors, 25.2
Election or appointment of directors, declaratory relief action, 24.3
Foreign corporations, service of process on, 31,22, 31.26
Homeowner corporation's declaratory relief action to determine validity of city ordinance, 24.8
Indemnification of director, declaratory relief action, 24.35
Interrogatories, question of general appearance, 31.12
Nonexistence of corporation, unsuitability of declaratory relief action to decree, 24.13
Reorganization, intervention resulting from, 25.2
Shares and shareholders
Consolidation of actions by dissident shareholders, 27.4
Declaratory relief action to determine shareholders' rights, 24.7
Dismissal of shareholder derivative action, 31.73
Equitable nature of derivative actions, 26.28
Intervention by creditor in action against shareholder, 25.2
Intervention by shareholders, 25.2, 25.16, 25.20, 25.58

CORRECTIONS. See Amended and Supplemental Pleadings; Amendments

COSTS
See also Fees
Agreed case, 32.1
Default proceedings, memorandum of costs in, 30.22, 30.27; *form*, 30.29

INDEX 568

COSTS—*cont.*
Dismissal of actions. *See* Dismissal of Actions
Settlement
   Advantages of settlement, 33.2
   Dismissal with prejudice, effect of, 33.29
   Nonappearance at conference, effect of, 33.17, 33.27
   Offer to allow judgment, effect of, 33.10, 33.12, 33.14
   Summary judgment proceedings, 29.73–29.74
Transfer fees and costs, dismissal for failure to pay. *See* Dismissal of Actions
Trial continuance, payment of costs to adverse party, 26.93, 26.99
Trial setting conference procedures, 26.46

COUNTERAFFIDAVITS. *See* Affidavits

COUNTERCLAIMS. *See* Cross-Complaints

COUNTERDECLARATIONS. *See* Declarations

COUNTS
   See also Causes of Action
Declaratory relief actions, use of separate counts, 24.31

COURT CALENDARS. *See* Calendars

COURT COMMISSIONERS
Consent judgment, authorization for entry of, 34.12
Dismissal motions, hearing, 31.52

COVENANT NOT TO SUE
Defined, 33.29

CREDITORS. *See* Claims; Debts

CRIMINAL ACTIONS
Assault and battery, 30.58
Declaratory relief, effect of availability of criminal action on, 24.13, 24.24

CROSS-COMPLAINTS
Consolidation of actions, 27.10
Declaratory relief. *See* Declaratory Relief
Default procedures, 30.2, 30.15–30.17
Dismissal of actions
   Affirmative relief, defendant seeking, 31.71–31.72, 31.80
   Use of cross-complaint generally, 31.5, 31.7, 31.9–31.12, 31.18, 31.34, 31.79
Equitable issues, effect on right to jury trial, 24.40
Intervention. *See* Intervention of Parties
Motion to strike by cross-complainant, 29.15
Readiness certificate, effect of filing, 26.19, 26.25
Severance of actions
   Generally, 27.3, 27.7
   Notice of motion, *form*, 27.18
   Order, *form*, 27.19
   Unanswered cross-complaint, severance of, 26.10
Summary judgment proceedings, 29.12, 29.15, 29.84

DAMAGES
Consolidation of actions, statutory authority for, 27.4
Declaratory relief actions, 24.27, 24.32
Default and default judgments. *See* Default and Default Judgments
Dismissal of fewer than all causes of action, 31.77
Insurance issues, exclusion of, 25.13
Jury trial, right to, 26.28
Notice in personal injury and wrongful death actions, 30.36

DAMAGES—*cont.*
Settlement conference, itemizing special and general damages prior to, 33.20–33.21
Severance of liability
 Generally, 27.5, 27.12
 Notice of motion, *form*, 27.18
 Order, *form*, 27.19
Summary judgment proceedings, statement of facts in, 29.43

DEATH
Continuance of trial due to death of attorney or witness, 26.87
Declaratory relief action to establish facts of birth or death, 24.3
Service of process, effect of, 31.9
Wrongful death. *See* Wrongful Death

DEBTS
Consent judgment, use of, 34.2, 34.5, 34.7
Default judgment by clerk, collection actions, 30.37–30.38, 30.45
General creditors, intervention by, 25.24
Judgment creditors, intervention by, 25.5, 25.14
Notes. *See* Notes

DECLARATIONS
 See also Affidavits
Advancing, specially setting, or resetting conferences or trial, declaration in support of motion, *form*, 26.82
Caption and introduction, 23.39, 23.50
Consent judgment, declaration supporting motion for entry of, 34.12
Consolidation of actions, declaration in support of, 27.13; *form*, 27.15
Constructive trust, declaration of, 26.28
Contents, 23.40–23.41
Coordination. *See* Coordination of Actions
Counterdeclarations
 Dismissal for lack of prosecution, declarations in opposition to, 31.51
 Opposition declarations generally, 23.50, 23.52, 23.54
 Summary judgment procedure, 29.8
Default and default judgments. *See* Default and Default Judgments
Dismissal of actions
 Just cause, showing by declaration, 31.88
 Lack of prosecution, declaration in support of motion based on, 31.46–31.48; *form*, 31.50
 Transfer fees and costs, declaration in support of motion to dismiss for failure to pay, *form*, 31.62
 Two-year trial requirement, declaration in support of motion to dismiss for noncompliance with, 31.57
Ex parte application for order, declaration form of, 23.66
Filing, effect of, 23.41
Form, declaration in support of motion, 23.37
Identity and competence of declarant, 23.40
Incorporation of document by reference in declaration, 23.44, 29.54
Intervention. *See* Intervention of Parties
Mistrial, declaration of, 26.2
Nature and purpose, 23.36, 23.57
New application following denial of order, declaration accompanying, 23.63
Notice of motion, declarations accompanying, 23.17, 23.19, 23.24

INDEX 570

DECLARATIONS—*cont.*
Open book account, declaration regarding, 30.37, 30.45
Opposition declarations. *See* Counterdeclarations, above
Opposition memorandum of points and authorities, 23.49
Personal Appearance at Trial Setting Conference, Stipulation/Declaration in Lieu of, 26.41, 26.46
Physician's declaration in support of allegation of illness, 26.88
Pleadings and papers, reference in declaration to, 23.44
Pretrial conference, declaration in support of motion for, 26.62
Severance of actions, declaration in support of, 27.18
Show cause order, declaration form of application for, 23.69
Signature, 23.36, 23.42
Special declaration, failure of parties to sign certificate of readiness, 26.21; *form*, 26.23–26.24
Submitted case. *See* Submitted Case
Summary judgment. *See* Summary Judgment
Supplemental affidavits and declarations, filing in summary judgment proceedings, 29.54, 29.68–29.69
Trial continuance, declaration in support of motion for, 26.95–26.96; *form*, 26.98

DECLARATORY RELIEF
Accrued cause of action, effect of, 24.14
Actual controversy, requirement of
Generally, 24.4, 24.8, 24.20, 24.30
Agreed case, analogy, 32.1
Defined, 24.9
Examples, 24.10
Lack of actual controversy, effect of, 24.17
Lack of actual controversy, examples of, 24.11
Administrative regulations, determining validity of, 24.7
Administrative remedies, effect of failure to exhaust, 24.21, 24.23
Advantages, 24.4
Answer, 24.34
Burden of proof, 24.41
Calendar precedence, 24.31, 24.39, 26.4
Coercive relief, power of court to award, 24.43
Complaints
Acts concluded before commencement of action, effect of, 24.25
Answer, 24.34
Contracts. *See* Contract, complaint on, below
Cross-complaints. *See* Cross-complaints, below
Demurrers to, 24.31, 24.36, 24.38
Essential elements, 24.30
Failure to state cause of action, effect of, 24.20, 24.36
Future controversy, likelihood of, 24.8
Health care contract, action for construction of, 24.19
Joinder of causes of action, 24.31, 24.33
Jurisdictional considerations, 24.27
Statutes and ordinances. *See* Statute or ordinance, complaint on, below
Construction and interpretation
Advantages of declaratory relief action, 24.4
Complaint, liberal construction of, 24.30
Cumulative nature of remedies, 24.12
Joinder of parties in action concerning interpretation of statute, 24.29
Judicial discretion to deny declaratory relief, 24.19

INDEX

DECLARATORY RELIEF—*cont.*
Construction—*cont.*

  Statutes and ordinances. *See*
    Statute or ordinance, complaint on, below
Contract, complaint on
  Examples, 24.10
  Form, complaint on written or oral contract, 24.32
  Jurisdiction, 24.27
  Statutory authority, 24.5, 24.8
Criminal action, effect of availability of, 24.13, 24.24
Cross-complaints
  Generally, 24.7, 24.27, 24.35, 24.39–24.40
  Severance from cross-complaint
    Notice of motion, *form*, 27.18
    Order, *form*, 27.19
Demurrers, 24.31, 24.36, 24.38
Denial, grounds for, 24.13–24.14, 24.16–24.26
Determination that party has no rights, effect of, 24.15
Full and complete declaration, duty of trial court to render, 24.42
Governmental entities, actions against, 24.29
Historical background, 24.1
Injunctions, 24.33, 24.43–24.44
Interpretation. *See* Construction and interpretation, above
Judgment
  Appeal, 24.45
  Essential elements, 24.43
  Form, 24.44
  Seeking judgment as distinguished from declaratory relief, 24.20
Judgment on the pleadings, obtaining declaratory judgment by, 24.37
Judicial discretion to deny, 24.2, 24.14, 24.19–24.21, 24.24, 24.35–24.36, 24.39, 24.41
Jurisdiction of courts, 24.6, 24.16, 24.27–24.29
Jury trial, 24.2, 24.40
Laches, 24.2, 24.19, 24.22
Nature of action, 24.2, 24.12

Oral and written contracts, 24.5
Other forums, effect of availability of, 24.13, 24.23
Other government branch or agency, matters within exclusive province of, 24.23
Other remedies, availability of, 24.12–24.15, 24.19, 24.21, 24.24–24.25
Other written instruments, 24.6, 24.8
Parties to action, 24.8, 24.16, 24.27, 24.29
Persons who may obtain relief, 24.6, 24.8
Pretrial motions generally, 24.38
Purposes generally, 24.4
Severance from cross-complaint. *See* Cross-complaints, above
Standing to bring action, effect of lack of, 24.18
Statute of limitations, 24.22, 24.34
Statute or ordinance, complaint on
  Generally, 24.7–24.9, 24.19, 24.23, 24.27, 24.29
  Cross-complaint, 24.35
  Form, 24.33
Statutory authority, 24.3
Summary judgment, obtaining declaratory judgment by, 24.37
Trial aspects, 24.2, 24.39–24.42
Venue, 24.28
Water rights, actions to determine, 24.7–24.9, 24.18, 24.29

DEEDS
Declaratory relief, 24.6, 24.8

DEFAMATION
Trial setting priority, 26.4

DEFAULT AND DEFAULT JUDGMENTS
Affidavits and declarations
  Attorney's fees, hearing on, 30.48
  Conflicting declarations, 30.70
  Counterdeclarations of defendant, 34.7
  Default judgment by court, requirements, 30.49–30.50, 30.52, 30.54

INDEX

DEFAULT—*cont.*

Judge's review of declarations, 30.51
Lost or destroyed records, declaration relating to, 30.43
Nonmilitary status, declaration of, 30.9, 30.22, 30.28; *form*, 30.29
Open book account, declaration regarding, 30.37, 30.45
Request for entry of default, declaration of mailing, 30.21, 30.26; *form*, 30.29
Setting aside default or default judgment
    Declaration in support of motion, 30.63; *form*, 30.65
    Declaration of merits, 30.60, 30.63; *form*, 30.66; 30.69, 30.74
    Lack of actual notice, procedure, 30.78
    Opposing declarations, 30.69–30.70
    Renewed motion, declaration in support of, 30.72
Stay of execution, declarations in support of motion for, 30.67
Transfer of action, affidavit in support of, 30.18
Venue provisions, declaration regarding, 30.21, 30.25; *form*, 30.29; 30.45
Amended complaint or amendment to complaint
    Default previously entered, effect of amended complaint on, 30.34
    Effect of amendment, 30.14
    Entry of default on amended complaint, 30.15–30.17
    Material amendment after entry of default, 30.2, 30.34
    Proof of service, amending complaint to conform to, 30.30–30.31, 30.44

Answers
    Amended complaint, answer to, 30.34
    Change of venue motion, answer to, 30.18
    Equitable motion for relief, inclusion of proposed answer with, 30.73
    Filing generally, 30.1–30.2, 30.7–30.8, 30.15–30.17
    Independent action in equity to set aside default or default judgment, filing procedure, 30.74
    Relief where no answer filed, 30.36
    Setting aside default or default judgment, moving papers, 30.63, 30.69
Appeals
    Relief from default or default judgment, policy of appellate courts, 30.60–30.61, 30.80
    Transfer of action, challenging order granting or denying, 30.18
Applications
    Generally, 30.2, 30.4–30.5, 30.20–30.21
    Attorney's fees, application for, 30.48
    Clerk's duties, entry of default, 30.32–30.33, 30.40
    Clerk's duties, entry of default judgment, 30.3–30.4, 30.27, 30.42
    Form of application for entry of default judgment, 30.42
    Request for entry of default, 30.5, 30.21, 30.23, 30.26–30.27; *form*, 30.29
    Service by publication, application for default judgment, 30.6, 30.53
Attorney's fees, 30.22, 30.25, 30.29, 30.37, 30.42, 30.48, 30.61
Cause of action, stating in complaint, 30.52

DEFAULT—*cont.*
CCP §585(3), default judgment under, 30.6, 30.35
Clerk of court
  Appealability of order setting aside clerk's entry of default, 30.80
  Application for clerk's entry of default judgment, 30.3–30.4, 30.27, 30.42
  Default judgment by clerk, 30.3–30.4, 30.27, 30.37–30.45; *form*, 30.46; 30.48
  Error in entering or denying default judgment, 30.40
Consent judgment, 34.7, 34.9
Contract action for money and damages
  Generally, 30.35–30.37
  Attorney's fees, 30.22, 30.48
  Default judgment by court, requirement, 30.47
  Denial of judgment for failure to establish damages, 30.52
  Entry of judgment, 30.4, 30.43
  Proof of service, 30.24
  Venue considerations, 30.25
Court, default judgment by
  Affidavits and declarations, 30.49–30.50, 30.52, 30.54
  Appealability of order, 30.80
  Attorney's fees, 30.22, 30.25, 30.29, 30.48
  Basic situations requiring, 30.47
  Form, 30.55
  Hearing
    Affidavits and declarations, use of, 30.50
    Basic rules, 30.52
    Service of summons by publication, procedure, 30.53–30.54
    Setting date, 30.51
  Papers required, 30.49–30.50
Damages
  Assessment of damages by jury, 30.52
  Contract action. *See* Contract action for money or damages, above

Declarations. *See* Affidavits and declarations, above
Defined, 30.1, 30.3
Demurrer, filing, 30.1–30.2, 30.7–30.8, 30.15–30.17, 30.34, 30.63, 30.69
Diligence of plaintiff in obtaining default judgment, 31.15
Discovery defaults, 30.7–30.8, 30.64
Dismissal of action, 30.7, 30.15, 30.18–30.19, 30.44, 31.10, 31.13, 31.16–31.17, 31.23
Entry of default as prerequisite to default judgment, 30.2, 30.4–30.5, 30.11, 30.20
Ethical considerations, 30.10
Extent of relief generally, 30.36
Fictitious name, obtaining default judgment against defendant under, 30.9, 30.30–30.31, 30.44
Five-year trial requirement, exception, 31.13, 31.23
Hearings
  Attorney's fees, hearing on application for, 30.48
  Court, default judgment by. *See* Court, default judgment by, above
  Motion to strike complaint, 30.17
  Setting aside default or default judgment, hearings on, 30.57, 30.60, 30.70, 30.76–30.77
  Stay of execution of judgment pending hearing, order for, 30.63, 30.67; *form*, 30.68
  Trial, proceedings constituting, 31.19
Insurers and sureties, conditions allowing intervention by, 25.13
Limited partner's intervention after entry of default, 25.16
Memorandum of costs, 30.22, 30.27; *form*, 30.29
Memorandum of points and authorities, motion to set aside default or default judgment, 30.63–30.64

INDEX

DEFAULT—*cont.*

Motions, notice of
  Entry of stipulated judgment, motion for, 34.7
  Name of party, motion for amendment to correct, 30.31
  Quashing service of summons, 30.15, 30.19
  Setting aside default or default judgment, 30.25, 30.62–30.63; *form*, 30.64; 30.67
  Setting aside default or default judgment, renewed motion for, 30.72
  Setting aside default or default judgment where service does not afford actual notice, 30.75, 30.77–30.78
  Stay or dismissal of action, 30.7, 30.15, 30.18–30.19
  Striking complaint, 30.15, 30.17
  Transfer of complaint, 30.15, 30.18

Moving papers for entry of default, 30.21–30.22

Moving papers for relief actions, 30.63, 30.78

Multiple causes of action, default judgment by clerk, 30.38

Notices
  Defaulting defendant, rights of, 30.2, 30.9–30.10
  Judgment, notice of entry of, 30.62
  Mandate, notice of petition for. 30.19
  Motions. *See* Motions, notice of, above
  Opposing counsel, notice to, 30.10
  Order overruling demurrer, notice of, 30.16
  Personal injury and wrongful death actions, notice of damages in, 30.36
  Request for entry of default, effect of nonreceipt of notice of, 30.26
  Service of process. *See* Service of process and papers, below

Orders
  Appeal of orders granting or denying relief, 30.80
  Clerk of court, default judgment by. *See* Clerk of court, above
  Court, default judgment by. *See* Court, default judgment by, above
  Demurrer, order overruling, 30.16
  Entry of default, order directing, 30.24
  Entry of judgment where records lost or destroyed, order for, 30.43
  Setting aside default and default judgment, 30.63; *form*, 30.71
  Setting aside default and default judgment where service does not afford actual notice, 30.79
  Stay of execution pending hearing, order for, 30.63, 30.67; *form*, 30.68
  Transfer of action, order granting or denying, 30.18

Papers required for clerk's default judgment, 30.41–30.46

Papers required for court's default judgment, 30.49–30.50

Plaintiff's failure to request entry of default, effect of, 30.13

Publication, service by
  Generally, 30.20, 30.47
  Affidavits, 30.26
  Application for default judgment, 30.6, 30.53
  Fees, 30.27
  Form, default judgment by court, 30.55
  Hearing, 30.53–30.54
  Time to respond, 30.12

Relief
  See also Setting aside, below
  Equitable motion, 30.59, 30.73, 30.76
  Extent of relief generally, 30.36
  Time factors, 30.57–30.59, 30.73–30.74, 30.77, 30.79

DEFAULT—*cont.*
Request for entry of default. *See* Applications, above
Restrictions on default judgments, 30.9
Service of process and papers
  Generally, 30.2
  Actual notice, service affording, 30.56–30.59
  Actual notice, service not affording, 30.75–30.79
  Amended complaint. *See* Amended complaint or amendment to complaint, above
  Conflicting declarations, 30.70
  Contract actions and judgment for damages, 30.4, 30.22, 30.24, 30.48
  Entry of judgment, notice of, 30.62
  False return, effect of filing, 31.10
  Fictitiously named defendant, 30.9, 30.30–30.31, 30.44
  General actions, 30.5
  Judgment, copy of, 30.46, 30.55
  Notice of damages in personal injury and wrongful death actions, 30.36
  Notice of motion to set aside, 30.64, 30.67
  Prerequisite to entry of default, service as, 30.11–30.12
  Proof of service of summons, 30.21, 30.24, 30.63, 31.10
  Publication. *See* Publication, service by, above
  Quashing service, 30.15, 30.19
  Time for response, specifying in summons, 30.12
Setting aside
  See also Relief, above
  Generally, 30.2
  Address of defendant, effect of failure to ascertain, 30.26
  Appeal of order granting or denying relief, 30.80
  Clerk's error in entering default judgment, 30.40

Setting aside—*cont.*
  Conditions, imposition by court, 30.61, 30.79
  Declaration in support of motion, 30.63; *form*, 30.65
  Declaration of merits, 30.60, 30.63; *form*, 30.66; 30.69, 30.74
  Ethical considerations, 30.10
  Excusable neglect, case examples, 30.58
  Hearings, 30.57, 30.60, 30.70, 30.76–30.77
  Independent action in equity, 30.74, 30.78
  Intervention by nonparty, 25.33
  Judicial policy, 30.60, 30.80
  Mistake, inadvertence, surprise, excusable neglect, and extrinsic fraud as grounds, 30.56–30.60, 30.62–30.65, 30.76
  Moving papers, 30.63, 30.78
  Notice of motion, 30.25, 30.62–30.63; *form*, 30.64; 30.67
  Notice of motion where service does not afford actual notice, 30.75, 30.77–30.78
  Notice of renewed motion, 30.72
  Notice of request for entry of default, effect of nonreceipt of, 30.26
  Notice to opposing counsel, effect of failure to give, 30.10
  Opposing papers, 30.69
  Order, 30.63; *form*, 30.71
  Order where service does not afford actual notice, 30.79
  Procedure where service affords actual notice, 30.56–30.59
  Procedure where service does not afford actual notice, 30.75–30.79
  Renewed motion after denial, 30.62, 30.70, 30.72
  Stay of execution and shortening of time, order for, 30.63, 30.67; *form*, 30.68

INDEX 576

DEFAULT—*cont.*
Setting aside—*cont.*
  Time factors generally, 30.57–30.59, 30.73–30.74
  Time for motion, 30.62, 30.72
  Trial, proceedings constituting, 31.19
  Unserved defendant, 30.11
Settlement agreement or stipulation for judgment, provisions for default in, 34.7, 34.9
Several defendants, action against, 30.29, 30.39
Stay of execution and shortening of time, order for, 30.63, 30.67; *form*, 30.68
Stay or dismissal of action, 30.7, 30.15, 30.18–30.19, 30.44, 31.10, 31.13, 31.16–31.17, 31.23
Striking complaint, notice of motion, 30.15, 30.17
Three-year requirement for entry of judgment, applicability, 31.16–31.17
Timely response, requirement, 30.7–30.8, 30.10, 30.12–30.18, 30.20, 30.56
Transfer of action, 30.15, 30.18
Types of default judgments, 30.35
Uncontested action, 30.7
Vacating. *See* Setting aside, above
Venue
  Declaration regarding venue, 30.21, 30.25; *form*, 30.29; 30.45
  Notice of motion to transfer action, 30.15, 30.18

DEFENSES
Equitable issues, effect on right to jury trial, 24.40
Setting aside default or default judgment, declaration of merits regarding meritorious defense, 30.60, 30.63; *form*, 30.66; 30.69
Summary judgment. *See* Summary Judgment

DEFINITIONS. *See* Words and Phrases

DEMAND FOR JURY TRIAL. *See* Juries and Verdicts

DEMURRERS
Declaratory relief actions, 24.31, 24.36, 24.38
Default proceedings, 30.1–30.2, 30.7–30.8, 30.15–30.17, 30.34, 30.63, 30.69
Dismissal of action after demurrer not sustained, 31.77
Dismissal of action after demurrer sustained without leave to amend, 31.75, 31.77
Dismissal of action for failure to amend after demurrer sustained, 31.41, 31.72
General appearance, demurrer as, 31.12
Hearing
  Agreed statement of facts, effect of, 32.6
  Trial, hearing on demurrer as not constituting, 31.19, 31.75
Intervention complaint, demurrer to, 25.48, 25.50, 25.56
New trial after demurrer overruled, 31.33
Summary judgment. *See* Summary Judgment

DEPOSIT IN COURT
Jury fees, 26.33–26.35

DEPOSITIONS
Authentication of depositions, 29.63
Authentication of documents by depositions, 29.55–29.56
Coordination petition, use of depositions at hearing on, 28.34
Incapacity of party or essential witness, deposition resulting from, 26.88
Intervenor, effect of depositions on, 25.58
Settlement conference, required documents, 33.21

DEPOSITIONS—*cont.*
Summary judgment proceedings, 29.38, 29.44, 29.63
Trial continuance, denial due to inadequacy of deposition, 26.89
Trial setting conference, use of depositions at, 26.41

DISCLOSURE
See also Confidentiality
Quiet title action, third party as undisclosed agent of plaintiff's husband, 25.26
Trial setting conference, disclosure of evidence at, 26.44
Witnesses, disclosing at pretrial conference, 26.66

DISCOVERY
Attorney's advice to court regarding status of discovery, 26.40
Authentication of documents, 29.55–29.56
Continuance of trial setting conference, need for further discovery as ground for, 26.50
Coordination motion judge, effect of assignment of, 28.22
Coordination trial judge, powers of, 28.42, 28.45
Declaratory relief actions, 24.38
Default and default judgments
  Discovery request, default judgment for failure to comply with, 30.7–30.8, 30.64
  Independent action in equity, advantages in filing, 30.74
Depositions. *See* Depositions
Interrogatories. *See* Interrogatories
Order for further discovery, inclusion in trial setting order, 26.42
Pretrial conference, 26.58, 26.60, 26.66
Readiness certificate, contents of, 26.22
Summary judgment
  Completion of discovery prior to filing motion, 29.31

Summary judgment—*cont.*
  Documents, 29.38, 29.44, 29.62–29.66
  Other discovery as alternative to, 29.5
  Request for time to conduct discovery, denial of, 29.13
  Time limitation, 26.3, 26.5, 26.22, 26.26, 26.66
  Witnesses, disclosing at pretrial conference, 26.66

DISCRETION OF COURT
Advancement or change in setting of conferences or trial, 26.79
Change in setting case for trial, 26.26
Consolidation of actions, 27.3, 27.11, 27.21
Declaratory relief actions
  Equitable issues, trial precedence of, 24.40
  Granting or denying, 24.2, 24.14, 24.19–24.21, 24.24, 24.35–24.36, 24.39, 24.41
  Judgment, nature of, 24.43
Default or default judgment, relief from, 30.61–30.62, 30.70–30.71, 30.80
Denial of motion, 31.38–31.39
  Foreclosure of mechanics' lien, 31.4
  Imposition of conditions as proper exercise of discretion, 31.58
  Party's failure to appear, effect of, 31.40
  Second motion to dismiss, granting, 31.38
  Two years, failure to try action within, 31.3–31.4, 31.20, 31.36–31.37, 31.58, 31.74
Discovery, procedure in superior court, 26.3
Dismissal of actions
  Appellate reversal, effect of, 31.33
  Hearing on motion, procedures at, 23.56–23.57

INDEX 578

DISCRETION OF COURT—*cont.*

Intervention and joinder of parties, 25.1–25.2, 25.4, 25.10
Joinder of causes of action, sustaining demurrer to, 24.31
Judgment creditor's lien on judgment debtor's cause of action and judgment, 25.5
Jury trial, right to, 26.12, 26.29, 26.36
Plaintiff's offer to allow judgment, recovery of augmented costs, 33.12
Pretrial conference, location of, 26.65
Pretrial conference order, modifying, 26.72
Readiness certificate, vacating, 26.26
Setting case for trial within five-year period, 31.20
Settlement conference, continuance of, 33.18
Several defendants, default judgment against, 30.39
Severance of actions, 27.2–27.3, 27.12, 27.21
Summary judgment
  Amendment of pleadings, 29.29
  Attorney's fees, adjustment of, 29.73
  Continuance of proceedings, 29.13, 29.31, 29.68
  Declarations, refusal of court to accept, 29.69
  Granting or denying motion, 29.6, 29.11
  Testimony, taking of, 29.70
Trial, continuance of, 26.89–26.90, 26.95, 26.102
Trial date, setting, 26.51, 26.74
Unsupported motion, hearing, 23.26

DISMISSAL OF ACTIONS
    See also Compromise; Settlement
Abandonment of case, dismissal for, 31.80, 31.82, 31.88
Abatement procedure, 27.10
Appeals
  Appellate reversal, effect of, 31.33
  Challenging demurrer, appeal from resulting judgment, 31.41
  Denial of motion, appellate review of, 31.39, 31.53, 31.55
  Dismissal without prejudice, effect of, 31.68
  Entry of dismissal, appealability, 31.89, 31.91
  Judgment following dismissal, appealability, 31.91
  Partial dismissal, effect of, 31.77
Appearances
  Adverse party, effect of absence of, 26.55, 26.74
  Failure of parties to appear, dismissal for, 25.3, 31.40
  General appearance, examples of, 31.12
  Indispensable party, dismissal for absence of, 25.3
  Joint defendants, 31.48
  Stipulation extending defendant's time to plead, effect of, 31.11–31.12
Attorney's fees. *See* Costs and attorney's fees, below
Class actions, 31.31, 31.73
Consent judgment, effect of, 34.2, 34.9
Consent of parties, dismissal on, 31.78, 31.81, 31.83–31.84, 31.87
Contrived case, 32.1
Costs and attorney's fees
  Defendant's right generally, 31.6, 31.68–31.69, 33.29
  Transfer costs and fees. *See* Transfer costs and fees, failure to pay, below
  Trial continuance, dismissal for failure to pay costs of, 26.99
  Voluntary dismissal by plaintiff on payment of costs, 31.71, 31.85–31.86, 31.89

DISMISSAL—cont.
Cross-complaints. *See* Cross-Complaints
Declaratory relief
  Appealing dismissal, 24.45
  Improper casting of action to obtain precedence on calendar, 24.39
  Joinder with other causes of action, effect of, 24.31
Default and default judgments, 30.7, 30.15, 30.18–30.19, 30.44, 31.10, 31.13, 31.16–31.17, 31.23
Demurrer, effect of sustaining with and without leave to amend, 31.41
Denial of motion
  Appeal, 31.39, 31.53, 31.55
  Conditional denial, 31.58
  Defendant's remedies, 31.53
  Second motion, making, 31.38, 31.53
Documents, dismissal for failure to file, 26.20, 26.46
Fewer than all causes of action, dismissal of, 31.77
Fewer than all defendants, dismissal against, 31.76
Five years, failure to try action within
  Generally, 26.51, 26.74, 26.76–26.77, 26.79, 31.2
  Admission by defendant, effect of, 31.30
  Appellate reversal, effect of, 31.33
  Basic requirements, 31.19
  Class actions, 31.31
  Defendant not amenable to process, 31.22
  Duty of court to set case, 31.20
  Estoppel to claim exception, 31.28–31.29
  Impossibility, impracticability, and futility as exceptions, 31.24–31.28
  New trial motion, effect of, 31.32–31.33

Five years, failure to try action with—*cont.*
  Running of period, 31.3, 31.18
  Stipulation extending time, 31.18, 31.21, 31.25, 31.29
  Suspension of jurisdiction, effect of, 31.23
Health care contract, action for construction of, 24.19
Impossibility, impracticability, or futility
  Five-year trial requirement, grounds for noncompliance with, 31.24–31.28
  Three-year requirement for entry of judgment, grounds for noncompliance with, 31.17
  Three-year requirement for service and return of summons, grounds for noncompliance with, 31.13
  Three-year trial requirement after mistrial, grounds for noncompliance with, 31.34
  Three-year trial requirement after new trial granted, grounds for noncompliance with, 31.32
  Two-year trial requirement, grounds for noncompliance with, 31.35
Inherent power of court, 31.44–31.45, 31.59
Intervention
  Applicability of dismissal statutes generally, 31.18, 31.65, 31.68, 31.72, 31.91
  Dismissal after intervention, 25.59–25.60
  Intervention after dismissal, 25.34
  Show cause order, effect of, 25.41
Judgment of dismissal. *See* Orders, below
Judicial attitude, 31.2, 31.58
Lack of prosecution, dismissal for
  Appeal, 31.39, 31.53, 31.55
  Counterdeclarations, 31.51
  Declaration in support of motion, 31.46–31.48; *form,* 31.50

DISMISSAL—*cont.*
Lack of prosecution—*cont.*
  Diligence in prosecution, requirement, 31.2, 31.44, 31.51
  Hearing motion, 31.52
  Inherent power of court, 31.44–31.45, 31.59
  Notice of motion, 31.46–31.48; *form,* 31.49
  Order, 31.53; *form,* 31.54; 31.55
  Plaintiff's remedies when dismissal granted, 31.55
  Stayed action, 28.27
Mandatory and discretionary dismissal, comparison of statutes (chart), 31.3
Motions, notice of
  Generally, 31.32, 31.34, 31.41
  Court's inherent power, motion to dismiss under, 31.59
  Lack of prosecution, dismissal for, 31.46–31.48; *form,* 31.49
  Service, time for, 23.9
  Transfer fees and costs, motion to dismiss for failure to pay, 31.42, 31.60; *form,* 31.61
  Two-year trial requirement, motion to dismiss for noncompliance with, 31.56–31.57
Nonsuit. *See* Nonsuit
Notice of dismissal, entry of, 31.89
Notice of motions. *See* Motions, notice of, above
Orders
  Abandonment, order dismissing action after, 31.80, 31.82, 31.88
  Consent of parties, order dismissing action on, 31.78, 31.81, 31.83–31.84, 31.87
  Denial of motion to dismiss, appealability of order, 31.53
  Filing, effect of, 31.64, 31.89–31.90
  Form, order of dismissal, 31.54
  Just cause, order dismissing action on showing of, 31.82

Orders—*cont.*
  New trial order, dismissal for failure to try action within three years of affirmation of, 31.3, 31.33
  Vacating, 31.55, 31.68, 31.71, 31.75, 31.91
Partial dismissal, 31.76–31.77
Plaintiff's duty to bring case to trial, 31.2
Prejudice, dismissal with
  Abandonment of case, 31.80, 31.82, 31.88
  Collateral attack, 31.91
  Defined, 33.29
  Dismissal without prejudice distinguished, 31.66
  Effect, 31.70
  Motion, requirement, 31.88
  Plaintiff's right to dismiss after commencement of trial, 31.79
  Time for making, 31.83
Prejudice, dismissal without
  Consent of parties, dismissal on, 31.81, 31.83–31.84, 31.87
  Costs and attorney's fees, defendant's right to, 31.68–31.69, 31.85
  Dismissal with prejudice distinguished, 31.66, 33.29
  Jurisdiction, effect on, 31.68
  Just cause, showing of, 31.82, 31.88
  Motion, requirement, 31.88
  New action following dismissal, 31.67, 31.77
  Pretrial conference, matters considered at, 26.66
  Request for dismissal, 31.83; *form,* 31.84
  Service of process. *See* Three years, failure to serve and return summons within, below
  Setting aside, 31.55, 31.68, 31.71, 31.75, 31.91
Settlement defined, 33.1
Sham actions, 29.3, 29.14, 31.2

DISMISSAL—cont.

"Speaking motion" to dismiss as superseded by motion for summary judgment, 29.14

Statutes
  Applicability of general dismissal statutes, 31.5
  Comparison (chart), 31.3
  Judicial attitude toward, 31.2, 31.58
  Mandatory and jurisdictional effects, 31.6
  Mechanics' lien, statutes applicable to, 31.4
  Purpose, 31.1
  Taxpayer's actions, statutes applicable to, 31.4
  Voluntary dismissal, statutes applicable to, 31.65
Stayed action, dismissal for lack of prosecution, 28.27
Summary judgment, effect of dismissal of undetermined causes of action on finality of, 29.83
Three years after mistrial, failure to try action within, 31.3, 31.34
Three years after new trial granted or new trial order affirmed, failure to try action within, 31.3, 31.32–31.33
Three years, failure to enter judgment within
  Basic rule, 31.15
  Default judgments, applicability to, 31.16–31.17
  Exceptions, 31.17
  Statutory bases, 31.3, 31.5
  Stipulation for extension of time, 31.15, 31.17
  Tolling of period, 31.3, 31.15
Three years, failure to serve and return summons within
  Declaration, 31.46–31.47
  Estoppel, 31.11, 31.14, 31.29
  General appearance, effect of, 31.12
  Impossibility, impracticability, or futility as exceptions, 31.13

Three years' failure—cont.
  Running and tolling of period, 31.9–31.10, 31.13
  Statutory and case authorities, 31.1, 31.3, 31.7–31.8
  Stipulation for extension of time, 31.11–31.12, 31.14
Transfer fees and costs, failure to pay
  Declaration in support of motion to dismiss, *form*, 31.62
  Estoppel to seek dismissal, 31.43, 31.74
  Notice of motion to dismiss, 31.42, 31.60; *form*, 31.61
  Order of dismissal, 31.64
  Stipulation, effect of, 31.63
Trial continuance, dismissal of action for failure to pay costs of, 26.99
Trial, dismissal after commencement of
  Abandonment of case, 31.80, 31.82, 31.88
  Consent of parties, dismissal on, 31.81, 31.83–31.84, 31.87
  Just cause, showing of, 31.82, 31.88
  Plaintiff's right to dismiss with prejudice, 31.79
Trial, dismissal before commencement of
  Consent of parties, dismissal on, 31.78, 31.83–31.84, 31.87
  Cross-complaint by defendant seeking affirmative relief, effect of, 31.71–31.72
  Estoppel, 31.74
  Fewer than all causes of action, dismissal of, 31.77
  Fewer than all defendants, dismissal against, 31.76
  Plaintiff as not sole party in interest, effect of, 31.65, 31.73
  Right of plaintiff generally, 31.71
  Time of commencement, 31.75
Two years, failure to try action within

DISMISSAL—cont.
Two years, failure to try within—cont.

   Denial of motion to dismiss, effect of, 31.38–31.39

   Discretion of court, 31.3–31.4, 31.20, 31.36–31.37, 31.58, 31.74

   Foreclosure of mechanics' lien, 31.4

   Good cause, duty of plaintiff to show, 31.36

   Matters considered by court, 31.37

   Notice of motion for dismissal, 31.56–31.57

   Ruling on motion, 31.58

   Statutory bases, 31.3, 31.35

   Unavoidability of two-year delay, 31.44

   Waiver of provisions, effect of, 31.29

   Venue change. *See* Transfer fees and costs, failure to pay, above

DISQUALIFICATION OF JUDGES. *See* Judges

DISSOLUTION OF CORPORATIONS. *See* Corporations

DISSOLUTION OF MARRIAGE
Amendment of substance, example, 30.33
Declaratory relief actions to determine validity and rights relating to divorce decree, 24.6–24.7, 24.11
Default procedures, 30.9, 30.21, 30.50
Dismissal, rule affecting, 31.17
Intervention in proceedings, 25.31

DOE DEFENDANTS
Dismissal of actions, 31.9, 31.68

DOMESTIC RELATIONS
See also Family Law Act
Application for orders, rule governing, 23.2
Dissolution of marriage. *See* Dissolution of Marriage
Parent and child. *See* Parent and Child
Show cause procedure, 23.6, 23.67

DOMICILE. *See* Residence and Domicile

DUE PROCESS
See also Constitutional Law
Summary judgment proceedings, continuance of, 29.13

EDUCATION
Affirmative action admission programs, intervention in litigation, 25.1, 25.22

ELECTIONS
Declaratory relief, 24.3, 24.7, 24.13
Intervention by voters, 25.19

EMERGENCIES
Settlement conference, continuance of, 33.18
Trial, continuance of, 26.84, 26.89, 26.92, 26.95

EMINENT DOMAIN
Condemnation. *See* Condemnation
Dismissal statutes, applicability, 31.5, 31.65, 31.72, 31.74
Jury fees, deposit of, 26.33
Offer to allow judgment, rule affecting eminent domain actions, 33.10
Special setting for pretrial conference and trial, 26.77
Trial setting priority, 26.4

EMPLOYERS AND EMPLOYEES
Answers to interrogatories, question of general appearance, 31.12
Civil service. *See* Civil Service
Consolidation of actions under workers' compensation laws, 27.4
Improper conclusions in declarations, examples, 29.51
Settlement of actions by injured workers against third parties, 33.1
Workers' Compensation. *See* Workers' Compensation

EMPLOYMENT AGREEMENTS
Declaratory relief, 24.5

ENVIRONMENTAL IMPACT REPORTS
Declaratory relief action to review or set aside decisions of public agencies, 24.3

ESCROW
Declaratory relief, 24.5

ESTOPPEL
Action for commission based on estoppel theory, equitable nature of, 26.28
Consent judgment, effect of, 34.3
Declaratory judgment, effect on application of collateral estoppel, 24.43
Default judgment, collateral estoppel effect of, 30.3
Dismissal of actions, 31.11, 31.14, 31.17, 31.28–31.29, 31.35, 31.43, 31.74
Offer to allow judgment in settlement negotiations, effect of, 33.10
Stay of proceedings, collateral estoppel effect of, 28.11, 28.26

ETHICS. *See* Legal Ethics

EVIDENCE
Actions in which default judgments prohibited, 30.9
Amicus, limitation on, 25.9
Best evidence rule, 29.57–29.58
Burden of proof. *See* Burden of Proof
Coordination petition, evidence at hearing on, 28.33–28.34
Declaration in support of motion, effect of filing, 23.41
Default judgment by court, basic rules, 30.52, 30.54
Depository of evidentiary materials, establishment by coordination trial judge, 28.45
Directed verdict, basis for, 29.18
Exhibits. *See* Exhibits
Hearsay
 Admissibility, 23.41, 23.44
 Business records as exception to hearsay rule, 29.52, 29.60–29.61
 Incorporation of documents by reference, propriety of, 29.54
 Statement of facts in stipulation for judgment, treatment of, 34.3
Motion proceedings, sources of evidence and facts in, 23.24, 23.36, 23.57
Settlement negotiations, 33.4–33.5, 33.19
Submitted case, 32.2, 32.6
Summary judgment. *See* Summary judgment
Trial, commencement on introduction of evidence, 31.75
Trial, continuance due to absence of evidence, 26.93, 26.96
Trial setting conference, disclosure of evidence at, 26.44

EXCUSABLE NEGLECT
Default or default judgment, excusable neglect as basis for relief from, 30.56–30.60, 30.62–30.65, 30.75, 30.78–30.79

INDEX 584

EXCUSABLE NEGLECT—*cont.*
Dismissal, setting aside, 31.91
Relief on ground of excusable neglect generally, 23.62
Summary judgment, review of, 29.80, 29.82, 29.88

EXECUTION
See also Signatures

EXECUTION OF DOCUMENTS.
See Signatures

EXECUTORS AND ADMINISTRATORS
Declaratory relief action, 24.3
Intervention as substitute parties, 25.12

EXHIBITS
Acceptance as evidence, 23.44, 23.57
Best evidence rule, 29.57–29.58
Pretrial conference order, listing exhibits in, 26.69
Summary judgment proceedings, 29.54–29.58
Trial setting conference, disclosure of exhibits at, 26.44

EX PARTE PROCEEDINGS
Consent judgment, ex parte application for entry of, 34.12
Default and default judgments
  Obtaining default judgment, 30.43, 30.50
  Stay of execution, motion for, 30.67
Dismissal, ex parte application for, 31.41
Ex parte application defined, 23.64
Ex parte application for order and order, *form*, 23.66
General court rules, 23.2, 31.41, 31.46
Intervention. *See* Intervention of Parties

Noncomplying application, setting aside order issued on, 23.63
Noticed motions and ex parte motions distinguished, 23.5
Procedure and conditions for obtaining order, 23.65
Show cause orders. *See* Show Cause Orders

EXPENSES AND EXPENDITURES
"Reasonable expenses," interpretation of, 29.74

EXPERT WITNESSES
Declarant as expert witness, 23.41, 29.49
Handwriting experts and nonexperts, authentication of documents by, 29.55–29.56
Qualification to give opinions, 29.51
Settlement actions, 33.12, 33.14, 33.20

EXTENSION OF TIME. *See* Time

FACT AND LAW QUESTIONS.
See Questions of Law and Fact

FAMILY LAW ACT
Coordination of actions, 28.2, 28.6

FEDERAL COURT ACTIONS AND PROCEEDINGS
Declaratory relief action, 24.27
State court action delayed by federal proceedings, 31.25

FEES
See also Costs
Attorney's fees. *See* Attorney's Fees
Deposit in court. *See* Deposit in Court
Intervention complaint, 25.55
Pretrial conference, reporter's fees, 26.65

FICTITIOUS DEFENDANTS. See Doe Defendants

FICTITIOUS NAMES. See Names

FINDINGS OF FACT AND CONCLUSIONS OF LAW
Agreed case. See Submitted case, below
Consolidation of actions, separate findings, 27.6
Declarations, statements in, 23.41
Default judgment, hearing on, 30.52, 30.70
Former summary judgment decisions, effect of legal conclusions on, 29.8
Personal knowledge, showing by fact and not by conclusion, 29.8, 29.49
Pretrial motion, granting or denying, 23.58
Submitted case
  Erroneous agreement on conclusion of law, effect of, 32.2
  Statement of agreed facts, effect of, 32.4, 32.6
Summarily adjudicated issues, treatment of, 29.7
Summary judgment
  Contents of order, 29.71
  Inadmissible conclusions, 29.50–29.51, 29.54

FINES
See also Penalties
Settlement conference, fine for failure to attend, 33.27

FIRES
Declaratory relief action by insurance company to determine liability under fire policy, 24.41

FORCIBLE ENTRY
Time to answer complaint, 30.12

FORECLOSURE
Intervention in proceedings, 25.25

FOREFEITURE
Settlement or continuance of trial, notice to clerk to avoid forfeiture of jury fees, 26.33
Stipulated judgment, effect of conditional provisions in, 34.7

FORM AND FORMAT OF COURT PAPERS
See also specific papers by name
Coordination proceedings, 28.21
Judicial Council forms, mandatory use of, 30.21, 31.83
Memorandum of points and authorities in format of appellate brief, 23.27
Title of action, effect of defect in, 23.39

FORM VERSUS SUBSTANCE
Amendments to complaints, 30.16, 30.34

FORUM
See also Venue
Declaratory relief, effect of availability of other forums on, 24.13, 24.23
Default procedures, dismissal of action on ground of inconvenient forum, 30.19

FRAUD
Default or default judgment, extrinsic fraud as basis for relief from, 30.56–30.59, 30.64, 30.76
General release obtained from injured person, time effect of, 33.29
Improper conclusions in declarations, examples, 29.51
Quiet title action, intervention of former owner of property, 25.26

INDEX 586

FRAUD—*cont.*
Summary judgment, extrinsic fraud as ground for relief from, 29.81, 29.88
Vacation of judgment obtained through extrinsic fraud, 25.33

FRIEND OF COURT
Intervention, restriction on, 25.9

GAMBLING
Declaratory relief action, 24.24

GAS. *See* Oil and Gas

GUARDIANSHIP AND CONSERVATORSHIP
Declaratory relief action by guardian, 24.3
Dismissal of action by plaintiff as matter of right, preventing, 31.73

HANDWRITING
See also Signatures
Authentication of documents, 29.55–29.56

HEALTH. *See* Illness

HEALTH CARE CONTRACTS
Declaratory relief action seeking construction of, 24.19

HEARINGS
Advancement. *See* Advancement of Proceedings
Certificate of readiness, hearing on dismissal for failure to file, 26.20
Common issues, joint hearing of, 27.6
Consent judgment, hearing prior to entry of, 34.12
Continuance. *See* Continuance
Coordination. *See* Coordination of Actions
Default and default judgments. *See* Default and Default Judgments
Demurrers. *See* Demurrers
Dismissal motions, 31.52
Filing applications for orders that request hearing, 23.4
Intervention
  Ex parte application, hearing on, 25.38
  Order granting leave to intervene after hearing on show cause order or noticed motion, *form*, 25.46
Jury trial, hearing on motion for, 26.29, 31.75
Motions generally, hearing on. *See* Motions
Notice, time for serving, 23.9
Noticed motions and ex parte motions distinguished, 23.5
Severance, hearing motion for, 27.17
Show cause procedure. *See* Show Cause Orders
Subpena duces tecum, hearing on motion to quash, 31.75
Summary judgment. *See* Summary Judgment
Transfer of action, hearing on, 28.49

HEARSAY. *See* Evidence

HEIRSHIP
Declaratory relief action to determine, 24.3
Intervention in heirship proceedings, 25.12, 25.30, 25.37

HIGHWAYS. *See* Streets, Roads, and Highways

HOLIDAYS. *See* Saturdays, Sundays, and Holidays

HOMEOWNERS' CORPORATION. *See* Corporations

HUSBAND AND WIFE
Community property. *See* Community Property
Dissolution of marriage. *See* Dissolution of Marriage

HYBRID ACTIONS
Jury trial, right to, 26.28

IDENTITY, ESTABLISHMENT OF
Declaratory relief action to establish facts of birth or death, 24.3

ILLNESS
Advancement of proceedings, poor health as ground for, 26.76–26.77
Continuance of trial due to illness of party, attorney, or witness, 26.88
Mental illness. *See* Mental Illness

IMPOSSIBILITY, IMPRACTICABILITY, OR FUTILITY DOCTRINE. *See* Dismissal of Actions

INADEQUACY OF LEGAL REMEDY. *See* Adequacy of Legal Remedy

INADVERTENCE
Default or default judgment, inadvertence as basis for relief from, 30.56–30.60, 30.62–30.65
Dismissal, setting aside, 31.91
Relief on ground of inadvertence generally, 23.62
Summary judgment, review of, 29.80, 29.82, 29.88

INCOME TAX, STATE
Declaratory relief action, determining residence for state income tax purposes, 24.3

INCOMPETENCY. *See* Insane and Incompetent Persons

INCORPORATION BY REFERENCE
Declaration incorporating documents by reference, 23.44, 29.54
Independent action in equity to set aside default or default judgment, filing procedure, 30.74
Intervention, complaint in, 25.53

INDEMNITY
Declaratory relief actions, cross-complaint in, 24.35
Release, terms of, 33.30

IN FORMA PAUPERIS PROCEEDINGS
Jury fees, payment of, 26.33

INJUNCTIONS
Application for preliminary injunction as not constituting trial, 31.19
Declaratory relief actions, 24.33, 24.43–24.44
Dismissal statute, applicability, 31.65
Preliminary injunction
  Show cause procedure, 23.6, 23.67
  Trial setting priority, 26.4

INSANE AND INCOMPETENT PERSONS
See also Mental Illness
Private settlements, 33.5

INSOLVENCY
See also Bankruptcy
General creditors, rule governing intervention by, 25.24

INSTALLMENT SALES
Default proceedings, declaration regarding venue, 30.18, 30.21, 30.25; *form*, 30.29

INDEX 588

INSURANCE
Discharged attorney's declaratory relief action against insurance company for fees, 24.8
Intervention in insurance actions, 25.13–25.14
Joinder of parties, declaratory relief action by insurer to determine, 24.29
Liability under fire policy, declaratory relief action by insurance company to determine, 24.41
Settlement actions, participation of insurer in, 33.1, 33.4, 33.9, 33.23, 33.26

INTENT
Default judgment, legislative intent requiring plaintiff to exercise diligence in obtaining, 31.15
Dismissal motion, intent of, 31.60, 31.88
General appearance, act constituting, 31.12
"Reasonable expenses," legislative intent, 29.74
Statement explaining loss of document without fraudulent intent, 29.57
Stipulation extending defendant's time to plead, 31.17

INTERLOCUTORY JUDGMENTS. See Judgments

INTERPLEADER
Consolidation compared, 27.10
Declaratory relief, 24.3
Dismissal statute, applicability, 31.65

INTERPRETATION. See Construction and Interpretation

INTERROGATORIES
Answers as not constituting general appearance, 31.12
Authentication of documents by interrogatories, 29.55–29.56
Coordination petition, answering interrogatories at hearing on, 28.34
Summary judgment proceedings, 29.38, 29.44, 29.55–29.56, 29.64

INTERVENTION OF PARTIES
See also Joinder of Parties
Adjoining landowners, intervention by, 25.18, 25.23
Affirmative action school admission programs, 25.1, 25.22
Appeals
  Appellate opinions, 25.1
  Reversal on appeal, intervention after, 25.35
  Review of orders denying or granting leave to intervene, 25.51–25.52
  Waiver of objections to intervention, effect of, 25.50
Applications
  Dismissal of action, effect of pendency of application on, 25.34
  Drafting, manner of, 25.10
  Ex parte application. See Ex parte application, below
  New trial, application by nonparty to intervene before commencement of, 25.35
  Opposition to, 25.48–25.49
  Statute of limitations, 25.37
  Timeliness, 25.1, 25.10, 25.32–25.37, 25.49
Attorney's fees, actions for collection of, 25.21
Burden of proof, 25.47
Class actions, 25.7
Complaints
  Affirmative relief, effect of defendant seeking, 31.72
  Answers and demurrers, 25.3, 25.48, 25.50, 25.56, 25.58
  Appearance fee, payment of, 25.55
  Cross-complaints. See Cross-complaints, below

INTERVENTION—*cont.*
Complaints—*cont.*

    Declaration, advantages of, 25.39
    Essential elements, 25.53
    Ex parte action by nonparty, 25.38
    Failure to state cause of action, assertion by intervenor, 25.58
    Filing, 25.4, 25.34, 25.37
    Five-year requirement for bringing action to trial, rule affecting, 31.18
    Form, 25.54
    Joinder of parties, 25.58
    Opposition procedures, 25.48–25.50
    Service, 25.55–25.56
    Statute of limitations, 25.37
    Statutory bases, 25.3
    Striking, 25.48, 25.51
Criteria for, 25.1, 25.10
Cross-complaints
    CCP §§387 and 389, filing under, 25.3
    Intervenor, cross-complaint against, 25.57
    Nonparty, cross-claim against, 25.58
Declarations
    Opposing declarations, 25.48–25.49
    Order granting leave to intervene, declaration for, 25.38; *form*, 25.39
    Show cause order re intervention, declaration for, *form*, 25.42
Default or default judgment, intervention to set aside, 25.33
Defined, 25.1, 25.10
Dismissal of actions. *See* Dismissal of Actions
Ex parte application
    Appeal by intervenor after striking of complaint, 25.51
    General procedure, 25.38
    Orders. *See* Orders, below

Foreclosure proceedings, intervention in, 25.25
General creditors, intervention by, 25.24
Heirship proceedings, intervention in, 25.12, 25.30, 25.37
Husband's or wife's intervention in actions concerning community property, 25.17
Impression of trust, intervention in actions for, 25.29
Incorporation of cities, intervention in proceedings for, 25.23
Insurance matters, 25.13–25.14
Intervenor as not indispensable party, 25.10
Judgment creditor, intervention by, 25.5, 25.14
Limited partner, intervention by, 25.16
Marriage dissolution proceedings, intervention in, 25.31
Motion, notice of
    Dismissal of action during pendency of noticed motion, 25.38, 25.44
    Form, 25.45
    Judgment creditor's motion to intervene, 25.5
    Order granting leave to intervene after hearing on motion, *form*, 25.46
Nonparty claimants, intervention by, 25.6, 25.15, 25.33
Notice of motion. *See* Motion, notice of, above
Opposition, procedure for presenting, 25.48–25.50
Orders
    Appeals. *See* Appeals, above
    Declaration for order granting leave to intervene and order, 25.38; *form*, 25.39
    Forms, orders granting leave to intervene, 25.39–25.40, 25.46
    Show cause order. *See* Show cause order, below

INTERVENTION—*cont.*

Quieting title, 25.21, 25.23, 25.26
Real or personal property, parties claiming interest in, 25.2, 25.4, 25.6, 25.10, 25.15, 25.23, 25.27–25.28, 25.31
Real party in interest, 25.11
Rights and remedies of intervenor, 25.58
Riparian rights, 25.23
Settlement of actions by injured workers on intervention of employer or insurer, 33.1
Shareholders, intervention by. *See* Corporations
Show cause order
   Declaration for order, *form*, 25.42
   Forms, orders to show cause why leave to intervene should not be granted, 25.42–25.43
   General procedure, 25.41
Special statutes, intervention under, 25.2
Statutory authority generally, 25.1, 25.4
Successors in interest, 25.12, 25.33
Sureties, intervention by, 25.13
Taxpayers, intervention by, 25.22
Voters, intervention by, 25.19
Will contests, intervention in, 25.12, 25.30, 25.37

INVOICES

Default judgment, supporting, 30.45

JOINDER OF CAUSES OF ACTION. *See* Causes of Action

JOINDER OF PARTIES

   See also Intervention of Parties
Generally, 25.1
Amended complaints
   Real or personal property, parties claiming interest in, 25.4
   Service and return of amended complaint adding new parties, 31.9

Applications
   Omitted party's application for joinder order, 25.3, 25.32
   Person claiming interest in real or personal property, application by, 25.4
Consolidation and permissive joinder compared, 27.10
Declaratory relief actions, 24.29
Dismissal of action against defendant joined as indispensable party, 31.76
Intervention complaint, joinder of parties in, 25.58
Personal injury case, joinder of third party in, 26.10
Service and return of amended complaint adding new parties, time effect, 31.9
Statutory authority, joinder of indispensable party, 25.3
Wrongful death action, 31.22–31.23

JUDGES

Consent judgment, function of judge, 34.12
Coordination. *See* Coordination of Actions
Default judgment, qualifications of judge granting, 30.2
Disqualification
   Coordination trial judge, challenge to assignment of, 28.41
   Intervenor, motion by, 25.58
Judicial discretion. *See* Discretion of Court
Misinformation from judge, nonappearance resulting from, 31.40
New trial following severed trial, issues tried before different judges, 27.20
Pretrial conference judge, duties of, 26.56
Settlement, role of judge, 33.2, 33.24
Trial setting conference, role of judge, 26.3, 26.47–26.48

JUDGMENT NOTWITHSTANDING VERDICT
Summary judgment compared, 29.18

JUDGMENT ON THE PLEADINGS
Appeal, effect on five-year trial requirement, 31.23
Declaratory judgment, obtaining, 24.37
Notice of motion, 29.16
Objection to introduction of all evidence, similarity, 29.17
Summary judgment motion as replacing "speaking motion for judgment on the pleadings," 29.3
Summary judgment motion combined with motion for, 29.45
Summary judgment motion compared with motion for, 29.16, 29.29

JUDGMENTS
Absence of adverse party from trial, effect of, 26.55
Abstracts. *See* Abstract of Judgment
Agreed case, judgment in, 32.1–32.2
CCP §631.8, motion for judgment under, 29.19
Consent judgment. *See* Consent Judgment
Consolidation of pleadings and rendering of single judgment, 27.6
Coordination of actions to avoid duplicate and inconsistent judgments, 28.5
Coordination motion judge, effect of assignment of, 28.22, 28.26
Declaratory judgment. *See* Declaratory Relief
Defined, 23.58
Final judgment
    Appealability of final and nonfinal judgments, 29.83–29.84, 29.89, 31.53, 31.55

Final judgment—*cont.*
    Findings, rule affecting, 23.58
Interlocutory judgments
    Pretrial conference order, interlocutory review of, 26.72
Intervention, qualification for, 25.10
Judgment creditor's lien on judgment debtor's cause of action and judgment, 25.5, 25.14
Offer to allow judgment. *See* Settlement
Prior judgment. *See* Res Judicata
Severance of actions where several judgments proper, 27.5
Severed issues, judgment after trial of, 27.20
Summary adjudication of issues. *See* Summary Judgment
Summary judgment. *See* Summary Judgment
Three years, failure to enter judgment within. *See* Dismissal of Actions

JUDICIAL COUNCIL
Mandatory use of forms, 30.21, 31.83

JUDICIAL DISCRETION. *See* Discretion of Court

JUDICIAL DISTRICTS
Determining population, declaratory relief action, 24.3

JUDICIAL NOTICE
Coordination petition, judicial notice of evidence presented at hearing on, 28.34
Court's notice of own file, 29.63
Defects in presentation of evidence, 29.33
Request, *form*, 23.45
Request in summary judgment proceedings, *form*, 29.47
Signatures, similarity of, 29.55
Summary judgment. *See* Summary Judgment

INDEX 592

JURIES AND VERDICTS
Absence of adverse party from trial, effect of, 26.55, 26.74
Actions in which jury trial not matter of right, advisory character of verdict, 26.29
Consolidation of actions, rendering of single verdict, 27.6
Declaratory relief action, jury trial, 24.2, 24.40
Demand for jury trial
  At-issue memorandum, demand in, 26.11–26.12, 26.15, 26.30–26.31
  Continuing nature, 26.31
  Court's discretion where no right exists, 26.12, 26.29
  Deciding whether to demand or retain jury, 26.30
  Deposit of fees and other expenses, 26.33–26.35
  Form, 26.32
  Intervenor, demand by, 25.58
  Motion, notice of, 26.11, 26.15, 26.29, 26.32
  Reliance on other party's demand, 26.34
  Right to jury, 26.11–26.12, 26.15, 26.28, 26.52, 30.74
  Waiver for failure to make timely demand, 26.31, 26.35
Directed verdict and summary judgment compared, 29.18
Empanelment of jury as constituting partial trial, 31.19
Evidence, motion to exclude, 29.16
Hearing on default judgment, jury's assessment of damages, 30.52
Hearing on motion for jury trial, effect of, 31.75
Judgment notwithstanding verdict. *See* Judgment Notwithstanding Verdict
Severance of actions, jury trial, 27.3, 27.11–27.12, 27.19–27.20
Submitted case, trying on statement of agreed facts, 32.6

Summarily adjudicated issues, incorporation into jury instructions, 29.7
Summary judgment, attacking on ground of denial of jury trial, 29.4
Trial continuance due to unavailability of jury, 26.93
Vacating setting for jury trial, 26.15, 26.52
Waiver of jury trial
  Acts resulting in waiver, 26.35
  Consent, waiver by, 26.12, 26.35
  Demand after previous waiver, 25.58, 26.32
  Deposit of jury fees, effect of failure to make, 26.33, 26.35
  Notice, 26.34
  Relief from waiver, 26.36–26.37
  Timely demand, waiver for failure to make, 26.31, 26.35

JURISDICTION
Agreed case, jurisdictional requirements, 32.1–32.2
Amount in controversy. *See* Amount in Controversy
Consolidation of actions, limit on court's authority, 27.1
Coordination petition, orders granting or denying, 28.35–28.36
Declaratory relief actions, 24.6, 24.16, 24.27–24.29
Default proceedings, 30.18–30.19, 30.52, 30.58–30.59, 30.74, 30.80
Dismissal statutes, jurisdictional nature of, 31.5, 31.68, 31.73, 31.77
Five-year trial requirement, effect of suspension of court's jurisdiction on, 31.23
General appearance, act indicating submission to court's jurisdiction as, 31.12
Intervenor, objection by, 25.58
Opposing motion on jurisdictional grounds, 23.51

JURISDICTION—cont.
Other states. *See* Other States
Pretrial conference, matters considered at, 26.66
Transfer of actions. *See* Transfer of Actions

JURY TRIAL. *See* Juries and Verdicts

JUSTICE COURTS
See also Jurisdiction; Venue
Continuances, basic requirement for, 26.86
Declaratory relief actions, 24.27
Default and default judgments
  Jurisdiction generally, 30.18–30.19, 30.58–30.59, 30.74, 30.80
  Stay of execution, duration of, 30.67
  Time limitations, 30.59
Jury fees, deposit of, 26.33–26.34
Jury trial, procedure for demanding, 26.31, 26.34
Notice of motion, rules relating to, 23.2, 23.19
Pretrial conferences, statutory authority, 26.57
Setting case for trial, 26.5

LABOR UNIONS
Declaratory relief actions, 24.7, 24.11

LACHES
Judicial discretion, 24.2, 24.19, 24.22
Notice of motion, delay in serving 23.11

LANDLORD AND TENANT
Declaratory relief action, 24.10

LAW AND FACT QUESTIONS
See Questions of Law and Fact

LAW LIBRARIES
Local rules relating to motion practice, availability of, 23.2

LEASES
Declaration of rights under sublease, status of parties, 24.29
Declaratory relief action to determine performance of lease option, 24.27

LEGAL ETHICS
Default procedures, standards provided by case law, 30.10

LEGISLATURE
Continuance of trial or proceeding resulting from membership in legislature, 26.93
Intent. *See* Intent

LIBEL AND SLANDER
Declaratory relief, 24.7
Dismissal of action, defendant's recovery of attorney's fees and costs, 31.69

LICENSES AND PERMITS
Consolidation of actions for suspension or revocation of contractor's license, 27.4
Declaratory relief actions, 24.8–24.9, 24.11

LIENS
Consent judgment, recording as lien against specific property, 34.2, 34.5
Consolidation of actions to foreclose loggers' liens, 27.4
Judgment creditor's lien on judgment debtor's cause of action and judgment, 25.5, 25.14
Mechanics' liens. *See* Mechanics' Liens

INDEX

LIMITATION OF ACTIONS
See also Time
Declaratory relief, 24.22, 24.34
Default or default judgment, relief from, 30.62
Dismissal statutes compared, 31.1–31.3, 31.10
Dismissal with and without prejudice distinguished, 31.66–31.67
Estoppel to raise statute of limitations defense as triable by court, 26.28
Intervention, complaint in, 25.37
Joinder of indispensable party, statutory provision, 25.32
Severance of statute of limitations
  Generally, 27.5, 27.12
  Notice of motion, *form*, 27.18
  Order, *form*, 27.19
Summary judgment proceedings, special defense in, 29.20, 29.24

LIMITED PARTNERSHIPS
Intervention by limited partner in action against limited partnership, 25.16

LITIGATION
Default and default judgments, effects of serving actual notice of litigation, 30.56–30.59
Dismissal statutes, effect of, 31.1
Intervention, statutory provisions, 25.1, 25.3, 25.22
Settlement
  Advantages of settlement, 33.3
  Offer to allow judgment, effect on relitigation, 33.10

LOST PAPERS
Default proceedings, effect of loss of original contract, 30.43
Reestablishment of destroyed land records, prohibition of default judgment, 30.9
Statements supporting introduction of secondary evidence, 29.58

MAIL
See also Addresses
Request for entry of default, declaration of mailing, 30.21, 30.26; *form*, 30.29
Service of process. See Service of Process

MALICIOUS PROSECUTION
Dismissal without prejudice, malicious prosecution action following, 31.67
Mutual release, terms of, 33.30

MALPRACTICE. See Medical Malpractice

MANDATE
Consolidation or severance of actions, review of order granting or denying, 27.21
Coordination of actions, review of orders granting or denying, 28.35, 28.37, 28.56
Declaratory relief, joinder of causes of action, 24.33
Default procedures, 30.9, 30.15, 30.18–30.19, 30.32, 30.40, 30.61, 30.80
Dismissal of actions, use of writ, 31.33, 31.53, 31.55, 31.89
Jury trial in mandamus proceedings, 26.29
Order granting or denying motion, review of, 23.62
Pretrial conference order, interlocutory review by mandamus, 26.72
Show cause order, application for, 23.67
Submission of agreed case, treatment as petition for writ, 32.2
Summary judgment
  Continuance of proceedings, review of decision, 29.68
  Order denying summary judgment, review of, 29.89

MANDATE—*cont.*
Summary judgment—*cont.*
Summary adjudication of issues, attacking by extraordinary writ, 29.88
Venue change, review of, 31.42

MARRIAGE
Declaratory relief action, testing validity of marriage, 24.3
Dissolution. *See* Dissolution of Marriage

MECHANICS' LIENS
Consolidation of actions to foreclose, 27.4
Dismissal of action to foreclose, 31.4

MEDICAL EXAMINATIONS
Settlement actions, use of medical reports in personal injury cases, 33.20–33.21
Summary judgment proceedings, use of reports in, 29.44, 29.66

MEDICAL MALPRACTICE
Severance of actions, 27.5

MEMORANDUM OF POINTS AND AUTHORITIES
Attaching to notice of motion, 23.17, 23.19, 23.24
Caption, 23.28, 23.49
Conclusion, 23.34
Contents, 23.23
Default or default judgment, setting aside, 30.63–30.64
Drafting, 23.27
Grounds for motion, memorandum as amplification of, 23.23
Headings of sections, 23.31, 23.49
Introduction, 23.29, 23.49
Judicial notice, request for, *form*, 23.45
Manner of presenting points and authorities, 23.32–23.33, 23.49
Opposition memorandum, 23.49, 23.52, 23.54
Pleadings and papers, reference in memorandum to, 23.44
Pretrial conference, matters considered at, 26.66
Purpose, 23.26
Signature, 23.35
Summary judgment motion, 29.41–29.43, 29.46, 29.69
Table of contents or index, 23.30, 23.49

MEMORANDUM TO SET. *See* Setting Case for Trial

MENTAL ILLNESS
See also Insane and Incompetent Persons
Summary judgment proceedings, use of reports in, 29.44, 29.66

MILITARY SERVICE. *See* Servicemen and Veterans

MINORS
Private settlements, 33.5

MISTAKES
Default or default judgment, mistake as basis for relief from, 30.56–30.60, 30.62–30.65, 30.76
Dismissal, setting aside, 31.91
Relief on ground of mistake generally, 23.62
Summary judgment, review of, 29.80–29.82, 29.88

MISTRIAL
Declaration of, 26.2
Dismissal for failure to try action within three years after mistrial, 31.3, 31.34

MODIFICATIONS. *See* Amended and Supplemental Pleadings; Amendments

INDEX 596

MOTIONS
  See also Orders
Affidavits. *See* Affidavits
Collateral response, opposition by, 23.51–23.62
Consolidation. *See* Consolidation of Actions
Declarations supporting and opposing. *See* Declarations
Defined, 23.1
Denial (generally)
  Findings, rule affecting pretrial motion, 23.58
  Grounds, failure to state, 23.23
  Memorandum of points and authorities, failure to file, 23.26
  Order granting or denying motion, *form*, 23.60
  Procedure after motion denied, 23.63
  Statutory or court rule requirements, nonconformance with, 23.1
Documents used in support of, 23.44
Granting (generally)
  Findings, rule affecting pretrial motion, 23.58
  Modification of ruling granting motion, 23.62
  Order, *form*, 23.60
  Procedure by moving party after motion granted, 23.61
  Procedure by opposing party after motion granted, 23.62
Hearing on motion
  Attendance, 23.55–23.56
  Date and place, specifying, 23.19, 23.21, 23.23, 23.28, 23.39
  Evidence generally, 23.24, 23.36, 23.57
  Extension of time
    Application for order and order, 23.14; *form*, 23.16
    Stipulation, 23.14; *form*, 23.15
  New points, oral presentation of, 23.54
  Notice, 23.9, 23.20

Hearing on motion—*cont.*
  Oral argument, 23.54, 23.56
  Procedural questions, 23.56
  Rulings. *See* Rulings, below
  Service of papers at hearing, effect of, 23.52
  Shortening time, application for order and order, 23.12; *form*, 23.13
  Statement by attorney opposing motion, 23.48
  Unsupported motion, hearing, 23.26
Local policies and rules, legal effect of, 23.2
Manner of making and determining, 23.1, 23.36, 23.55
Nonparties, motions made by, 23.3
Notice. *See* Motions, Notice of
Opposition procedures generally, 23.48, 23.52, 23.54
Opposition without declaration, 23.50
Place of application, 23.4
Renewed motions
  Default or default judgments, renewed motion for relief from, 30.62, 30.70, 30.72
  Summary judgment motion, 29.90
Reply and supplemental papers, filing, 23.54
ulings
  Effectiveness of oral ruling, 23.58
  Modification of ruling granting motion, 23.62
  Notice, 23.58; *form*, 23.59
  Notice, waiver of, 23.61
  Tentative rulings, 23.48, 23.53, 23.58
Severance. *See* Severance of Actions
Statutes and rules governing motion procedures, 23.1–23.2
Summary judgment, effect of granting to nonmoving party, 29.6
Tactical and economic considerations, 23.7

MOTIONS, NOTICE OF
Advancing, specially setting, or resetting conferences or trial, 26.49–26.50, 26.80; *form,* 26.81
Caption and introduction, 23.17, 23.19
Consent judgment, motion for entry of, 34.7, 34.9, 34.12
Consolidation of actions, motion for, 27.13; *form,* 27.14
Coordination of actions, motion for, *form,* 28.13
Copies of allegations and papers, attaching, 23.44
Declaratory relief actions, trial precedence of, 24.39
Default and default judgments. *See* Default and Default Judgments
Dismissal of actions. *See* Dismissal of Actions
Ex parte motions and noticed motions distinguished, 23.5
Filing. *See* Service and filing, below
Form, 23.18
General court rules, 23.2, 23.6
Grounds for motion, statement of, 23.23
Intervention. *See* Intervention of Parties
Judgment on the pleadings, motion for, 29.16
Judicial notice, request for, *form,* 23.45
Jury trial, motion for, 26.11, 26.15, 26.29, 26.32
Jury trial, motion to vacate setting for, 26.15
Jury waiver, relief from, 26.37
Nature of order sought, 23.19, 23.22
Pretrial conference, requesting after filing of at-issue memorandum, 26.62
Procedural checklist, 23.8
Service and filing
Generally, 23.6, 23.8, 23.17, 23.24

Service and filing—*cont.*
Date of service, 23.25
Effect of filing, 23.1, 23.55
Extension of time
Application for order and order, 23.14; *form,* 23.16
Stipulation, 23.14; *form,* 23.15
Laches, 23.11
Mail, service by, 23.10, 23.25, 23.47
Memorandum of points and authorities, 23.26
Proof of service, 23.47
Shortening time for hearing, application for order and order, 23.12; *form,* 23.13
Summary judgment motion, 29.12
Time limitations generally, 23.9–23.11
Setting case for trial, motion to change, 26.25–26.27, 26.51
Settlement conference, motion for continuance of, 33.18
Severance of actions, motion for, 27.17; *form,* 27.18
Show cause procedure as alternative to noticed motion, 23.67
Signature, 23.25, 23.27
Summary judgment. *See* Summary Judgment
Supporting papers, 23.17, 23.24
Trial continuance, motion for, 26.96; *form,* 26.97
Trial date, motion to shorten time for, 26.51, 26.74

MOTIONS TO STRIKE
Answers, striking, 29.3, 29.15
At-issue memorandum, striking, 26.14, 26.25
Declaratory relief, applicability, 24.38
Default procedures, 30.15, 30.17
General appearance, notice as, 31.12
Insufficient pleadings, raising defect by motion to strike, 29.16, 29.31

INDEX 598

MOTIONS TO STRIKE—*cont.*
Intervention complaint, striking, 25.48, 25.51
Purpose, 29.15
Readiness certificate, striking, 26.14, 26.25
Service and filing, time limitation, 23.9
Sham defenses, striking, 29.3, 29.15

MULTIPLE PARTIES
See also Joinder of Parties; Multiplicity of Actions
Coordination of actions, 28.6, 28.10
Default, entry against several defendants, 30.29
Default judgment by clerk, 30.39
Designation of opposing party in notice of motion, 29.35
Dismissal motion by joint defendant, 31.48
Fewer than all defendants, dismissal against, 31.76
Five-year trial requirement, exception to, 31.27
Rulings on motions, recitals required, 23.59
Service and return in actions involving several defendants, 31.8
Settlement actions, multiple plaintiffs and defendants in, 33.12, 33.14, 33.26, 33.32
Severance of actions against several defendants, 27.5

MULTIPLICITY OF ACTIONS
See also Multiple Parties
Consolidation, factor favoring, 27.11
Default judgment by clerk, multiple causes of action, 30.38
Personal injury case, joinder of third party to avoid piecemeal litigation, 26.10

MUNICIPAL COURTS
See also Jurisdiction; Venue
Continuances, basic requirement for, 26.86
Coordination of actions, 28.6
Declaratory relief actions, 24.27

Default and default judgments
Jurisdiction generally, 30.18–30.19, 30.58–30.59, 30.74, 30.80
Time limitations, 30.59
Venue, 30.18
Jury fees, deposit of, 26.33–26.34
Jury trial, procedure for demanding, 26.31, 26.34
Notice of motion, rules relating to, 23.2, 23.19
Pretrial conferences, statutory authority, 26.57
Setting case for trial, 26.5
Settlement conference, obtaining, 33.16

NAMES
Declarations, names in, 23.39, 28.15, 28.19
Default judgment, obtaining against defendant under fictitious name, 30.9, 30.30–30.31, 30.44
Service of process, effect of different or incorrect names, 30.24, 30.30–30.31

NEGLECT. *See* Excusable Neglect

NEGLIGENCE. *See* Contributory Negligence

NEW TRIAL
Demand for jury trial, continuing nature of, 26.31
Dismissal for failure to try action within three years after new trial granted or new trial order affirmed, 31.3, 31.32–31.33
Intervention by nonparty before commencement of new trial, 25.35
Joinder of state as indispensable party, 25.3
Severed trial, motion for new trial following, 27.20
Summary judgment decision, motion for new trial after, 29.79, 29.82

NONRESIDENTS. *See* Residence and Domicile

NONSUIT
See also Dismissal of Actions
Declaratory relief actions, 24.42
Summary judgment compared, 29.18

NOTARIES
Affidavits, oath before notary, 29.48
Duties, 23.36, 23.39, 23.43

NOTES
Consent judgment, use of, 34.2
Signatures, judicial notice of, 29.55

NOTICES
Appeals. *See* Appeals
Appearance, notice of, 31.12
Class action under Consumer Legal Remedies Act, notice of proposed dismissal of, 31.73
Consolidation of actions by persons who have given stop notices, 27.4
Coordination. *See* Coordination of Actions
Default and default judgments. *See* Default and Default Judgments
Dismissal of action, entry of notice of, 31.89
Dismissal of action on consent of parties, notice of, 31.78, 31.81, 31.83–31.84, 31.87
Eminent domain proceedings, notice of abandonment of, 31.72, 31.74
Ex parte application for orders, notice of, 23.65
Intervention, granting ex parte applications for orders without notice to adverse parties, 25.38
Judicial notice. *See* Judicial Notice
Jury trial, notice of, 26.31
Jury trial, notice of waiver of, 26.34
Motions. *See* Motions, Notice of
Opposing motion on ground of insufficient notice, 23.51
Pretrial conference, notice of, 26.64, 26.76
Pretrial conference order, notice of correction or modification of, 26.70
Readiness, certificate of
 Eligibility to file, notice of, 26.18–26.20, 26.25
 Filing after notification by court, 26.1
Ruling on motion, notice of, 23.58; *form*, 23.59
Ruling on motion, waiver of notice of, 23.61
Service. *See* Service of Process and Papers
Settlement. *See* Settlement
Show cause order, notice of application for, 23.68
Small claims proceedings, notice of continuance of, 26.6
Statutory basis, 23.2
Summary judgment. *See* Summary Judgment
Transfer of actions
 Costs and fees, notice of order for payment of, 31.42–31.43
 Hearing, notice of, 28.49
Trial, notice of, 26.3, 26.5, 26.54–26.55, 26.74, 30.2, 30.7, 31.40
Trial setting conference, notice of, 26.49, 26.76

OATH AND AFFIRMATION
See also Notaries
Affidavits, formal requirements of, 29.48
Default proceedings
 Costs, oath verifying, 30.27
 Summons served by publication, examining plaintiff under oath, 30.54
Trial, commencement on administration of oath or affirmation, 31.75

INDEX 600

OBSCENE MATERIALS
Declaratory relief action, 24.24

OFFER TO ALLOW JUDGMENT. *See* Settlement

OIL AND GAS
Slant-drilling causing subsurface trespass, intervention by adjoining landowners, 25.18

OPINIONS
Admissibility as evidence, 29.51
Memorandum of points and authorities, citing court opinions in, 23.33

ORDERS
See also Motions
Appeals generally, 23.62
Consent judgment, orders for entry of, *forms*, 34.10–34.11
Consolidation. *See* Consolidation of Actions
Continuance and order removing case from calendar distinguished, 26.83
Coordination. *See* Coordination of Actions
Default and default judgments. *See* Default and Default Judgments
Defined, 23.1, 23.58
Dismissal of actions. *See* Dismissal of Actions
Effectiveness, time of, 23.58
Ex parte. *See* Ex Parte Proceedings
Hearing on motion, application for order and order extending time for, 23.14; *form*, 23.16
Hearing on motion, application for order and order shortening time for, 23.12; *form*, 23.13
Intervention. *See* Intervention of Parties
Joinder of parties. *See* Joinder of Parties
Motion, order granting or denying, *form*, 23.60
Moving papers, attaching proposed order to, 23.46
Nature of order sought, statement in notice of motion, 23.19, 23.22
New trial order, dismissal for failure to try action within three years of affirmation of, 31.3, 31.33
Party status of applicant, 23.3
Pretrial conference orders. *See* Setting Case for Trial
Readiness certificate, order vacating, 26.26
Removal of case from calendar, order for, 26.86
Removal of case from civil active list, order for, 26.66
Severance. *See* Severance of Actions
Show cause orders. *See* Show Cause Orders
Statutory basis, 23.2
Stop work orders. *See* Stop Work Orders
Summary judgment. *See* Summary Judgment
Transfer fees and costs, order for payment of, 31.42–31.43
Trial continuance motion, obtaining order shortening time for service of, 26.97
Trial continuance, order for, 26.50, 26.91
Trial continuance, relief from order denying, 26.102
Trial date, order setting, 26.52–26.55
Trial setting order, inclusion of order for further discovery in, 26.42
Vacating. *See* Vacating and Setting Aside

OTHER STATES
Declarations and affidavits, use of, 23.36
Declaratory relief action relating to real property outside state, 24.27–24.28

OTHER STATES—*cont.*

Reports of other jurisdictions, presenting in memorandum of points and authorities, 23.33

OWNERSHIP AND POSSESSION

Declaratory relief action, 24.13
Default procedures, actions relating to real or personal property, 30.54, 30.62
Intervention in actions relating to real or personal property, 25.2, 25.4, 25.6, 25.10, 25.15, 25.23, 25.27–25.28, 25.31

PARENT AND CHILD

Consolidation of actions to recover damages and for wrongful death, 27.4
Declaratory relief, 24.3, 24.7

PARTIES

Adverse parties
  Absence from trial, effect of, 26.55, 26.74
  Appearance, effect of, 23.6
  Ex parte applications, effect of, 23.5, 25.38
  Ex parte orders, notice by adverse party of opposition to, 23.65
  Excusable neglect, delay affecting adverse party, 30.62, 30.65
  Grounds of motions, defining issues for adverse party and court, 23.23
  Notice of motion, designation of opposing party in, 29.35
  Oral ruling on motion, serving on adverse party, 23.61
  Settlement negotiations. *See* Settlement
  Show cause order, notice to adverse party of application for, 23.68
  Striking pleadings in default proceedings, notice to adverse party, 30.17

Adverse parties—*cont.*
  Trial continuance, payment of costs to adverse party, 26.93, 26.99
Appearances. *See* Appearances
Consent. *See* Consent; Consent Judgment
Continuance of trial due to illness or unavailability of party, 26.88–26.89, 26.91, 26.93
Coordination of actions for convenience of parties, 28.5
Declaratory relief actions, 24.8, 24.16, 24.27, 24.29
Defined, 28.29
Intervention. *See* Intervention of Parties
Joinder. *See* Joinder of Parties
Jury trial, reliance on other party's demand, 26.34
Multiple parties. *See* Multiple Parties
Orders, party status of applicants for, 23.3
Sole party in interest, effect on dismissal, 31.65, 31.73

PARTNERSHIPS

Declaratory relief action, determining creation of partnership by, 24.8
Limited partnerships. *See* Limited Partnerships

PAYMENT

See also Costs; Fees
Jury fees in in forma pauperis proceedings, 26.33
Nonsettling defendants, relief against overpayment, 33.32
Settlement agreement, terms of payment in, 34.9
Statements in declarations for introduction of business records, 29.61
Transfer fees and costs, failure to pay. *See* Dismissal of Actions

INDEX 602

PENALTIES
Settlement conference, sanctions for nonappearance at, 33.17, 33.22–33.23, 33.27
Summary judgment proceedings, sanctions for bad faith affidavits in, 29.8, 29.30, 29.74
Trial setting conference, sanctions for disregarding rules of, 26.45–26.46

PENDING ACTIONS AND PROCEEDINGS
Consolidation through coordination procedure, 27.1, 27.10
Coordination proceeding, transmittal and service of papers during pendency of, 28.7–28.9
Intervention, dismissal of action during pendency of noticed motion for, 25.38, 25.44

PERFORMANCE
Lease option, declaratory relief action to determine performance of, 24.27
Specific performance. *See* Specific Performance

PERMITS. *See* Licenses and Permits

PERSONAL INJURIES
Consolidation of actions, 27.4, 31.25
Coordination of actions, 28.6
Declaratory relief actions, 24.7, 24.27, 24.35
Default, conditions for, 30.36
Factual statements in release, 33.30
Five-year trial requirement, exception, 31.22, 31.24
General release obtained from injured person, time effect of, 33.29
Jury trial, right to, 26.28
Settlement, factors affecting, 33.1, 33.3–33.4, 33.20–33.21, 33.29–33.30

Severance of actions, 27.5
Severance of cross-complaint from main action, 26.10

PERSONAL PROPERTY
Declaratory relief, 24.3
Defined, 24.8
Intervention in actions relating to personal property, 25.4, 25.6, 25.10, 25.15, 25.27, 25.31
Ownership and possession. *See* Ownership and Possession
Recovery action, right to jury trial, 26.28
Third party claims, 25.6

PERSONAL REPRESENTATIVES
Personal injury action, appointment of personal representative in, 31.22
Service of process on, 31.9

PETITIONS
Coordination. *See* Coordination of Actions
Mandate. *See* Mandate
Prohibition. *See* Prohibition

PHYSICAL EXAMINATIONS. *See* Medical Examinations

POINTS AND AUTHORITIES. *See* Memorandum of Points and Authorities

POLICE. *See* Sheriffs and Other Peace Officers

PORNOGRAPHY. *See* Obscene Materials

POSTPONEMENT OF PROCEEDINGS. *See* Continuance

PRAYERS
Declaratory relief action, contents of prayer, 24.30

PREJUDICE

Bias and prejudice. *See* Bias and Prejudice

Dismissal of actions. *See* Dismissal of Actions

PRESUMPTIONS

Declarations made on personal knowledge, 29.49

Directed verdict, use of legitimate inferences, 29.18

General release obtained from injured person, time effect of, 33.29

Service of process, effect of different names, 30.24

Settlement, authority of attorney, 33.6, 34.6

Several defendants, default judgment against, 30.39

Summary judgment motion, ruling on, 29.10, 29.18

Written instruments, presumption of truth of recitals in, 29.60

PRETRIAL PROCEEDINGS

Conferences. *See* Setting Case for Trial

Coordination of Actions. *See* Coordination of Actions

Declaratory relief actions generally, 24.38

Informal severance motions, judicial attitude toward, 27.17

Setting case for trial. *See* Setting Case for Trial

Summary judgment motion, value of, 29.2

PRINCIPAL AND AGENT

Attorney-client relationship, effect on settlement, 33.6, 33.25

Quiet title action, third party as undisclosed agent of plaintiff's husband, 25.26

PRIOR JUDGMENT. *See* Res Judicata

PROBATE

See also Heirship; Wills

Dismissal statute, applicability, 31.65, 31.73

PROHIBITION

Default proceedings, use of writ, 30.9, 30.32, 30.40

Dismissal of actions, use of writ, 31.53, 31.71, 31.89

Jury trial in prohibition proceedings, 26.29

Pretrial conference order, interlocutory review by prohibition, 26.72

Trial continuance, relief from order denying, 26.102

PUBLIC WORKS

Declaratory relief action to determine validity of contracts, 24.3

PUBLICATION

Service by. *See* Default and Default Judgments

QUASHING. *See* Service of Process and Papers

QUESTIONS OF LAW AND FACT

Absence of adverse party from trial, effect of, 26.55, 26.74

Amicus, limitation on, 25.9

Consolidation of actions involving common questions, 27.1, 27.8, 27.11, 27.13–27.16

Coordination of actions, 25.8, 27.10, 28.1, 28.5, 28.15, 28.52

Declaratory relief actions, resolution of disputes in, 24.40, 24.43

Five-year trial requirement, effect of admission by defendant, 31.30

Intervention in cases involving common questions, 25.10

INDEX 604

QUESTIONS OF LAW AND FACT—*cont.*

Pretrial conference, statement of factual and legal contentions, 26.58, 26.69
Summary judgment motion, use of, 29.3–29.4, 29.6–29.7, 29.9, 29.16, 29.19–29.20, 29.79, 29.85

QUIETING TITLE TO REAL PROPERTY

Consolidation of actions, 27.4
Declaratory relief, 24.3
Default judgments, 30.9, 30.27
Equitable action, 26.28
Intervention of parties, 25.21, 25.23, 25.26

QUO WARRANTO

Declaratory relief, 24.3, 24.13, 24.26

READINESS, CERTIFICATE OF. *See* Setting Case for Trial

REAL PARTY IN INTEREST

Intervention, right of, 25.11

REAL PROPERTY

Access rights. *See* Access Rights
Adjoining landowners. *See* Adjoining Landowners
Consent judgment, recording as lien against specific property, 34.2, 34.5
Coordination of actions, 28.6
Declaratory relief actions, 24.3, 24.7, 24.10–24.11, 24.27–24.29
Defined, 24.8
Eminent domain. *See* Eminent Domain
Intervention in actions relating to, 25.2, 25.4, 25.15, 25.23, 25.27–25.28
Ownership and possession. *See* Ownership and Possession

Quieting title. *See* Quieting Title to Real Property
Recovery action, right to jury trial, 26.28
Reestablishment of destroyed land records, prohibition of default judgment, 30.9
Title. *See* Title

RECORDS AND RECORDINGS

See also Reports
Authentication of documents, 29.55–29.56, 29.63
Best evidence rule, 29.57–29.58
Books, documents, and records, notice to produce in summary judgment proceedings, 29.57; *form*, 29.59
Business records as exception to hearsay rule, 29.52, 29.60–29.61
Business records, statements for introduction of, 29.61
Consent judgment, recording as lien against specific property, 34.2, 34.5
Default judgment by clerk, papers required for, 30.41–30.46
Depository of evidentiary materials, establishment by coordination trial judge, 28.45
Judicial notice of public records and documents, 23.45, 29.46
Lost. *See* Lost Papers
Pretrial conference, recording agreements and stipulations at, 26.39, 26.56
Reestablishment of destroyed land records, prohibition of default judgment, 30.9
Summary judgment proceedings, identifying supporting papers in, 29.38

REES-LEVERING ACT

Default proceedings, declaration regarding venue, 30.18, 30.21, 30.25; *form*, 30.29

REFEREES
Pretrial conference, matters considered at, 26.66

RELEASE
Defined, 33.29
Drafting, 33.30
Settlement. *See* Settlement
Summary judgment proceedings, special defense, 29.24

REMEDIES. *See* Adequacy of Legal Remedy

REMITTITUR
Dismissal for failure to try case within three years of filing, 31.2–31.3

RENEWED MOTIONS. *See* Motions

REPORTER'S TRANSCRIPTS. *See* Transcripts

REPORTS
See also Records and Recordings
Coordination determination, reporting delay in, 28.38
Settlement actions, use of medical reports in personal injury cases, 33.20–33.21
Summary judgment proceedings, reports of physical or mental examinations in, 29.44, 29.66

RESCISSION AND RESTITUTION
Equitable action, 26.28
Release as subject to rescission, 33.29

RESETTING CASE FOR TRIAL. *See* Setting Case for Trial

RESIDENCE AND DOMICILE
Access rights. *See* Access Rights
Nonresidents
  Default proceedings, 30.54
  Small claims defendants residing outside county of filing, 26.6
Tax questions, use of declaratory relief, 24.3, 24.7

RES JUDICATA
Consent judgment, effect of, 34.3
Declaratory judgment, effect of, 24.43
Default judgment, court's decision on motion to set aside, 30.72
Default judgment defined, 30.3
Dismissal statutes, judgments rendered under, 31.6, 31.67, 31.70
Filing late pleading, effect of res judicata, 26.19
Intervention determination, appellate review of, 25.51
Stay of proceedings, res judicata effect of, 28.11, 28.26
Summary judgment proceedings, special defense in, 29.20, 29.24

RETRIAL
Intervention by nonparty before retrial, 25.35

RIPARIAN RIGHTS
Intervention of parties, 25.23

ROADS. *See* Streets, Roads, and Highways

RULINGS ON MOTIONS. *See* Motions

SANCTIONS. *See* Penalties

SATURDAYS, SUNDAYS, AND HOLIDAYS
Notice of motion, calculating time within which to serve, 23.9

INDEX

SEPARATE TRIAL. See Severance of Actions

SERVICE OF PROCESS AND PAPERS
Default and default judgments. See Default and Default Judgments
Dismissal statutes, effect of, 31.1
Foreign corporation as defendant, 31.22, 31.26
Mail, service by
Notice of motions, 23.10, 23.25, 23.47
  Statutory construction, 29.67
Notices and other papers
  At-issue memorandum, 26.13, 26.20, 26.31
  At-issue memorandum, countermemoranda to, 26.14, 26.31
  Certificate of readiness, 26.24
  Certificate of readiness, notice of eligibility to file, 26.18, 26.20
  Certificate of readiness, notice of motion to vacate, 26.27
  Change in setting case, notice of motion for, 26.27
  Coordination of actions, papers relating to, 28.7–28.9, 28.16–28.18, 28.22–28.23, 28.25–28.26, 28.29, 28.33, 28.37, 28.39–28.41, 28.55–28.56
  Coordination of add-on case, papers relating to, 28.53–28.54
  Dismissal motion, papers relating to, 31.56–31.57
  Ex parte orders, applications for, 23.65–23.66
  Intervention complaint and related papers, 25.55–25.56
Jury trial, demand for, 26.34
Jury trial, notice of motion for, 26.15, 26.29
  Memorandum of points and authorities, 23.26, 23.52, 23.54
  Memorandum to set, 26.5, 26.34

Jury trial, demand for—*cont.*
  Motions generally, notice of. See Motions, Notice of
  Offers to allow judgment in settlement actions, papers relating to, 33.11–33.14
  Opposition papers, 23.52, 23.54
  Pretrial conference order, 26.70
  Proof of service, 23.47
  Ruling on motion, notice of, 23.58–23.59, 23.61
  Show cause order, 23.67–23.69
  Small claims court, order to appear, 26.6
  Summary judgment motion, 23.9, 29.12, 29.67
  Summary judgment motion, motion to amend, 29.29
  Summary judgment proceedings, service of subpena duces tecum, 29.57
  Transfer order, 28.50
  Trial, notice of, 26.3
  Trial setting conference service of, 26.97
  Trial, notice of, 26.3
  Trial setting conference memorandum, 26.53–26.54
  Trial setting conference, notice of, 26.49
  Trial setting order, 26.54–26.55
Pretrial conference, determining parties not served, 26.66
Quashing service
  Default proceedings, 30.15, 30.19
  Opposing motion on merits, alternative to, 23.8
Substituted service on concealed defendant, 31.22
Three years, failure to service and return summons within. See Dismissal of Actions

SERVICEMEN AND VETERANS
Default proceedings, declaration of nonmilitary status in, 30.9, 30.22, 30.28; *form*, 30.29
Trial continuance or delay, party in armed forces, 26.93, 31.25

SETTING ASIDE. *See* Vacating and Setting Aside

SETTING CASE FOR TRIAL
See also Pretrial Proceedings
Advancing. *See* Advancement of Proceedings
At-issue memorandum
  Amending, 26.2
  Combined at-issue memorandum and certificate of readiness, 26.18, 26.23
  Countermemoranda, 26.14–26.15, 26.31, 26.61
  Essential elements, 26.10
  Filing, 26.1–26.2, 26.9, 26.18, 26.20, 26.62, 31.35–31.36
  Form, 26.13
  Jury trial, demand for, 26.11–26.12, 26.15, 26.30–26.31
  Nature and function, 26.8
  New memorandum, filing after removal of case from civil active list, 26.45–26.46, 26.78
  Pretrial conference, requesting, 26.61–26.62
  Severing unanswered cross-complaint before filing, 26.10
  Striking, 26.14, 26.25
Basic steps, superior court trials, 26.1
Certificate of readiness. *See* Readiness, Certificate of, below
Changing setting on noticed motion, 26.25–26.27, 26.51
  Manner of selecting cases, 26.18–26.20, 26.25, 26.48, 26.59, 26.63
  Municipal and justice courts, procedure in, 26.5
  Nonappearance at trial setting conference, removal of case for, 26.40, 26.45
  Order at pretrial conference removing case from list, 26.66
  Priorities, 26.4–26.5, 26.18–26.20, 26.25, 26.48, 26.63, 26.74, 26.77–26.78, 26.84

Changing setting on noticed motion—*cont.*
  Purpose, 26.9
  Removal of case resulting from motion to strike at-issue memorandum, 26.14
  Smaller counties, trial setting process, 26.3
  Superior court rules, placing case on civil active list, 26.1
Continuance. *See* Continuance
Coordination of actions. *See* Coordination of Actions
Date of trial, setting
  Advancing, 26.76
  Basic considerations, 26.43, 26.84
  Notice of trial date, 26.3, 26.5, 26.74
  Order, 26.52–26.55
  Pretrial conference, setting for trial after, 26.74
  Pretrial order, stating time and place of trial in, 26.69
  Restrictions, 26.51
Declaratory relief actions, 24.39
Five-year requirement for bringing case to trial, basic requirements, 31.19–31.20
Informal severance motions, judicial attitude toward, 27.17
Jury trial, demand for. *See* Juries and Verdicts
Memorandum to set
  Filing and serving, 26.5, 26.34
  Municipal and justice courts, procedure in, 26.5
Mistrial. *See* Mistrial
Municipal and justice courts, 26.5
Notices. *See* Notices
Preliminary trial conference. *See* Coordination of Actions
Pretrial conference
  At-issue memorandum, requesting conference after filing of, 26.62
  At-issue memorandum, requesting conference in, 26.61
  Certificate of readiness, effect of filing, 26.19–26.20, 26.25

SETTING CASE—*cont.*
Pretrial conference—*cont.*
  Conduct, 26.65
  Continuance. *See* Continuance
  Coordination proceedings. *See* Coordination of Actions
  Countermemorandum, requesting conference by, 26.14
  Date of trial, setting. *See* Date of trial, setting, above
  Jury trial, raising issue of, 26.15
  Local variations and changes, 26.3, 26.7, 26.57–26.59, 26.62, 26.66
  Matters considered at conference, 26.66
  Notice, 26.64, 26.76
  Orders
    Generally, 26.39, 26.56, 26.59, 26.65
    Content, 26.69
    Corrections and modifications, 26.70, 26.72–26.73
    Noncompliance, effect of, 26.71
    Preparation, 26.68
    Review, 26.72–26.73
    Service and filing, 26.70
    Subsequent proceedings, effect on, 26.73
  Preparing for, 26.58
  Purpose, 26.39, 26.56, 26.73
  Reference at trial, restriction on, 26.73
  Requesting after receipt of notice of trial setting conference, 26.49
  Resetting. *See* Resetting, below
  Sanctions for disregard of rules, 26.58
  Selecting cases, 26.59–26.63
  Short cause exemption, 26.1–26.2, 26.38, 26.57
  Shortening of time for. *See* Advancement of Proceedings
  Specially setting. *See* Specially setting, below
  Statutory authority, 26.57

Pretrial conference—*cont.*
  Summary judgment, alternative to, 26.60, 29.5
  Superior court rules, 26.1, 26.57
  Trial-ready list, priority established by, 26.19, 26.25
  Trial setting conference, relationship to, 26.39, 26.43, 26.48, 26.56, 26.59
Readiness, certificate of
  Combined at-issue memorandum and certificate of readiness, 26.18, 26.23
  Counties where required, 26.17
  Curing deficiencies of prematurely filed certificate, 26.26
  Eligibility to file, notice of, 26.18–26.20, 26.25
  Essential elements, 26.22
  Filing, 26.1, 26.9, 26.11, 26.16, 26.18–26.21, 26.24–26.25
  Form, 26.23
  Local variations and changes, 26.22
  Nature and purpose, 26.16
  Persons who may prepare, 26.21
  Pretrial conference, requesting, 26.62
  Smaller counties, procedure in, 26.3
  Striking, 26.14, 26.25
  Vacating, 26.25–26.27
Resetting
  Generally, 26.76, 26.78–26.79
  Declaration in support of motion, *form*, 26.82
  Notice of motion, 26.50, 26.80; *form*, 26.81
  Priority, 26.84
Settlement conference. *See* Settlement
Short causes
  Agreed statement of facts, effect of, 32.6
  Defined, 26.2
  Exemption from conferences, 26.1–26.2, 26.38, 26.57
  Local variations and changes, 26.3, 26.38

SETTING CASE—*cont.*

Small claims courts, 26.6
Specially setting
  Generally, 26.76–26.77, 26.79
  Declaration in support of motion, *form*, 26.82
  Motions to advance and to specially set distinguished, 26.77
  Notice of motion, 26.50, 26.80; *form*, 26.81
  Priority, 26.5
Superior courts, 26.1–26.4
Trial-ready list, 26.19, 26.25
Trial setting conference
  Advancing. *See* Advancement of Proceedings
  Appearance by parties and counsel, 26.40–26.42, 26.45–26.46, 26.48, 26.78
  Certificate of readiness, effect of filing, 26.19–26.20, 26.25
  Combined notice of trial setting conference and invitation to attend settlement conference, 26.49
  Conflicts between original memorandum and counter-memorandum, resolving, 26.14
  Continuance, 26.50
  Date of conference, setting, 26.48
  Date of trial, setting. *See* Date of trial, setting, above
  Jury trial, raising issue of, 26.15
  Local variations and changes, 26.3, 26.7, 26.38, 26.41–26.42, 26.46–26.47, 26.81
  Matters considered at conference, 26.43–26.44
  Notice, 26.49
  Order, 26.52–26.55
  Pretrial conference, relationship to, 26.39, 26.43, 26.48, 26.56, 26.59
  Procedures generally, 26.47
  Purpose, 26.38, 26.39
  Resetting. *See* Resetting, above

Trial setting conference—*cont.*
  Sanctions for disregard of rules, 26.45–26.46
  Short cause exemption, 26.1–26.2, 26.38, 26.57
  Shortening of time for. *See* Advancement of Proceedings
  Specially setting. *See* Specially setting, above
  Superior court rules, 26.1
  Trial-ready list, priority established by, 26.19
Trial setting conference memorandum, 26.53–26.54

SETTLEMENT
  See also Compromise
Advantages, 33.2
Adverse counsel, negotiations with, 33.8, 33.13
Adverse party, direct negotiations with, 33.7, 33.9
Agreement
  Client's repudiation of attorney's agreement, 33.6
  Consent judgment, 33.28, 34.2, 34.5, 34.8–34.9
  Continuance of trial setting conference to consummate agreement, 26.50
  Essential elements, 33.1, 33.28
  Judge, role of, 33.24
  Notification to court, 33.31
  Preliminary agreement, 33.26
  Release and dismissal. *See* Release and dismissal, below
  Sliding scale agreement with fewer than all defendants, 33.32
Attorney's authority, 33,1, 33.6, 33.19, 34.6
Class action under Consumer Legal Remedies Act, settlement of, 31.73
Conference
  Generally, 26.1
  Attorneys for plaintiff and defendant, duties of, 33.25–33.26

INDEX

SETTLEMENT—*cont.*
Conference—*cont.*
  Authority, Rules of Court, 26.75, 33.16
  Combined notice of trial setting conference and invitation to attend settlement conference, 26.49
  Conduct of conference generally, 33.23–33.26
  Continuance, 33.18
  Good faith discussions prior to conference, 33.19
  Information and documents required, 33.21
  Judge, limitation on disclosures to, 33.6, 33.25
  Judge, role of, 33.2, 33.24
  Mandatory conference, 26.43, 26.47, 26.57, 26.60, 26.75, 33.16–33.18
  Nonappearance, sanctions for, 33.17, 33.22–33.23, 33.27
  Preparation by attorney, 33.19
  Reading settlement into minutes, 33.3
  Short cause exemption, 26.2
  Time for setting, 26.43, 26.52, 26.60, 33.16–33.17
  Voluntary conference, 33.16
  Written statement of special and general damages, 33.20–33.21
Confidentiality, 33.5–33.6, 33.25
Consent judgment. *See* Consent Judgment
Coordination of actions, effect of, 28.5
Default, provision in settlement agreement for, 34.7
Defined, 33.1
Delaying factors, 33.3
Deposited jury fees, refund of, 26.33
Dismissal of action. *See* Release and dismissal, below
Evaluation factors, 33.4
Fewer than all defendants, settlement with, 33.32
Judgment creditor's lien, effect on compromise or settlement, 25.5, 25.14
Notices
  Duty to notify court of settlement, 33.31
  Forfeiture of jury fees, notice to clerk to avoid, 26.33
  Offer to allow judgment, notice of acceptance of, 33.11
  Settlement conference, notice of acceptance of invitation to, 33.16
  Settlement conference, notification of inability to attend, 33.23
Offer to allow judgment
  Defendant's offer, 33.10, 33.14; *form,* 33.15
  Plaintiff's offer, 33.10, 33.12; *form,* 33.13
  Service and filing of papers, 33.11–33.14
  Statutory authority, 33.10
Pretrial conference, matters considered at, 26.66
Pretrial order, reference to settlement in, 26.69
Release and dismissal
  Defined, 33.29
  Drafting release, 33.30
  Fewer than all defendants, settlement with, 33.32
  Private settlements, 33.5
  Settlement defined, 33.1
Stipulation that trial go off calendar, settlement as precondition to, 26.92
Summary judgment, settlement as alternative to, 29.5
Trial setting conference, informal settlement negotiations at, 26.42
Written statements and brochures, use of, 33.9

SEVERANCE OF ACTIONS
  See also Consolidation of Actions
Coordination petition, granting in part, 28.35
Coordination trial judge, powers of, 28.42
Cross-complaints. *See* Cross-Complaints
Five-year trial requirement, action involving multiple defendants, 31.27
Hybrid actions, jury trial on severable legal issues, 26.28
Judgment, entry of, 27.20
Judicial attitude, 27.9
Judicial discretion, 27.2–27.3, 27.12, 27.21
Liability issue. *See* Damages
Mandatory severance, examples, 27.5
Motion for severance
  Declaration in support of, 27.18
  Notice of, 27.17; *form*, 27.18
  Order granting motion, 27.5, 27.17; *form*, 27.19
  Preliminary determinations, 27.12
Nature and purpose, 27.2
Orders
  Appealability of order granting or denying, 27.21
  Motion for severance, order granting, 27.5, 27.17; *form*, 27.19
  Summary judgment, effect of severance order on, 29.83
  Vacation of, 27.11
Posttrial procedure, 27.20
Severed issues, treatment of, 27.7
Statute of limitations. *See* Limitation of Actions
Statutory authority, 27.3, 27.5, 27.7
Summary judgment, effect of severance order on finality of, 29.83
Trial continuance, severance as alternative to, 26.101

SHAM ACTIONS
Dismissal, 29.3, 29.14, 31.2
Summary judgment procedure, 29.3, 29.14–29.15, 29.23, 29.51

SHARES AND SHAREHOLDERS. *See* Corporations

SHERIFFS AND OTHER PEACE OFFICERS
Police officers as expert witnesses, 33.12, 33.14

SHORT CAUSES. *See* Setting Case for Trial

SHORTENING OF TIME. *See* Advancement of Proceedings; Time

SHOW CAUSE ORDERS
Application for order and order, *form*, 23.69
Basic procedure, 23.67–23.68
Dismissal of case for failure to file required documents, 26.20, 26.46
Intervention. *See* Intervention of Parties
Notice of application, 23.68
Purpose, 23.6, 23.8

SIGNATURES
Affidavits, 23.36, 23.43
Agreed case, submission of, 32.4
Authentication of documents by witnesses and experts, 29.55–29.56
Declarations, 23.36, 23.42
Depositions, 29.63
Memorandum of points and authorities, 23.35
Notice of motion, 23.25, 23.27
Orders, 23.46, 23.60–23.61
Readiness, certificate of, 26.21
Settlement actions
  Offers and acceptances, 33.6, 33.13

SIGNATURES—*cont.*
Settlement actions—*cont.*

Release, 33.30
Request for dismissal, 33.29
Stipulation for entry of judgment, 34.6, 34.9

SMALL CLAIMS COURTS
Default judgment, prohibition of, 30.9
Setting case for trial, 26.6

SPECIAL APPEARANCE. *See* Appearances

SPECIALLY SETTING CASE FOR TRIAL. *See* Setting Case for Trial

SPECIAL PROCEEDINGS
Dismissal statutes, applicability, 31.5, 31.65

SPECIFIC PERFORMANCE
Declaratory relief action, 24.43
Equitable action, 26.28

STANDING, DOCTRINE OF
Declaratory relief, effect of lack of standing to bring action, 24.18

STAY OF EXECUTION
Default judgment, order for stay of execution pending hearing, 30.63, 30.67; *form,* 30.68

STAY OF PROCEEDINGS
Coordination. *See* Coordination of Actions
Default procedures, 30.15, 30.18–30.19
Intervenor's request for stay, 25.38, 25.41

STIPULATED JUDGMENT. *See* Consent Judgment

STIPULATIONS
At-issue memorandum and certificate of readiness, stipulation affecting, 26.14, 26.25
Consent judgment. *See* Consent Judgment
Consolidation of actions, stipulation for, 27.13
Continuance of trial, stipulation for, 26.92–26.93, 26.96
Court commissioner, hearing of contested matters by, 31.52
Default procedures, 30.12, 30.16, 30.18
Extension of time, stipulations for. *See* Time
Jury trial, stipulation for, 26.31, 26.52
Motion, stipulation setting new hearing date on, 23.14; *form,* 23.15
Notice of motion, stipulation extending time to serve, 23.14; *form,* 23.15
Personal Appearance at Trial Setting Conference, Stipulation/Declaration in Lieu of, 26.41, 26.46
Pretrial conference, stipulations at, 26.39, 26.56, 26.58, 26.60, 26.66
Removal of case from calendar, stipulation for, 26.86
Settlement conference, rule affecting stipulation for continuance of, 33.18
Settlement discussion stipulations as alternative to summary judgment, 29.5
Submitted case. *See* Submitted Case
Summary judgment proceedings, 29.21, 29.44–29.45, 29.83
Three-year trial requirement, 31.33
Transfer of action, effect of stipulation on payment of transfer fees and costs, 31.63
Trial date, shortening by stipulation, 26.3

STIPULATIONS—*cont.*

Trial date, stipulation waiving notice of, 26.55

Two-year trial requirement, stipulation waiving, 31.29

STOP WORK ORDERS

Consolidation of actions by persons who have given stop notices, 27.4

STREETS, ROADS, AND HIGHWAYS

Declaratory relief, 24.3

STRIKING. *See* Motions to Strike

SUBMITTED CASE

Agreed case, submission of, 32.2; *form*, 32.4

Agreed statement of facts and agreed case distinguished, 32.6

Appeal rights, 32.1–32.2, 32.4

Declaration of good faith
 Form, 32.5
 Nature of requirement, 32.1, 32.3

Five-year trial requirement, 31.30

Judgment, entry of, 32.1–32.2

Jurisdictional requirements, 32.1–32.2

Nonstatutory nature of procedure, submission after action filed, 32.6

Statement of agreed facts, 31.30, 32.2, 32.6

Statutory authority, submission without filing action, 32.1

Stipulations
 Agreed facts, stipulation to, 32.2, 32.6; *form*, 32.7
 Procedural and remedial matters, 32.4

SUBPENAS

Documents controlled by nonparties, obtaining by subpena duces tecum, 23.44

Hearing on motion to quash subpena duces tecum, effect of, 31.75

Summary judgment proceedings, service of subpena duces tecum, 29.57

SUBROGATION

Insurer as prospective subrogee, effect on intervention, 25.13

SUBSTANCE, FORM VERSUS.
See Form Versus Substance

SUCCESSORS IN INTEREST

Intervention by, 25.12

SUMMARY ADJUDICATION OF ISSUES. *See* Summary Judgment

SUMMARY JUDGMENT

Adjudication of specific issues. *See* Summary adjudication of issues, below

Admissibility of evidence. *See* Evidence, below

Admissions
 Authentication of documents by admissions, 29.55–29.56
 Best evidence rule, overcoming by admissions, 29.57
 Credibility, 29.11, 29.21
 Requests for admissions, 29.5, 29.64
 Use generally, 29.29, 29.31, 29.44–29.45

Affidavits and declarations
 Authentication of documents, examples of statements in declarations, 29.56
 Bad faith affidavits and declarations, sanctions for, 29.8, 29.30, 29.74
 Best evidence rule, compliance of declarations with, 29.57–29.58

SUMMARY JUDGMENT—*cont.*
Affidavits and declarations—*cont.*
  Business records, statements in declarations for introduction of, 29.61
  Competence and personal knowledge requirements, 29.8, 29.49, 29.55
  Continuance, declarations in support of, 29.68
  Contradictory or inconsistent declarations, effect of, 29.44
  Counteraffidavits, 29.10, 29.25
  Counterdeclarations, 29.8, 29.29
  Court rules governing declarations, 23.40–23.41
  Defective pleading, correcting by declaration, 29.29
  Defects in, 29.33, 29.50, 29.86
  Denial or continuance of motion, declaration by opposing party, 29.28
  Different action, use of declaration filed in, 29.46
  Formal requirements, 29.48, 29.50
  General use, 29.3, 29.8, 29.11, 29.13, 29.16, 29.29, 29.44
  Identification of documents after filing supplemental or reply affidavit, 29.54
  Inadmissible conclusions in declarations, 29.50–29.51
  Inadmissible hearsay rule, 29.52
  Incorporation of document by reference in declaration, 29.54
  Statement of facts, reference to affidavits in, 29.42
  Supplemental affidavits and declarations, filing, 29.54, 29.68–29.69
Alternatives to, 26.60, 29.5, 29.14–29.20
Amendment of pleadings
  Continuance on ground of, 29.28–29.29, 29.31, 29.68
  Opposing party, action by, 29.28–29.29

Answers
  Generally, 29.31, 29.44, 29.64
  Amending, 29.29
  Judicial admissions, denials constituting, 29.45
  Motion to strike compared, 29.15
  Purpose, 29.12
  Unverified answer, effect of, 29.45
Appeals
  Generally, 29.16, 29.18, 29.38, 29.71
  Evidentiary objections, 29.86
  Final and nonfinal judgments, 29.83–29.84, 29.89
  New trial, effect of motion for, 29.79
  Nonmoving party, action by, 29.87
  Notice of appeal from order, construction of, 29.83
  Order denying summary judgment, review of, 29.89–29.90
  Rules, 29.85
  Statutory basis, 29.83
  Summary adjudication of issues, appealability, 29.88
Bibliography, 29.1
Bill of particulars, 29.5, 29.66
Burden of proof
  Defendant's burden, 29.22, 29.24
  Moving parties generally, 29.22, 29.25–29.27, 29.29
  Plaintiff's burden, 29.22–29.23
CCP §437, significant elements of, 29.2, 29.6–29.13
Complaints
  Amending, 29.29
  Materiality of facts. *See* Materiality of facts, below
Constitutionality, 29.4
Continuance of proceedings
  Generally, 29.28–29.29, 29.31
  Conditions for, 29.13
  Motion, manner of making, 29.68
Costs and attorneys' fees, 29.73–29.74
Cross-complaints, 29.12, 29.15, 29.84

SUMMARY JUDGMENT—*cont.*

Cross-motion, filing by opposing party, 29.27, 29.87
Declarations. *See* Affidavits and declarations, above
Declaratory judgment, obtaining, 24.37
Defenses
  Affirmative defenses generally, 29.22–29.24, 29.26
  Special defenses, 29.20, 29.24
Demurrers
  Defective pleadings, use of demurrer, 29.16, 29.29, 29.31
  Summary judgment motion as replacing "speaking demurrer," 29.3
Denial
  Affidavits and declarations, noncompliance with requirements of, 29.48
  Beneficial side effect, 29.30
  Continuance or amendment of pleadings, objective of opposing party, 29.28
  Information gained by discovery, use at trial, 29.31
  Lack of credibility as ground, 29.4, 29.11
  New trial, motion for, 29.79, 29.82
  Order denying summary judgment and granting summary adjudication of issues, *form*, 29.76
  Review of order, 29.89–29.90
  Statutory basis, 29.13
Depositions, use of, 29.38, 29.44, 29.63
Directed verdict compared, 29.18
Discovery. *See* Discovery
Documents (generally)
  Authentication, 29.55–29.56, 29.63
  Books, documents, and records, notice to produce, 29.57; *form*, 29.59
  Common problems, 29.53

Documents (generally)—*cont.*
  Defects in supporting papers, 29.33
  Identifying documents in notice of motion, 29.38, 29.54
  Incorporation of document by reference in declaration, 29.54
  Types of supporting papers, 29.3, 29.44
Evidence
  Admissible evidence standard, 29.8, 29.10, 29.21–29.26, 29.46, 29.50–29.52
  Authentication of documents, 29.55–29.56, 29.63
  Best evidence rule, compliance with, 29.57
  Burden of proof. *See* Burden of proof, above
  Continuance for purpose of obtaining additional evidence, 29.13, 29.68
  Defects, 29.33, 29.50, 29.86
  Effect of summary adjudications on evidence presented at trial, 29.7
  Hearsay
    Business records as exception to hearsay rule, 29.52, 29.60–29.61
    Incorporation by reference of documents containing hearsay statements, 29.54
  Inadmissible conclusions and opinions, 29.50–29.51, 29.54
  Inadmissible methods of proving facts, 29.44
  Inferences deducible from evidence, 29.10, 29.18
  Materiality of facts. *See* Materiality of facts, below
  New trial motion based on newly discovered evidence, 29.79
  Objections, asserting on appeal, 29.86
  Objections to introduction of all evidence, 29.16–29.17

INDEX

SUMMARY JUDGMENT—*cont.*
Evidence—*cont.*
  Secondary evidence, statements supporting introduction of, 29.58
  Statement of facts, 29.42–29.43, 29.46, 29.49
Facts
  Impermissible methods of proof, 29.44
  Materiality. *See* Materiality of facts, below
  Statement of facts, 29.42–29.43, 29.46, 29.49
Finality of judgment, 29.83–29.84, 29.89
Fraud as ground for relief from judgment, 29.81, 29.88
Granting motion as constituting trial, 31.19
Grounds, statement of, 29.36
Hearing on motion
  See also Notice of motion, below
  Agreed statement of facts, effect of, 32.6
  Amendment opposing motion, hearing on, 29.29
  Continuance. *See* Continuance of proceedings, above
  Original documents, examination of, 29.57
  Time, 29.12, 29.29, 29.57, 29.59
Interrogatories, use of, 29.38, 29.44, 29.64
Judgment notwithstanding verdict compared, 29.18
Judgment on the pleadings compared, 29.16, 29.29
Judgment on the pleadings, summary motion combined with, 29.45
Judgment under CCP §631.8 compared, 29.19
Judicial notice
  Generally, 29.33, 29.44
  Mandatory and permissible notice, 29.46

Request for, *form*, 29.47
Signatures, similarity of, 29.55
Late filings, 29.69
Materiality of facts
  Disputes, 29.9, 29.16, 29.20–29.21
  Gathering facts, 29.30, 29.87
  No triable issue of material fact as ground for granting motion, 29.3, 29.6, 29.11, 29.15, 29.19, 29.21, 29.23–29.26, 29.85
Medical reports, use of, 29.44, 29.66
Memorandum of points and authorities, 29.41–29.43, 29.46, 29.69
Methods of making motion, 29.7
Mistake, inadvertence, surprise, or excusable neglect as grounds for relief from judgment, 29.80–29.82, 29.88
New trial, motion for, 29.79, 29.82
Nonstatutory motions for relief from judgment, improper use of, 29.82
Nonsuit compared, 29.18
Notice of motion
  Defects in, 29.32
  Documents supporting motion, identification of, 29.38, 29.54, 29.69
  Essential elements, 29.34
  Memorandum of points and authorities, filing, 29.41–29.43, 29.46, 29.69
  Nature of order sought, specifying, 29.37
  Opposing party, designation of, 29.35
  Reopening submitted matter, 29.69
  Service and filing, 23.9, 29.12, 29.67
  Summary adjudication of issues, 29.3, 29.7; *forms*, 29.39–29.40

SUMMARY JUDGMENT—*cont.*
Notice of motion—*cont.*
Summary judgment or summary adjudication of issues, 29.3, 29.7; *form*, 29.39
Notices
Books, documents, and records, notice to produce, 29.57; *form*, 29.59
Judicial notice. *See* Judicial notice, above
Motions. *See* Notice of motion, above
Orders, construction of notice of appeal from, 29.83
Objectives of moving party, 29.21
Oral argument, permissibility, 29.70
Orders and judgments
Appeals. *See* Appeals, above
CCP §437c, judgment by court under, *form*, 29.78
Contents, 29.71
Denying summary judgment and granting summary adjudication of issues, *form*, 29.76
Entry of summary judgment, order for, *form*, 29.75
Nature of order sought, specifying, 29.37
Summary adjudication of issues, orders granting, 29.3, 29.7, 29.22, 29.37; *forms*, 29.76–29.77
Types of judgments, 29.72
Vacating or setting aside, 29.79–29.82, 29.88
Partial summary judgment, 29.3, 31.19
Personal knowledge requirements, 29.8, 29.49, 29.55
Pretrial conference compared, 26.60, 29.5
Purposes of motion, 29.3
Renewal of motion, 29.90
Reopening submitted matter, motion for, 29.69

Res judicata as special defense, 29.20, 29.24
Review of pleadings. *See* Amendment of pleadings, above
Sanctions for bad faith declarations, 29.8, 29.30, 29.74
Sham actions, proving, 29.3, 29.14–29.15, 29.23, 29.51
Special defenses, use of, 29.20, 29.24
Statute of limitations as special defense, 29.20, 29.24
Statutory nature, 29.2
Stipulations, use of, 29.21, 29.44–29.45
Substantial controversy, issues without. *See* Summary adjudication of issues, below
Summary adjudication of issues
Generally, 29.25–29.27
Appealability, 29.88
Identification of issues in minute order, 29.71
Notices of motion, *forms*, 29.39–29.40
Oral argument, 29.70
Orders granting, 29.3, 29.7, 29.22, 29.37; *forms*, 29.76–29.77
Testimony, rules governing, 29.8, 29.44, 29.54, 29.70
Time for making motion, 29.12, 29.31
Vacating or setting aside, 29.79–29.82, 29.88

SUPERIOR COURTS
See also Jurisdiction; Venue
Continuances, basic requirement for, 26.86
Declaratory relief actions, jurisdiction of court, 24.6, 24.27
Default and default judgments, jurisdictional considerations, 30.18–30.19, 30.58–30.59, 30.74, 30.80
Discovery, time limitation, 26.3

INDEX

SUPERIOR COURTS—cont.
Judges. See Judges
Jury fees, deposit of, 26.33–26.34
Jury trial, demand for, 26.31, 26.34
Mandatory settlement conferences, adoption of local rules, 33.17
Notice of motion, rules relating to, 23.2
Pretrial conferences, statutory authority, 26.1, 26.57
Setting case for trial. See Setting Case for Trial

SUPPLEMENTAL PLEADINGS. See Amended and Supplemental Pleadings

SUPREME COURT. See California Supreme Court

SURETYSHIP
Intervention by sureties, 25.13

SURPRISE
Default or default judgment, surprise as basis for relief from, 30.56–30.60, 30.62–30.65
Dismissal, setting aside, 31.91
Relief on ground of surprise generally, 23.62
Summary judgment, review of, 29.80, 29.82, 29.88

SURVIVAL OF ACTIONS
Wrongful death, statutory authority for survival action arising from, 27.4

TAXES AND ASSESSMENTS
Abstract of judgment as protection against tax lien, 34.5
Declaratory relief actions, 24.3, 24.7, 24.11, 24.26
Dismissal statutes, applicability to tax actions, 31.4
Consolidation of actions to recover assessments, 27.4
Income tax, state. See Income Tax, State
Intervention by taxpayers in actions involving validity of legislation, 25.22

TAXPAYER'S ACTIONS
Enjoining waste of public funds, trial setting priority, 26.4

TESTIMONY
See also Hearings; Witnesses
Coordination petition, testimony at hearing on, 28.34
Declarations and affidavits as substitutes for sworn oral testimony, 23.36
Declarations as aid to understanding testimony, 23.41
Default and default judgments
  Attorney's fees, hearing on, 30.48
  Hearing on default judgment by court, 30.50, 30.52, 30.54
  Independent action in equity to set aside default or default judgment, 30.74
  Introduction of testimony by plaintiff, 30.7
  Setting aside, hearing on, 30.70
Hearing on motion, oral arguments and oral testimony at, 23.56–23.57
Hearsay testimony. See Evidence
Pretrial conference, admission of testimony not conforming to pretrial statement, 26.73
Summary judgment proceedings, 29.8, 29.44, 29.54–29.56, 29.70

THIRD PARTIES
Consolidation of actions against third party under workers' compensation laws, 27.4
Intervention by employer or employee in action against third party, 25.2

THIRD PARTIES—*cont.*

Judgment debtor granting third party lien on cause of action, 25.5, 25.14

Personal property, third party claims to, 25.6

Quiet title action, third party as undisclosed agent of plaintiff's husband, 25.26

Real property, third party claims to, 25.15

Settlement of actions by injured workers against third parties, 33.1, 33.30

Summary judgment proceedings, service of subpena duces tecum on third party, 29.57

Unanswered cross-complaint, severance of, 26.10

TIME

Abandonment of eminent domain proceedings, time of motion for, 31.74

Abstract of judgment, filing prior to debtor's declaration of bankruptcy, 34.5

Advancement of proceedings. *See* Advancement of Proceedings

At-issue memoranda, filing and serving countermemoranda to, 26.14

Change in setting case, notice of motion for, 26.27

Civil active list, preparation of, 26.9

Continuance of proceedings, stipulation for, 26.93

Coordination of actions

    Add-on case, notice of opposition to coordination of, 28.53

    Affidavits supporting or opposing petition, service of, 28.29

    Opposition to petition, serving notice of, 28.17

    Petition, timing of, 28.18

    Preliminary trial conference, holding, 28.43

    Reporting delay in determination, 28.38

Coordination of actions—*cont.*

    Review of order by mandate, time for filing petition, 28.37, 28.56

    Stay of related actions pending petition for coordination, duration of, 28.10, 28.12

    Stay order issued without hearing, termination of, 28.27

    Stay order, termination on denial of petition for coordination, 28.55

    Stay order, timing of application and opposition papers, 28.24–28.25

Courtroom facilities for trial, providing, 31.20

Default and default judgments

    Actual notice of litigation, time effects of, 30.56–30.59

    Declaration of nonmilitary status, filing, 30.28

    Discovery request, noncompliance with, 30.8

    Entry of default for failure to respond timely to process, 30.10, 30.12–30.18, 30.20, 30.56

    Entry of default, judgment following, 30.7

    Military service, voiding default judgment against defendant in, 30.28

    Motion or renewed motion to set aside, time for, 30.62, 30.72

    Relief, time factors affecting, 30.57–30.59, 30.62, 30.72–30.74, 30.77, 30.79

    Staying execution and shortening time (order), 30.63, 30.67; *form*, 30.68

Discovery, superior court rule, 26.3, 26.5, 26.22, 26.26, 26.66

Dismissal of actions

    Cost bill, filing by defendant, 31.69, 31.90

INDEX 620

TIME—*cont.*
Dismissal of actions—*cont.*
  Lack of prosecution, dismissal for, 31.44
  Prejudice, time for dismissal with, 31.83
  Setting aside, 31.91
  Tolling of time (chart) 31.3
  Transfer fees and costs, dismissal for failure to pay, 31.74
Extension
  Amended or supplemental complaint, effect of service and return of, 31.9
  Five-year requirement for bringing action to trial, stipulation extending time for, 31.18, 31.21, 31.25, 31.29
  General rules, 23.2
  Hearing on motion, application for order and order setting new date for, 23.14; *form*, 23.16
  Notice of motion, application for order and order extending time to serve, 23.14; *form*, 23.16
  Notice of motion, stipulation extending time to serve, 23.14; *form*, 23.15
  Service and return of process, stipulation extending time for, 31.11–31.12, 31.14
  Service of process, extension of time to respond to, 30.12–30.13, 30.19
  Three-year requirement for entry of judgment, stipulation extending time for, 31.15, 31.17
  Transfer fees and costs, payment of, 31.42
Five years, failure to try action within. *See* Dismissal of Actions
General release obtained from injured person, time effect of, 33.29

Intervention
  Application, timing of, 25.1, 25.10, 25.32–25.37, 25.49
  Dismissal after intervention, 25.59–25.60
  Responses to complaint, time for filing and serving, 25.56
Judgment on the pleadings, time for making, 29.16
Jury fees, deposit of, 26.33–26.34
Jury trial
  Demand, time for, 26.31
  Filing motion to vacate setting for, 26.15
  Filing notice of motion for, 26.11, 26.29
  Waiver, notice of, 26.34
Laches. *See* Laches
Motion denial, commencement of time period after, 23.63
Motions, hearing on. *See* Motions
Municipal and justice court trials, choosing cases from civil active list, 26.5
Order, effectiveness of, 23.58
Pretrial conference
  Filing orders, 26.70
  Notice, 26.64
  Preparation of orders, 26.68
  Setting, 26.63
Readiness, certificate of
  Filing, 26.1, 26.18, 26.20
  Signing, 26.24
  Vacating certificate, notice of motion, 26.27
Service of process and papers
  Motions, notice of, 23.9–23.16
  Offer to allow judgment in settlement action, papers relating to, 33.11–33.14
  Opposition memoranda of points and authorities and declarations, 23.52, 23.54
Settlement actions
  Damages, itemizing, 33.20
  Demands and offers, conveying prior to conference. 33.19

TIME—*cont.*
Settlement actions—*cont.*

   Documents, delivery to judge, 33.20

   Nonappearance at conference, notification of, 33.23

   Offer to allow judgment, service of papers relating to, 33.11–33.14

Settlement conference, acceptance of, 26.49, 33.16

Settlement conference, setting, 26.43, 26.52, 26.60, 33.16–33.17

Severance, notice of motion for, 27.17

Short causes defined, 26.2

Shortening

   Default judgment, order staying execution and shortening time, 30.63, 30.67; *form*, 30.68

   Dismissal, service and filing of notice of motion for, 31.56

   Hearing on motion, application for order and order shortening time for, 23.12; *form*, 23.13

   Pretrial conference, 26.64, 26.76

   Summary judgment motion, 29.12, 29.31

   Trial continuance motion, obtaining order shortening time for service of, 26.97

   Trial date, notice of, 26.3

   Trial date, setting, 26.51, 26.74

   Trial setting conference, 26.76

Small claims court proceedings, 26.6

Statute of limitations. *See* Limitation of Actions

Stay of proceedings. *See* Coordination of actions, above

Stipulations for extension. *See* Extension, above

Summary judgment

   Late filings, 29.69

Summary judgment—*cont.*

   Motion, serving and filing notice of, 23.9, 29.12, 29.67

   Motion, time for hearing, 29.12, 29.29, 29.57, 29.59

   Motion, time for making, 29.12, 29.31

   New trial motion, 29.79

   Relief from order on grounds of mistake, inadvertence, surprise, or excusable neglect, 29.80

   Request for time to conduct discovery, denial of, 29.13

Tentative rulings on motions, availability of, 23.53

Three years after mistrial, dismissal for failure to try action within, 31.3, 31.34

Three years after new trial granted or new trial order affirmed, dismissal for failure to try action within 31.3, 31.32–31.33

Three years, failure to enter judgment within. *See* Dismissal of Actions

Three years, failure to serve and return summons within. *See* Dismissal of Actions

Trailing cases, 26.100

Transfer fees and costs, payment of, 31.42

Trial commencement, 31.75

Trial date, notice of, 26.3

Trial date, setting. *See* Setting Case for Trial

Trial, notice of, 26.55, 31.40

Trial setting conference

   Date, setting, 26.48

   Filing document in lieu of appearance at, 26.41

   Notice 26.49

Two years, failure to try action within. *See* Dismissal of Actions

Unavailability of attorney, time of motion, 26.89

TITLE
Default judgment hearing, cases affecting title to real property, 30.54
Defect in title of action, effect of, 23.39
Nonparty trying question of title, 25.6
Quieting title. *See* Quieting Title to Real Property

TRANSCRIPTS
Oral argument on motion, arranging transcript of, 23.56
Pretrial conference, 26.65

TRANSFER OF ACTIONS
See also Jurisdiction; Venue
Abatement procedure, 27.10
Coordination trial judge, powers of, 28.42, 28.48
Declaratory relief action, 24.27
Default procedures, 30.15, 30.18
Defined, 28.48
Dismissal for failure to pay transfer fees and costs. *See* Dismissal of Actions
General appearance, notice of motion as, 31.12
Notice and hearing, 28.49
Order, 28.50; *form*, 28.51
Severance, effect of, 27.7
Voluntary dismissal of action by plaintiff, rule affecting, 31.71

TRESPASS
Adjoining landowners' intervention in trespass action, 25.18

TRIAL
Absence of adverse party, effect of, 26.55, 26.74
Advancing. *See* Advancement of Proceedings
Calendars. *See* Calendars
Compelling trial on merits, policy of appellate courts, 30.60
Consolidation of actions. *See* Consolidation of Actions
Continuance
　Alternative procedures, 26.100–26.102
　Declaration in support of motion, 26.95–26.96; *form*, 26.98
　Defaulting defendant, request by, 30.2
　Defined, 26.83
　Good cause
　　Basic requirement, 26.84, 26.86, 26.92, 26.95
　　Examples, 26.87–26.91, 26.93
　Grounds, 26.84–26.85, 26.93
　Inherent power of court, 26.94
　Judicial discretion, 26.89–26.90, 26.95, 26.102
　Notice of motion, 26.96; *form*, 26.97
　Order, 26.50, 26.91
　Policy against continuances, 26.84–26.85, 26.92
　Striking at-issue memorandum, trial postponement resulting from, 26.14
　Trailing cases, 26.92–26.93, 26.100
　Waiver of jury trial, continuance for insufficient notice of, 26.34
Coordination motion judge, effect of assignment of, 28.22, 28.26
Declaratory relief actions, 24.39–24.42
Five years, failure to try action within. *See* Dismissal of Actions
Imminence of trial, effect of delay in petitioning for coordination, 28.18, 28.32
Intervention during trial, 25.32
Jury trial. *See* Juries and Verdicts
Mistrial. *See* Mistrial
New trial. *See* New Trial
Notice of, 26.3, 26.5, 26.54–26.55, 26.74, 30.2, 30.7, 31.40
Partial trial, satisfying five-year requirement for bringing action to trial, 31.19

TRIAL—*cont.*

Plaintiff's duty to bring case to trial, 31.2
Pretrial conference, references at trial, 26.73
Retrial. *See* Retrial
Separate trial. *See* Severance of Actions
Setting case. *See* Setting Case for Trial
Summary judgment motion, beneficial effect of preparing for, 29.30–29.31
Two years, failure to try action within. *See* Dismissal of Actions

TRUSTS

Declaration of constructive trust, equitable action, 26.28
Impression of trust, intervention in actions for, 25.29

UNCLEAN HANDS DOCTRINE

Judicial discretion, 24.2, 24.19

UNDERTAKINGS. *See* Bonds and Undertakings

UNIONS. *See* Labor Unions

UNLAWFUL DETAINER

Notice of trial, 26.55
Time to answer complaint, 30.12
Trial setting priority, 26.4
Vacation of default, case example, 30.10

UNRUH ACT

Default proceedings, declaration regarding venue, 30.18, 30.21, 30.25; *form*, 30.29

VACATING AND SETTING ASIDE

Consolidation order, vacation of, 27.12
Default and default judgments. *See* Default and Default Judgments
Dismissal order, 31.55, 31.68, 31.71, 31.75, 31.91
Environmental impact reports, declaratory relief action to set aside, 24.3
Extrinsic fraud, court's inherent power to vacate judgment on ground of, 25.33
Jury trial, motion to vacate setting for, 26.15, 26.52
Orders on granted motions, bases for vacation of, 23.23, 23.62–23.63
Readiness certificate, vacation of, 26.25–26.27
Severance order, vacation of, 27.11
Special setting of case for trial, order vacating, 31.20
Summary judgment, vacation of, 29.79–29.82, 29.88

VENUE

See also Transfer of Actions
Affidavits, statement in, 23.39
Change
   Declaration supporting, question of general appearance, 31.12
   Default proceedings, notice of motion to transfer action in, 30.15, 30.18
   Intervenor, motion by, 25.58
   Jurisdictional considerations, 31.23
   Review of order, 31.42
   Transfer fees and costs, failure to pay. *See* Dismissal of Actions
   Trial delay, grounds for, 31.25–31.26
Declaratory relief, 24.28
Default proceedings. *See* Default and Default Judgments

VERDICTS. *See* Judgment Notwithstanding Verdict; Juries and Verdicts

VERIFICATION

Pleading, need for verification of, 23.44
Signatures, judicial notice of, 29.55
Summary judgment proceedings, effect of unverified answer in, 29.45

VETERANS. *See* Servicemen and Veterans

VOTING. *See* Elections

WAIVERS

Appearance, waiver of notice by, 23.6
Consent judgment, effect of, 34.4–34.5
Consent judgment, waiver of hearing prior to entry of, 34.12
Costs as part of settlement agreement, waiver of, 33.29
Default procedures, waiver of requirements applicable to military personnel, 30.28
Dismissal motion, timeliness of, 31.56
Dismissal, waiver of right, 31.11, 31.21
Evidentiary objections, rule governing review of summary judgments, 29.86
Intervention, waiver of objections to, 25.50
Jury trial. *See* Juries and Verdicts
Notice of trial requirement, waiver of, 26.55
Opposing motion, failure as waiver, 23.48
Order overruling demurrer, waiver of notice of, 30.16
Ruling of motion, waiver of notice of, 23.61
Submitted case, rule covering waiver of findings in, 32.4
Three-year trial requirement, 31.33
Two-year trial requirement, 31.29

WATER

Declaratory relief actions, 24.7–24.9, 24.18, 24.29
Reference to hearing officer of water rights controversy as ground for trial delay, 31.25
Riparian rights. *See* Riparian Rights

WILLS

Contest
  Dismissal statute, applicability, 31.65, 31.73
  Intervention in, 25.12, 25.30, 25.37
Declaratory relief, 24.6, 24.8, 24.13

WITNESSES

See also Hearings; Testimony
Continuance of trial
  Avoiding continuance by substitution of witnesses, 26.95
  Death, illness, or unavailability of witness as grounds, 26.87–26.89, 26.93, 26.96, 26.98
  Testimony of material and necessary witness, continuance to hear, 26.94
Coordination of actions for convenience of witnesses, 28.5
Default judgment proceedings, obtaining key witness, 30.61
Expert. *See* Expert Witnesses
Opinions of nonexpert witnesses, 29.51
Partial trial, swearing of one witness, 31.19
Pretrial conference, disclosing witnesses at, 26.66
Qualifications, 23.40, 29.49
Settlement, factors affecting, 33.4, 33.12, 33.19
Severance of actions for convenience of witnesses, order for, 27.5, 27.17; *form*, 27.19
Summary judgment proceedings
  Declaration by sole witness, effect of, 29.11
  Discovery, value where witness unavailable, 29.31
Transfer of actions, considering convenience of witnesses, 28.49

WORDS AND PHRASES
Action, 31.77
Actual controversy, 24.9
Affidavits, 23.36, 29.48
Application, 23.1
Assigned judge, 28.4
Book account, 30.37
Cause of action, 31.77
Certificate of readiness, 26.16
Certify, 23.42
Civil active list, 26.9
Collateral estoppel, 34.3
Compromise settlement, 33.10
Consent judgment, 34.1–34.2
Consolidation, 27.1
Continuance of trial, 26.83
Coordinated action, 28.4
Coordination judge, 28.4
Covenant not to sue, 33.29
Declare, 23.42
Declarations, 23.36
Default, 30.1
Default judgment, 30.3
Demand, 33.1
Dismissal with and without prejudice, 31.66, 33.29
Excusable neglect, 30.58
Ex parte application, 23.64
Extrinsic fraud or mistake, 30.59
General appearance, 29.12
Hybrid actions, 26.28
If no appeal has been taken, 31.32
Included action, 28.4
Inferences and presumptions, 29.10
Interested person, 24.8
Intervention, 25.1, 25.10
Judgment, 23.58
Jurat, 23.43
Jurisdiction, 24.27
Motion, 23.1
Offer, 33.1
Order, 23.1, 23.58
Party, 28.29
Person entitled to declaratory relief, 24.8
Petition to coordinate an add-on case, 28.52
Points, 23.32
Place (of hearing motion), 23.21
Proceeding in a court, 26.93
Property, 24.8

Release, 33.29
Responsive paper, 30.15
Retransfer, 28.48
Retraxit, 33.29
Settlement, 33.1
Severance, 27.2
Short causes, 26.2
Sole witness, 29.11
Summary judgment, 29.79
Supporting papers, 29.3
Transfer, 28.48
Triable issue as to any material fact, 29.9

WORKERS' COMPENSATION
Consolidation of actions against third party under workers' compensation laws, 27.4
Intervention in proceedings, 25.2, 25.37
Release by workers' compensation insurer, 33.30
Settlement of actions by injured workers against third parties, 33.1, 33.30

WRITS. *See* Mandate; Prohibition

WRITTEN INSTRUMENTS
See also Handwriting; Records and Recordings; Reports
Best evidence rule, compliance with, 29.57
Contracts. *See* Contracts
Statements supporting introduction of secondary evidence, 29.58

WRONGFUL DEATH
Consolidation of actions, 27.4, 31.25
Default, conditions for, 30.36
Factual statements in release, 33.30
Joinder of parties, 31.22–31.23
Settlement offer prior to conference, 33.20

ZONING
Adjoining landowners' intervention in enforcement actions, 25.18
Declaratory relief, 24.11, 24.23, 24.29